Residence of the late A. J. Downing. Newburgh, on the Hudson

Rural Essays

BY

A. J. Downing

THE LIBRARY: RESIDENCE OF THE LATE A. J. DOWNING.

NEW YORK:

LEAVITT & ALLEN.

1858.

RURAL ESSAYS.

BY

A. J. DOWNING.

EDITED, WITH A MEMOIR OF THE AUTHOR,

BY

GEORGE WILLIAM CURTIS,

AND

A LETTER TO HIS FRIENDS,

BY

FREDERIKA BREMER.

NEW YORK:
LEAVITT & ALLEN,
379 BROADWAY.

JOHN F. TROW,
PRINTER AND STEREOTYPER,
379 Broadway.

PREFACE.

THIS posthumous volume completes the series of Mr. Downing's works. It comprises, with one or two exceptions, all his editorial papers in the "Horticulturist." The Editor has preferred to retain their various temporary allusions, because they serve to remind the reader of the circumstances under which the articles were prepared. Mr. Downing had designed a work upon the Shade-Trees of the United States, but left no notes upon the subject.

In the preparation of the memoir, the Editor has been indebted to a sketch in the Knickerbocker Magazine, by Mrs. Monell, of Newburgh, to Mr. Wilder's eulogy before the Pomological Congress, and to an article in the "New-York Quarterly," by Clarence Cook, Esq.

The tribute to the genius and character of Downing

by Miss Bremer, although addressed to all his friends, has the unreserved warmth of a private letter. No man has lived in vain who has inspired such regard in such a woman.

NEW-YORK, April, 1853.

CONTENTS.

LANDSCAPE GARDENING.

RURAL ARCHITECTURE.

TREES.

AGRICULTURE.

FRUIT.

LETTERS FROM ENGLAND.

MEMOIR

MEMOIR.

ANDREW JACKSON DOWNING was born at Newburgh, upon the Hudson, on the spot where he always lived, and which he always loved more than any other, on the 30th of October, 1815. His father and mother were both natives of Lexington, Massachusetts, and, upon their marriage, removed to Orange County, New-York, where they settled, some thirty or forty miles from Newburgh. Presently, however, they came from the interior of the county to the banks of the river. The father built a cottage upon the highlands of Newburgh, on the skirts of the town, and there his five children were born. He had begun life as a wheelwright, but abandoned the trade to become a nurseryman, and after working prosperously in his garden for twenty-one years, died in 1822.

Andrew was born many years after the other children. He was the child of his parents' age, and, for that reason, very dear. He began to talk before he could walk, when he was only nine months old, and the wise village gossips shook their heads in his mother's little cottage, and prophesied a bright career for the precocious child. At eleven months that career manifestly began, in the gossips' eyes, by his walking bravely about the room: a handsome, cheerful, intelligent child, but quiet and thoughtful, petted by the elder brothers and sister, standing sometimes in the door, as he grew older, and watching the shadows of the clouds chase each other over the Fishkill mountains upon the opposite side of the river ; soothed by the universal silence of the country, while the constant occupation of the father, and of the brother who worked with him in the nursery, made the boy serious, by necessarily leaving him much alone.

In the little cottage upon the Newburgh highlands, looking down upon the broad bay which the Hudson river there makes, before winding in a narrow stream through the highlands of West Point, and looking eastward across the river to the Fishkill hills, which rise gradually from the bank into a gentle mountain boldness, and northward, up the river, to shores that do not obstruct the horizon,—passed the first years of the boy's life, thus early befriending him with one of the loveliest of landscapes. While his father and brother were pruning and grafting their trees, and the other brother was busily at work in the comb factory, where he was employed, the young Andrew ran alone about the garden, playing his solitary games in the presence of the scene whose influence helped to mould his life, and which, even so early, filled his mind with images of rural beauty. His health, like that of most children born in their parents' later years, was not at all robust. The father, watching the slight form glancing among his trees, and the mother, aware of her boy sitting silent and thoughtful, had many a pang of apprehension, which was not relieved by the ominous words of the gossips that it was "hard to raise these smart children,"—the homely modern echo of the old Greek fancy, "Whom the gods love die young."

The mother, a thrifty housekeeper and a religious woman, occupied with her many cares, cooking, mending, scrubbing, and setting things to rights, probably looked forward with some apprehension to the future condition of her sensitive Benjamin, even if he lived. The dreamy, shy ways of the boy were not such as indicated the stern stuff that enables poor men's children to grapple with the world. Left to himself, his will began to grow imperious. The busy mother could not severely scold her ailing child; but a sharp rebuke had probably often been pleasanter to him than the milder treatment that resulted from affectionate compassion, but showed no real sympathy. It is evident, from the tone in which he always spoke of his childhood, that his recollections of it were not altogether agreeable. It was undoubtedly clouded by a want of sympathy, which he could not understand at the time, but which appeared plainly enough when his genius came into play. It is the same kind of clouded childhood that so often occurs in literary biography, where there was great mutual affection and no ill feeling, but a lack of that instinctive apprehension of motives and aims, which makes each one perfectly tolerant of each other.

When Andrew was seven years old, his father died, and his elder brother succeeded to the management of the nursery business. Andrew's developing tastes led him to the natural sciences, to botany and mineralogy. As he grew older he began to read the treatises upon these favorite subjects, and went, at length, to an academy at Montgomery, a town not far from Newburgh, and in the same county. Those who remember him here, speak of him as a thoughtful, reserved boy, looking fixedly out of his large, dark brown eyes, and carrying his brow a little inclined forward, as if slightly defiant. He was a poor boy, and very proud. Doubtless that indomitable will had already resolved that he should not be the least of the men that he and his schoolfellows would presently become. He was shy, and made few friends among the boys. He kept his own secrets, and his companions do not remember that he gave any hint, while at Montgomery Academy, of his peculiar power. Neither looking backward nor forward, was the prospect very fascinating to his dumb, and probably a little dogged, ambition. Behind were the few first years of childhood, sickly, left much alone in the cottage and garden, with nothing in those around him (as he felt without knowing it) that strictly sympathized with him; and yet, as always in such cases, of a nature whose development craved the most generous sympathy: these few years, too, cast among all the charms of a landscape which the Fishkill hills lifted from littleness, and the broad river inspired with a kind of grandeur; years, which the universal silence of the country, always so imposing to young imaginations, and the rainbow pomp of the year, as it came and went up and down the river-banks and over the mountains, and the general solitude of country life, were not very likely to enliven. Before, lay a career of hard work in a pursuit which rarely enriches the workman, with little apparent promise of leisure to pursue his studies or to follow his tastes. It is natural enough, that in the midst of such prospects, the boy, delicately organized to appreciate his position, should have gone to his recitations and his play in a very silent—if not stern—manner, all the more reserved and silent for the firm resolution to master and not be mastered. It is hard to fancy that he was ever a blithe boy. The gravity of maturity came early upon him. Those who saw him only in later years can, probably, easily see the boy at Montgomery Academy, by fancying him quite as they knew him, less twenty or twenty-five years. One by one, the boys went from the academy to college, or into business, and when Andrew was sixteen years old, he also left the academy and returned home.

He, too, had been hoping to go to college; but the family means forbade. His mother, anxious to see him early settled, urged him, as his elder brothers were both doing well in business—the one as a nurseryman, and the other, who had left the comb factory, practising ably and prosperously as a physician—to enter as a clerk into a drygoods store. That request explains the want of delight with which he remembered his childhood: because it shows that his good, kind mother, in the midst of her baking, and boiling, and darning the children's stockings, made no allowance—as how should she, not being able to perceive them—for the possibly very positive tastes of her boy. Besides, the first duty of each member of the poor household was, as she justly conceived, to get a living; and as Andrew was a delicate child, and could not lift and carry much, nor brave the chances of an out-door occupation, it was better that he should be in the shelter of a store. He, however, a youth of sixteen years, fresh from the studies, and dreams, and hopes of the Montgomery Academy, found his first duty to be the gentle withstanding of his mother's wish; and quite willing to "settle," if he could do it in his own way, joined his brother in the management of the nursery. He had no doubt of his vocation. Since it was clear that he must directly do something, his fine taste and exquisite appreciation of natural beauty, his love of natural forms, and the processes and phenomena of natural life, immediately determined his choice. Not in vain had his eyes first looked upon the mountains and the river. Those silent companions of his childhood claimed their own in the spirit with which the youth entered upon his profession. To the poet's eye began to be added the philosopher's mind; and the great spectacle of Nature which he had loved as beauty, began to enrich his life as knowledge. Yet I remember, as showing that with all his accurate science he was always a poet, he agreed in many conversations that the highest enjoyment of beauty was quite independent of use; and that while the pleasure of a botanist who could at once determine the family and species of a plant, and detail all the peculiarities and fitness of its structure, was very great and inappreciable, yet that it was upon a lower level than the instinctive delight in the beauty of the same flower. The botanist could not have the highest pleasure in the flower if he were not a poet. The poet would increase the variety of his pleasure, if he were a botanist. It was this constant subjection of science to the sentiment of beauty that made him an artist, and did not leave him an artisan; and his science was always most accurate and profound, because the very depth and delicacy of his feeling for beauty gave him the utmost patience to learn, and the greatest rapidity to adapt, the means of organizing to the eye the ideal image in his mind.

About this time the Baron de Liderer, the Austrian Consul General, who had a summer retreat in Newburgh, began to notice the youth, whose botanical and mineralogical tastes so harmonized with his own. Nature keeps fresh the feelings of her votaries, and the Baron, although an old man, made hearty friends with Downing; and they explored together the hills and lowlands of the neighborhood, till it had no more vegetable nor mineral secrets from the enthusiasts. Downing always kept in the hall of his house, a cabinet, containing mineralogical specimens collected in these excursions. At the house of the Baron, also, and in that of his wealthy neighbor, Edward Armstrong, Downing discovered how subtly cultivation refines men as well as plants, and there first met that polished society whose elegance and grace could not fail to charm him as essential to the most satisfactory intercourse, while it presented the most entire contrast to the associations of his childhood. It is not difficult to fancy the lonely child, playing unheeded in the garden, and the dark, shy boy, of the Montgomery Academy, meeting with a thrill of satisfaction, as if he had been waiting for them, the fine gentlemen and ladies at the Consul General's, and the wealthy neighbor's, Mr. Armstrong, at whose country-seat he was introduced to Mr. Charles Augustus Murray, when, for the first time, he saw one of the class that he never ceased to honor for their virtues and graces—the English gentleman. At this time, also, the figure of Raphael Hoyle, an English landscape painter, flits across his history. Congenial in taste and feeling, and with varying knowledge, the two young men rambled together over the country near Newburgh, and while Hoyle caught upon canvas the colors and forms of the flowers, and the outline of the landscape, Downing instructed him in their history and habits, until they wandered from the actual scene into discussions dear to both, of art, and life, and beauty; or the artist piqued the imagination of his friend with stories of English parks, and of Italian vineyards, and of cloud-capped Alps, embracing every zone and season, as they rose,—while the untravelled youth looked across the river to the Fishkill hills, and imagined Switzerland. This soon ended. Raphael Hoyle died. The living book of travel and romantic experience, in which the youth who had wandered no farther than to Montgomery Academy and to the top of the South Beacon,—the highest hill of the Fishkill range,—had so deeply read of scenes and a life that suited him, was closed forever.

Little record is left of these years of application, of work, and study. The Fishkill hills and the broad river, in whose presence he had always lived, and the quiet country around Newburgh, which he had so thoroughly explored, began to claim some visible token of their influence. It is pleasant to know that his first literary works were recognitions of their charms. It shows the intellectual integrity of the man that, despite glowing hopes and restless ambition for other things, his first essay was written from his experience; it was a description of the "Danskamer," or Devil's Dancing-Ground — a point on the Hudson, seven miles above Newburgh—published in the *New-York Mirror*. A description of Beacon Hill followed.

He wrote, then, a discussion of novel-reading, and some botanical papers, which were published in a Boston journal. Whether he was discouraged by the ill success of these attempts, or perceived that he was not yet sufficient master of his resources to present them properly to the public, does not appear, but he published nothing more for several years. Perhaps he knew that upon the subjects to which his natural tastes directed his studies, nothing but experience spoke with authority. Whatever the reason of his silence, however, he worked on unyieldingly, studying, proving, succeeding; finding time, also, to read the poets and the philosophers, and to gain that familiarity with elegant literature which always graced his own composition. Of this period of his life, little record, but great results, remain. With his pen, and books, and microscope, in the red house, and his pruning-knife and sharp eye in the nursery and garden, he was learning, adapting, and triumphing,—and also, doubtless, dreaming and resolving. If any stranger wishing to purchase trees at the nursery of the Messrs. Downing, in Newburgh, had visited that pleasant town, and transacted business with the younger partner, he would have been perplexed to understand why the younger partner with his large knowledge, his remarkable power of combination, his fine taste, his rich cultivation, his singular force and precision of expression, his evident mastery of his profession, was not a recognized authority in it, and why he had never been heard of. For it was remarkable in Downing, to the end, that he always attracted attention and excited speculation. The boy of the Montgomery Academy carried that slightly defiant head into the arena of life, and seemed always too much a critical observer not to challenge wonder, sometimes, even, to excite distrust. That was the eye which in the vegetable world had scanned the law through the appearance, and followed through the landscape the elusive line of beauty. It was a full, firm, serious eye. He did not smile with his eyes as many do, but they held you as in a grasp, looking from under their cover of dark brows.

The young man, now twenty years old or more, and hard at work, began to visit the noble estates upon the banks of the Hudson, to extend his experience, and confirm his nascent theories of art in landscape-gardening. Studying in the red cottage, and working in the nursery upon the Newburgh highlands, he had early seen that in a new, and unworked, and quite boundless country, with every variety of kindly climate and available soil, where fortunes arose in a night, an opportunity was offered to Art, of achieving a new and characteristic triumph. To touch the continent lying chaotic, in mountain, and lake, and forest, with a finger that should develop all its resources of beauty, for the admiration and benefit of its children, seemed to him a task worthy the highest genius. This was the dream that dazzled the silent years of his life in the garden, and inspired and strengthened him in every exertion. As he saw more and more of the results of this spirit in the beautiful Hudson country-seats, he was, naturally, only the more resolved. To lay out one garden well, in conformity with the character of the surrounding landscape, in obedience to the truest taste, and to make a man's home, and its grounds, and its accessories, as genuine works of art as any picture or statue that the owner had brought over the sea, was, in his mind, the first step toward the great result.

At the various places upon the river, as he visited them from time to time, he was received as a gentleman, a scholar, and the most practical man of the party, would necessarily be welcomed. He sketched, he measured; "in a walk he plucks from an overhanging bough a single leaf, examines its color, form and structure; inspects it with his microscope, and, having recorded his observations, presents it to his friend, and invites him to study it, as suggestive of some of the first principles of rural architecture and economy." No man enjoyed society more, and none ever lost less time. His pleasure trips from point to point upon the river were the excursions of the honey-bee into the flower. He returned richly laden; and the young partner, feeling from childhood the necessity of entire self-dependence, continued to live much alone, to be reserved, but always affable and gentle. These travels were usually brief, and strictly essential to his education. He was wisely getting ready; it would be so fatal to speak without authority, and authority came only with much observation and many years.

But, during these victorious incursions into the realms of experience, the younger partner had himself been conquered. Directly opposite the red cottage, upon the other side of the river, at Fishkill Landing, lay, under blossoming locust trees, the estate and old family mansion of John P. De Wint, Esq. The place had the charms of a "moated grange," and was quite the contrast of the elegant care and incessant cultivation that marked the grounds of the young man in Newburgh. But the fine old place, indolently lying in luxuriant decay, was the seat of boundless hospitality and social festivity. The spacious piazzas, and the gently sloping lawn, which made the foreground of one of the most exquisite glimpses of the Hudson, rang all summer long with happy laughter. Under those blossoming locust trees were walks that led to the shore, and the moon hanging over Cro' Nest recalled to all loiterers along the bank the loveliest legends of the river. In winter the revel shifted from the lawn to the frozen river. One such gay household is sufficient nucleus for endless enjoyment. From the neighboring West Point, only ten miles distant came gallant young officers, boating in summer, and skating in winter, to serenade under the locusts, or join the dance upon the lawn. Whatever was young and gay was drawn into the merry maelstrom, and the dark-haired boy from Newburgh, now grown, somehow, to be a gentleman of quiet and polished manners, found himself, even when in the grasp of the scientific coils of Parmentier, Repton, Price, Loudon, Lindley, and the rest,—or busy with knife, clay, and grafts,—dreaming of the grange beyond the river, and of the Marianna he had found there.

Summer lay warm upon the hills and river; the landscape was yet untouched by the scorching July heats; and on the seventh of June, 1838,—he being then in his twenty-third year,—Downing was married to Caroline, eldest daughter of J. P. De Wint, Esq. At this time, he dissolved the business connection with his elder brother, and continued the nursery by himself. There were other changes also. The busy mother of his childhood was busy no longer. She had now been for several years an invalid, unable even to walk in the garden. She continued to live in the little red cottage which Downing afterwards removed to make way for a green-house. Her sons were men now, and her daughter a woman. The necessity for her own exertion was passed, and her hold upon life was gradually loosened, until she died in 1839.

Downing now considered himself ready to begin the career for which he had so long been preparing; and very properly his first work was his own house, built in the garden of his father, and only a few rods from the cottage in which he was born. It was a simple house, in an Elizabethan style, by which he designed to prove that a beautiful, and durable, and convenient mansion, could be built as cheaply as a poor and tasteless temple, which seemed to be, at that time, the highest American conception of a fine residence. In this design he entirely succeeded. His house, which did not, however, satisfy his maturer eye, was externally very simple, but extremely elegant; indeed, its chief impression was that of elegance. Internally it was spacious and convenient, very gracefully proportioned and finished, and marked every where by the same spirit. Wherever the eye fell, it detected that a wiser eye had been before it. All the forms and colors, the style of the furniture, the frames of the mirrors and pictures, the patterns of the carpets, were harmonious, and it was a harmony as easily achieved by taste as discord by vulgarity. There was no painful conformity, no rigid monotony, there was nothing finical nor foppish in this elegance—it was the necessary result of knowledge and skill. While the house was building, he lived with his wife at her father's. He personally superintended the work, which went briskly forward. From the foot of the Fishkill hills beyond the river, other eyes superintended it, also, scanning, with a telescope, the Newburgh garden and growing house; and, possibly, from some rude telegraph, as a white cloth upon a tree, or a blot of black paint upon a smooth board, Hero knew whether at evening to expect her Leander.

The house was at length finished. A graceful and beautiful building stood in the garden, higher and handsomer than the little red cottage—a very pregnant symbol to any poet who should chance that way and hear the history of the architect.

Once fairly established in his house, it became the seat of the most gracious hospitality, and was a beautiful illustration of that "rural home" upon whose influence Downing counted so largely for the education and intelligent patriotism of his countrymen. His personal exertions were unremitting. He had been for some time projecting a work upon his favorite art of Landscape Gardening, and presently began to throw it into form. His time for literary labor was necessarily limited by his superintendence of the nursery. But the book was at length completed, and in the year 1841, the Author being then twenty-six years old, Messrs. Wiley & Putnam published in New-York and London, "A Treatise on the Theory and Practice of Landscape Gardening, adapted to North America, with a view to the Improvement of Country Residences. With

Remarks on Rural Architecture. By A. J. Downing." The most concise and comprehensive definition of Landscape Gardening that occurs in his works, is to be found in the essay, "Hints on Landscape Gardening." "It is an art," he says, "which selects from natural materials that abound in any country its best sylvan features, and by giving them a better opportunity than they could otherwise obtain, brings about a higher beauty of development and a more perfect expression than nature herself offers." The preface of the book is quite without pretence. "The love of country," says our author, with a gravity that overtops his years, "is inseparably connected with the love of home. Whatever, therefore, leads man to assemble the comforts and elegancies of life around his habitation, tends to increase local attachments, and render domestic life more delightful; thus, not only augmenting his own enjoyment, but strengthening his patriotism, and making him a better citizen. And there is no employment or recreation which affords the mind greater or more permanent satisfaction than that of cultivating the earth and adorning our own property. 'God Almighty first planted a garden; and, indeed, it is the parent of human pleasures,' says Lord Bacon. And as the first man was shut out from the garden, in the cultivation of which no alloy was mixed with his happiness, the desire to return to it seems to be implanted by nature, more or less strongly, in every heart."

This book passed to instant popularity, and became a classic, invaluable to the thousands in every part of the country who were waiting for the master-word which should tell them what to do to make their homes as beautiful as they wished. Its fine scholarship in the literature and history of rural art; its singular dexterity in stating the great principles of taste, and their application to actual circumstances, with a clearness that satisfied the dullest mind; its genial grace of style, illuminated by the sense of that beauty which it was its aim to indicate, and with a cheerfulness which is one of the marked characteristics of Downing as an author; the easy mastery of the subject, and its intrinsic interest;—all these combined to secure to the book the position it has always occupied. The testimony of the men most competent to speak with authority in the matter was grateful, because deserved, praise. Loudon, the editor of "Repton's Landscape Gardening," and perhaps at the time the greatest living critic in the department of rural art, at once declared it "a masterly work;" and after quoting freely from its pages, remarked: "We have quoted largely from this work, because in so doing we think we shall give a just idea of the great merit of the author." Dr. Lindley, also, in his "Gardener's Chronicle," dissented from "some minor points," but said: "On the whole, we know of no work in which the fundamental principles of this profession are so well or so concisely expressed:" adding, "No English landscape gardener has written so clearly, or with so much real intensity."

The "quiet, thoughtful, and reserved boy" of the Montgomery Academy had thus suddenly displayed the talent which was not suspected by his school-fellows. The younger partner had now justified the expectation he aroused; and the long, silent, careful years of study and experience insured the permanent value of the results he announced. The following year saw the publication of the "Cottage Residences," in which the principles of the first volume were applied in detail. For the same reason it achieved a success similar to the "Landscape Gardening."

Rural England recognized its great value. Loudon said: "It cannot fail to be of great service." Another said: "We stretch our arm across the 'big water' to tender our Yankee coadjutor an English shake and a cordial recognition." These welcomes from those who knew what and why they welcomed, founded Downing's authority in the minds of the less learned, while the simplicity of his own statements confirmed it. From the publication of the "Landscape Gardening" until his death, he continued to be the chief American authority in rural art.

European honors soon began to seek the young gardener upon the Hudson. He had been for some time in correspondence with Loudon, and the other eminent men of the profession. He was now elected corresponding member of the Royal Botanic Society of London, of the Horticultural Societies of Berlin, the Low Countries, &c. Queen Anne of Denmark sent him "a magnificent ring," in acknowledgment of her pleasure in his works. But, as the years slowly passed, a sweeter praise saluted him than the Queen's ring, namely, the gradual improvement of the national rural taste, and the universal testimony that it was due to Downing. It was found as easy to live in a handsome house as in one that shocked all sense of propriety and beauty. The capabilities of the landscape began to develop themselves to the man who looked at it from his windows, with Downing's books in his hand. Mr. Wilder says that a gentleman "who is eminently qualified to form an enlightened judgment," declared that much of the improvement that has taken place in this country during the last twelve years, in rural architecture and in ornamental gardening and planting, may be ascribed to him. Another gentleman, "speaking of suburban cottages in the West," says: "I asked the origin of so much taste, and was told it might principally be traced to 'Downing's Cottage Residences' and the 'Horticulturist.'" He was naturally elected an honorary member of most of the Horticultural Societies in the country; and as his interest in rural life was universal, embracing no less the soil and cultivation, than the plant, and flower, and fruit, with the residence of the cultivator, he received the same honor from the Agricultural Associations.

Meanwhile his studies were unremitting; and in 1845 Wiley & Putnam published in New-York and London "The Fruits and Fruit Trees of America," a volume of six hundred pages. The duodecimo edition had only lineal drawings. The large octavo was illustrated with finely colored plates, executed in Paris, from drawings made in this country from the original fruits. It is a masterly resumé of the results of American experience in the history, character, and growth of fruit, to the date of its publication. The fourteenth edition was published in the year 1852.

It was in May of the year 1846 that I first saw Downing. A party was made up under the locusts to cross the river and pass the day at "Highland Gardens," as his place was named. The river at Newburgh is about a mile wide, and is crossed by a quiet country ferry, whence the view downward toward the West Point Highlands, Butter-Hill, Sugar-Loaf, Cro' Nest, and Skunnymunk, is as beautiful a river view as can be seen upon a summer day. It was a merry party which crossed, that bright May morning, and broke, with ringing laughter, the silence of the river. Most of us were newly escaped from the city, where we had been blockaded by the winter for many months, and although often tempted by the warm days that came in March, opening the windows on Broadway and ranging the blossoming plants in them, to believe that summer had fairly arrived, we had uniformly found the spring to be that laughing lie which the poets insist it is not. There was no doubt longer, however. The country was so brilliant with the tender green that it seemed festally adorned, and it was easy enough to believe that human genius could have no lovelier nor loftier task than the development of these colors, and forms, and opportunities, into their greatest use and adaptation to human life. "God Almighty first planted a garden, and, indeed, it is the first of human pleasures." Lord Bacon said it long ago, and the bright May morning echoed it, as we crossed the river.

I had read Downing's books; and they had given me the impression, naturally formed of one who truly said of himself, "Angry volumes of politics have we written none: but peaceful books, humbly aiming to weave something more into the fair garland of the beautiful and useful that encircles this excellent old earth."

His image in my mind was idyllic. I looked upon him as a kind of pastoral poet. I had fancied a simple, abstracted cultivator, gentle and silent. We left the boat and drove to his house. The open gate admitted us to a smooth avenue. We had glimpses of an Arbor-Vitæ hedge,—a small and exquisite lawn—rare and flowering trees, and bushes beyond—a lustrous and odorous thicket—a gleam of the river below—"a feeling" of the mountains across the river—and were at the same moment alighting at the door of the elegant mansion, in which stood, what appeared to me a tall, slight Spanish gentleman, with thick black hair worn very long, and dark eyes fixed upon me with a searching glance. He was dressed simply in a costume fitted for the morning hospitalities of his house, or for the study, or the garden. His welcoming smile was reserved, but genuine,—his manner singularly hearty and quiet, marked by the easy elegance and perfect *savoir faire* which would have adorned the Escurial. We passed into the library. The book-shelves were let into the wall, and the doors covered with glass. They occupied only part of the walls, and upon the space above each was a bracket with busts of Dante, Milton, Petrarch, Franklin, Linnæus, and Scott. There was a large bay window opposite the fireplace. The forms and colors of this room were delightful. It was the retreat of an elegantly cultivated gentleman. There were no signs of work except a writing-table, with pens, and portfolios, and piles of letters.

Here we sat and conversed. Our host entered into every subject gayly and familiarly, with an appreciating deference to differences of opinion, and an evident tenacity of his own, all the while, which surprised me, as the peculiarity of the most accomplished man of the world. There was a certain aristocratic *hauteur* in his manner, a constant sense of personal dignity, which comported with the reserve of his smile and the quiet welcome. His intellectual attitude seemed to be one of curious criticism, as if he were sharply scrutinizing all that his affability of manner drew forth. No one had a readier generosity of acknowledgment, and there was a negative flattery in his address and attention, which was very subtle and attractive. In all allusions to rural affairs, and matters with which he was entirely familiar, his conversation was not in the slightest degree pedantic, nor positive. He spoke of such things with the simplicity of a child talking of his toys. The workman, the author, the artist, were entirely subjugated in him to the gentleman. That was his favorite idea. The *gentleman* was the full flower, of which all the others were suggestions and parts. The *gentleman* is, to the various powers and cultivations of the man, what the tone is to the picture, which lies in no single color, but in the harmony of the whole. The gentleman is the final bloom of the man. But no man could be a gentleman without original nobleness of feeling and genuineness of character. Gentleness was developed from that by experience and study, as the delicate tinge upon precious fruits, by propitious circumstances and healthy growth.

In this feeling, which was a constituent of his character, lay the secret of the appearance of *hauteur* that was so often remarked in him, to which Miss Bremer alludes, and which all his friends perceived, more or less distinctly. Its origin was, doubtless, twofold. It sprang first from his exquisite mental organization, which instinctively shrunk from whatever was coarse or crude, and which made his artistic taste so true and fine. That easily extended itself to demand the finest results of men, as of trees, and fruits, and flowers; and then committed the natural error of often accepting the appearance of this result, where the fact was wanting. Hence he had a natural fondness for the highest circles of society—a fondness as deeply founded as his love of the best possible fruits. His social tendency was constantly toward those to whom great wealth had given opportunity of that ameliorating culture,—of surrounding beautiful homes with beautiful grounds, and filling them with refined and beautiful persons, which is the happy fortune of few. Hence, also, the fact that his introduction to Mr. Murray was a remembered event, because the mind of the boy instantly recognized that society to which, by affinity, he belonged; and hence, also, that admiration of the character and life of the English gentleman, which was life-long with him, and which made him, when he went to England, naturally and directly at home among them. From this, also, came his extreme fondness for music, although he had very little ear; and often when his wife read to him any peculiarly beautiful or touching passage from a book, he was quite unable to speak, so much was he mastered by his emotion. Besides this delicacy of organization, which makes aristocrats of all who have it, the sharp contrast between his childhood and his mature life doubtlessly nourished a kind of mental protest against the hard discomforts, want of sympathy, and misunderstandings of poverty.

I recall but one place in which he deliberately states this instinct of his, as an opinion. In the paper upon "Improvement of Vegetable Races," April, 1852, he says: "We are not going to be led into a physiological digression on the subject of the inextinguishable rights of a superior organization in certain men, and races of men, which Nature every day reaffirms, notwithstanding the socialistic and democratic theories of our politicians." But this statement only asserts the difference of organization. No man was a truer American than Downing; no man more opposed to all kinds of recognition of that difference in intellectual organization by a difference of social rank. That he considered to be the true democracy which asserted the absolute equality of opportunity;—and, therefore, he writes from Warwick Castle, a place which in every way could charm no man more than him: "but I turned my face at last westward toward my native land, and with uplifted eyes thanked the good God that, though to England, the country of my ancestors, it had been given to show the growth of man in his highest development of class or noble, to America has been reserved the greater blessing of solving for the world the true problem of all humanity,—that of the abolition of all castes, and the recognition of the divine rights of every human soul." On that May morning, in the library, I remember the conversation, drifting from subject to subject, touched an essay upon "Manners," by Mr. Emerson, then recently published; and in the few words that Mr. Downing said, lay the germ of what I gradually discovered to be his feeling upon the subject. This *hauteur* was always evident in his personal intercourse. In his dealings with workmen, with publishers, with men of affairs of all kinds, the same feeling, which they called "stiffness," coldness," "pride," "haughtiness," or "reserve," revealed itself. That first morning it only heightened in my mind the Spanish impression of the dark, slim man, who so courteously welcomed us at his door.

It was May, and the magnolias were in blossom. Under our host's guidance, we strolled about his grounds, which, although they comprised but some five acres, were laid out in a large style, that greatly enhanced their apparent extent. The town lay at the bottom of the hill, between the garden and the water, and there was a road just at the foot of the garden. But so skilfully were the trees arranged, that all suspicion of town or road was removed. Lying upon the lawn, standing in the door, or sitting under the light piazza before the parlor windows, the enchanted visitor saw only the garden ending in the thicket, which was so dexterously trimmed as to reveal the loveliest glimpses of the river, each a picture in its frame of foliage, but which was not cut low enough to betray the presence of road or town. You fancied the estate extended to the river; yes, and probably owned the river as an ornament, and included the mountains beyond. At least, you felt that here was a man who knew that the best part of the landscape could not be owned, but belonged to every one who could appropriate it. The thicket seemed not only to conceal, but to annihilate, the town. So sequestered and satisfied was the guest of that garden, that he was quite careless and incurious of the world beyond. I have often passed a week there without wishing to go outside the gate, and entirely forgot that there was any town near by. Sometimes, at sunset or twilight, we stepped into a light wagon, and turning up the hill, as we came out of the grounds, left Newburgh below, and drove along roads hanging over the river, or, passing Washington's Head Quarters, trotted leisurely along the shore.

Within his house it was easy to understand that *the home* was so much the subject of his thought. Why did he wish that the landscape should be lovely, and the houses graceful and beautiful, and the fruit fine, and the flowers perfect, but because these were all dependencies and ornaments of home, and home was the sanctuary of the highest human affection. This was the point of departure of his philosophy. Nature must serve man. The landscape must be made a picture in the gallery of love. Home was the pivot upon which turned all his theories of rural art. All his efforts, all the grasp of genius, and the cunning of talent, were to complete, in a perfect home, the apotheosis of love. It is in this fact that the permanence of his influence is rooted. His works are not the result of elegant taste, and generous cultivation, and a clear intellect, only; but of a noble hope that inspired taste, cultivation, and intellect. This saved him as an author from being wrecked upon formulas. He was strictly scientific, few men in his department more so; but he was never rigidly academical. He always discerned the thing signified through the expression; and, in his own art, insisted that if there was nothing to say, nothing should be said. He knew perfectly well that there is a time for discords, and a place for departures from rule, and he understood them when they came,—which was peculiar and very lovely in a man of so delicate a nervous organization. This led him to be tolerant of all differences of opinion and action, and to be sensitively wary of injuring the feelings of those from whom he differed. He was thus scientific in the true sense. In his department he was wise, and we find him writing from Warwick Castle again, thus: "Whoever designed this front, made up as it is of lofty towers and irregular walls, must have been a poet as well as architect, for its composition and details struck me as having the proportions and congruity of a fine scene in nature, which we feel is not to be measured and defined by the ordinary rules of art."

His own home was his finest work. It was materially beautiful, and spiritually bright with the purest lights of affection. Its hospitality was gracious and graceful. It consulted the taste, wishes, and habits of the guest, but with such unobtrusiveness, that the favorite flower every morning by the plate upon the breakfast-table, seemed to have come there as naturally, in the family arrangements, as the plate itself. He held his house as the steward of his friends. His social genius never suffered a moment to drag wearily by. No man was so necessarily devoted to his own affairs,—no host ever seemed so devoted to his guests. Those guests were of the most agreeable kind, or, at least, they seemed so in that house. Perhaps the interpreter of the House Beautiful, she who—in the poet's natural order—was as "moonlight unto sunlight," was the universal solvent. By day, there were always books, conversation, driving, working, lying on the lawn, excursions into the mountains across the river, visits to beautiful neighboring places, boating, botanizing, painting,—or whatever else could be done in the country, and done in the pleasantest way. At evening, there was music,—fine playing and singing, for the guest was thrice welcome who was musical, and the musical were triply musical there,—dancing, charades, games of every kind,—never suffered to flag, always delicately directed,—and in due season some slight violation of the Maine Law. Mr. Downing liked the Ohio wines, with which his friend, Mr. Longworth, kept him supplied, and of which he said, with his calm good sense, in the "Horticulturist," August, 1850,—"We do not mean to say that men could not live and breathe just as well if there were no such thing as wine known; but that since the time of Noah men will not be contented with merely living and breathing; and it is therefore better to provide them with proper and wholesome food and drink, than to put improper aliments within their reach." Charades were a favorite diversion, in which several of his most frequent guests excelled. He was always ready to take part, but his reserve and self-consciousness interfered with his success. His social enjoyment was always quiet. He rarely laughed loud. He preferred rather to sit with a friend and watch the dance or the game from a corner, than to mingle in them. He wrote verses, but never showed them. They were chiefly rhyming letters, clever and graceful, to his wife, and her sisters, and some intimate friends, and to a little niece, of whom he was especially fond. One evening, after vainly endeavoring to persuade a friend that he was mistaken in the kind of a fruit, he sent him the following characteristic lines:

"TO THE DOCTOR, ON HIS PASSION FOR THE 'DUCHESS OF OLDENBURGH.'"

"Dear Doctor, I write you this little effusion,
On learning you're still in that fatal delusion
Of thinking the object you love is a Duchess,
When 'tis only a milkmaid you hold in your clutches;
Why, 'tis certainly plain as the spots in the sun,
That the creature is only a fine *Dutch Mignonne.*
She is *Dutch*—there is surely no question of that,—
She's so large and so ruddy—so plump and so fat;
And that she's a Mignonne—a beauty—most moving,
Is equally proved by your desperate loving;
But that she's a Duchess I flatly deny,
There's such a broad twinkle about her deep eye;
And glance at the russety hue of her skin—
A lady—a noble—would think it a sin!
Ah no, my dear Doctor, upon my own honor,
I must send you a dose of the *true Bella donna!*"

I had expressed great delight with the magnolia, and carried one of the flowers in my hand during our morning stroll. At evening he handed me a fresh one, and every day while I remained, the breakfast-room was perfumed by the magnolia that was placed beside my plate. This delicate thoughtfulness was universal with him. He knew all the flowers that his friends especially loved; and in his notes to me he often wrote, "the magnolias are waiting for you," as an irresistible allurement—which it was very apt to prove. Downing was in the library when I came down the morning after our arrival. He had the air of a man who has been broad awake and at work for several hours. There was the same quiet greeting as before—a gay conversation, glancing at a thousand things—and breakfast. After breakfast he disappeared; but if, at any time, an excursion was proposed,—to climb some hill, to explore some meadows rich in rhododendron, to visit some lovely lake,—he was quite ready, and went with the same unhurried air that marked all his actions. Like Sir Walter Scott, he was producing results implying close application and labor, but without any apparent expense of time or means. His step was so leisurely, his manner so composed, there was always such total absence of weariness in all he said and did, that it was impossible to believe he was so diligent a worker.

But this composure, this reticence, this leisurely air, were all imposed upon his manner by his regal will. He was under the most supreme self-control. It was so absolute as to deprive him of spontaneity and enthusiasm. In social intercourse he was like two persons: the one conversed with you pleasantly upon every topic, the other watched you from behind that pleasant talk, like a sentinel. The delicate child, left much to himself by his parents, naturally grew wayward and imperious. But the man of shrewd common sense, with his way to make in the world, saw clearly that that waywardness must be sternly subjugated. It was so, and at the usual expense. What the friend of Downing most desired in him was a frank and unreserved flow of feeling, which should drown out that curious, critical self-consciousness. He felt this want as much as any one, and often playfully endeavored to supply it. It doubtless arose, in great part, from too fine a nervous organization. Under the mask of the finished man of the world he concealed the most feminine feelings, which often expressed themselves with pathetic intensity to the only one in whom he unreservedly confided.

This critical reserve behind the cordial manner invested his whole character with mystery. The long dark hair, the firm dark eyes, the slightly defiant brow, the Spanish mien, that welcomed us that May morning, seemed to me always afterward, the symbols of his character. A cloud wrapped his inner life. Motives, and the deeper feelings, were lost to view in that obscurity. It seemed that within this cloud there might be desperate struggles, like the battle of the Huns and Romans, invisible in the air, but of which no token escaped into the experience of his friends. He confronted circumstances with the same composed and indomitable resolution, and it was not possible to tell whether he were entertaining angels, or wrestling with demons, in the secret chambers of his soul. There are passages in letters to his wife which indicate, and they only by implication, that his character was tried and tempered by struggles. Those most intimate letters, however, are full of expressions of religious faith and dependence, sometimes uttered with a kind of clinging earnestness, as if he well knew the value of the peace that passes understanding. But nothing of all this appeared in his friendly intercourse with men. He had, however, very few intimate friends among men. His warmest and most confiding friendships were with women. In his intercourse with them, he revealed a rare and beautiful sense of the uses of friendship, which united him very closely to them. To men he was much more inaccessible. It cannot be denied that the feeling of mystery in his character affected the impression he made upon various persons. It might be called as before, "haughtiness," "reserve," "coldness," or "hardness," but it was quite the same thing. It repelled many who were otherwise most strongly attracted to him by his books. In others, still, it begot a slight distrust, and suspicion of self-seeking upon his part.

I remember a little circumstance, the impression of which is strictly in accordance with my feeling of this singular mystery in his character. We had one day been sitting in the library, and he had told me his intention of building a little study and working-room, adjoining the house: "but I don't know," he said, "where or how to connect it with the house." But I was very well convinced that he would arrange it in the best possible manner, and was not surprised when he afterward wrote me that he had made a door through the wall of the library into the new building. This door occupied just the space of one of the book-cases let into the wall, and, by retaining the double doors of the book-case precisely as they were, and putting false books behind the glass of the doors, the appearance of the library was entirely unaltered, while the whole apparent book-case, doors and all, swung to and fro, at his will, as a private door. During my next visit at his house, I was sitting very late at night in the library, with a single candle, thinking that every one had long since retired, and having quite forgotten, in the perfectly familiar appearance of the room, that the little change had been made, when suddenly one of the book-cases flew out of the wall, turning upon noiseless hinges, and, out of the perfect darkness behind, Downing darted into the room, while I sat staring like a benighted guest in the Castle of Otranto. The moment, the place, and the circumstance, were entirely harmonious with my impression of the man.

Thus, although, upon the bright May morning, I had crossed the river to see a man of transparent and simple nature, a lover and poet of rural beauty, a man who had travelled little, who had made his own way into polished and cultivated social relations, as he did into every thing which he mastered, being altogether a self-made man—I found the courteous and accomplished gentleman, the quiet man of the world, full of tact and easy dignity, in whom it was easy to discover that lover and poet, though not in the form anticipated. His exquisite regard for the details of life, gave a completeness to his household, which is nowhere surpassed. Fitness is the first element of beauty, and every thing in his arrangement was appropriate. It was hard not to sigh, when contemplating the beautiful results he accomplished by taste and tact, and at comparatively little pecuniary expense, to think of the sums elsewhere squandered upon an insufficient and shallow splendor. Yet, as beauty was, with Downing, life, and not luxury, although he was, in feeling and by actual profession, the Priest of Beauty, he was never a Sybarite, never sentimental, never weakened by the service. In the dispositions of most men devoted to beauty, as artists and poets, there is a vein of languor, a leaning to luxury, of which no trace was even visible in him. His habits of life were singularly regular. He used no tobacco, drank little wine, and was no gourmand. But he was no ascetic. He loved to entertain Sybarites, poets, and the lovers of luxury: doubtless from a consciousness that he had the magic of pleasing them more than they had ever been pleased. He enjoyed the pleasure of his guests. The various play of different characters entertained him. Yet with all his fondness for fine places, he justly estimated the tendency of their influence. He was not enthusiastic, he was not seduced into blindness by his own preferences, but he maintained that cool and accurate estimate of things and tendencies which always made his advice invaluable. Is there any truer account of the syren influence of a superb and extensive country-seat than the following from the paper: "A Visit to Montgomery Place." "It is not, we are sure, the spot for a man to plan campaigns of conquest, and we doubt, even, whether the scholar whose ambition it is

"to scorn delights,
And live laborious days,"

would not find something in the air of this demesne so soothing as to dampen the fire of his great purposes, and dispose him to believe that there is more dignity in repose, than merit in action."

So, certainly, I believed, as the May days passed, and found me still lingering in the enchanted garden.

In August, 1846, "The Horticulturist" was commenced by Mr. Luther Tucker, of Albany, who invited Mr. Downing to become the editor, in which position he remained, writing a monthly leader for it, until his death. These articles are contained in the present volume. Literature offers no more charming rural essays. They are the thoughtful talk of a country gentleman, and scholar, and practical workman, upon the rural aspects and interests of every month in the year. They insinuate instruction, rather than directly teach, and in a style mellow, mature, and cheerful, adapted to every age and every mood. By their variety of topic and treatment, they are, perhaps, the most complete memorial of the man. Their genial simplicity fascinated all kinds of persons. A correspondence which might be called affectionate, sprang up between the editor and scores of his readers. They wanted instruction and advice. They confided to him their plans and hopes; to him—the personally unknown "we" of their monthly magazine—the reserved man whom publishers and others found "stiff," and "cold," and "a little haughty," and whose fine points of character stood out, like sunny mountain peaks against a mist. These letters, it appears, were personal, and full of feeling. The writers wished to know the man, to see his portrait, and many requested him to have it published in the "Horticulturist." When in his neighborhood, these correspondents came to visit him. They were anxious "to see the man who had written books which had enabled them to make their houses beautiful,—which had helped their wives in the flower-garden, and had shown them how, with little expense, to decorate their humble parlors, and add a grace to the barrenness of daily life." All this was better than Queen Anne's "magnificent ring."

Meanwhile, business in the nursery looked a little threatening. Money was always dropping from the hospitable hand of the owner. Expenses increased—affairs became complicated. It is not the genius of men like Downing to manage the finances very skilfully. "Every tree that he sold for a dollar, cost him ten shillings;"—which is not a money-making process. He was perhaps too lavish, too careless, too sanguine. "Had his income been a million a minute, he would always have been in debt," says one who knew him well. The composed manner was as unruffled as ever; the regal will preserved the usual appearance of things, but in the winter of 1846–7 Mr. Downing was seriously embarrassed. It was a very grave juncture, for it was likely that he would be obliged to leave his house and begin life again. But his friends rallied to the rescue. They assured to him his house and grounds; and he, without losing time, without repining, and with the old determination, went to work more industriously than ever. His attention was unremitting to the "Horticulturist," and to all the projects he had undertaken. His interest in the management of the nursery, however, decreased, and he devoted himself with more energy to rural architecture and landscape gardening, until he gradually discontinued altogether the raising of trees for sale. His house was still the resort of the most brilliant society; still—as it always had been, and was, until the end—the seat of beautiful hospitality. He was often enough perplexed in his affairs—hurried by the monthly recurring necessity of "the leader," and not quite satisfied at any time until that literary task was accomplished. His business confined and interested him; his large correspondence was promptly managed; but he was still sanguine, under that Spanish reserve, and still spent profusely. He had a thousand interests; a State agricultural school, a national agricultural bureau at Washington, designing private and public buildings, laying out large estates, pursuing his own scientific and literary studies, and preparing a work upon Rural Architecture. From his elegant home he was scattering, in the Horticulturist, pearl-seed of precious suggestion, which fell in all kinds of secluded and remote regions, and bore, and are bearing, costly fruit.

In 1849, Mr. John Wiley published "Hints to Young Architects, by George Wightwick, Architect; with Additional Notes and Hints to Persons about Building in this Country, by A. J. Downing." It was a work preparatory to the original one he designed to publish, and full of most valuable suggestions. For in every thing he was American. His sharp sense of propriety as the primal element of beauty, led him constantly to insist that the place, and circumstances, and time, should always be carefully considered before any step was taken. The satin shoe was a grace in the parlor, but a deformity in the garden. The Parthenon was perfect in a certain climate, under certain conditions, and for certain purposes. But the Parthenon as a country mansion in the midst of American woods and fields was unhandsome and offensive. His aim in building a house was to adapt it to the site, and to the means and character of the owner.

It was in the autumn of 1849 that Frederika Bremer came to America. She had been for several years in intimate correspondence with Mr. Downing, and was closely attracted to him by a profound sympathy with his view of the dignity and influence of the *home*. He received Miss Bremer upon her arrival, and she went with him to his house, where she staid several weeks, and wrote there the introduction to the authorized American edition of her works. It is well for us, perhaps, that as she has written a work upon "The Homes of the United States," she should have taken her first impression of them from that of Mr. Downing. During all her travels in this country she constantly corresponded with him and his wife, to whom she was very tenderly attached. Her letters were full of cheerful humor and shrewd observation. She went bravely about alone, and was treated, almost without exception, with consideration and courtesy. And after her journey was over, and she was about to return home, she came to say farewell where she had first greeted America, in Downing's garden.

In this year he finally resolved to devote himself entirely to architecture and building, and, in order to benefit by the largest variety of experience in elegant rural life, and to secure the services of an accomplished and able architect, thoroughly trained to the business he proposed, Mr. Downing went to England in the summer of 1850, having arranged with Messrs. D. Appleton & Co. for the publication of "The Architecture of Country Houses; including Designs for Cottages, Farm-houses, and Villas."

Already in correspondence with the leading Englishmen in his department, Mr. Downing was at once cordially welcomed. He showed the admirable, and not the unfriendly, qualities of his countrymen, and was directly engaged in a series of visits to the most extensive and remarkable of English country seats, where he was an honored guest. The delight of the position was beyond words to a man of his peculiar character and habits. He saw on every hand the perfection of elegant rural life, which was his ideal of life. He saw the boundless parks, the cultivated landscape, the tropics imprisoned in glass; he saw spacious Italian villas, more Italian than in Italy; every various triumph of park, garden, and country-house. But with these, also, he met in the pleasantest way much fine English society, which was his ideal of society. There was nothing wanting to gratify his fine and fastidious taste; but the passage already quoted from his letter at Warwick Castle shows how firmly his faith was set upon his native land, while his private letters are full of affectionate longing to return. It is easy to figure him moving with courtly grace through the rooms of palaces, gentle, respectful, low in tone, never exaggerating, welcome to lord and lady for his good sense, his practical knowledge, his exact detail; pleasing the English man and woman by his English sympathies, and interesting them by his manly and genuine, not boasting, assertions of American genius and success. Looking at the picture, one remembers again that earlier one of the boy coming home from Montgomery Academy, in Orange County, and introduced at the wealthy neighbor's to the English gentleman. The instinct that remembered so slight an event secured his appreciation of all that England offered. No American ever visited England with a mind more in tune with all that is nobly characteristic of her. He remarked, upon his return, that he had been much impressed by the quiet, religious life and habits which he found in many great English houses. It is not a point of English life often noticed, nor presupposed, but it was doubly grateful to him, because he was always a Christian believer, and because all parade was repugnant to him. His letters before his marriage, and during the last years of his life, evince the most genuine Christian faith and feeling.

His residence in England was very brief—a summer trip. He crossed to Paris and saw French life. Fortunately, as his time was short, he saw more in a day than most men in a month, because he was prepared to see, and knew where to look. He found the assistant he wished in Mr. Calvert Vaux, a young English architect, to whom he was introduced by the Secretary of the Architectural Association, and with whom, so mutual was the satisfaction, he directly concluded an agreement. Mr. Vaux sailed with him from Liverpool in September, presently became his partner in business, and commanded, to the end, Mr. Downing's unreserved confidence and respect.

I remember a Christmas visit to Downing in 1850, after his return from Europe, when we all danced to a fiddle upon the marble pavement of the hall, by the light of rustic chandeliers wreathed with Christmas green, and under the antlers, and pikes, and helmets, and breastplates, and plumed hats of cavaliers, that hung upon the walls. The very genius of English Christmas ruled the revel.

During these years he was engaged in superintending the various new editions of his works, and looking forward to larger achievements with maturer years. He designed a greatly enlarged edition of the "Fruit-Trees," and spoke occasionally of the "Shade-Trees," as a work which would be of the greatest practical value. He was much interested in the establishment of the Pomological Congress, was chairman of its fruit committee from the beginning, and drew up the "Rules of American Pomology." Every moment had its work. There was not a more useful man in America; but his visitor found still the same quiet host, leisurely, disengaged; picking his favorite flowers before breakfast; driving here and there, writing, studying, as if rather for amusement; and at twilight stepping into the wagon for a loitering drive along the river.

His love of the country and faith in rural influences were too genuine for him not to be deeply interested in the improvement of cities by means of public parks and gardens. Not only for their sanitary use, but for their elegance and refining influence, he was anxious that all our cities should be richly endowed with them. He alluded frequently to the subject in the columns of his magazine, and when it was resolved by Congress to turn the public grounds in Washington, near the Capitol, White House, and Smithsonian Institute, into a public garden and promenade, Downing was naturally the man invited by the President, in April, 1851, to design the arrangement of the grounds and to superintend their execution. All the designs and much of the work were completed before his death. This new labor, added to the rest, while it increased his income, consumed much of his time. He went once every month to Washington, and was absent ten or twelve days.

He was not suffered to be at peace in this position. There were plenty of jealousies and rivalries, and much sharp questioning about the $2500 annually paid to an accomplished artist for laying out the public grounds of the American Capital, in a manner worthy the nation, and for reclaiming many acres from waste and the breeding of miasma. At length the matter was discussed in Congress.

On the 24th March, 1852, during a debate upon various appropriations, Mr. Jones, of Tennessee, moved to strike out the sum of $12,000, proposed to complete the improvements around the President's house; complained that there were great abuses under the proviso of this appropriation, and declared, quite directly, that Mr. Downing was overpaid for his services. Mr. Stanton, of Kentucky, replied:—"It is astonishing to my mind—and I have no doubt to the minds of others—with what facility otherwise intelligent and respectable gentlemen on this floor can deal out wholesale denunciations of men about whom they know nothing, and will not inform themselves; and how much the legislation of the country is controlled by prejudices thus invoked and clamor thus raised." After speaking of the bill under which the improvements were making, he continued: "The President was authorized to appoint some competent person to superintend the carrying out of the plan adopted. He appointed Mr. Downing. And who is he? One of the most accomplished gentlemen in his profession in the Union; a man known to the world as possessing rare skill as a 'rural architect' and landscape gardener, as well as a man of great scientific intelligence. * * * * I deny that he has neglected his duties, as the gentleman from Tennessee has charged. Instead of being here only three days in the month, he has been here vigilantly discharging his duties at all times when those duties required him to be here. He has superintended, directed, and carried out the plan adopted, as fully as the funds appropriated have enabled him to do. If all the officers of the Government had been as conscientious and scrupulous in the discharge of their duties as he has been since his appointment, there would be no ground for reproaches against those who have control of the Government"

Mr. Downing was annoyed by this continual carping and bickering, and anxious to have the matter definitely arranged, he requested the President to summon the Cabinet. The Secretaries assembled, and Mr. Downing was presented. He explained the case as he understood it, unrolled his plans, stated his duties, and the time he devoted to them, and the salary he received. He then added, that he wished the arrangement to be clearly understood. If the President and Cabinet thought that his requirements were extravagant, he was perfectly willing to roll up his plans, and return home. If they approved them, he would gladly remain, but upon the express condition that he was to be relieved from the annoyances of the quarrel. The President and Cabinet agreed that his plans were the best, and his demands reasonable; and the work went on in peace from that time.

The year 1852 opened upon Downing, in the garden where he had played and dreamed alone, while the father tended the trees; and to which he had clung, with indefeasible instinct, when the busy mother had suggested that her delicate boy would thrive better as a drygoods clerk. He was just past his thirty-sixth birth-day, and the Fishkill mountains, that had watched the boy departing for the academy where he was to show no sign of his power, now beheld him, in the bloom of manhood, honored at home and abroad—no man, in fact, more honored at home than he. Yet the honor sprang from the work that had been achieved in that garden. It was there he had thought, and studied, and observed. It was to that home he returned from his little excursions, to ponder upon the new things he had seen and heard, to try them by the immutable principles of taste, and to test them by rigorous proofs. It was from that home that he looked upon the landscape which, as it allured his youth, now satisfied his manhood. The mountains, upon whose shoreward slope his wife was born under the blossoming locusts on the very day on which he was born in the Newburgh garden, smiled upon his success and shared it. He owed them a debt he never disavowed. Below his house flowed the river of which he so proudly wrote in the preface to the "Fruit-Trees"—"A man born on the banks of one of the noblest and most fruitful rivers in America, and whose best days have been spent in gardens and orchards, may perhaps be pardoned for talking about fruit-trees." Over the gleaming bay which the river's expansion at Newburgh forms, glided the dazzling summer days; or the black thunder-gusts swept suddenly out from the bold highlands of West Point; or the winter landscape lay calm around the garden. From his windows he saw all the changing glory of the year. New-York was of easy access by the steamers that constantly passed to and from Albany and the river towns, and the railroad brought the city within three hours of his door. It brought constant visitors also, from the city and beyond; and scattered up and down the banks of the Hudson were the beautiful homes of friends, with whom he was constantly in the exchange of the most unrestrained hospitality. He added to his house the working-room communicating with the library by the mysterious door, and was deeply engaged in the planning and building of country-houses in every direction. Among these I may mention, as among the last and finest, the summer residence of Daniel Parish, Esq., at Newport, R. I. Mr. Downing knew that Newport was the great social exchange of the country, that men of wealth and taste yearly assembled there, and that a fine house of his designing erected there would be of the greatest service to his art. This house is at once simple, massive, and graceful, as becomes the spot. It is the work of an artist, in the finest sense, harmonious with the bare cliff and the sea. But even where his personal services were not required, his books were educating taste, and his influence was visible in hundreds of houses that he had never seen. He edited, during this year, Mrs. Loudon's Gardening for Ladies, which was published by Mr. John Wiley. No man was a more practically useful friend to thousands who did not know him. Yet if, at any time, while his house was full of visitors, business summoned him, as it frequently did, he slipped quietly out of the gate, left the visitors to a care as thoughtful and beautiful as his own, and his house was made their home for the time they chose to remain. Downing was in his thirty-seventh year, in the fulness of his fame and power. The difficulties of the failure were gradually disappearing behind him like clouds rolling away. He stood in his golden prime, as in his summer garden; the Future smiled upon him like the blue Fishkill hills beyond the river. That Future, also, lay beyond the river.

At the end of June, 1852, I went to pass a few days with him. He held an annual feast of roses with as many friends as he could gather and his house could hold. The days of my visit had all the fresh sweetness of early summer, and the garden and the landscape were fuller than ever of grace and beauty. It was an Arcadian chapter, with the roses and blossoming figs upon the green-house wall, and the music by moonlight, and reading of songs, and tales, and games upon the lawn, under the Warwick vase. Boccaccio's groups in their Fiesole garden, were not gayer; nor the blithe circle of a summer's day upon Sir Walter Vivian's lawn. Indeed it was precisely in Downing's garden that the poetry of such old traditions became fact—or rather the fact was lifted into that old poetry. He had achieved in it the beauty of an extreme civilization, without losing the natural, healthy vigor of his country and time.

One evening—the moon was full—we crossed in a rowboat to the Fishkill shore, and floated upon the gleaming river under the black banks of foliage to a quaint old country-house, in whose small library the Society of the Cincinnati was formed, at the close of the Revolution, and in whose rooms a pleasant party was gathered that summer evening. The doors and windows were open. We stood in the rooms or loitered upon the piazza, looking into the unspeakable beauty of the night. A lady was pointed out to me as the heroine of a romantic history—a handsome woman, with the traces of hard experience in her face, standing in that little peaceful spot of summer moonlight, as a child snatching a brief dream of peace between spasms of mortal agony. As we returned at midnight across the river, Downing told us more of the stranger lady, and of his early feats of swimming from Newburgh to Fishkill; and so we drifted homeward upon the oily calm with talk, and song, and silence—a brief, beautiful voyage upon the water, where the same summer, while yet unfaded, should see him embarked upon a longer journey. In these last days he was the same generous, thoughtful, quiet, effective person I had always found him. Friends peculiarly dear to him were in his house. The Washington work was advancing finely: he was much interested in his Newport plans, and we looked forward to a gay meeting there in the later summer. The time for his monthly trip to Washington arrived while I was still his guest. "We shall meet in Newport," I said. "Yes," he an swered, "but you must stay and keep house with my wife until I return."

I was gone before he reached home again, but, with many who wished to consult him about houses they were building, and with many whom he honored and wished to know, awaited his promised visit at Newport.

Mr. Downing had intended to leave Newburgh with his wife upon Tuesday, the 27th of July, when they would have taken one of the large river steamers for New-York. But his business prevented his leaving upon that day, and it was postponed to Wednesday, the 28th of July, on which day only the two smaller boats, the "Henry Clay" and the "Armenia" were running. Upon reaching the wharf, Mr. and Mrs. Downing met her mother, Mrs. De Wint, with her youngest son and daughter, and the lady who had been pointed out as the heroine of a tragedy. But this morning she was as sunny as the day, which was one of the loveliest of summer.

The two steamers were already in sight, coming down the river, and there was a little discussion in the party as to which they would take. But the "Henry Clay" was the largest and reached the wharf first. Mr. Downing and his party embarked, and soon perceived that the two boats were desperately racing. The circumstance was, however, too common to excite any apprehension in the minds of the party, or even to occasion remark. They sat upon the deck enjoying the graceful shores that fled by them—a picture on the air. Mr. Downing was engaged in lively talk with his companion, who had never been to Newport and was very curious to see and share its brilliant life. They had dined, and the boat was within twenty miles of New-York, in a broad reach of the river between the Palisades and the town of Yonkers, when Mrs. Downing observed a slight smoke blowing toward them from the centre of the boat. She spoke of it, rose, and said they had better go into the cabin. Her husband replied, no, that they were as safe where they then were as any where. Mrs. Downing, however, went into the cabin where her mother was sitting, knitting, with her daughter by her side. There was little time to say any thing. The smoke rapidly increased ; all who could reach it hurried into the cabin. The thickening smoke poured in after the crowd, who were nearly suffocated.

The dense mass choked the door, and Mr. Downing's party instinctively rushed to the cabin windows to escape. They climbed through them to the narrow passage between the cabin and the bulwarks of the boat, the crowd pressing heavily, shouting, crying, despairing, and suffocating in the smoke that now fell upon them in black clouds. Suddenly Mr. Downing said, "They are running her ashore, and we shall all be taken off." He led them round to the stern of the boat, thinking to escape more readily from the other side, but there saw a person upon the shore waving them back, so they returned to their former place. The flames began now to crackle and roar as they crept along the woodwork from the boiler, and the pressure of the throng toward the stern was frightful. Mr. Downing was seen by his wife to step upon the railing, with his coat tightly buttoned, ready for a spring upon the upper deck. At that moment she was borne away by the crowd and saw him no more. Their friend, who had been conversing with Mr. Downing, was calm but pale with alarm. "What will become of us?" said one of these women, in this frightful extremity of peril, as they held each other's hands and were removed from all human help. "May God have mercy upon us," answered the other.

Upon the instant they were separated by the swaying crowd, but Mrs. Downing still kept near her mother, and sister, and brother. The flames were now within three yards of them, and her brother said, "We must get overboard." Yet she still held some books and a parasol in her hand, not yet able to believe that this was Death creeping along the deck. She turned and looked for her husband. She could not see him and called his name. Her voice was lost in that wild whirl and chaos of frenzied despair, and her brother again said to her, "You must get overboard." In that moment the daughter looked upon the mother—the mother, who had said to her daughter's husband when he asked her hand, "She has been the comfort of her mother's heart, and the solace of her hours," and she saw that her mother's face was "full of the terrible reality and inevitable necessity" that awaited them. The crowd choked them, the flames darted toward them; the brother helped them upon the railing and they leaped into the water.

Mrs. Downing stretched out her hands, and grasped two chairs that floated near her, and lying quietly upon her back, was buoyed up by the chairs; then seizing another that was passing her, and holding two in one hand and one in the other, she floated away from the smoking and blazing wreck, from the shrieking and drowning crowd, past the stern of the boat that lay head in to the shore, past the blackened fragments, away from the roaring death struggle into the calm water of the river, calling upon God to save her. She could see the burning boat below her, three hundred yards, perhaps, but the tide was coming in, and after floating some little distance up the river, a current turned her directly toward the shore. Where the water was yet too deep for her to stand, she was grasped by a man, drawn toward the bank, and there, finding that she could stand, she was led out of the water by two men. With the rest of the bewildered, horror-stunned people, she walked up and down the margin of the river looking for her husband. Her brother and sister met her as she walked here—a meeting more sad than joyful. Still the husband did not come, nor the mother, nor that friend who had implored the mercy of God. Mrs. Downing was sure that her husband was safe. He had come ashore above—he was still floating somewhere—he had been picked up—he had swam out to some sloop in the river—he was busy rescuing the drowning—he was doing his duty somewhere—he could not be lost.

She was persuaded into a little house, where she sat at a window until nightfall, watching the wreck and the confusion. Then she was taken home upon the railroad. The neighbors and friends came to her to pass the night. They sat partly in the house and partly stood watching at the door and upon the piazza, waiting for news from the messengers who came constantly from the wreck. Mr. Vaux and others left directly for the wreck, and remained there until the end. The wife clung to her hope, but lay very ill, in the care of the physician. The day dawned over that blighted garden, and in the afternoon they told her that the body of her husband had been found, and they were bringing it home. A young woman who had been saved from the wreck and sat trembling in the house, then said what until then it had been impossible for her to say, that, at the last moment, Mr. Downing had told her how to sustain herself in the water, but that before she was compelled to leap, she saw him struggling in the river with his friend and others clinging to him. Then she heard him utter a prayer to God, and saw him no more.

Another had seen him upon the upper deck, probably just after his wife lost sight of him, throwing chairs into the river to serve as supports; nor is it too improbable that the chairs upon which his wife floated to shore were among those he had so thoughtfully provided.

In the afternoon, they brought him home, and laid him in his library. A terrific storm burst over the river and crashed among the hills, and the wild sympathy of nature surrounded that blasted home. But its master lay serene in the peace of the last prayer he uttered. Loving hands had woven garlands of the fragrant blossoms of the Cape jessamine, the sweet clematis, and the royal roses he loved so well. The next morning was calm and bright, and he was laid in the graveyard, where his father and mother lie. The quiet Fishkill mountains, that won the love of the shy boy in the garden, now watch the grave of the man, who was buried, not yet thirty-seven years old, but with great duties done in this world, and with firm faith in the divine goodness.

"Unwatch'd, the garden bough shall sway,
The tender blossom flutter down,
Unloved, that beech will gather brown,
This maple burn itself away;

"Unloved, the sun-flower, shining fair
Ray round with flame her disk of seed,
And many a rose-carnation feed
With summer spice the humming air.

"Unloved, by many a sandy bar
The brook shall babble down the plain,
At noon, or when the lesser wain
Is twisting round the polar star;

"Uncared for, gird the windy grove,
And flood the haunts of hern and crake;

Or into silver arrows break,
The sailing moon in creek and cove;

"Till from the garden and the wild,
A fresh association blow,
And year by year, the landscape grow
Familiar to the stranger's child;

"As, year by year, the laborer tills
His wonted glebe, or lops the glades;
And year by year our memory fades
From all the circle of the hills."

A LETTER FROM MISS BREMER.

TO THE FRIENDS OF A. J. DOWNING.

STOCKHOLM, November, 1852.

HERE, before me, are the pages on which a noble and refined spirit has breathed his mind. He is gone, he breathes no more on earth to adorn and ennoble it ; but in these pages his mind still speaks to us—his eye, his discerning spirit still guides and directs us. Thank God, there is immortality even on earth ! Thank God, the work of the good, the word of the noble and intelligent, has in it seeds of eternal growth !

Friends of my friend, let us rejoice, while we weep, that we still have so much of him left, so much of him with us, to learn by, to beautify our homes, our loves, our lives !

Let us be thankful that we can turn to these pages, which bear his words and works, and again there enjoy his conversation—the peculiar glances of his mind and eye at the objects of life ; let us thank the Giver of all good things for the gift of such a mind as his to this imperfect world ; for he understood and knew *the perfect*, and worked for perfection wherever his word or work could reach. But not as that personage ascribed to Shakspeare, to whom it is said : " You seem to me somewhat surly and critical," and who answers, "It is that I have early seen the perfect beauty."

Our friend had—even he—early seen the perfect beauty, but he was not surly when he saw what was not so. His criticism, unflinching as was his eye, looked upon things imperfect or mistaken with a quiet rebuke, more of commiseration than of scorn. A smile of gentle, good-humored sarcasm, or a simple, earnest statement of the truth, were his modes of condemnation, and the beauty of the Ideal and his faith in its power would, as a heavenly light, pierce through his frown. So the real diamond will, by a ray of superior power, criticize the false one, and make it darken and shrink into nothingness.

Oh! let me speak of my friend to you, his friends, though you saw him more and knew him for a longer time than I, the stranger, who came to his home and went, as a passing bird. Let me speak of him to you, for, though you saw him more and knew him longer, I loved him better than all, save *one*—the sweet wife who made all his days days of peace and pleasantness. And the eye of love is clairvoyant. Let me plead also with you my right as a *stranger;* for the stranger comes to a new world with fresh eyes, as those accustomed to snowy climates would be more alive to the peculiar beauty of tropical life, than those who see it every day. And it was so that, when I saw him, our departed friend, I became aware of a kind of individual beauty and finish, that I had little anticipated to find in the New World, and indeed, had never seen before, any where.

At war with the elegant refinements and beauties of life, to which I was secretly bound by strong sympathies, but which I looked upon as Samson should have looked upon Delilah, and in love with the ascetic severities of life, with

St John and St. Theresa,—I used to have a little pride in my disdain of things that the greater part of the world look upon as most desirable. Still, I could not but believe that things beautiful and refined—yea, even the luxuries of life, had a right to citizenship in the kingdom of God. And I had said to myself, as the young Quakeress said to her mother, when reproached by her for seeking more the gayeties of this world than the things made of God;

"*He* made the flowers and the rainbow."

But again, the saints and the Puritans after them, had said, "Beauty is Temptation," and so it has been at all times.

When I came to the New World, I was met on the shore by A. J. Downing, who had invited me to his house. By some of his books that I had seen, as well as by his letters, I knew him to be a man of a refined and noble mind. When I saw him, I was struck, as we are by a natural object of uncommon cast or beauty. He took me gently by the hand, and led me to his home. That he became to me as a brother,—that his discerning eye and mind guided my untutored spirit with a careless grace, but not the less impressively, to look upon things and persons most influential and leading in the formation of the life and mind of the people of the United States, was much to me; that he became to me a charming friend, whose care and attention followed me every where during my pilgrimage,—that he made a new summer life, rich with the charm of America's Indian summer, come in my heart, though the affection with which he inspired me, was much to me; yet what was still more, was, that in him I learned to understand a new nature, and through him, to appreciate a new realm of life.

You will understand this easily from what I have just stated, and when you think of him, and look on these pages where he has written down his individual mind; for if ever writer incarnated his very nature in his work, truly and entirely, it was done by A. J. Downing. And if his words and works have won authority all over the United States, wherever the mind of the people has risen to the sphere of intelligence and beauty; if under the snowy roofs of Concord in the Pilgrim State, as under the orange and oak groves of South Carolina, I heard the same words—"Mr. Downing has done much for this country;" if even in other countries I hear the same appreciation of his works, and not a single contradiction; it is that his peculiar nature and talent were so one and whole, so in one gush out of the hand of the Creator, that he won authority and faith by the force of those primeval laws to which we bow by a divine necessity as we recognize in them the mark of divine truth.

God had given to our friend to understand the true beauty; Christianity had elevated the moral standard of his mind; the spirit of the New World had breathed on him its enlarging influence; and so he became a judge of beauty in a new sense. The beauty that he saw, that inspired him, was no more the Venus Anadyomene of the heathen world still living on through all ages, even in the Christian one, mingling the false with the true and carrying abominations under her golden mantle. It was the Venus Urania, radiant with the pure glory of the Virgin, mother of divinity on earth. The beauty that inspired him was in accordance with all that was true and good, nor would he ever see the first severed from the two others. It was the beauty at home in the Kingdom of God.

In Mr. Downing's home on the Hudson I was impressed

with the chastity in forms and colors, as well as with the perfect grace and nobleness even in the slightest things. A soul, a pure and elevated soul, seemed to have breathed through them, and modelled them to expressions of its innermost life and taste. How earnest was the home-spirit breathing throughout the house and in every thing there, and yet how cheerful, how calm, and yet how full of life; how silent and yet how suggestive, how full of noble teaching!

When I saw the master of the house in the quiet of his home, in every day life, I ceased to think of his art, but I began to admire his nature. And his slight words, his smile, even his silence, became to me as revelations of new truths. You must see it also, you must recognize it in these pages, through which he still speaks to us; you must recognize in them a special gift, a power of *inspired*, not acquired, kind; what is acquired, others may acquire also, but what is given by the grace of God is the exclusive property of the favored one.

When I saw how my friend worked, I saw how it was with him. For he worked not as the workman does; he worked as the lilies in the field, which neither toil nor spin, but unconsciously, smilingly, work out their glorious robes and breathe forth their perfumes.

To me it is a labor to write a letter, especially on business; he discharged every day, ten or twelve letters, as easily as the wind carries flower-seeds on its wings over the land.

He never spoke of business—of having much to do; he never seemed to have much to do. With a careless ease and grace, belonging naturally to him, he did many things as if they were nothing, and had plenty of leisure and pleasantness for his friends. He seemed quietly and joyfully, without any effort, to breathe forth the life and light given him. It was his nature. In a flower-pot arranged by his hand, there was a silent lecture on true taste, applicable to all objects and arrangements in life. His slight and delicately formed hand, "la main âme," as Vicomte d'Agincourt would have named it, could not touch things to arrange them without giving them a soul of beauty.

Though commonly silent and retired, there was in his very presence something that made you feel a secret influence, a secret speaking, in appreciation or in criticism—that made you feel that *the Judge* was there; yea, though kind and benevolent, still *the Judge*, severe to the thing, the expression, though indulgent to the individual. Often when travelling with him on his beloved Hudson, and in deep silence sitting by his side, a glance of his eye, a smile, half melancholy, half arch, would direct my looks to some curious things passing, or some words would break the silence, slightly spoken, without accent, yet with meaning and power enough never to be forgotten. His appreciation of things always touched the characteristic points. He could not help it, it was his nature.

And so, while I became impressed with that nature, as a peculiar finished work of God, and the true spirit and aim of the refinements and graces of civilized life became through him more clear to me, I felt a very great joy to see that the New World—the world of my hopes—had in him a leading mind, through which its realm of beauty might rise out of the old heathenish chaos and glittering falsities, to the pure region where beauty is connected with what is chaste, and noble, and dignified in every form and application.

A new conception of beauty and refinement, in all

realms of life, belongs to the New World, the new home of the people of peoples, and it was given through A. J. Downing.

I am not sure of being right in my observation, but it seemed to me that in the course of no long time, the mind of my friend had undergone a change in some views that to me seem of importance. When I knew him at first he seemed to me a little too exclusive, a little aristocratic, as I even told him, and used to taunt him with, half in earnest, half in play—and we had about that theme some skirmishings, just good to stir up a fresh breeze over the smooth waters of daily life and intercourse. I thought that he still wanted a baptizing of a more Christian, republican spirit. Later I thought the baptizing had come, gentle and pure as heavenly dew.

And before my leaving America I enjoyed to see the soul of my friend rise, expand, and become more and more enlarged and universal. It could not be otherwise, a soul so gifted must scatter its divine gifts as the sun its rays, and the flower its seeds, over the whole land, for the whole people, for one and for all. The good and gifted man would not else be a true republican. It was with heartfelt delight that I, on my last visit to the home of my friend, did read in the August number of the Horticulturist these words in a leading article by him, on the New-York Park.

"Social doubters, who intrench themselves in the citadel of exclusiveness in republican America, mistake our people and its destiny. If we would but have listened to them, our magnificent river and lake steamers, those real palaces of the million, would have no velvet couches, no splendid mirrors, no luxurious carpets; such costly and rare appliances of civilization, they would have told us, could only be rightly used by the privileged families of wealth, and would be trampled upon and utterly ruined by the democracy of the country, who travel one hundred miles for half a dollar. And yet these our floating palaces, and our monster hotels, with their purple and fine linen, are they not respected by the majority who use them as truly as other palaces by their rightful sovereigns? Alas, for the faithlessness of the few who possess, regarding the capacity for culture of the many who are wanting.

"Even upon the lower platform of liberty and education that the masses stand in Europe, we see the elevating influences of a wide popular enjoyment of galleries of art, public libraries, parks and gardens, which have raised the people in social civilization and social culture, to a far higher level than we have yet attained in republican America. And yet this broad ground of popular refinement *must* be taken in republican America, for it belongs of right more truly here than elsewhere. It is republican in its very idea and tendency. It takes up popular education where the common school and ballot-box leave it, and raises up the working man to the same level of enjoyment with the man of leisure and accomplishment. The higher social and artistic elements of every man's nature lie dormant within him, and every laborer is a possible gentleman; not by the possession of money or fine clothes, but through the refining influence of intelligent and moral culture. Open wide therefore the doors of your libraries and picture-galleries, all ye true republicans! Build halls where knowledge shall be freely diffused among men, and not shut up within the narrow walls of narrower institutions. Plant spacious parks in your cities, and unloose their gates as wide as the gates of the morning, to the whole people. As there are no dark places at noonday, so education and culture—the true sunshine of the soul—will banish the plague-spots of democracy; and the dread of the ignorant exclusive who has no faith in the refinement of a republic, will stand abashed in the next century, before a whole people whose system of voluntary education embraces (combined with perfect individual freedom) not only common schools and rudimentary knowledge, but common enjoyments for all classes in the higher realms of art, letters, science, social recreations and enjoyments. Were our legislators wise enough to understand to-day the destinies of the New World, the gentility of Sir Philip Sidney made universal, would be not half so much a miracle fifty years hence in America, as the idea of a whole nation of laboring men reading and writing was, in his day, in England."

In one of my latest conversations with my friend, as he followed me down to the sea-shore, he spoke with great satisfaction of Miss Cooper's work, "Rural Hours," just published, and expressed again a hope I had heard him express more than once, that the taste for rural science and occupations would more and more be cultivated by the women of America. It was indeed a thing for which I felt most grateful, and that marked my friend as a true American man, namely, the interest he took in the elevation of woman's culture and social influence.

His was a mind alive to every thing good and beautiful and true, in every department of life, and he would fain have made them all, and every species of excellence, adorn his native country.

Blessed be his words and works, on the soil of the New World. As he was to his stranger friend, so may he be to millions yet to come in his land, a giver of Hesperian fruits, a sure guide through the wilderness!

When I was in Cuba, I remember being strongly impressed with a beauty of nature and existence, of which I hitherto had formed no idea, and that enlarged my conceptions of the realms of nature as well as of art. I remember writing of it to Mr. Downing, saying (if not exactly in the same words, at least to the same purport):

"You must come here, my brother, you must see these trees and flowers, these curves and colors, and take into your soul the image of this earthly paradise, while you are still on earth; and then, when God shall call you to that other world, to be there a gardener of His own, and you will have a star of your own to plant and perfect—as of course you will have—then you will mingle the palms and bamboo groves of Cuba with your own American oaks and elms, and taking models out of the beautiful objects of all nature and all climates, you will build houses and temples of which even 'The Seven Lamps of Architecture' give but distant ideas. You will build a cathedral, where every plant and every creature will be as a link rising upwards, joining in one harmonious Apocalypse revealing the glory of the Creator."

And now, when the call has come, and my friend is taken away, and much of the charm of this world is taken from me with him, I solace my fancy with the vision I thus anticipated. I see my friend working in some more perfect world, out of more perfect matter, the ideas of beauty and perfection which were life of his life, so to make it a fit abode for pure and heavenly spirits.

Why should it not be so? I think it *must* be so, as God's gifts are of immortal cost as well as the individual spirit to whom they were given. Is not all that is beautiful in nature, true and charming in art, based upon laws and affinities as eternal as the Spirit which recognizes them? Are these laws not manifested through the whole universe, from planet to planet, from sun to sun?

Verily, the immortal Spirit will ever reproduce its inward world, even if the scene of action is changed, and the stuff for working is changed. Every man will, as it was said by the prophet of old, "*awake in his own part*, when the days (of sublunary life) will be ended!"

I know that in my final hopes beyond this world, I shall look forward in prayer and hope, to a home among trees and flowers planted by the hand of my friend, there to see him again and with him to adore a new world—with him to adore!

FREDERIKA BREMER.

HORTICULTURE.

HORTICULTURE.

I.

INTRODUCTORY.

July, 1846.

BRIGHT and beautiful June! Embroidered with clusters of odorous roses, and laden with ruddy cherries and strawberries; rich with the freshness of spring, and the luxuriance of summer,—leafy June! If any one's heart does not swell with the unwritten thoughts that belong to this season, then is he only fit for "treasons, stratagems and spoils." He does not practically believe that "God made the *country*."

Flora and Pomona, from amid the blossoming gardens and orchards of June, smile graciously as we write these few introductory words to their circle of devotees. Happy are we to know that it is not to us a new or strange circle, but to feel that large numbers of our readers are already congenial and familiar spirits. Angry volumes of politics have we written none; but peaceful books, humbly aiming to weave something more into the fair garland of the beautiful and useful, that encircles this excellent old Earth.

To the thousands, who have kindly made our rural volumes part of their household library, we offer this new production, which begins to unfold itself now, in the midsummer of the year. In its pages, from month to month, we shall give them a collection of all that can most interest those whose feelings are firmly rooted in the soil, and its kindred avocations. The garden and the orchard; the hot-house and the conservatory; the park and the pleasure-grounds, all, if we can read them rightly, shall be made to preach useful lessons in our pages. All fruitful and luxuriant grounds shall we revel in, and delight to honor. Blooming trees, and fruitful vines, we shall open our lips to praise. And if nature has been over-partial to any one part of the globe, either in good gardens, fair flowers, or good fruits,—if she has any where lavished secret vegetable treasures that our cultivators have not yet made prizes of, we promise our readers to watch closely, and to give a faithful account of them. Skilful cultivators promise to make these sheets the repository of their knowledge. Sound practice, and ingenious theory will be continually developed and illustrated. The humblest cottage kitchen garden, as well as the most extended pleasure-grounds, will occupy the attention of the pens in our service. Beautiful flowers shall picture themselves in our columns, till even our sterner utilitarians shall be tempted to admire and cultivate them; and the honeyed, juicy gifts of Pomona shall be treated of till every one who reads shall discover that the most delicious products of our soil are no longer *forbidden* fruits.

Fewer, perhaps, are there, who have watched as closely as ourselves the zeal and enthusiasm which the last five years have begotten in American Horticulture. Every where, on both sides of the Alleghanies, are our friends rapidly turning the fertile soil into luxuriant gardens, and crying out loudly for more light and more knowledge. Already do the readers of rural works in the United States number more than in any cisatlantic country, except gardening England. Already do our orchards cover more acres than those of any other country. Already are the banks of the Ohio becoming famous for their delicate wines. Already are the suburbs of our cities, and the banks of our broad and picturesque rivers, studded with the tasteful villa and cottage, where a charming taste in ornamental gardening is rapidly developing itself. The patient toil of the pioneer and settler has no sooner fairly ceased, than our people begin to enter with the same zeal and spirit into the refinements and enjoyments which belong to a country life, and a country home. A fortunate range of climate—lands fertile and easily acquired, tempt persons even of little means and leisure into the delights of gardening. Where peaches and melons, the richest fruits of the tropics, are raised without walls—where apples and pears, the pride of the temperate zones, are often grown with little more than the trouble of planting them—who would not be tempted to join in the enthusiasm of the exclamation,

"Allons mes amis, il faut cultiver nos jardins."

Behold us then, with all this growing zeal of our countrymen for our beautiful and favorite art, unable to resist the temptation of commencing new labors in its behalf. Whatever our own feeble efforts can achieve, whatever our more intelligent correspondents can accomplish, shall be done to render worthy this monthly record of the progress of horticulture and its kindred pursuits. If it is a laudable ambition to "make two blades of grass grow where only one grew before," we shall hope for the encouragement, and assistance, and sympathy of all those who would see our vast territory made smiling with gardens, and rich in all that makes one's country worth living and dying for.

II.

HINTS ON FLOWER-GARDENS.

April, 1847.

WE are once more unlocked from the chilling embraces of the Ice-King! APRIL, full of soft airs, balm-dropping showers, and fitful gleams of sunshine, brings life and animation to the millions of embryo leaves and blossoms, that, quietly folded up in the bud, have slept the mesmeric sleep of a northern winter—APRIL, that first gives us of the Northern States our proper spring flowers, which seem to succeed almost by magic to the barrenness of the month gone by. A few pale snowdrops, sun-bright crocuses, and timidly blushing mezereums, have already gladdened us, like the few faint bars of golden and ruddy light that usher in the full radiance of sunrise; but APRIL scatters in her train as she goes out, the first richness and beauty that really belong to a temperate spring. Hyacinths, and daffodils, and violets, bespread her lap and fill the air with fragrance, and the husbandman beholds with joy his orchards gay with the thousand blossoms—beautiful harbingers of luscious and abundant crops.

All this resurrection of sweetness and beauty, inspires us with a desire to look into the *Flower-Garden*, and to say a few words about it and the flowers themselves. We trust there are none of "our parish," who, though they may not make flower-gardens, can turn away with impatient or unsympathizing hearts from flowers themselves. If there are such, we must, at the very threshhold of the matter, borrow a homily for them from that pure and eloquent preacher, Mary Howitt:

"God might have made the earth bring forth
Enough for great and small,
The oak tree and the cedar tree,
Without a flower at all.

"Our outward life requires them not—
Then wherefore had they birth?
To minister delight to man,
To beautify the earth.

"To comfort man, to whisper hope
Whene'er his faith is dim;
For who so careth for the flowers,
Will much more care for him!"

Now, there are many genuine lovers of flowers who have attempted to make flower-gardens—in the simplicity of their hearts believing it to be the easiest thing in the world to arrange so many beautiful annuals and perennials into "a living knot of wonders"—who have quite failed in realizing all that they conceived of and fairly expected when they first set about it. It is easy enough to draw upon paper a pleasing plan of a flower-garden, whether in the *geometric*, or the *natural*, or the "*gardenesque*" style, that shall satisfy the eye of the beholder. But it is far more difficult to plant and arrange a garden of this kind in such a way as to afford a *constant succession* of beauty, both in blossom and leaf. Indeed, among the hundreds of avowed flower-gardens which we have seen in different parts of the country, public and private, we cannot name half-a-dozen which are in any considerable degree *satisfactory*.

The two leading faults in all our flower-gardens, are the *want* of *proper selection* in *the plants themselves*, and a *faulty arrangement*, by which as much surface of *bare soil meets the eye* as is clothed with verdure and blossoms.

Regarding the first effect, it seems to us that the entire beauty of a flower-garden almost depends upon it. However elegant or striking may be the design of a garden, that design is made poor or valueless, when it is badly planted so as to conceal its merits, or filled with a selection of unsuitable plants, which, from their coarse or ragged habit of growth, or their remaining in bloom but a short time, give the whole a confused and meagre effect. A flower-garden, deserving the name, should, if possible, be as rich as a piece of embroidery, during the whole summer and autumn. In a botanical garden, or the collection of a curious amateur, one expects to see *variety of species*, plants of all known forms, at the expense of every thing else. But in a flower-garden, properly so called, the whole object of which is to afford a continual display of beautiful colors and delicious odors, we conceive that every thing should be rejected (or only most sparingly introduced), which does not combine almost perpetual blooming, with neat and agreeable habit of growth.

The passion for novelty and variety among the lovers of flowers, is as great as in any other enthusiasts. But as some of the greatest of the old painters are said to owe the success of their masterpieces to the few colors they employed, so we are confident the most beautiful flower-gardens are those where but few species are introduced, and those only such as possess the important qualities we have alluded to.

Thus among flowering shrubs, taking for illustration the tribe of *Roses*, we would reject, in our choice flower-garden, nearly all the old class of roses, which are in bloom for a few days and but once a year, and exhibit during the rest of the season, for the most part, meagre stems and dingy foliage. We would supply their place by Bourbons, Perpetuals, Bengals, etc., roses which offer an abundance of blossoms and fine fresh foliage during the whole growing season. Among *annuals*, we would reject every thing short-lived, and introduce only those like the *Portulaccas*, *Verbenas*, *Petunias*, *Mignonette*, *Phlox Drummondii*, and the like, which are always in bloom, and fresh and pretty in habit.*

After this we would add to the effect of our selection of perpetual blooming plants, by abandoning altogether the old method of *intermingling* species and varieties of all colors and habits of growth,

* Some of the most beautiful of the perpetual blooming plants for the flower-garden, are the *Salvias*, *Bouvardias*, Scarlet Geraniums, &c., properly green-house plants, and requiring protection in a pit or warm cellar in winter. "Bedded out" in May, they form rich flowing masses till the frosts of autumn.

and substitute for it the opposite mode of *grouping* or *massing* colors and particular species of plants. Masses of crimson and white, of yellow and purple, and the other colors and shades, brought boldly into contrast, or disposed so as to form an agreeable harmony, will attract the eye, and make a much more forcible and delightful impression, than can ever be produced by a confused mixture of shades and colors, nowhere distinct enough to give any decided effect to the whole. The effect of thus collecting masses of colors in a flower-garden in this way, is to give it what the painters call *breadth of effect*, which in the other mode is entirely frittered away and destroyed.

This arranging plants in patches or masses, each composed of the same species, also contributes to do away in a great degree with the second fault which we have alluded to as a grievous one in most of our flower-gardens—that of the exhibition of bare surface of soil—parts of beds not covered by foliage and flowers.

In a hot climate, like that of our summers, nothing is more unpleasing to the eyes or more destructive to that expression of softness, verdure, and gayety, that should exist in the flower-garden, than to behold the surface of the soil in any of the beds or parterres unclothed with plants. The dryness and parched appearance of such portions goes far to impair whatever air of freshness and beauty may be imparted by the flowers themselves. Now whenever beds are planted with a heterogeneous mixture of plants, tall and short, spreading and straggling, it is nearly impossible that considerable parts of the surface of the soil should not be visible. On the contrary, where species and varieties of plants, chosen for their excellent habits of growth and flowering, are planted in masses, almost every part of the surface of the beds may be hidden from the eye, which we consider almost a *sine qua non* in all good flower-gardens.

Following out this principle—on the whole perhaps the most important in all flower-gardens in this country—that there should, if possible, be no bare surface soil visible, our own taste leads us to prefer the modern English style of laying out flower-gardens upon a *groundwork of grass* or turf, kept scrupulously short. Its advantage over a flower-garden composed only of beds with a narrow edging and gravel walks, consists in the greater softness, freshness and verdure of the green turf, which serves as a *setting* to the flower beds, and heightens the brilliancy of the flowers themselves. Still, both these modes have their merits, and each is best adapted to certain situations, and harmonizes best with its appropriate scenery.

There are two other defects in many of our flower-gardens, easily remedied, and about which we must say a word or two in passing.

One of these is the common practice, brought over here by gardeners from England, of forming raised *convex* beds for flowering plants. This is a very unmeaning and injurious practice in this country, as a moment's reference to the philosophy of the thing will convince any one. In a *damp* climate, like that of England, a bed with a high convex surface, by throwing off the superfluous water, keeps the plants from suffering by excess of wet, and the form is an excellent one. In this country, where most frequently our flower-gardens fail from drouth, what sound reason can be given for forming the beds with a raised and rounded surface of six inches in every three feet, so as to throw off four-fifths of every shower? The true mode, as a little reflection and experience will convince any one, is to form the surface of the bed nearly level, so that it may retain its due proportion of the rains that fall.

Next to this is the defect of not keeping the walks in flower-gardens *full* of gravel. In many instances that we could name, the level of the gravel in the walk is six inches below that of the adjoining bed or border of turf. This gives a harsh and ditch-like character to the walks, quite at variance with the smoothness and perfection of details which ought especially to characterize so elegant a portion of the grounds as this in question. "Keep the walks brimful of gravel," was one of the maxims most strongly insisted on by the late Mr. Loudon, and one to which we fully subscribe.

We insert here a copy of the plan of the celebrated flower-garden of Baron Von Hügel, near Vienna. This gentleman is one of the most enthusiastic devotees to Horticulture in Germany. In the *Algemeine Garten Zeitung*, a detailed account is given, by the Secretary of the Imperial Horticultural Society of Vienna, of the residence and grounds of the Baron, from which we gather that they are not surpassed in the richness and variety of their botanical treasures by any private collection on the Continent. "A forest of Camellias almost makes one believe that he is in Japan." Some of these are 22 feet high, and altogether the collection numbers 1000 varieties. The hot-house devoted to *orchids*, or air plants, contains 200 varieties, and the various green-houses include equally rich collections of the exotics of various climates. Regarding the Baron's flower-garden itself, we quote the words of M. Peinter.

"But still another most delightful scene is reserved, which is a mosaic picture of flowers, a so-called Rococo garden. We have to thank Baron Von Hügel for giving the first example of a style, since pretty largely copied, both here and in the adjacent country. A garden, laid out in this manner, demands much cleverness and skill in the gardener, both in the choice and the arrangement of the flowers. He must also take care that, during the whole summer, there are no portions destitute of flowering plants. It is but justice to the Baron's head gardener, to affirm that he has completely accomplished this task, and has been entirely successful in carrying out the design or purpose of this garden. The connoisseur does not indeed see the usual collection of ornamental plants in this sea of flowers, but a great many varieties; and, in short, here, as everywhere else, the æsthetic taste of the Baron predominates. Beautiful is this garden within a garden, and hence it has become the model garden of Austria. Around it the most charming landscape opens to the view, gently swelling hills, interspersed with pretty villages, gardens and grounds."

In the plan of the garden, *a* and *b* are masses of shrubs; *c*, circular beds, separated by a border or belt of turf, *e*, from the serpentine bed, *d*. The whole of this running pattern is surrounded by a border of turf, *f*; *g* and *h* are gravel walks; *i*, beds, with pedestal and statue in the centre; *k*, small oval beds, separated from the bed, *l*, by a border of turf; *m*, *n*, *o*, *p*, irregular or arabesque beds, set in turf.

As a good deal of the interest of such a flower-garden as this, depends on the plan itself, it is evident that the beds should be filled with groups or masses, composed mostly of *low growing* flowers, as tall ones would interfere with, or break up its effect as a whole. Mr. Loudon, in some criticisms on this garden, in the *Gardener's Magazine*, says, that the running chain pattern of beds, which forms the outer border to the design, was originated in England, by the Duchess of Bedford, about the year 1800. "It is," he remarks, "capable of producing a very brilliant effect, by planting the circular beds, *c*, with bright colors, each alternating with white. For example, beginning at *c*, and proceeding to the right, we might have dark red, *white*, blue, *white*, yellow, *white*, scarlet, *white*, purple, *white*, and so on. The interlacing beds, *d*, might be planted on exactly the same principle, but omitting white. Proceeding to the right from the bed, *d*, which may be yellow, the next may be crimson, the next purple, the next orange, and so on."

This plan is by no means faultless, yet as it is admirably planted with ever-blooming flowers, and kept in the highest order, it is said to attract universal admiration, and is worthy of the examination of our floral friends. We should imagine it much inferior, in design and general effect, to the very beautiful new flower-garden at *Montgomery Place*, the seat of Mrs. Edward Livingston, on the Hudson, which is about double its size, and is undoubtedly one of the most beautiful and most tastefully managed examples of a flower-garden in America.

III.

INFLUENCE OF HORTICULTURE.

July, 1847.

THE multiplication of Horticultural Societies is taking place so rapidly of late, in various parts of the country, as to lead one to reflect somewhat on their influence, and that of the art they foster, upon the character of our people.

Most persons, no doubt, look upon them as performing a work of some usefulness and elegance, by promoting the culture of fruits and flowers, and introducing to all parts of the country the finer species of vegetable productions. In other words, they are thought to add very considerably to the amount of physical gratifications which every American citizen endeavors, and has a right to endeavor, to assemble around him.

Granting all the foregoing, we are inclined to claim also, for horticultural pursuits, a political and moral influence vastly more significant and important than the mere gratification of the senses. We think, then, in a few words, that Horticulture and its kindred arts, tend strongly to fix the habits, and elevate the character, of our whole rural population.

One does not need to be much of a philosopher to remark that one of the most striking of our national traits, is the SPIRIT OF UNREST. It is the grand energetic element which leads us to clear vast forests, and settle new States, with a rapidity unparalleled in the world's history; the spirit, possessed with which, our yet comparatively scanty people do not find elbow-room enough in a territory already in their possession, and vast enough to hold the greatest of ancient empires; which drives the emigrant's wagon across vast sandy deserts to California, and over Rocky Mountains to Oregon and the Pacific; which builds up a great State like Ohio in 30 years, so populous, civilized and productive, that the bare recital of its growth sounds like a genuine miracle to European ears; and which overruns and takes possession of a whole empire, like that of Mexico, while the cabinets of old monarchies are debating whether or not it is necessary to interfere and restore the balance of power in the new world as in the old.

This is the grand and exciting side of the picture. Turn it in another light, and study it, and the effect is by no means so agreeable to the reflective mind. The *spirit of unrest*, followed into the bosom of society, makes of man a feverish being, in whose Tantalus' cup *repose* is the unattainable drop. Unable to take root any where, he leads, socially and physically, the uncertain life of a tree transplanted from place to place, and shifted to a different soil every season.

It has been shrewdly said that what qualities we do not possess, are always in our mouths. Our countrymen, it seems to us, are fonder of no one Anglo-Saxon word than the term *settle.** It was the great object of our forefathers to find a proper spot to settle. Every year, large numbers of our population from the older States go west to settle; while those already west, *pull up*, with a kind of desperate joy, their yet new-set *stakes*, and go farther west to settle again. So truly national is the word, that all the business of the country, from State debts to the products of a "truck farm," are not satisfactorily adjusted till they are "settled;" and no sooner is a passenger fairly on board one of our river steamers, than he is politely and emphatically invited by a sable representative of its executive power, to "call at the captain's office *and settle!*"

Yet, as a people, we are never settled. It is one of the first points that strikes a citizen of the old world, where something of the dignity of repose, as well as the value of action, enters into their ideal of life. De Tocqueville says, in speaking of our national trait:

* Anglo-Saxon *sath-lian*, from the verb *settan*, to set, to cease from motion, to fix a dwelling-place, to repose, etc.

"At first sight, there is something surprising in this strange unrest of so many happy men, restless in the midst of abundance. The spectacle itself is, however, as old as the world. The novelty is to see *a whole people* furnish an exemplification of it.

"In the United States a man builds a house to spend his latter years in, and sells it before the roof is on; he brings a field into tillage, and leave other men to gather the crops; he embraces a profession, and gives it up; he settles in a place, which he soon after leaves, in order to carry his changeable longings elsewhere. If his private affairs leave him any leisure he instantly plunges into the vortex of politics; and if at the end of a year of unremitting labor, he finds he has a few days' vacation, his eager curiosity whirls him over the vast extent of the United States, and he will travel fifteen hundred miles in a few days, to shake off his happiness."

Much as we admire the energy of our people, we value no less the love of order, the obedience to law, the security and repose of society, the love of home, and the partiality to localities endeared by birth or association, of which it is in some degree the antagonist. And we are therefore deeply convinced that whatever tends, without checking due energy of character, but to develope along with it certain virtues that will keep it within due bounds, may be looked upon as a boon to the nation.

Now the difference between the son of Ishmael, who lives in tents, and that man who has the strongest attachment to the home of his fathers, is, in the beginning, one mainly of outward circumstances. He whose sole property is a tent and a camel, whose ties to one spot are no stronger than the cords which confine his habitation to the sandy floor of the desert, who can break up his encampment at an hour's notice, and choose a new and equally agreeable site, fifty miles distant, the next day—such a person is very little likely to become much more strongly attached to any one spot of earth than another.

The condition of a western emigrant is not greatly dissimilar. That long covered wagon, which is the Noah's ark of his preservation, is also the concrete essence of house and home to him. He emigrates, he "squats," he "locates," but before he can be fairly said to have a fixed home, the spirit of unrest besets him; he sells his "diggins" to some less adventurous pioneer, and, *tackling* the wagon of the wilderness, migrates once more.

It must not be supposed, large as is the infusion of restlessness in our people that there are not also large exceptions to the general rule. Else there would never be growing villages and prosperous towns. Nay, it cannot be overlooked by a careful observer, that the tendency "to settle" is slowly but gradually on the increase, and that there is, in all the older portions of the country, growing evidence that the Anglo-Saxon love of home is gradually developing itself out of the Anglo-American love of change.

It is not difficult to see how strongly horticulture contributes to the development of local attachments. In it lies the most powerful *philtre* that civilized man has yet found to charm him to one spot of earth. It transforms what is only a tame meadow and a bleak aspect, into an Eden of interest and delights. It makes all the difference between "Araby the blest," and a pine barren. It gives a bit of soil, too insignificant to find a place in the geography of the earth's surface, such an importance in the eyes of its possessor, that he finds it more attractive than countless acres of unknown and unexplored "territory." In other words, it contains the mind and soul of the man, materialized in many of the fairest and richest forms of nature, so that he looks upon it as tearing himself up, root and branch, to ask him to move a mile to the right or the left. Do we need to say more, to prove that it is the panacea that really "settles" mankind?

It is not, therefore, without much pleasurable emotion, that we have had notice lately of the formation of five new Horticultural societies, the last at St. Louis, and most of them west of the Alleghanies. Whoever lives to see the end of the next cycle of our race, will see the great valleys of the West the garden of the world; and we watch with interest the first development, in the midst of the busy fermentation of its active masses, of that beautiful and quiet spirit, of the joint culture of the earth and the heart, that is destined to give a tone to the future character of its untold millions.

The increased love of home and the garden, in the older States, is a matter of every-day remark; and it is not a little curious, that just in proportion to the intelligence and *settled* character of its population, is the amount of interest manifested in horticulture. Thus, the three most settled of the original States, we suppose to be Massachusetts, New-York and Pennsylvania; and in these States horticulture is more eagerly pursued than in any others. The first named State has now seven horticultural societies; the second, seven; the third, three. Following out the comparison in the cities, we should say that Boston had the most settled population, Philadelphia the next, and New-York the least so of any city in the Union; and it is well known that the horticultural society of Boston is at this moment the most energetic one in the country, and that it is stimulated by the interest excited by societies in all its neighboring towns. The Philadelphia society is exceedingly prosperous; while in New-York, we regret to say, that the numerous efforts that have been made to establish firmly a society of this kind have not, up to this time, resulted in any success whatever. Its mighty tide of people is as yet too much possessed with the spirit of business and of unrest."*

* "The New-York Horticultural Society" was organized in the spring of 1852, and is already in a flourishing condition.—Ed.

IV.

A TALK WITH FLORA AND POMONA.

September, 1847.

WE beg leave to inform such of our readers as may be interested, that we have lately had the honor of a personal interview with the distinguished deities that preside over the garden and the orchard, Flora and Pomona.

The time was a soft balmy August night; the scene was a leafy nook in our own grounds, where, after the toils of the day, we were enjoying the *dolce far niente* of a hammock, and wondering at the necessity of any thing fairer or diviner than rural nature, and such moonlight as then filled the vaulted heaven, bathed the tufted foreground of trees, the distant purple hills, and

"Tipt with silver all the fruit tree tops."

It was a scene for an artist; yet, as we do not write for the Court Journal, we must be pardoned for any little omission in the costumes or equipages of the divinities themselves. Indeed, we were so thoroughly captivated with the immortal candor and freshness of the goddesses, that we find many of the accessories have escaped our memory. Pomona's breath, however, when she spoke, filled the air with the odor of ripe apricots, and she held in her left hand a fruit, which we immediately recognized as one of the golden apples of the Hesperides, (of which she knew any gardener upon earth would give his right hand for a slip,) and which in the course of our interview, she acknowledged was the only sort in the mythological gardens which excels the Newtown Pippin. Her lips had the dewy freshness of the ruddiest strawberries raised by Mr. Longworth's favorite old Cincinnati market woman; and there was a bright sparkle in her eye, that assured us there is no trouble with the curculio in the celestial orchards.

But if we were charmed with the ruddy beauty of Pomona, we were still more fascinated by the ideal freshness and grace of Flora. She wore on her head a kind of fanciful crown of roses, which were not only dewy moss roses, of the loveliest shades imaginable, but the colors themselves changed every moment, as she turned her head, in a manner that struck us quite speechless with admiration. The goddess observing this, very graciously remarked that these roses were the *true perpetuals*, since they not only really bloomed always, but when plucked, they retained their brilliancy and freshness for ever. Her girdle was woven in a kind of green and silver pattern of jasmine leaves and starry blossoms, but of a species far more lovely than any in Mr. Paxton's Magazine. She held a bouquet in her hand, composed of sweet scented camellias, and violets as dark as sapphire, which she said her gardener had brought from the new planet Neptune; and unique and fragrant blossoms continually dropped from her robe, as she walked about, or raised her arms in gestures graceful as the swinging of a garland wooed by the west wind.

After some stammering on our own part, about the honor conferred on an humble mortal like ourselves—rare visits of the goddesses to earth, etc., they, understanding, probably, what Mr. Beecher calls our "amiable fondness for the Hudson," obligingly put us at our ease, by paying us some compliments on the scenery of the Highlands, as seen at that moment from our garden seat, comparing the broad river, radiant with the chaste light of the moon, to some favorite lake owned by the immortals, of whose name, we are sorry to say, we are at this moment entirely oblivious.

Our readers will not, of course, expect us to repeat all that passed during this enchanting interview. But, as we are obliged to own that the visit was not altogether on our own behalf, or rather that the turn of the discourse held by our immortal guests showed that it was chiefly intended to be laid before the readers of the Horticulturist, we lose no time in putting the latter *en rapport*.

Pomona opened the discourse by a few graceful remarks, touching the gratification it gave them that the moderns, down to the present generation, had piously recognized her guardian rights and those of her sister Flora, even while those of many of the other Olympians, such as Jupiter, Pan, Vulcan, and the like, were nearly forgotten. The wonderful fondness for fruits and flowers, growing up in the western world, had, she declared, not escaped her eye, and it received her warmest approbation. She said something that we do not quite remember, in the style of that good old phrase, of "making the wilderness blossom like the rose," and declared that Flora intended to festoon every cottage in America with double Michigan roses, Wistarias, and sweet-scented vines. For her own part, she said, her people were busy enough in their invisible superintendence of the orchard planting now going on at such a gigantic rate in America, especially in the Western States. Such was the fever in some of those districts, to get large plantations of fruit, that she could not, for the life of her, induce men to pause long enough to select their ground or the proper sorts of fruit to be planted. As a last resort, to keep them a little in check, she was obliged, against her better feelings, to allow the blight to cut off part of an orchard now and then. Otherwise the whole country would be filled up with poor miserable odds and ends from Europe—"Beurrés and Bergamots, with more sound in their French names, than flavor under their skins."

These last words, we confess, startled us so much, that we opened our eyes rather widely, and called upon the name of Dr. Van Mons, the great Belgian—spoke of the gratitude of the pomological world, etc. To our surprise, Pomona declared that she had her doubts about the Belgian professor—she said he was a very crotchety man, and although he had devoted his life to her service, yet he had such strange whims and caprices about *improving* fruits by a regular system of degeneration or running them out, that she could make nothing of him. "Depend upon it," she said, "many of his sorts are worthless,—most of them have sickly constitutions, and," she added, with some emphasis, snapping her fingers as she spoke, "I would not give one sound healthy seedling pear, springing up under natural culture in your American soil, for all that Dr. Van Mons ever raised!" [We beg our readers to understand that these were Pomona's words and not ours.] She gave us, after this, very special charge to impress it upon her devotees in the United States, not to be too much smitten with the love of new names, and great collections. It gave her more satisfaction to see the orchards and fruit room of one of her liege subjects teeming with the abundance of the few sorts of real golden merit, than to see whole acres of new varieties that have no other value than that of novelty. She said too, that it was truly amazing how this passion for collecting fruits—a genuine monomania—grew upon a poor mortal, when he was once attacked by it; so that indeed, if he could not add every season at least fifty new sorts from the continent, with some such outlandish names, (which she said she would never recognize,) as *Beurré bleu d'été nouveau de Scrowsywowsy*, etc., he would positively hang himself in a fit of the blues!

Pomona further drew our attention in some sly remarks that were half earnest and half satire, to the figure that many of these "Belgian pericarps" cut at those handsome levees, which her votaries among us hold in the shape of the great September exhibitions. She said it was really droll to see, at such shows as those of our two large cities, where there was a profusion of ripe and luscious fruit, that she would have been proud of in her own celestial orchards—to see there intermingled some hundred or so mean looking, hard green pears, that never had ripened, or never did, would, or could ripen, so as to be palatable to any but a New Zealander. "Do solicit my friends there, for the sake of my feelings," said she, "to give the gentlemen who take such pleasure in exhibiting this degenerate foreign squad, a separate 'green room' for themselves." To this remark we smiled and bowed low, though we would not venture to carry out her suggestion for the world.

We had a delightful little chat with Flora, about some new plants which she told us grew in certain unknown passes in the Rocky Mountains, and mountainous parts of Mexico, that will prove quite hardy with us, and which neither Mr. Fortune nor the London Horticultural Society know any thing about. But she finally informed us, that her real object in making herself visible on the earth at present, with Madam Pomona, was to beg us to enter her formal and decided protest against the style of decorations called after her name, and which had, for several years past, made the otherwise brilliant AUTUMNAL HORTICULTURAL SHOWS in our quarter of the globe so disagreeable an offering to her. "To call the monstrous formations, which, under the name of temples, stars, tripods, and obelisks—great bizarre masses of flowers plastered on wooden frames—to call these after her name, 'Floral designs,' was," she said, "even more than the patience of a goddess could bear." If those who make them are sincerely her devoted admirers, as they profess to be, she begged us to say to them, that, unless they had designs upon her flow of youth and spirits, that had hitherto been eternal, she trusted they would hereafter desist.

We hereupon ventured to offer some apology for the offending parties, by saying they were mostly the work of the "bone and sinew" of the gardening profession, men with blunt fingers but earnest souls, who worked for days upon what they fancied was a worthy offering to be laid upon her altars. She smiled, and said the intention was accepted, but not its results, and hinted something about the same labor being performed under the direction of the more tasteful eye of ladies, who should invent and arrange, while the fingers of honest toil wrought the ruder outline only.

Flora then hinted to us, how much more beautiful flowers were when arranged in the simplest forms, and said, when combined or moulded into shapes or devices, nothing more elaborate or artificial than a *vase-form* is really pleasing. *Baskets*, moss-covered and flower-woven, she said, were thought elegant enough for Paradise itself. "There are not only baskets," continued she, "that are beautiful lying down, and showing inside a rich mosaic of flowers—each basket, large or small, devoted perhaps, to some one choice flower in its many varieties; but baskets on the tops of mossy pedestals, bearing tasteful emblems interwoven on their sides; and baskets hanging from ceilings, or high festooned arches—in which case they display in the most graceful and becoming manner, all manner of drooping and twining plants, the latter stealing out of the nest or body of the basket, and waving to and fro in the air they perfume." "Then there is the *garland*," continued our fair guest; "it is quite amazing, that since the days of those clever and harmonious people, the Greeks, no one seems to know any thing of the beauty of the garland. Now in fact nothing is more beautiful or becoming than flowers woven into tasteful garlands or chaplets. The form a *circle*—that emblem of eternity, so full of dread and mystery to you mortals—and the size is one that may be carried in the hand or hung up, and it always looks lovely. Believe me, nothing is prettier in my eyes, which, young as they look, have had many thousands of your years of experience, than a fresh, green garland woven with bright roses."

As she said this, she seized a somewhat common basket that lay near us, and passing her delicate fingers over it, as she plucked a few flowers from the surrounding plants, she held it, a picture of magical verdure and blossoms, aloft in the air over our heads, while on her arm she hung a garland as exquisitely formed and proportioned as if cut in marble, with, at the same time, all the airiness which only flowers can have. The effect was ravishing! simplicity, delicacy, gracefulness, and perfume. The goddess moved around us with an air and in an attitude compared with which the glories of Titian and Raphael seem tame and cold, and as the basket was again passing over our head, we were just reaching out our hand to detain the lovely vision, when, unluckily, the parti-colored dog that guards our demesne, broke into a loud bark; Pomona hastily seized her golden apple; Flora dropped our basket (which fell to the ground in its wonted garb of plain willow), and both vanished into the dusky gloom of the night shadows; at that moment, suddenly rising up in our hammock, we found we had been—dreaming.

V.

A CHAPTER ON ROSES.

August, 1848.

A FRESH bouquet of midsummer roses stands upon the table before us. The morning dew-drops hang, heavy as emeralds, upon branch and buds; soft and rich colors delight the eye with their lovely hues, and that rose-odor, which, every one feels, has not lost any thing of its divine sweetness since the first day the flower bloomed in that heaven-garden of Eve, fills the air. Yes, the flowers have it; and if we are not fairly forced to say something this month in behalf of roses, then was Dr. Darwin mistaken in his theory of vegetable magnetism.

We believe it was that monster, the Duke of Guise, who always made his escape at the sight of a rose. If there are any "outside barbarians" of this stamp among the readers of our "flowery land," let them glide out while the door is open. They deserve to be drowned in a butt of attar of rose—the insensibles! We can well afford to let them go, indeed; for we feel that we have only to mention the name of a rose, to draw more closely around us the thousands of the fairer and better part of our readers, with whom it is the type of every thing fair and lovely on earth.

"Dear flower of heaven and love! thou glorious thing
That lookest out the garden nooks among;
Rose, that art ever fair and ever young;
Was it some angel on invisible wing
Hover'd around thy fragrant sleep, to fling
His glowing mantle of warm sunset hues

O'er thy unfolding petals, wet with dews,
Such as the flower-fays to Titania bring?
O flower of thousand memories and dreams,
That take the heart with faintness, while we gaze
On the rich depths of thy inwoven maze;
From the green banks of Eden's blessed streams
I dream'd thee brought, of brighter days to tell
Long pass'd, but promised yet with us to dwell."

If there is any proof necessary that the rose has a diviner origin than all other flowers, it is easily found in the unvarying constancy of mankind to it for so many long centuries. Fashions there have been innumerable, in ornaments of all sorts, from simple sea-shells, worn by Nubian maidens, to costly diamonds, that heightened the charms of the proudest court beauty—silver, gold, precious stones—all have their season of favor, and then again sink into comparative neglect; but a simple rose has ever been and will ever be the favorite emblem and adornment of beauty.

"Whatsoe'er of beauty
Yearns, and yet reposes,
Blush, and bosom, and sweet breath,
Took a shape in roses." LEIGH HUNT.

Now the secret of this perpetual and undying charm about the rose, is not to be found in its color—there are bright lilies, and gay tiger-flowers, and dazzling air-plants, far more rich and vivid: it is not alone in fragrance,—for there are violets and jasmines with "more passionate sighs of sweetness;" it is not in foliage, for there are laurels and magnolias, with leaves of richer and more glossy green. Where, then, does this secret of the world's six thousand years' homage lie?

In its being a type of *infinity*. Of infinity! says our most innocent maiden reader, who loves roses without caring why, and who does *not* love infinity, because she does not understand it. Roses, a type of infinity, says our theological reader, who has been in the habit of considering all flowers of the field, aye, and the garden, too, as emblems of the short-lived race of man—"born to trouble as the sparks fly upward." Yes, we have said it, and for the honor of the rose we will prove it, that the secret of the world's devotion to the rose,—of her being the queen of flowers by acclamation always and for ever, is that the rose is a type of infinity.

In the first place, then, the rose is a type of infinity, because there is no limit to the variety and beauty of the forms and colors which it assumes. From the *wild rose*, whose sweet, faint odor is wasted in the depths of the silent wood, or the eglantine, whose wreaths of fresh sweet blossoms embroider even the dusty road sides,

"Starring each bush in lanes and glades,"

to that most perfect, full, rounded, and odorous flower, that swells the heart of the florist as he beholds its richness and symmetry, what an innumerable range of shades, and forms, and colors! And, indeed, with the hundreds and thousands of roses of modern times, we still know little of all the varied shapes which the plant has taken in by-gone days, and which have perished with the thousand other refinements and luxuries of the nations who cultivated and enjoyed them.*

All this variety of form, so far from destroying the admiration of mankind for the rose, actually increases it. This very character of infinity, in its beauty, makes it the symbol and interpreter of the

* Many of our readers may not be aware to what perfection the culture of flowers was once carried in Rome. During Cæsar's reign, so abundant had forced flowers become in that city, that when the Egyptians, intending to compliment him on his birthday, sent him roses in midwinter, they found their present almost valueless from the profusion of roses in Rome. The following translation of *Martial's* Latin Ode to Cæsar upon this present, will give some idea of the state of floriculture then. There can scarcely be a doubt that there were hundreds of sorts of roses known to, and cultivated by the Romans, now entirely lost.

"The ambitious inhabitants of the land, watered by the Nile, have sent thee, O Cæsar, the roses of winter, as a present, valuable for its novelty. But the boatman of Memphis will laugh at the gardens of Pharaoh as soon as he has taken one step in thy capital city; for the spring in all its charms, and the flowers in their fragrance and beauty, equal the glory of the fields of Pæstum. Wherever he wanders, or casts his eyes, every street is brilliant with garlands of roses. And thou, O Nile! must yield to the fogs of Rome. Send us thy harvests, and we will send thee roses."

affections of all ranks, classes, and conditions of men. The poet, amid all the perfections of the parterre, still prefers the scent of the woods and the air of freedom about the original blossom, and says—

"Far dearer to me is the wild flower that grows
Unseen by the brook where in shadow it flows."

The *cabbage-rose*, that perfect emblem of healthful rural life, is the pride of the cottager; the *daily China rose*, which cheats the window of the crowded city of its gloom, is the joy of the daughter of the humblest day laborer; the delicate and odorous *tea-rose*, fated to be admired and to languish in the drawing-room or the boudoir, wins its place in the affections of those of most cultivated and fastidious tastes; while the *moss-rose* unites the admiration of all classes, coming in as it does with its last added charm, to complete the circle of perfection.

Again, there is the *infinity of associations* which float like rich incense about the rose, and that, after all, bind it most strongly to us; for they represent the accumulated wealth of joys and sorrows, which has become so inseparably connected with it in the human heart.

"What were life without a rose!"

seems to many, doubtless, to be a most extravagant apostrophe; yet, if this single flower were to be struck out of existence, what a chasm in the language of the heart would be found without it! What would the poets do? They would find their finest emblem of female loveliness stolen away. Listen, for instance, to old Beaumont and Fletcher:

———"Of all flowers,
Methinks a Rose is best;
It is the very emblem of a maid;
For when the west wind courts her gently,
How modestly she blows and paints the sun
With her chaste blushes! When the north wind comes near her,
Rude and impatient, then, like chastity,
She locks her beauties in her bud again,
And leaves him to base briars."

What would the lovers do? What tender confessions, hitherto uttered by fair half-open buds and bouquets, more eloquent of passion than the *Nouvelle Heloise*, would have to be stammered forth in miserable clumsy *words!* How many doubtful suits would be lost—how many bashful hearts would never venture—how many rash and reckless adventurers would be shipwrecked, if the tender and expressive language of the rose were all suddenly lost and blotted out! What could we place in the hands of childhood to mirror back its innocent expression so truly? What blossoms could bloom on the breast of the youthful beauty so typical of the infinity of hope and sweet thoughts, that lie folded up in her own heart, as fair young rose-buds? What wreath could so lovingly encircle the head of the fair young bride as that of white roses, full of purity and grace? And, last of all, what blossom, so expressive of human affections, could we find at the bier to take the place of the rose; the rose, sacred to this purpose for so many ages, and with so many nations,

> ———"because its breath
> Is rich beyond the rest; and when it dies
> It doth bequeath a charm to sweeten death."
>
> BARRY CORNWALL.

The rose is not only infinite in its forms, hues, types, and associations, but it *deserves an infinite number of admirers.* This is the explanation of our desire to be eloquent in its behalf. There are, unfortunately, some persons who, however lovely, beautiful, or perfect a thing may be in itself, will never raise their eyes to look at it, or open their hearts to admire it, unless it is incessantly talked about.

We have always observed, however, that the great difficulty with those who like to talk about fruits and flowers is, when once talking, to stop. There is no doubt whatever, that we might go on, therefore, and fill this whole number with roses, rosariums, rosaries, and rose-water, but that some of our western readers, who are looking for us to give them a cure for the pear-blight, might cry out—"a blight on your roses!" We must, therefore, grow more systematic and considerate in our remarks.

We thought some years ago that we had seen that *ultima thule* —"a perfect rose." But we were mistaken! Old associates, familiar names, and long cherished sorts have their proper hold on our affections; but—we are bound to confess it—modern florists have coaxed and teased nature till she has given them roses more perfect in form, more airy, rich and brilliant in color, and more delicate and exquisite in perfume, than any that our grandfathers knew or dreamed of. And, more than all, they have produced roses—in abundance, as large and fragant as June roses—that blossom all the year round. If this unceasingly renewed perpetuity of charms does not complete the claims of the rose to *infinity*, as far as any plant can express that quality, then are we no metaphysician.

There is certainly something instinctive and true in that favorite fancy of the poets—that roses are the type or symbol of female loveliness—

"Know you not our only
Rival flower—the human?
Loveliest weight, on lightest foot—
Joy-abundant woman,"

sings Leigh Hunt for the roses. And, we will add, it is striking and curious that refined and careful culture has the same effect on the outward conformation of the rose that it has on feminine beauty. The *Tea* and the *Bourbon roses* may be taken as an illustration of this. They are the last and finest product of the most perfect culture of the garden; and do they not, in their graceful airy forms, their subdued and bewitching odors, and their refined and delicate colors, body forth the most perfect symbol of the most refined and cultivated Imogen or Ophelia that it is possible to conceive? We claim the entire merit of pointing this out, and leave it for some poet to make himself immortal by!

There are odd, crotchety persons among horticulturists, who correspond to old bachelors in society, that are never satisfied to love any thing in particular, because they have really no affections of their own to fix upon any object, and who are always, for instance, excusing their want of devotion to the rose, under the pretence that among so many beautiful varieties it is impossible to choose.

Undoubtedly there is an *embarras de richesses* in the multitude of beautiful varieties that compose the groups and subdivisions of the rose family. So many lovely forms and colors are there, dazzling the eye, and attracting the senses, that it requires a man or woman of nerve as well as taste, to decide and select. Some of the great rose-growers continually try to confuse the poor amateur by their long catalogues, and by their advertisements about "acres of roses." (Mr. Paul, an English nurseryman, published, in June last, that he had 70,000 plants in bloom at once!) This is puzzling enough, even to one that has his eyes wide open, and the sorts in full blaze of beauty before them. What, then, must be the quandary in which the novice, not yet introduced into the aristocracy of roses, whose knowledge only goes up to a "cabbage-rose," or a "maiden's blush," and who has in his hand a long list of some great collector—what, we say, must be his perplexity, when he suddenly finds amidst all the renowned names of old and new world's history, all the aristocrats and republicans, heroes and heroines of past and present times—Napoleon, Prince Esterhazy, Tippoo Saib, Semiramis, Duchess of Sutherland, Princesse Clementine, with occasionally such touches of sentiment from the French rose-growers, as *Souvenir d'un Ami*, or *Nid d'Amour* (nest of love!) &c. &c. In this whirlpool of rank, fashion, and sentiment, the poor novitiate rose-hunter is likely enough to be quite wrecked; and instead of looking out for a *perfect rose*, it is a thousand to one that he finds himself confused amid the names of princes, princesses, and lovely duchesses, a vivid picture of whose charms rises to his imagination as he reads the brief words "pale flesh, wax-like, superb," or "large, perfect form, beautiful," or "pale blush, very pretty;" so that it is ten to one that Duchesses, not Roses, are all the while at the bottom of his imagination!

Now, the only way to help the rose novices out of this difficulty, is for all the initiated to confess their favorites. No doubt it will be a hard task for those who have had butterfly fancies,—coquetting firs with one family and then with another. But we trust these horticultural flirts are rare among the more experienced of our gardening readers,—persons of sense, who have laid aside such follies, as only becoming to youthful and inexperienced amateurs.

We have long ago invited our correspondents to send us their "confessions," which, if not as mysterious and fascinating as those of Rousseau, would be found far more innocent and wholesome to our readers. Mr. Buist (whose new nursery grounds, near Philadelphia, have, we learn, been a paradise of roses this season), has already sent us his list of favorites, which we have before made public, to the great satisfaction of many about to form little rose-gardens. Dr. Valk, also, has indicated his preferences. And to encourage other devotees—more experienced than ourselves—we give our own list of favorites, as follows:

First of all roses, then, in our estimation, stands the BOURBONS (the only branch of the family, not repudiated by republicans). The most perpetual of all perpetuals, the most lovely in form, of all colors, and many of them of the richest fragrance; and, for us northerners, most of all, *hardy* and *easily cultivated*, we cannot but give them the first rank. Let us, then, say—

HALF A DOZEN BOURBON ROSES.

Souvenir de Malmaison, *pale flesh color.*
Paul Joseph, *purplish crimson.*
Hermosa, *deep rose.*
Queen, *delicate fawn color.*
Dupetit Thouars, *changeable carmine.*
Acidalie, *white.*

Souvenir de Malmaison is, take it altogether,—its constant blooming habit, its large size, hardiness, beautiful form, exquisite color, and charming fragrance,—our favorite rose; the rose which, if we should be condemned to that hard penance of cultivating but one variety, our choice would immediately settle upon. Its beauty suggests a blending of the finest sculpture and the loveliest feminine complexion.

Second to the BOURBONS, we rank the REMONTANTES, as the French term them; a better name than the English one—*perpetuals;* for they are by no means perpetual in their blooming habit, when compared with the Bourbons, China, or Tea roses. They are, in fact, June roses, that bloom two or three times in the season, whenever strong new shoots spring up; hence, no name so appropriate as *Remontante*,—sending up new flower shoots. We think this class of roses has been a little overrated by rose-growers. Its great merit is the true, old-fashioned rose character of the blossoms, —large and fragrant as a damask or Provence rose. But in this climate, *Remontantes* cannot be depended on for a constant supply of flowers, like Bourbon roses. Here are our favorite:

HALF A DOZEN REMONTANTES.

La Reine, *deep rose, very large.*
Duchess of Sutherland, *pale rose.*
Crimson Perpetual, *light crimson.*
Aubernon, *brilliant crimson.*
Lady Alice Peel, *fine deep pink.*
Madame Dameme, *dark crimson.*

Next to these come the CHINA ROSES, less fragrant, but *everlastingly* in bloom, and with very bright and rich colors.

HALF A DOZEN CHINA ROSES.

Mrs. Bosanquet, *exquisite pale flesh color.*
Madame Breon, *rose.*
Eugene Beauharnais, *bright crimson.*
Clara Sylvain, *pure white.*
Cramoisie Superieure, *brilliant crimson.*
Virginale, *blush.*

The TEA ROSES, most refined of all roses, unluckily, require considerable shelter and care in winter, in this climate; but they so richly repay all, that no rose-lover can grudge them this trouble. Tea roses are, indeed, to the common garden varieties what the finest porcelain is to vulgar crockery ware.

HALF A DOZEN TEA ROSES.

Safrano, *the buds rich deep fawn.*
Souvenir d'un Ami, *salmon, shaded with rose.*
Goubault, *bright rose, large and fragrant.*

Devoniensis, *creamy white.*
Bougere, *glossy bronze.*
Josephine Malton, *beautiful shaded white.*

We thought to give NOISETTES the go-by; but the saucy, rampant little beauties climb up and thrust their clusters of bright blossoms into our face, and will be heard. So here they are:

HALF A DOZEN NOISETTES.

Solfaterre, *bright sulphur, large.*
Jaune Desprez, *large bright fawn.*
Cloth of Gold, *pure yellow, fine.*
Aimee Vibert, *pure white, very free bloomer.*
Fellenberg, *brilliant crimson.*
Joan of Arc, *pure white.*

"Girdle of Venus! does he call this a select list?" exclaims some leveller, who expected us to compress all rose perfections into half a dozen sorts; when here we find, on looking back, that we have *thirty*, and even then, there is not a single moss rose, climbing rose, Provence rose, damask rose, to say nothing of "musk roses," "microphylla roses," and half a dozen other divisions that we boldly shut our eyes upon! Well, if the truth must come out, we confess it boldly, that we are worshippers of the EVERBLOOMING roses. Compared with them, beautiful as all other roses may be and are (we can't deny it), they have little chance of favor with those that we have named, which are a perpetual garland of sweetness. It is the difference between a smile once a year, and a golden temper, always sweetness and sunshine. Why, the everblooming roses make a garden of themselves! Not a day without rich colors, delicious perfume, luxuriant foliage. No, take the lists as they are—too small by half; for we cannot cut a name out of them.

And yet, there are a few other roses that *ought to be* in the smallest collection. That finest of all rose-gems, the *Old Red Moss*, still at the head of all moss roses, and its curious cousin, the *Crested Moss*, must have their place. Those fine hardy climbers, that in northern gardens will grow in any exposure, and cover the highest walls or trellises with garlands of beauty,—the *Queen of the Prairies* and *Baltimore Belle* (or, for southern gardens, say—*Laure Davoust*, and *Greville*, and *Ruga Ayrshire*); that finest and richest of all yellow roses, the double *Persian Yellow*, and half a dozen of the gems among the hybrid roses, such as *Chénédole*, *George the Fourth*, *Village Maid*, *Great Western*, *Fulgeus*, *Blanchefleur*; we should try, at least, to make room for these also.

If we were to have but three roses, for our own personal gratification, they would be—

Souvenir de Malmaison,
Old Red Moss,
Gen. Dubourg.

The latter is a Bourbon rose, which, because it is an old variety, and not very double, has gone out of fashion. We, however, shall cultivate it as long as we enjoy the blessing of olfactory nerves; for it gives us, all the season, an abundance of flowers, with the most perfect rose scent that we have ever yet found; in fact, the true *attar of Rose.*

There are few secrets in the cultivation of the rose in this climate. First of all, make the soil *deep;* and, if the subsoil is not quite dry, let it be well drained. Then remember, that what the rose delights to grow in is *loam* and *rotten manure*. Enrich your soil, therefore, with well-decomposed stable manure; and if it is too sandy, mix fresh loam from an old pasture field; if it is too clayey, mix river or pit sand with it. The most perfect *specific stimulus* that we have ever tried in the culture of the rose, is what Mr. Rivers calls *roasted turf*, which is easily made by paring sods from the lane sides, and half charring them. It acts like magic upon the little spongioles of the rose; making new buds and fine fresh foliage start out very speedily, and then a succession of superb and richly colored flowers. We commend it, especially, to all those who cultivate roses in old gardens, where the soil is more or less worn out.

And now, like the Persians, with the hope that our fair readers "may sleep upon roses, and the dew that falls may turn into rose-water," we must end this rather prolix chapter upon roses.

Plan of a Greenhouse.

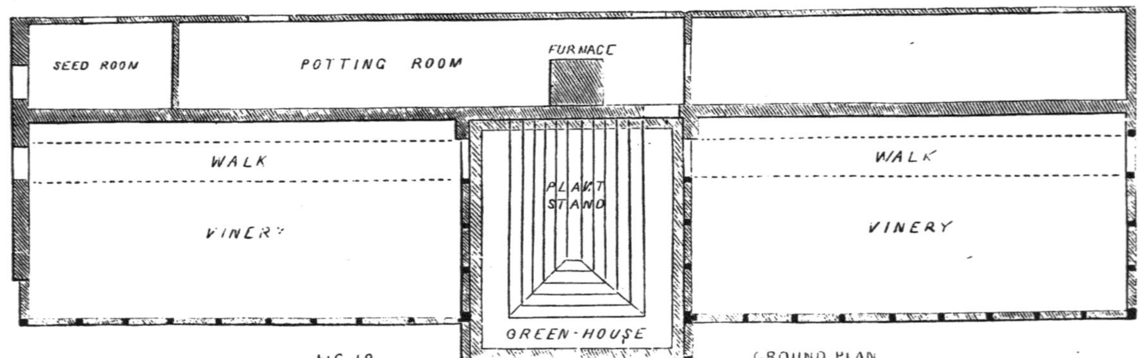

FIG. 18.

GROUND PLAN

VI.

A CHAPTER ON GREEN-HOUSES.

December, 1848.

DECEMBER, here in the north, is certainly a cold month. Yes, one does not look for primroses under the hedges, nor gather violets in the valleys, often, at this season. One must be content to enjoy a bright sky over head, and a frosty walk under foot; one must find pleasure in the anatomy of trees, and the grand outline of hills and mountains half covered with snow. And then, to be sure, there are the *evergreens*. What a pleasant thing it is to see how bravely they stand their ground, and bid defiance even to zero; especially those two fine old veterans, the *Hemlock* and the *White Pine*. They, indeed, smile defiance at all the attacks of the Ice King. It is not easy to make a winter landscape dull or gloomy where they stand, ready as they are at all times with such a sturdy look of wholesome content in every bough.

That must be an insipid climate, depend upon it, where there is "summer all the year round." In an ideal point of view,—that is, for angels and "beatitudes"—it is, nay, it must be, quite perfect. Their sensations never wear out. But to us, poor mortals, compounded as we are of such a moiety of clay, and alas, too many of us full of inconstancy,—always demanding variety—always looking for a change—wearying, as the angels do not, of things which ought to satisfy any reasonable creature for ever; no, even perpetual summer will not do for us. Winter, keen and frosty winter, comes to brace up our languid nerves. It acts like a long night's sleep, after a day full of exciting events. Spring comes back again to us like a positively new miracle! To watch all these black and leafless trees suddenly become draped with green again, to see the ice-bound and snow-clad earth, now so dead and cold, absolutely bud and grow warm with new life,—that, certainly, is a joy which never animates the soul of our fellow-beings of the equator.

"But the winter, the long winter—without verdure—without foliage—without flowers—all so bleak and barren." Softly, warm weather friend, open this little glazed door, out of the parlor, even now, while the icicles hang from the eaves, and what do you see? Truly a cheering and enlivening prospect, we think; a little miniature tropical scene, separated from the outer frost-world only by a few panes of glass, and yet as gay and blooming as the valley of Cashmere in June. What can be purer than these pure, spotless double white,—what richer than these rich, parti-colored Camellias? What more delicate than these Heaths, with their little fairy-like bells? What more fresh and airy than these Azaleas? What more delicious than these Daphnes, and Neapolitan Violets? Why, one can spend an hour here, every day, in studying these curious and beautiful strangers—belles of other climes, that turn winter into summer, to repay us for a little warmth and shelter. Is there not something exciting and gratifying in this little spectacle of our triumph of art over nature? this holding out a little garden of the most delicate plants in the very face of winter, stern as he is, and bidding him defiance to his teeth? Truly yes; and therefore, to one who has enough of vegetable sympathy in his nature to love flowers with all his or her heart—to love them enough to watch over them, to care for all their wants, and to feel an absolute thrill of joy as the first delicate bit of color mounts into the cheek of every blushing bud as it is about to burst open,—to such of our readers, we say, a GREEN-HOUSE is a great comfort and consolation!

There are many of our readers who enjoy the luxury of green-houses, hot-houses, and conservatories,—large, beautifully constructed, heated with hot water pipes, paved with marble, and filled with every rare and beautiful exotic worth having, from the birdlike air plants of Guiana to the jewel-like Fuchsias of Mexico. They have taste, and much "money in their purses." They want no advice from us; they have only to say "let us have green-houses," and they have them.

But we have also other readers, many thousands of them, who have quite as much natural taste, and not an hundredth part as much of the "needful" with which to gratify it. Yes, many, who look upon a green-house as a sort of crystal palace, which it requires a great deal of skill to construct, and untold wealth to pay for and keep in order. The little conversation that we hold to-day must be considered as addressed to this latter class; and we don't propose to show even them, how to build a green-house for nothing,—but how it may be built cheaply, and so simply that it is not necessary to send for the architect of Trinity Church to give them a plan for its construction.

The idea that comes straightway into one's head, when a green-house is mentioned, is something with a half roof stuck against a wall, and glazed all over,—what gardeners call a lean-to or shed-roofed green-house. This is a very good form where economy alone is to be thought of; but not in the least will it please the eye of taste. We dislike it, because there is something incomplete about it; it is, in fact, only half a green-house.

We must have, then, the idea, in a complete form, by having the whole roof—what in garden architecture is called a "span-roof"—which, indeed, is nothing more than the common form of the roof of a house, sloping both ways from the ridge pole to the eaves.

A green-house may be of any size, from ten to as many hundred feet; but let us now, for the sake of having something definite before us, choose to plan one 15 by 20 feet. We will suppose it at tached to a cottage in the country, extending out 20 feet, either on the south, or the east, or the west side; for, though the south is the best aspect, it will do in this bright and sunny climate very well in either of the others, provided it is fully exposed to the sun, and not concealed by trees at the sunny time of day.

Taking *fig.* 2 as the ground-plan, you will see that by cutting down the window in the parlor, so as to make a glazed door of it, you have the opening precisely where you want it for convenience, and exactly where there will be a fine vista down the walk as you sit in the parlor. Now, by having this house a little wider than usual, with an open roof, our plants have the light on all sides; consequently they are never *drawn*. Besides this, instead of a single walk down the front of the house, at the end of which you are forced to wheel about, like a grenadier, and return; you have the agreeable variety of making the entire circuit of the house, reaching the same spot again, with something new before you at every step. This walk is 2½ feet wide. The stage for the tall plants is a parallelogram, in the middle of the house, *c*, 7 feet wide; the shelf, which borders the margin of the house, *d*, is about 18 inches wide. This will hold all the small pots, the more delicate growing plants, the winter-flowering bulbs, and all those little favorites which of themselves like best to be near the light, and which one likes to have near the eye. It is quite incredible what a number of dozen of small plants this single shelf, running nearly all round, will hold.

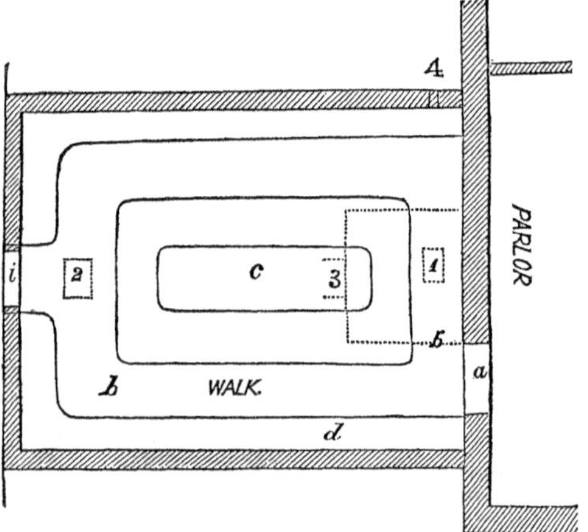

Fig. 2.—Plan of a small Green-House.

Now let us take a glance at the plan of the *section* of the greenhouse, *fig.* 3, which may be supposed to be a *slice* down through the end of it. The sides of the house are 8 feet high. They consist of a row of sashes (*f*), 3½ feet high, placed just below the plate that supports the roof, and a wall, *h*, on which these sashes stand. This may be a wall of brick or stone (if of the former, 8 inches thick is sufficient); or it may, when it is to be attached to a wooden dwelling, be built of wood—good cedar posts being set as supports 3½ feet deep, and lined with weather-boarding on each side, leaving a space of 12 inches wide, to be filled very compactly with charcoal dust, or dry tan.

FIG. 8. Section of the Same.

At the farther end of the house is a door, *i*.

The roof may rise in the middle so as to be from 12 to 15 feet high (in our plan, it is shown 12 feet). It is wholly glazed,—the sashes on either side *sliding* down in the rafters, so as to admit air when necessary. The rafters themselves to be placed about 4 feet apart. Is it not a neat little green-house—this structure that we have conjured up before you? It is particularly light and airy; and do you not observe that the great charm about it is, that every plant is within reach—always inviting attention, always ready to be enjoyed? Truly, it is not like those tall houses, with stages running up like stairs, entirely out of the reach of one's nose, arms or fingers. Do you not see, also, that you can very well water and take care of every plant yourself, if you are really fond of such things? Very well; now let us look a little into the way in which we are to keep this little place of pleasure always warm and genial for the plants themselves.

In the first place, we must inform our reader that we are not to have either a furnace with brick flues, or a boiler with hot water pipes. They are both excellent things; but we must have, at present, something simpler and more economical.

Every body, in the northern States, very well knows what an *air-tight stove* is; a most complete and capital little machine, whether for wood or coal; most easily managed, and giving us almost the whole possible amount of caloric to be got out of hickory or anthracite.

Now we mean to heat our little green-house with an air-tight stove, of good size; and we mean to heat it, too, in the latest and most approved system—nothing less than what the English call *Polmaise* —by which we are able to warm every part of the house alike; by which we shall be able to create a continual circulation of the warm air from one end of it, quite over the plants, to the other; and which, no doubt, they will mistake for a West India current of air every evening.

In order to bring this about, we must have an *air-chamber*. This also must be below the level of the green-house floor. It is not important under what part it is placed; it may be built wherever it is most convenient. In our plan (*fig.* 2), as there is a cellar under the parlor, we will put it next the cellar wall, so that there may be a door to enter it from this cellar. This air-chamber must be built of brick, say about 7 or 8 feet square (as represented by the dotted lines around *b*). The wall of this air-chamber should be two bricks thick at the sides and one brick at the ends, and all smoothly plastered on the inside. The top should be covered with large flagging stones; and upon the top of these, a course of bricks should be laid, which will form part of the floor of the walk in the green-house above. Or, if flagging is not to be had, then cover the whole with a low arch of brick work.

In this air-chamber we will place our air-tight stove, the smoke pipe of which must be brought back into the cellar again, so as to be carried into one of the chimney flues of the house. There must be a large sheet-iron or cast-iron door to the air-chamber, to enable us to feed the fire in the stove; and, in the top or covering of the air-chamber, directly in the middle of the walk (at 1), must be an opening 18 inches in diameter, covered with a grating, or register. Through this the hot air will rise into the house.

Now, both that we may heat the house easily and quickly, and also that we may have that continual *circulation* of air which is so wholesome for the plants, we must also have what is called a "*cold-air drain;*" it must lead from that end of the house farthest from the hot-air chamber, and therefore the coldest end, directly to the bottom of the air-chamber itself. We will put the mouth of this drain in the middle of the walk near the door, at 2, with a grating over it also. This drain shall be simply a long box, made of boards; and we will have it 1 foot by 2 feet, inside. From the mouth, 2, it shall lead along, in a straight line, just below the level of the floor, to B, where it descends so as to enter on a level with the floor of the hot-air chamber. We will also have a smaller box, or drain, for *fresh air*, leading from the bottom of the air-chamber to the open air through the foundation wall, at 4, to supply the house with fresh air. This air-pipe should be six inches in diameter, and there should be a *slide* in it to enable us to shut it up, whenever the weather is too cold to admit of its being open, without lowering the temperature of the house too much.

Now let us suppose all is ready, and that a fire is lighted in our air-tight stove. The air in the air-chamber becoming heated, it rises rapidly and passes into the green-house through the grated opening at 1. Very quickly, then, in order to supply the deficiency caused in the air-chamber, the air rushes through the cold-air drain. This makes a current from the coolest part of the house, at 2, towards the air-chamber; and, to make good again the lost air carried off from that end of the house, the warm stream which rises through the opening at 1, immediately flows over the tops of the plants towards the opposite end of the house, and, as it becomes cold again, descends and enters the mouth of the cold-air drain, at 2. By taking advantage of this simple and beautiful principle, that is to say the *rising* of warm air, we are able in this way to heat every part of the house alike, and have a constant bland zephyr passing over the plants.*

It is not easy to find any thing simpler or more easily managed than this way of heating a small green-house. In this latitude, a couple of cords of wood or a couple of tons of anthracite, will be sufficient for the whole winter; for, it must be remembered, that no matter how cold the day, the moment the sun shines there is not the slightest need of a fire; the temperature will then immediately begin to rise. Usually after bright days, which are abundant in our coldest winter months, we shall not need to light a fire till one,

* When a *coal* air-tight stove is used, there should be a water pan suspended over it. For a wood air-tight it is not necessary.

two, or sometimes three hours after sunset; and if our air-tight is one of good size, and constructed as it should be, so as to maintain a good fire for a long time, our last replenishing in the evening need not usually be later than ten o'clock; but we must, in this case, give a full supply of fuel for the night's consumption.

Every sensible person will, of course, use light outside shutters, for the roof and side glass of such a house as this. We slide them on at sunset, and take them off at sunrise; and by this means we not only save one-third of our fuel, but keep up a pleasant greenhouse temperature, without cold draughts at night. It is worth while to remember, too, that in glazing the roof, the most useful possible size for the glass is 4 by 6 inches, or, at the largest, 6 by 8 inches. The former answers the purpose perfectly, and is not only much less costly than large glass, but is also far less expensive to keep in repair; neither hail nor frost breaking the small panes, as they do the large ones.

As to the minor details, we will have a small cistern under the floor, into which the water from the roof can be conveyed for watering the plants. Beneath the centre stage (which may be partly concealed with lattice work), we may keep our dahlia roots, and a dozen other sorts of half hardy plants for the summer border, now dormant, and snugly packed quite out of sight.

We did intend, when we sat down, to give our novices a great deal of exceedingly valuable advice about the sorts of plants that they ought to cultivate in this glazed flower-garden. But we see that we are getting beyond the limits of a leader, and must not, therefore, weary those of our subscribers, who take no more interest in geraniums than we do in Irish landlords, with too long a parley on exotics.

We must have space enough, however, for a word or two more to beginners. Let them take our word for it—if they prefer an abundance of beautiful flowers to a *pot-pourri*, of every imaginable species that can be grown under glass, they had better confine themselves to a few really worthy and respectable genera. If they only want winter-blooming plants, then let them take *Camellias* and *Chinese Azaleas*, as the groundwork of their collection, filling in the interstices with daphnes, heaths, sweet-scented violets, and choice bulbs. For the spring, rely on everblooming roses,* and geraniums. If they also wish to have the green-house gay in summer, they must *shade* it (or wash the under side of the roof-glass with whiting), and grow *Fuchsias* and *Achimenes.* In this way, they will never be without flowers in abundance, while their neighbors, who collect every new thing to be heard of under the sun, will have more tall stalks and meagre foliage, than bright blossoms and odorous bouquets for their trouble.

* Nothing is more satisfactory than those fine Noisette roses, the *Lamarque* and *Cloth of Gold*, planted in an inside border, and trained up under the rafters of the green-house. In this way they grow to great size, and give a profusion of roses.

VII.

ON FEMININE TASTE IN RURAL AFFAIRS.

April, 1849.

WHAT a very little fact sometimes betrays the national character; and what an odd thing this national character is! Look at a Frenchman. He eats, talks, lives in public. He is only happy when he has spectators. In town, on the boulevards, in the *cafe*, at places of public amusement, he is all enjoyment. But in the country—ah, there he never goes willingly; or else, he only goes to sentimentalize, or to entertain his town friends. Even the natural born country people seem to find nature and solitude *ennuyant*, and so collect in little villages to keep each other in spirits! The Frenchman eats and sleeps almost any where; but he is never "at home but when he is abroad."

Look, on the other hand, at John Bull. He only lives what he feels to be a rational life, when he lives in the country. His country place is to him a little Juan Fernandez island; it contains his own family, his own castle, every thing that belongs to him. He hates the smoke of town; he takes root in the soil. His horses, his dogs, his trees, are not separate existences; they are parts of himself. He is social with a reservation. Nature is nearer akin to him than strange men. His dogs are truly attached to him; he doubts if his fellows are. People often play the hypocrite; but the trees in his park never deceive him. Home is to him the next best place to heaven.

And only a little narrow strait of water divides these two nations!

Shall *we* ever have a distinct national character? Will a country, which is settled by every people of the old world,—a dozen nations, all as distinct as the French and the English,—ever crystallize into a symmetrical form—something distinct and homogeneous? And what will that national character be?

Certainly no one, who looks at our comparative isolation—at the broad ocean that separates us from such external influences—at the mighty internal forces of new government and new circumstances, which continually act upon us,—and, above all, at the mighty vital force of the Yankee Constitution, which every year swallows hundreds of thousands of foreigners, and *digests* them all; no one can look reflectingly on all this, and not see that there is a national type, which will prevail over all the complexity, which various origin, foreign manners, and different religions bring to our shores.

The English are, perhaps, the most distinct of civilized nations, in their nationality. But they had almost as mixed an origin as ourselves,—Anglo-Saxon, Celts, Roman, Danish, Norman; all these apparently discordant elements, were fused so successfully into a great and united people.

That a hundred years hence will find us quite as distinct and quite as developed, in our national character, we cannot doubt. What that character will be, in all its phases, no one at present can precisely say; but that the French and English elements will largely influence it in its growth, and yet, that in morals, in feeling, and in heart, we shall be entirely distinct from either of those nations, is as clear to us as a summer noon.

We are not going into a profound philosophical dissertation on the political or the social side of national character. We want to touch very slightly on a curious little point that interests us; one that political philosophers would think quite beneath them; one that moralists would not trouble themselves about; and one that we are very much afraid nobody else will think worth notice at all; and therefore we shall set about it directly.

What is the reason American ladies don't love to work in their gardens?

It is of no use whatever, that some fifty or a hundred of our fair readers say, "we do." We have carefully studied the matter, until it has become a fact past all contradiction. They may love to "potter" a little. Three or four times in the spring they take a fancy to examine the color of the soil a few inches below the surface; they sow some China Asters, and plant a few Dahlias, and it is all over. Love flowers, with all their hearts, they certainly do. Few things are more enchanting to them than a fine garden; and *bouquets on their centre tables* are positive necessities, with every lady, from Maine to the Rio Grande.

Now, we certainly have all the *love of nature* of our English forefathers. We love the country; and a large part of the millions, earned every year by our enterprise, is spent in creating and embellishing country homes. But, on the contrary, our wives and daughters only love gardens as the French love them—for the results. They love to walk through them; they enjoy the beauty and perfume of their products, but only as amateurs. They know no more of that intense enjoyment of her who plans, creates, and daily watches the growth of those gardens or flowers,—no more of that absolute, living enjoyment, which the English have in out-of-door pursuits, than a mere amateur, who goes through a fine gallery of pictures, knows of the intensified emotions which the painters of those pictures experienced in their souls, when they gazed on the gradual growth and perfected splendor of their finest master-pieces.

As it is plain, from our love of the country, that we are not French at heart, this manifestation that we complain of, must come from our natural tendency to copy the social manners of the most polished nation in the world. And it is indeed quite wonderful how, being scarcely in the least affected by the *morale*, we still borrow almost instinctively, and entirely without being aware of it, so much from *la Belle France.* That our dress, mode of life, and intercourse, is largely tinged with French taste, every traveller notices. But it goes farther. Even the plans of our houses become more and more decidedly French. We have had occasion, lately, to make considerable explorations in the domestic architecture of France and England, and we have noticed some striking national peculiarities. One of these relates to the connection of the principal apartments. In a French house, the beau ideal is to have every thing *ensuite;*

all the rooms open into each other; or, at least, as many of the largest as will produce a fine effect. In an English house, every room is complete in itself. It may be very large, and very grand, but it is all the worse for being connected with any other room; for that destroys the privacy which an Englishman so much loves.

Does any one, familiar with the progress of building in the United States for the last ten years, desire to be told which mode we have followed? And yet, there are very few who are aware that our love of folding-doors, and suites of apartments, is essentially French.

Now our national taste in gardening and out-door employments, is just in the process of formation. Honestly and ardently believing that the loveliest and best women in the world are those of our own country, we cannot think of their losing so much of their own and nature's bloom, as only to enjoy their gardens by the *results*, like the French, rather than through the *development*, like the English. We would gladly show them how much they lose. We would convince them, that only to pluck the full-blown flower, is like a first introduction to it, compared with the life-long friendship of its mistress, who has nursed it from its first two leaves; and that the real zest of our enjoyment of nature, even in a garden, lies in our looking at her, not like a spectator who admires, but like a dear and intimate friend, to whom, after long intimacy, she reveals sweets wholly hidden from those who only come to her in full dress, and in the attitude of formal visitors.

If any one wishes to know how completely and intensely English women enter into the spirit of gardening, he has only to watch the wife of the most humble artisan who settles in any of our cities. She not only has a pot of flowers—her back-yard is a perfect curiosity-shop of botanical rarities. She is never done with training, and watering, and caring for them. And truly, they reward her well; for who ever saw such large geraniums, such fresh daisies, such ruddy roses! Comparing them with the neglected and weak specimens in the garden of her neighbor, one might be tempted to believe that they had been magnetized by the charm of personal fondness of their mistress, into a life and beauty not common to other plants.

Mr. Colman, in his European Tour, seems to have been struck by this trait, and gave so capital a portrait of rural accomplishments in a lady of rank he had the good fortune to meet, that we cannot resist the temptation of turning the picture to the light once more:

"I had no sooner, then, entered the house, where my visit had been expected, than I was met with an unaffected cordiality, which at once made me at home. In the midst of gilded halls, and hosts of liveried servants, of dazzling lamps and glittering mirrors, redoubling the highest triumphs of art and of taste; in the midst of books, and statues, and pictures, and all the elegancies and refinements of luxury; in the midst of titles, and dignitaries, and ranks allied to regal grandeur,—there was one object which transcended and eclipsed them all, and showed how much the nobility of character surpassed the nobility of rank, the beauty of refined and simple manners all the adornments of art, the scintillations of the soul, beaming from the eyes, the purest gems that ever glittered in a princely diadem. In person, in education and improvement, in quickness of perception, in facility and elegance of expression, in accomplishments and taste, in a frankness and gentleness of manner, tempered by a modesty which courted confidence and inspired respect, and in a high moral tone and sentiment, which, like a bright halo, seemed to encircle the whole person,—I confess the fictions of poetry became substantial, and the *beau ideal* of my youthful imagination was realized.

"In the morning I first met her at prayers; for, to the honor of England, there is scarcely a family, among the hundreds whose hospitality I have shared, where the duties of the day are not preceded by family worship; and the master and the servant, the parent and the child, the teacher and the taught, the friend and the stranger, come together to recognize and strengthen the sense of their common equality, in the presence of their common Father, and to acknowledge their equal dependence upon his care and mercy. She was then kind enough to tell me, after her morning's arrangements, she claimed me for the day. She first showed me her children, whom, like the Roman mother, she deemed her brightest jewels, and arranged their studies and occupations for the day. She then took me two or three miles on foot, to visit a sick neighbor; and, while performing this act of kindness, left me to visit some of the cottages upon the estate, whose inmates I found loud in the praises of her kindness and benefactions. Our next excursion was to see some of the finest, and largest, and most aged trees in the park, the size of which was truly magnificent; and I sympathized in the veneration which she expressed for them, which was like that with which one recalls the illustrious memory of a remote progenitor. Our next visit was to the green-houses and gardens; and she explained to me the mode adopted there, of managing the most delicate plants, and of cultivating, in the most economical and successful manner, the fruits of a warmer region. From the garden we proceeded to the cultivated fields; and she informed me of the system of husbandry pursued on the estate, the rotation of crops, the management and application of manures, the amount of seed sown, the ordinary yield, and the appropriation of the produce, with a perspicuous detail of the expenses and results. She then undertook to show me the yards and offices, the byres, the feeding stalls, the plans for saving, increasing, and managing the manure; the cattle for feeding, for breeding, the milking stock, the piggery, the poultry-yard, the stables, the harness-rooms, the implement-rooms, the dairy. She explained to me the process of making the different kinds of cheese, and the general management of the milk, and the mode of feeding the stock; and then, conducting me into the bailiff's house, she exhibited to me the Farm Journal, and the whole systematic mode of keeping the accounts and making the returns, with which she seemed as familiar as if they were the accounts of her own wardrobe. This did not finish our grand tour; for, on my return, she admitted me into her boudoir, and showed me the secrets of her own admirable housewifery, in the exact accounts which she kept of every thing connected with the dairy, the market, the table, and the drawing-room, and the servants' hall. All this was done with a simplicity and a frankness, which showed an absence of all consciousness of any extraordinary merit in her own department, and which evidently sprang solely from a kind desire to gratify a curiosity on my part, which, I hope, under such circumstances, was not unreasonable.

"A short hour after this brought us into another relation; for the dinner bell summoned us, and this same lady was found presiding over a brilliant circle of the highest rank and fashion, with an ease, elegance, wit, intelligence, and good humor, with a kind attention to every one's wants, and an unaffected concern for every one's comfort, which would lead one to suppose that this was her only and her peculiar sphere. Now I will not say how many mud-puddles we had waded through, and how many manure heaps we had crossed, and what places we had explored, and how every farming topic was discussed; but I will say that she pursued her object without any of that fastidiousness and affected deli-

4

cacy, which pass with some persons for refinement, but which, in many cases, indicate a weak, if not a corrupt mind. * * * *

"Now I do not say that the lady to whom I have referred was herself the manager of the farm; that rested entirely with her husband; but I have intended simply to show how gratifying to him must have been the lively interest and sympathy which she took in concerns which necessarily so much engaged his time and attention; and how the country would be divested of that dulness and *ennui*, so often complained of as inseparable from it, when a cordial and practical interest is taken in the concerns which belong to rural life. I meant also to show—and this and many other examples, which have come under my observation, emphatically do show—that an interest in, and familiarity with, even the most humble occupations of agricultural life, are not inconsistent with the highest refinements of taste, the most improved cultivation of the mind, and elegance, and dignity of manners, unsurpassed in the highest circles of society."

This picture is thoroughly English; and who do our readers suppose this lady was? Mr. Colman puts his finger on his lips, and declares that however much he may be questioned by his fair readers at home, he will make no disclosures. But other people recognize the portrait; and we understand it is that of the Duchess of Portland.

Now, as a contrast to this, here is a little fragment—a mere bit—but enough to show the French feeling about country life. It is from one of Madame de Sevigne's charming letters; and, fond of society as she was, she certainly had as much of love of the country as belongs to her class and sex on her side of the channel. It is part of a letter written from her country home. She is writing to her daughter, and speaking of an expected visit from one of her friends:

"It follows that, after I have been to see her, she will come to see me, when, of course, I shall wish her to find my garden in good order; my walks in good order—those fine walks, of which you are so fond. Attend also, if you please, to a little suggestion *en passant*. You are aware that haymaking is going forward. Well, I have no haymakers. I send into the neighboring fields to press them into my service; there are none to be found; and so all my own people are summoned to make nay instead. But do you know what haymaking is? I will tell you. *Haymaking is the prettiest thing in the world. You play at turning the grass over in a meadow; and as soon as you know that, you know how to make hay.*"

Is it not capital? We italicize her description of haymaking, it is so *Française*, and so totally unlike the account that the Duchess would have given Mr. Colman. Her garden, too; she wanted to have it *put in order before her friend arrived.* She would have shown it, not as an English woman would have done, to excite an interest in its rare and beautiful plants, and the perfection to which they had grown under her care, but that it might give her friend a pleasant promenade.

Now we have not the least desire, that American wives and daughters should have any thing to do with the *rough toil* of the farm or the garden, beyond their own household province. We delight in the chivalry which pervades this whole country, in regard to the female character, and which even foreigners have remarked as one of the strongest national characteristics.* But we would gladly have them seize on that happy medium, between the English passion for every thing out of doors, and the French taste for nothing beyond the drawing-room. Every thing which relates to the garden, the lawn, the pleasure-grounds, should claim their immediate interest. And this, not merely to walk out occasionally and enjoy it; but to know it by heart; to do it, or see it all done; to know

* M. Chevalier, one of the most intelligent of recent French travellers, says, in his work on this country—"Not only does the American mechanic and farmer relieve, as much as possible, his wife from all severe labor, all disagreeable employments, but there is also, in relation to them, and to women in general, a disposition to oblige, that is unknown among us, even in men who pique themselves upon cultivation of mind and literary education." * * * * * * *

"We buy our wives with our fortunes, or we sell ourselves to them for their dowries. The American chooses her, or rather he offers himself to her for her beauty, her intelligence, and the qualities of her heart; it is the only dowry which he seeks. Thus, while we make of that which is most sacred a matter of business, these traders affect a delicacy, and an elevation of sentiment, which would have done honor to the most perfect models of chivalry" the history of any plant, shrub, or tree, from the time it was so small as to be invisible to all but their eyes, to the time when every passer-by stops to admire and enjoy it; to live, in short, not only the in-door but the out-of-door life of a true woman in the country. Every lady may not be "born to love pigs and chickens" (though that is a good thing to be born to); but, depend upon it, she has been cut off by her mother nature with less than a shilling's patrimony, if she does not love trees, flowers, gardens, and nature, as if they were all part of herself.

We half suspect, if the truth must be told, that there is a little affectation or coquetry among some of our fair readers, in this want of hearty interest in rural occupation. We have noticed that it is precisely those who have the smallest gardens, and, therefore, who ought most naturally to wish to take the greatest interest in their culture themselves,—it is precisely those who depend entirely upon their gardener. They rest with such entire faith on the chivalry of our sex, that they gladly permit every thing to be done for them, and thus lose the greatest charm which their garden could give—that of a delightful personal intimacy.

Almost all the really enthusiastic and energetic lady gardeners that we have the pleasure of knowing, belong to the wealthiest class in this country. We have a neighbor on the Hudson, for instance, whose pleasure-grounds cover many acres, whose flower-garden is a miracle of beauty, and who keeps six gardeners at work all the season. But there is never a tree transplanted that she does not see its roots carefully handled; not a walk laid out that she does not mark its curves; not a parterre arranged that she does not direct its colors and grouping, and even assist in planting it. No matter what guests enjoy her hospitality, several hours every day are thus spent in out-of-door employment; and from the zeal and enthusiasm with which she always talks of every thing relating to her country life, we do not doubt that she is far more rationally happy now, than when she received the homage of a circle of admirers at one of the most brilliant of foreign courts.

On the table before us, lies a letter from a lady of fortune in Philadelphia, whose sincere and hearty enthusiasm in country life always delights us. She is one of those beings who animate every thing she touches, and would make a heart beat in a granite rock, if it had not the stubbornness of all "facts before the flood." She is in a dilemma now about the precise uses of lime (which has staggered many an old cultivator, by the way), and tells the story of her doubts with an earnest directness and eloquence that one seeks for in vain in the essays of our male chemico-horticultural correspondents. We are quite sure that there will be a meaning in every fruit and flower which this lady plucks from the garden, of which our fair friends, who are the disciples of the Sevigne school, have not the feeblest conception.

There are, also, we fear, those who fancy that there is something rustic, unfeminine and unrefined, about an interest in country out-of-door matters. Would we could present to them a picture which rises in our memory, at this moment, as the finest of all possible denials to such a theory. In the midst of the richest agricultural region of the northern States, lives a lady—a young, unmarried lady; mistress of herself; of some thousands of acres of the finest lands; and a mansion which is almost the *ideal* of taste and refinement. Very well. Does this lady sit in her drawing-room all day, to receive her visitors? By no means. You will find her, in the morning, either on horseback or driving a light carriage with a pair of spirited horses. She explores every corner of the estate; she visits her tenants, examines the crops, projects improvements, directs repairs, and is thoroughly mistress of her whole demesne. Her mansion opens into the most exquisite garden of flowers and fruits, every one of which she knows by heart. And yet this lady, so energetic and spirited in her enjoyment and management in out-of-door matters, is, in the drawing-room, the most gentle, the most retiring, the most refined of her sex.

A word or two more, and upon what ought to be the most important argument of all. EXERCISE, FRESH AIR, HEALTH,—are they not almost synonymous? The exquisite bloom on the cheeks of American girls, fades, in the matron, much sooner here than in England,—not alone because of the softness of the English climate, as many suppose. It is because exercise, so necessary to the maintenance of health, is so little a matter of habit and education here, and so largely insisted upon in England; and it is because exercise, when taken here at all, is taken too often as a matter of duty; that it is then only a lifeless duty, and has no soul in it; while the English woman, who takes a living interest in her rural employments, inhales new life in every day's occupation, and plants perpetual roses in her cheeks, by the mere act of planting them in her garden.

"But, Mr. Downing, think of the hot sun in this country, and our complexions!"

Yes, yes, we know it. But get up an hour earlier, fair reader; put on your broadest sun-bonnet, and your stoutest pair of gloves, and try the problem of health, enjoyment and beauty, before the sun gets too ardent. A great deal may be done in this way; and after a while, if your heart is in the right place for ruralities, you will find the occupation so fascinating that you will gradually find yourself able to enjoy keenly what was at first only a very irksome sort of duty.

VIII.

ECONOMY IN GARDENING.

May, 1849.

MR. COLMAN, in his Agricultural Tour, remarks, that his observations abroad convinced him that the Americans are the most extravagant people in the world; and the truth of the remark is corroborated by the experience of every sensible traveller that returns from Europe. The much greater facility of getting money here, makes us more regardless of system in its expenditure; and the income of many an estate abroad, amounting to twenty thousand dollars, is expended with an exactness, and nicety of calculation, that would astonish persons in this country, who have only an income of twenty hundred dollars. Abroad, it is the study of those who have, how to save; or, in the case of spending, how to get the most for their money. At home, it seems to be the desire of every body to get—and, having obtained wealth, to expend it in the most lavish and careless manner.

There are, again, many who wish to be economical in their disbursements, but find, in a country where labor is one of the dearest of commodities, that every thing which is attained by the expenditure of labor, costs so much more than they had supposed, that moderate "improvements"—as we call all kinds of building and gardening in this country—in a short time consume a handsome competence.

The fact, that in no country is labor better paid for than in ours, is one that has much to do with the success and progress of the country itself. Where the day-laborer is so poorly paid, that he must, of necessity, always be a day-laborer, it follows, inevitably, that the condition of the largest number of human beings in the State must remain nearly stationary. On the other hand, in a community where the industrious, prudent, and intelligent day-laborer can certainly rise to a more independent position, it is equally evident that the improvement of national character, and the increase of wealth, must go on rapidly together.

But, just in proportion to the ease with which men accumulate wealth, will they desire to spend it; and, in spending it, to obtain the utmost satisfaction which it can produce. Among the most rational modes of doing this, in the country, are building and gardening; and hence, every year, we find a greater number of our citizens endeavoring to realize the pleasures of country life.

Now *building* is sufficiently cheap with us. A man may build a *cottage ornée* for a few hundred dollars, which abroad would cost a few thousands. But the moment he touches a spade to the ground, to plant a tree, or to level a hillock, that moment his farm is taxed three or four times as heavily as in Europe; and as he builds in a year, but " gardens" all his life, it is evident that his out-of-door expenses must be systematized, or economized, or he will find his income greatly the loser by it. Many a citizen, who has settled in the country with the greatest enthusiasm, has gone back to town in disgust at the unsuspected cost of country pleasures.

And yet, there are ways in which economy and satisfactory results may be combined in country life. There are always two ways of arriving at a result; and, in some cases, that mode least usually pursued is the better and more satisfactory one.

The price of the cheapest labor in the country generally, averages 80 cents to $1 per day. Now we have no wish whatever to lower the price of labor; we would rather feel that, by and by, we could afford to pay even more. But we wish either to avoid unnecessary expenditure for labor in producing a certain result, or to arrive at some mode of insuring that the dollar a day, paid for labor, shall be fairly and well earned.

Four-fifths of all the gardening labor performed in the eastern and middle States is performed by Irish emigrants. Always accustomed to something of oppression on the part of landlords and em ployers, in their own country, it is not surprising that their old habits stick close to them here; and as a class, they require far more *watching* to get a fair day's labor from them than many of our own people. On the other hand, there is no workman who is more stimulated by the consciousness of working on his own account than an Irishman. He will work stoutly and faithfully, from early to late, to accomplish a "job" of his own seeking, or which he has fairly contracted for, and accomplish it in a third less time than if working by the day.

The deduction which experienced employers in the country draw from this, is, never to employ "rough hands," or persons whose ability and steadiness have not been well proved, by the day or month, but always by contract, piece or job. The saving to the employer is large; and the laborer, while he gets fairly paid, is induced, by a feeling of greater independence, or to sustain his own credit, to labor faithfully and without wasting the time of his employer.

We saw a striking illustration of this lately, in the case of two neighbors,—both planting extensive orchards, and requiring, therefore, a good deal of extra labor. One of them had all the holes for his trees dug by contract, of good size, and two spades deep, for six cents per hole. The other had it executed by the day, and by the same class of labor,—foreigners, newly arrived. We had the curiosity to ask a few questions, to ascertain the difference of cost in the two cases; and found, as we expected, that the cost in the day's work system was about ten cents per hole, or more than a third beyond what it cost by the job.

Now, whether a country place is large or small, there is always, in the course of the season, more or less *extra work* to be performed. The regular gardener, or workman, must generally be hired by the day or month; though we know instances of every thing being done by contract. But all this extra work can, in almost all cases, be done by contract, at a price greatly below what it would otherwise cost. Trenching, subsoiling, preparing the ground for orchards or kitchen gardens, or even ploughing, and gathering crops, may be done very much cheaper by contract than by day's labor.

In Germany, the whole family, including women and children,

work in the gardens and vineyards; and they always do the same here when they have land in their own possession. Now in every garden, vineyard, or orchard, there is a great deal of light work, that may be as well performed by the younger members of such a family as by any others. Hence, we learn that the Germans, in the large vineyards now growing on the Ohio, are able to cultivate the grape more profitably than other persons; and hence, German families, accustomed to this kind of labor, may be employed by contract in doing certain kinds of horticultural labors, at a great saving to the employer.

Another mode of economizing, in this kind of expenditure, is by the use of all possible *labor-saving machines.* One of our correspondents—a practical gardener—recommended, in our last number, that the kitchen garden, in this country, in places of any importance, should always be placed near the stables, to save trouble and time in carting manure; and should be so arranged as to allow the plough and cultivator to be used, instead of the spade and hoe. This is excellent and judicious advice, and exactly adapted to this country. In parts of Europe where garden labor can be had for 20 cents a day, the kitchen garden may properly be treated with such nicety that not only good vegetables, but something ornamental shall be attained by it. But here, where the pay is as much for one man's labor as that of five men's labor is worth in Germany, it is far better to cheapen the cost of vegetables, and pay for ornamental work where it is more needed.

So, too, with regard to every instance, where the more cheap and rapid working of an improved machine, or implement, may be substituted for manual labor. In several of the largest country seats on the Hudson, where there is so great an extent of walks and carriage road, that several men would be employed almost constantly in keeping them in order, they are all cleaned of weeds in a day by the aid of the horse hoe for gravel walks, described in the appendix to our Landscape Gardening. In all such cases as these, the proprietor not only gets rid of the trouble and care of employing a large number of workmen, but of the annoyance of paying more than their labor is fairly worth for the purpose in question.

There are many modes of economizing in the expenditures of a country place, which time, and the ingenuity of our countrymen will suggest, with more experience. But there is one which has frequently occurred to us, and which is so obvious that we are surprised that no one has adopted it. We mean the substitution, in country places of tolerable size, of fine *sheep*, for the scythe, in keeping the lawn in order.

No one now thinks of considering his place in any way ornamental, who does not keep his lawn well mown,—not once or twice a year, for grass, but once or twice a month, for "velvet." This, to be sure, costs something; but, for general effect, the beauty of a good lawn and trees is so much greater than that of mere flowers, that no one, who values them rightly, would even think of paying dearly for the latter, and neglecting the former.

Now, half a dozen or more *sheep*, of some breed serviceable and ornamental, might be kept on a place properly arranged, so as to do the work of two mowers, always keeping the lawn close and short, and not only without expense, but possibly with some profit. No grass surface, except a short lawn, is neater than one cropped by sheep; and, for a certain kind of country residence, where the picturesque or pastoral, rather than the studiously elegant, is desired, sheep would heighten the interest and beauty of the scene.

In order to use sheep in this way, the place should be so arranged that the flower-garden and shrubbery shall be distinct from the lawn. In many cases in England, a small portion, directly round the house, is inclosed with a wire fence, woven in a pretty pattern (worth three or four shillings a yard). This contains the flowers and shrubs, on the parlor side of the house, with a small portion of lawn dressed by the scythe. All the rest is fed by the sheep, which are folded regularly every night, to prevent accident from dogs. In this way, a beautiful lawn-like surface is maintained without the least annual outlay. We commend the practice for imitation in this country.

IX.

A LOOK ABOUT US.

April, 1850.

IN the old-fashioned way of travelling, "up hill and down dale," by post-coaches, it was a great gratification (altogether lost in swift and smooth railroads), to stop and rest for a moment on a hill-top and survey the country behind and about us.

Something of this retrospect is as refreshing and salutary in any other field of progress. Certainly, nothing will carry us on with such speed as to look neither to the right or left, to concentrate all our powers to this undeviating straight-forward line. But, on the other hand, as he who travels in a rail-car knows little or nothing of the country, except the points of departure and arrival, so, if we do not occasionally take a slight glance at things about us, we shall be comparatively ignorant of many interesting features, not in the straight line of "onward march."

One of the best signs of the times for country people, is the increase of agricultural papers in number, and the still greater increase of subscribers. When the Albany Cultivator stood nearly alone in the field, some fifteen years ago, and boasted of twenty thousand subscribers, it was thought a marvellous thing—this interest in the intellectual part of farming; and there were those who thought it "could not last long." Now that there are dozens of agricultural journals, with hundreds of thousands of readers, the interest in "book farming" is at last beginning to be looked upon as something significant; and the agricultural press *begins* to feel that it is of some account in the *commonwealth*. When it does something more—

when it rouses the farming class to a sense of its rights in the state, its rights to good education, to agricultural schools, to a place in the legislative halls; when farmers shall not only be talked about in complimentary phrase as "honest yeomen," or the "bone and sinew of the country," but see and feel by the comparison of power and influence with the commercial and professional classes that they are such, then we shall not hear so much about the dangers of the republic, but more of the intelligence and good sense of the people.

Among the good signs of the times, we notice the establishment of an Agricultural Bureau at Washington. At its head has been placed, for the present, at least, Dr. Lee, the editor of the Genesee Farmer—a man thoroughly alive to the interests of the cultivators of the soil, and awake to the unjust estimation practically placed upon farmers, both by themselves and the country at large. If he does his duty, as we think he will, in collecting and presenting statistics and other information showing the importance and value of the agriculture of the United States, we believe this Agricultural Bureau will be of vast service, if only in showing the farmers their own strength for all good purposes, if they will only first educate and then use their powers.

In our more immediate department—horticulture—there are the most cheering signs of improvement in every direction. In all parts of the country, but especially at the West, horticultural societies are being formed. We think Ohio alone numbers five at this moment; and as the bare formation of such societies shows the existence of a little more than private zeal on the part of the inhabitants, in gardening matters, we may take it for granted that the culture of gardens is making progress at the West, with a rapidity commensurate to the wonderful growth there in other respects.

It is now no longer a question, indeed, that horticulture, both for profit and pleasure, is destined to become of far more consequence here than in any part of Europe. Take, for example, the matter of fruit culture. In no part of Europe has the planting of orchards been carried to the same extent as it has already been in the United States. There is no single peach orchard in France, Italy, or Spain, that has produced the owner over $10,000 in a single year, like one in Delaware. There is no apple orchard in Germany or northern Europe, a single crop of which has yielded $12,000, like that of Pelham farm on the Hudson. And these, though unusual examples of orchard cultivation by single proprietors, are mere fractions of the aggregate value of the products of the orchards, in all the northern States. The dried fruits—apples and peaches alone, of western New-York, amount in value to very large sums annually. And, if we judge of what we hear, orchard culture, especially of the finer market fruits, has only just commenced.

We doubt if, at any horticultural assemblage that ever convened in Europe, there has been the same amount of practical knowledge of pomology brought together as at the congress of fruitgrowers, last October, in New-York. An intelligent nurseryman, who has just returned from a horticultural tour through Great Britain, assures us, that at the present moment that country is astonishingly behind us, both in interest in, and knowledge of fruits. This he partly explains by the fact, that only half a dozen sorts of each fruit are usually grown in England, where we grow twenty or thirty; but mainly by the inferiority of their climate, which makes the culture of pears, peaches, &c., without walls, an impossibility, except in rare cases. Again, the fact that in this country, there are so many landholders of intelligence among all classes of society—all busy in improving their places—whether they consist of a rood or a mile square—causes the interest in fine fruits to become so multiplied, that it assumes an importance here that is not dreamed of for it, on the other side of the water.

With this wide-spread interest, and the numberless experiments that large practice will beget, we trust we shall very soon see good results in the production of *best native* varieties of the finer fruits. Almost every experienced American horticulturist has become convinced that we shall never fairly "touch bottom," or rest on a solid foundation, till we get a good assortment of first-rate pears, grapes, &c., raised from seeds in this country; sorts with sound constitutions, adapted to our climate and soil. With great respect for the unwearied labors of Van Mons, and others who have followed his plan of obtaining varieties, we have not the least faith in the vital powers of varieties so originated. They will, in the end, be entirely abandoned in this country for sound healthy seedlings, raised directly from vigorous parents.

Far as we are in advance of Europe, at this moment, in the matter of pomology, we are a long way behind in all that relates to ornamental gardening. Not that there is not a wonderfully growing taste for ornamental gardening, especially in the northern and eastern States. Not, indeed, that we have not a number of country places that would be respectable in point of taste and good cultivation every where. But the popular feeling has not fairly set in this direction, and most persons are content with a few common trees, shrubs, and plants, when they might adorn their lawns and gardens with species of far greater beauty.

One of the greatest drawbacks to the satisfaction of pleasure-grounds, in this country, is the want of knowledge as to how they should be arranged to give rapid growth and fine verdure. The whole secret, as we have again and again stated, is the *deep soil;* if not naturally such, then made so by deep culture. Even the best English gardeners (always afraid, in their damp climate, of canker, if the roots go downwards) are discouraged, and fail in our pleasure-grounds, from the very fineness and dryness of our climate, because they will not *trench—trench—trench!* as we all must do, to have satisfactory lawns or pleasure-grounds.

And this reminds us that a great want in the country, at the present time, is a sort of practical school for gardeners; not so much to teach them from the outset—for ninety-nine hundredths of all our gardeners are Europeans—as to *naturalize* their knowledge in this country. If one of the leading horticultural societies, with ready means (that of Boston, for example), would start an experimental garden, and making, by an agency abroad, some arrangement with deserving gardeners wishing to emigrate, take these *freshmen* on their arrival, and carry them through a season's practice in the experimental garden, and let them out at the end of a year really good gardeners for our climate, they would do an incal culable service to the cause of horticulture, and to thousands of employers, besides getting their own gardens (like that of the London Horticultural Society) cultivated at a little cost.

It may be said that gardeners would not enter such a preparatory garden, since they could find places at once. We reply to this, that if they found, after they had had their year's practice in this garden, and could show its certificate of character and abilities, they could readily get $50 or $100 a year more—as we are confident they could—there would be no difficulty on this head.

The Belgian government has just established such a school, and placed it under the direction of M. Van Houtte, the well-known horticulturist of Ghent. Something of the sort has been contemplated here, in connection with the agricultural college proposed by this State. Considering the scarcity, nay, absolute dearth of good gardeners among us at the present moment,—the supply not half equal to the demand,—it seems to us that some plan might be adopted by which we should not be at the mercy of those who only call themselves gardeners, but who also know little beyond the mysteries of cultivating that excellent plant, the *Solanum tuberosum*, commonly known as the potato.

X.

A SPRING GOSSIP.

May, 1850.

"IF any man feels no joy in the spring, then has he no warm blood in his veins!" So said one of the old dramatists, two hundred years ago; and so we repeat his very words in this month of May, eighteen hundred and fifty. Not to feel the sweet influences of this young and creative season, is indeed like being blind to the dewy brightness of the rainbow, or deaf to the rich music of the mocking-bird. Why, every thing feels it; the gushing, noisy brook; the full-throated robin; the swallows circling and sailing through the air. Even the old rocks smile, and look less hard and stony; or at least try to by the help of the moss, lately grown green in the rain and sunshine of April. And, as Lowell has so finely said,

"Every clod feels a stir of might,
An instinct within it that reaches and towers;
And grasping blindly above it for light,
Climbs to a soul in grass and flowers."

From the time when the maple hangs out its little tufts of ruddy threads on the wood side, or the first crocus astonishes us with its audacity in embroidering the ground with gold almost before the snow has left it, until June flings us her first garlands of roses to tell us that summer is at hand, all is excitement in the country—real poetic excitement—some spark of which even the dullest souls that follow the oxen must feel.

'No matter how barren the past may haye been,
'Tis enough for us now that the leaves are green."

And you, most sober and practical of men, as you stand in your orchard and see the fruit trees all dressed in spring robes of white, and pink, and blush, and immediately set about divining what a noble crop you will have, "if nothing happens"—meaning, thereby, if every thing happens as nature for the most part makes it happen —you, too, are a little of a poet in spite of yourself. You imagine— you hope—you believe—and, from that delicate gossamer fabric of peach-blossoms, you conjure out of the future, bushels of downy, ripe, ruddy, and palpable, though melting rareripes, every one of which is such as was never seen but at prize exhibitions, when gold medals bring out horticultural prodigies. If this is not being a poet —a practical one, if you please, but still a poet—then are there no gay colors in peacocks' tails.

And as for our lady readers in the country, who hang over the sweet firstlings of the flowers that the spring gives us, with as fresh and as pure a delight every year as if the world (and violets) were just new born, and had not been convulsed, battered, and torn by earthquakes, wars, and revolutions, for more than six thousand years; why, we need not waste time in proving them to be poets, and their lives—or at least all that part of them passed in delicious rambles in the woods, or sweet toils in the garden—pure poetry. However stupid the rest of creation may be, they, at least, see and understand that those early gifts of the year, yes, and the very spring itself, are types of fairer and better things. They, at least, feel that this wonderful resurrection of life and beauty out of the death-sleep of winter, has a meaning in it that should bring glad tears into our eyes, being, as it is, a foreshadowing of that transformation and awakening of us all in the spiritual spring of another and a higher life.

The flowers of spring are not so gay and gorgeous as those of summer and autumn. Except those flaunting gentlemen-ushers the Dutch tulips (which, indeed, have been coaxed into gay liveries since Mynheer fell sick of flori-mania), the spring blossoms are delicate, modest, and subdued in color, and with something more of freshness and vivacity about them than is common in the lilies, roses, and dahlias of a later and hotter time of the year. The fact that the *violet* blooms in the spring, is of itself enough to make the season dear to us. We do not now mean the pansy, or three-colored violet—the "Johnny-jump-up" of the cottager—that little, roguish coquette of a blossom, all animation and boldness—but the true violet of the poets; the delicate, modest, retiring violet, dim,

> "But sweeter than the lids of Juno's eyes,
> Or Cytherea's breath."

The flower that has been loved, and praised, and petted, and cultivated, at least three thousand years, and is not in the least spoiled by it; nay, has all the unmistakable freshness still, of a nature ever young and eternal.

There is a great deal, too, in the associations that cluster about spring flowers. Take that early yellow flower, popularly known as "Butter and Eggs," and the most common bulb in all our gardens, though introduced from abroad. It is not handsome, certainly, although one always welcomes its hardy face with pleasure; but when we know that it suggested that fine passage to Shakspeare—

> "Daffodils
> That come *before the swallow dares*, and take
> The winds of March with beauty"—

we feel that the flower is for ever immortalized; and though not half so handsome as our native blood-root, with its snowy petals, or our wood anemone, tinged like the first blush of morning, yet still the daffodil, embalmed by poesy, like a fly in amber, has a value given it by human genius that causes it to stir the imagination more than the most faultless and sculpture-like camellia that ever bloomed in marble conservatory.

A pleasant task it would be to linger over the spring flowers, taking them up one by one, and inhaling all their fragrance and poetry, leisurely—whether the cowslips, hyacinths, daisies, and hawthorns of the garden, or the honeysuckles, trilliums, wild moccasins, and liverworts of the woods. But we should grow garrulous on the subject and the season, if we were to wander thus into details.

Among all the flowers of spring, there are, however, few that surpass in delicacy, freshness, and beauty, that common and popular thing, an *apple blossom.* Certainly, no one would plant an apple-tree in his park or pleasure ground; for, like a hard day-laborer, it has a bent and bowed-down look in its head and branches, that ill accord with the graceful bending of the elm, or the well-rounded curve of the maple. But as the day-laborer has a soul, which at one time or another must blossom in all its beauty, so too has the apple-tree a flower that challenges the world to surpass it, whether for the delicacy with which the white and red are blended—as upon the cheek of fairest maiden of sixteen—or the wild grace and symmetry of its cinquefoil petals, or the harmony of its coloring heightened by the tender verdure of the bursting leaves that surround it. We only mention this to show what a wealth of beauty there is in common and familiar objects in the country; and if any of our town readers are so unfortunate as never to have seen an apple orchard in full bloom, then have they lost one of the fairest sights that the month of April has in her kaleidoscope.

Spring, in this country, is not the tedious jade that she is in England,—keeping one waiting from February till June, while she makes her toilet, and fairly puts her foot on the daisy-spangled turf. For the most part, she comes to us with a quick bound; and, to make amends for being late, she showers down such a wealth of blossoms, that our gardens and orchards, at the end of April, look as if they were turned into fairy parterres, so loaded are they—especially the fruit trees—with beauty and promise. An American spring may be said to commence fairly with the blossom of the apricot or the elm tree, and end with the ripening of the first strawberries.

To end with *strawberries!* What a finale to one's life. More sanguinary, perhaps (as there is a stain left on one's fingers sometimes), but not less delicious than to

"Die of a rose in aromatic pain."

But it is a fitting close to such a beautiful season to end with such a fruit as this. We believe, indeed, that strawberries, if the truth could be known, are the most popular of fruits. People always affect to prefer the peach, or the orange, or perhaps the pear; but this is only because these stand well in the world—are much talked of —and can give "the most respectable references." But take our word for it, if the secret preference, the concealed passion, of every lover of fruit could be got at, without the formality of a public trial, the strawberry would be found out to be the little betrayer of hearts. Was not Linnæus cured of the gout by them? And did not even that hard-hearted monster, Richard the III., beseech "My Lord of Ely" to send for some of "the good strawberries" from his garden at Holborn? Nay, an Italian poet has written a whole poem, of nine hundred lines or more, entirely upon strawberries. "Strawberries and sugar" are to him what "sack and sugar" was to Falstaff—"the indispensable companion—the sovereign remedy for all evil—the climax of good." In short, he can do no more in wishing a couple of new married friends of his the completest earthly happiness, than to say—

> "E a dire che ogni cosa lieta vada,
> Su le Fragole il zucchero le cada."
>
> In short, to sum up all that earth can prize,
> May they have sugar to their strawberries!

There are few writers who have treated of the spring and its influences more fittingly than some of the English essayists; for the English have the key to the poetry of rural life. Indeed, we cannot perhaps give our readers greater pleasure than by ending this article with the following extract from one of the papers of that genial and kindly writer, Leigh Hunt:

"The lightest thoughts have their roots in gravity; and the most fugitive colors of the world are set off by the mighty background of eternity. One of the greatest pleasures of so light and airy a thing as the vernal season, arises from the consciousness that the world is young again; that the spring has come round; that we shall not all cease, and be no world. Nature has begun again, and not begun for nothing. One fancies somehow that she could not have the heart to put a stop to us in April or May. She may pluck away a poor little life here and there; nay, many blossoms of youth, —but not all,—not the whole garden of life. She prunes, but does not destroy. If she did,—if she were in the mind to have done with us,—to look upon us as a sort of experiment not worth going on with, as a set of ungenial and obstinate compounds, which refused to co-operate in her sweet designs, and could not be made to answer in the working,—depend upon it, she would take pity on our incapability and bad humors, and conveniently quash us in some dismal, sullen winter's day, just at the natural dying of the year, most likely in November; for Christmas is a sort of spring itself—a winter flowering. We care nothing for arguments about storms, earthquakes, or other apparently unseasonable interruptions of our pleasures. We imitate, in that respect, the magnanimous indifference, or what appears to be such, of the great mother herself, knowing that she means us the best in the *gross;* and also that we may all get our remedies for these evils in time, if we will only co-operate. People in South America, for instance, may learn from experience, and *build* so as to make a comparative nothing of those rockings of the ground. It is of the *gross* itself that we speak; and sure we are, that with an eye to *that*, Nature does not feel as Pope ventures to say she does, or sees 'with *equal* eye'—

> Atoms or systems into ruin hurl'd,
> And now a bubble burst, and now a world.'

"He may have flattered himself that he should think it a fine thing for his little poetship to sit upon a star, and look grand in his own eyes, from an eye so very dispassionate; but Nature, who is the author of passion, and joy, and sorrow, does not look upon animate and inanimate, depend upon it, with the same want of sympathy. 'A world' full of hopes, and loves, and endeavors, and of her own life and loveliness, is a far greater thing in her eyes, rest assured, than a 'bubble;' and, *à fortiori*, many worlds, or a 'system,' far greater than the 'atom,' talked of with so much complacency by this divine little whipper-snapper. *Ergo*, the moment the kind mother gives promise of a renewed year, with these green and budding signals, be certain she is not going to falsify them; and that being sure of April, we are sure as far as November. As for an existence any further, that, we conceive, depends somewhat upon how we behave ourselves; and therefore we would exhort everybody to do their best for the earth, and all that is upon it, in order that it and they may be thought worth continuance.

"What! Shall we be put into a beautiful garden, and turn up our noses at it, and call it a 'vale of tears,' and all sorts of bad names (helping thereby to make it so), and yet confidently reckon that nature will never shut it up, and have done with it, or set about forming a better stock of inhabitants? Recollect, we beseech you, dear 'Lord Worldly Wiseman,' and you, 'Sir Having,' and my 'Lady Greedy,' that there is reason for supposing that man was not always an inhabitant of this very fashionable world, and somewhat larger globe; and that perhaps the chief occupant before him was only an inferior species to ourselves (odd as you may think it), who could not be brought to know what a beautiful place he lived in, and so had a different chance given him in a different shape. Good heavens! If there were none but *mere* ladies and gentlemen, and city-men, and soldiers, upon earth, and no poets, readers, and milkmaids, to remind us that there is such a thing as Nature, we really should begin to tremble for Almacks and Change Alley (the upper ten' and Wall-street), about the 20th of next October."

XI.

THE GREAT DISCOVERY IN VEGETATION.

April, 1851.

IT is one of the misfortunes of an editor to be expected to answer all questions, as if he were an oracle. It is all pleasant enough, when his correspondent is lost in the woods, and he can speedily set him right, or when he is groping in some dark passage that only needs the glimmer of his farthing candle of experience, to make the way tolerably clear to him. But correspondents are often unreasonable, and ask for what is little short of a miracle. It is clear that an editor is not only expected to know every thing, but that he is not to be allowed the comfort of belonging to any secret societies, or any of those little fraternities where such a charming air of mystery is thrown over the commonest subjects.

We are brought to these reflections by a letter that has just come before us, and which runs as follows:

DEAR SIR:—I have been expecting in the last two numbers, to hear from you on the subject of the great discovery in vegetation, which was laid before the committee of the State Agricultural Society at its annual meeting in January last. You were, if I mistake not, a member of that committee, and of course, the fullest disclosures of the secret of the gentleman who claims to have found out a new "principle in vegetation," were laid before you. No formal report has, I think, been published by the Society. The public are, therefore, in the dark still. Is this right, when the discoverer is now urging the Legislature of this State to pass a bill giving him a bonus of $150,000 to make his secret public, for the benefit of all cultivators of the soil? Either the thing is pure humbug, or there is something in it worthy of attention. Pray enlighten us on this subject. Yours, &c.

Yes, we were upon that committee, and nothing would give us greater pleasure than to unburden our heart to the public on this subject, and rid our bosom of this "perilous stuff" that has weighed upon us ever since. But alas! this gentleman who has been urging his great discovery upon the attention of Congress and the Legislature for ten or twelve years past, put all the committee under a solemn vow of secrecy, though we protested at the time against his expecting that a horticultural editor should preserve silence touching any thing that is told him *sub rosa*.

And yet we would not treat our correspondent rudely; for his letter only expresses what a good many others have expressed to us verbally. We shall, therefore, endeavor to console him for the want of the learned dissertation on vegetable physiology which he no doubt expected, by telling him a story.

Once on a time there was a little spaniel, who lived only for the good of his race. He had a mild countenance, and looked at the first, enough like other dogs. But for all that, he was an oddity. Year in and year out, this little spaniel wandered about with a wise look, like the men that gaze at the stars through the great telescopes. The fact was, he had taken it into his head that he was a philosopher, and had discovered a great secret. This was no less than the secret of *instinct* by which dogs do so many wonderful things, that some men with all their big looks, their learning, yes, and even their wonderful knack of talking, cannot do.

It was curious to see how the little spaniel who had turned philosopher, gave himself up to this fancy that had got into his head. He had a comfortable kennel, where he might have kept house, barked, looked after trespassers, where he might have been well fed, and had a jolly time of it like other dogs.

But no, he was far too wise for that. He had, as he said, found out something that would alter the whole "platform" on which dogs stood, something that would help them to carry their heads higher than many men he could name, instead of being obliged to play second fiddle to the horse. If the community of dogs in general would but listen to him, he would teach them not only how to be always wise and rich, how to be strong and hearty, but above all, how to preserve their scent—for the scent is a pleasure that dogs prize as much as some old ladies who take snuff. In short, the knowledge of this wonderful discovery would bring about a canine millennium—for he assured them that not only was every one of them entitled to his "day," but that "a good time was coming," even for dogs.

And why, you will say, did not our philosopher divulge for the benefit of the whole family of dogs? "It is so pleasant to do something for the elevation of our race," as the travelled monkey thought when he was teaching his brothers to walk on their hind legs. All the dogs in the country could not but owe him a debt of gratitude, since they would soon become so wise that they might even teach their masters something of instinct. And then they would be so happy—since there would not be a downcast tail in all the land—for the whole country would be in one perpetual wag of delight.

Ah! dear reader, we see that you, who put such questions, know nothing either of philosophy, or the world. As if the people who discover why the world turns round, and the stars shine, throw their knowledge into the street for every dog to trample on. No, indeed! They will have a patent for it, or a great sum of money from the government, or something of that sort. It would be a sorry fellow who should think that every new thing found out is to be given away to every body for nothing at all, in that manner. To be sure, it would, perhaps, benefit mankind all the more; but that is only half the question. "If you think the moon is made of green cheese," said our curly philosopher to his friends, "you are greatly mistaken. I am well satisfied, for my part, that that is only a vulgar error. If it had been, John Bull would have eaten it up for lunch a long time ago."

So our philosopher went about among his fellow-dogs, far and near, and spent most of his little patrimony in waiting on distinguished mastiffs, Newfoundlands, and curs of high degree. He went, also, to all conventions or public assemblies, where wise terriers were in the habit of putting their heads together for the public good. Wherever he went, you would see him holding some poor victim by the button, expounding his great secret, and showing how the progress, yes, the very existence of dogs, depended upon the knowledge of his *secret*—since it would really explain in a moment every thing that had been dark since the days when their great-grandfathers were kept from drowning in the ark. Only let the congress of greyhounds agree to pay him a million of money, and he would make known principles that would make the distemper cease, and all the other ills that dog-flesh is heir to, fade clean out of memory.

Some of the big dogs to whom he told his secret (always, remember, in the strictest confidence), shook their heads, and looked wise; others, to get rid of his endless lectures, gave him a certificate, saying that Solomon was wrong when he said there was nothing new under the sun; and all agreed that there was no denying that there is *something* in it, though they could not exactly say it was a new discovery.

Finally, after a long time spent in lobbying, and after wise talks with all the members that would listen to him, yes, and after exhibiting to every dog that had an hour to give him, his collection of dogs' bones that had died solely because of the lamentable ignorance of his secret in dogdom, he found a committee that took hold of his doctrine in good earnest—quite determined to do justice to him, and vote him a million if he deserved it, but, nevertheless, quite determined not to be humbugged by any false doggerel, however potent it might have been to terriers less experienced in this current commodity of many modern philosophers.

It was a long story that the committee were obliged to hear, and there were plenty of hard words thrown in to puzzle terriers who might not have had a scientific education in their youth. But the dogs on the committee were not to be puzzled; they seized hold of the fundamental principle of the philosophic spaniel, tossed it, and worried it, and shook it, till it stood out, at last, quite a simple truth (how beautiful is deep philosophy), and it was this—

THE GREAT SECRET *of perfect instinct in dogs, is* TO KEEP THEIR NOSES COOL.

Of course, the majority of the committee were startled and delighted with the novelty and grandeur of the discovery. There were, to be sure, a few who had the foolhardiness to remark, that the thing was *not* new, and had been acted upon, time out of mind, in all good kennels. But the philosopher soon put down such nonsense, by observing that the fact might, perchance, have been known to a few, but who, before him, had ever shown the PRINCIPLE of the thing?

And now, we should like to see that cur who shall dare to say the canine philosopher who has spent his life in studying nature and the books, to such good results, shall not have a million for his discoverv

XII.

STATE AND PROSPECTS OF HORTICULTURE.

December, 1851.

A RETROSPECTIVE glance over the journey we have travelled, is often both instructive and encouraging. We not only learn what we have really accomplished, but we are better able to overcome the obstacles that lie in our onward way, by reviewing the difficulties already overcome.

The progress of the last five years in Horticulture, has been a remarkable one in the United States. The rapid increase of population, and the accumulation of capital, has very naturally led to the multiplication of private gardens and country-seats, and the planting of orchards and market gardens, to an enormous extent. The facility with which every man may acquire land in this country, naturally leads to the formation of separate and independent homes, and the number of those who are in some degree interested in the culture of the soil is thus every day being added to. The very fact, however, that a large proportion of these little homes are *new* places, and that the expense of building and establishing them is considerable, prevents their owners from doing much more for the first few years, than to secure the more useful and necessary features of the establishment. Hence, the ornamental still appears neglected in our country homes and gardens, generally, as compared with those of the more civilized countries abroad. The shrubs, and flowers, and vines, that embellish almost every where the rural homes of England, are as yet only rarely seen in this country—though in all the older sections of the Union the taste for ornamental gardening is developing itself anew every day. On the other hand, the great facility with which excellent fruits and vegetables are grown in this climate, as compared with the North of Europe, makes our gardens compare most favorably with theirs in respect to these two points. The tables of the United States are more abundantly supplied with peaches and melons, than those of the wealthiest classes abroad—and the display of culinary vegetables of the North of Europe, which is almost confined to the potatoes, peas, French beans, and cauliflowers, makes but a sorry comparison with the abundant bill of fare within the daily reach of all Americans. The traveller abroad from this side of the Atlantic, learns to value the tomatoes, Indian corn, Lima beans, egg-plants, okra, sweet potatoes, and many other half-tropical products, which the bright sun of his own land offers him in such abundance, with a new relish; and putting these and the delicious fruits, which are so cheaply and abundantly produced, into the scale against the smooth lawns and the deep verdure of Great Britain, he is more than consoled for the superiority of the latter country in these finer elements of mere embellishment.

In the useful branches of gardening, the last ten years have largely increased the culture of all the fine culinary vegetables, and our markets are now almost every where abundantly supplied with them. The tomato, the egg-plant, salsify, and okra, from being rarities have become almost universally cultivated. The tomato affords a singular illustration of the fact that an article of food not generally relished at first, if its use is founded in its adaptation to the nature of the climate, may speedily come to be considered indispensable to a whole nation. Fifteen years ago it would have been difficult to find this vegetable for sale in five market towns in America. At the present moment, it is grown almost every where, and there are hundreds of acres devoted to its culture for the supply of the New-York market alone. We are certain that no people at the present moment, use so large a variety of fine vegetables as the people of the United States. Their culture is so remarkably easy and the product so abundant.

We have no means of knowing the precise annual value of the products of the orchards of the United States. The Commissioner of Patents, from the statistics in his possession, estimates it at ten millions of dollars. The planting of orchards and fruit-gardens within the last five years has been more than three times as great as in any previous five years, and as soon as these trees come into bearing, the annual value of their products cannot fall short of twenty-five or thirty millions of dollars. American apples are universally admitted to be the finest in the world, and our pippins and Baldwins have taken their place among the regular exports of the country. In five years more we confidently expect to see our fine late pears taking the same rank, and from the great success which has begun to attend their extensive culture in Western New-York, there can be little doubt that that region will come to be considered the centre of the pear culture of this country.

The improvements of the last few years in fruit-tree culture have been very great, and are very easily extended. From having been pursued in the most careless and slovenly manner possible, it is now perhaps the best understood of any branch of horticulture in America. The importance of deep trenching, mulching, a correct system of pruning, and the proper manures, have come to be pretty generally acknowledged, so that our horticultural shows, especially, and the larger markets, to a certain extent, begin to show decided evidences of progress in the art of raising good fruits. Our nurserymen and amateurs, after having made trial of hundreds of highly rated foreign sorts, and found but few of them really valuable, are turning their attention to the propagation and dissemination of those really good, and to the increase of the number mainly by selections from the numerous good native varieties now springing into existence.

The greatest acquisition to the amateur's fruit garden, within the last few years, has been the *cold vinery*,—a cheap glass structure by the aid of which, without any fire heat, the finest foreign grapes can be fully ripened, almost to the extreme northern parts of the Union. These vineries have astonishingly multiplied within the last four years, so that instead of being confined to the gardens of the very wealthy, they are now to be found in the environs of all our larger towns—and a necessary accompaniment to every considerable country place. As a matter of luxury, in fruit gardening, they perhaps afford more satisfaction and enjoyment than any other single feature whatever, and the annual value of the grapes, even to the market-gardener, is a very satisfactory interest on the outlay made in the necessary building.

Now that the point is well settled that the foreign grapes cannot be successfully grown without the aid of glass, our most enterprising experimentalists are busy with the production of new hybrid varieties—the product of a cross between the former and our native varieties—which shall give us fine flavor and adaptation to open air culture, and some results lately made public, would lead us to the belief that the desideratum may soon be attained. In the mean time the native grapes, or at least one variety—the Catawba—has taken its rank—no longer disputed—as a fine wine grape; and the hundreds of acres of vineyards which now line the banks of the Ohio, and the rapid sale of their vintages, show conclusively that we can at least make the finest light wines on this side of the Atlantic.

In ornamental gardening, many and beautiful are the changes of the last few years. Cottages and villas begin to embroider the country in all directions, and the neighborhood of our three or four largest cities begins to vie with the environs of any of the old world capitals in their lovely surroundings of beautiful gardens and grounds. The old and formal style of design, common until within a few years, is almost displaced by a more natural and graceful style of curved lines, and graceful plantations. The taste for ornamental planting has extended so largely, that much as the nurseries have increased, they are not able to meet the demand for rare trees and shrubs—especially evergreens—so that hundreds of thousands of fine species are annually imported from abroad. Though by no means so favorable a climate for lawns as that of England, ours is a far better one for deciduous trees, and our park and pleasure-ground scenery (if we except evergreens) is marked even now by a greater variety of foliage than one easily finds in any other temperate climate.

A peculiar feature of what may be called the scenery of ornamental grounds in this country, at the present moment, is, as we have before remarked, to be found in our rural cemeteries. They vary in size, from a few to three or four hundred acres, and in character, from pretty shrubberies and pleasure-grounds to wild sylvan groves, or superb parks and pleasure-grounds—laid out and kept in the highest style of the art of landscape gardening. There is nothing in any part of the world which equals in all respects, at the present moment, Greenwood Cemetery, near New-York—though it has many rivals. We may give some idea of the extent and high keeping of this lovely resting-place of the dead, by saying that about three hundred persons were constantly employed in the care, improvement, and preservation of its grounds, this season. The Cemetery of the Evergreens, also near New-York, Mount Auburn at Boston, Laurel Hill at Philadelphia, and the cemeteries of Cincinnati, Albany, Salem, and several others of the larger towns, are scarcely less interesting in many respects—while all have features of interest and beauty peculiar to themselves.

From cemeteries we naturally rise to public parks and gardens. As yet our countrymen have almost entirely overlooked the sanitary value and importance of these breathing places for large cities, or the powerful part which they may be made to play in refining, elevating, and affording enjoyment to the people at large. A more rapid and easy communication with Europe is, however, beginning to awaken us to a sense of our vast inferiority in this respect, and the inhabitants of our largest cities are beginning to take a lively interest in the appropriation of sufficient space—while space may be obtained—for this beautiful and useful purpose. The government has wisely taken the lead in this movement, by undertaking the improvement (on a comprehensive plan given by us) of a large piece of public ground—150 acres or more—lying almost in the heart of Washington. A commencement has been made this season, and we hope the whole may be completed in the course of three or four years. The plan embraces four or five miles of carriage-drive—walks for pedestrians—ponds of water, fountains and statues—picturesque groupings of trees and shrubs, and a complete collection of all the trees that belong to North America. It will, if carried out as it has been undertaken, undoubtedly give a great impetus to the popular taste in landscape-gardening and the culture of ornamental trees; and as the climate of Washington is one peculiarly adapted to this purpose—this national park may be made a sylvan museum such as it would be difficult to equal in beauty and variety in any part of the world.

As a part of the same movement, we must not forget to mention that the city of New-York has been empowered by the State legislature to buy 160 acres of land, admirably situated in the upper part of the city, and improve and embellish it for a public park. A similar feeling is on foot in Philadelphia, where the Gratz estate and the Lemon Hill estate are, we understand, likely to be purchased by the city for this purpose. It is easy to see from these signs of the times, that gardening—both as a practical art and an art of taste—is advancing side by side with the steady and rapid growth of the country—and we congratulate our readers that they live in an age and nation where the whole tendency is so healthful and beautiful, and where man's destiny seems to grow brighter and better every day.

XIII.

AMERICAN vs. BRITISH HORTICULTURE.

June, 1852.

WHEN a man goes into a country without understanding its language—merely as a traveller—he is likely to comprehend little of the real character of that country; when he settles in it, and persists in not understanding its language, manners, or customs, and stubbornly adheres to his own, there is little probability of his ever being a contented or successful citizen. In such a country as this, its very spirit of liberty and progress, its freedom from old prejudices, and the boundless life and energy that make the pulses of its true citizens—either native or adopted—beat with health and exultation, only serve to vex and chafe that alien in a strange land, who vainly tries to live in the new world, with all his old-world prejudices and customs.

We are led into this train of reflection by being constantly reminded, as we are in our various journeyings through the country, of the heavy impediment existing—the lion lying in the path of our progress in horticulture, all over the country, in the circumstance that our practical gardening is almost entirely in the hands of foreign gardeners. The statistics of the gardening class, if carefully collected, would, we imagine, show that not three per cent. of all the working gardeners in the United States, are either native or naturalized citizens. They are, for the most part, natives of Ireland, with a few Scotchmen, and a still smaller proportion of English and Germans.

We suppose we have had as much to do, for the last sixteen or eighteen years, with the employment of gardeners, as almost any person in America, and we never remember an instance of an American offering himself as a professional gardener. Our own rural workmen confine themselves wholly to the farm, knowing nothing, or next to nothing, of the more refined and careful operations of the garden. We may, therefore, thank foreigners for nearly all the gardening skill that we have in the country, and we are by no means inclined to underrate the value of their labors. Among them there are, as we well know, many most excellent men, who deserve the highest commendation for skill, taste, and adaptation—though, on the other hand, there are a great many who have been gardeners (if we may trust their word for it), to the Duke of ——, and the Marquis of ——, but who would make us pity his grace or his lordship, if we could believe he ever depended on Paddy for any other exotics than potatoes and cabbages.

But taking it for granted that our gardeners are wholly foreigners, and mostly British, they all have the disadvantage of coming to us, even the best educated of them, with their practice wholly *founded upon a climate the very opposite of ours.* Finding how little the "natives" know of their favorite art, and being, therefore, by no means disposed to take advice of them, or unlearn any of their old-world knowledge here, are they not, as a class, placed very much in the condition of the aliens in a foreign country, we have just alluded to, who refuse, for the most part, either to learn its language, or adapt themselves to the institutions of that country? We think so; for in fact, no two languages can be more different than the gardening tongues of England and America. The ugly words of English gardening, are *damp, wet, want of sunshine, canker.* Our bugbears are *drought, hot sunshine, great stimulus to growth, and blights and diseases resulting from sudden checks.* An English gardener, therefore, is very naturally taught, as soon as he can lisp, to avoid cool and damp aspects, to nestle like a lizard, on the sunny side of south walls, to be perpetually guarding the roots of plants against wet, and continually opening the heads of his trees and shrubs, by thinning out the branches, to let the light in. He raises even his flower-beds, to shed off the too abundant rain; trains his fruit-trees upon trellises, to expose every leaf to the sunshine, and is continually endeavoring to extract "sunshine from cucumbers," in a climate where nothing grows golden and ripe without coaxing nature's smiles under glass-houses!

For theorists, who know little of human nature, it is easy to answer—"well, when British gardeners come to a climate totally different from their own—where sunshine is so plenty that they can raise melons and peaches as easily as they once did cauliflowers and gooseberries—why, they will open their eyes to such glaring facts, and alter their practice accordingly." Very good reasoning, indeed. But anybody who knows the effect of habit and education on character, knows that it is as difficult for an Irishman to make due allowance for American sunshine and heat, as for a German to forget sour-krout, or a Yankee to feel an instinctive reverence for royalty. There is a whole lifetime of education, national habit, daily practice, to overcome, and reason seldom has complete sway over the minds of men rather in the habit of practising a system, than referring to principles, in their every-day labors.

Rapid as the progress of horticulture is at the present time in the United States, there can be no doubt that it is immensely retarded by this disadvantage, that all our gardeners have been educated in the school of British horticulture. It is their misfortune, since they have the constant obstacle to contend with, of not understanding the necessities of our climate, and therefore endeavoring to carry out a practice admirably well suited where they learned it—but most ill suited to the country where they are to practise it. It is our misfortune, because we suffer doubly by their mistakes—first, in the needless money they spend in their failures—and second, in the discouragement they throw upon the growing taste for gardening among us. A gentleman who is himself ignorant of gardening, establishes himself at a country-seat. He engages the best gardener he can find. The latter fails in one half that he attempts, and the proprietor, knowing nothing of the reason of the failures, attributes to the difficulties of the thing itself, what should be attributed to the want of knowledge, or experience of the soil and climate, in the gardener.

A case of this kind, which has recently come under our notice, is too striking an illustration not to be worth mentioning here. In one of our large cities south of New-York, where the soil and climate are particularly fine for fruit-growing—where the most delicious peaches, pears, and apricots grow almost as easily as the apple at the north, it was confidently stated to us by several amateurs, that the foreign grape could not be cultivated in vineries there—"several had tried it and failed." We were, of course, as incredulous as if we had been told that the peach would not ripen in Persia, or the fig in Spain. But our incredulity was answered by a promise to show us the next day, that the thing had been well tried.

We were accordingly shown: and the exhibition, as we suspected, amounted to this. The vineries were in all cases placed and treated, in that bright, powerful sunshine, just as they would have been placed and treated in Britain—that is, facing due south, and generally under the shelter of a warm bank. Besides this, not half provision enough was made, either for ventilation or water. The result was perfectly natural. The vines were burned up by excess of light and heat, and starved for want of air and water. We pointed out how the same money (no small amount, for one of the ranges was 200 feet long), applied in building a span-roofed house, on a perfectly open exposure, and running on a *north and south*, instead of an east and west line, and treated by a person who would open his eyes to the fact, that he was no longer gardening in the old, but the new world—would have given *tons* of grapes, where only pounds had been obtained.

The same thing is seen on a smaller scale, in almost every fruit garden that is laid out. Tender fruit trees are planted on the south side of fences or walls, for sun, when they ought always to be put on the north, for shade; and foliage is constantly thinned out, to let the sun in to the fruit, when it ought to be encouraged to grow thicker, to protect it from the solar rays.*

But, in fact, the whole routine of practice in American and British horticulture, is, and must be essentially different. We give to Boston, Salem, and the eastern cities, the credit of bearing off the

* If we were asked to say what practice, founded on *principle*, had been most beneficially introduced into our horticulture—we should answer *mulching*—mulching suggested by the need of moisture in our dry climate, the difficulty of preserving it about the roots of plants.

palm of horticultural skill; and we must not conceal the fact, that the superiority of the fruits and flowers there, in a climate more un favorable than that of the middle States, has been owing, not to the superiority of the foreign gardeners which they employ—but to the greater knowledge and interest in horticulture taken there by the proprietors of gardens themselves. There is really a native school of horticulture about Boston, and even foreign gardeners there are obliged to yield to its influence.

We have spoken out our thoughts on this subject plainly, in the hope of benefiting both gardeners and employers among us. Every right-minded and intelligent foreign gardener, will agree with us in deploring the ignorance of many of his brethren, and we hope will, by his influence and example, help to banish it. The evil we complain of has grown to be a very serious one, and it can only be cured by continually urging upon gardeners that British horticulture will not suit America, without great modification, and by continually insisting upon employers learning for themselves, the principles of gardening as it *must* be practised, to obtain any good results. This sowing good seed, and gathering tares, is an insult to Providence, in a country that, in its soil and climate, invites a whole population to a feast of Flora and Pomona.

XIV.

ON THE DRAPERY OF COTTAGES AND GARDENS.

February, 1849.

OUR readers very well know that, in the country, whenever any thing especially tasteful is to be done, when a church is to be "dressed for Christmas," a public hall festooned for a fair, or a saloon decorated for a horticultural show, we have to entreat the assistance of the fairer half of humanity. All that is most graceful and charming in this way, owes its existence to female hands. Over the heavy exterior of man's handiwork, they weave a fairy-like web of enchantment, which, like our Indian summer haze upon autumn hills, spiritualizes and makes poetical, whatever of rude form or rough outlines may lie beneath.

Knowing all this, as we well do, we write this leader especially for the eyes of the ladies. They are naturally mistresses of the art of embellishment. Men are so stupid, in the main, about these matters, that, if the majority of them had their own way, there would neither be a ringlet, nor a ruffle, a wreath, nor a nosegay left in the world. All would be as stiff and as meaningless as their own meagre black coats, without an atom of the graceful or romantic about them; nothing to awaken a spark of interest or stir a chord of feeling; nothing, in short, but downright, commonplace matter-of-fact. And they undertake to defend it—the logicians—on the ground of utility and the spirit of the age! As if trees did not bear lovely blossoms as well as good fruit; as if the sun did not give us rainbows as well as light and warmth; as if there were not still mocking-birds and nightingales as well as ducks and turkeys.

But enough of that. You do not need any arguments to prove that *grace* is a quality as positive as electro-magnetism. Would that you could span the world with it as quickly as Mr. Morse with his telegraph. To come to the point, we want to talk a little with you about what we call the *drapery* of cottages and gardens; about those beautiful vines, and climbers, and creepers, which nature made on purpose to cover up every thing ugly, and to heighten the charm of every thing pretty and picturesque. In short, we want your aid and assistance in dressing, embellishing, and decorating, not for a single holiday, fair, or festival, but for years and for ever, the *out-sides* of our simple cottages, and country homes; wreathing them about with such perennial festoons of verdure, and starring them over with such bouquets of delicious odor, that your husbands and brothers would no more think of giving up such houses, than they would of abandoning you (as that beggarly Greek, Theseus, did the lovely Ariadne) to the misery of solitude on a desolate island.

And what a difference a little of this kind of rural drapery, tastefully arranged, makes in the aspect of a cottage or farm house in the country! At the end of the village, for instance, is that old-fashioned stone house, which was the homestead of Tim Steady. First and last, that family lived there two generations; and every thing about them had a look of some comfort. But with the exception of a coat of paint, which the house got once in ten years, nothing was ever done to give the place the least appearance of taste. An old, half decayed ash-tree stood near the south door, and a few decrepit and worn-out apple-trees behind the house. But there was not a lilac bush, nor a syringo, not a rose-bush nor a honey-suckle about the whole premises. You would never suppose that a spark of affection for nature, or a gleam of feeling for grace or beauty, in any shape, ever dawned within or around the house.

Well, five years ago the place was put up for sale. There were some things to recommend it. There was a "good well of water;" the house was in excellent repair; and the location was not a bad one. But, though many went to see it, and "liked the place tolerably well," yet there seemed to be a want of heart about it, that made it unattractive, and prevented people from buying it.

It was a good while in the market; but at last it fell into the hands of the Widow Winning and her two daughters. They bought it at a bargain, and must have foreseen its capabilities.

What that house and place is now, it would do your heart good to see. A porch of rustic trellis-work was built over the front doorway, simple and pretty hoods upon brackets over the windows, the door-yard was all laid out afresh, the worn-out apple-trees were dug up, a nice bit of lawn made around the house, and pleasant groups of shrubbery (mixed with two or three graceful elms) planted about it. But, most of all, what fixes the attention, is the lovely profusion of flowering vines that enrich the old house, and transform what was a soulless habitation, into a home that captivates all eyes. Even the old and almost leafless ash-tree is almost overrun with a creeper, which is stuck full of gay trumpets all summer, that seem to blow many a strain of gladness to the passers by. How many sorts of honeysuckle, clematises, roses, etc., there are on wall or trellis about that cottage, is more than we can tell. Certain it is, however, that half the village walks past that house of a summer night, and inwardly thanks the fair inmates for the fragrance that steals through the air in its neighborhood: and no less certain is it that this house is now the "admired of all admirers," and that the Widow Winning has twice refused double the sum it went begging at when it was only the plain and meagre home of Tim Steady.

Many of you in the country, as we well know, are compelled by circumstances to live in houses which some one else built, or which have, by ill-luck, an ugly expression in every board or block of stone, from the sill of the door to the peak of the roof. Paint won't hide it, nor cleanliness disguise it, however goodly and agreeable things they are. But vines will do both; or, what is better, they will, with their lovely, graceful shapes, and rich foliage and flowers, give a new character to the whole exterior. However ugly the wall, however bald the architecture, only give it this fair drapery of leaf and blossom, and nature will touch it at once with something of grace and beauty.

"What are our favorite vines?" This is what you would ask of us, and this is what we are most anxious to tell you; as we see, already, that no sooner will the spring open, than you will immediately set about the good work.

Our two favorite vines, then, for the adornment of cottages, in the Northern States, are the double *Prairie Rose*, and the *Chinese Wistaria.* Why we like these best is, because they have the greatest number of good qualities to recommend them. In the first place, they are hardy, thriving in all soils and exposures; in the second place, they are luxuriant in their growth, and produce an effect in a very short time—after which, they may be kept to the limits of a single pillar on the piazza, or trained over the whole side of a cottage; in the last place, they are rich in the foliage, and beautiful in the blossom.

Now there are many vines more beautiful than these in some respects, but not for this purpose, and taken altogether. For cottage drapery, a *popular* vine must be one that will grow anywhere, with little care, and must need no shelter, and the least possible attention, beyond seeing that it has something to run on, and a looking over, pruning, and tying up once a year—say in early spring. This is precisely the character of these two vines; and hence we think they deserve to be planted from one end of the Union to the other. They will give the greatest amount of beauty, with the least care, and in the greatest number of places.

The Prairie roses are, no doubt, known to most of you. They have been raised from seeds of the wild rose of Michigan, which clambers over high trees in the forests, and are remarkable for the profusion of their very double flowers (so double, that they always look like large pouting buds, rather than full-blown roses), and their extreme hardiness and luxuriance of growth,—shoots of twenty feet, in a single year, being a not uncommon sight. Among all the sorts yet known, the Queen of the Prairies (deep pink), and Superba (nearly white), are the best.

We wish we could give our fair readers a glance at a Chinese Wistaria in our grounds, as it looked last April. It covered the side of a small cottage completely. If they will imagine a space of 10 by 20 feet, completely draped with Wistaria shoots, on which hung, thick as in a flower pattern, at least 500 clusters of the most delicate blossoms, of a tint between pearl and lilac, each bunch of bloom shaped like that of a locust tree, but eight inches to a foot long, and most gracefully pendant from branches just starting into tender green foliage; if, we say, they could see all this, as we saw it, and not utter exclamations of delight, then they deserve to be classed with those women of the nineteenth century, who are thoroughly "fit for sea-captains."

For a cottage climber, that will take care of itself better than almost any other, and embower door and windows with rich foliage and flowers, take the common *Boursault* Rose. Long purplish shoots, foliage always fresh and abundant, and bright purplish blossoms in June, as thick as stars in a midnight sky,—all belong to this plant. Perhaps the richest and prettiest Boursault, is the one called by the nurserymen *Amadis*, or *Elegans;* the flower a bright cherry-color, becoming crimson purple as it fades, with a delicate stripe of white through an occasional petal.

There are two very favorite climbers that belong properly to the middle States, as they are a little tender, and need protection to the North or East. One of them is the Japan Honeysuckle (*Lonicera japonica*, or *flexuosa**); the species with very dark, half evergreen leaves, and a profusion of lovely delicate white and fawn-colored blossoms. It is the queen of all honeysuckles for cottage walls, or veranda pillars; its foliage is always so rich; it is entirely free from the white aphis (which is the pest of the old sorts), and it blooms (as soon as the plant gets strong) nearly the whole summer, affording a perpetual feast of beauty and fragance. The other, is the Sweet-scented Clematis (*C. flammula*), the very type of delicacy and grace, whose flowers are broidered like pale stars over the whole vine in midsummer, and whose perfume is the most spiritual, impalpable, and yet far-spreading of all vegetable odors.

All the honeysuckles are beautiful in the garden, though none of them, except the foregoing, and what are familiarly called the "trumpet honeysuckles," are fit for the walls of a cottage, because they harbor insects. Nothing, however, can well be prettier than the Red and Yellow Trumpet Honeysuckles, when planted together and allowed to interweave their branches, contrasting the delicate straw-color of the flower tubes of one, with the deep coral-red hue of those of the other; and they bloom with a welcome prodigality from April to December.

* The "Chinese twining," of some gardens.

Where you want to produce a bold and picturesque effect with a vine, nothing will do it more rapidly and completely than our native grapes. They are precisely adapted to the porch of the farm-house, or to cover any building, or part of a building, where expression of strength rather than of delicacy is sought after. Then you will find it easy to smooth away all objections from the practical soul of the farmer, by offering him a prospect of ten bushels of fine Isabella or Catawba grapes a year, which you, in your innermost heart, do not value half so much as five or ten months of beautiful drapery!

Next to the grape-vine, the boldest and most striking of hardy vines is the Dutchman's pipe (*Aristolochia sipho*). It is a grand twining climber, and will canopy over a large arbor in a short time, and make a shade under it so dense that not a ray of pure sunshine will ever find its way through. Its gigantic circular leaves, of a rich green, form masses such as delight a painter's eye,—so broad and effective are they; and as for its flowers, which are about an inch and a half long,—why, they are so like a veritable *meer-schaum*—the pipe of a true Dutchman from "Faderland"—that you cannot but laugh outright at the first sight of them. Whether Daphne was truly metamorphosed into the sweet flower that bears her name, as Ovid says, we know not; but no one can look at the blossom of the Dutchman's pipe vine, without being convinced that nature has punished some inveterately lazy Dutch smoker by turning him into a vine, which loves nothing so well as to bask in the warm sunshine, with its hundred pipes, dangling on all sides.

And now, having glanced at the best of the climbers and twiners, properly so called (all of which need a little training and supporting), let us take a peep at those climbing shrubs that seize hold of a wall, building, or fence, of themselves, by throwing out their little *rootlets* into the stone or brick wall as they grow up, so that it is as hard to break up any attachments of theirs, when they get fairly established, as it was to part Hector and Andromache. The principal of these are the true Ivy of Europe, the Virginia Creeper, or American Ivy, and the "Trumpet Creepers" (*Bignonias* or *Tecomas*).

These are all fine, picturesque vines, not to be surpassed for certain effects by any thing else that will grow out of doors in our climate. You must remember, however, that, as they are wedded for life to whatever they cling to, they must not be planted by the sides of wooden cottages, which are to be kept in order by a fresh coat of paint now and then. Other climbers may be taken down, and afterwards tied back to their places; but constant, indissoluble intimacies like these must be let alone. You will therefore always take care to plant them where they can fix themselves permanently on a wall of some kind, or else upon some rough wooden building, where they will not be likely to be disturbed.

Certainly the finest of all this class of climbers is the European Ivy. Such rich masses of glossy, deep green foliage, such fine contrasts of light and shade, and such a wealth of associations, is possessed by no other plant; the Ivy, to which the ghost of all the storied past alone tells its tale of departed greatness; the confidant of old ruined castles and abbeys; the bosom companion of solitude itself,—

> "Deep in your most sequestered bower
> Let me at last recline,
> Where solitude, mild, modest flower,
> Leans on her *ivy'd* shrine."

True to these instincts, the Ivy does not seem to be naturalized so easily in America as most other foreign vines. We are yet too young—this country of a great future, and a little past.

The richest and most perfect specimen of it that we have seen, in the northern States, is upon the cottage of Washington Irving, on the Hudson, near Tarrytown. He, who as you all know, lingers over the past with a reverence as fond and poetical as that of a pious Crusader for the walls of Jerusalem—yes, he has completely won the sympathies of the Ivy, even on our own soil, and it has garlanded and decked his antique and quaint cottage, "Sunnyside," till its windows peep out from amid the wealth of its foliage, like the dark eyes of a Spanish Senora from a shadowy canopy of dark lace and darker tresses.

The Ivy is the finest of climbers, too, because it is so perfectly *evergreen*. North of New-York it is a little tender, and needs to be sheltered for a few years, unless it be planted on a north wall, quite out of the reach of the winter sun); and north of Albany, we think it will not grow at all. But all over the middle States it should be planted and cherished, wherever there is a wall for it to cling to, as the finest of all cottage drapery.

After this plant, comes always our Virginia Creeper, or American Ivy, as it is often called (*Ampelopsis*). It grows more rapidly than the Ivy, clings in the same way to wood or stone, and makes rich and beautiful festoons of verdure in summer, dying off in autumn, before the leaves fall, in the finest crimson. Its greatest beauty, on this account, is perhaps seen when it runs up in the centre of a dark cedar, or other evergreen,—exhibiting in October the richest contrast of the two colors. It will grow any where, in the coldest situations, and only asks to be planted, to work out its own problem of beauty without further attention. This and the European Ivy are the two climbers, above all others, for the exteriors of our rural stone churches; to which they will give a local interest greater than that of any carving in stone, at a millionth part of the cost.

The common Trumpet Creeper all of you know by heart. It is rather a wild and rambling fellow in its habits; but nothing is better to cover old outside chimneys, stone out-buildings, and rude walls and fences. The sort with large cup-shaped flowers (*Tecoma grandiflora*), is a most showy and magnificent climber in the middle States, where the winters are moderate, absolutely glowing in July with its thousands of rich orange-red blossoms, like clusters of bright goblets.

We might go on, and enumerate dozens more of fine twining shrubs and climbing roses; but that would only defeat our present object, which is not to give you a garden catalogue, but to tell you of half a dozen hardy shrubby vines, which we implore you to make popular; so that wherever we travel, from Maine to St. Louis, we shall see no rural cottages shivering in their chill nudity of bare walls or barer boards, but draped tastefully with something fresh, and green, and graceful: let it be a hop-vine if nothing better,—but roses, and wistaria, and honeysuckles, if they can be had. How much this apparently trifling feature, if it could be generally carried out, would alter the face of the whole country, you will not at once be able to believe. What summer foliage is to a naked forest, what rich tufts of ferns are to a rock in a woodland dell, what "hyacinthine locks" are to the goddess of beauty, or wings to an angel, the drapery of climbing plants is to cottages in the country.

One word or two about vines in the gardens and pleasure-grounds before we conclude. How to make *arbors* and *trellises* is no mystery, though you will, no doubt, agree with us, that the less formal and the more rustic the better. But how to manage single specimens of fine climbers, in the lawn or garden, so as to display them to the best advantage, is not quite so clear. Small fanciful frames are pretty, but soon want repairs; and stakes, though ever so stout, will rot off at the bottom, and blow down in high winds, to your great mortification; and that, too, perhaps, when your plant is in its very court dress of bud and blossom.

Now the best mode of treating single vines, when you have not a tree to festoon them upon, is one which many of you will be able to attain easily. It is nothing more than getting from the woods the trunk of a cedar-tree, from ten to fifteen feet high, shortening-in all the side branches to within two feet of the trunk (and still shorter near the top), and setting it again, as you would a post, two or three feet deep in the ground.*

Cedar is the best; partly because it will last for ever, and partly because the regular disposition of its branches forms naturally a fine trellis for the shoots to fasten upon.

Plant your favorite climber, whether rose, wistaria, or honeysuckle, at the foot of this tree. It will soon cover it, from top to bottom, with the finest pyramid of verdure. The young shoots will ramble out on its side branches, and when in full bloom, will hang most gracefully or picturesquely from the ends.

The advantage of this mode is that, once obtained, your support lasts for fifty years; it is so firm that winds do not blow it down; it presents every side to the kindly influences of sun and air,

* We owe this hint to Mr. Alfred Smith, of Newport, a most intelligent and successful amateur, in whose garden we first saw fine specimens of this mode of treating climbers.

and permits every blossom that opens, to be seen by the admiring spectator. How it looks at first, and afterwards, in a complete state, we have endeavored to give you a faint idea in this little sketch.

"What shall those of us do who have neither cottages nor gardens?—who, in short, are confined to a little front and back yard of a town life, and yet who love vines and climbing plants with all our hearts?"

Movable Trellis.

That is a hard case, truly. But, now we think of it, that ingenious and clever *horticulteur*, Monsieur Van Houtte, of Ghent, has contrived the very thing for you.* Here it is. He calls it a "Trellis Mobile;" and if we mistake not, it will be quite as valuable for the ornament and defence of cities, as the *Garde Mobile* of the Parisians. It is nothing more than a good strong wooden box, upon wooden rollers. The box is about three feet long, and the double trellis may be eight or ten feet high. In this box the finer sorts of exotic climbers, such as passion flowers, everblooming roses, maurandias, ipomea learii, and the like, may be grown with a charming effect. Put upon wheels, as this itinerant bower is, it may be transported, as Mr. Van Houtte says, "wherever fancy dictates, and even into the apartments of the house itself." And here, having fairly escorted you back to your apartments, after our long

* *Flore des Serres.*

talk about out-door drapery, we leave you to examine the *Trellis Mobile*, and wish you a good morning.

Climbing Plants on Cedar Trunks.

LANDSCAPE GARDENING.

LANDSCAPE GARDENING.

I.

THE PHILOSOPHY OF RURAL TASTE.

August, 1849.

ALL travellers agree, that while the English people are far from being remarkable for their taste in the arts generally, they are unrivalled in their taste for landscape gardening. So completely is this true, that wherever on the continent one finds a garden, conspicuous for the taste of its design, one is certain to learn that it is laid out in the "English style," and usually kept by an English gardener.

Not, indeed, that the south of Europe is wanting in magnificent gardens, which are as essentially national in their character as the parks and pleasure-grounds of England. The surroundings of the superb villas of Florence and Rome, are fine examples of a species of scenery as distinct and striking as any to be found in the world; but which, however splendid, fall as far below the English gardens in interesting the imagination, as a level plain does below the finest mountain valley in Switzerland. In the English landscape garden, one sees and feels every where the spirit of *nature*, only softened and refined by art. In the French or Italian garden, one sees and feels only the effects of *art*, slightly assisted by nature. In one, the free and luxuriant growth of every tree and shrub, the widening and curving of every walk, suggests perhaps even a higher ideal of nature,—a miniature of a primal paradise, as we would imagine it to have been by divine right; in the other, the prodigality of works of art, the variety of statues and vases, terraces and balustrades, united with walks marked by the same studied symmetry and artistic formality, and only mingled with just foliage enough to constitute a garden,—all this suggests rather a statue gallery in the open air,—an accompaniment to the fair architecture of the mansion, than any pure or natural ideas of landscape beauty.

The only writer who has ever attempted to account for this striking distinction of national taste in gardening, which distinguishes the people of northern and southern Europe, is Humboldt. In his last great work—*Cosmos*—he has devoted some pages to the consideration of the study of nature, and the description of natural scenery,—a portion of the work in the highest degree interesting to every man of taste, as well as every lover of nature.

In this portion he shows, we think, very conclusively, that certain races of mankind, however great in other gifts, are deficient in their perceptions of natural beauty; that northern nations possess the love of nature much more strongly than those of the south; and that the Greeks and Romans, richly gifted as they were with the artistic endowments, were inferior to other nations in a profound feeling of the beauty of nature.

Humboldt also shows that our enjoyment of natural landscape gardening, which many suppose to have originated in the cultivated and refined taste of a later age, is, on the contrary, purely a matter of national organization. The parks of the Persian monarchs, and the pleasure-gardens of the Chinese, were characterized by the same spirit of natural beauty which we see in the English landscape gardens, and which is widely distinct from that elegant formality of the geometric gardens of the Greeks and Romans of several centuries later. To prove how sound were the principles of Chinese taste, ages ago, he gives us a quotation from an ancient Chinese writer, Lieu-tscheu, which might well be the text of the most tasteful improver of the present day, and which we copy for the study of our own readers.

"What is it," says Lieu-tscheu, "that we seek in the pleasures of a garden? It has always been agreed that these plantations *should make men amends for living at a distance from what would be their more congenial and agreeable dwelling-place—in the midst of nature,* free and unconstrained. The art of laying out gardens consists, therefore, in combining cheerfulness of prospect, luxuriance of growth, shade, retirement and repose; so that the rural aspect may produce an illusion. Variety, which is the chief merit in the natural landscape, must be sought by the choice of ground, with alternation of hill and dale, flowing streams and lakes, covered with aquatic plants. *Symmetry is wearisome; and a garden where every thing betrays constraint and art, becomes tedious and distasteful.*"

We shall seek in vain, in the treatises of modern writers, for a theory of rural taste more concise and satisfactory than this of the Chinese landscape garden.

Looking at this instinctive love of nature as a national characteristic, which belongs almost exclusively to distinct races, Humboldt asserts, that while the "profoundest feeling of nature speaks forth in the earliest poetry of the Hebrews, the Indians, and the Semitic and Indo-Germanic nations, it is comparatively wanting in the works of the Greeks and Romans."

"In Grecian art," says he, "all is made to concentrate within the sphere of *human* life and feeling. The description of nature, in her manifold diversity, as a distinct branch of poetic literature, was altogether foreign to the ideas of the Greeks. With them, the landscape is always the mere background of a picture, in the foreground of which human figures are moving. Passion, breaking forth in action, invited their attention almost exclusively; the agitation of politics, and a life passed chiefly in public, withdrew men's minds from enthusiastic absorption in the tranquil pursuit of nature."

On the other hand, the poetry of Britain, from a very early period, has been especially remarkable for the deep and instinctive love of natural beauty which it exhibits. And here lies the explanation of the riddle of the superiority of English taste in rural embellishment; that people enjoying their gardens the more as they embodied the spirit of nature, while the Italians, like the Greeks, enjoyed them the more as they embodied the spirit of art.

The Romans, tried in the alembic of the great German *savan*, are found still colder in their love of nature's charms than the Greeks. "A nation which manifested a marked predilection for agriculture and rural life might have justified other hopes; but with all their capacity for practical activity, the Romans, in their cold gravity and measured sobriety of understanding, were, as a people, far inferior to the Greeks in the perception of beauty, far less sensitive to its influence, and much more devoted to the realities of every-day life, than to an idealizing contemplation of nature."

Judging them by their writings, Humboldt pronounces the great Roman writers to be comparatively destitute of real poetic feeling for nature. Livy and Tacitus show, in their histories, little or no interest in natural scenery. Cicero describes landscape without poetic feeling. Pliny, though he rises to true poetic inspiration when describing the great moving causes of the natural universe, "has few individual descriptions of nature." Ovid, in his exile, saw little to charm him in the scenery around him; and Virgil, though he often devoted himself to subjects which prompt the enthusiasm of a lover of nature, rarely glows with the fire of a true worshipper of her mysterious charms. And not only were the Romans indifferent to the beauty of natural landscape which daily surrounded them, but even to the sublimity and magnificence of those wilder and grander scenes, into which their love of conquest often led them. The following striking paragraph, from Humboldt's work, is at once eloquent and convincing on this point:

"No description of the eternal snows of the Alps, when tinged in the morning or evening with a rosy hue,—of the beauty of the blue glacier ice, or of any part of the grandeur of the scenery in Switzerland,—have reached us from the ancients, although statesmen and generals, with men of letters in their train, were constantly passing from Helvetia into Gaul. All these travellers think only of complaining of the difficulties of the way; the romantic character of the scenery seems never to have engaged their attention. It is even known that Julius Cæsar, when returning to his legions, in Gaul, employed his time while passing over the Alps in preparing a grammatical treatise, 'De Analogia.'"

The corollary to be drawn from this learned and curious investigation of the history of national sensibility and taste, is a very clear and satisfactory one, viz., that as success, in "the art of composing a landscape" (as Humboldt significantly calls landscape-gardening), depends on appreciation of nature, the taste of an individual as well as that of a nation, will be in direct proportion to the profound sensibility with which he perceives the Beautiful in natural scenery.

Our own observation not only fully confirms this theory, but it also leads us to the recognition of the fact, that among our countrymen, at the present day, there are two distinct classes of taste in rural art; first, the poetic or northern taste, based on a deep, instinctive feeling for nature; and second, the artistic or symmetric taste, based on a perception of the Beautiful, as embodied in works of art.

The larger part of our countrymen inherit the northern or Anglo-Saxon love of nature, and find most delight in the natural landscape garden; but we have also not a few to whom the classic villa, with its artistic adornments of vase and statue, urn and terrace, is an object of much more positive pleasure than the most varied and seductive gardens, laid out with all the witchery of nature's own handiwork.

It is not part of our philosophy to urge our readers to war against their organizations, to whichever path, in the "Delectable Mountains," they may be led by them; but those who have not already studied *Cosmos* will, we trust, at least thank us for giving them the key to their natural bias towards one or the other of the two world-wide styles of ornamental gardening.

II.

THE BEAUTIFUL IN GROUND.

March, 1852.

WE have sketched, elsewhere, the elements of the beautiful in a tree. Let us glance for a few moments at the beautiful in ground.

We may have readers who think themselves not devoid of some taste for nature, but who have never thought of looking for beauty in the mere surface of the earth—whether in a natural landscape, or in ornamental grounds. Their idea of beauty is, for the most part, attached to the foliage and verdure, the streams of water, the high hills and the deep valleys, that make up the landscape. A meadow is to them but a meadow, and a ploughed field is but the same thing in a rough state. And yet there is a great and enduring interest, to a refined and artistic eye, in the mere surface of the ground. There is a sense of pleasure awakened by the pleasing lines into which yonder sloping bank of turf steals away from the eye, and a sense of ugliness and harshness, by the raw and broken outline of the abandoned quarry on the hill-side, which hardly any one can be so obtuse as not to see and feel. Yet the finer gradations are nearly overlooked, and the charm of beautiful surface in a lawn is seldom or never considered in selecting a new site or improving an old one.

We believe artists and men of taste have agreed that all forms of acknowledged beauty are composed of *curved lines*; and we may add to this, that the more gentle and gradual the curves, or rather, the farther they are removed from those hard and forcible lines which denote violence, the more beautiful are they. The principle applies as well to the surface of the earth as to other objects. The most beautiful shape in ground is that where one undulation melts gradually and insensibly into another. Every one who has observed scenery where the foregrounds were remarkable for beauty, must have been struck by this prevalence of curved lines; and every landscape gardener well knows that no grassy surface is so captivating to the eye, as one where these gentle swells and undulations rise and melt away gradually into one another. Some poet, happy in his fancy, has called such bits of grassy slopes and swells, "earth's smiles;" and when the effect of the beauty and form of outline is heightened by the pleasing gradation of light and shade, caused by the sun's light, variously reflected by such undulations of lawn, the simile seems strikingly appropriate. With every change of position the outlines vary, and the lights and shades vary with them, so that the eye is doubly pleased by the beauty of form and chiaro-oscuro, in a lawn with gracefully undulating surface.

A flat or *level* surface is considered beautiful by many persons, though it has no beauty in itself. It is, in fact, chiefly valued because it evinces art. Though there is no positive beauty in a straight or level line, it is often interesting as expressive of *power*, and we feel as much awed by the boundless prairie or desert, as by the lofty snow-capped hill. On a smaller scale, a level surface is sometimes agreeable in the midst of a rude and wild country by way of contrast, as a small, level garden in the Alps will sometimes attract one astonishingly, that would be passed by, unnoticed, in the midst of a flat and cultivated country.

Hence, as there are a thousand men who value power, where there is one who can feel beauty, we see all ignorant persons who set about embellishing their pleasure-grounds, or even the site for a home, immediately commence *levelling* the surface. Once brought to this level, improvement can go no further, according to their views, since to subjugate or level, is the whole aim of man's ambition. Once levelled, you may give to grounds, or even to a whole landscape, according to their theory, as much beauty as you like. It is only a question of expense.

This is a fearful fallacy, however; fearful, oftentimes, to both the eye and the purse. If a dead level were the thing needful to constitute beauty of surface—then all Holland would be the Arcadia of Landscape Painters; and while Claude, condemned to tame Italy, would have painted the interior of inns, and groups of boors drinking (vide the Dutch School of Art), Teniers, living in the dead level of his beautiful nature, would have bequeathed to the world pictures of his native land, full of the loveliness of meadows smooth as a carpet, or enlivened only by pollard willows and stagnant canals. It is not the less fearful to see, as we have often seen in this country, where new places are continually made, a finely varied outline of ground utterly spoiled by being graded for the mansion and its surrounding lawn, at an expense which would have curved all the walks, and filled the grounds with the finest trees and shrubs, if their surface had been left nearly or quite as nature formed it. Not much better, or even far worse, is the foolish fancy many persons have of *terracing* every piece of sloping ground—as a mere matter of ornament, where no terrace is needed. It may be pretty safely said, that a terrace is always ugly, unless it is on a large scale, and is treated with dignity, so as to become part of the building itself, or more properly be supposed to belong to it than to the grounds—like the fine, architectural terraces which surround the old English mansions. But little gardens thrown up into terraces, are devoid of all beauty whatever—though they may often be rendered more useful or available in this way.

The surface of ground is rarely *ugly* in a state of nature—because all nature leans to the beautiful, and the constant action of the elements goes continually to soften and wear away the harshness and violence of surface. What cannot be softened, is hidden and rounded by means of foliage, trees and shrubs, and creeping vines, and so the tendency to the curve is always greater and greater. But man often forms ugly surfaces of ground, by breaking up all natural curves, without recognizing their expression, by distributing lumps of earth here and there, by grading levels in the midst of undulations, and raising mounds on perfectly smooth surfaces; in short, by regarding only the little he wishes to do in his folly, and not studying the larger part that nature has already done in her wisdom. As a common, though accidental illustration of this, we may notice that the mere routine of tillage on a farm, has a tendency to destroy natural beauty of surface, by ridging up the soil at the outsides of the field, and thus breaking up that continuous flow of line which delights the eye.

Our object in these remarks, is simply to ask our readers to think in the beginning, before they even commence any improvements on the surface of ground which they wish to embellish—to think in what natural beauty really consists, and whether in grading, they are not wasting money, and losing that which they are seeking. It will be better still, if they will consider the matter seriously, when they are about buying a place, since, as we have before observed, no money is expended with so little to show for it, and so little satisfaction, as that spent in changing the original surface of the ground.

Practically—the rules we would deduce are the following: To select, always, if possible, a surface varied by gentle curves and undulations. If something of this character already exists, it may often be greatly heightened or improved at little cost. Very often, too, a nearly level surface may, by a very trifling addition—only adding a few inches in certain points, be raised to a character of positive beauty—by simply following the hints given by nature.

When a surface is quite level by nature, we must usually content ourselves with trusting to planting, and the arrangement of walks, buildings, &c., to produce beauty and variety; and we would always, in such cases, rather expend money in introducing beautiful vases, statues, or other works of positive artistic merit, than to terrace and unmake what character nature has stamped on the ground.

Positively ugly and forbidding surfaces of ground, may be rendered highly interesting and beautiful, only by changing their character, entirely, by planting. Such ground, after this has been done, becomes only the skeleton of the fair outside of beauty and verdure that covers the forbidding original. Some of the most picturesque ravines and rocky hill-sides, if stripped entirely of their foliage, would appear as ugly as they were before beautiful; and while this may teach the improver that there is no situation that may not be rendered attractive, if the soil will yield a growth of trees, shrubs, and vines, it does not the less render it worth our attention in choosing or improving a place, to examine carefully beforehand, in what really consists the Beautiful in ground, and whether we should lose or gain it in our proposed improvements.

III.

HINTS TO RURAL IMPROVERS.

July, 1848.

ONE of the most striking proofs of the progress of refinement, in the United States, is the rapid increase of taste for ornamental gardening and rural embellishment in all the older portions of the northern and middle States.

It cannot be denied, that the tasteful improvement of a country residence is both one of the most agreeable and the most natural recreations that can occupy a cultivated mind. With all the interest and, to many, all the excitement of the more seductive amusements of society, it has the incalculable advantage of fostering only the purest feelings, and (unlike many other occupations of business men) refining, instead of hardening the heart.

The great German poet, Goethe, says—

> "Happy the man who hath escaped the town,
> Him did an angel bless when he was born."

This apostrophe was addressed to the devotee of country life as a member of a *class*, in the old world, where men, for the most part, are confined to certain walks of life by the limits of caste, to a degree totally unknown in this country.

With us, country life is a leading object of nearly all men's desires. The wealthiest merchant looks upon his country-seat as the best ultimatum of his laborious days in the counting-house. The most indefatigable statesman dates, in his retirement, from his "Ashland," or his "Lindenwold." Webster has his "Marshfield," where his scientific agriculture is no less admirable than his profound eloquence in the Senate. Taylor's well-ordered plantation is not less significant of the man, than the battle of Buena Vista. Washington Irving's cottage, on the Hudson, is even more poetical than any chapter of his Sketch Book; and Cole, the greatest of our landscape painters, had his rural home under the very shadow of the Catskills.

This is well. In the United States, nature and domestic life are better than society and the manners of towns. Hence all sensible men gladly escape, earlier or later, and partially or wholly, from the turmoil of the cities. Hence the dignity and value of country life is every day augmenting. And hence the enjoyment of landscape or ornamental gardening—which, when in pure taste, may properly be called *a more refined kind of nature*,—is every day becoming more and more widely diffused.

Those who are not as conversant as ourselves with the statistics of horticulture and rural architecture, have no just idea of the rapid multiplication of pretty cottages and villas in many parts of North America. The vast web of railroads which now interlaces the continent, though really built for the purposes of trade, cannot wholly escape doing some duty for the Beautiful as well as the Useful. Hundreds and thousands, formerly obliged to live in the crowded streets of cities, now find themselves able to enjoy a country cottage, several miles distant,—the old notions of time and space being half annihilated; and these suburban cottages enable the busy citizen to breathe freely, and keep alive his love for nature, till the time shall come when he shall have wrung out of the nervous hand of commerce enough means to enable him to realize his ideal of the "retired life" of an American landed proprietor.

The number of our country residences which are laid out, and kept at a high point of ornamental gardening, is certainly not very large, though it is continually increasing. But we have no hesitation in saying that the aggregate sum annually expended in this way, for the last five years, in North America, is not exceeded in any country in the world save one.

England ranks before all other countries in the perfection of its landscape gardening; and enormous, almost incredible sums have been expended by her wealthier class upon their rural improvements.

But the taste of England is, we have good reasons for believing, at its maximum; and the expenditure of the aristocracy is, of late, chiefly devoted to *keeping up* the existing style of their parks and pleasure-grounds. In this country, it is quite surprising how rapid is the creation of new country residences, and how large is the aggregate amount continually expended in the construction of houses and grounds, of a character more or less ornamental.

Granting all this, it cannot be denied that there are also, in the United States, large sums of money—many millions of dollars—annually, most unwisely and injudiciously expended in these rural improvements. While we gladly admit that there has been a surprising and gratifying advance in taste within the last ten years, we are also forced to confess that there are countless specimens of *bad taste*, and hundreds of examples where a more agreeable and satisfactory result *might have been attained at one-half the cost.*

Is it not, therefore, worth while to inquire a little more definitely what are the obstacles that lie in the way of forming satisfactory, tasteful, and agreeable country residences?

The common reply to this question, when directly put in the face of any signal example of failure is—"Oh, Mr. —— is a man of no *taste!*" There is, undoubtedly, often but too much truth in this clean cut at the *æsthetic* capacities of the unlucky improver. But it by no means follows that it is always true. A man may have taste, and yet if he trusts to his own powers of direction, signally fail in tasteful improvements.

We should say that two grand errors are the fertile causes of all the failures in the rural improvements of the United States at the present moment.

The first error lies in supposing that good taste is a natural gift, which springs heaven-born into perfect existence—needing no cultivation or improvement. The second is in supposing that taste alone is sufficient to the production of extensive or complete works in architecture or landscape gardening.

A lively *sensibility to the Beautiful*, is a natural faculty, mistaken by more than half the world for good taste itself. But good taste, in the true meaning of the terms, or, more strictly, correct taste, only exists where sensibility to the Beautiful, and good judgment, are combined in the same mind. Thus, a person may have a delicate organization, which will enable him to receive pleasure from every thing that possesses grace or beauty, but with it so little power of discrimination as to be unable to select among many pleasing objects, those which, under given circumstances, are the most beautiful, harmonious, or fitting. Such a person may be said to have natural sensibility, or fine perceptions, but not good taste; the latter belongs properly to one who, among many beautiful objects, rapidly compares, discriminates, and gives due rank to each, according to its merit.

Now, although that delicacy of organization, usually called taste, is a natural gift, which can no more be acquired than hearing can be by a deaf man, yet, in most persons, this sensibility to the Beautiful may be cultivated and ripened into good taste by the study and comparison of beautiful productions in nature and art.

This is precisely what we wish to insist upon, to all persons about to commence rural embellishments, who have not a cultivated or just taste; but only sensibility, or what they would call a natural taste.

Three-fourths of all the building and ornamental gardening of America, hitherto, have been *amateur* performances—often the productions of persons who, with abundant natural sensibility, have taken no pains to cultivate it and form a correct, or even a good taste, by studying and comparing the best examples already in existence in various parts of this or other countries. Now the study of the best productions in the fine arts is not more necessary to the success of the young painter and sculptor than that of buildings and grounds to the amateur or professional improver, who desires to improve a country residence well and tastefully. In both cases comparison, discrimination, the use of the reasoning faculty, educate the natural delicacy of perception into taste, more or less just and perfect, and enable it not only to arrive at Beauty, but to select the most beautiful for the end in view.

There are at the present moment, without going abroad, opportunities of cultivating a taste in landscape-gardening, quite sufficient to enable any one of natural sensibility to the Beautiful, combined with good reasoning powers, to arrive at that point which may be

8

considered good taste. There are, indeed, few persons who are aware how instructive and interesting to an amateur, a visit to all the *finest* country residences of the older States, would be at the present moment. The study of books on taste is by no means to be neglected by the novice in rural embellishment; but the practical illustrations of different styles and principles, to be found in the best cottage and villa residences, are far more convincing and instructive to most minds, than lessons taught in any other mode whatever.

We shall not, therefore, hesitate to commend a few of the most interesting places to the study of the tasteful improver. By the expenditure of the necessary time and money to examine and compare thoroughly such places, he will undoubtedly save himself much unnecessary outlay; he will be able to seize and develope many beauties which would otherwise be overlooked; and, most of all, he will be able to avoid the exhibition of that crude and uncultivated taste, which characterizes the attempts of the majority of beginners, who rather know how to *enjoy* beautiful grounds than how to go to work to *produce* them.

For that species of suburban cottage or villa residence which is most frequent within the reach of persons of moderate fortunes, the environs of Boston afford the finest examples in the Union. Averaging from five to twenty acres, they are usually laid out with taste, are well planted with a large variety of trees and shrubs, and above all, are exquisitely kept. As a cottage ornée, there are few places in America more perfect than the grounds of Colonel Perkins, or of Thos. Lee, Esq., at Brookline, near Boston. The latter is especially remarkable for the beauty of the lawn, and the successful management of rare trees and shrubs, and is a most excellent study for the suburban landscape-gardener. There are many other places in that neighborhood abounding with interest; but the great feature of the gardens of Boston lies rather in their horticultural than their artistical merit. In forcing and skilful cultivation, they still rank before any other of the country. Mr. Cushing's residence, near Watertown, has long been celebrated in this respect.

An amateur who wishes to study trees, should visit the fine old places in the neighborhood of Philadelphia. A couple of days spent at the *Bartram Garden*, the *Hamilton Place*, and many of the old estates bordering the Schuylkill, will make him familiar with rare and fine trees, such as *Salisburias*, *Magnolias*, *Virgilias*, etc., of a size and beauty of growth that will not only fill him with astonishment, but convince him what effects may be produced by planting. As a specimen of a cottage residence of the first class, exquisitely kept, there are also few examples in America more perfect than Mrs. Camac's grounds, four or five miles from Philadelphia.

For landscape gardening, on a large scale, and in its best sense, there are no places in America which compare with those on the east bank of the Hudson, between Hyde Park and the town of Hudson. The extent of the grounds, and their fine natural advantages of wood and lawn, combined with their grand and beautiful views, and the admirable manner in which these natural charms are heightened by art, place them far before any other residences in the United States in picturesque beauty. In a strictly *horticultural* sense, they are, perhaps, as much inferior to the best places about Boston as they are superior to them in the beauty of landscape gardening and picturesque effect.

Among these places, those which enjoy the highest reputation, are *Montgomery Place*, the seat of Mrs. Edward Livingston, *Blithewood*, the seat of R. Donaldson, Esq., and *Hyde Park*, the seat of W. Langdon, Esq. The first is remarkable for its extent, for the wonderful variety of scenery—wood, water, and gardenesque—which it embraces, and for the excellent general keeping of the grounds. The second is a fine illustration of great natural beauty,—a mingling of the graceful and grand in scenery,—admirably treated and heightened by art. Hyde Park is almost too well known to need more than a passing notice. It is a noble site, greatly enhanced in interest lately, by the erection of a fine new mansion.

The student or amateur in landscape gardening, who wishes to examine two places as remarkable for breadth and dignity of effect as any in America, will not fail to go to the *Livingston Manor*, seven miles east of Hudson, and to *Rensselaerwyck*, a few miles from Albany, on the eastern shore. The former has the best kept and most extensive lawn in the Union; and the latter, with five or six miles of gravelled walks and drives, within its own boundaries, exhibits some of the cleverest illustrations of practical skill in *laying out* grounds that we remember to have seen.*

If no person, about to improve a country residence, would expend a dollar until he had visited and carefully studied, at least *twenty places* of the character of these which we have thus pointed out, we think the number of specimens of bad taste, or total want of taste, would be astonishingly diminished. We could point to half a dozen examples within our own knowledge, where ten days spent by their proprietors in examining what had already been done in some of the best specimens of building and gardening in the country, could not but have prevented their proprietors from making their places absolutely hideous, and throwing away ten, twenty, or thirty thousand dollars. Ignorance is *not* bliss, nor is it economy, in improving a country-seat.

We think, also, there can scarcely be a question that an examination of the best examples of taste in rural improvement at home, is far more instructive to an American, than an inspection of the finest country places in Europe; and this, chiefly, because a really successful example at home is based upon republican modes of life, enjoyment, and expenditure,—which are almost the reverse of those of an aristocratic government. For the same reason, we think those places most instructive, and best worthy general study in this country, which realize most completely our ideal of refined country life in America. To do this, it is by no means necessary to have baronial possessions, or a mansion of vast extent. No more should be attempted than can be done well, and in perfect harmony with our habits, mode of life, and domestic institutions. Hence, smaller suburban residences, like those in the neighborhood of Boston, are, perhaps, better models, or studies for the public generally, than our grander and more extensive seats; mainly because they are more expressive of the means and character of the majority of

* We should apologize for thus pointing out private places, did we not know that the liberal proprietors of those just named, are persons who take the liveliest interest in the progress of good taste, and will cheerfully allow their places to be examined by those who visit them with such motives as we here urge,—very different from idle curiosity.

those of our countrymen whose intelligence and refinement lead them to find their happiness in country life. It is better to attempt a small place, and attain perfect success, than to fail in one of greater extent.

Having pointed out what we consider indispensable to be done, to assist in forming, if possible, a correct taste in those who have only a natural delicacy of organization, which they miscall taste, we may also add that good taste, or even a perfect taste, is often by no means sufficient for the production of really *extensive* works of rural architecture or landscape-gardening.

"Taste," says Cousin, in his Philosophy of the Beautiful, "is a faculty indolent and passive; it reposes tranquilly in the contemplation of the Beautiful in Nature. *Genius* is proud and free; genius creates and reconstructs."

He, therefore (whether as amateur or professor), who hopes to be successful in the highest degree, in the arts of refined building or landscape-gardening, must possess not only *taste* to appreciate the Beautiful, but genius to produce it. Do we not often see persons who have for half their lives enjoyed a reputation for correct taste, suddenly lose it when they attempt to embody it in some practical manner? Such persons have only the "indolent and passive," and not the "free and creative faculty." Yet there are a thousand little offices of supervision and control, where the taste alone may be exercised with the happiest results upon a country place. It is by no means a small merit to prevent any violations of good taste, if we cannot achieve any great work of genius. And we are happy to be able to say that we know many amateurs in this country who unite with a refined taste a creative genius, or practical ability to carry beautiful improvements into execution, which has already enriched the country with beautiful examples of rural residences; and we can congratulate ourselves that, along with other traits of the Anglo-Saxon mind, we have by no means failed in our inheritance of that fine appreciation of rural beauty, and the power of developing it, which the English have so long possessed.

We hope the number of those who are able to enjoy this most refined kind of happiness will every day grow more and more numerous; and that it may do so, we are confident we can give no better advice than again to commend beginners, before they lay a corner stone, or plant a tree, to visit and study at least a dozen or twenty of the acknowledged best specimens of good taste in America.

IV.

A FEW HINTS ON LANDSCAPE GARDENING.

November, 1851.

NOVEMBER is, above all others, the tree-planting month over the wide Union. Accordingly, every one who has a rood of land, looks about him at this season, to see what can be done to improve and embellish it. Some have bought new places, where they have to build and create every thing in the way of home scenery, and they, of course, will have their heads full of shade trees and fruit trees, ornamental shrubs and evergreens, lawns and walks, and will tax their imagination to the utmost to see in the future all the varied beauty which they mean to work out of the present blank fields that they have taken in hand. These, look for the most rapid-growing and effective materials, with which to hide their nakedness, and spread something of the drapery of beauty over their premises, in the shortest possible time. Others, have already a goodly stock of foliage and shade, but the trees have been planted without taste, and by thinning out somewhat here, making an opening there, and planting a little yonder, they hope to break up the stiff boundaries, and thus magically to convert awkward angles into graceful curves, and harmonious outlines. Whilst others, again, whose gardens and pleasure-grounds have long had their earnest devotion, are busy turning over the catalogues of the nurseries, in search of rare and curious trees and shrubs, to add still more of novelty and interest to their favorite lawns and walks. As the pleasure of creation may be supposed to be the highest pleasure, and as the creation of scenery in landscape gardening is the nearest approach to the matter that we can realize in a practical way, it is not difficult to see that November, dreary as it may seem to the cockneys who have rushed back to gas-lights and the paved streets of the city, is full of interest, and even excitement, to the real lover of the country.

It is, however, one of the characteristics of the human mind to overlook that which is immediately about us, however admirable, and to attach the greatest importance to whatever is rare, and difficult to be obtained. A remarkable illustration of the truth of this, may be found in the ornamental gardening of this country, which is noted for the strongly marked features made in its artificial scenery by certain poorer sorts of foreign trees, as well as the almost total neglect of finer native materials, that are indigenous to the soil. We will undertake to say, for example, that almost one-half of all the deciduous trees that have been set in ornamental plantations for the last ten years, have been composed, for the most part, of two very indifferent foreign trees—the ailantus and the silver poplar. When we say indifferent, we do not mean to say that such trees as the ailantus and the silver poplar, are not valuable trees in their way—that is, that they are rapid growing, will thrive in all soils, and are transplanted with the greatest facility—suiting at once both the money-making grower and the ignorant planter—but we do say, that when such trees as the American elms, maples and oaks, can be raised with so little trouble—trees as full of grace, dignity, and beauty, as any that grow in any part of the world—trees, too, that go on gathering new beauty with age, instead of throwing up suckers that utterly spoil lawns, or that become, after the first few years, only a more intolerable nuisance every day—it is time to protest against the indiscriminate use of such sylvan materials—no matter how much of "heavenly origin," or "silvery" foliage, they may have in their well sounding names.

It is by no means the fault of the nurserymen, that their nurseries abound in ailantuses and poplars, while so many of our fine forest trees are hardly to be found. The nurserymen are bound to pursue their business so as to make it profitable, and if people ignore oaks and ashes, and adore poplars and ailantuses, nurserymen cannot be expected to starve because the planting public generally are destitute of taste.

What the planting public need is to have their attention called to the study of *nature*—to be made to understand that it is in our beautiful woodland slopes, with their undulating outlines, our broad river meadows studded with single trees and groups allowed to grow and expand quite in a state of free and graceful development, our steep hills, sprinkled with picturesque pines and firs, and our deep valleys, dark with hemlocks and cedars, that the real lessons in the beautiful and picturesque are to be taken, which will lead us to the appreciation of the finest elements of beauty in the embellishment of our country places—instead of this miserable rage for "trees of heaven" and other fashionable tastes of the like nature. There are, for example, to be found along side of almost every sequestered lawn by the road-side in the northern States, three trees that are strikingly remarkable for beauty of foliage, growth or flower, viz.: the tulip-tree, the sassafras, and the pepperidge. The first is, for stately elegance, almost unrivalled among forest trees: the second, when planted in cultivated soil and allowed a fair chance, is more beautiful in its diversified laurel-like foliage than almost any foreign tree in our pleasure-grounds: and the last is not surpassed by the orange or the bay in its glossy leaves, deep green as an emerald in summer, and rich red as a ruby in autumn—and all of them freer from the attacks of insects than either larches, lindens, or elms, or a dozen other favorite foreign trees,—besides being unaffected by the summer sun where horse-chestnuts are burned brown, and holding their foliage through all the season like native-born Americans, when foreigners shrivel and die; and yet we could name a dozen nurseries where there is a large collection of ornamental trees of foreign growth, but neither a sassafras, nor a pepperidge, nor perhaps a tulip-tree could be had for love or money.

There is a large spirit of inquiry and a lively interest in rural taste, awakened on every side of us, at the present time, from Maine to the valley of the Mississippi—but the great mistake made by most novices is that they study *gardens* too much, and *nature* too little. Now gardens, in general, are stiff and graceless, except just so far as nature, ever free and flowing, re-asserts her rights, in spite of man's want of taste, or helps him when he has endeavored to work in her own spirit. But the fields and woods are full of instruction, and in such features of our richest and most smiling and diversified country must the best hints for the embellishment of rural homes always be derived. And yet it is not any portion of the woods and fields that we wish our finest pleasure-ground scenery precisely to resemble. We rather wish to *select* from the finest sylvan features of nature, and to recompose the materials in a choicer manner—by rejecting any thing foreign to the spirit of elegance and refinement which should characterize the landscape of the most tasteful country residence—a landscape in which all that is graceful and beautiful in nature is preserved—all her most perfect forms and most harmonious lines—but with that added refinement which high keeping and continual care confer on natural beauty, without impairing its innate spirit of freedom, or the truth and freshness of its intrinsic character. A planted elm of fifty years, which stands in the midst of the smooth lawn before yonder mansion—its long graceful branches towering upwards like an antique classical vase, and then sweeping to the ground with a curve as beautiful as the falling spray of a fountain, has all the freedom of character of its best prototypes in the wild woods, with a refinement and a perfection of symmetry which it would be next to impossible to find in a wild tree. Let us take it then as the type of all true art in landscape gardening—which selects from natural materials that abound in any country, its best sylvan features, and by giving them a better opportunity than they could otherwise obtain, brings about a higher beauty of development and a more perfect expression than nature itself offers. Study landscape in nature more, and the gardens and their catalogues less,—is our advice to the rising generation of planters, who wish to embellish their places in the best and purest taste.

V.

ON THE MISTAKES OF CITIZENS IN COUNTRY LIFE.

January, 1849.

NO one loves the country more sincerely, or welcomes new devotees to the worship of its pure altars more warmly, than ourselves. To those who bring here hearts capable of understanding the lessons of truth and beauty, which the Good Creator has written so legibly on all his works; to those in whose nature is implanted a sentiment that interprets the tender and the loving, as well as the grand and sublime lessons of the universe, what a life full of joy, and beauty, and inspiration, is that of the country; to such,

—— "The deep recess of dusky groves,
Or forest where the deer securely roves,
The fall of waters and the song of birds,
And hills that echo to the distant herds,
Are luxuries, excelling all the glare
The world can boast, and her chief fav'rites share."

There are those who rejoice in our Anglo-Saxon inheritance of the love of conquest, and the desire for boundless territory,—who exult in the "manifest destiny" of the race, to plant the standard of the eagle or the lion in every soil, and every zone of the earth's surface. We rejoice much more in the love of country life, the enjoyment of nature, and the taste for rural beauty, which we also inherit from our Anglo-Saxon forefathers, and to which, more than all else, they owe so many of the peculiar virtues of the race.

With us, as a people, retirement to country life, must come to be the universal pleasure of the nation. The successful statesman, professional man, merchant, trader, mechanic,—all look to it as the only way of enjoying the *otium cum dignitate;* and the great beauty and extent of our rural scenery, as well as the absence of any great national capital, with its completeness of metropolitan life, must render the country the most satisfactory place for passing a part of every man's days, who has the power of choice.

It is not to be denied, however, that "retirement to the country," which is the beau ideal of all the busy and successful citizens of our towns, is not always found to be the elysium which it has been fondly imagined. No doubt there are good reasons why nothing in this world should afford perfect and uninterrupted happiness.

"The desire of the moth for the star"

might cease, if parks and pleasure-grounds could fill up the yearnings of human nature, so as to leave no aspirations for futurity.

But this is not our present meaning. What we would say is, that numbers are disappointed with country life, and perhaps leave it in disgust, without reason, either from mistaken views of its nature, of their own incapacities for enjoying it, or a want of practical ability to govern it.

We might throw our views into a more concrete shape, perhaps, by saying that the disappointments in country life arise chiefly from two causes. The first is, from *expecting too much.* The second, from *undertaking too much.*

There are, we should judge from observation, many citizens who retire to the country, after ten or twenty years' hard service in the business and society of towns, and who carry with them the most romantic ideas of country life. They expect to pass their time in wandering over daisy-spangled meadows, and by the side of meandering streams. They will listen to the singing of birds, and find a perpetual feast of enjoyment in the charm of hills and mountains. Above all, they have an *extravagant* notion of the purity and the simplicity of country life. All its intercourse, as well as all its pleasures, are to be so charmingly pure, pastoral, and poetical!

What a disappointment to find that there is *prose* even in country life,—that meadows do not give up their sweet incense, or corn-fields wave their rich harvests without care,—that "work-folks" are often unfaithful, and oxen stubborn, even an hundred miles from the smoke of towns, or the intrigues of great cities.

Another, and a large class of those citizens, who expect too much in the country, are those who find, to their astonishment, that the country is *dull.* They really admire nature, and love rural life; but, though they are ashamed to confess it, they are "bored to death," and leave the country in despair.

This is a mistake which grows out of their want of knowledge of themselves, and, we may add, of human nature generally. Man is a *social,* as well as a reflective and devout being. He must have friends to share his pleasures, to sympathize in his tastes, to enjoy with him the delights of his home, or these become wearisome and insipid. Cowper has well expressed the want of this large class, and their suffering, when left wholly to themselves:—

> "I praise the Frenchman, his remark was shrewd,—
> How sweet, how passing sweet, is solitude!
> *But give me still a friend, in my retreat,*
> *Whom I may whisper—solitude is sweet.*

The mistake made by this class, is that of thinking only of the beauty of the *scenery* where they propose to reside, and leaving out of sight the equal charms of good society. To them, the latter, both by nature and habit, is a *necessity,* not to be wholly waived for converse of "babbling brooks." And since there are numberless localities where one *may* choose a residence in a genial and agreeable country neighborhood, the remedy for this species of discontent is as plain as a pike-staff. One can scarcely expect friends to follow one into country seclusion, if one will, for the sake of the picturesque, settle on the banks of the Winipissiogee. These latter spots are for poets, artists, naturalists; men, between whom and nature there is an intimacy of a wholly different kind, and who find in the structure of a moss or the flight of a water fowl, the text to a whole volume of inspiration.

The third class of the disappointed, consists of those who are astonished at the *cost* of life in the country. They left town not only for the healthful breezes of the hill-tops, but also to make a small income do the business of a large one. To their great surprise, they find the country *dear*. Every thing they grow on their land costs them as much as when bought (because they produce it with *hired* labor); and every thing they do to improve their estate, calls for a mint of money, because with us labor is always costly. But, in fact, the great secret of the matter is this; they have brought as many as possible of their town habits into the country, and find that a moderate income, applied in this way, gives less here than in town. To live economically in the country, one must adopt the rustic habits of country life. Labor must be understood, closely watched, and even shared, to give the farm products at a cost likely to increase the income; and *patés de foie gras*, or *perigord pies* must be given up for boiled mutton and turnips. (And, between them and us, it is not so difficult as might be imagined, when the mistress of the house is a woman of genius, to give as refined an expression to country life with the latter as the former. The way of doing things is, in these matters, as important as the means.)

Now a word or two, touching the second source of evil in country life,—undertaking too much.

There is, apparently, as much fascination in the idea of a large landed estate as in the eye of a serpent. Notwithstanding our institutions, our habits, above all the continual distribution of our fortunes, every thing, in short, teaching us so plainly the folly of improving large landed estates, human nature and the love of distinction, every now and then, triumph over all. What a homily might there not be written on the extravagance of Americans! We can point at once to half a dozen examples of country residences, that have cost between one and two hundred thousand dollars; and every one of which either already has been, or soon will be, enjoyed by others than those who constructed them. This is the great and glaring mistake of our wealthy men, ambitious of taste,—that of supposing that only by large places and great expenditures can the problem of rural beauty and enjoyment be solved. The truth is, that with us, a large fortune does not and cannot (at least at the present time) produce the increased enjoyment which it does abroad. Large estates, large houses, large establishments, only make slaves of their possessors; for the service, to be done daily by those who must hold aloft this dazzling canopy of wealth, is so indifferently performed, servants are so time-serving and unworthy in this country, where intelligent labor finds independent channels for itself, that the lord of the manor finds his life overburdened with the drudgery of watching his drudges.

Hence, the true philosophy of living in America, is to be found in moderate desires, a moderate establishment, and moderate expenditures. We have seen so many more examples of success in those of even less moderate size, that we had almost said, with Cowley "a little cheerful house, a little company, and a very little feast."

But among those who undertake too much, by far the largest class is that whose members do so through *ignorance* of what is to be done.

Although the world is pretty well aware of the existence of professional builders and planters, still the majority of those who build and plant, in this country, do it without the advice of experienced persons. There is, apparently, a latent conviction at the bottom of every man's heart, that he can build a villa or a cottage, and lay out its grounds in a more perfect, or, at least, a *much more* satisfactory manner than any of his predecessors or contemporaries. Fatal delusion! One may plead his own case in law, or even write a lay sermon, like Sir Walter Scott, with more chance of success than he will have in realizing, in solid walls, the *perfect model* of beauty and convenience that floats dimly in his head. We mean this to apply chiefly to the production as a work of art.

As a matter of economy, it is still worse. If the improver selects an experienced architect, and contracts with a responsible and trustworthy builder, he knows within twenty per cent., at the farthest, of what his edifice will cost. If he undertakes to play the amateur, and corrects and revises his work, as most amateurs do, while the house is in progress, he will have the mortification of paying twice as much as he should have done, without any just satisfaction at last.

What is the result of this course of proceeding of the new resident in the country? That he has obtained a large and showy house, of which, if he is alive to improvement, he will live to regret the bad taste; and that he has laid the foundation of expenditures far beyond his income.

He finds himself now in a dilemma, of which there are two horns. One of them is the necessity of laying out and keeping up large pleasure-grounds, gardens, &c., to correspond to the style and character of his house. The other is to allow the house to remain in the midst of beggarly surroundings of meadow and stubble; or, at the most, with half executed and miserably kept grounds on every side of it.

Nothing can be more unsatisfactory than either of these positions. If he is seduced into expenditures *en grand seigneur*, to keep up the style in which the mansion or villa has been erected, he finds that instead of the peace of mind and enjoyment which he expected to find in the country, he is perpetually nervous about the tight place in his income,—constantly obliged to make an effort to maintain that which, when maintained, gives no more real pleasure than a residence on a small scale.

If, on the other hand, he stops short, like a prudent man, at the mighty show of figures at the bottom of the builder's accounts, and leaves all about in a crude and unfinished condition, then he has the mortification, if possessed of the least taste, of knowing that all the grace with which he meant to surround his country home, has eluded his grasp; that he lives in the house of a noble, set in the fields of a sluggard. This he feels the more keenly, after a walk over the grounds of some wiser or more fortunate neighbor, who has been able to sweep the whole circle of taste, and better advised, has realized precisely that which has escaped the reach of our unfortunate improver. Is it any marvel that the latter should find himself disappointed in the pleasures of a country life?

Do we thus portray the mistakes of country life in order to dissuade persons from retiring? Far from it. There is no one who would more willingly exhibit its charms in the most glowing colors. But we would not lure the traveller into an Arcadia, without telling him that there are not only golden fruits, but also others, which may prove Sodom-apples if ignorantly plucked. We would not hang garlands of flowers over dangerous pits and fearful chasms. It is rather our duty and pleasure loudly to warn those who are likely to fall into such errors, and to open their eyes to the danger that lies in their paths; for the country is really full of interest to those who are fitted to understand it; nature is full of beauty to those who approach her simply and devoutly; and rural life is full of pure and happy influences, to those who are wise enough rightly to accept and enjoy them.

What most retired citizens need, in country life, are objects of real interest, society, occupation.

We place first, something of permanent interest; for, after all, this is the great desideratum. All men, with the fresh breath of the hay-fields of boyhood floating through their memory, fancy that *farming* itself is the grand occupation and panacea of country life. This is a profound error. There is no *permanent* interest in any pursuit which we are not successful in; and farming, at least in the older States, is an art as difficult as navigation. We mean by this, *profitable* farming, for there is no constant satisfaction in any other; and though some of the best farmers in the Union are retired citizens, yet not more than one in twenty succeeds in making his land productive. It is well enough, therefore, for the citizen about retiring, to look upon this resource with a little diffidence.

If our novice is fond of horticulture, there is some hope for him. In the first place, if he pursues it as an amusement, it is inexhaustible, because there is no end to new fruits and flowers, or to the combinations which he may produce by their aid. And besides this, he need not draw heavily on his banker, or purchase a whole township to attain his object. Only grant a downright taste for fruits and flowers, and a man may have occupation and amusement for years, in an hundred feet square of good soil.

Among the happiest men in the country, as we have hinted, are those who find an intense pleasure in nature, either as artists or naturalists. To such men, there is no weariness; and they should choose a country residence, not so much with a view to what can be made by improving it, as to *where* it is, what grand and beautiful scenery surrounds it, and how much inspiration its neighborhood will offer them.

Men of society, as we have already said, should, in settling in the country, never let go the cord that binds them to their fellows.

A suburban country life will most nearly meet their requirements; or, at least, they should select a site where some friends of congenial minds have already made a social sunshine in the "wilderness of woods and forests."

Above all, we should counsel all persons not to *underrate* the cost of building and improving in the country. Do not imagine that a villa, or even a cottage ornée, takes care of itself. If you wish for rural beauty, at a cheap rate, either on the grand or the moderate scale, choose a spot where the two features of home scenery are trees and grass. You may have five hundred acres of natural park—that is to say, fine old woods, tastefully opened, and threaded with walks and drives, for less cost, in preparation and annual outlay, than it will require to maintain five acres of artificial pleasure-grounds. A pretty little natural glen, filled with old trees and made alive by a clear perennial stream, is often a cheaper and more unwearying source of enjoyment than the gayest flower-garden. Not that we mean to disparage beautiful parks, pleasure-grounds, or flower-gardens; we only wish our readers about settling in the country to understand that they do not constitute the highest and most expressive kind of rural beauty,—as they certainly do the most *expensive*.

It is so hard to be content with simplicity! Why, we have seen thousands expended on a few acres of ground, and the result was, after all, only a showy villa, a green-house, and a flower-garden, —not half so captivating to the man of true taste as a cottage embosomed in shrubbery, a little park filled with a few fine trees, a lawn kept short by a flock of favorite sheep, and a knot of flowers woven gayly together in the green turf of the terrace under the parlor windows. But the man of wealth so loves to astonish the admiring world by the display of riches, and it is so rare to find those who comprehend the charm of grace and beauty in their simple dress!

VI.

CITIZENS RETIRING TO THE COUNTRY.

February, 1852.

IN a former volume we offered a few words to our readers on the subject of choosing a country-seat. As the subject was only slightly touched upon, we propose to say something more regarding it now.

There are few or no *magnificent* country-seats in America, if we take as a standard such residences as Chatsworth, Woburn, Blenheim, and other well known English places—with parks a dozen miles round, and palaces in their midst larger than our largest public buildings. But any one who notices in the suburbs of our towns and cities, and on the borders of our great rivers and railroads, in the older parts of the Union, the rapidity with which cottages and villa residences are increasing, each one of which costs from three, to thirty or forty thousand dollars, will find that the aggregate amount of money expended in American rural homes, for the last ten years, is perhaps larger than has been spent in any part of the world. Our Anglo-Saxon nature leads our successful business men always to look forward to a home out of the city; and the ease with which freehold property may be obtained here, offers every encouragement to the growth of the natural instinct for landed proprietorship.

This large class of citizens turning country-folk, which every season's revolution is increasing, which every successful business year greatly augments, and every fortune made in California helps to swell in number, is one which, perhaps, spends its means more freely, and with more of the feeling of getting its full value, than any other class.

But do they get its full value? Are there not many who are disgusted with the country after a few years' trial, mainly because they find country places, and country life, as they have tried them, more expensive than a residence in town? And is there not something that may be done to warn the new beginners of the dangers of the voyage of pleasure on which they are about to embark, with the fullest faith that it is all smooth water?

We think so: and as we are daily brought into contact with precisely this class of citizens, seeking for and building country places, we should be glad to be able to offer some useful hints to those who are not too wise to find them of value.

Perhaps the foundation of all the miscalculations that arise, as to expenditure in forming a country residence, is, that citizens are in the habit of thinking every thing in the country *cheap*. Land in the town is sold by the foot, in the country by the acre. The price of a good house in town is, perhaps, three times the cost of one of the best farms in the country. The town buys every thing: the country raises every thing. To live on your own estate, be it one acre or a thousand, to have your own milk, butter and eggs, to raise your own chickens and gather your own strawberries, with nature to keep the account instead of your grocer and market-woman, that is something like a rational life; and more than rational, it must be cheap. So argues the citizen about retiring, not only to enjoy his *otium cum dignitate*, but to make a thousand dollars of his income, produce him more of the comforts of life than two thousand did before.

Well; he goes into the country. He buys a farm (run down with poor tenants and bad tillage). He builds a new house, with his own ignorance instead of architect and master-builder, and is cheated roundly by those who take advantage of this masterly ignorance in the matter of bricks and mortar; or he repairs an old house at the full cost of a new one, and has an unsatisfactory dwelling for ever afterwards. He undertakes high farming, and knowing nothing of the practical economy of husbandry, every bushel of corn that he raises costs him the price of a bushel and a half in the market. Used in town to a neat and orderly condition of his premises, he is disgusted with old tottering fences, half drained fields and worn-out pastures, and employs all the laboring force of the neighborhood to put his grounds in good order.

Now there is no objection to all this for its own sake. On the contrary, good buildings, good fences, and rich pasture fields are what especially delight us in the country. What then is the reason that, as the country place gets to wear a smiling aspect, its citizen owner begins to look serious and unhappy? Why is it that country life does not satisfy and content him? Is the *country*, which all poets and philosophers have celebrated as the Arcadia of this world,—is the country treacherous? Is nature a cheat, and do seed-time and harvest conspire against the peace of mind of the retired citizen?

Alas! It is a matter of *money*. Every thing seems to be a matter of money now-a-days. The country life of the old world, of the poets and romancers, is cheap. The country life of our republic is *dear*. It is for the good of the many that labor should be high, and it is high labor that makes country life heavy and oppressive to such men—only because it shows a balance, increasing year after year, on the wrong side of the ledger. Here is the source of all the trouble and dissatisfaction in what may be called the country life of gentlemen amateurs, or citizens, in this country—"it don't pay." Land is cheap, nature is beautiful, the country is healthy, and all these conspire to draw our well-to-do citizen into the country. But labor is dear, experience is dearer, and a series of experiments in unprofitable crops the dearest of all; and our citizen friend, himself, as we have said, is in the situation of a man who has set out on a delightful voyage, on a smooth sea, and with a cheerful ship's company; but who discovers, also, that the ship has sprung a leak—not large enough to make it necessary to call all hands to the pump—not large enough perhaps to attract any body's attention but his own, but quite large enough to make it certain that he must leave her or be swamped—and quite large enough to make his voyage a serious piece of business.

Every thing which a citizen does in the country, costs him an incredible sum. In Europe (heaven save the masses), you may have the best of laboring men for twenty or thirty cents a day. Here you must pay them a dollar, at least our amateur must, though the farmers contrive to get their labor for eight or ten dollars a month and board. The citizen's home once built, he looks upon all heavy expenditures as over; but how many hundreds—perhaps thousands, has he not paid for out-buildings, for fences, for roads, &c. Cutting down yonder hill, which made an ugly blotch in the view,—it looked like a trifling task; yet there were $500 swept clean out of his bank account, and there seems almost nothing to show for it. You would not believe now that any hill ever stood there—or at least that nature had not arranged it all (as you feel she ought to have done), just as you see it. Your favorite cattle and horses have died, and the flock of sheep have been sadly diminished by the dogs, all to be replaced—and a careful account of the men's time, labor and manure on the grain fields, shows that for some reason that you cannot understand, the crop—which is a fair one, has actually cost you a trifle more than it is worth in a good market.

To cut a long story short, the larger part of our citizens who retire upon a farm to make it a country residence, are not aware of the fact, that capital cannot be profitably employed on land in the Atlantic States *without a thoroughly practical knowledge of farming.* A close and systematic economy, upon a good soil, may enable, and does enable some gentlemen farmers that we could name, to make a good profit out of their land—but citizens who launch boldly into farming, hiring farm laborers at high prices, and trusting operations to others that should be managed under the master's eye—are very likely to find their farms a sinking fund that will drive them back into business again.

To be happy in any business or occupation (and country life on a farm is a matter of business), we must have some kind of *success* in it; and there is no success without profit, and no profit without practical knowledge of farming.

The lesson that we would deduce from these reflections is this; that no mere amateur should buy a large farm for a country residence, with the expectation of finding pleasure and profit in it for the rest of his life, unless, like some citizens that we have known—rare exceptions—they have a genius for all manner of business, and can master the whole of farming, as they would learn a running-hand in six easy lessons. Farming, in the older States, where the natural wealth of the soil has been exhausted, is *not* a profitable business for amateurs—but quite the reverse. And a citizen who has a sufficient income without farming, had better not damage it by engaging in so expensive an amusement.

"But we must have something to do; we have been busy near all our lives, and cannot retire into the country to fold our hands and sit in the sunshine to be idle." Precisely so. But you need not therefore ruin yourself on a large farm. Do not be ambitious of being great landed proprietors. Assume that you need occupation and interest, and buy a small piece of ground—a few acres only—as *few* as you please—but without any regard for profit. Leave that to those who have learned farming in a more practical school. You think, perhaps, that you can find nothing to do on a few acres of ground. But that is the greatest of mistakes. A half a dozen acres, the capacities of which are fully developed, will give you more pleasure than five hundred poorly cultivated. And the advantage for you is, that you can, upon your few acres, spend just as little or just as much as you please. If you wish to be prudent, lay out your little estate in a simple way, with grass and trees, and a few walks, and a single man may then take care of it. If you wish to indulge your taste, you may fill it with shrubberies, and arboretums, and conservatories, and flower-gardens, till every tree and plant and fruit in the whole vegetable kingdom, of really superior beauty and interest, is in your collection. Or, if you wish to turn a penny, you will find it easier to take up certain fruits or plants and grow them to high perfection so as to command a profit in the market, than you will to manage the various operations of a large farm. We could point to ten acres of ground from which a larger income has been produced than from any farm of five hundred acres in the country. Gardening, too, offers more variety of interest to a citizen than farming; its operations are less rude and toilsome, and its pleasures more immediate and refined. Citizens, ignorant of farming, should, therefore, buy small places, rather than large ones, if they wish to consult their own true interest and happiness.

But some of our readers, who have tried the thing, may say that it is a very expensive thing to settle oneself and get well established, even on a small place in the country. And so it is, if we proceed upon the fallacy, as we have said, that every thing in the *country* is cheap. Labor is dear; it costs you dearly to-day, and it will cost you dearly to-morrow, and the next year. Therefore, in selecting a site for a home in the country, always remember to choose a site where nature has done as much as possible for you. Don't say to yourself as many have done before you—"Oh! I want occupation, and I rather like the new place—raw and naked though it may be. *I will create a paradise for myself.* I will cut down yonder hill that intercepts the view, I will level and slope more gracefully yonder rude bank, I will terrace this rapid descent, I will make a lake in yonder hollow." Yes, all this you may do for occupation, and find it very delightful occupation too, if you have the income of Mr. Astor. Otherwise, after you have spent thousands in creating your paradise, and chance to go to some friend who has bought all the graceful undulations, and sloping lawns, and sheets of water, natural, ready made—as they may be bought in thousands of purely natural places in America, for a few hundred dollars, it will give you a species of pleasure-ground-dyspepsia to see how foolishly you have wasted your money. And this, more especially, when you find, as the possessor of the most finished place in America finds, that he has no want of occupation, and that far from being finished, he has only begun to elicit the highest beauty, keeping and completeness of which his place is capable.

It would be easy to say a great deal more in illustration of the mistakes continually made by citizens going into the country; of their false ideas of the cost of doing every thing; of the profits of farming; of their own talent for making an income from the land, and their disappointment, growing out of a failure of all their theories and expectations. But we have perhaps said enough to cause some of our readers about to take the step, to consider whether they mean to look upon country life as a luxury they are willing to pay so much a year for, or as a means of adding something to their incomes. Even in the former case, they are likely to underrate the cost of the luxury, and in the latter they must set about it with the frugal and industrial habits of the real farmer, or they will fail. The safest way is to attempt but a modest residence at first, and let the more elaborate details be developed, if at all, only when we have learned how much country life costs, and how far the expenditure is a wise one. Fortunately, it is *art*, and not nature, which costs money in the country, and therefore the beauty of lovely scenery and fine landscapes (the right to enjoy miles of which may often be had for a trifle), in connection with a very modest and simple place, will give more lasting satisfaction than gardens and pleasure-grounds innumerable. Persons of moderate means should, for this reason, always secure, in their fee simple, as much as possible of natural beauty, and undertake the elaborate improvement of only small places, which will not become a burden to them. Millionnaires, of course, we leave out of the question. They may do what they like. But most Americans, buying a country place, may take it for their creed, that

> Man wants but *little* land below,
> Nor wants that little *dear*.

VII.

A TALK ABOUT PUBLIC PARKS AND GARDENS.

October, 1848.

EDITOR. I am heartily glad to see you home again. I almost fear, however, from your long residence on the continent, that you have become a foreigner in all your sympathies.

Traveller. Not a whit. I come home to the United States more thoroughly American than ever. The last few months' residence in Europe, with revolutions, tumult, bloodshed on every side, people continually crying for liberty—who mean by that word, the privilege of being responsible to neither God nor governments—*ouvriers*, expecting wages to drop like manna from heaven, not as a reward for industry, but as a sign that the millennium has come; republics, in which every other man you meet is a soldier, sworn to preserve "liberty, fraternity, equality," at the point of the bayonet; from all this unsatisfactory movement—the more unsatisfactory because its aims are almost beyond the capacities of a new nation, and entirely impossible to an old people—I repeat, I come home again to rejoice most fervently that "I, too, am an *American*."

Ed. After five years expatriation, pray tell me what strikes you most on returning?

Trav. Most of all, the wonderful, extraordinary, unparalleled growth of our country. It seems to me, after the general, steady, quiet torpor of the old world (which those great convulsions have only latterly broken), to be the moving and breathing of a robust young giant, compared with the crippled and feeble motions of an exhausted old man. Why, it is difficult for me to "catch up" to

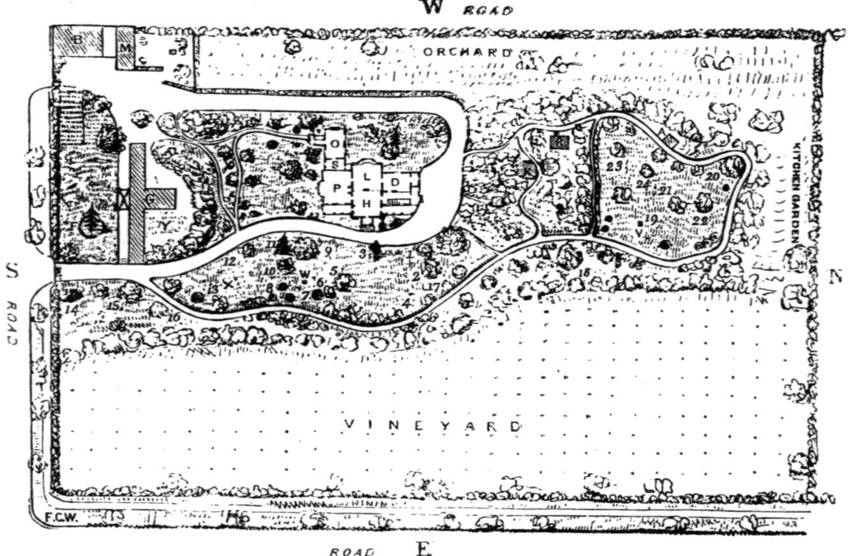

Mr Downing's Residence: Plan of House and Grounds.

my countrymen, or to bridge over the gap which five years have made in the condition of things. From a country looked upon with contempt by monarchists, and hardly esteemed more than a third-rate power by republicans abroad, we have risen to the admitted first rank every where. To say, on the continent, now, that you are from the "United States," is to dilate the pupil of every eye with a sort of glad welcome. The gates of besieged cities open to you, and the few real republicans who have just conceptions of the ends of government, take you by the hand as if you had a sort of liberty-magnetism in your touch. A country that exports, in a single year, more than fifty-three millions worth of bread stuffs, that conquers a neighboring nation without any apparent expenditure of strength, and swallows up a deluge of foreign emigrants every season,—turning all that "raw material," by a sort of wonderful vital force, into good citizens,—such a country, I say, is felt to have an *avoirdupois* about it, that weighs heavily in the scale of nations.

Ed. I am glad to see you so sound and patriotic. Very few men who go abroad, like yourself, to enjoy the art and antiquities of the old world, come home without "turned heads." The greatness of the past, and the luxury and completeness of the present forms of civilization abroad, seize hold of them, to the exclusion of every thing else; and they return home lamenting always and for ever the "purple and fine linen" left behind.

Trav. "Purple and fine linen," when they clothe forms of lifeless majesty, are far inferior, in the eyes of any sensible person, to linsey-woolsey, enwrapping the body of a free, healthy man. But there are some points of civilization—good points, too—that we do not yet understand, which are well understood abroad, and which are well worth attention here at home, at the present moment. In fact, I came here to talk a little, about one or two of these, to-day.

Ed. Talk on, with all my heart.

Trav. I dare say you will be surprised to hear me say that the French and Germans—difficult as they find it to be republican, in a political sense—are practically far more so, in many of the customs of *social* life, than Americans.

Ed. Such as what, pray?

Trav. Public enjoyments, open tc all classes of people, provided at public cost, maintained at public expense, and enjoyed daily and hourly, by all classes of persons.

Ed. Picture galleries, libraries, and the like, I suppose you allude to?

Trav. Yes; but more especially at the present moment, I am thinking of PUBLIC PARKS and GARDENS—those salubrious and wholesome breathing places, provided in the midst of, or upon the suburbs of so many towns on the continent—full of really grand and beautiful trees, fresh grass, fountains, and, in many cases, rare plants, shrubs, and flowers. Public picture galleries, and even libraries, are intellectual luxuries; and though we must and will have them, as wealth accumulates, yet I look upon public parks and gardens, which are great social enjoyments, as naturally coming first. Man's social nature stands before his intellectual one in the *order* of cultivation.

Ed. But these great public parks are mostly the appendages of royalty, and have been created for purposes of show and magnificence, quite incompatible with our ideas of republican simplicity.

Trav. Not at all. In many places these parks were made for royal enjoyment; but, even in these days, they are, on the continent, no longer held for royal use, but are the pleasure-grounds of the public generally. Look, for example, at the Garden of the Tuileries—spacious, full of flowers, green lawns, orange-trees, and rare plants, in the very heart of Paris, and all open to the public, without charge. Even in third-rate towns, like the Hague, there is a royal park of two hundred acres, filled with superb trees, rich turf, and broad pieces of water—the whole exquisitely kept, and absolutely and entirely at the enjoyment of every well-disposed person that chooses to enter.

Ed. Still, these are not parks or gardens made for the public; but are the result, originally, of princely taste, and afterwards given up to the public.

Trav. But Germany, which is in many respects a most instructive country to Americans, affords many examples of public gardens, in the neighborhood of the principal towns, of extraordinary size and beauty, originally made and laid out solely for the general use. The public garden at Munich, for example, contains above five hundred acres, originally laid out by the celebrated Count Rumford, with five miles of roads and walks, and a collection of all the trees and shrubs that will thrive in that country. It combines the beauty of a park and a garden.

Ed. And Frankfort?

Trav. Yes, I was coming to that, for it is quite a model of this kind of civilization. The public garden of Frankfort is, to my mind, one of the most delightful sights in the world. Frankfort deserves, indeed, in this respect, to be called a "free town;" for I doubt if we are yet ready to evince the same capacity for self-government and non-imposition of restraint as is shown daily by the good citizens of that place, in the enjoyment of this beautiful public garden. Think of a broad belt, about *two miles long*, surrounding the city on all sides but one (being built upon the site of the old ramparts), converted into the most lovely pleasure-grounds, intersected with all manner of shady walks and picturesque glades, planted not only with all manner of fine trees and shrubs, but beds of the choicest flowers, roses, carnations, dahlias, verbenas, tuberoses, violets, &c., &c.

Ed. And well guarded, I suppose, by *gen-d'armes*, or the police!

Trav. By no means. On the contrary, it is open to every man, woman, and child in the city; there are even no gates at the various entrances. Only at these entrances are put up notices, stating that as the garden was made for the public, and is kept up at its expense, the town authorities commit it to the protection of all good citizens. Fifty thousand souls have the right to enter and enjoy these beautiful grounds; and yet, though they are most thoroughly enjoyed, you will no more see a bed trampled upon, or a tree injured, than in your own private garden here at home!

Ed. There is truly a democracy in that, worth imitating in our more professedly democratic country.

Trav. Well, out of this common enjoyment of public grounds, by all classes, grows also a *social freedom*, and an easy and agreeable intercourse of all classes, that strikes an American with surprise and delight. Every afternoon, in the public grounds of the German towns, you will meet thousands of neatly-dressed men, women, and children. All classes assemble under the shade of the same trees,

—the nobility (even the king is often seen among them), the wealthy citizens, the shopkeepers, and the artisans, &c. There they all meet, sip their tea and coffee, ices, or other refreshments, from tables in the open air, talk, walk about, and listen to bands of admirable music, stationed here and there throughout the park. In short, these great public grounds are the pleasant drawing-rooms of the whole population; where they gain health, good spirits, social enjoyment, and a frank and cordial bearing towards their neighbors, that is totally unknown either in England or America.

Ed. There appears a disinclination in the Anglo-Saxon race to any large social intercourse, or unrestrained public enjoyment.

Trav. It is not difficult to account for such a feeling in England. But in this country, it is quite unworthy of us and our institutions. With large professions of equality, I find my countrymen more and more inclined to raise up barriers of class, wealth, and fashion, which are almost as strong in our social usages, as the law of caste is in England. It is quite unworthy of us, as it is the meanest and most contemptible part of aristocracy; and we owe it to ourselves and our republican professions, to set about establishing a larger and more fraternal spirit in our social life.

Ed. Pray, how would you set about it?

Trav. Mainly by establishing refined public places of resort, parks and gardens, galleries, libraries, museums, &c. By these means, you would soften and humanize the rude, educate and enlighten the ignorant, and give continual enjoyment to the educated. Nothing tends to beat down those artificial barriers, that false pride, which is the besetting folly of our Anglo-Saxon nature, so much as a community of rational enjoyments. Now there is absolutely no class of persons in this country whose means allow them the luxury of great parks, or fine concerts of instrumental music within their own houses. But a trifling yearly contribution from all the inhabitants of even a small town, will enable all those inhabitants to have an excellent band, performing every fair afternoon through the whole summer. Make the public parks or pleasure-grounds attractive by their lawns, fine trees, shady walks, and beautiful shrubs and flowers, by fine music, and the certainty of "meeting every body," and you draw the whole moving population of the town there daily.

Ed. I am afraid the natural *gêne* of our people would keep many of those at home who would most enjoy such places, and that they would be given up to those who would abuse the privilege and despoil the grounds. Do you think it would be possible, for instance, to preserve fine flowers in such a place, as in Germany?

Trav. I have not the slightest doubt of it. How can I have, after going on board such magnificent steamboats as the Isaac Newton or the Bay State, all fitted up with the same luxury of velvet ottomans, rich carpets, mirrors, and the costliest furniture, that I have found in palaces abroad, and all at the use of millions of every class of American travellers, from the chimney-sweep to the President, and yet this profuse luxury not abused in the slightest manner!

Ed. But the more educated of our people—would they, think you, resort to public pleasure-grounds daily, for amusement? Would not the natural exclusiveness of our better-halves, for instance, *taboo* this medley of "all sorts of people that we don't know?"

Trav. I trust too much in the good sense of our women to believe it. Indeed, I find plenty of reasons for believing quite the opposite. I see the public watering-places filled with all classes of society, partaking of the same pleasures, with as much zest as in any part of the world; and you must remember that there is no *forced* intercourse in the daily reunions in a public garden or park. There is room and space enough for pleasant little groups or circles of all tastes and sizes, and no one is necessarily brought into contact with uncongenial spirits; while the daily meeting of families, who *ought* to sympathize, from natural congeniality, will be more likely to bring them together than any other social gatherings. Then the advantage to our fair countrywomen in health and spirits, of exercise in the pure open air, amid the groups of fresh foliage and flowers, in a chat with friends, and pleasures shared with them, as compared with a listless lounge upon a sofa at home, over the last new novel or pattern of embroidery! When I first returned home, I assure you, I was almost shocked at the extreme delicacy, and apparent universal want of health in my countrywomen, as compared with the same classes abroad. It is, most clearly, owing to the many sedentary, listless hours which they pass within doors; no out-of-door occupations—walking considered irksome and fatiguing—and almost no parks, pleasure-grounds, or shaded avenues, to tempt fair pedestrians to this most healthful and natural exercise.

Ed. Enough. I am fully satisfied of the benefits of these places of healthful public enjoyment, and of their being most completely adapted to our institutions. But how to achieve them? What do we find among us to warrant a belief that public parks, for instance, are within the means of our people?

Trav. Several things: but most of all, the condition of our public *cemeteries* at the present moment. Why, twenty years ago, such a thing as an embellished, rural cemetery, was unheard of in the United States; and, at the present moment, we surpass all other nations in these beautiful resting-places for the dead. Greenwood, Mount Auburn, and Laurel Hill, are as much superior to the far-famed *Père la Chaise* of Paris, in natural beauty, tasteful arrangement, and all that constitutes the charm of such a spot, as St. Peter's is to the Boston State House. Indeed, these cemeteries are the only places in the country that can give an untravelled American any idea of the beauty of many of the public parks and gardens abroad. Judging from the crowds of people in carriages, and on foot, which I find constantly thronging Greenwood and Mount Auburn, I think it is plain enough how much our citizens, of all classes, would enjoy public parks on a similar scale. Indeed, the only draw back to these beautiful and highly kept cemeteries, to my taste, is the gala-day air of *recreation* they present. People seem to go there to enjoy themselves, and not to indulge in any serious recollections or regrets. Can you doubt that if our large towns had suburban pleasure-grounds, like Greenwood (excepting the monuments), where the best music could be heard daily, they would become the constant resort of the citizens, or that being so, they would tend to soften and allay some of the feverish unrest of business which seems to have possession of most Americans, body and soul?

Ed. But the *modus operandi?* Cemeteries are, in a measure, private speculations; hundreds are induced to buy *lots* in them from fashion or personal pride, besides those whose hearts are touched by the beauiful sentiment which they involve; and thus a large fund is produced, which maintains every thing in the most perfect order.

Trav. Appeal to the public liberality. We subscribe hundreds of thousands of dollars to give food to the Irish, or to assist the needy inhabitants of a burnt-out city, or to send missionaries to South Sea Islands. Are there no dollars in the same generous pockets for a public park, which shall be the great wholesome breathing zone, social mass-meeting, and grand out-of-door concert-room of all the inhabitants daily? Make it praiseworthy and laudable for wealthy men to make bequests of land, properly situated, for this public enjoyment, and commemorate the public spirit of such men by a statue or a beautiful marble vase, with an inscription, telling all succeeding generations to whom they are indebted for the beauty and enjoyment that constitute the chief attraction of the town. Let the ladies gather money from young and old by fairs, and "tea parties," to aid in planting and embellishing the grounds. Nay, I would have life-members, who on paying a certain sum, should be the owners in "fee simple" of certain fine trees, or groups of trees; since there are some who will never give money but for some tangible and visible property.

Ed. It is, perhaps, not so difficult to get the public park or garden, as to meet all the annual expenses required to keep it in the requisite condition.

Trav. There is, to my mind, but one effectual and rational mode of doing this—by a voluntary taxation on the part of all the inhabitants. A few shillings each person, or a small per centage on the value of all the property in a town, would keep a park of a hundred or two acres in admirable order, and defray all the incidental expenses. Did you ever make a calculation of the sum voluntarily paid in towns like this, of nine thousand inhabitants, for pew rent in churches and places of worship?

Ed. No.

Trav. Very well; I have had the curiosity lately to do so, and find that in a town of nine thousand souls, and with ten "meeting-houses" of various sects, more than ten thousand dollars are voluntarily paid every year for the privilege of sitting in these churches. Does it appear to you impossible that half that sum (a few shillings a year each) would be willingly paid every year for the privilege of a hundred acres of beautiful park or pleasure-grounds, where every man, woman, and child in the community could have, for a few shillings, all the soft verdure, the umbrageous foliage, the lovely flowers, the place for exercise, recreation, repose, that Victoria has in her Park of Windsor?

Ed. Not at all, if our countrymen could be made to look upon the matter in the same light as yourself. But while no men contribute money so willingly and liberally as we Americans for the support of religion, or indeed for the furtherance of any object of moral good, we are slow to understand the value and influence of beauty of this material kind, on our daily lives.

Trav. But we *must* believe it, because the BEAUTIFUL is no less eternal than the TRUE and the GOOD. And it is the province of the press—of writers who have the public ear—to help those to see (who are slow to perceive it), how much these outward influences have to do with bettering the condition of a people, as good citizens, patriots, men. Nay, more; what an important influence these public resorts, of a rational and refined character, must exert in elevating the national character, and softening the many little jealousies of social life by a community of enjoyments. A people will have its pleasures, as certainly as its religion or its laws; and whether these pleasures are poisonous and hurtful, or innocent and salutary, must greatly depend on the interest taken in them by the directing minds of the age. Get some country town of the first class to set the example by making a public park or garden of this kind. Let our people once see for themselves the influence for good which it would effect, no less than the healthful enjoyment it will afford, and I feel confident that the taste for public pleasure-grounds, in the United States, will spread as rapidly as that for cemeteries has done. If my own observation of the effect of these places in Germany is worth any thing, you may take my word for it that they will be better preachers of temperance than temperance societies, better refiners of national manners than dancing-schools, and better promoters of general good feeling than any lectures on the philosophy of happiness ever delivered in the lecture-room. In short, I am in earnest about the matter, and must therefore talk, write, preach, do all I can about it, and beg the assistance of all those who have public influence, till some good experiment of the kind is fairly tried in this country.

Ed. I wish you all success in your good undertaking; and will, at least, print our conversation for the benefit of the readers of the Horticulturist.

VIII.

THE NEW-YORK PARK.

August, 1851.

THE leading topic of town gossip and newspaper paragraphs just now, in New-York, is the new park proposed by Mayor Kingsland. Deluded New-York has, until lately, contented itself with the little door-yards of space—mere grass-plats of verdure, which form the squares of the city, in the mistaken idea that they are parks. The fourth city in the world (with a growth that will soon make it the second), the commercial metropolis of a continent spacious enough to border both oceans, has not hitherto been able to afford sufficient land to give its citizens (the majority of whom live there the whole year round) any breathing space for pure air, any recreation ground for healthful exercise, any pleasant roads for riding or driving, or any enjoyment of that lovely and refreshing natural beauty from which they have, in leaving the country, reluctantly expatriated themselves for so many years—perhaps for ever. Some few thousands, more fortunate than the rest, are able to escape for a couple of months, into the country, to find repose for body and soul, in its leafy groves and pleasant pastures, or to inhale new life on the refreshing sea-shore. But in the mean time the city is always full. Its steady population of five hundred thousand souls is always there; always on the increase. Every ship brings a live cargo from over-peopled Europe, to fill up its over-crowded lodging-houses; every steamer brings hundreds of strangers to fill its thronged thoroughfares. Crowded hotels, crowded streets, hot summers, business pursued till it becomes a game of excitement, pleasure followed till its votaries are exhausted, where is the quiet reverse side of this picture of town life, intensified almost to distraction?

Mayor Kingsland spreads it out to the vision of the dwellers in this arid desert of business and dissipation—a green oasis for the refreshment of the city's soul and body. He tells the citizens of that feverish metropolis, as every intelligent man will tell them who knows the cities of the old world, that New-York, and American cities generally, are voluntarily and ignorantly living in a state of complete forgetfulness of nature, and her innocent recreations. That, because it is needful in civilized life for men to live in cities,—yes, and unfortunately too, for children to be born and educated without a daily sight of the blessed horizon,—it is not, therefore, needful for them to be so miserly as to live utterly divorced from all pleasant and healthful intercourse with gardens, and green fields. He informs them that cool umbrageous groves have not forsworn themselves within town limits, and that half a million of people have a *right* to ask for the "greatest happiness" of parks and pleasure-grounds, as well as for paving stones and gas-lights.

Now that public opinion has fairly settled that a park is necessary, the parsimonious declare that the plot of one hundred and sixty acres proposed by Mayor Kingsland is extravagantly large. Short-sighted economists! If the future growth of the city were confined to the boundaries their narrow vision would fix, it would soon cease to be the commercial emporium of the country. If they were the purveyors of the young giant, he would soon present the sorry spectacle of a robust youth magnificently developed, but whose extremities had outgrown every garment that they had provided to cover his nakedness.

These timid tax-payers, and men nervous in their private pockets of the municipal expenditures, should take a lesson from some of their number to whose admirable foresight we owe the unity of materials displayed in the New-York City-Hall. Every one familiar with New-York, has wondered or smiled at the apparent perversity of taste which gave us a building—in the most conspicuous part of the city, and devoted to the highest municipal uses, three sides of which are pure white marble, and the fourth of coarse, brown stone. But few of those who see that incongruity, know that it was dictated by the narrow-sighted frugality of the common council who were its building committee, and who determined that it would be useless to waste marble on the rear of the City-Hall, "*since that side would only be seen by persons living in the suburbs.*"

Thanking Mayor Kingsland most heartily for his proposed new park, the only objection we make to it is that it is *too small.* One hundred and sixty acres of park for a city that will soon contain three-quarters of a million of people! It is only a child's play-ground. Why London has over six thousand acres either within its own limits, or in the accessible suburbs, open to the enjoyment of its population—and six thousand acres composed too, either of the grandest and most lovely park scenery, like Kensington and Richmond, or of luxuriant gardens, filled with rare plants, hot-houses, and hardy shrubs and trees, like the National Garden at Kew. Paris has its Garden of the Tuileries, whose alleys are lined with orange-trees two hundred years old, whose parterres are gay with the brightest flowers, whose cool groves of horse-chestnuts, stretching out to the Elysian Fields, are in the very midst of the city. Yes, and on its outskirts are Versailles (three thousand acres of imperial groves and gardens there also), and Fontainbleau, and St. Cloud, with all the rural, scenic, and palatial beauty that the opulence of the most profuse of French monarchs could create, all open to the *people* of Paris. Vienna has its great *Prater*, to make which, would swallow up most of the "unimproved" part of New-York city. Munich has a superb pleasure-ground of five hundred acres, which makes the Arcadia of her citizens. Even the smaller towns are provided with public grounds to an extent that would beggar the imagination of our short-sighted economists, who would deny "a greenery" to New-York; Frankfort, for example, is skirted by the most beautiful gardens, formed upon the platform which made the old ramparts of the city—gardens filled with the loveliest plants and shrubs, tastefully grouped along walks over *two miles* in extent.

Looking at the present government of the city as about to provide, in the People's Park, a breathing zone, and healthful place for exercise for a city of half a million of souls, we trust they will not be content with the limited number of acres already proposed. *Five hundred acres* is the smallest area that should be reserved for the future wants of such a city, *now*, while it may be obtained. Five hundred acres may be selected between Thirty-ninth-street and the Harlem River, including a varied surface of land, a good deal of which is yet waste area, so that the whole may be purchased at something like a million of dollars. In that area there would be space enough to have broad reaches of park and pleasure-grounds, with a real feeling of the breadth and beauty of green fields, the perfume and freshness of nature. In its midst would be located the great distributing reservoirs of the Croton aqueduct, formed into lovely lakes of limpid water, covering many acres, and heightening the charm of the sylvan accessories by the finest natural contrast. In such a park, the citizens who would take excursions in carriages or on horseback, could have the substantial delights of country roads and country scenery, and forget, for a time the rattle of the pavements and the glare of brick walls. Pedestrians would find quiet and secluded walks when they wished to be solitary, and broad alleys filled with thousands of happy faces, when they would be gay. The thoughtful denizen of the town would go out there in the morning, to hold converse with the whispering trees, and the weary tradesmen in the evening, to enjoy an hour of happiness by mingling in the open space with "all the world."

The many beauties and utilities that would gradually grow out of a great park like this, in a great city like New-York, suggest themselves immediately and forcibly. Where would be found so fitting a position for noble works of art, the statues, monuments, and buildings commemorative at once of the great men of the nation, of the history of the age and country, and the genius of our highest artists? In the broad area of such a verdant zone would gradually grow up, as the wealth of the city increases, winter gardens of glass, like the great Crystal Palace, where the whole people could luxuriate in groves of the palms and spice trees of the tropics, at the same moment that sleighing parties glided swiftly and noiselessly over the snow-covered surface of the country-like avenues of the wintry park without. Zoological Gardens, like those of London and Paris, would gradually be formed by private subscription or public funds, where thousands of old and young would find daily pleasure in studying natural history, illustrated by all the wildest and strangest animals of the globe, almost as much at home in their paddocks and jungles, as if in their native forests; and Horticultural and Industrial Societies would hold their annual shows there, and great expositions of the arts would take place in spacious buildings within the park, far more fittingly than in the noise and din of the crowded streets of the city.

We have said nothing of the *social* influence of such a great park in New-York. But this is really the most interesting phase of the whole matter. It is a fact not a little remarkable, that, ultra democratic as are the political tendencies of America, its most intelligent social tendencies are almost wholly in a contrary direction. And among the topics discussed by the advocates and opponents of the new park, none seem so poorly understood as the social aspect of the thing. It is, indeed, both curious and amusing to see the stand taken on the one hand by the million, that the park is made for the "upper ten," who ride in fine carriages, and, on the other hand, by the wealthy and refined, that a park in this country will be "usurped by rowdies and low people." Shame upon our republican compatriots who so little understand the elevating influences of the beautiful in nature and in art, when enjoyed in common by thousands and hundreds of thousands of all classes without distinction! They can never have seen, how all over France and Germany, the whole population of the cities pass their afternoons and evenings together, in the beautiful public parks and gardens. How they enjoy together the same music, breathe the same atmosphere of art, enjoy the same scenery, and grow into social freedom by the very influences of easy intercourse, space and beauty that surround them. In Germany, especially, they have never seen how the highest and the lowest partake alike of the common enjoyment—the prince seated beneath the trees on a rush-bottomed chair, before a little wooden table, supping his coffee or his ice, with the same freedom from state and pretension as the simplest subject. Drawing-room conventionalities are too narrow for a mile or two of spacious garden landscape, and one can be happy with ten thousand in the social freedom of a community of genial influences, without the unutterable pang of not having been *introduced* to the company present.

These social doubters who thus intrench themselves in the sole citadel of *exclusiveness* in republican America, mistake our people and their destiny. If we would but have listened to them, our magnificent river and lake steamers, those real palaces of the million, would have had no velvet couches, no splendid mirrors, no luxurious carpets. Such costly and rare appliances of civilization, they would have told us, could only be rightly used by the privileged families of wealth, and would be trampled upon and utterly ruined by the democracy of the country, who travel one hundred miles for half a dollar. And yet these, our floating palaces and our monster hotels, with their purple and fine linen, are they not respected by the majority who use them, as truly as other palaces by their rightful sovereigns? Alas, for the faithlessness of the few, who possess, regarding the capacity for culture of the many, who are wanting. Even upon the lower platform of liberty and education that the masses stand in Europe, we see the elevating influences of a wide popular enjoyment of galleries of art, public libraries, parks and gardens, which have raised the people in *social* civilization and social culture to a far higher level than we have yet attained in republican America. And yet this broad ground of popular refinement *must* be taken in republican America, for it belongs of right more truly here, than elsewhere. It is republican in its very idea and tendency. It takes up popular education where the common school and ballot-box leave it, and raises up the working-man to the same level of enjoyment with the man of leisure and accomplishment. The higher social and artistic elements of every man's nature lie dormant within him, and every laborer is a possible gentleman, not by the possession of money or fine clothes—but through the refining influence of intellectual and moral culture. Open wide, therefore, the doors of your libraries and picture galleries, all ye true republicans! Build halls where knowledge shall be freely diffused among men, and not shut up within the narrow walls of narrower institutions. Plant spacious parks in your cities, and unloose their gates as wide as the gates of morning to the whole people. As there are no dark places at noon day, so education and culture—the true sunshine of the soul—will banish the plague spots of democracy; and the dread of the ignorant exclusive who has no faith in the refinement of a republic, will stand abashed in the next century, before a whole people whose system of voluntary education embraces (combined with perfect individual freedom), not only common schools of rudimentary knowledge, but common enjoyments for all classes in the higher realms of art, letters, science, social recreations, and enjoyments. Were our legislators but wise enough to understand, to-day, the destinies of the New World, the gentility of Sir Philip Sidney, made universal, would be not half so much a miracle fifty years hence in America, as the idea of a whole nation of laboring-men reading and writing, was, in his day, in England.

IX.

PUBLIC CEMETERIES AND PUBLIC GARDENS.

July, 1849.

ONE of the most remarkable illustrations of the popular taste, in this country, is to be found in the rise and progress of our rural cemeteries.

Twenty years ago, nothing better than a common grave-yard, filled with high grass, and a chance sprinkling of weeds and thistles, was to be found in the Union. If there were one or two exceptions, like the burial ground at New Haven, where a few willow trees broke the monotony of the scene, they existed only to prove the rule more completely.

Eighteen years ago, Mount Auburn, about six miles from Boston, was made a rural cemetery. It was then a charming natural site, finely varied in surface, containing about 80 acres of land, and admirably clothed by groups and masses of native forest trees. It was tastefully laid out, monuments were built, and the whole highly embellished. No sooner was attention generally roused to the charms of this first American cemetery, than the idea took the public mind by storm. Travellers made pilgrimages to the Athens of New England, solely to see the realization of their long cherished dream of a resting-place for the dead, at once sacred from profanation, dear to the memory, and captivating to the imagination.

Not twenty years have passed since that time; and, at the present moment, there is scarcely a city of note in the whole country that has not its rural cemetery. The three leading cities of the north, New-York, Philadelphia, Boston, have, each of them, besides their great cemeteries,—Greenwood, Laurel Hill, Mount Auburn,—many others of less note; but any of which would have astonished and delighted their inhabitants twenty years ago. Philadelphia has, we learn, nearly twenty rural cemeteries at the present moment,—several of them belonging to distinct societies, sects or associations, while others are open to all.*

The great attraction of these cemeteries, to the mass of the community, is not in the fact that they are burial-places, or solemn places of meditation for the friends of the deceased, or striking exhibitions of monumental sculpture, though all these have their influence. All these might be realized in a burial-ground, planted with straight lines of willows, and sombre avenues of evergreens. The true secret of the attraction lies in the natural beauty of the sites, and in the tasteful and harmonious embellishment of these sites by art. Nearly all these cemeteries were rich portions of forest land, broken by hill and dale, and varied by copses and glades, like Mount Auburn and Greenwood, or old country-seats, richly wooded with fine planted trees, like Laurel Hill. Hence, to an inhabitant of the town, a visit to one of these spots has the united charm of nature and art,—the double wealth of rural and moral associations. It awakens at the same moment, the feeling of human sympathy and the love of natural beauty, implanted in every heart. His must be a dull or a trifling soul that neither swells with emotion, or rises with admiration, at the varied beauty of these lovely and hallowed spots.

Indeed, in the absence of great public gardens, such as we must surely one day have in America, our rural cemeteries are doing a great deal to enlarge and educate the popular taste in rural embellishment. They are for the most part laid out with admirable taste; they contain the greatest variety of trees and shrubs to be found in the country, and several of them are kept in a manner seldom equalled in private places.†

* We made a rough calculation from some data obtained at Philadelphia lately, by which we find that, including the cost of the lots, more than a million and a half of dollars have been expended in the purchase and decoration of cemeteries in that neighborhood alone.

† Laurel Hill is especially rich in rare trees. We saw, last month, almost every procurable species of hardy tree and shrub growing there,—among

The character of each of the three great cemeteries is essentially distinct. *Greenwood*, the largest, and unquestionably the finest, is grand, dignified, and park-like. It is laid out in a broad and simple style, commands noble ocean views, and is admirably kept. *Mount Auburn* is richly picturesque, in its varied hill and dale, and owes its charm mainly to this variety and intricacy of sylvan features. *Laurel Hill* is a charming *pleasure-ground*, filled with beautiful and rare shrubs and flowers; at this season, a wilderness of roses, as well as fine trees and monuments.*

To enable the reader to form a correct idea of the influence

others, the Cedar of Lebanon, the Deodar Cedar, the Paulownia, the Araucaria, etc. Rhododendrons and Azaleas were in full bloom; and the purple Beeches, the weeping Ash, rare Junipers, Pines, and deciduous trees were abundant in many parts of the grounds. Twenty acres of new ground have just been added to this cemetery. It is a better *arboretum* than can easily be found elsewhere in the country.

* Few things are perfect; and beautiful and interesting as our rural cemeteries now are,—more beautiful and interesting than any thing of the same kind abroad, we cannot pass by one feature in all, marked by the most violent bad taste; we mean the hideous *ironmongery*, which they all more or less display. Why, if the separate lots *must* be inclosed with iron railings, the railings should not be of simple and unobtrusive patterns, we are wholly unable to conceive. As we now see them, by far the greater part are so ugly as to be positive blots on the beauty of the scene. Fantastic conceits and gimcracks in iron might be pardonable as adornments of the balustrade of a circus or a temple of Comus; but how reasonable beings can tolerate them as inclosures to the quiet grave of a family, and in such scenes of sylvan beauty, is mountain high above our comprehension.

But this is not all; as if to show how far human infirmity can go, we noticed lately several lots in one of these cemeteries, not only inclosed with a most barbarous piece of *irony*, but the gate of which was positively ornamented with the coat of arms of the owner, accompanied by a brass doorplate, on which was engraved the owner's name, and city residence! All the world has amused itself with the epitaph on a tombstone in Père la Chaise, erected by a wife to her husband's memory; in which, after recapitulating the many virtues of the departed, the bereaved one concludes with —"his disconsolate widow still continues the business, No. —, Rose-street, Paris." We really have some doubts if the disconsolate widow's epitaph advertisement is not in better taste than the cemetery brass doorplate immortality of our friends at home.

which these beautiful cemeteries constantly exercise on the public mind, it is only necessary to refer to the rapidity with which they have increased in fifteen years, as we have just remarked. To enable them to judge how largely they arouse public curiosity, we may mention that at Laurel Hill, four miles from Philadelphia, an account was kept of the number of visitors during last season; and the sum total, as we were told by one of the directors, was nearly 30,000 persons, who entered the gates between April and December, 1848. Judging only from occasional observations, we should imagine that double that number visit Greenwood, and certainly an equal number, Mount Auburn, in a season.

We have already remarked, that, in the absence of public gardens, rural cemeteries, in a certain degree, supplied their place. But does not this general interest, manifested in these cemeteries, prove that public gardens, established in a liberal and suitable manner, near our large cities, would be equally successful? If 30,000 persons visit a cemetery in a single season, would not a large public garden be equally a matter of curious investigation? Would not such gardens educate the public taste more rapidly than any thing else? And would not the progress of horticulture, as a science and an art, be equally benefited by such establishments? The passion for rural pleasures is destined to be the predominant passion of all the more thoughtful and educated portion of our people; and any means of gratifying their love for ornamental or useful gardening, will be eagerly seized by hundreds of thousands of our countrymen.

Let us suppose a joint-stock company, formed in any of our cities, for the purpose of providing its inhabitants with the luxury of a public garden. A site should be selected with the same judgment which has already been shown by the cemetery companies. It should have a varied surface, a good position, sufficient natural wood, with open space and good soil enough for the arrangement of all those portions which require to be newly planted.

Such a garden might, in the space of fifty to one hundred acres, afford an example of the principal modes of laying out grounds,—thus teaching practical landscape-gardening. It might contain a collection of all the hardy trees and shrubs that grow in this climate, each distinctly labelled,—so that the most ignorant visitor could not fail to learn something of trees. It might have a botanical arrangement of plants, and a lecture-room where, at the proper season, lectures on botany could be delivered, and the classes which should resort there could study with the growing plants under their eyes. It might be laid out so as, in its wooded position, to afford a magnificent drive for those who chose so to enjoy it; and it might be furnished with suitable ices and other refreshments, so that, like the German gardens, it would be the great promenade of all strangers and citizens, visitors, or inhabitants of the city of whose suburbs it would form a part. But how shall such an establishment be supported? Cemeteries are sustained by the prices paid for lots, which, though costing not a large sum each, make an enormous sum in the aggregate.

We answer, by a small admission fee. Only those who are shareholders would (like those owning lots in a cemetery) have entrance for their horses and carriages. This privilege alone would tempt hundreds to subscribe, thus adding to the capital, while the daily resort of citizens and strangers would give the necessary income; for no traveller would leave a city, possessing such a public garden as we have described, without seeing that, its most interesting feature. The finest band of music, the most rigid police, the certainty of an agreeable promenade and excellent refreshments, would, we think, as surely tempt a large part of the better class of the inhabitants of our cities to such a resort here as in Germany. If the road to Mount Auburn is now lined with coaches, continually carrying the inhabitants of Boston by thousands and tens of thousands, is it not likely that such a garden, full of the most varied instruction, amusement, and recreation, would be ten times more visited? Fêtes might be held there, horticultural societies would make annual exhibitions there, and it would be the general holiday-ground of all who love to escape from the brick walls, paved streets, and stifling atmosphere of towns.

Would such a project pay? This is the home question of all the calculating part of the community, who must open their purse-strings to make it a substantial reality.

We can only judge by analogy. The mere yearly rent of Barnum's Museum in Broadway is, we believe, about $10,000 (a sum more than sufficient to meet all the annual expenses of such a garden); and it is not only paid, but very large profits have been made there. Now, if hundreds of thousands of the inhabitants of cities, like New-York, will pay to see stuffed boa-constrictors and *un*-human Belgian giants, or incur the expense and trouble of going five or six miles to visit Greenwood, we think it may safely be estimated that a much larger number would resort to a public garden, at once the finest park, the most charming drive, the most inviting pleasure-ground, and the most agreeable promenade within their reach. That such a project, carefully planned, and liberally and judiciously carried out, would not only *pay*, in money, but largely civilize and refine the national character, foster the love of rural beauty, and increase the knowledge of and taste for rare and beautiful trees and plants, we cannot entertain a reasonable doubt.

It is only necessary for one of the three cities which first opened cemeteries, to set the example, and the thing once fairly seen, it becomes universal. The true policy of republics, is to foster the taste for great public libraries, sculpture and picture galléries, parks, and gardens, which *all* may enjoy, since our institutions wisely forbid the growth of private fortunes sufficient to achieve these desirable results in any other way.

X.

HOW TO CHOOSE A SITE FOR A COUNTRY-SEAT.

December, 1847.

HOW to choose the site for a country house, is a subject now occupying the thoughts of many of our countrymen, and therefore is not undeserving a few words from us at the present moment.

The greater part of those who build country-seats in the United States, are citizens who retire from the active pursuits of town to enjoy, in the most rational way possible, the fortunes accumulated there—that is to say, in the creation of beautiful and agreeable rural homes.

Whatever may be the natural taste of this class, their avocations have not permitted them to become familiar with the difficulties to be encountered in making a *new* place, or the most successful way of accomplishing all that they propose to themselves. Hence, we not unfrequently see a very complete house surrounded, for years, by very unfinished and meagre grounds. Weary with the labor and expense of levelling earth, opening roads and walks, and clothing a naked place with new plantations, all of which he finds far less easily accomplished than building brick walls in the city, the once sanguine improver often abates his energy, and loses his interest in the embellishment of his grounds, before his plans are half perfected.

All this arises from a general disposition to underrate the difficulty and cost of making plantations, and laying the groundwork of a complete country residence. Landscape gardening, where all its elements require to be newly arranged, where the scenery of a place requires to be almost wholly created, is by no means either a cheap or rapid process. Labor and patience must be added to taste, time and money, before a bare site can be turned into smooth lawns and complete pleasure-grounds.

The best advice which the most experienced landscape gardener can give an American about to select ground for a country residence, is, therefore, to choose a site where there is *natural wood*, and where nature offers the greatest number of good features ready for a basis upon which to commence improvements.

We have, already, so often descanted on the superiority of trees and lawns to all other features of ornamental places united, that our readers are not, we trust, slow to side with us in a thorough appreciation of their charms.

Hence, when a site for a country place is to be selected (after health and good neighborhood), the first points are, if possible, to secure a position where there is some existing wood, and where the ground is so disposed as to offer a natural surface for a fine lawn. These two points secured, half the battle is fought, for the framework or background of foliage being ready grown, immediate shelter, shade, and effect is given as soon as the house is erected; and a surface well shaped for a lawn (or one which requires but trifling alterations) once obtained, all the labor and cost of grading is avoided, and a single season's thorough preparation gives you velvet to walk about upon.

Some of our readers, no doubt, will say this is excellent advice, but unfortunately not easily followed. So many are forced to build on a bare site, "and begin at the beginning."

This is no doubt occasionally true, but in nine cases out of ten, in this country, our own observation has convinced us that the choice of a poor location is the result of local prejudice, or want of knowledge of the subject, rather than of necessity.

How frequently do we see men paying large prices for indifferent sites, when at a distance of half a mile there are one or more positions on which nature has lavished treasures of wood and water, and spread out undulating surfaces, which seem absolutely to court the finishing touches of the rural artist. Place a dwelling in such a site, and it appropriates all nature's handiwork to itself in a moment.

The masses of trees are easily broken into groups that have immediately the effect of old plantations, and all the minor details of shrubbery, walks, and flower and fruit gardens, fall gracefully and becomingly into their proper positions. Sheltered and screened, and brought into harmony with the landscape, these finishing touches serve in turn to enhance the beauty and value of the original trees themselves.

We by no means wish to deter those who have an abundance of means, taste, enthusiasm and patience, from undertaking the creation of entire new scenery in their country residences. There are few sources of satisfaction more genuine and lasting than that of walking through extensive groves and plantations, all reared by one's own hands—to look on a landscape which one has transformed into leafy hills and wood-embowered slopes. We scarcely remember more real delight evinced by any youthful devotee of our favorite art, in all the fervor of his first enthusiasm, than has been expressed to us by one of our venerable ex-Presidents, now in a ripe old age, when showing us, at various times, fine old forest trees, oaks, hickories, etc., which have been watched by him in their entire cycle of development, from the naked seeds deposited in the soil by his own hands, to their now furrowed trunks and umbrageous heads!

But it must be confessed, that it is throwing away a large part of one's life—and that too, more especially, when the cup of country pleasures is not brought to the lips till one's meridian is well nigh past—to take the whole business of making a landscape from the invisible carbon and oxygen waiting in soil and atmosphere, to be turned by the slow alchemy of ten or twenty summers' growth into groves of weeping elms, and groups of overshadowing oaks!

Those, therefore, who wish to start with the advantage of a good patrimony from nature, will prefer to examine what mother Earth has to offer them in her choicest nooks, before they determine on taking hold of some meagre scene, where the woodman's axe and the ploughman's furrow have long ago obliterated all the original beauty of the landscape. If a place cannot be found well wooded, perhaps a fringe of wood or a background of forest foliage can be taken advantage of. These will give shelter, and serve as a groundwork to help on the effects of the ornamental planter. We have seen a cottage or a villa site dignified, and rendered attractive for ever, by the possession of even three or four fine trees of the original growth, judiciously preserved, and taken as the nucleus of a whole series of belts and minor plantations.

There is another most striking advantage in the possession of considerable wooded surface, properly located, in a country residence. This is the seclusion and privacy of the walks and drives, which such bits of woodland afford. Walks, in open lawn, or even amid belts of shrubbery, are never felt to have that seclusion and comparative solitude which belong to the wilder aspect of woodland scenes. And no contrast is more agreeable than that from the open sunny brightness of the lawn and pleasure-grounds, to the retirement and quiet of a woodland walk.

Again, it is no small matter of consideration to many persons settling in the country, the production of picturesque effect, the working out of a realm of beauty of their own, without any serious inroads into their incomes. One's private walks and parterres, unluckily, cannot be had at the cost of one's daily bread and butter—though the Beautiful overtops the useful, as stars outshine farthing candles. But the difference of cost between keeping up a long series of walks, in a place mainly composed of flower-garden, shrubbery, and pleasure-grounds, compared with another, where there are merely lawns and sylvan scenery, is like that between maintaining a chancery suit, or keeping on pleasant terms with your best friend or favorite country neighbor. Open walks must be scrupulously neat, and broad sunshine and rich soil make weeds grow faster than a new city in the best "western diggins," and your gardener has no sooner put the series of walks in perfect order, than he looks over his shoulder, and beholds the enemy is there, to be conquered over again. On the other hand, woodland walks are swept and repaired in the spring, and like some of those gifted individuals, "born neat," they require no more attention than the rainbow, to remain fresh and bright till the autumn leaves begin to drop again.

Our citizen reader, therefore, who wishes to enjoy his country-seat as an elegant sylvan retreat, with the greatest amount of beauty and enjoyment, and the smallest care and expenditure, will choose a place naturally well wooded, or where open glades and bits of lawn alternate with masses or groups, and, it may be, with extensive tracts of well-grown wood. A house once erected on such a site, the whole can very easily be turned into a charming labyrinth of beautiful and secluded drives and walks. And as our improver cultivates his eye and his taste, nature will certainly give him fresh hints; she will tell him how by opening a glade here, and piercing a thicket there, by making underwood occasionally give place to soft turf, so as to show fine trunks to the greatest advantage, and thereby bringing into more complete contrast some wilder and more picturesque dell, all the natural charms of a place may be heightened into a beauty far more impressive and significant than they originally possessed.

Why man's perception of the Beautiful seems clouded over in most uncultivated natures, and is only brought out by a certain process of refining and mental culture, as the lapidary brings out, by polishing, all the rich play of colors in a stone that one passes by as a common pebble, we leave to the metaphysicians to explain. Certain it is, that we see, occasionally, lamentable proofs of the fact in the treatment of nature's best features, by her untutored children. More than one instance do we call to mind, of settlers, in districts of country where there are masses and great woods of trees, that the druids would have worshipped for their grandeur, sweeping them all down mercilessly with their axes, and then planting with the supremest satisfaction, a straight line of paltry saplings before their doors! It is like exchanging a neighborhood of proud and benevolent yeomanry, honest and free as the soil they spring from, for a file of sentinels or *gens-d'armes*, that watch over one's outgoings and incomings, like a chief of police!

Most happily for our country, and its beautiful rural scenery, this spirit of destruction, under the rapid development of taste that is taking place among us, is very fast disappearing. "Woodman, spare that tree," is the choral sentiment that should be instilled and taught at the agricultural schools, and re-echoed by all the agricultural and horticultural societies in the land. If we have neither old castles nor old associations, we have at least, here and there, old trees that can teach us lessons of antiquity, not less instructive and poetical than the ruins of a past age.

Our first hint, therefore, to persons about choosing a site for a country place, is, in all possible cases, to look for a situation where there is some natural wood. With this for the warp—strong, rich, and permanent—you may embroider upon it all the gold threads of fruit and floral embellishment with an effect equally rapid and successful. Every thing done upon such a groundwork will tell at once; and since there is no end to the delightful task of perfecting a country place, so long as there are thirty thousand species of plants known, and at least thirty millions of varied combinations of landscape scenery possible, we think there is little fear that the possessor of a country place will not find time enough to employ his time, mind, and purse, if he really loves the subject, even though he find himself in possession of a fee-simple of a pretty number of acres of fine wood.

But we have already exhausted our present limits, and must leave the discussion of other points to be observed in choosing a country place until a future number.

XI.

HOW TO ARRANGE COUNTRY PLACES.

March, 1850.

HOW to lay out a country place? That is a question about which we and our readers might have many a long conversation, if we could be brought on familiar terms, colloquially speaking, with all parts of the Union where rural improvements are going on. As it is, we shall touch on a few leading points this month, which may be considered of universal application.

These cardinal points within the bounds of a country residence, are (taking health and pleasant locality for granted), *convenience, comfort*—or social enjoyment—and *beauty;* and we shall touch on them in a very rambling manner.

Innumerable are the mistakes of those novices in forming country places, who reverse the order of these three conditions,—and placing beauty first (as, intellectually considered, it deserves to be), leave the useful, convenient, and comfortable, pretty much to themselves; or, at least, consider them entitled only to a second place in their consideration. In the country places which they create, the casual visitor may be struck with many beautiful effects; but when a trifling observation has shown him that this beauty is not the result of a harmony between the real and the ideal,—or, in other words, between the surface of things intended to be seen and the things themselves, as they minister to our daily wants,—then all the pleasure vanishes, and the opposite feeling takes its place.

To begin at the very root of things, the most defective matter in laying out our country places (as we know from experience), is the want of forethought and plan, regarding the location of what is called the *kitchen offices.* By this, we refer, of course, to that wing or portion of a country house containing the kitchen, with its store-room, pantry, scullery, laundry, wood-house, and whatever else, more or less, may be included under this head.

Our correspondent, Jeffreys, has, in his usual bold manner, pointed out how defective, in all cases (where the thing is not impossible), is a country house with a kitchen below stairs; and we have but lamely apologized for the practice in some houses by the greater *economy* of such an arrangement. But, in truth, we quite agree with him, that no country house is complete unless the kitchen offices are on the same level as the principal floor containing the living apartments.

At first thought, our inexperienced readers may not see precisely what this has to do with laying out the grounds of a country place. But, indeed, it is the very starting point and fundamental substratum on which the whole thing rests. There can be no complete country place, however large or small, in which the greatest possible amount of privacy and seclusion is not attained within its grounds, especially within that part intended for the enjoyment of the family. Now it is very clear, that there can be no seclusion where there is no separation of uses, no shelter, no portions set apart for especial purposes, both of utility and enjoyment. First of all, then, in planning a country place, the house should be so located that there shall be at least two sides; an entrance side, which belongs to the living, or best apartments of the house; and a kitchen side (or "*blind side*"), complete in itself, and more or less shut out from all observation from the remaining portions of the place.

This is as indispensable for the comfort of the inmates of the kitchen as those of the parlor. By shutting off completely one side of the house by belts or plantations of trees and shrubbery from the rest, you are enabled to make that part more extensive and complete in itself. The kitchen yard, the clothes-drying ground, the dairy, and all the structures which are so practically important in a country house, have abundant room and space, and the domestics can perform their appointed labors with ease and freedom, without disturbing the different aspect of any other portion of the grounds. There are few new sites where there is not naturally a " blind side" indicated; a side where there is a fringe of wood, or some natural disposition of surface, which points it out as the spot where the kitchen offices should be placed, in order to have the utmost shelter and privacy,—at the same time leaving the finer glades, openings, and views, for the more refined, social and beautiful portions of the residence. Wherever these indications are wanting, they must be created, by artificial planting of belts, and groups of trees and shrubs,—not in stiff and formal lines like fences, but in an irregular and naturally varied manner, so as to appear as if formed of a natural copse, or, rather, so as not to attract special attention at all.

We are induced to insist upon this point the more strenuously, because, along with the taste for the architecture of Pericles (may we indulge the hope that he is not permitted to behold the *Greek* architecture of the new world!) which came into fashion in this country fifteen or twenty years ago, came also the fashion of sweeping away every thing that was not temple-like about the house. Far from recognizing that man lives a domestic life,—that he cooks, washes, bakes and churns in his country house, and, therefore, that kitchen offices (tastefully concealed if you please, but still ample) are a necessary, and therefore truthful part of his dwelling,—they went upon the principle that if man had fallen, and was no longer one of the gods, he might still live in a temple dedicated to the immortals. A clear space on all sides—pediments at each end, and perhaps a colonnade all round; this is the undomestic, uncomfortable ideal of half the better country houses in America.

Having fixed upon and arranged the blind side of the house—which, of course, will naturally be placed so as to connect itself directly with the stable and other out-buildings,—the next point of attack is the *kitchen garden.* This is not so easily disposed of as many imagine. All persons of good taste agree that however necessary, satisfactory, and pleasant a thing a good kitchen garden is, it is not, æsthetically, considered a beautiful thing; and it never accords well with the ornamental portions of a country place, where the latter is large enough to have a lawn, pleasure-grounds, or other portions that give it an ornamental character. The fruit trees (and we include now, for the sake of conciseness, kitchen and fruit garden), the vegetables, and all that makes the utility of the kitchen garden, never harmonize with the more graceful forms of ornamental scenery. Hence, the kitchen garden, in a complete country place, should always form a scene by itself, and should, also, be shut out from the lawn or ornamental grounds by plantations of trees and shrubs. A good locality, as regards soil, is an important point to be considered in determining its site; and it will usually adjoin the space given to the kitchen offices, or that near the stable or barns, or, perhaps lie between both, so that it also is kept on the blind side of the house.

After having disposed of the useful and indispensable portions of the place, by placing them in the spots at once best fitted for them, and least interfering with the convenience and beauty of the remaining portions, let us now turn to what may properly be called the ornamental portion of the place.

This may be confined to a mere bit of lawn, extending a few feet in front of the parlor windows, or it may cover a number of acres, according to the extent of the place, and the taste and means of the owner.

Be that as it may, the groundwork of this part should, in our judgment, always be lawn. There is in the country no object which at all seasons and times gives the constant satisfaction of the green turf of a nicely kept lawn. If your place is large, so much larger and broader is the good effect of the lawn, as it stretches away, over gentle undulations, alternately smiling and looking serious, in the play of sunshine and shade that rests upon it. If it is small—a mere bit of green turf before your door—then it forms the best and most becoming setting to the small beds and masses of ever-blooming roses, verbenas, and gay annuals, with which you embroider it, like a carpet.

Lawn there must be, to give any refreshment to the spirit of man in our country places; for nothing is so intolerable to the eye as great flower-gardens of parched earth, lying half baked in the meridian sun of an American summer. And though no nation under the sun may have such lawns as the British, because Britain lies in the lap of the sea, with a climate always more or less humid, yet green and pleasant lawns most persons may have in the Northern States, who will make the soil *deep* and keep the grass well mown.

To mow a large surface of lawn—that is to say, many acres—is a thing attempted in but few places in America, from the high price of labor. But a happy expedient comes in to our aid, to save labor and trouble, and produce all the good effect of a well-mown lawn. We mean sheep and wire fences. Our neighbor and correspondent, Mr. Sargent, of Wodenethe, on the Hudson, who passed a couple of years abroad, curiously gleaning all clever foreign notions that were really worth naturalizing at home, has already told our readers how wire fences may be constructed round lawns or portions of the pleasure-grounds, so that only a strip round the house need be mown, while the extent of the lawn is kept short by sheep. This fence, which costs less than any tolerable looking fence of other materials, is abundantly strong to turn both sheep and cattle, and is invisible at the distance of 40 or 50 rods. Mr. Sargent is not a theorist, but has actually inclosed his own lawn of several acres in this way; and those who have examined the plan are struck with the usefulness and economy of the thing, in all ornamental country places of considerable extent.

We have said nothing, as yet, of the most important feature of all country places—trees. A country place without trees, is like a caliph without his beard; in other words, it is not a country place. We shall assume, therefore, that all proprietors who do not already possess this indispensable feature, will set about planting with more ardor than Walter Scott ever did. It is the one thing needful for them; and deep trenching, plentiful manuring, and sufficient mulching, are the powerful auxiliaries to help them forward in the good work.

It is, of course, impossible for us to tell our readers how to arrange trees tastefully and well, under all circumstances, in this short chapter. We can offer them, however, two or three hints as to arrangement, which they may perhaps profit by.

The first principle in ornamental planting, is to study the *character of the place* to be improved, and to plant in accordance with it. If your place has breadth, and simplicity, and fine open views, plant in groups, and rather sparingly, so as to heighten and adorn the landscape, not shut out and obstruct the beauty of prospect which nature has placed before your eyes. *Scattered groups*, with continuous reaches or vistas between, produce the best effect in such situations. In other and more remote parts of the place, greater density of foliage may serve as a contrast.

In residences where there is little or no distant view, the contrary plan must be pursued. Intricacy and variety must be created by planting. Walks must be led in various directions, and concealed from each other by thickets, and masses of shrubs and trees, and occasionally rich masses of foliage; not forgetting to heighten all, however, by an occasional contrast of broad, unbroken surface of lawn.

In all country places, and especially in small ones, a great object to be kept in view in planting, is to produce as perfect seclusion and privacy within the grounds as possible. We do not entirely feel that to be our own, which is indiscriminately enjoyed by each passer-by, and every man's individuality and home-feeling is invaded by the presence of unbidden guests. Therefore, while you preserve the beauty of the view, shut out, by boundary belts and thickets, all eyes but those that are fairly within your own grounds. This will enable you to feel at home all over your place, and to indulge your individual taste in walking, riding, reciting your next speech or sermon, or wearing any peculiarly rustic costume, without being suspected of being a "queer fellow" by any of your neighbors; while it will add to the general beauty and interest of the country at large,—since, in passing a fine place, we always *imagine* it finer than it is, if a boundary plantation, by concealing it, forces us to depend wholly on the imagination.

XII.

THE MANAGEMENT OF LARGE COUNTRY PLACES.

March, 1851.

COUNTRY places that may properly be called ornamental, are increasing so fast, especially in the neighborhood of the large cities, that a word or two more, touching their treatment, will not be looked upon as out of place here.

All our country residences may readily be divided into two classes. The first and largest class, is the suburban place of from five to twenty or thirty acres; the second is the country-seat, properly so called, which consists of from thirty to five hundred or more acres.

In all suburban residences, from the limited extent of ground, and the desire to get the utmost beauty from it, the whole, or at least a large part of the ornamental portion, must be considered only as pleasure-grounds—a term used to denote a garden scene, consisting of trees, shrubs, and flowers, generally upon a basis of lawn, laid out in walks of different styles, and kept in the highest order. The aim, in this kind of residence, is to produce the greatest possible variety within a given space, and to attain the utmost beauty of gardening as an *art*, by the highest keeping and culture which the means of the proprietor will permit.

Of this kind of pleasure-ground residence, we have numberless excellent examples—and perhaps nowhere more admirable specimens than in the neighborhood of Boston. Both in design and execution, these little places will, at the present moment, bear very favorable comparison with many in older countries. The practical management of such places is also very well understood, and they need no especial mention in these remarks.

But in the larger country places there are ten instances of failure for one of success. This is not owing to the want of natural beauty, for the sites are picturesque, the surface varied, and the woods and plantations excellent. The failure consists, for the most part, in a certain incongruity and want of distinct character in the treatment of the place as a whole. They are too large to be kept in order as pleasure-grounds, while they are not laid out or treated as parks. The grass which stretches on all sides of the house, is partly mown, for lawn, and partly for hay; the lines of the farm and the ornamental portion of the grounds, meet in a confused and unsatisfactory manner, and the result is a residence pretending to be much superior to a common farm, and yet not rising to the dignity of a really tasteful country-seat.

It appears to us that a species of country places particularly adapted to this country, has not, as yet, been attempted, though it offers the largest possible satisfaction at the least cost.

We mean a place which is a *combination of the park-like and pastoral* landscape. A place in which the chief features should be fine forest trees, either natural or planted, and scattered over a surface of grass, kept short by the pasturage of fine cattle. A place, in short, where sylvan and pastoral beauty, added to large extent and great facility of management, would cost no more than a much smaller demesne, where a large part is laid out, planted, and kept in an expensive though still unsatisfactory manner.

There are sites of this kind, already prettily wooded, which may be had in many desirable localities, at much cheaper rates than the improved sites. On certain portions of the Hudson, for instance, we could purchase, to-day, finely wooded sites and open glades, in the midst of fine scenery—in fact what could, with very trifling expense be turned into a natural park—at $60 per acre, while the im proved sites will readily command $200 or $300 per acre.

Considerable familiarity with the country-seats on the Hudson enables us to state that, for the most part, few persons keep up a fine country place, counting all the products of the farm-land attached to it, without being more or less out of pocket at the end of the year. And yet there are very few of the large places that can be looked upon as examples of tolerable keeping.

The explanation of this lies in the high price of all kinds of labor—which costs us nearly double or treble what it does on the other side of the Atlantic, and the comparatively small profits of land managed in the expensive way common on almost all farms attached to our Atlantic country-seats. The remedy for this unsatisfactory condition of the large country places is, we think, a very simple one—that of turning a large part of their areas into park meadow, and *feeding* it, instead of mowing and cultivating it.

The great and distinguishing beauty of England, as every one knows, is its parks. And yet the English parks are only very large meadows, studded with oaks and elms—and grazed—*profitably grazed*, by deer, cattle, and sheep. We believe it is a commonly received idea in this country, with those who have not travelled abroad, that English parks are portions of highly-dressed scenery—at least that they are kept short by frequent mowing, etc. It is an entire mistake. The mown lawn with its polished garden scenery, is confined to the pleasure-grounds proper—a spot of greater or less size, immediately surrounding the house, and wholly separated from the park by a terrace wall, or an iron fence, or some handsome architectural barrier. The park, which generally comes quite up to the house on one side, receives no other attention than such as belongs to the care of the animals that graze in it. As most of these parks afford excellent pasturage, and though apparently one wide, unbroken surface, they are really subdivided into large fields, by wire or other invisible fences, they actually pay a very fair income to the proprietor, in the shape of good beef, mutton, and venison.

Certainly, nothing can be a more beautiful sight in its way, than the numerous herds of deer, short-horned cattle and fine sheep, which embroider and give life to the scenery of an English country home of this kind.* There is a quiet pastoral beauty, a spacious-

* All attempts to render our native deer really tame in home grounds have, so far as we know, failed among us—though with patience the thing may doubtless be done. It would be well worth while to import the finer breeds of the English deer, which are thoroughly domesticated in their habits, and the most beautiful animals for a park.

ness and dignity, and a simple feeling of nature about it which no highly decorated pleasure-grounds or garden scenery can approach, as the continual surrounding of a country residence. It is, in fact, the poetical idea of Arcadia, a sort of ideal nature—softened, refined, and ennobled, without being made to look artificial.

Of course, any thing like English parks, so far as regards *extent*, is almost out of the question here; simply because land and fortunes are widely divided here, instead of being kept in large bodies, intact, as in England. Still, as the first class country-seats of the Hudson now command from $50,000 to $75,000, it is evident that there is a growing taste for space and beauty in the private domains of republicans. What we wish to suggest now, is, simply, that the greatest beauty and satisfaction may be had here, as in England—(for the plan really suits our limited means better), by treating the bulk of the ornamental portion as open park pasture—and thus getting the greatest space and beauty at the least original expenditure, and with the largest annual profit.

To some of our readers who have never seen the thing, the idea of a park, pastured by animals almost to the very door, will seem at variance with all decorum and elegance. This, however, is not actually the case. The house should either stand on a raised terrace of turf, which, if it is a fine mansion, may have a handsome terrace wall, or if a cottage, a pretty rustic or trellis fence, to separate it from the park. Directly around the house, and stretching on one or more sides, in the rear, lie the more highly dressed portions of the scene, which may be a flower-garden and shrubbery set in a small bit of lawn kept as short as velvet—or may be pleasure-grounds, fruit, and kitchen-gardens, so multiplied as to equal the largest necessities of the place and family. All that is to be borne in mind is, that the park may be as large as you can afford to purchase—for it may be kept up at a profit—while the pleasure-grounds and garden scenery, may, with this management, be compressed into the smallest space actually deemed necessary to the place—thereby lessening labor, and bestowing that labor, in a concentrated space, where it will tell.

The practical details of keeping the stock upon such a place, are familiar to almost every farmer. Of course, in a country place, only comely animals would be kept, and a preference would be given to breeds of fine stock that "take on flesh" readily, and command the best price in the market. In cases where an interest is taken in breeding cattle, provision must be made, in the shape of hay and shelter, for the whole year round; but we imagine the most profitable, as well as least troublesome mode, to the majority of gentlemen proprietors, would be to buy the suitable stock in the spring, put it in good condition, and sell it again in the autumn. The sheep would also require to be folded at night to prevent the flocks from being ravaged by dogs.

With this kind of arrangement and management of a country place, the owner would be in a position to reap the greatest enjoyment with the least possible care. To country gentlemen ignorant of farming, such an extent of park, with its drives and walks, along with its simplicity of management, would be a relief from a multitude of embarrassing details; while to those who have tried, to their cost, the expenses of keeping a large place in high order, it would be an equal relief to the debtor side of the cash account.

XIII.

COUNTRY PLACES IN AUTUMN.

December, 1850.

NOVEMBER, which is one of the least interesting months to those who come into the country to admire the freshness of spring or the fulness of summer and early autumn, is one of the most interesting to those who live in the country, or who have country places which they wish to improve.

When the leaves have all dropped from the trees, when the enchantment and illusion of summer are over, and "the fall" (our expressive American word for autumn) has stripped the glory from the sylvan landscape, then the rural improver puts on his spectacles, and looks at his demesne with practical and philosophical eyes. Taking things at their worst, as they appear now, he sets about finding out what improvements can be made, and how the surroundings which make his home, can be so arranged as to offer a fairer picture to the eye, or a larger share of enjoyments and benefits to the family, in the year that is to come.

The end of autumn is the best month to buy a country place, and the best to improve one. You see it then in the barest skeleton expression of ugliness or beauty—with all opportunity to learn its defects, all its weak points visible, all its possible capacities and suggestions for improvement laid bare to you. If it satisfy you now, either in its present aspect, or in what promise you see in it of order and beauty after your moderate plans are carried out, you may buy it, with the full assurance that you will not have cause to repent when you learn to like it better as seen in the fresher and fairer aspect of its summer loveliness.

As a season for rural improvements, the fall is preferable to the spring, partly because the earth is dryer, and more easily moved and worked, and partly because there is more time to do *well* what we undertake. In the middle States, fine autumnal weather is often continued till the middle of December; and as long as the ground is open and mellow, the planting of hardy trees may be done with the best chances of success. The surface may be smoothed, drains made, walks and roads laid out, and all the heavier operations on the surface of the earth—so requisite as a groundwork for lawns and pleasure-grounds, kitchen or flower-gardens—may be carried on more cheaply and efficiently than amid the bustle and hurry of spring. And when sharp frosty nights fairly set in, then is the time to commence the grander operations of transplanting. Then is the time for moving *large trees*—elms, maples, etc.; a few of which will give more effect to a new and bare site than thousands of the young things, which are the despair of all improvers of little faith and ardent imaginations. With two or three "hands," a pair of horses or oxen, a "stone boat," or low sled, and some ropes or "tackle," the removal of trees twenty-five feet high, and six or eight inches in the diameter of the stem, is a very simple and easy process. A little practice will enable a couple of men to do it most perfectly and efficiently; and if only free-growing trees, like elms, maples, lindens, or horse-chestnuts, are chosen, there is no more doubt of success than in planting a currant bush. Two or three points we may, however, repeat, for the benefit of the novice, viz., to prepare the soil thoroughly by digging a large hole, trenching it two-and-a-half feet deep, and filling it with rich soil; to take up the tree with a good mass of roots, inclosed in a ball of frozen earth;* and to reduce the *ends* of the limbs, evenly all over the top, in order to lessen the demand for sustenance, made on the roots the first summer after removal.

This is not only the season to plant very hardy trees; it is also

* This is easily done by digging a trench all round, leaving a ball about four or five feet in diameter; undermining it well, and leaving it to freeze for one or two nights. Then turn the tree down, place the uplifted side of the ball upon the "stone boat;" right the trunk, and get the whole ball firmly upon the sled, and then the horses will drag it easily to its new position.

the time to *feed* those which are already established, and are living on too scanty an income. And how many trees are there upon lawns and in gardens—shade trees and fruit trees—that are literally so *poor* that they are *starving to death!* Perhaps they have once been luxuriant and thrifty, and have borne the finest fruit and blossoms, so that their owners have smiled, and said pleasant words in their praise, as they passed beneath their boughs. Then they had a good subsistence; the native strength of the soil passed into their limbs, and made them stretch out and expand with all the vigor of a young Hercules. Now, alas, they are mossy and decrepit—the leaves small—the blossoms or fruit indifferent. And yet they are not old. Nay, they are quite in the prime of life. If they could speak to their master or mistress, they would say—"First of all, give us something to eat. Here are we, tied hand and foot to one spot, where we have been feeding this dozen or twenty years, until we are actually reduced to our last morsel. What the gardener has occasionally given us, in his scanty top-dressing of manure, has been as a mere crust thrown out to a famished man. If you wish us to salute you next year with a glorious drapery of green leaves—the deepest, richest green, and start into new forms of luxuriant growth—*feed us.* Dig a trench around us, at the extremity of our roots, throw away all the old worn-out soil you find there, and replace it with some fresh soil from the lower corner of some rich meadow, where it has lain fallow for years, growing richer every day. Mingle this with some manure, some chopped sods—any thing that can allay our thirst and satisfy our hunger for three or four years to come, and see what a new leaf—yes, what volumes of new leaves we will turn over for you next year. We are fruit trees, perhaps, and you wish us to bear fair and excellent fruit. Then you must also feed us. The soil is thin, and contains little that we can digest; or it is old, and 'sour' for the want of being aired. Remove all the earth for several yards about us, baring some of our roots—and perhaps shortening a few. Trench the ground, when our new roots will ramble, next year, twenty inches deep. Mingle the top and bottom soil, rejecting the worst parts of it, and making the void good—*very good*—by manure, ashes, and decaying leaves. Then you shall have bushels of fair and fine pears and apples, where you now have pecks of spotted and deformed fruit."

Such is the sermon which the "tongues in trees" preach to those who listen to them at this season of the year. We do not mean to poets, or lovers of nature (for to them, they have other and more romantic stories to tell); but to the earnest, practical, working owners of the soil,—especially to those who grudge a little food and a little labor, in order that the trees may live contented, healthy, beautiful, and fruitful lives. We have written it down here, in order that our readers, when they walk round their gardens and grounds, and think "the work of the season is all done," may not be wholly blind and deaf to the fact that the trees are as capable, in their way, of hunger and thirst, as the cattle in the farm-yards; and since, at the oftenest, they only need feeding once a year, now is the cheapest and the best time for doing it. The very frosts of winter creep into the soil, loosened by stirring at this season, and fertilize, while they crumble and decompose it. Walk about, then, and listen to the sermon which your hungry trees preach.

XIV.

A CHAPTER ON LAWNS.

November, 1846.

LANDSCAPE GARDENING embraces, in the circle of its perfections, many *elements* of beauty; certainly not a less number than the modern chemists count as the simplest conditions of matter. But with something of the feeling of the old philosophers, who believed that earth, air, fire and water, included every thing in nature, we like to go back to plain and simple facts, of breadth and importance enough to embrace a multitude of little details. The great elements then, of landscape gardening, as we understand it, are TREES and GRASS.

TREES—delicate, beautiful, grand, or majestic trees—pliantly answering to the wooing of the softest west wind, like the willow; or bravely and sturdily defying centuries of storm and tempest, like the oak—they are indeed the great "princes, potentates, and people," of our realm of beauty. But it is not to-day that we are permitted to sing triumphal songs in their praise.

In behalf of the grass—the turf, the lawn,—then, we ask our readers to listen to us for a short time. And by this we do not mean to speak of it in a moral sense, as did the inspired preacher of old, when he gravely told us that "all flesh is grass;" or in a style savoring of the vanities of costume, as did Prior, when he wrote the couplet,

> "Those limbs in *lawn* and softest silk arrayed,
> From sunbeams guarded, and of winds afraid."

Or with the keen relish of the English jockey, whose only idea of "the turf," is that of the place nature has specially provided him upon which to race horses.

Neither do we look upon grass, at the present moment, with the eyes of our friend Tom Thrifty, the farmer, who cuts "three tons to the acre." We have, in our present mood, no patience with the tall and gigantic *fodder*, by this name, that grows in the fertile bottoms of the West, so tall that the largest Durham is lost to view while walking through it.

No—we love most the soft turf which, beneath the flickering shadows of scattered trees, is thrown like a smooth natural carpet over the swelling outline of the smiling earth. Grass, not grown into tall meadows, or wild bog tussocks, but softened and refined by the frequent touches of the patient mower, till at last it becomes a perfect wonder of tufted freshness and verdure. Such grass, in short, as Shakspeare had in his mind, when he said, in words since echoed ten thousand times,

> "How sweet the moonlight sleeps upon that bank;"

or Ariosto, in his Orlando—

> "The approaching night, not knowing where to pass,
> She checks her reins, and on the *velvet grass*,
> Beneath the umbrageous trees, her form she throws,
> To cheat the tedious hours with brief repose."

In short, the ideal of grass is a *lawn*, which is, to a meadow, what "Bishop's lawn" is to homespun Irish linen.

With such a lawn, and large and massive trees, one has indeed the most enduring sources of beauty in a country residence. Perpetual neatness, freshness and verdure in the one; ever expanding beauty, variety and grandeur in the other—what more does a reasonable man desire of the beautiful about him in the country? Must we add flowers, exotic plants, fruits? Perhaps so, but they are all, in an ornamental light, secondary to trees and grass, where these can be had in perfection. Only one other grand element is needed to make our landscape garden complete—*water*. A river, or a lake, in which the skies and the "tufted trees" may see themselves reflected, is ever an indispensable feature to a perfect landscape.

How to obtain a fine lawn, is a question which has no doubt already puzzled many of our readers. They have thought, perhaps, that it would be quite sufficient to sow with grass seeds, or lay down neatly with sods, any plat of common soil, to mow it occasionally, to be repaid by the perpetual softness and verdure of an "English lawn."

They have found, however, after a patient trial in several seasons, that an American summer, so bright and sunny as to give us, in our fruits, almost the ripeness and prodigality of the tropics, does not, like that of Britain, ever moist and humid, naturally favor the condition of fine lawns.

Beautiful as our lawns usually are in May, June, September, and October, yet in July and August, they too often lose that freshness and verdure which is for them what the rose-bloom of youth is to a beauty of seventeen—their most captivating feature.

There are not wanting admirers of fine lawns, who, witnessing this summer *searing*, have pronounced it an impossible thing to produce a fine lawn in this country. To such an opinion we can never subscribe—for the very sufficient reason that we have seen, over and over again, admirable lawns wherever they have been properly treated. Fine lawns are therefore possible in all the northern half of the Union. What then are the necessary conditions to be observed—what the preliminary steps to be taken in order to obtain them? Let us answer in a few words—*deep soil*, *the proper kinds of grasses*, and *frequent mowing*.

First of all, for us, *deep soil*. In a moist climate, where showers or fogs give all vegetable nature a weekly succession of baths, one may raise a pretty bit of turf on a bare board, with half an inch of soil. But here it does not require much observation or theory to teach us, that if any plant is to maintain its verdure through a long and bright summer, with alternate periods of wet and drouth, it must have a deep soil in which to extend its roots. We have seen the roots of common clover, in trenched soil, which had descended to the depth of four feet! A surface drouth, or dry weather, had little power over a plant whose little fibres were in the cool moist understratum of that depth. And a lawn which is well established on thoroughly trenched soil, will remain, even in midsummer, of a fine dark vèrdure, when upon the same soil untrenched, every little period of dryness would give a brown and faded look to the turf.

The most essential point being a deep soil, we need not say that in our estimation, any person about to lay down a permanent lawn, whether of fifty acres or fifty feet square, *must* provide himself against failure by this *groundwork* of success.

Little plats of ground are easily trenched with the spade. Large lawn surfaces are only to be managed (unless expense is not a consideration), with the subsoil plough. With this grand developer of resources, worked by two yoke of oxen, let the whole area to be laid down be thoroughly moved and broken up two feet deep. The autumn or early winter is the best season for performing this, because the surface will have ample time to settle, and take a proper shape before spring.

After being ploughed, subsoiled and harrowed, let the whole surface be entirely cleared of even the smallest stone. It is quite impossible to *mow* a lawn well that is not as smooth as ground can be made. Manure, if necessary, should be applied while subsoiling. We say, if necessary, for if the land is strong and in good heart, it is not needed. The object in a lawn, it will be remembered, is not to obtain a heavy crop of hay, but simply to maintain perpetual verdure. *Rich* soil would defeat our object by causing a rank growth and coarse stalks, when we wish a short growth and soft herbage. Let the soil, therefore, be good, but not rich; depth, and the power of retaining moisture, are the truly needful qualities here. If the land is very light and sandy (the worst naturally), we would advise a mixture of loam or clay; which indeed subsoiling, when the substratum is heavy, will often most readily effect.

The soil, thus prepared, lies all winter to mellow and settle, with the kindly influences of the atmosphere and frost upon it.

As early in the spring, as it is in friable working condition, stir it lightly with the plough and harrow, and make the surface as smooth as possible- -we do not mean level, for if the ground is not a flat, nothing is so agreeable as gentle swells or undulations. But *quite smooth* the surface must be.

Now for the sowing; and here a farmer would advise you to "seed down with oats," or some such established agricultural precept. Do not listen to him for a moment! What you desire is a close turf, and therefore sow nothing but grass; and do not suppose you are going to assist a weak growing plant by sowing along with it a coarser growing one to starve it.

Choose, if possible, a calm day, and sow your seed as evenly as you can. The seed to be sown is a mixture of red-top (*Agostis vulgaris*) and white clover (*Trifolium repens*), which are hardy short grasses, and on the whole make the best and most enduring lawn for this climate.* The proportion should be about three-fourths red-top to one-fourth white clover. The seed should be perfectly clean; then sow *four bushels* of it *to the acre;* not a pint less as you hope to walk upon velvet! Finish the whole by rolling the surface evenly and neatly.

A few soft vernal showers, and bright sunny days, will show you a coat of verdure bright as emerald. By the first of June, you will find it necessary to look about for your mower.

And this reminds us to say a word about a lawn scythe. You must not suppose, as many ignorant people do, that a lawn can be mown with a brush hook, or a common meadow scythe for cutting hay in the fastest possible manner. It can only be done with a broad-bladed scythe, of the most perfect temper and quality, which will hold an edge like a razor. The easiest way to get such an article is to inquire at any of the agricultural warehouses in the great cities, for an "English lawn scythe." When used, it should be set low, so as to be level with the plane of the grass; when the mower is erect, he will mow without leaving any marks, and with the least possible exertion.

After your lawn is once fairly established, there are but two secrets in keeping it perfect—frequent mowing and rolling. Without the first, it will soon degenerate into a coarse meadow; the

* We learn the blue-grass of Kentucky makes a fine lawn at the West, but with this we have no experience.

latter will render it firmer, closer, shorter, and finer every time it is repeated.

A good lawn must be mown every ten days or fortnight. The latter may be assumed as the proper average time in this climate. Ten days is the usual limit of growth for the best kept lawns in England, and it is surprising how soon a coarse and wiry bit of sward will become smooth turf, under the magic influences of regular and oft repeated mowing and rolling.

Of course, a lawn can only be cut when the grass is damp, and rolling is best performed directly after rain. The English always roll a few hours before using the scythe. On large lawns, a donkey or light horse may be advantageously employed in performing this operation.

There are but few good lawns yet in America; but we have great pleasure in observing that they are rapidly multiplying. Though it may seem a heavy tax to some, yet no expenditure in ornamental gardening is, to our mind, productive of so much beauty as that incurred in producing a well-kept lawn. Without this feature, no place, however great its architectural beauties, its charms of scenery, or its collections of flowers and shrubs, can be said to deserve consideration in point of landscape gardening; and with it the humble cottage grounds will possess a charm which is, among pleasure-grounds, what a refined and graceful manner is in society —a universal passport to admiration.

There are two residences in this country which so far surpass all others in the perfection of their lawns, that we hope to be pardoned for holding them up to commendation. These are the UPPER LIVINGSTON MANOR, the seat of Mrs. Mary Livingston, about seven miles from Hudson, N. Y., and the CAMAC COTTAGE, near Philadelphia.*

The lawn at the Livingston Manor is very extensive and park-like—certainly the largest well-kept lawn in America, and we wish all our readers who are skeptical regarding an American lawn, could see and feel its many excellent perfections. They would only

* See Downing's "Landscape Gardening," pp. 45, 58.

be still more surprised when they were told how few men keep so large a surface in the highest order.

The Camac Cottage is a gem of neatness and high keeping. We hope Pennsylvanians at least, who, we think, have perhaps our best lawn climate, will not fail to profit by so admirable an example as they will find there, of what SPENSER quaintly and prettily calls "*the grassie ground.*"

XV.

MR. TUDOR'S GARDEN AT NAHANT.

August, 1847.

A FEW miles east of Boston, boldly jutting into the Atlantic, lies the celebrated promontory of NAHANT. Nature has made it remarkable for the grandeur and bleakness of its position. It is a headland of a hundred acres, more or less, sprinkled with a light turf, and girded about with bold cliffs of rock, against which the sea dashes with infinite grandeur and majesty. No tree anciently deigned to raise its head against the rude breezes that blow here in winter, as if tempest-driven by Boreas himself; and that, even in summer, make of Nahant, with its many cottages and hotels, a refrigerator, for the preservation of the dissolving souls and bodies of the exhausted population of Boston, in the months of July and August.

At the present moment, the interesting feature at Nahant, after the Ocean itself, is, strange to say, one of the most remarkable gardens in existence. We mean the grounds of the private residence of Frederic Tudor, Esq., a gentleman well known in the four quarters of the world, as the originator of the present successful mode of shipping ice to the most distant tropical countries; and, we may here add, for the remarkable manner in which he has again triumphed over nature, by transforming some acres of her bleakest and most sterile soil into a spot of luxuriant verdure, fruitfulness, and beauty.

To appreciate the difficulties with which this gentleman had to contend, or, as we might more properly say, which stimulated all his efforts, we must recall to mind that, frequently, in high winds, the salt spray drives over the whole of Nahant; that, until Mr. Tudor began his improvements, not even a bush grew naturally on the whole of its area, and that the east winds, which blow from the Atlantic in the spring, are sufficient to render all gardening possibilities in the usual way nearly as chimerical as cultivating the volcanoes of the moon.

Mr. Tudor's residence there now, is a curious and striking illustration of the triumph of art over nature, and as it involves some points that we think most instructive to horticulturists, we trust he will pardon us for drawing the attention of our readers to it at the present time. Our first visit to his grounds was made in July, 1845, one of the driest and most unfavorable seasons for the growth of trees and plants that we remember. But at that time, perhaps the best possible one to test the merits of the mode of cultivation adopted, we found Mr. Tudor's garden in a more flourishing condition than any one of the celebrated places about Boston. The average growth of the thriftiest standard fruit-trees about Boston, at that time, was little more than six inches to a foot. In this Nahant garden it was two feet, and we measured shoots on some of the standard trees three feet in length. By far the largest and finest cherries we tasted that season, were from trees growing there; and there was an apparent health and vigor about every species within its boundary, which would have been creditable any where, but which at Nahant, and in a season so unfavorable, quite astonished us.

The two strong points in this gentleman's gardening operations at Nahant, appear to us to be the following: First, the employment of screens to break the force of the wind, producing thereby an artificial climate; and second, the thorough preparation of the soil by trenching and manuring.

Of course, even the idea of a place worthy of the name of a garden in this bald, sea-girt cape, was out of the question, unless some mode of overcoming the violence of the gales, and the bad effects of the salt spray, could be devised. The plan Mr. Tudor has adopted is, we believe, original with him, and is at once extremely simple, and perfectly effective.

It consists merely of two, or at most three, parallel rows of high open fences, made of rough slats or palings, nailed in the common vertical manner, about three inches wide, and a space of a couple of inches left between them. These paling fences are about sixteen feet high, and usually form a double row (on the most exposed side a triple row), round the whole garden. The distance between that on the outer boundary and the next interior one is about four feet. The garden is also intersected here and there by tall trellis fences of the same kind, all of which help to increase the shelter, while some of those in the interior serve as frames for training trees upon.

The effect of this double or triple barrier of high paling is marvellous. Although like a common paling, apparently open and permitting the wind free passage, yet in practice it is found entirely to rob the gales of their violence, and their saltness. To use Mr. Tudor's words, "it completely sifts the air." After great storms, when the outer barrier will be found covered with a coating of salt, the foliage in the garden is entirely uninjured. It acts, in short, like a rustic veil, that admits just so much of the air, and in such a manner as most to promote the growth of the trees, while it breaks and wards off all the deleterious influences of a genuine ocean breeze—so pernicious to tender leaves and shoots.

Again, regarding the luxuriant growth, which surprised us in a place naturally a sterile gravel, we were greatly struck with the additional argument which it furnished us with in support of our favorite theory of the value of trenching in this climate. Mr. Tudor has, at incredible labor, trenched and manured the soil of his garden three feet deep. The consequence of this is, that, although it is mainly of a light, porous texture, yet the depth to which it has been stirred and cultivated, renders it proof against the effects of drouth. In the hottest and driest seasons, the growth here is luxuriant, and no better proof can be desired of the great value of thoroughly trenching, as the first and indispensable foundation of all good culture, even in thin and poor soils.

It is worthy of record, among the results of Mr. Tudor's culture, that, two years after the principal plantation of his fruit-trees was made, he carried off the second prize for pears, at the annual exhibition of the Massachusetts Horticultural Society, among dozens of zealous competitors, and with the fruit most carefully grown in that vicinity.

We have observed also, and noted as indicative of no small degree of practical skill, that in various quarters of the garden are standard trees, apples and pears especially, that have been transplanted from Boston, with large heads and trunks, six or eight inches in diameter, and are now in a state of complete luxuriance and fruitfulness.

There are, of course, but few individuals who have the desire and the means thus to weave a spell of freshness and beauty over a spot which nature has created so stern and bald; perhaps there are still fewer who would have the courage to plan and carry out improvements of this kind, to the attainment of so beautiful a result, in the very teeth of the elements. But there are many who may learn something valuable from Mr. Tudor's labor in the cause of Horticulture. There are, for example, hundreds along the sea-coasts, to whom gardening of any sort is nearly impossible, from the injurious effects of breezes loaded with salt water. There are, again, many beautiful sites that we could name on the shores of some of our great inland lakes, and the number is every day increasing, sites where the soil is deep and excellent, and the skies warm and bright, but the violence of the vernal and autumnal winds is such, that the better culture of the orchard and garden makes little progress.

In all such sites, Mr. Tudor's Nahant screens for sifting the air, will at once obviate all the difficulty, temper the wind to the tender buds, and make for the spot a soft climate in a naturally harsh and bleak aspect.

XVI.

A VISIT TO MONTGOMERY PLACE.

October, 1847.

THERE are few persons, among what may be called the travelling class, who know the beauty of the finest American country-seats. Mary are ignorant of the very existence of those rural gems that embroider the landscapes here and there, in the older and wealthier parts of the country. Held in the retirement of private life, they are rarely visited, except by those who enjoy the friendship of their possessors. The annual tourist by the railroad and steamboat, who moves through wood and meadow and river and hill, with the celerity of a rocket, and then fancies he knows the country, is in a state of total ignorance of their many attractions; and those whose taste has not led them to seek this species of pleasure, are equally unconscious of the landscape-gardening beauties that are developing themselves every day, with the advancing prosperity of the country.

It has been our good fortune to know a great number of the finest of these delightful residences, to revel in their beauties, and occasionally to chronicle their charms. If we have not sooner spoken at large of Montgomery Place, second as it is to no seat in America, for its combination of attractions, it has been rather that we were silent—like a devout gazer at the marvellous beauty of the Apollo—from excess of enjoyment, than from not deeply feeling all its varied mysteries of pleasure-grounds and lawns, wood and water.

Montgomery Place is one of the superb old seats belonging to the Livingston family, and situated in that part of Dutchess county bordering on the Hudson. About one hundred miles from New-York, the swift river steamers reach this part of the river in six hours; and the guest, who leaves the noisy din of the town in the early morning, finds himself, at a little past noon, plunged amid all the seclusion and quiet of its leafy groves.

And this *accessible* perfect seclusion is, perhaps, one of the most captivating features in the life of the country gentleman, whose lot is cast on this part of the Hudson. For twenty miles here, on the eastern shore, the banks are nearly a continuous succession of fine seats. The landings are by no means towns, or large villages, with the busy air of trade, but quiet stopping places, serving the convenience of the neighboring residents. Surrounded by extensive pleasure-grounds, fine woods or parks, even the adjoining estates are often concealed from that part of the grounds around the house, and but for the broad Hudson, which forms the grand feature in all these varied landscapes—the Hudson always so full of life in its numberless bright sails and steamers—one might fancy himself a thousand miles from all crowded and busy haunts of men.

Around Montgomery Place, indeed, this air of quiet and seclusion lurks more bewitchingly than in any other seat whose hospitality we have enjoyed. Whether the charm lies in the deep and mysterious wood, full of the echo of water-spirits, that forms the Northern boundary, or whether it grows out of a profound feeling of completeness and perfection in foregrounds of old trees, and distances of calm serene mountains, we have not been able to divine; but certain it is that there is a spell in the very air, which is fatal to the energies of a great speculation. It is not, we are sure, the spot for a man to plan campaigns of conquest, and we doubt even whether the scholar, whose ambition it is

> "To scorn delights,
> And live laborious days,"

would not find something in the air of this demesne, so soothing as to dampen the fire of his great purposes, and dispose him to believe that there is more dignity in repose, than merit in action.

There is not wanting something of the charm of historical association here. The estate derives its name from Gen. Montgomery, the hero and martyr of Quebec (whose portrait, among other fine family pictures, adorns the walls of the mansion). Mrs. Montgomery, after his lamented death on the heights of Abraham, resided here during the remainder of her life. At her death, she bequeathed it to her brother, the Hon. Edward Livingston, our late Minister to France. Here this distinguished diplomatist and jurist passed, in elegant retirement, the leisure intervals of a life largely devoted to the service of the State, and here still reside his family, whose greatest pleasure seems to be to add, if possible, every year, some admirable improvement, or elicit some new charm of its extraordinary natural beauty.

The age of Montgomery Place heightens its interest in no ordinary degree. Its richness of foliage, both in natural wood and planted trees, is one of its marked features. Indeed, so great is the variety and intricacy of scenery, caused by the leafy woods, thickets and bosquets, that one may pass days and even weeks here, and not thoroughly explore all its fine points—

> "Milles arbres, de ces lieux ondoyante parure
> Charme de l'odorat, de gout et des regards,
> Elégamment groupés, négligemment épars,
> Se fuyaient, s'approchaient, quelquefois à la vue
> Ouvraient dans la lointain un scène imprévue;
> Ou, tombant jusqu'à terre, et recourbant leurs bras
> Venaient d'un doux obstacle embarrasser leurs pas
> Ou pendaient sur leur tête en festons de verdure,
> Et de fleurs, en passant, semaient leur chevelure.
> Dirai-je ces forêts d'arbustes, d'arbrisseaux,
> Entrelaçant en voûte, en alcove, en berceaux,
> Leurs bras voluptueux, et leurs tiges fleuries?"

About four hundred acres comprise the estate called Montgomery Place, a very large part of which is devoted to pleasure-grounds and ornamental purposes. The ever-varied surface affords the finest scope for the numerous roads, drives, and walks, with which it abounds. Even its natural boundaries are admirable. On the west is the Hudson, broken by islands into an outline unusually varied and picturesque. On the north, it is separated from

Blithewood, the adjoining seat, by a wooded valley, in the depths of which runs a broad stream, rich in waterfalls. On the south is a rich oak wood, in the centre of which is a private drive On the east it touches the post road. Here is the entrance gate and from it leads a long and stately avenue of trees, like the approach to an old French chateau. Half-way up its length, the lines of planted trees give place to a tall wood, and this again is succeeded by the lawn, which opens in all its stately dignity, with increased effect after the deeper shadows of this vestibule-like wood. The eye is now caught at once by the fine specimens of hemlock, lime, ash and fir, whose proud heads and large trunks form the finest possible accessories to a large and spacious mansion, which is one of the best specimens of our manor houses. Built many years ago, in the most substantial manner, the edifice has been retouched and somewhat enlarged within a few years, and is at present both commodious, and architectural in character.

Without going into any details of the interior, we may call attention to the unique effect of the *pavilion*, thirty feet wide, which forms the north wing of this house. It opens from the library and drawing-room by low windows. Its ribbed roof is supported by a tasteful series of columns and arches, in the style of an Italian arcade. As it is on the north side of the dwelling, its position is always cool in summer; and this coolness is still further increased by the abundant shade of tall old trees, whose heads cast a pleasant gloom, while their tall trunks allow the eye to feast on the rich landscape spread around it.*

To attempt to describe the scenery, which bewitches the eye, as it wanders over the wide expanse to the west from this pavilion, would be but an idle effort to make words express what even the pencil of the painter often fails to copy. As a foreground, imagine a large lawn waving in undulations of soft verdure, varied with fine groups, and margined with rich belts of foliage. Its base is washed by the river, which is here a broad sheet of water, lying like a long lake beneath the eye. Wooded banks stretch along its margin. Its bosom is studded with islands, which are set like emeralds on its

* See Downing's "Landscape Gardening,' p. 47.

pale blue bosom. On the opposite shores, more than a mile distant, is seen a rich mingling of woods and corn-fields. But the crowning glory of the landscape is the background of mountains. The Kaatskills, as seen from this part of the Hudson, are, it seems to us, more beautiful than any mountain scenery in the middle States. It is not merely that their outline is bold, and that the summit of Roundtop, rising three thousand feet above the surrounding country, gives an air of more grandeur than is usually seen, even in the Highlands; but it is the *color* which renders the Kaatskills so captivating a feature in the landscape here. Never harsh or cold, like some of our finest hills, Nature seems to delight in casting a veil of the softest azure over these mountains—immortalized by the historian of Rip Van Winkle. Morning and noon, the shade only varies from softer to deeper blue. But the hour of sunset is the magical time for the fantasies of the color-genii of these mountains. Seen at this period, from the terrace of the pavilion of Montgomery Place, the eye is filled with wonder at the various dyes that bathe the receding hills—the most distant of which are twenty or thirty miles away. Azure, purple, violet, pale grayish-lilac, and the dim hazy hue of the most distant cloud-rift, are all seen distinct, yet blending magically into each other in these receding hills. It is a spectacle of rare beauty, and he who loves tones of color, soft and dreamy as one of the mystical airs of a German maestro, should see the sunset fade into twilight from the seats on this part of the Hudson.

THE MORNING WALK.

Leaving the terrace on the western front, the steps of the visitor, exploring Montgomery Place, are naturally directed towards the river bank. A path on the left of the broad lawn leads one to the fanciful rustic-gabled seat, among a growth of locusts at the bottom of the slope. Here commences a long walk, which is the favorite morning ramble of guests. Deeply shaded, winding along the thickly wooded bank, with the refreshing sound of the tide-waves gently dashing against the rocky shores below, or expending themselves on the beach of gravel, it curves along the bank for a great distance. Sometimes overhanging cliffs, crested with pines, frown darkly over it; sometimes thick tufts of fern and mossy-carpeted rocks border it, while at various points, vistas or long reaches of the beautiful river scenery burst upon the eye. Half-way along this morning ramble, a rustic seat, placed on a bold little plateau, at the base of a large tree, eighty feet above the water, and fenced about with a rustic barrier, invites you to linger and gaze at the fascinating river landscape here presented. It embraces the distant mountains, a sylvan foreground, and the broad river stretching away for miles, sprinkled with white sails. The *coup-d'œil* is heightened by its being seen through a dark framework of thick leaves and branches, which open here just sufficiently to show as much as the eye can enjoy or revel in, without change of position.

A little farther on, we reach a flight of stony steps, leading up to the border of the lawn. At the top of these is a rustic seat with a thatched canopy, curiously built round the trunk of an aged tree.

Passing these steps, the morning walk begins to descend more rapidly toward the river. At the distance of some hundred yards, we found ourselves on the river shore, and on a pretty jutting point of land stands a little *rustic pavilion*, from which a much lower and wider view of the landscape is again enjoyed. Here you find a boat ready for an excursion, if the spirit leads you to reverse the scenery, and behold the leafy banks from the water.

THE WILDERNESS.

Leaving the morning walk, we enter at once into "The Wilderness." This is a large and long wooded valley. It is broad, and much varied in surface, swelling into deep ravines, and spreading into wide hollows. In its lowest depths runs a large stream of water, that has, in portions, all the volume and swiftness of a mountain torrent. But the peculiarity of "The Wilderness," is in the depth and massiveness of its foliage. It is covered with the native growth of trees, thick, dark and shadowy, so that once plunged in its recesses, you can easily imagine yourself in the depths of an old forest, far away from the haunts of civilization. Here and there, rich thickets of the kalmia or native laurel clothe the surface of the ground, and form the richest underwood.

But the wilderness is by no means savage in the aspect of its beauty; on the contrary, here as elsewhere in this demesne, are evidences, in every improvement, of a fine appreciation of the natural charms of the locality. The whole of this richly wooded valley is threaded with walks, ingeniously and naturally conducted so as to penetrate to all the most interesting points; while a great variety of rustic seats, formed beneath the trees, in deep secluded thickets, by the side of the swift rushing stream, or on some inviting eminence, enables one fully to enjoy them.

There are a couple of miles of these walks, and from the depth and thickness of the wood, and the varied surface of the ground, their intricacy is such that only the family, or those very familiar with their course, are at all able to follow them all with any thing like positive certainty as to their destination. Though we have threaded them several seasons, yet our late visit to Montgomery Place found us giving ourselves up to the pleasing perplexity of choosing one at random, and trusting to a lucky guess to bring us out of the wood at the desired point.

Not long after leaving the *rustic pavilion*,* on descending by one of the paths that diverges to the left, we reach a charming little covered resting-place, in the form of a rustic porch. The roof is prettily thatched with thick green moss. Nestling under a dark canopy of evergreens in the shelter of a rocky fern-covered bank, an hour or two may be whiled away within it, almost unconscious of the passage of time.

THE CATARACT.

But the stranger who enters the depths of this dusky wood by this route, is not long inclined to remain here. His imagination is excited by the not very distant sound of waterfalls.

> "Above, below, aërial murmurs swell,
> From hanging wood, brown heath and bushy dell;
> A thousand gushing rills that shun the light,
> Stealing like music on the ear of night."

He takes another path, passes by an airy-looking rustic bridge, and plunging for a moment into the thicket, emerges again in full view

* See Downing's "Landscape Gardening," p. 48.

of the first cataract. Coming from the solemn depths of the wood, he is astonished at the noise and volume of the stream, which here rushes in wild foam and confusion over a rocky fall, forty feet in depth. Ascending a flight of steps made in the precipitous banks of the stream, we have another view, which is scarcely less spirited and picturesque.

This waterfall, beautiful at all seasons, would alone be considered a sufficient attraction to give notoriety to a rural locality in most country neighborhoods. But as if Nature had intended to lavish her gifts here, she has, in the course of this valley, given two other cataracts. These are all striking enough to be worthy of the pencil of the artist, and they make this valley a feast of wonders to the lovers of the picturesque.

There is a secret charm which binds us to these haunts of the water spirits. The spot is filled with the music of the falling water. Its echoes pervade the air, and beget a kind of dreamy revery. The memory of the world's toil gradually becomes fainter and fainter, under the spell of the soothing monotone; until at last one begins to doubt the existence of towns and cities, full of busy fellow-beings, and to fancy the true happiness of life lies in a more simple existence, where man, the dreamy silence of thick forests, the lulling tones of babbling brooks, and the whole heart of nature, make one sensation, full of quiet harmony and joy.

THE LAKE.

That shadowy path, that steals away so enticingly from the neighborhood of the cataract, leads to a spot of equal, though a different kind of loveliness. Leaving the border of the stream, and following it past one or two distracting points, where other paths, starting out at various angles, seem provokingly to tempt one away from the neighborhood of the water, we suddenly behold, with a feeling of delight, the lake.*

Nothing can have a more charming effect than this natural mirror in the bosom of the valley. It is a fine expansion of the same stream, which farther down forms the large cataract. Here

* See Downing's "Landscape Gardening," p. 49.

it sleeps, as lazily and glassily as if quite incapable of aught but reflecting the beauty of the blue sky, and the snowy clouds, that float over it. On two sides, it is overhung and deeply shaded by the bowery thickets of the surrounding wilderness; on the third is a peninsula, fringed with the graceful willow, and rendered more attractive by a *rustic temple;* while the fourth side is more sunny and open, and permits a peep at the distant azure mountain tops.

This part of the grounds is seen at the most advantage, either towards evening, or in moonlight. Then the effect of contrast in light and shadow is most striking, and the seclusion and beauty of the spot are more fully enjoyed than at any other hour. Then you will most certainly be tempted to leave the curious rustic seat, with its roof wrapped round with a rude entablature like Pluto's crown; and you will take a seat in ***Psyche's boat***, on whose prow is poised a giant butterfly, that looks so mysteriously down into the depths below as to impress you with a belief that it is the metempsychosis of the spirit of the place, guarding against all unhallowed violation of its purity and solitude.

The peninsula, on the north of the lake, is carpeted with the dry leaves of the thick cedars that cover it, and form so umbrageous a resting-place that the sky over it seems absolutely dusky at noonday. On its northern bank is a rude sofa, formed entirely of stone. Here you linger again, to wonder afresh at the novelty and beauty of the *second cascade.* The stream here emerges from a dark thicket, falls about twenty feet, and then rushes away on the side of the peninsula opposite the lake. Although only separated by a short walk and the mass of cedars on the promontory, from the lake itself, yet one cannot be seen from the other; and the lake, so full of the very spirit of repose, is a perfect opposite to this foaming, noisy little waterfall.

Farther up the stream is another cascade, but leaving that for the present, let us now select a path leading, as near as we can judge, in the direction of the open pleasure-grounds near the house. Winding along the sides of the valley, and stretching for a good distance across its broadest part, all the while so deeply immersed, however, in its umbrageous shelter, as scarcely to see the sun, or indeed to feel very certain of our whereabouts, we emerge in the neighborhood of the CONSERVATORY.*

This is a large, isolated, glazed structure, designed by Mr. Catherwood, to add to the scenic effect of the pleasure-grounds. On its northern side are, in summer, arranged the more delicate green-house plants; and in front are groups of large oranges, lemons, citrons, Cape jasmines, eugenias, etc., in tubs—plants remarkable for their size and beauty. Passing under neat and tasteful archways of wirework, covered with rare climbers, we enter what is properly

THE FLOWER-GARDEN.

How different a scene from the deep sequestered shadows of the Wilderness! Here all is gay and smiling. Bright parterres of brilliant flowers bask in the full daylight, and rich masses of color seem to revel in the sunshine. The walks are fancifully laid out, so as to form a tasteful whole; the beds are surrounded by low edgings of turf or box, and the whole looks like some rich oriental pattern or carpet of embroidery. In the centre of the garden stands a large vase of the Warwick pattern; others occupy the centres of parterres in the midst of its two main divisions, and at either end is a fanciful light summer-house, or pavilion, of Moresque character. The whole garden is surrounded and shut out from the lawn, by a belt of shrubbery, and above and behind this, rises, like a noble framework, the background of trees of the lawn and the Wilderness. If there is any prettier flower-garden scene than this *ensemble* in the country, we have not yet had the good fortune to behold it.

It must be an industrious sight-seer who could accomplish more than we have here indicated of the beauties of this residence, in a day. Indeed there is enough of exercise for the body, and enjoyment for the senses in it, for a week. But another morning may be most agreeably passed in a portion of the estate quite apart from that which has met the eye from any point yet examined. This is

THE DRIVE.

On the southern boundary is an oak wood of about fifty acres.

* See Downing's "Landscape Gardening," p. 453.

It is totally different in character from the Wilderness on the north, and is a nearly level or slightly undulating surface, well covered with fine Oak, Chestnut, and other timber trees. Through it is laid out the DRIVE; a sylvan route as agreeable for exercise in the carriage, or on horseback, as the "Wilderness," or the "Morning Walk," is for a ramble on foot. It adds no small additional charm to a country place in the eyes of many persons, this secluded and perfectly private drive, entirely within its own limits.

Though MONTGOMERY PLACE itself is old, yet a spirit ever new directs the improvements carried on within it. Among those more worthy of note, we gladly mention an *arboretum*, just commenced on a fine site in the pleasure-grounds, set apart and thoroughly prepared for the purpose. Here a scientific arrangement of all the most beautiful hardy trees and shrubs, will interest the student, who looks upon the vegetable kingdom with a more curious eye than the ordinary observer.

The whole extent of the private roads and walks, within the precincts of MONTGOMERY PLACE, is between *five and six miles.* The remarkably natural beauty which it embraces, has been elicited and heightened every where, in a tasteful and judicious manner. There are numberless lessons here for the landscape gardener; there are an hundred points that will delight the artist; there are meditative walks and a thousand suggestive aspects of nature for the poet; and the man of the world, engaged in a feverish pursuit of its gold and its glitter, may here taste something of the beauty and refinement of rural life in its highest aspect, and be able afterwards understandingly to wish that

> "One fair asylum from the world *he* knew,
> One chosen seat, that charms the various view.
> Who boasts of more, (believe the serious strain,)
> Sighs for a home, and sighs, alas! in vain.
> Thro' each he roves, the tenant of a day,
> And with the swallow wings the year away."
>
> ROGERS.

RURAL ARCHITECTURE.

I.

A FEW WORDS ON RURAL ARCHITECTURE.

July, 1850.

NO one pretends that we have, as yet, either a national architecture or national music in America; unless our Yankee clapboard house be taken as a specimen of the first, and "Old Susannah" of the second fine art. But there is, on the other hand, perhaps, no country where there is more building or more "musicianing," such as they are, at the present moment. And as a perfect taste in arts is no more to be expected in a young nation, mainly occupied with the practical wants of life, than a knowledge of geometry is in an infant school, we are content with the large promise that we find in the present, and confidently look forward for fulfilment to the future.

In almost every other country, a few landlords own the land, which a great many tenants live upon and cultivate. Hence the general interest in building is confined to a comparatively small class, improvements are made in a solid and substantial way, and but little change takes place from one generation to another in the style of the dwelling and the manner of living.

But in this country we are, comparatively, all landlords. In the country, especially, a large part of the rural population own the land they cultivate, and build their own houses. Hence it is a matter of no little moment to them, to avail themselves of every possible improvement in the manner of constructing their dwellings, so as to secure the largest amount of comfort, convenience, and beauty, for the moderate sum which an American landholder has to spend. While the rural proprietors of the other continent are often content to live in the same houses, and with the same inconveniences as their forefathers, no one in our time and country, who has any of the national spirit of progress in him, is satisfied unless, in building a new house, he has some of the "modern improvements" in it.

This is a good sign of the times; and when we see it coupled with another, viz., the great desire to make the dwelling agreeable and ornamental as well as comfortable, we think there is abundant reason to hope, so far as the country is concerned, that something like a national taste will come in due time.

What the popular taste in building seems to us to require, just now, is not so much *impulse* as right *direction*. There are numberless persons who have determined, in building their new home in the country, that they "will have something pretty;" but precisely what character it shall have, and whether there is any character, beyond that of a "pretty cottage" or a "splendid house," is not perhaps very clear to their minds.

We do not make this statement to find fault with the condition of things; far from it. We see too much good in the newly awakened taste for the Beautiful, to criticize severely its want of intelligence as to the exact course it should take to achieve its object—or perhaps its want of definiteness as to what that object is—beyond providing an agreeable home. But we allude to it to show that, with a little direction, the popular taste now awakened in this particular department, may develop itself in such a manner as to produce the most satisfactory and beautiful results.

Fifteen years ago there was but one idea relating to a house in the country. It must be a Grecian temple. Whether twenty feet or two hundred feet front, it must have its columns and portico. There might be comfortable rooms behind them or not; that was a matter which the *severe* taste of the classical builder could not stoop to consider. The roof might be so flat that there was no space for comfortable servants' bedrooms, or the attic so hot that the second story was uninhabitable in a midsummer's day. But of what consequence was that, if the portico were copied from the Temple of Theseus, or the columns were miniature imitations in wood of those of Jupiter Olympus?

We have made a great step onward in that short fifteen years. There is, to be sure, a *fashion* now in building houses in the country—almost as prevalent and despotic as its pseudo-classical predecessor, but it is a far more rational and sensible one, and though likely to produce the same unsatisfactory effect of all other fashions—that is, to substitute sameness and monotony for tasteful individuality—yet we gladly accept it as the next step onward.

We allude, of course, to the Gothic or English cottage, with steep roofs and high gables—just now the ambition of almost every person building in the country. There are, indeed, few things so beautiful as a cottage of this kind, well designed and tastefully placed. There is nothing, all the world over, so truly rural and so unmistakably country-like as this very cottage, which has been developed in so much perfection in the rural lanes and amidst the picturesque lights and shadows of an English landscape. And for this reason, because it is essentially rural and country-like, we gladly welcome its general naturalization (with the needful variation of the veranda, &c., demanded by our climate), as the type of most of our country dwellings.

But it is time to enter a protest against the absolute and indiscriminate employment of the Gothic cottage in *every* site and situation in the country—whether appropriate or inappropriate—whether suited to the grounds or the life of those who are to inhabit it, or the contrary.

We have endeavored, in our work on "COUNTRY-HOUSES," just issued from the press, to show that rural architecture has more significance and a deeper meaning than merely to afford a "pretty cottage," or a "handsome house," for him who can afford to pay for it. We believe not only that a house may have an absolute beauty of its own, growing out of its architecture, but that it may have a relative beauty no less interesting, which arises from its expressing the life and occupation of those who build or inhabit it. In other words, we think the home of every family, possessed of character may be made to express that character, and will be most beautiful (supposing the character good), when in addition to architectural beauty it unites this significance or individuality.

We have not the space to go into detail on this subject here; and to do so would only be repeating what we have already said in the work in question. But the most casual reader will understand from our suggestion, that if a man's house can be made to express the best traits of his character, it is undeniable that a large source of beauty and interest is always lost by those who copy each other's homes without reflection, even though they may be copying the most faultless *cottage ornée.*

We would have the cottage, the farm-house, and the larger country-house, all marked by a somewhat distinctive character of their own, so far as relates to making them complete and individual of their kind; and believing as we do, that the beauty and force of every true man's life or occupation depend largely on his pursuing it frankly, honestly, and openly, with all the individuality of his character, we would have his house and home help to give significance to, and dignify that daily life and occupation, by harmonizing with them. For this reason, we think the farmer errs when he copies the filagree work of the retired citizen's cottage, instead of showing that rustic strength and solidity in his house which are its true elements of interest and beauty. For this reason, we think he who builds a simple and modest cottage in the country, fails in attaining that which he aims at by copying, as nearly as his means will permit, the parlors, folding doors, and showy furniture of the newest house he has seen in town.

We will not do more at present than throw out these suggestions, in the hope that those about to build in the country will reflect that an entirely satisfactory house is one in which there are not only pretty forms and details, but one which has some *meaning* in its beauty, considered in relation to their own position, character, and daily lives.

II.

MORAL INFLUENCE OF GOOD HOUSES.

February, 1848.

A VERY little observation will convince any one that, in the United States, a new era, in *Domestic Architecture*, is already commenced. A few years ago, and all our houses, with rare exceptions, were built upon the most meagre plan. A shelter from the inclemencies of the weather; space enough in which to eat, drink and sleep; perhaps some excellence of mechanical workmanship in the details; these were the characteristic features of the great mass of our dwelling-houses—and especially country houses—a few years ago.

A dwelling-house, for a civilized man, built with no higher aspirations than these, we look upon with the same feelings that inspire us when we behold the Indian, who guards himself against heat and cold by that primitive, and, as he considers it, sufficient costume—a blanket. An unmeaning pile of wood, or stone, serves as a shelter to the bodily frame of man; it does the same for the brute animals that serve him; the blanket covers the skin of the savage from the harshness of the elements, as the thick shaggy coat protects the beasts he hunts in the forest. But these are only manifestations of the grosser wants of life; and the mind of the civilized and cultivated man as naturally manifests itself in fitting, appropriate, and beautiful forms of habitation and costume, as it does in fine and lofty written thought and uttered speech.

Hence, as society advances beyond that condition, in which the primary wants of human nature are satisfied, we naturally find that literature and the arts flourish. Along with great crators and inspired poets, come fine architecture, and tasteful grounds and gardens.

Let us congratulate ourselves that the new era is fairly commenced in the United States. We by no means wish to be understood, that all our citizens have fairly passed the barrier that separates utter indifference, or peurile fancy, from good taste. There are, and will be, for a long time, a large proportion of houses built without any definite principles of construction, except those of the most downright necessity. But, on the other hand, we are glad to perceive a very considerable sprinkling over the whole country—from the Mississippi to the Kennebec—of houses built in such a manner, as to prove at first glance, that the ideal of their owners has risen above the platform of mere animal wants: that they perceive the intellectual superiority of a beautiful design over a meaningless and uncouth form; and that a house is to them no longer a comfortable shelter merely, but an expression of the intelligent life of man, in a state of society where the soul, the intellect, and the heart, are all awake, and all educated.

There are, perhaps, few persons who have examined fully the effects of a general diffusion of good taste, of well being, and a love of order and proportion, upon the community at large. There are, no doubt, some who look upon fine houses as fostering the pride of the few, and the envy and discontent of the many; and—in some transatlantic countries, where wealth and its avenues are closed to all but a few—not without reason. But, in this country, where integrity and industry are almost always rewarded by more than the means of subsistence, we have firm faith in the *moral* effects of the fine arts. We believe in the bettering influence of beautiful cottages and country houses—in the improvement of human nature necessarily resulting to all *classes*, from the possession of lovely gardens and fruitful orchards.

We do not know how we can present any argument of this matter, if it requires one, so good as one of that long-ago distinguished man—Dr. Dwight. He is describing, in his *Travels in America*, the influence of good architecture, as evinced in its effects on the manners and character of the inhabitants in a town in New England:

"There is a kind of symmetry in the thoughts, feelings, and efforts of the human mind. Its taste, intelligence, affections, and conduct, are so intimately related, that no preconcertion can prevent them from being mutually causes and effects. The first thing powerfully operated upon, and, in its turn, proportionately operative, is the taste. The *perception* of beauty and deformity, of refinement and grossness, of decency and vulgarity, of propriety and indecorum, is the first thing which influences man to attempt an escape from a grovelling, brutish character; *a character in which morality is chilled, or absolutely frozen.* In most persons, this perception is awakened by what may be called the *exterior* of society, particularly by the mode of building. Uncouth, mean, ragged, dirty houses, constituting the body of any town, will regularly be accompanied by coarse, grovelling manners. The dress, the furniture, the mode of living, and the manners, will all correspond with the appearance of the buildings, and will universally be, in every such case, of a vulgar and debased nature. On the inhabitants of such a town, it will be difficult, if not impossible, to work a conviction that intelligence is either necessary or useful. Generally, they will regard both learning and science only with contempt. Of morals, except in the coarsest form, and that which has the least influence on the heart, they will scarcely have any apprehensions. The rights enforced by municipal law, they may be compelled to respect, and the corresponding duties they may be necessitated to perform; but the rights and obligations which lie beyond the reach of magistracy, in which the chief duties of morality are found, and from which the chief enjoyments of society spring, will scarcely gain even their passing notice. They may pay their debts, but they will neglect almost every thing of value in the education of their children.

"The very fact, that men see good houses built around them, will, more than almost any thing else, awaken in them a sense of superiority in those by whom such houses are inhabited. The same sense is derived, in the same manner, from handsome dress, furniture, and equipage. The sense of beauty is necessarily accompanied by a perception of the superiority which it possesses over deformity; and is instinctively felt to confer this superiority on those who can call it their own, over those who cannot.

"This, I apprehend, is the manner in which coarse society is first started towards improvement; for no objects, but those which are sensible, can make any considerable impression on coarse minds."

The first motive which leads men to build good houses is, no doubt, that of increasing largely their own comfort and happiness. But it is easy to see that, in this country, where so many are able to achieve a home for themselves, he who gives to the public a more beautiful and tasteful model of a habitation than his neighbors, is a benefactor to the cause of morality, good order, and the improvement of society where he lives. To place before men reasonable objects of ambition, and to dignify and exalt their aims, cannot but be laudable in the sight of all. And in a country where it is confessedly neither for the benefit of the community at large, nor that of the succeeding generation, to amass and transmit great fortunes, we would encourage a taste for beautiful and appropriate architecture, as a means of promoting public virtue and the general good.

We have said beautiful and *appropriate* architecture—not without desiring that all our readers should feel the value of this latter qualification as fully as we do. Among the many strivings after architectural beauty, which we see daily made by our countrymen, there are, of course, some failures, and only now and then examples of perfect success. But the rock on which all novices split—and especially all men who have thought little of the subject, and who are satisfied with a feeble imitation of some great example from other countries—this dangerous rock is *want of fitness*, or *propriety*. Almost the first principle, certainly the grand principle, which an apostle of architectural progress ought to preach in America, is, "keep in mind PROPRIETY." Do not build your houses like temples, churches, or cathedrals. Let them be, characteristically, dwelling-houses. And more than this; always let their individuality of purpose be fairly avowed; let the cottage be a cottage—the farm-house a farm-house—the villa a villa, and the mansion a mansion. Do not attempt to build a dwelling upon your farm after the fashion of the town-house of your friend, the city merchant; do not attempt to give the modest little cottage the ambitious air of the ornate villa. Be assured that there is, if you will search for it, a peculiar beauty that belongs to each of these classes of dwellings that heightens and adorns it almost magically; while, if it borrows the ornaments of the other, it is only debased and falsified in character and expression. The most expensive and elaborate structure, overlaid with costly ornaments, will fail to give a ray of pleasure to the mind of real taste, if it is not appropriate to the purpose in view, or the means or position of its occupant; while the simple farm-house, rustically and tastefully adorned, and ministering beauty to hearts that answer to the spirit of the beautiful, will weave a spell in the memory not easily forgotten.

III.

A FEW WORDS ON OUR PROGRESS IN BUILDING.

June, 1851.

THE "Genius of Architecture," said Thomas Jefferson, some fifty years ago, "has shed its malediction upon America." Jefferson, though the boldest of democrats, had a secret respect and admiration for the magnificent results of aristocratic institutions in the arts, and had so refined his taste in France, as to be shocked, past endurance, on his return home, with the raw and crude attempts at building in the republic.

No one, however, can accuse the Americans with apathy or want of interest in architecture, at the present moment. Within ten years past, the attention of great numbers has been turned to the improvement and embellishment of public and private edifices; many foreign architects have settled in the Union; numerous works—especially upon domestic architecture—have been issued from the press, and the whole community, in town and country, seem at the present moment to be afflicted with the building mania. The upper part of New-York, especially, has the air of some city of fine houses in all styles, rising from the earth as if by enchantment, while in the suburbs of Boston, rural cottages are springing up on all sides, as if the "Genius of Architecture" had sown, broadcast, the seeds of *ornée* cottages, and was in a fair way of having a fine harvest in that quarter.

There are many persons who are as discontented with this new hot-bed growth of architectural beauty, as Jefferson was with the earlier and ranker growth of deformity in his day. Some denounce "fancy houses,"—as they call every thing but a solid square block—altogether. Others have become weary of "Gothic" (without, perhaps, ever having really seen one good specimen of the style), and suggest whether there be not something barbarous in a lancet window to a modern parlor; while the larger number go on building vigorously in the newest style they can find, determined to have something, if not better and more substantial than their neighbors, at least more extraordinary and uncommon.

There is still another class of our countrymen who put on a hypercritical air, and sit in judgment on the progress and development of the building taste in this country. They disclaim every thing foreign. They will have no Gothic mansions, Italian villas, or Swiss cottages. Nothing will go down with them but an entirely new "order," as they call it, and they berate all architectural writers (we have come in for our share) for presenting certain more or less meritorious modifications of such foreign styles. What they demand, with their brows lowered and their hands clenched, is an "American style of architecture!" As if an architecture sprung up like the after-growth in our forests, the natural and immediate consequence of clearing the soil. As if a people not even indigenous to the country, but wholly European colonists, or their descendants, a people who have neither a new language nor religion, who wear the fashions of Paris, and who, in their highest education, hang upon the skirts of Greece and Rome, were likely to invent (as if it were a new plough) an original and altogether novel and satisfactory style of architecture.

A *little* learning, we have been rightly told, is one of the articles to be labelled "dangerous." Our hypercritical friends prove the truth of the saying, by expecting what never did, and never will happen. An original style in architecture or any other of the arts, has never yet been invented or composed outright; but all have been modifications of previously existing modes of building. Late discoverers have proved that Grecian Architecture was only perfected in Greece—the models of their temples were found in older Egypt.*

* According to the last conclusions of the *savans*, Solomon's Temple was a pure model of Greek Architecture.

The Romans composed their finest structures out of the very ruins of public edifices brought from Greece, and the round arch had its rise from working with these fragments instead of masses of stone. The Gothic arch, the origin of which has been claimed as an invention of comparatively modern art, Mr. Ruskin has proved to be of purely Arabic origin, in use in Asia long before Gothic architecture was known, and gradually introduced into Europe by architects from the East. And whoever studies Oriental art, will see the elements of Arabic architecture, the groundwork of the style, abounding in the ruins of Indian temples of the oldest date known on the globe.

It is thus, by a little research, that we find there has never been such a novelty as the invention of a positively new style in building. What are now known as the Grecian, Gothic, Roman and other styles, are only those local modifications of the styles of the older countries, from which the newer colony borrowed them, as the climate, habits of the people, and genius of the architects, *acting upon each other through a long series of years*, gradually developed into such styles. It is, therefore, as absurd for the critics to ask for the *American style of architecture*, as it was for the English friends of a Yankee of our acquaintance to request him (after they were on quite familiar terms) to do them the favor to put on his savage dress and talk a little American! This country is, indeed, too distinct in its institutions, and too vast in its territorial and social destinies, not to shape out for itself a great national type in character, manners and art; but the development of the finer and more intellectual traits of character are slower in a nation than they are in a man, and only time can develope them healthily in either case.

In the mean time, we are in the midst of what may be called the experimental stage of architectural taste. With the passion for novelty, and the feeling of independence that belong to this country, our people seem determined to *try every thing*. A proprietor on the lower part of the Hudson, is building a stone castle, with all the towers clustered together, after the fashion of the old robber strongholds on the Rhine. We trust he has no intention of levying toll on the railroad that runs six trains a day under his frowning battlements, or exacting booty from the river craft of all sizes forever floating by. A noted New-Yorker has erected a villa near Bridgeport, which looks like the minareted and domed residence of a Persian *Shah*—though its orientalism is rather put out of countenance by the prim and puritanical dwellings of the plain citizens within rifle shot of it. A citizen of fortune dies, and leaves a large sum to erect a "large plain building" for a school to educate orphan boys —which the building committee consider to mean a superb marble temple, like that of Jupiter Olympus; a foreigner liberally bequeaths his fortune to the foundation of an institution "for the diffusion of knowledge among men"—and the regents erect a college in the style of a Norman monastery—with a relish of the dark ages in it, the better to contrast with its avowed purpose of diffusing light. On all sides, in our large towns, we have churches built after Gothic models, and though highly fitting and beautiful as churches, i. e., edifices for purely devotional purposes—are quite useless as places to hear sermons in, because the preacher's voice is inaudible in at least one-half of the church. And every where in the older parts of the country, private fortunes are rapidly crystallizing into mansions, villas, country-houses and cottages, in all known styles supposed to be in any way suitable to the purposes of civilized habitations.

Without in the least desiring to apologize for the frequent violations of taste witnessed in all this fermentation of the popular feeling in architecture, we do not hesitate to say that we rejoice in it. It is a fermentation that shows clearly there is no apathy in the public mind, and we feel as much confidence as the vintner who walks through the wine cellar in full activity, that the froth of foreign affectations will work off, and the impurities of vulgar taste settle down, leaving us the pure spirit of a better national taste at last. Rome was not built in a day, and whoever would see a national architecture, must be patient till it has time to rise out of the old materials, under the influences of a new climate, our novel institutions and modified habits.

In domestic architecture, the difficulties that lie in the way of achieving a pure and correct taste, are, perhaps, greater than in civil or ecclesiastical edifices. There are so many private *fancies*, and personal vanities, which seek to manifest themselves in the house of the ambitious private citizen, and which are defended under the shield of that miserable falsehood, "there is no disputing about *tastes.*" (If the proverb read *whims*, it would be gospel truth.) Hence we see numberless persons who set about building their own house without the aid of an architect, who would not think of being their own lawyer, though one profession demands as much study and capacity as the other; and it is not to this we object, for we hold that a man may often build his own house and plead his own rights to justice satisfactorily—but it must be done in both instances, in the simplest and most straightforward manner. If he attempts to go into the discussion of Blackstone on the one hand, or the mysteries of Vitruvius and Pugin on the other, he is sure to get speedily swamped, and commit all sorts of follies and extravagancies quite out of keeping with his natural character.

The two greatest trials to the architect of taste, who desires to see his country and age making a respectable figure in this branch of the arts, are to be found in that class of travelled smatterers in *virtu*, who have picked up here and there, in the tour from Liverpool to Rome, certain ill-assorted notions of art, which they wish combined in one sublime whole, in the shape of their own domicil; and that larger class, who ambitiously imitate in a small cottage, all that belongs to palaces, castles and buildings of princely dimensions.

The first class is confined to no country. Examples are to be found every where, and we do not know of a better hit at the folly of these *cognoscenti*, than in the following relation of experiences by one of the cleverest of English architectural critics:

"The architect is requested, perhaps, by a man of great wealth, nay, of established taste in some points, to make a design for a villa in a lovely situation. The future proprietor carries him up stairs to his study, to give him what he calls his 'ideas and materials,' and, in all probability, begins somewhat thus: 'This, sir, is a slight note; I made it on the spot; approach to Villa Reale, near Puzzuoli. Dancing nymphs, you perceive; cypresses, shell fountain. I think I should like something like this for the approach; classical you perceive, sir; elegant, graceful. Then, sir, this is a sketch by an American friend of mine; Whe-whaw-Kantamaraw's wigwam, king of the —— Cannibal Islands; I think he said, sir. Log, you observe; scalps, and boa constrictor skins; curious. Something like this, sir, would look neat, I think, for the front door; don't you?

Then the lower windows, I'm not quite decided upon; but what would you say to Egyptian, sir? I think I should like my windows Egyptian, with hieroglyphics, sir; storks and coffins, and appropriate mouldings above; I brought some from Fountain's Abbey the other day. Look here, sir; angel's heads putting their tongues out, rolled up in cabbage leaves, with a dragon on each side riding on a broomstick, and the devil looking out from the mouth of an alligator, sir.* Odd, I think; interesting. Then the corners may be turned by octagonal towers, like the centre one in Kenilworth Castle; with Gothic doors, portcullis, and all, quite perfect; with cross slits for arrows, battlements for musketry, machiolations for boiling lead, and a room at the top for drying plums; and the conservatory at the bottom, sir, with Virginia creepers up the towers; door supported by sphinxes, holding scrapers in their fore paws, and having their tails prolonged into warm-water pipes, to keep the plants safe in winter, &c.'"

We have seen buildings in England, where such Bedlam suggestions of taste have not only been made, but accepted either wholly or partly by the architect, and where the result was, of course, both ludicrous and absurd. There is less dictation to architects in this country on one hand, and more independence of any class on the other, to bring such examples of architectural salmagundies into existence—though there are a few in the profession weak enough to prostitute their talents to any whim or caprice of the employer.

But by far the greater danger at the present moment lies in the inordinate *ambition* of the builders of ornamental cottages. Not contented with the simple and befitting decoration of the modest veranda, the bracketed roof, the latticed window, and the lovely accessories of vines and flowering shrubs, the builder of the *cottage ornée* in too many cases, attempts to ingraft upon his simple story of a habitation, all the tropes and figures of architectural rhetoric which belong to the elaborate oratory of a palace or a temple.

We have made a point of enforcing the superior charm of simplicity—and the *realness* of the beauty which grows out of it, in

* This grotesque device is actually carved on one of the groins of Roslin Castle, Scotland.

our late work on Country Houses. We even went so far as to give a few examples of farm-houses studiously made simple and rural in character, though not without a certain beauty of expression befitting their locality, and the uses to which they were destined. But, judging from some criticisms on these farm-houses in one of the western papers, we believe it will not be an easy task to convince the future proprietors of farm-houses and rural cottages, that truthful simplicity is better than borrowed decorations, in their country homes. Our critic wonders why farmers should not be allowed to live in as handsome houses (confounding mere decorations with beauty) as any other class of our citizens, if they can afford it—and claims for them the use of the most ornamental architecture in their farm-houses. We have only to answer to this, that the simplest expression of beauty which grows out of a man's life, ranks higher for him than the most elaborate one borrowed from another's life or circumstances. We will add, by way of illustration, that there is no moral or political objection, that we know, of a farmer's wearing a general's uniform in his corn-fields, if he likes it better than plain clothes; but to our mind, his costume—undoubtedly handsomer in the right place—would be both absurd and ugly, behind the harrow.

We are glad to find, however, that our feeling of the folly of this exaggerated pretension in cottage architecture, is gradually finding its expression in other channels of the public press—a sure sign that it will eventually take hold of public opinion. The following satire on the taste of the day in this overloaded style of "carpenter's gothic," from the pen of one of the wittiest and cleverest of American poets, has lately appeared (as part of a longer satire on another subject), in one of our popular magazines. But it is too good to be lost sight of by our readers, and we recommend it to a second perusal. A thought or two upon its moral, as applied to the taste of the country, will help us on most essentially in this, our experimental age of architecture.

THE RURAL COT OF MR. KNOTT.

BY LOWELL.

My worthy friend, A. Gordon Knott,
  From business snug withdrawn,
Was much contented with a lot
Which would contain a Tudor cot
'Twixt twelve feet square of garden-plot
  And twelve feet more of lawn.

He had laid business on the shelf
  To give his taste expansion,
And, since no man, retired with pelf,
  The building mania can shun,
Knott being middle-aged himself,
Resolved to build (unhappy elf!)
  A mediæval mansion.

He called an architect in counsel;
  "I want," said he, "a—you know what,
  (You are a builder, I am Knott,)
  A thing complete from chimney-pot
Down to the very groundsel;
  Here's a half acre of good land;
  Just have it nicely mapped and planned,
And make your workmen drive on;
  Meadow there is, and upland too,
  And I should like a water-view,
D' you think you could contrive one?
  (Perhaps the pump and trough would do,
  If painted a judicious blue?)
  The woodland I've attended to;"
  (He meant three pines stuck up askew,
Two dead ones and a live one.)
  "A pocket-full of rocks 'twould take
To build a house of freestone,
  But then it is not hard to make
What now-a-days is *the* stone;
  The cunning painter in a trice
  Your house's outside petrifies,
  And people think it very gneiss
Without inquiring deeper;

My money never shall be thrown
Away on such a deal of stone,
When stone of deal is cheaper."

And so the greenest of antiques
Was reared for Knott to dwell in;
The architect worked hard for weeks
In venting all his private peaks
Upon the roof, whose crop of leaks
Had satisfied Fluellen.
Whatever anybody had
Out of the common, good or bad,
Knott had it all worked well in,
A donjon keep where clothes might dry,
A porter's lodge that was a sty,
A campanile slim and high,
Too small to hang a bell in;
All up and down and here and there,
With Lord-knows-what of round and square
Stuck on at random every where;
It was a house to make one stare,
All corners and all gables;
Like dogs let loose upon a bear,
Ten emulous styles *staboyed* with care,
The whole among them seemed to bear
And all the oddities to spare,
Were set upon the stables.

Knott was delighted with a pile
Approved by fashion's leaders,
(Only he made the builder smile,
By asking, every little while,
Why that was called the Twodoor style,
Which certainly had *three* doors!)
Yet better for this luckless man
If he had put a downright ban
Upon the thing *in limine;*
For, though to quit affairs his plan,
Ere many days, poor Knott began
Perforce accepting draughts that ran
All ways—except up chimney:
The house, though painted stone to mock,
With nice white lines round every block,
Some trepidation stood in,

When tempests (with petrific shock,
So to speak) made it really rock,
  Though not a whit less wooden;
And painted stone, howe'er well done,
Will not take in the prodigal sun
Whose beams are never quite at one
  With our terrestrial lumber;
So the wood shrank around the knots,
And gaped in disconcerting spots,
And there were lots of dots and rots
  And crannies without number,
Where though, as you may well presume,
The wind, like water through a flume,
  Came rushing in ecstatic,
Leaving in all three floors, no room
  That was not a rheumatic;
And what, with points and squares and rounds,
  Grown shaky on their poises,
The house at night was full of pounds,
Thumps, bumps, creaks, scratchings, raps,—till—"zounds,"
Cried Knott, "this goes beyond all bounds,
I do not deal in tongues and sounds,
Nor have I let my house and grounds,
  To a family of Noyeses."

IV.

COCKNEYISM IN THE COUNTRY.

September, 1849.

WHEN a farmer, who visits the metropolis once a year, stares into the shop windows in Broadway, and stops now and then with an indefinite curiosity at the corners of the streets, the citizens smile, with the satisfaction of superior knowledge, at the awkward airs of the countryman in town.

But how shall we describe the conduct of the true *cockneys* in the country? How shall we find words to express our horror and pity at the cockneyisms with which they deform the landscape? How shall we paint, without the aid of Hogarth and Cruikshanks, the ridiculous insults which they often try to put upon nature and truth in their cottages and country-seats?

The countryman in town is at least modest. He has, perhaps, a mysterious though mistaken respect for men who live in such prodigiously fine houses, who drive in coaches with liveried servants, and pay thousands for the transfer of little scraps of paper, which they call stocks.

But the true cit is brazen and impertinent in the country. Conscious that his clothes are designed, his hat fabricated, his tilbury built, by the only *artists* of their several professions on this side of the Atlantic, he pities and despises all who do not bear the outward stamp of the same coinage. He comes in the country to rusticate, (that is, to recruit his purse and his digestion,) very much as he turns his horse out to grass; as a means of gaining strength sufficient to go back again to the only arena in which it is worth while to exhibit his powers. He wonders how people can live in the country from choice, and asks a solemn question, now and then, about passing the winter there, as he would about a passage through Behring's Straits, or a pic-nic on the borders of the Dead Sea.

But this is all very harmless. On their own ground, country folks have the advantage of the cockneys. The scale is turned then; and knowing perfectly well how to mow, cradle, build stone walls and drive oxen,—undeniably useful and substantial kinds of knowledge,—they are scarcely less amused at the fine airs and droll ignorances of the cockney in the country, who does not know a bullrush from a butternut, than the citizens are in town at their ignorance of an air of the new opera, or the step of the last redowa.

But if the cockney visitor is harmless, the cockney resident is not. When the downright citizen retires to the country,—not because he has any taste for it, but because it is the fashion to have a country house,—he often becomes, perhaps for the first time in his life, a dangerous member of society. There is always a certain influence about the mere possessor of wealth, that dazzles us, and makes us see things in a false light; and the cockney has wealth. As he builds a house which costs five times as much as that of any of his country neighbors, some of them, who take it for granted that wealth and taste go together, fancy the cockney house puts their simple, modest cottages to the blush. Hence, they directly go to imitating it in their moderate way; and so, a quiet country neighborhood is as certainly tainted with the malaria of cockneyism, as it would be by a ship-fever, or the air of the Pontine marshes.

The cockneyisms which are fatal to the peace of mind, and more especially to the right feeling of persons of good sense and propriety in the country, are those which have perhaps a real meaning and value in town; which are associated with excellent houses and people there; and which are only absurd and foolish when transplanted, without the least reflection or adaptation, into the wholly different and distinct condition of things in country life.

It would be too long and troublesome a task to give a catalogue of these sins against good sense and good taste, which we every day see perpetrated by people who come from town, and who, we are bound to say, are far from always being cockneys; but who, nevertheless, unthinkingly perpetrate these ever to be condemned cockneyisms. Among them, we may enumerate, as illustrations,—building large houses, only to shut up the best rooms and live in the basement; placing the first story so high as to demand a long flight of steps to get into the front door; placing the dining-room below stairs, when there is abundant space on the first floor; using the iron railings of street doors in town to porches and piazzas in the country; arranging suites of parlors with folding doors, precisely like a town house, where other and far more convenient arrangements could be made; introducing plate glass windows, and ornate stucco cornices in cottages of moderate size and cost; building large parlors for display, and small bed-rooms for daily use; placing the house so near the street (with acres of land in the rear) as to destroy all seclusion, and secure all possible dust; and all the hundred like expedients, for producing the utmost *effect* in a small space in town, which are wholly unnecessary and uncalled for in the country.

We remember few things more unpleasant than to enter a cockney house in the country. As the highest ideal of beauty in the mind of its owner is to reproduce, as nearly as possible, a fac-simile of a certain kind of town house, one is distressed with the entire want of fitness and appropriateness in every thing it contains. The furniture is all made for display, not for use; and between a profusion of gilt ornaments, embroidered white satin chairs, and other like finery, one feels that one has no rest for the sole of his foot.

We do not mean, by these remarks, to have it understood that we do not admire really beautiful, rich and tasteful furniture, or ornaments and decorations belonging to the interior and exterior of houses in the country. But we only admire them when they are introduced in the right manner and the right place. In a country house of large size—a mansion of the first class—where there are rooms in abundance for all purposes, and where a feeling of comfort, luxury, and wealth, reigns throughout, there is no reason why the most beautiful and highly finished decorations should not be seen in its drawing-room or saloon,—always supposing them to be tasteful and appropriate; though we confess our feeling is, that a certain *soberness* should distinguish the richness of the finest mansion in the country from that in town. Still, in a villa or mansion, where all the details are carefully elaborated, where there is no neglect of essentials in order to give effect to what first meets the eye, where every thing is substantial and genuine, and not trick and tinsel,—there one expects to see more or less of the luxury of art in its best apartments.

But all this pleasure vanishes in the tawdry and tinsel *imitation* of costly and expensive furniture, to be found in cockney country houses. Instead of a befitting harmony through the whole house, one sees many minor comforts visibly sacrificed to produce a little extra show in the parlor; mock "fashionable" furniture, which, instead of being really fine, has only the look of finery, usurps in the principal room the place of the becoming, unpretending and modest fittings that belong there; and one is constantly struck with the *effort* which the cottage is continually making to look like the town house, rather than to wear its own more appropriate and becoming modesty of expression.

The pith of all that should be said on this subject, lies in a few words, viz., that *true taste lies in the union of the beautiful and the significant.* Hence, as a house in the country is quite distinct in character and uses, in many respects, from a house in town, it should always be built and furnished upon a widely different principle. It is far better, in a country house, to have an abundance of space, as many rooms as possible on a floor, the utmost convenience of arrangement, and a thorough realization of comfort throughout, than a couple of very fine apartments, loaded with showy furniture, "in the latest style," at the expense of the useful and convenient every where else.

And we may add to this, that the superior charm of significance or appropriateness is felt instantly by every one, when it is attained —though *display* only imposes on vulgar minds. We have seen a cottage where the finest furniture was of oak in simple forms, where every thing like display was unknown, where every thing costly was eschewed, but where you felt, at a glance, that there was a prevailing taste and fitness, that gave a meaning to all, and brought all into harmony; the furniture with the house, the house with the grounds, and all with the life of its inmates. This cottage, we need scarcely say, struck all who entered it with a pleasure more real and enduring than that of any costly mansion in the land. The plea sure arose from the feeling that all was significant; that the cottage, its arrangement, its furniture, and its surroundings, were all in keeping with the country, with each other and with their uses; and that no cockneyisms, no imitations of city splendor, had violated the simplicity and modesty of the country.

There must with us be progress in all things; and an American cannot but be proud of the progress of taste in this country. But as a great portion of the improvements, newly made in the country, are made by citizens, and not unfrequently by citizens whose time has been so closely occupied with business, that they have had no opportunity to cultivate a taste for rural matters, it is not surprising that we should continually see transplanted, as unexceptionable things, the ideas in houses, furniture, and even in gardens, which have been familiar to them in cities.

As, however, it is an indisputable axiom, that there are laws of taste which belong to the country and country life, quite distinct from those which belong to town, the citizen always runs into cockneyisms when he neglects these laws. And what we would gladly insist upon, therefore, is that it is only what is appropriate and significant in the country, (or what is equally so in town and country,) that can be adopted, without insulting the natural grace and freedom of umbrageous trees and green lawns.

He who comes from a city, and wishes to build himself a country-seat, would do well to *forget* all that he considers the standard of excellence in houses and furniture in town, (and which are, perhaps, really excellent there,) and make a pilgrimage of inspection to the best country houses, villas and cottages, with their grounds, before he lays a stone in his foundation walls, or marks a curve of his walks. If he does this, he will be certain to open his eyes to the fact, that, though there are good models in town, for town life, there are far better models in the country, for country life.

V.

ON THE IMPROVEMENT OF COUNTRY VILLAGES.

June, 1849.

"IF you, or any man of taste, wish to have a fit of the blues, let him come to the village of ——. I have just settled here; and all my ideas of rural beauty have been put to flight by what I see around me every day. Old wooden houses out of repair, and looking rickety and dejected; new wooden houses, distressingly lean in their proportions, chalky white in their clapboards, and *spinachy* green in their blinds. The church is absolutely hideous,— a long box of card-board, with a huge pepper-box on the top. There is not a tree in the streets; and if it were not for fields of refreshing verdure that surround the place, I should have the ophthalmia as well as the blue-devils. Is there no way of instilling some rudiments of taste into the minds of dwellers in remote country places?"

We beg our correspondent, from whose letter we quote the above paragraph, not to despair. There are always wise and good purposes hidden in the most common events of life; and we have no doubt Providence has sent *him* to the village of ——, as an APOSTLE OF TASTE, to instil some ideas of beauty and fitness into the minds of its inhabitants.

That the aspect of a large part of our rural villages, out of New England, is distressing to a man of taste, is undeniable. Not from want of means; for the inhabitants of these villages are thriving, industrious people, and poverty is very little known there. Not from want of materials; for both nature and the useful arts are ready to give them every thing needful, to impart a cheerful, tasteful, and inviting aspect to their homes; but simply from a poverty of ideas, and a dormant sense of the enjoyment to be derived from orderly, tasteful, and agreeable dwellings and streets, do these villages merit the condemnation of all men of taste and right feeling.

The first duty of an inhabitant of forlorn neighborhoods, like the village of ——, is to use all possible influence to have the *streets planted with trees.* To plant trees, costs little trouble or expense to each property holder; and once planted, there is some assurance that, with the aid of time and nature, we can at least cast a graceful veil over the deformity of a country home, if we cannot wholly remodel its features. Indeed, a village whose streets are bare of trees, ought to be looked upon as in a condition not less pitiable than a community without a schoolmaster, or a teacher of religion; for certain it is, when the affections are so dull, and the domestic virtues so blunt that men do not care how their own homes and villages look, they care very little for fulfilling any moral obligations not made compulsory by the strong arm of the law; while, on the other hand, show us a Massachusetts village, adorned by its avenues of elms, and made tasteful by the affection of its inhabitants, and you also place before us the fact, that it is there where order, good character, and virtuous deportment most of all adorn the lives and daily conduct of its people.

Our correspondents who, like the one just quoted, are apostles of taste, must not be discouraged by lukewarmness and opposition on the part of the inhabitants of these GRACELESS VILLAGES. They must expect sneers and derision from the ignorant and prejudiced; for, strange to say, poor human nature does not love to be shown that it is ignorant and prejudiced; and men who would think a cow-shed good enough to live in, if only *their* wants were concerned, take pleasure in pronouncing every man a visionary whose ideas rise above the level of their own accustomed vision. But, as an offset to this, it should always be remembered that there are two great principles at the bottom of our national character, which the apostle of taste in the most benighted, GRACELESS VILLAGE, may safely count upon. One of these is the *principle of imitation*, which will never allow a Yankee to be outdone by his neighbors; and the other, the *principle of progress*, which will not allow him to stand still when he discovers that his neighbor has really made an improvement.

Begin, then, by planting the first half-dozen trees in the public streets. "They will grow," as Sir Walter observed, "while you sleep;" and once fairly settled in their new congregation, so that they get the use of their arms, and especially of their tongues, it is quite extraordinary what sermons they will preach to those dull and tasteless villagers. Not a breeze that blows, but you will hear these tongues of theirs (which some look upon merely as *leaves*), whispering the most eloquent appeals to any passer by. There are some, doubtless, whose auriculars are so obtuse they they do not understand this language of the trees; but let even one of these walk home in a hot July day, when the sun that shines on the American continent has a face brighter than California gold, and if he does not return thanks devoutly for the cool shade of our half-dozen trees, as he approaches them and rests beneath their cool boughs, then is he a worse heathen than any piratical Malay of the Indian Ocean. But even such a man is sometimes convinced, by an appeal to the only chord that vibrates in the narrow compass of his soul,—that of utility,—when he sees with surprise a fine row of trees in a village, stretching out their leafy canopy as a barrier to a destructive fire, that otherwise would have crossed the street and burnt down the other half of the best houses in the village.

The next step to improve the GRACELESS VILLAGE, is to persuade some of those who are erecting new buildings, to adopt more tasteful models. And by this we mean, not necessarily what builders call a "fancy house," decorated with various ornaments that are supposed to give beauty to a cottage; but rather to copy some design, or some other building, where good proportions, pleasing form, and fitness for the use intended, give the beauty sought for, without calling in the aid of ornaments, which may heighten but never create beauty. If you cannot find such a house ready built to copy from, procure works where such designs exist, or, still better, a rough and cheap sketch from a competent architect, as a guide. Persuade your neighbor, who is about to build, that even if his house is to cost but $600, there is no economy that he can practise in the expenditure of that sum so indisputable, or which he will so completely realize the value of afterwards, as $10 or $20 worth of advice, with a few pen or pencil marks, to fix the ideas, upon paper, from an architect of acknowledged taste and judgment. Whether the house is to look awkward and ugly, or whether it is to be comfortable and pleasing for years, all depend upon the *idea* of that house which previously exists in *somebody's mind*,—either architect, owner, or mechanic,—whoever, in short, conceives what that house shall be, before it becomes " a local habitation," or has any name among other houses already born in the hitherto GRACELESS VILLAGE.

It is both surprising and pleasant, to one accustomed to watch the development of the human soul, to see the gradual but certain effect of building one really good and tasteful house in a graceless village. Just as certain as there is a dormant spark of the love of beauty, which underlays all natures extant, in that village, so certain will it awaken at the sight of that house. You will hear nothing about it; or if you do, perhaps you may, at first, even hear all kinds of facetious comments on Mr. ——'s new house. But next year you will find the old mode abandoned by him who builds a new house. He has a new idea; he strives to make his dwelling manifest it; and this process goes on, till, by-and-by, you wonder what new genius has so changed the aspect of this village, and turned its neglected, bare, and lanky streets into avenues of fine foliage, and streets of neat and tasteful houses.

It is an old adage, that " a cobbler's family has no shoes." We are forced to call the adage up for an explanation of the curious fact, that in five villages out of six in the United States, there does not appear to have been room enough in which properly to lay out the streets or place the houses. Why, on a continent so broad that the mere public lands amount to an area of fifty acres for every man, woman, and child, in the commonwealth, there should not be found space sufficient to lay out country towns, so that the streets shall be wide enough for avenues, and the house-lots broad enough to allow sufficient trees and shrubbery to give a little privacy and seclusion, is one of the unexplained phenomena in the natural history of our continent, which, along with the boulders and glaciers, we leave to the learned and ingenious Professor Agassiz. Certain it is, our ancestors did not bring over this national trait from England; for in that small, and yet great kingdom, not larger than one of our largest states, there is one city—London—which has more acres devoted to *public parks*, than can be numbered for this purpose in all America.

It may appear too soon to talk of village greens, and village squares, or small parks planted with trees, and open to the common enjoyment of the inhabitants, in the case of GRACELESS VILLAGES, where there is yet not a shade-tree standing in one of the streets. But this will come gradually; and all the sooner, just in proportion as the apostles of taste multiply in various parts of the country. Persons interested in these improvements, and who are not aware of what has been done in some parts of New England, should immediately visit New Haven and Springfield. The former city is a bower of elms; and the inhabitants who now walk beneath spacious avenues, of this finest of American trees, speak with gratitude of the energy, public spirit and taste of the late Mr. Hillhouse, who was the great apostle of taste for that city, years ago, when the streets were as bare as those of the most graceless villages in the land. And what stranger has passed through Springfield, and not recognized immediately a superior spirit in the place, which long since suggested and planted the pretty little square which now ornaments the town?

But we should be doing injustice to the principle of progress, to which we have already referred, if we did not mention here the signs of the times, which we have lately noticed; signs that prove the spirit of rural improvement is fairly awake over this broad continent. We have received accounts, within the last month, of the doings of *ornamental tree associations*, lately formed in five different states, from New Hampshire to Tennessee.* The object of these associations is to do precisely what nobody in particular thinks it his business to do; that is, to rouse the public mind to the impor-

* We cannot deny ourselves the pleasure of commending the public spirit of a gentleman in one of the villages in western New York, who, by offering a bounty for all trees planted in the village where he lives, has induced many to set about the work in good earnest.

tance of embellishing the streets of towns and villages, and to induce everybody to plant trees in front of his own premises.

While we are writing this, we have received the printed report of one of these associations,—*The Rockingham Farmers' Club*, of Exeter, New Hampshire. The whole report is so much to the point, that we republish it entire in our Domestic Notices of the month; but there is so much earnest enthusiasm in the first paragraph of the report, and it is so entirely apposite to our present remarks, that we must also introduce it here:

"Why are not the streets of all our villages shaded and adorned with trees? Why are so many of our dwellings still unprotected from the burning heat of summer, and the 'pelting of the pitiless storms' of winter? Is it because in New England hearts, hurried and pressed as they are by care and business, there is no just appreciation of the importance of the subject? Or is it that failure in the attempt, which almost every man has made, once in his life, in this way to ornament his home, has led many to the belief that there is some mystery, passing the comprehension of common men, about this matter of transplanting trees? The answer may be found, we apprehend, partly in each of the reasons suggested. Ask your neighbor why he has not more trees about his home, and he will tell you that they are of no great *use*, and, besides, that it is very difficult to make them grow; that he has tried it once or twice, and they have all died. Now these, the common reasons, are both ill-founded. It *is* of *use* for every man to surround himself with objects of interest, to cultivate a taste for the beautiful in all things, and especially in the works of nature. It is of use for every family to have a *home*, a pleasant, happy home, hallowed by purifying influences. It *is* of use, that every child should be educated, not only in sciences, and arts, and *dead* languages, but that his affections and his *taste* should be developed and refined; that the book of nature should be laid open to him; and that he should learn to read her language in the flower and the leaf, written everywhere, in the valley and on the hill-side, and hear it in the songs of birds, and the murmuring of the forest. If you would keep pure the heart of your child, and make his youth innocent and happy, surround him with objects of interest and beauty at home. If you would prevent a restless spirit, if you would save him from that lowest species of idolatry, 'the love of money,' and teach him to 'love what is lovely,' adorn your dwellings, your places of worship, your school-houses, your streets and public squares, with trees and hedges, and lawns and flowers, so that his heart may early and ever be impressed with the love of Him who made them all." * *

What more can we add to this eloquent appeal from the committee of a farmers' club in a village of New Hampshire? Only to entreat other farmers' clubs to go and do likewise; other ornamental tree societies to carry on the good work of adorning the country; other apostles of taste not to be discouraged, but to be unceasing in their efforts, till they see the clouds of ignorance and prejudice dispersing; and, finally, all who live in the country and have an affection for it, to take hold of this good work of rural improvement, till not a GRACELESS VILLAGE can be found from the Penobscot to the Rio Grande, or a man of intelligence who is not ashamed to be found living in such a village.

VI.

OUR COUNTRY VILLAGES.

June, 1850.

WITHOUT any boasting, it may safely be said, that the natural features of our common country (as the speakers in Congress call her), are as agreeable and prepossessing as those of any other land—whether merry England, *la belle France*, or the German fatherland. We have greater lakes, larger rivers, broader and more fertile prairies than the old world can show; and if the Alleghanies are rather dwarfish when compared to the Alps, there are peaks and summits, "castle hills" and volcanoes, in our great back-bone range of the Pacific—the Rocky Mountains—which may safely hold up their heads along with Mont Blanc and the Jungfrau.

Providence, then, has blessed this country—our country—with "natural born" features, which we may look upon and be glad. But how have we sought to deform the fair landscape here and there by little, miserable shabby-looking towns and villages; not miserable and shabby-looking from the poverty and wretchedness of the inhabitants—for in no land is there more peace and plenty—but miserable and shabby-looking from the absence of taste, symmetry, order, space, proportion,—all that constitutes beauty. Ah, well and truly did Cowper say,

> "God made the country, but *man* made the town."

For in the one, we every where see utility and beauty harmoniously combined, while the other presents us but too often the reverse; that is to say, the marriage of utility and deformity.

Some of our readers may remind us that we have already preached a sermon from this text. No matter; we should be glad to preach fifty; yes, or even establish a sect,—as that seems the only way of making proselytes now,—whose duty it should be to convert people living in the country towns to the true faith; we mean the true rural faith, viz., that it is immoral and uncivilized to live in mean and uncouth villages, where there is no poverty, or want of intelligence in the inhabitants; that there is nothing laudable in having a piano-forte and mahogany chairs in the parlor, where the streets outside are barren of shade trees, destitute of side-walks, and populous with pigs and geese.

We are bound to admit (with a little shame and humiliation,—being a native of New-York, the "Empire State"), that there is one part of the Union where the millennium of country towns, and good government, and rural taste has not only commenced, but is in full domination. We mean, of course, Massachusetts. The traveller may go from one end of that State to the other, and find flourishing villages, with broad streets lined with maples and elms, behind which are goodly rows of neat and substantial dwellings, full of evidences of order, comfort and taste. Throughout the whole State, no animals are allowed to run at large in the streets of towns and villages. Hence so much more cleanliness than elsewhere; so much more order and neatness; so many more pretty rural lanes; so many inviting flower-gardens and orchards—only separated from the passer-by by a low railing or hedge, instead of a formidable board fence. Now, if you cross the State line into New-York—a State of far greater wealth than Massachusetts, as long settled and nearly as populous—you feel directly that you are in the land of "pigs and poultry," in the least agreeable sense of the word. In passing through villages and towns, the truth is still more striking, as you go to the south and west; and you feel little or nothing of that sense, of "how pleasant it must be to live here," which the traveller through Berkshire, or the Connecticut valley, or the pretty villages about Boston, feels moving his heart within him. You are rather inclined to wish there were two new commandments, viz.: thou shalt plant trees, to hide the nakedness of the streets; and thou shalt not keep pigs—except in the back yard! *

Our more reflective and inquiring readers will naturally ask, why is this better condition of things—a condition that denotes better citizens, better laws, and higher civilization—confined almost wholly to Massachusetts? To save them an infinite deal of painstaking, research and investigation, we will tell them in a few words. *That State is better educated than the rest.* She sees the advantage, morally and socially, of orderly, neat, tasteful villages; in producing better citizens, in causing the laws to be respected, in making homes dearer and more sacred, in making domestic life and the enjoyment of property to be more truly and rightly estimated.

And these are the legitimate and natural results of this kind of improvement we so ardently desire in the outward life and appearance of rural towns. If our readers suppose us anxious for the building of good houses, and the planting of street avenues, solely that the country may look more beautiful to the eye, and that the taste shall be gratified, they do us an injustice. This is only the external sign by which we would have the country's health and beauty known, as we look for the health and beauty of its fair daughters in the presence of the rose on their cheeks. But as the latter only blooms lastingly there, when a good constitution is joined with healthful habits of mind and body, so the tasteful appearance which we long for in our country towns, we seek as the outward mark of education, moral sentiment, love of home, and refined cultivation, which makes the main difference between Massachusetts and Madagascar.

We have, in a former number, said something as to the practical manner in which "graceless villages" may be improved. We have urged the force of example in those who set about improving

* We believe we must lay this latter sin at the doors of our hard-working emigrants from the Emerald Isle. Wherever they settle, they cling to their ancient fraternity of porkers; and think it "no free country where pigs can't have their liberty." Newburgh is by no means a well-planned village, though scarcely surpassed for scenery; but we believe it may claim the credit of being the only one among all the towns, cities and villages of New-York, where pigs and geese have not the freedom of the streets.

their own property, and shown the influence of even two or three persons in giving an air of civilization and refinement to the streets and suburbs of country towns. There is not a village in America, however badly planned at first, or ill-built afterwards, that may not be redeemed, in a great measure, by the aid of shade trees in the streets, and a little shrubbery in the front yards, and it is never too late or too early to project improvements of this kind. Every spring and every autumn should witness a revival of associated efforts on the part of select-men, trustees of corporations, and persons of means and influence, to adorn and embellish the external condition of their towns. Those least alive to the result as regards beauty, may be roused as to the effects of increased value given to the property thus improved, and villages thus rendered attractive and desirable as places of residence.

But let us now go a step further than this. In no country, perhaps, are there so many *new* villages and towns laid out every year as in the United States. Indeed, so large is the number, that the builders and projectors are fairly at a loss for names,—ancient and modern history having been literally worn threadbare by the godfathers, until all association with great heroes and mighty deeds is fairly beggared by this re-christening going on in our new settlements and future towns, as yet only populous to the extent of six houses. And notwithstanding the apparent vastness of our territory, the growth of new towns and new States is so wonderful—fifteen or twenty years giving a population of hundreds of thousands, where all was wilderness before—that the plan and arrangement of new towns ought to be a matter of national importance. And yet, to judge by the manner in which we see the thing done, there has not, in the whole duration of the republic, been a single word said, or a single plan formed, calculated to embody past experience, or to assist in any way the laying out of a village or town.

We have been the more struck by this fact in observing the efforts of some companies who have lately, upon the Hudson, within some twenty or more miles of New-York, undertaken to lay out rural villages, with some pretension to taste and comfort; and aim, at least, at combining the advantages of the country with easy railroad access to them.

Our readers most interested in such matters as this (and, taking our principal cities together, it is a pretty large class), will be interested to know what is the beau-ideal of these companies, who undertake to buy tracts of land, lay them out in the best manner, and form the most complete and attractive rural villages, in order to tempt those tired of the wayworn life of sidewalks, into a neighborhood where, without losing society, they can see the horizon, breathe the fresh air, and walk upon elastic greensward.

Well, the beau-ideal of these newly-planned villages is not down to the zero of dirty lanes and shadeless roadsides; but it rises, we are sorry to say, no higher than streets, lined on each side with shade-trees, and bordered with rows of houses. For the most part, those houses—cottages, we presume—are to be built on fifty-feet lots; or if any buyer is not satisfied with that amount of elbow room, he may buy two lots, though certain that his neighbor will still be within twenty feet of his fence. And this is the sum total of the rural beauty, convenience, and comfort, of the latest plan for a rural village in the Union.* The buyer gets nothing more than he has in town, save his little patch of back and front yard, a little peep down the street, looking one way at the river, and the other way at the sky. So far from gaining any thing which all inhabitants of a village should gain by the combination, one of these new villagers actually loses; for if he were to go by himself, he would buy land cheaper, and have a fresh landscape of fields and hills around him, instead of houses on all sides, almost as closely placed as in the city, which he has endeavored to fly from.

Now a rural village—newly planned in the suburbs of a great city, and planned, too, specially for those whose circumstances will allow them to own a tasteful cottage in such a village—should present attractions much higher than this. It should aim at something higher than mere rows of houses upon streets crossing each other at right angles, and bordered with shade-trees. Any one may find as good shade-trees, and much better houses, in certain streets of the city which he leaves behind him; and if he is to give up fifty con-

* We say *plan*, but we do not mean to include in this such villages as Northampton, Brookline, &c., beautiful and tasteful as they are. But they are in Massachusetts!

veniences and comforts, long enjoyed in town, for the mere fact of fresh air, he had better take board during the summer months in some snug farmhouse as before.

The indispensable desiderata in rural villages of this kind, are the following: 1st, a large open space, common, or park, situated in the middle of the village—not less than twenty acres; and better if fifty or more in extent. This should be well planted with groups of trees, and kept as a lawn. The expense of mowing it would be paid by the grass in some cases; and in others, a considerable part of the space might be inclosed with a wire fence, and fed by sheep or cows, like many of the public parks in England.

This park would be the nucleus or *heart of the village*, and would give it an essentially rural character. Around it should be grouped all the best cottages and residences of the place; and this would be secured by selling no lots fronting upon it of less than one-fourth of an acre in extent. Wide streets, with rows of elms or maples, should diverge from the park on each side, and upon these streets smaller lots, but not smaller than one hundred feet front, should be sold for smaller cottages.

In this way, we would secure to our village a permanent rural character; first, by the possession of a large central space, always devoted to park or pleasure-ground, and always held as joint property, and for the common use of the whole village; second, by the imperative arrangement of cottages or dwellings around it, in such a way as to secure in all parts of the village sufficient space, view, circulation of air, and broad, well-planted avenues of shade-trees.

After such a village was built, and the central park planted a few years, the inhabitants would not be contented with the mere meadow and trees, usually called a park in this country. By submitting to a small annual tax per family, they could turn the whole park, if small, or considerable portions, here and there, if large, into pleasure-grounds. In the latter, there would be collected, by the combined means of the village, all the rare, hardy shrubs, trees, and plants, usually found in the private grounds of any amateur in America. Beds and masses of ever-blooming roses, sweet-scented climbers, and the richest shrubs, would thus be open to the enjoyment of all during the whole growing season. Those who had

16

neither the means, time, nor inclination, to devote to the culture of private pleasure-grounds, could thus enjoy those which belonged to all. Others might prefer to devote their own garden to fruits and vegetables, since the pleasure-grounds, which belonged to all, and which all would enjoy, would, by their greater breadth and magnitude, offer beauties and enjoyments which few private gardens can give.

The next step, after the possession of such public pleasure-grounds, would be the social and common enjoyment of them. Upon the well-mown glades of lawn, and beneath the shade of the forest-trees, would be formed rustic seats. Little arbors would be placed near, where in midsummer evenings ices would be served to all who wished them. And, little by little, the musical taste of the village (with the help of those good musical folks—the German emigrants) would organize itself into a band, which would occasionally delight the ears of all frequenters of the park with popular airs.

Do we overrate the mental and moral influences of such a common ground of entertainment as this, when we say that the inhabitants of such a village—enjoying in this way a common interest in flowers, trees, the fresh air, and sweet music, daily—would have something more healthful than the ordinary life of cities, and more refining and elevating than the common gossip of country villages?

"Ah! I see, Mr. Editor, you are a bit of a communist." By no means. On the contrary, we believe, above all things under heaven, in the power and virtue of the *individual home.* We devote our life and humble efforts to raising its condition. But people *must* live in towns and villages, and therefore let us raise the condition of towns and villages, and especially of rural towns and villages, by all possible means!

But we are *republican;* and, shall we confess it, we are a little vexed that as a people generally, we do not see how much in America we lose by not using the advantages of republicanism. We mean now, for refined culture, physical comfort, and the like. Republican *education* we are now beginning pretty well to understand the value of; and it will not be long before it will be hard to find a native citizen who cannot read and write. And this comes by making every man see what a great moral and intellectual good comes from cheerfully bearing a part in the burden of popular education. Let us next take up popular refinement in the arts, manners, social life, and innocent enjoyments, and we shall see what a virtuous and educated republic can really become.

Besides this, it is the proper duty of the state—that is, *the people* —to do in this way what the reigning power does in a monarchy. If the kings and princes in Germany, and the sovereign of England, have made magnificent parks and pleasure-gardens, and thrown them wide open for the enjoyment of all classes of the people (the latter, after all, having to pay for it), may it not be that our sovereign *people* will (far more cheaply, as they may) make and support these great and healthy sources of pleasure and refinement for themselves in America? We believe so; and we confidently wait for the time when public parks, public gardens, public galleries, and tasteful villages, shall be among the peculiar features of our happy republic.

VII.

ON SIMPLE RURAL COTTAGES.

September, 1846.

THE simple rural cottage, or *the Working Man's Cottage*, deserves some serious consideration, and we wish to call the attention of our readers to it at this moment. The pretty suburban cottage, and the ornamented villa, are no longer vague and rudimentary ideas in the minds of our people. The last five years have produced in the environs of all our principal towns, in the Eastern and Middle States, some specimens of tasteful dwellings of this class, that would be considered beautiful examples of rural architecture in any part of the world. Our attention has been called to at least a dozen examples lately, of rural edifices, altogether charming and in the best taste.

In some parts of the country, the inhabitants of the suburbs of towns appear, indeed, almost to have a mania on the subject of ornamental cottages. Weary of the unfitness and the uncouthness of the previous models, and inspired with some notions of rural Gothic, they have seized it with a kind of frenzy, and carpenters, distracted with *verge-boards* and *gables*, have, in some cases, made sad work of the picturesque. Here and there we see a really good and well-proportioned ornamental dwelling. But almost in the immediate neighborhood of it, soon spring up tasteless and meagre imitations, the absurdity of whose effect borders upon a caricature.

Notwithstanding this deplorably bad taste, rural architecture is making a progress in the United States that is really wonderful. Among the many failures in cottages, there are some very successful attempts, and every rural dwelling, really well designed and executed, has a strong and positive effect upon the good taste of the whole country.

There is, perhaps, a more intuitive judgment—we mean a natural and instinctive one—in the popular mind, regarding architecture, than any other one of the fine arts. We have known many men, who could not themselves design a good common gate, who yet felt truly, and at a glance, the beauty of a well-proportioned and tasteful house, and the deformity of one whose proportions and details were bad. Why then are there so many failures in building ornamental cottages?

We imagine the answer to this lies plainly in the fact, that the most erroneous notions prevail respecting the proper use of DECORATION in rural architecture.

It is the most common belief and practice, with those whose taste is merely borrowed, and not founded upon any clearly defined principles, that it is only necessary to adopt the *ornaments* of a certain building, or a certain style of building, to produce the best effect of the style or building in question. But so far is this from being the true mode of attaining this result, that in every case where it is adopted, as we perceive at a glance, the result is altogether unsatisfactory.

Ten years ago the mock-Grecian fashion was at its height. Perhaps nothing is more truly beautiful than the pure and classical Greek temple—so perfect in its proportions, so chaste and harmonious in its decorations. It is certainly not the best style for a country house; but still we have seen a few specimens in this country, of really beautiful villas, in this style—where the proportions of the whole, and the admirable completeness of all the parts, executed on a fitting scale, produced emotions of the highest pleasure.

But, alas! no sooner were there a few specimens of the classical style in the country, than the Greek temple mania became an epidemic. Churches, banks, and court-houses, one could very well bear to see *Vitruvianized.* Their simple uses and respectable size bore well the honors which the destiny of the day forced upon them. But to see the five orders applied to every other building, from the rich merchant's mansion to the smallest and meanest of all edifices, was a spectacle which made even the warmest admirers of Vitruvius sad, and would have made a true Greek believe that the gods who preside over beauty and harmony, had for ever abandoned the new world!

But the Greek temple disease has passed its crisis. The people have survived it. Some few buildings of simple forms, and convenient arrangements, that stood here and there over the country, uttering silent rebukes, perhaps had something to do with bringing us to just notions of fitness and propriety. Many of the perishable wooden porticoes have fallen down; many more will soon do so; and many have been pulled down, and replaced by less pretending piazzas or verandas.

Yet we are now obliged to confess that we see strong symptoms manifesting themselves of a second disease, which is to disturb the architectural growth of our people. We feel that we shall not be able to avert it, but perhaps, by exhibiting a *diagnosis* of the symptoms, we may prevent its extending so widely as it might otherwise do.

We allude to the mania just springing up for a kind of *spurious* rural Gothic cottage. It is nothing more than a miserable wooden thing, tricked out with flimsy verge-boards, and unmeaning gables. It has nothing of the true character of the cottage it seeks to imitate. It bears the same relation to it that a child's toy-house does to a real and substantial habitation.

If we inquire into the cause of these architectural abortions, either Grecian or Gothic, we shall find that they always arise from a poverty of ideas on the subject of *style* in architecture. The novice in architecture always supposes, when he builds a common house, and decorates it with the showiest *ornaments* of a certain style, that he has erected an edifice in that style. He deludes himself in the same manner as the schoolboy who, with his gaudy paper cap and tin sword, imagines himself a great general. We build a miserable shed, make one of its ends a portico with Ionic columns, and call it a temple in the Greek style. At the same time, it has none of the proportions, nothing of the size, solidity, and perfection of details, and probably few or none of the remaining decorations of that style.

So too, we now see erected a wooden cottage of a few feet in length, *gothicized* by the introduction of three or four pointed windows, little gables enough for a residence of the first class, and a profusion of thin, scolloped verge-boards, looking more like card ornaments, than the solid, heavy, carved decorations proper to the style imitated.

Let those who wish to avoid such exhibitions of bad taste, recur to some just and correct principles on this subject.

One of the soundest maxims ever laid down on this subject, by our lamented friend Loudon, (who understood its principles as well as any one that ever wrote on this subject), was the following: "*Nothing should be introduced into any cottage design, however ornamental it may appear, that is at variance with propriety, comfort, or sound workmanship.*"

The chiefest objection that we make to these over-decorated cottages of very small size, (which we have now in view,) is that the introduction of so much ornament is evidently a violation of the principles of *propriety.*

It cannot be denied by the least reflective mind, that there are several classes of dwelling-houses in every country. The mansion of the wealthy proprietor, which is filled with pictures and statues, ought certainly to have a superior architectural character to the cottage of the industrious workingman, who is just able to furnish a comfortable home for his family. While the first is allowed to display even an ornate style of building, which his means will enable him to complete and render somewhat perfect—the other cannot adopt the same ornaments without rendering a cottage, which might be agreeable and pleasing, from its fitness and genuine simplicity, offensive and distasteful through its ambitious, borrowed decorations.

By adopting such ornaments they must therefore violate propriety, because, architecturally, it is not fitting that the humble cottage should wear the decorations of a superior dwelling, any more than that the plain workingman should wear the same diamonds that represent the superfluous wealth of his neighbor. In a cottage of the smallest size, it is evident, also, that, if its tenant is the owner, he must make some sacrifice of comfort to produce effect; and he waives the principle which demands sound workmanship, since to adopt any highly ornamental style, the possessor of small means is obliged to make those ornaments flimsy and meagre, which ought to be substantial and carefully executed.

Do we then intend to say, that the humble cottage must be left bald and tasteless? By no means. We desire to see every rural dwelling in America tasteful. When the intelligence of our active-minded people has been turned in this direction long enough, we are confident that this country will more abound in beautiful rural dwellings than any other part of the world. But we wish to see the workingman's cottage made tasteful in a simple and fit manner. We wish to see him eschew all ornaments that are inappropriate and unbecoming, and give it a simple and pleasing character by the use of truthful means.

For the cottage of this class, we would then entirely reject all attempts at columns or verge-boards.* If the owner can afford it, we would, by all means, have a veranda (piazza), however small; for we consider that feature one affording the greatest comfort. If the cottage is of wood, we would even build it with strong *rough* boards, painting and sanding the same.

We would, first of all, give our cottage the best *proportions*. It should not be too narrow; it should not be too high. These are the two prevailing faults with us. After giving it an agreeable proportion—which is the highest source of all material beauty—we would give it something more of character as well as comfort, by extending the roof. Nothing is pleasanter to the eye than the shadow afforded by a projecting eave. It is nearly impossible that a house should be quite ugly, with an amply projecting roof: as it is difficult to render a simple one pleasing, when it is narrow and *pinched* about the eaves.

After this, we would bestow a little character by a bold and simple dressing, or facing, about the windows and doors. The

* Of course, these remarks regarding decorations do not apply strictly to the case of cottages for the tenants, gardeners, farmers, etc., of a large estate. In that case, such dwellings form parts of a highly finished whole. The means of the proprietor are sufficient to render them complete of their kind. Yet even in this case, we much prefer a becoming *simplicity* in the cottages of such a desmesne.

chimneys may next be attended to. Let them be less clumsy and heavy, if possible, than usual.

This would be character enough for the simplest class of cottages. We would rather aim to render them striking and expressive by a good outline, and a few simple details, than by the imitation of the ornaments of a more complete and highly finished style of building.

In figs. 1 and 2, we have endeavored to give two views of a workingman's cottage, of humble means.*

Whatever may be thought of the effect of these designs, (and we assure our readers that they appear much better when built than upon paper,) we think it will not be denied, that they have not the defects to which we have just alluded. The style is as economical as the cheapest mode of building; it is expressive of the simple wants of its occupant; and it is, we conceive, not without some tasteful character.

Last, though not least, this mode of building cottages is well adapted to our country. The material—wood—is one which must, yet for some years, be the only one used for small cottages. The projecting eaves partially shelter the building from our hot sun and violent storms; and the few simple details, which may be said to confer something of an ornamental character, as the rafter brackets and window dressings, are such as obviously grow out of the primary conveniences of the house—the necessity of a roof for shelter, and the necessity of windows for light.

Common narrow *siding*, (*i. e.* the thin *clap-boarding* in general use,) we would not employ for the exterior of this class of cottages—nor, indeed, for any simple rural buildings. What we greatly prefer, are good strong and sound boards, from ten to fourteen inches wide, and one to one and a fourth inches thick. These should be tongued and grooved so as to make a close joint, and nailed to the frame of the house in a *vertical* manner. The joint should be covered on the outside with a narrow strip of inch board, from two to three inches wide. The accompanying cut, fig. 3, *a*,

* We do not give the interior plan of these, at present. Our only object now is to call attention to the exteriors of dwellings of this class.

showing a section of this mode of weather-boarding will best explain it to the reader.

We first pointed out this mode of covering, in our "Cottage Residences." A great number of gentlemen have since adopted it, and all express themselves highly gratified with it. It is by far the most expressive and agreeable mode of building in wood for the country; it is stronger, equally cheap and much more durable than the thin *siding;* and it has a character of strength and permanence, which, to our eye, narrow and thin boards never can have. When *filled in* with cheap soft brick, it also makes a very warm house.

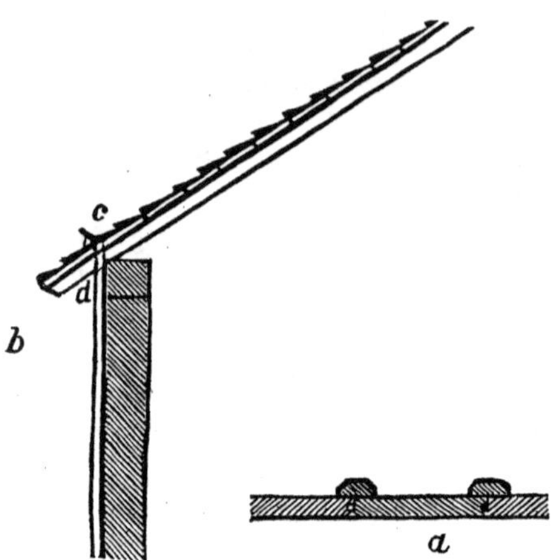

Fig. 3. Cottage Siding and Roofing.

The rafters of these two cottages are stout joists, placed two feet apart, which are allowed to extend beyond the house two feet, to answer the purpose of *brackets*, for the projecting eaves. Fig. 3, *b*, will show, at a glance, the mode of rafter boarding and shingling over these rafters, so as to form the simplest and best kind of roof.*

The window dressings, which should have a bold and simple character, and made by nailing on the weather boarding stout

* The simplest mode of forming an eave gutter on a projecting roof like this, is shown in the cut, fig. 3 at *c*. It consists merely of a tin trough, fastened to the roof by its longer portion, which extends up under one layer of shingles. This lies close upon the roof. The trough being directly over the line of the outer face of the house, the leader *d*, which conveys away the water, passes down in a straight line, avoiding the angles necessary in the common mode.

strips, four inches wide, fig. 4, *a*, of plank, one inch and a half in thickness. The coping piece, *b*, is of the same thickness, and six to eight inches wide, supported by a couple of pieces of joists, *c*, nailed under it for brackets.

We have tried the effect of this kind of exterior, using *unplaned* boards, to which we have given two good coats of paint, *sanding* the second coat. The effect we think much more agreeable—because it is in better keeping with a rustic cottage, than when the more expensive mode of using planed boards is resorted to.

Fig. 4. Cottage Window Dressing.

Some time ago, we ventured to record our objections to *white* as a universal color for country houses. We have had great satisfaction, since that time, in seeing a gradual improvement taking place with respect to this matter. Neutral tints are, with the best taste, now every where preferred to strong glaring colors. Cottages of this class, we would always paint some soft and pleasing shade of drab or fawn color. These are tints which, on the whole, harmonize best with the surrounding hues of the country itself.

These two little designs are intended for the simplest cottages, to cost from two to five hundred dollars. Our readers will not understand us as offering them as complete models of a workingman's cottage. They are only partial examples of our views and taste in this matter. We shall continue the subject, from time to time, with various other examples.

VIII.

ON THE COLOR OF COUNTRY HOUSES.

May, 1847.

CHARLES DICKENS, in that unlucky visit to America, in which he was treated like a spoiled child, and left it in the humor that often follows too lavish a bestowal of sugar plums on spoiled children, made now and then a remark in his characteristic vein of subtle perceptions. Speaking of some of our wooden villages—the houses as bright as the greenest blinds and the whitest weather-boarding can make them—he said it was quite impossible to believe them real, substantial habitations. They looked "as if they had been put up on Saturday night, and were to be taken down on Monday morning!"

There is no wonder that any tourist, accustomed to the quiet and harmonious color of buildings in an English landscape, should be shocked at the glare and rawness of many of our country dwellings. Brown, the celebrated English landscape gardener, used to say of a new red brick house, that it would "put a whole valley in a fever!" Some of our freshly painted villages, seen in a bright summer day, might give a man with weak eyes a fit of the ophthalmia.

We have previously ventured a word or two against this national passion for white paint, and it seems to us a fitting moment to look the subject boldly in the face once more.

In a country where a majority of the houses are built of wood, the use of some paint is an absolute necessity in point of economy. What the colors of this paint are, we consider a matter no less important in point of taste.

Now, genuine white lead (the color nominally used for most exteriors) is one of the dearest of paints.* It is not, therefore, economy which leads our countrymen into such a dazzling error. Some mistaken notions, touching its good effect, in connection with the country, is undoubtedly at the bottom of it. "Give me," says a retired citizen, before whose eyes red brick and dusty streets have been the only objects for years, "give me a white house with bright green blinds in the country." To him, white is at once the newest, cleanest, smartest, and most conspicuous color which it is possible to choose for his cottage or villa. Its freshness and newness he prizes as a clown does that of his Sunday suit, the more the first day after it comes from the tailor, with all the unsullied gloss and glitter of gilt buttons. To possess a house which has a quiet air, as though it might have been inhabited and well taken care of for years, is no pleasure to him. He desires every one to know that he, Mr. Broadcloth, has come into the country and built a NEW house. Nothing will give the stamp of newness so strongly as white paint. Besides this, he does not wish his light to be hidden under a bushel. He has no idea of leading an obscure life in the country. Seclusion and privacy are the only blue devils of his imagination. He wishes every passer-by on the river, railroad, or highway, to see and know that this is Mr. Broadcloth's villa. It must be *conspicuous*—therefore it is painted WHITE.

Any one who has watched the effect of example in a country neighborhood, does not need to be told that all the small dwellings that are built the next season after Mr. Broadcloth's new house, are painted, if possible, a shade whiter, and the blinds a little more intensely verdant—what the painters triumphantly call "French green." There is no resisting the fashion; those who cannot afford paint use whitewash; and whole villages, to borrow Miss Miggs's striking illustration, look like "whitenin' and supelters."

Our first objection to *white*, is, that it is too glaring and con-

* We say *genuine* white lead, for it is notorious that four-fifths of the white paint sold under this name in the United States, is only an imitation of it, composed largely of *whiting*. Though the first cost of the latter is little, yet as it soon rubs off and speedily repuires renewal, it is one of the dearest colors in the end.

spicuous. We scarcely know any thing more uncomfortable to the eye, than to approach the sunny side of a house in one of our brilliant midsummer days, when it revels in the fashionable purity of its color. It is absolutely painful. Nature, full of kindness for man, has covered most of the surface that meets his eye in the country, with a soft green hue—at once the most refreshing and most grateful to the eye. These habitations that we have referred to, appear to be colored on the very opposite principle, and one needs, in broad sunshine, to turn his eyes away to relieve them by a glimpse of the soft and refreshing shades that every where pervade the trees, the grass, and the surface of the earth.

Our second objection to white is, that it does not harmonize with the country, and thereby mars the effect of rural landscapes. Much of the beauty of landscape depends on what painters call *breadth of tone*—which is caused by broad masses of colors that harmonize and blend agreeably together. Nothing tends to destroy breadth of tone so much as any object of considerable size, and of a brilliant white. It stands harshly apart from all the soft shades of the scene. Hence landscape painters always studiously avoid the introduction of white in their buildings, and give them instead, some neutral tint—a tint which unites or contrasts agreeably with the color of trees and grass, and which seems to blend into other parts of natural landscape, instead of being a discordant note in the general harmony.

There is always, perhaps, something not quite agreeable in objects of a dazzling whiteness, when brought into contrast with other colors. Mr. Price, in his essays on the Beautiful and Picturesque, conceived that very white teeth gave a silly expression to the countenance—and brings forward, in illustration of it, the well-known *soubriquet* which Horace Walpole bestowed on one of his acquaintances—" the gentleman with the foolish teeth."

No one is successful in rural improvements, who does not study nature, and take her for the basis of his practice. Now, in natural landscape, any thing like strong and bright colors is seldom seen, except in very minute portions, and least of all pure white—chiefly appearing in small objects like flowers. The practical rule which should be deduced from this, is, to avoid all those colors which nature avoids. In buildings, we should copy those that she offers chiefly to the eye—such as those of the soil, rocks, wood, and the bark of trees,—the materials of which houses are built. These materials offer us the best and most natural study from which harmonious colors for the houses themselves should be taken.

Wordsworth, in a little volume on the Scenery of the Lakes, remarks that the objections to white as a color, in large spots or masses, in landscapes, are insurmountable. He says it destroys the *gradations* of distances, haunts the eye, and disturbs the repose of nature. To leave some little consolation to the lovers of white lead, we will add that there is one position in which their favorite color may not only be tolerated, but often has a happy effect. We mean in the case of a country house or cottage, deeply imbowered in trees. Surrounded by such a mass of foliage as Spenser describes,

> "In whose *enclosed shadow* there was set
> A fair pavilion *scarcely to be seen*,"

a white building often has a magical effect. But a landscape painter would quickly answer, if he were asked the reason of this exception to the rule, "It is because the building does not appear white." In other words, in the shadow of the foliage by which it is half concealed, it loses all the harshness and offensiveness of a white house in an open site. We have, indeed, often felt, in looking at examples of the latter, set upon a bald hill, that the building itself would, if possible, cry out,

> "Hide me from day's *garish eye*."

Having entered our protest against the general use of white in country edifices, we are bound to point out what we consider suitable shades of color.

We have said that one should look to nature for hints in color. This gives us, apparently, a wide choice of shades, but as we ought properly to employ modified shades, taken from the colors of the materials of which houses are constructed, the number of objects is brought within a moderate compass. Houses are not built of grass, or leaves, and there is, therefore, not much propriety in painting a dwelling green. Earth, stone, bricks, and wood, are the substances that enter mostly into the structure of our houses, and from these we would accordingly take suggestions for painting them.

Sir Joshua Reynolds, who was full of an artistical feeling for the union of a house with its surrounding scenery, once said, "If you would fix upon the best color for your house, turn up a stone, or pluck up a handful of grass by the roots, and see what is the color of the soil where the house is to stand, and let that be your choice." This rule was not probably intended to be exactly carried into general practice, but the feeling that prompted it was the same that we are endeavoring to illustrate—the necessity of a unity of color in the house and country about it.

We think, in the beginning, that the color of all buildings in the country should be of those *soft and quiet shades*, called neutral tints, such as fawn, drab, gray, brown, &c., and that all postive colors, such as white, yellow, red, blue, black, &c., should always be avoided; neutral tints being those drawn from nature, and harmonizing best with her, and positive colors being most discordant when introduced into rural scenery.

In the second place, wo would adapt the shade of color, as far as possible, to the expression, style, or character of the house itself. Thus, a large mansion may very properly receive a somewhat sober hue, expressive of dignity; while a country house, of moderate size, demands a lighter and more pleasant, but still quiet tone; and a small cottage should, we think, always have a cheerful and lively tint. Country houses, thickly surrounded by trees, should always be painted of a lighter shade than those standing exposed. And a new house, entirely unrelieved by foliage, as it is rendered conspicuous by the very nakedness of its position, should be painted several shades darker than the same building if placed in a well wooded site. *In proportion as a house is exposed to view, let its hue be darker, and where it is much concealed by foliage, a very light shade of color is to be preferred.*

Wordsworth remarks, in speaking of houses in the Lake country, that many persons who have heard white condemned, have erred by adopting a *cold slaty* color. The dulness and dimness of hue in some dark stones, produces an effect quite at variance with the cheerful expression which small houses should wear. "The flaring yellow," he adds, "runs into the opposite extreme, and is still more censurable. Upon the whole, the safest color, for general use, is something between a cream and a dust color.

This color, which Wordsworth recommends for general use, is the hue of the English freestone, called *Portland stone*—a *quiet fawn* color, to which we are strongly partial, and which harmonizes perhaps more completely with all situations in the country than any other that can be named. Next to this, we like a *warm gray*, that is, a drab mixed with a very little red and some yellow. *Browns* and *dark grays* are suitable for barns, stables, and outbuildings, which it is desirable to render inconspicuous—but for dwellings, unless very light shades of these latter colors are used, they are apt to give a dull and heavy effect in the country.*

A very slight admixture of a darker color is sufficient to remove the objections to white paint, by destroying the *glare of white*, the only color which reflects *all* the sun's rays. We would advise the use of soft shades, not much removed from white, for small cottages, which should not be painted of too dark a shade, which would give them an aspect of *gloom* in the place of *glare*. It is the more necessary to make this suggestion, since we have lately observed that some persons newly awakened to the bad effect of white, have rushed into the opposite extreme, and colored their country houses of such a sombre hue that they give a melancholy character to the whole neighborhood around them.

A species of monotony is also produced by using the same neutral tint for every part of the exterior of a country house. Now there are features, such as window facings, blinds, cornices, etc., which confer the same kind of expression on a house that the eyes, eyebrows, lips, &c. of a face, do upon the human countenance. To

* It is very difficult to convey any proper idea of shades of color by words. In our "*Cottage Residences*," we have attempted to do so by a plate showing some of the tints. We would suggest to persons wishing to select accurately, shades for their painter to copy, to go into a stationer's and examine a stock of tinted papers. A great variety of shades in agreeable neutral tints, will usually be found, and a selection once made, the color can be imitated without risk of failure.

paint the whole house plain drab, gives it very much the same dull and insipid effect that colorless features (white hair, pale eyebrows, lips, &c., &c.) do the face. A certain sprightliness is therefore always bestowed on a dwelling in a neutral tint, by painting the bolder projecting features of a different shade. The simplest practical rule that we can suggest for effecting this, in the most satisfactory and agreeable manner, is the following: Choose paint of some neutral tint that is quite satisfactory, and let the facings of the windows, cornices, &c., be painted several shades darker, of the same color. The blinds may either be a still darker shade than the facings, or else the darkest green.* This variety of shades will give a building a cheerful effect, when, if but one of the shades were employed, there would be a dulness and heaviness in the appearance of its exterior. Any one who will follow the principles we have suggested cannot, at least, fail to avoid the gross blunders in taste which most common house-painters and their employers have so long been in the habit of committing in the practice of painting country houses.

Uvedale Price justly remarked, that many people have a sort of *callus* over their organs of light, as others over those of hearing; and as the callous hearers feel nothing in music but kettle-drums and trombones, so the callous seers can only be moved by strong opposition of black and white, or by fiery reds. There are, we may add, many house-painters who appear to be equally benumbed to any delicate sensation in *shades* of color. They judge of the beauty of colors upon houses as they do in the raw pigment, and we verily believe would be more gratified to paint every thing chrome yellow, indigo blue, pure white, vermilion red, and the like, than with the most fitting and delicate mingling of shades to be found under the

* Thus, if the color of the house be that of Portland stone (a fawn shade), let the window casings, cornices, etc. be painted a light brown, the color of our common red freestone—and make the necessary shade by mixing the requisite quantity of brown with the color used in the body of the house. There is an excellent specimen of this effect in the exterior of the *Delavan House*, Albany. Very *dark* green is quite unobjectionable as a color for the venetian blinds, so much used in our country—as it is quite unobtrusive. Bright green is offensive to the eye, and vulgar and flashy in effect.

wide canopy of heaven. Fortunately *fashion*, a more powerful teacher of the multitude than the press or the schools, is now setting in the right direction. A few men of taste and judgment, in city and country, have set the example by casting off all connection with harsh colors. What a few leaders do at the first, from a nice sense of harmony in colors, the many will do afterwards, when they see the superior beauty of neutral tints, supported and enforced by the example of those who build and inhabit the most attractive and agreeable houses, and we trust, at no very distant time, one may have the pleasure of travelling over our whole country, without meeting with a single habitation of glaring and offensive color, but every where see something of harmony and beauty.

IX.

A SHORT CHAPTER ON COUNTRY CHURCHES.

January, 1851.

WHAT, among all the edifices that compose a country town or village, is that which the inhabitants should most love and reverence,—should most respect and admire among themselves, and should feel most pleasure in showing to a stranger?

We imagine the answer ready upon the lips of every one of our readers in the country, and rising at once to utterance, is—the VILLAGE CHURCH.

And yet, are our village churches winning and attractive in their exterior and interior? Is one drawn to admire them at first sight, by the beauty of their proportions, the expression of holy purpose which they embody, the feeling of harmony with GOD and man, which they suggest? Does one get to love the very stones of which they are composed, because they so completely belong to a building, which looks and is the home of Christian worship, and stands as the type of all that is firmest and deepest in our religious faith and affections?

Alas! we fear there are very few country churches in our land that exert this kind of spell,—a spell which grows out of making stone, and brick, and timber, obey the will of the living soul, and express a religious sentiment. Most persons, most committees, selectmen, vestrymen, and congregations, who have to do with the building of churches, appear indeed wholly to ignore the fact, that the form and feature of a building may be made to express religious, civil, domestic, or a dozen other feelings, as distinctly as the form and features of the human face;—and yet this is a fact as well known by all true architects, as that joy and sorrow, pleasure and pain, are capable of irradiating or darkening the countenance. Yes, and we do not say too much, when we add, that right expression in a building for religious purposes, has as much to do with awakening devotional feelings, and begetting an attachment in the heart, as the unmistakable signs of virtue and benevolence in our fellow-creatures, have in awakening kindred feeling in our own breasts.

We do not, of course, mean to say, that a beautiful rural church will make all the population about it devotional, any more than that sunshine will banish all gloom; but it is one of the influences that prepare the way for religious feeling, and which we are as unwise to neglect, as we should be to abjure the world and bury ourselves like the ancient troglodytes, in caves and caverns.

To speak out the truth boldly, would be to say that the ugliest church architecture in Christendom, is at this moment to be found in the country towns and villages of the United States. Doubtless, the hatred which originally existed in the minds of our puritan ancestors, against every thing that belonged to the Romish Church, including in one general sweep all beauty and all taste, along with all the superstitions and errors of what had become a corrupt system of religion, is a key to the bareness and baldness, and absence of all that is lovely to the eye in the primitive churches of New England—which are for the most part the type-churches of all America.

But, little by little, this ultra-puritanical spirit is wearing off. Men are not now so blinded by personal feeling against great spiritual wrongs, as to identify for ever, all that blessed boon of harmony, grace, proportion, symmetry and expression, which make what we call Beauty, with the vices, either real or supposed, of any particular creed. In short, as a people, our eyes are opening to the perception of influences that are good, healthful, and elevating to the soul, in all ages, and all countries—and we separate the vices of men from the laws of order and beauty, by which the universe is governed.

The first step which we have taken to show our emancipation from puritanism in architecture, is that of building our churches with *porticoes*, in a kind of shabby imitation of Greek temples. This has been the prevailing taste, if it is worthy of that name, of the Northern States, for the last fifteen or twenty years. The form of these churches is a parallelogram. A long row of windows, square or round-headed, and cut in two by a gallery on the inside; a clumsy portico of Doric or Ionic columns in front, and a cupola upon the top, (usually stuck in the only place where a cupola should never be—that is, directly over the pediment or portico)—such are the *chef d'œuvres* of ecclesiastical architecture, standing, in nine cases out of ten, as the rural churches of the country at large.

Now, *architecturally*, we ought not to consider these, *churches* at all. And by churches, we mean no narrow sectarian phrase—but a place where Christians worship God. Indeed, many of the congregations seem to have felt this, and contented themselves with calling them "meeting-houses." If they would go a step farther, and turn them into *town meeting-houses*—or at least would, in future, only build such edifices for town meetings, or other civil purposes, then the building and its purpose would be in good keeping, one with the other.

Not to appear presumptive and partial in our criticism, let us glance for a moment at the opposite purposes of the Grecian or classical, and the Gothic or pointed styles of architecture—as to what they really mean;—for our readers must not suppose that all architects are men who merely put together certain pretty lines and ornaments, to produce an agreeable effect and please the popular eye.

In these two styles, which have so taken root that they are employed at the present moment, all over Europe and America, there is something more than a mere conventional treatment of doors and windows; the application of columns in one case, and the introduction of pointed arches in the other. In other words, there is an intrinsic meaning or expression involved in each, which, not to understand, or vaguely to understand, is to be working blindly, or striving after something in the dark.

The leading idea of the Greek architecture, then, is in its horizontal lines—the unbroken level of its cornice, which is the "*level line of rationality.*" In this line, in the regular division of spaces, both of columns and windows, we find the elements of order, law, and human reason, fully and completely expressed. Hence, the fitness of classical architecture for the service of the state, for the town hall, the legislative assembly, the lecture room, for intellectual or scientific debate, and in short, for all civil purposes where the reason of man is supreme. So, on the other hand, the leading idea of Gothic architecture is found in its upward lines—its aspiring tendencies. No weight of long cornices, or flat ceilings, can keep it down; upward, higher and higher, it soars, lifting every thing, even heavy, ponderous stones, poising them in the air in vaulted ceilings, or piling them upwards towards Heaven, in spires, and steeples, and towers, that, in the great cathedrals, almost seem to pierce the sky. It must be a dull soul that does not catch and feel something of this upward tendency in the vaulted aisles, and high, open, pointed roofs of the interior of a fine Gothic church, as well as its subdued and mellow light, and its suggestive and beautiful forms: forms, too, that are rendered more touching by their associations with Christian worship in so many ages, not, like the Greek edifices, by associations with heathen devotees.

Granting that the Gothic cathedral expresses, in its lofty, aspiring lines, the spirit of that true faith and devotion which leads us to look upward, is it possible, in the narrow compass of a village church which costs but a few hundred, or at most, a few thousand dollars, to preserve this idea?

We answer, yes. A drop of water is not the ocean, but it is still a type of the infinite; and a few words of wisdom may not penetrate the understanding so deeply as a great volume by a master of the human heart, but they may work miracles, if fitly spoken. For it is not the magnitude of things that is the measure of their excellence and power; and there is space enough for the architect to awaken devotional feelings, and lead the soul upward, so far as material form can aid in doing this, though in a less degree, in the little chapel that is to hold a few hundred, as in the mighty minster where thousands may assemble.

And the *cost* too, shall not be greater; that is, if a substantial building is to be erected, and not a flimsy frame of boards and plaster. Indeed, we could quote numberless instances where the sums expended in classical buildings, of false proportions but costly execution,* which can never raise other than emotions of pride in the human heart, would have built beautiful rural churches, which every inhabitant of the town where they chanced to stand, would remember with feelings of respect and affection, to the end of all time.

And in truth, we would not desire to make the country church other than simple, truthful, and harmonious. We would avoid all pretensions to elaborate architectural ornament; we would depend upon the right proportions, forms, outlines, and the true expression Above all, we would have the country church rural and expressive, by placing it in a spot of green lawn, surrounding it with our beautiful natural shade trees, and decorating its *walls* (for no church built in any but the newest settlements, where means are utterly wanting, should be built of so perishable a material as wood)—with climbing plants—the ivy, or where that would not thrive, the Virginia creeper. And so we would make the country church, in its very forms and outlines, its walls and the vines that enwreath them, its shady green and the elms that overhang it, as well as in the lessons of goodness and piety that emanate from its pulpit, something to become a part of the affections, and touch and better the hearts of the whole country about it.

* We have seen with pain, lately, one of those great temple churches erected in a country town on the Hudson, at a cost of $20,000. It looks outside and inside, no more like a church, than does the Custom House. And yet this sum would have built the most perfect of devotional edifices for that congregation.

Plan of a School House.

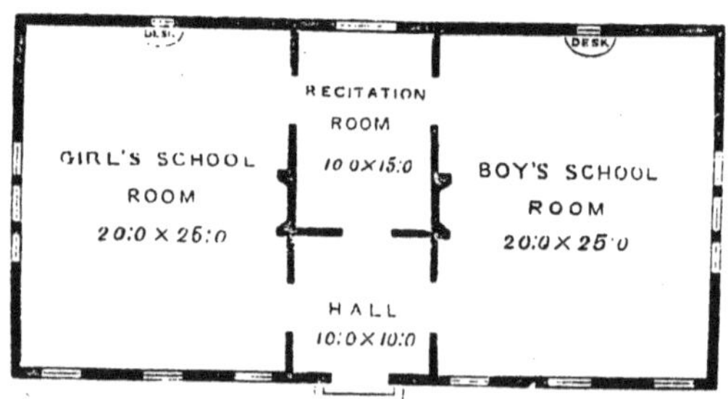

X.

A CHAPTER ON SCHOOL-HOUSES.

March, 1848.

IF there is any one thing on which the usefulness, the true greatness, and the permanence, of a free government depends more than another, it is Education.

Hence, it is not without satisfaction that we look upon our free schools, whose rudimentary education is afforded to so many at very small rates, or often entirely without charge. It is not without pleasure that we perceive new colleges springing up, as large cities multiply, and the population increases; it is most gratifying to see, in the older portions of the country, men of wealth and intelligence founding new professorships, and bequeathing the best of legacies to their successors—the means of acquiring knowledge easily and cheaply.

There is much to keep alive this train of thought, in the very means of acquiring education. The fertile invention of our age, and its teachers, seems to be especially devoted to removing all possible obstacles, and throwing all possible light on the once difficult and toilsome paths to the temple of science. Class-books, text-books, essays and treatises, written in clear terms, and illustrated with a more captivating style, rob learning of half is terrors to the beginner, and fairly allure those who do not come willingly into the charmed circle of educated minds.

All this is truly excellent. This broad basis of education, which is laid in the hearts of our people, which the States publicly maintain, which private munificence fosters, to which even men in foreign lands delight to contribute, must be cherished by every American as the key-stone of his liberty; it must be rendered still firmer and broader, to meet the growing strength and the growing dangers of the country; it must be adapted to the character of our people,—different and distinct as we believe that character to be from that of all other nations; and, above all, without teaching creeds or doctrines, it must be pervaded by profound and genuine moral feeling, more central, and more vital, than that of any narrow sectarianism.

Well, will any of our readers believe that this train of thought has grown out of our having just seen a most shabby and forbidding-looking school-house! Truly, yes! and, as in an old picture of Rembrandt's, the stronger the lights, the darker also the shadows, we are obliged to confess that, with so much to be proud of in our system of common schools, there is nothing so beggarly and disgraceful as the *externals* of our country school-houses themselves.

A traveller through the Union, is at once struck with the general appearance of comfort in the houses of our rural population. But, by the way-side, here and there, he observes a small, one story edifice, built of wood or stone in the most meagre mode,—dingy in aspect, and dilapidated in condition. It is placed in the barest and most forbidding site in the whole country round. If you fail to recognize it by these marks, you can easily make it out by the broken fences, and tumble-down stone walls that surround it; by the absence of all trees, and by the general expression of melancholy, as if every lover of good order and beauty in the neighborhood had abandoned it to the genius of desolation.

This condition of things is almost universal. It must, therefore, be founded in some deep-rooted prejudices, or some mistaken idea of the importance of the subject.

That the wretched condition of the country school-houses is owing to a general license of what the phrenologists would call the organs of destructiveness in boys, we are well aware. But it is in giving this license that the great error of teachers and superintendents of schools lies. There is also, God be thanked, a principle of order and a love of beauty implanted in every human mind; and the degree to which it may be cultivated in children is quite unknown to those who start leaving such a principle wholly out of sight. To be convinced of this, it is only necessary to inquire, and it will be found that in the homes of many of the pupils of the forlorn-looking school-house, the utmost propriety, order, and method reigns. Nay, even *within* the school-house itself, "heaven's first law" is obeyed, perhaps to the very letter. But to look at the exterior, it would appear that the "abbot of unreason," and not the "school-master," was "abroad." The truth seems to be simply this. The school-master does not himself appreciate the beautiful in rural objects; and, content with doing what he conceives his duty to the heads of his pupils, while they are within the school-house, he abandons its externals to the juvenile "reign of terror."

Nothing is so convincing on these subjects as example. We saw, last summer, in Dutchess County, New-York, a *free school*, erected to fulfil more perfectly the mission of an ordinary district school-house, which had been built by a gentleman, whose taste and benevolence seem, like sunshine, to warm and irradiate his whole neighborhood. It was a building simple enough, after all. A projecting roof, with slightly ornamented brackets, a pretty porch, neat chimney tops; its color a soft neutral tint; these were its leading features. But a single glance at it told, in a moment, that the *evil spirit had been cast out*, and the good spirit had taken its place. The utmost neatness and cleanliness appeared in every part. Beautiful vines and creepers climbed upon the walls, and hung in festoons over the windows. Groups of trees, and flowering shrubs, were thriving within its inclosure. A bit of neat lawn surrounded the building, and was evidently an object of care and respect with the pupils themselves. Altogether, it was a picture of a common district school which, compared with that we before described, and which one every day sees, was a foretaste of the millenium. If any stubborn pedagogue doubts it, let him come to us, and we will direct him on a pilgrimage to this Mecca, which is only eight miles from us.

It appears to us that a great error has taken deep root in the minds of most parents and teachers, regarding the influence of order and beauty on the youthful mind. Ah! it is precisely at that age—in youth—when the heart is most sensitive, when the feelings are more keenly alive than at any other; it is precisely at that age that the soul opens itself most to visions of beauty—that the least measure of harmony—the most simple notions of the graceful and symmetrical—fill it with joy. The few yards square, in which the child is permitted to realize his own vague ideal of a garden—does it not fill his heart more completely than the great Versailles of monarchs that of the mature man? Do we not forever remember with what transport of delight we have first seen the grand old trees, the beautiful garden, the favorite landscape, from the hill-top of our childhood? What after pictures, however grand—however magnificent—however perfect to the more educated eye, are ever able to efface these first daguerreotypes, printed on the fresh pages of the youthful soul?

It is rather because teachers misunderstand the nature of man, and more especially of boyhood, that we see so much to deplore in the exteriors of the houses in which they are taught. They forget, that in human natures there are not only intellects to acquire knowledge, but also hearts to feel and senses to enjoy life. They forget that all culture is one-sided and short-sighted, which does not aim to develop human nature completely, fully.

We have an ideal picture, that refreshes our imagination, of common school-houses, scattered all over our wide country; not wild bedlams, which seem to the traveller plague-spots on the fair country landscape; but little nests of verdure and beauty; embryo arcadias, that beget tastes for lovely gardens, neat houses, and well cultivated lands; spots of recreation, that are play-grounds for the memory, for many long years after all else of childhood is crowded out and effaced for ever.

Let some of our readers who have an influence in this matter, try to work a little reform in their own districts. Suppose, in the first place, the school-house itself is rendered agreeable to the eye. Suppose a miniature park of elms and maples is planted about it. Suppose a strip of ground is set apart for little gardens, to be given as premiums to the successful pupils; and which they are only to hold so long as both they and their gardens are kept up to the topmost standard. Suppose the trees are considered to be the property and under the protection of certain chiefs of the classes. And, suppose that, besides all this little arrangement for the growth of a love of order and beauty in the youthful heart and mind, there is an ample play-ground provided for the expenditure of youthful activity; where wild sports and gymnastics may be indulged to the utmost delight of their senses, and the utmost benefit of their constitutions. Is this Utopian? Does any wise reader think it is not worthier of the consideration of the State, than fifty of the projects which will this year come before it?

For ourselves, we have perfect faith in the future. We believe in the millennium of schoolboys. And we believe that our countrymen, as soon as they comprehend fully the value and importance of external objects on the mind—on the heart—on the manners—on the life of all human beings—will not be slow to concentrate all beautiful, good, and ennobling influences around that primary nursery of the intellect and sensations—the district school.

There is a strong illustration of our general acknowledgment of this influence of the beautiful, to be found, at the present moment, in this country more than in any other. We allude to our *Rural Cemeteries*, and our *Insane Asylums*. It is somewhat curious, but not less true, that no country-seats, no parks or pleasure-grounds, in America, are laid out with more care, adorned with more taste, filled with more lovely flowers, shrubs and trees, than some of our principal cemeteries and asylums. Is it not surprising that only when touched with sorrow, we, as a people, most seek the gentle and refining influence of nature? Ah! many a man, whose life was hard and stony, reposes, *after death*, in those cemeteries, beneath a turf covered with violets and roses; but for him, it is too late! Many a fine intellect, overtasked and wrecked in the too ardent pursuit of power or wealth, is fondly courted back to reason, and more quiet joys, by the dusky, cool walks of the asylum, where peace and rural beauty do not refuse to dwell. But, alas, too often their mission is fruitless!

How much better, to distil these "gentle dews of heaven" into the *young* heart, to implant, even in the schoolboy days, a love of trees; of flowers; of gardens; of the country; of home;—of all those pure and simple pleasures, which are, in the after life—even if they exist only in the memory—a blessed panacea, amid the dryness and dustiness of so many of the paths of life—politics—commerce—the professions—and all other busy, engrossing occupations, whose cares become, else, almost a fever in the veins of our ardent, enterprising people.

ORNAMENTAL ICE HOUSE ABOVE GROUND.

ORNAMENTAL ICE HOUSE ABOVE GROUND.

XI.

HOW TO BUILD ICE-HOUSES.

December, 1846.

THE ICE-HOUSE and the HOT-HOUSE, types of Lapland and the Tropics, are two contrivances which civilization has invented for the comfort or luxury of man. A native of the Sandwich Islands, who lives, as he conceives, in the most delicious climate in the world, and sleeps away the best part of his life in that happy state which the pleasure-loving Italians call "*dolce far niente*," (sweet do nothing)—smiles and shudders when he hears of a region where his familiar trees must be kept in glass houses, and the water turns, now and then, into solid, cold crystal!

Yet, if happiness, as some philosophers have affirmed, consists in a *variety* of sensations, we denizens of temperate latitudes have greatly the advantage of him. What surprise and pleasure awaits the Sandwich Islander, for example, like that we experience on entering a spacious hot-house, redolent of blossoms and of perfume, in mid-winter, or on refreshing our exhausted frames with one of "Thomson and Weller's" vanilla creams, or that agreeable compound of the vintage of Xeres, pounded ice, etc., that bears the humble name of "sherry-cobbler;" but which, having been introduced lately from this country into London, along with our "American ice," has sent into positive ecstasies all those of the great metropolis, who depend upon their *throats* for sensations.

Our business at the present moment, is with the *ice-house*,—as a necessary and most useful appendage to a country residence. Abroad, both the ice-house and the hot-house are portions of the wealthy man's establishment solely. But in this country, the ice-house forms part of the comforts of every substantial farmer. It is not for the sake of ice-creams and cooling liquors, that it has its great value in his eyes, but as a means of preserving and keeping in the finest condition, during the summer, his meat, his butter, his delicate fruit, and, in short, his whole perishable stock of provisions. Half a dozen correspondents, lately, have asked us for some advice on the construction of an ice-house, and we now cheerfully offer all the information in our possession.

To build an ice-house in *sandy or gravelly soils*, is one of the easiest things in the world. The drainage there is perfect, the dry and porous soil is of itself a sufficiently good *non-conductor*. All that it is necessary to do, is to dig a pit, twelve feet square, and as many deep, line it with logs or joists faced with boards, cover it with a simple roof on a level with the ground, and fill it with ice. Such ice-houses, built with trifling cost, and entirely answering the purpose of affording ample supply for a large family, are common in various parts of the country.

Fig. 8. The common Ice-house below ground.

But it often happens that one's residence is upon a strong loamy or clayey soil, based upon clay or slate, or, at least, rocky in its substratum. Such a soil is retentive of moisture, and even though it be well drained, the common ice-house, just described, will not preserve ice half through the summer in a locality of that kind. The clayey or rocky soil is always damp—it is always an excellent conductor, and the ice melts in it in spite of all the usual precautions.

Something more than the common ice-house is therefore needed in all such soils. "How shall it be built?" is the question which has been frequently put to us lately.

To enable us to answer this question in the most satisfactory manner, we addressed ourselves to Mr. N. J. Wyeth of Cambridge, Mass., whose practical information on this subject is probably fuller and more complete than that of any other person in the country, he, for many years, having had the construction and management of the enormous commercial ice-houses, near Boston—the largest and most perfect known.*

We desired Mr. Wyeth's hints for building an ice-house for family use, both above ground and below ground.

In the beginning we should remark that the great ice-houses of our ice companies are usually built above ground; and Mr. Wyeth in his letter to us remarks, "*we now never build or use an ice-house under ground;* it never preserves ice as well as those built above ground, and costs much more. I, however, send you directions for the construction of both kinds, with slight sketches in explanation." The following are Mr. Wyeth's directions for building:

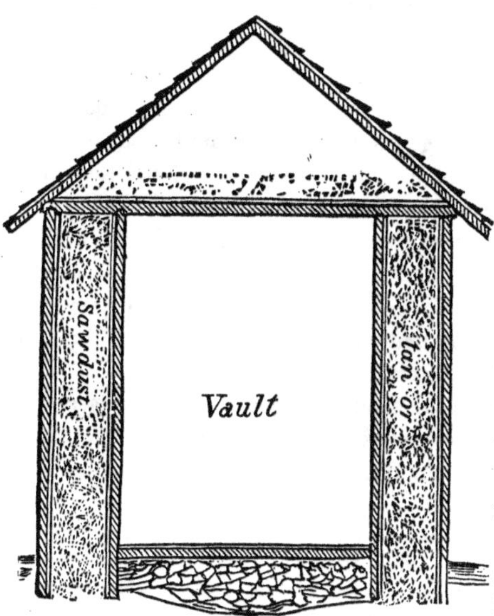

Fig 4. Section of the Ice-house above ground.

"1*st. An ice-house above ground.* An ice-house above ground should be built upon

* Few of our readers are aware of the magnitude which the business of supplying foreign countries with ice has attained in New England. Millions of dollars worth have been shipped from the port of Boston alone, within

the plan of having a double partition, with the hollow space between filled with some non-conducting substance.

"In the first place, the frame of the sides should be formed of two ranges of upright *joists*, 6 by 4 inches; the lower ends of the joists should be put into the ground *without any sill*, which is apt to let air pass through. These two ranges of joists should be about two feet and one-half apart at the bottom, and two feet deep at the top. At the top these joists should be mortised into the cross-beams, which are to support the upper floor. The joists in the two ranges should be placed each opposite another. They should then be lined or faced on one side, with rough boarding, which need not be very tight. This boarding should be nailed to those edges of the joists nearest each other, so that one range of joists shall be outside the building, and the other inside the ice-room or vault. (Fig. 5.)

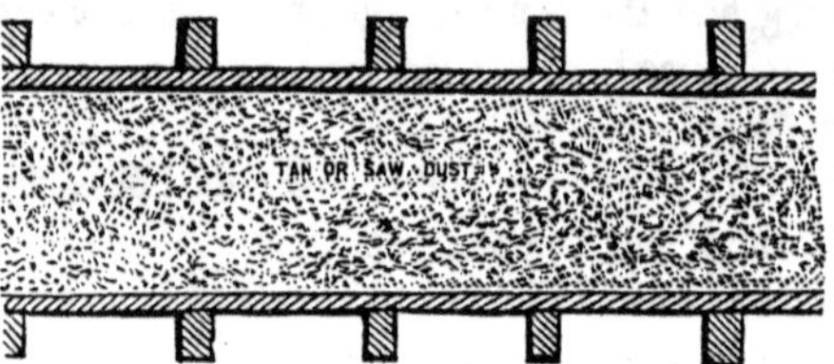

FIG. 5. Manner of nailing the boards to the joists.

"The space between these boardings or partitions should be filled with wet tan, or sawdust, whichever is cheapest or most easily obtained. The reason for using *wet* material for filling this space is that during winter it freezes, and until it is again thawed, little or no ice will melt at the sides of the vault.

"The bottom of the ice vault should be filled about a foot deep with small blocks of wood; these are levelled and covered with wood shavings, over which a strong plank floor should be laid to receive the ice.

the last eight years; and the East and West Indies, China, England, and the South, are constantly supplied with ice from that neighborhood. *Wenham Lake* is now as well known in London for its ice, as Westphalia for its hams. This enterprise owes its success mainly to the energy of Frederick Tudor, Esq., of Boston. The ice-houses of this gentleman, built, we believe, chiefly by Mr. Wyeth, are on a more gigantic scale than any others in the world. An extra whole year's supply is laid up in advance, to guard against the accident of a mild winter, and a railroad several miles in length, built expressly for the purpose, conveys the ice to the ships lying in the harbor.

"Upon the beams above the vault, a pretty tight floor should also be laid, and this floor should be covered several inches deep with dry tan or sawdust. The roof of the ice-house should have considerable pitch, and the space between the upper floor and the roof should be ventilated by a lattice window at each gable end or something equivalent, to pass out the warm air which will accumulate beneath the roof. A door must be provided in the side of the vault to fill and discharge it; but it should always be closed up higher than the ice, and when not in use should be kept closed altogether.

"2*d*. *An Ice-house below ground.* This is only thoroughly made by building up the sides of the pit with a good brick or stone wall, lain in mortar. Inside of this wall set joists, and build a light wooden partition against which to place the ice. A good floor should be laid over the vault as just described, and this should also be covered with dry tan or sawdust. In this floor the door must be cut to give access to the ice.

"As regards the bottom of the vault, the floor, the lattice windows in the gables for ventilation, etc., the same remarks will apply that have just been given for the ice-house above ground, with the addition that in one of the *gables*, in this case, must be the door for filling the house with ice.

"If the ground where ice-houses of either kind are built, is not porous enough to let the melted ice drain away, then there should be a waste pipe to carry it off, which should be slightly bent, so as always to retain enough water in it to prevent the passage of air upwards into the ice-house."

These plain and concise hints by Mr. Wyeth, will enable our readers, who have failed in building ice-houses in the common way, to remedy their defects, or to construct new ones on the improved plan just given. The main points, it will be seen, are, to place a sufficient non-conducting medium of tan or sawdust, if above ground, or of wall and wood partition, if below ground, to prevent the action of the air, or the damp soil, on the body of ice inclosed in the vault.

Mr. Wyeth has not told us how large the dimensions of an ice-house built in either of these modes should be to provide for the use of an ordinary family through a season; but we will add as to this point, that a cube of twelve or fourteen feet—that is, a house the vault of which will measure about twelve to fourteen feet "in the clear," every way, will be quite large enough, if properly constructed. An ice-house, the vault of which is a cube of twelve feet, will hold about fifty tons of ice. One of this size, near Boston, filled last January, is still half full of ice, after supplying the wants of a family all the season.

In the ice-house above ground, the opening being in the side, it will be best to have a double door, one in each partition, opposite each other. The outer one may be entire, but the inner one should be in two or three parts. The upper part may be opened first, so that only so much of the ice may be exposed at once, as is necessary to reach the topmost layers.

Fig. 6. Double Door of the Ice-house.

An ice-house below ground is so inconspicuous on object, that it is easily kept out of sight, and little or no regard may be paid to its exterior appearance. On the contrary, an ice-house above ground is a building of sufficient size to attract the eye, and in many country residences, therefore, it will be desirable to give its exterior a neat or tasteful air.

It will frequently be found, however, that an *ice-house above ground* may be very conveniently constructed under the same roof as the wood-house, tool-house, or some other necessary out-building, following all the necessary details just laid down, and continuing one roof and the same kind of exterior over the whole building.

In places of a more ornamental character, where it is desirable to place the elevated ice-house at no great distance from the dwelling, it should, of course, take something of an ornamental or picturesque character.

In figures 1 and 2, are shown two designs for ice-houses above ground, in picturesque styles. Figure 1 is built in a circular form, and the roof neatly thatched. The outside of this ice-house is roughly weather-boarded, and then ornamented with rustic work, or covered with strips of bark neatly nailed on in panels or devices. Two small gables with blinds ventilate the space under the roof.

Fig. 2 is a square ice-house, with a roof projecting three or four feet, and covered with shingles, the lower ends of which are cut so as to form diamond patterns when laid on the roof. The rustic brackets which support this roof, and the rustic columns of the other design, will be rendered more durable by stripping the bark off, and thoroughly painting them some neutral or wood tint.*

* The projecting roof will assist in keeping the building cool. In filling the house, back up the wagon loaded with ice, and slide the squares of ice to their places on a plank serving as an inclined plane.

XII.

THE FAVORITE POISON OF AMERICA.

November, 1850.

ONE of the most complete and salutary reforms ever, perhaps, made in any country, is the temperance reform of the last fifteen years in the United States. Every body, familiar with our manners and customs fifteen or twenty years ago, very well knows that though our people were never positively intemperate, yet ardent spirits were, at that time, in almost as constant daily use, both in public and private life, as tea and coffee are now; while at the present moment, they are seldom or never offered as a means of civility or refreshment—at least in the older States. The result of this higher civilization or temperance, as one may please to call it, is that a large amount of vice and crime have disappeared from amidst the laboring classes, while the physical as well as moral condition of those who labor too little to be able to bear intoxicating drinks, is very much improved.

We have taken this consolatory glance at this great and salutary reform of the habits of a whole country, because we need something to fortify our faith in the possibility of new reforms; for our countrymen have, within the last ten years, discovered a new poison, which is used wholesale, both in public and private, all over the country, till the national health and constitution are absolutely impaired by it.

"A national poison? Do you mean slavery, socialism, abolition, mormonism?" Nothing of the sort. "Then, perhaps, tobacco, patent medicines, or coffee?" Worse than these. It is a foe more insidious than these; for, at least, one very well knows what one is about when he takes copious draughts of such things. Whatever his own convictions may be, he knows that some of his fellow creatures consider them deleterious.

But the national poison is not thought dangerous. Far from it. On the contrary, it is made almost synonymous with domestic comfort. Old and young, rich and poor, drink it in with avidity, and without shame. The most tender and delicate women and children are fondest of it, and become so accustomed to it, that they gradually abandon the delights of bright sunshine, and the pure air of heaven, to take it in large draughts. What matter if their cheeks become as pale as the ghosts of Ossian; if their spirits forsake them, and they become listless and languid! Are they not well housed and *comfortable?* Are not their lives virtuous, and their affairs prosperous? Alas, yes! But they are not the less guilty of poisoning themselves daily, though perhaps unconscious of it all the time.

The national poison that we allude to, is nothing less than the vitiated air of *close stoves*, and the unventilated apartments which accompany them!

"Stoves"—exclaim a thousand readers in the same breath—"stoves poisonous? Nonsense! they are perfectly healthy, as well as the most economical, convenient, labor-saving, useful, and indispensable things in the world. Besides, are they not real Yankee inventions? In what country but this is there such an endless variety of stoves—cooking stoves, hall stoves, parlor stoves, air-tight stoves, cylinders, salamanders, etc.? Why, it is absolutely the national invention—this stove—the most useful result of universal Yankee ingenuity."

We grant it all, good friends and readers; but must also have our opinion—our calmly considered and carefully matured opinion—which is nothing more nor less than this, that stoves—as now used—are the national curse; the secret poisoners of that blessed air, bestowed by kind Providence as an elixir of life,—giving us new vigor and fresh energy at every inspiration; and we, ungrateful beings, as if the pure breath of heaven were not fit for us, we reject it, and breathe instead—what?—the air which passes over a surface of hot iron, and becomes loaded with all the vapor of arsenic and sulphur, which that metal, highly heated, constantly gives off!

If in the heart of large cities—where there is a large population crowded together, with scanty means of subsistence—one saw a few persons driven by necessity into warming their small apartments by little close stoves of iron, liable to be heated red-hot, and thereby to absolutely destroy the purity of the air, one would not be so much astonished at the result, because it is so difficult to preserve the poorest class from suffering, in some way or other, in great cities. But it is by no means only in the houses of those who have slender means of subsistence, that this is the case. It is safe to say that nine-tenths of all the houses in the northern States, whether belonging to rich or poor, are entirely unventilated, and heated at the present moment by close stoves!

It is absolutely a matter of *preference* on the part of thousands, with whom the trifling difference between one mode of heating and another is of no account. Even in the midst of the country, where there is still wood in abundance, the farmer will sell that wood and buy coal, so that he may have a little *demon*—alias a black, cheerless close stove—in the place of that genuine, hospitable, wholesome *friend* and comforter, an open wood fireplace.

And in order not to leave one unconverted soul in the wilderness, the stove inventors have lately brought out "a new article," for forest countries, where coal is not to be had either for love or barter—an "air-tight stove for burning wood." The seductive, convenient, monstrous thing! "It consumes one-fifth of the fuel which was needed by the open chimney—is so neat and clean, makes no dust, and gives no trouble." All quite true, dear, considerate housewife—all quite true; but that very stove causes your husband to pay twice its savings to the family doctor before two winters are past, and gives you thrice as much trouble in nursing the sick in your family, as you formerly spent in taking care of the fire in your chimney corner,—besides depriving you of the most delightful of all household occupations.

Our countrymen generally have a vast deal of national pride, and national sensitiveness, and we honor them for it. It is the warp and woof, out of which the stuff of national improvement is woven,

When a nation has become quite indifferent as to what it has done, or can do, then there is nothing left but for its prophets to utter lamentations over it.

Now there is a curious but indisputable fact (somebody *must* say it), touching our present condition and appearance, as a nation of men, women and children, in which we Americans compare most unfavorably with the people of Europe, and especially with those of northern Europe—England and France, for example. It is neither in religion or morality, law or liberty. In these great essentials, every American feels that his country is the birthplace of a larger number of robust and healthy souls than any other. But in the bodily condition, the *signs of physical health*, and all that constitutes the outward aspect of the men and women of the United States, our countrymen, and especially countrywomen, compare most unfavorably with all but the absolutely starving classes, on the other side of the Atlantic. So completely is this the fact, that, though we are unconscious of it at home, the first thing (especially of late years) which strikes an American, returning from abroad, is the pale and sickly countenances of his friends, acquaintances, and almost every one he meets in the streets of large towns,—every other man looking as if he had lately recovered from a fit of illness. The men look so pale and the women so delicate, that his eye, accustomed to the higher hues of health, and the more vigorous physical condition of transatlantic men and women, scarcely credits the assertion of old acquaintances, when they assure him that they were "never better in their lives."

With this sort of impression weighing disagreeably on our mind, on returning from Europe lately, we fancied it worth our while to plunge two hundred or three hundred miles into the interior of the State of New-York. It would be pleasant, we thought, to see, not only the rich forest scenery opened by the new railroad to Lake Erie, but also (for we felt confident they were there) some good, hearty, fresh-looking lads and lasses among the farmers' sons and daughters.

We were for the most part disappointed. Certainly the men, especially the young men, who live mostly in the open air, are healthy and robust. But the daughters of the farmers—they are as delicate and pale as lilies of the valley, or fine ladies of the Fifth Avenue. If one catches a glimpse of a rose in their cheeks, it is the pale rose of the hot-house, and not the fresh glow of the garden damask. Alas, we soon discovered the reason. They, too, live for seven months of the year in unventilated rooms, heated by close stoves! The fireplaces are closed up, and ruddy complexions have vanished with them. Occasionally, indeed, one meets with an exception; some bright-eyed, young, rustic Hebe, whose rosy cheeks and round, elastic figure would make you believe that the world has not all grown "delicate;" and if you inquire, you will learn, probably, that she is one of those whose natural spirits force them out continually, in the open air, so that she has, as yet, in that way escaped any considerable doses of the national poison.

Now that we are fairly afloat on this dangerous sea, we must unburthen our heart sufficiently to say, that neither in England nor France does one meet with so much beauty—certainly not, so far as charming eyes and expressive faces go towards constituting beauty—as in America. But alas, on the other hand, as compared with the elastic figures and healthful frames abroad, American beauty is as evanescent as a dissolving view, contrasting with a real and living landscape. What is with us a sweet dream, from sixteen to twenty-five, is there a permanent reality till forty-five or fifty.

We should think it might be a matter of *climate*, were it not that we saw, as the most common thing, even finer complexions in France—yes, in the heart of Paris, and especially among the peasantry, who are almost wholly in the open air—than in England.

And what, then, is the mystery of fine physical health, which is so much better understood in the old world than the new?

The first transatlantic secret of health, is a much longer time passed daily in the open air, by all classes of people; the second, the better modes of heating and ventilating the rooms in which they live.

Regular daily exercise in the open air, both as a duty and a pleasure, is something looked upon in a very different light on the two different sides of the Atlantic. On this side of the water, if a person—say a professional man, or a merchant—is seen regularly devoting a certain portion of the day to exercise, and the preservation of his bodily powers, he is looked upon as a valetudinarian,—

an invalid, who is *obliged* to take care of himself, poor soul! and his friends daily meet him with sympathizing looks, hoping he "feels better," etc. As for ladies, if there is not some *object* in taking a walk, they look upon it as the most stupid and unmeaning thing in the world.

On the other side of the water, a person who should neglect the pleasure of breathing the free air for a couple of hours, daily, or should shun the duty of exercise, is suspected of slight lunacy; and ladies who should prefer continually to devote their leisure to the solace of luxurious cushions, rather than an exhilarating ride or walk, are thought a little *tête montée*. What, in short, is looked upon as a virtue there, is only regarded as a matter of fancy here. Hence, an American generally shivers, in an air that is only grateful and bracing to an Englishman, and looks blue in Paris, in weather when the Parisians sit with the casement windows of their saloons wide open. Yet it is, undoubtedly, all a matter of habit; and we Yankees, (we mean those of us not forced to "rough it,") with the toughest natural constitutions in the world, nurse ourselves, as a people, into the least robust and most susceptible *physiques* in existence.

So much for the habit of exercise in the open air. Now let us look at our mode of warming and ventilating our dwellings; for it is here that the national poison is engendered, and here that the ghostly expression is begotten.

However healthy a person may be, he can neither *look* healthy nor remain in sound health long, if he is in the habit of breathing impure air. As sound health depends upon *pure blood*, and there can be no pure blood in one's veins if it is not repurified continually by the action of pure air upon it, through the agency of the lungs (the whole purpose of breathing being to purify and vitalize the blood), it follows, that if a nation of people *will*, from choice, live in badly ventilated rooms, full of impure air, they must become pale and sallow in complexions. It may not largely affect the health of the *men*, who are more or less called into the open air by their avocations, but the health of women (*ergo* the constitutions of children), and all those who are confined to rooms or offices heated in this way, must gradually give way under the influence of the poison. Hence, the delicacy of thousands and tens of thousands of the sex in America.

"And how can you satisfy me," asks some blind lover of stoves, "that the air of a room heated by a close stove is deleterious?" Very easily indeed, if you will listen to a few words of reason.

It is well established that a healthy man must have about a pint of air at a breath; that he breathes above a thousand times in an hour; and that, as a matter beyond dispute, he requires about *fifty-seven hogsheads* of air in twenty four hours.

Besides this, it is equally well settled, that as common air consists of a mixture of two gases, one healthy (oxygen), and the other unhealthy (nitrogen), the air we have once breathed, having, by passing through the lungs, been deprived of the most healthful gas, is little less than unmixed poison (nitrogen).

Now, a room warmed by an open fireplace or grate, is necessarily more or less ventilated, by the very process of combustion going on; because, as a good deal of the air of the room goes up the chimney, besides the smoke and vapor of the fire, a corresponding amount of fresh air comes in at the windows and door crevices to supply its place. The room, in other words, is tolerably well supplied with fresh air for breathing.

But let us take the case of a room heated by a close stove. The chimney is stopped up, to begin with. The room is shut up. The windows are made pretty tight to keep out the cold; and as there is very little air carried out of the room by the stove-pipe, (the stove is perhaps on the air-tight principle,—that is, it requires the minimum amount of air,) there is little fresh air coming in through the crevices to supply any vacuum. Suppose the room holds 300 hogsheads of air. If a single person requires 57 hogsheads of fresh air per day, it would last four persons but about twenty-four hours, and the stove would require half as much more. But, as a man renders noxious as much again air as he expires from his lungs, it actually happens that in four or five hours all the air in this room has been either breathed over, or is so mixed with the impure air which has been breathed over, that it is all thoroughly poisoned, and unfit for *healthful* respiration. A person with his senses unblunted, has only to go into an ordinary unventilated room, heated by a stove, to perceive at once, by the effect on the lungs, how dead, stifled, and destitute of all elasticity the air is.

And this is the air which four-fifths of our countrymen and countrywomen breathe in their homes,—not from necessity, but from choice.*

This is the air which those who travel by hundreds of thousands in our railroad cars, closed up in winter, and heated with close stoves, breathe for hours—or often entire days.†

This is the air which fills the cabins of closely packed steamboats, always heated by large stoves, and only half ventilated; the air breathed by countless numbers—both waking or sleeping.

This is the air—no, this is even salubrious compared with the air—that is breathed by hundreds and thousands in almost all our crowded lecture-rooms, concert-rooms, public halls, and private assemblies, all over the country. They are nearly all heated by stoves or furnaces, with very imperfect ventilation, or no ventilation at all.

Is it too much to call it the national poison, this continual atmosphere of close stoves, which, whether travelling or at home, we Americans are content to breathe, as if it were the air of Paradise?

We very well know that we have a great many readers who abominate stoves, and whose houses are warmed and ventilated in an excellent manner. But they constitute no appreciable fraction of the vast portion of our countrymen who love stoves—fill their houses with them—are ignorant of their evils, and think ventilation and fresh air physiological chimeras, which may be left to the speculations of doctors and learned men.

* We have said that the present generation of stove-reared farmers' daughters are pale and delicate in appearance. We may add that the most healthy and blooming looking American women, are those of certain families where exercise, and fresh air, and ventilation, are matters of conscience and duty here as in Europe.

† Why the ingenuity of clever Yankees has not been directed to warming railroad cars (by means of steam conveyed through metal tubes, running under the floor, and connected with flexible coupling pipes,) we cannot well understand. It would be at once cheaper than the present mode, (since waste steam could be used,) and far more wholesome. Railroad cars have, it is true, ventilators at the top for the escape of foul air, but no apertures in the floor for the inlet of fresh air! It is like emptying a barrel without a vent.

And so, every other face that one meets in America, has a ghostly paleness about it, that would make a European stare.*

What is to be done? "Americans will have stoves." They suit the country, especially the new country; they are cheap, labor-saving, clean. If the more enlightened and better informed throw them aside, the great bulk of the people will not. Stoves are, we are told, in short, essentially democratic and national.

We answer, let us *ventilate our rooms*, and learn to live more in the open air. If our countrymen will take poison in, with every breath which they inhale in their houses and all their public gatherings, let them *dilute it* largely, and they may escape from a part at least of the evils of taking it in such strong doses.

We have not space here to show in detail the best modes of ventilating now in use. But they may be found described in several works, especially devoted to the subject, published lately. In our volume on COUNTRY HOUSES, we have briefly shown, not only the principles of warming rooms, but the most simple and complete modes of ventilation,—from Arnott's chimney valve, which may for a small cost be easily placed in the chimney flue of any room, to Emerson's more complete apparatus, by which the largest apartments, or every room in the largest house, may be warmed and ventilated at the same time, in the most complete and satisfactory manner.

We assure our readers that we are the more in earnest upon this subject, because they are so apathetic. As they would shake a man about falling into that state of delightful numbness which precedes freezing to death, all the more vigorously in proportion to his own indifference and unconsciousness to his sad state, so we are the more emphatic in what we have said, because we see the national poison begins to work, and the nation is insensible.

Pale countrymen and countrywomen, rouse yourselves! Consider that GOD has given us an atmosphere of pure, salubrious, health-giving air, 45 miles high, and—*ventilate your houses.*

* We ought not, perhaps, to include the Germans and Russians. They also love stoves, and the poison of bad air indoors, and therefore have not the look of health of other European nations, though they live far more in the open air than we do.

TREES.

THE NORWAY SPRUCE FIR.

Full grown tree at Studley, 132 feet high; diam. of the trunk, 6½ ft.; and of the head, 39 ft

[*Scale* 1 *in. to* 24 *ft.*]

TREES.

I.

THE BEAUTIFUL IN A TREE.

February, 1851.

IN what does the beauty of a tree consist? We mean, of course, what may strictly be called an ornamental tree—not a tree planted for its fruit in the orchard, or growing for timber in the forest, but standing alone in the lawn or meadow—growing in groups in the pleasure-ground, overarching the roadside, or bordering some stately avenue.

Is it not, first of all, that such a tree, standing where it can grow untouched, and develop itself on all sides, is one of the finest pictures of symmetry and proportion that the eye can any where meet with? The tree may be young, or it may be old, but if left to nature, it is sure to grow into some form that courts the eye and satisfies it. It may branch out boldly and grandly, like the oak; its top may be broad and stately, like the chestnut, or drooping and elegant, like the elm, or delicate and airy like the birch, but it is sure to grow into the type form—either beautiful or picturesque—that nature stamped upon its species, and which is the highest beauty that such tree can possess. It is true, that nature plants some trees, like the fir and pine, in the fissures of the rock, and on the edge of the precipice; that she twists their boughs and gnarls their stems, by storms and tempests—thereby adding to their *picturesque* power in sublime and grand scenery; but as a general truth, it may be clearly stated that the *Beautiful*, in a tree of any kind, is never so fully developed as when, in a genial soil and climate, it stands quite alone, stretching its boughs upward freely to the sky, and outward to the breeze, and even downward towards the earth—almost touching it with their graceful sweep, till only a glimpse of the fine trunk is had at its spreading base, and the whole top is one great globe of floating, waving, drooping, or sturdy luxuriance, giving one as perfect an idea of symmetry and proportion, as can be found short of the Grecian Apollo itself.

We have taken the pains to present this *beau-ideal* of a fine ornamental tree to our readers, in order to contrast it with another picture, *not* from nature—but by the hands of quite another master.

This master is the man whose passion is to *prune trees.* To his mind, there is nothing comparable to the satisfaction of trimming a tree. A tree in a state of nature is a no more respectable object than an untamed savage. It is running to waste with leaves and branches, and has none of the look of civilization about it. Only let him use his saw for a short time, upon any young specimen just growing into adolescence, and throwing out its delicate branches like a fine fall of drapery, to conceal its naked trunk, and you shall see how he will *improve* its appearance. Yes, he will trim up those branches till there is a tall, naked stem, higher than his head. That shows that the tree has been taken care of—has been trimmed—*ergo*, trained and educated into a look of respectability. This is his great point—the fundamental law of sylvan beauty in his mind—*a bare pole with a top of foliage at the end of it.* If he cannot do this, he may content himself with thinning out the branches to let in the light, or clipping them at the ends to send the head upwards, or cutting out the leader to make it spread laterally. But though the trees formed by these latter modes of pruning, are well enough, they never reach that exalted standard, which has for its type, a pole as bare as a ship's mast, with only a flying studding-sail of green boughs at the end of it.*

We suppose this very common pleasure—for it must be a pleasure—which so many persons find in trimming up ornamental

* Some of our readers may not be aware that to cut off the side branches on a young trunk, actually lessens the growth in diameter of that trunk at once.

trees, is based on a feeling that trees, growing quite in the natural way, must be capable of some amelioration by art; and as pruning is usually acknowledged to be useful in developing certain points in a fruit tree, a like good purpose will be reached by the use of the knife upon an ornamental tree. But the comparison does not hold good—since the objects aimed at are essentially different. Pruning—at least all useful pruning—as applied to fruit trees, is applied for the purpose of adding to, diminishing, or otherwise regulating the *fruitfulness* of the tree; and this, in many cases, is effected at the acknowledged diminution of the growth, luxuriance and beauty of the trees–so far as spread of branches and prodigality of foliage go. But even here, the pruner who prunes only for the sake of using the knife (like heartless young surgeons in hospitals), not unfrequently goes too far, injures the perfect maturity of the crop, and hastens the decline of the tree, by depriving it of the fair proportions which nature has established between the leaf and the fruit.

But for the most part, we imagine that the practice we complain of is a want of perception of what is truly beautiful in an ornamental tree. It seems to us indisputable, that no one who has any perception of the beautiful in nature, could ever doubt for a moment, that a fine single elm or oak, such as we may find in the valley of the Connecticut or the Genesee, which has never been touched by the knife, is the most perfect standard of sylvan grace, symmetry, dignity, and finely balanced proportions, that it is possible to conceive. One would no more wish to touch it with saw or axe (unless to remove some branch that has fallen into decay), than to give a nicer curve to the rainbow, or add freshness to the dew-drop. If any of our readers, who still stand by the pruning-knife, will only give themselves up to the study of such trees as these—trees that have the most completely developed forms that nature stamps upon the species, they are certain to arrive at the same conclusions. For the beautiful in nature, though not alike visible to every man, never fails to dawn, sooner or later, upon all who seek her in the right spirit.

And in art too—no great master of landscape, no Claude, or Poussin, or Turner, paints mutilated trees; but trees of grand and majestic heads, full of health and majesty, or grandly stamped with the wild irregularity of nature in her sterner types. The few Dutch or French artists who are the exceptions to this, and have copied those emblems of pruned deformity—the pollard trees that figure in the landscapes of the Low Countries—have given local truthfulness to their landscapes, at the expense of every thing like sylvan loveliness. A pollard willow should be the very type and model of beauty in the eye of the champion of the pruning saw. Its finest parallels in the art of mending nature's proportions for the sake of beauty, are in the flattened heads of a certain tribe of Indians, and the deformed feet of Chinese women. What nature has especially shaped for a delight to the eye, and a fine suggestion to the spiritual sense, as a beautiful tree, or the human form divine, man should not lightly undertake to remodel or clip of its fair proportions.

II.

HOW TO POPULARIZE THE TASTE FOR PLANTING.

July, 1852.

HOW to popularize that taste for rural beauty, which gives to every beloved home in the country its greatest outward charm, and to the country itself its highest attraction, is a question which must often occur to many of our readers. A traveller never journeys through England without lavishing all the epithets of admiration on the rural beauty of that gardenesque country; and his praises are as justly due to the way-side cottages of the humble laborers (whose pecuniary condition of life is far below that of our numerous small householders), as to the great palaces and villas. Perhaps the loveliest and most fascinating of the "cottage homes," of which Mrs. Hemans has so touchingly sung, are the clergymen's dwellings in that country; dwellings, for the most part, of very moderate size, and no greater cost than are common in all the most thriving and populous parts of the Union—but which, owing to the love of horticulture, and the taste for something above the merely useful, which characterizes their owners, as a class, are, for the most part, radiant with the bloom and embellishment of the loveliest flowers and shrubs.

The contrast with the comparatively naked and neglected country dwellings that are the average rural tenements of our country at large, is very striking. Undoubtedly, this is, in part, owing to the fact that it takes a longer time, as Lord Bacon said a century ago, "to garden finely than to build stately." But the newness of our civilization is not sufficient apology. If so, we should be spared tne exhibition of gay carpets, fine mirrors and furniture in the "front parlor," of many a mechanic's, working-man's, and farmer's comfort able dwelling, where the "bare and bald" have pretty nearly supreme control in the "front yard."

What we lack, perhaps, more than all, is, not the capacity to perceive and enjoy the beauty of ornamental trees and shrubs—the rural embellishment alike of the cottage and the villa, but we are deficient in the knowledge and the opportunity of knowing how beautiful human habitations are made by a little taste, time, and means, expended in this way.

Abroad, it is clearly seen, that the taste has descended from the palace of the noble, and the public parks and gardens of the nation, to the hut of the simple peasant; but here, while our institutions have wisely prevented the perpetuation of accumulated estates, that would speedily find their expression in all the luxury of rural taste, we have not yet risen to that general diffusion of culture and competence which may one day give to the many, what in the old world belongs mainly to the favored few. In some localities, where that point has in some measure been arrived at already, the result that we anticipate has, in a good degree, already been attained. And there are, probably, more pretty rural homes within ten miles of Boston, owned by those who live in them, and have made them, than ever sprung up in so short a space of time, in any part of the world. The taste once formed there, it has become contagious, and is diffusing itself among all conditions of men, and gradually elevating and making beautiful, the whole neighborhood of that populous city.

In the country at large, however, even now, there cannot be said to be any thing like a general taste for gardening, or for embellishing the houses of the people. We are too much occupied with *making a great deal*, to have reached that point when a man or a people thinks it wiser to understand how to enjoy a little well, than to exhaust both mind and body in getting an indefinite *more*. And there are also many who would gladly do something to give a sentiment to their houses, but are ignorant both of the materials and the way to set about it. Accordingly, they plant *odorous* ailanthuses and filthy poplars, to the neglect of graceful elms and salubrious maples.

The influence of commercial gardens on the neighborhood where they are situated, is one of the best proofs of the growth of taste—that our people have no obtuseness of faculty, as to what is beautiful, but only lack information and example to embellish with the heartiest good will. Take Rochester, N. Y., for instance—which, at the present moment, has perhaps the largest and most active nurseries in the Union. We are confident that the aggregate planting of fruits and ornamental trees, within fifty miles of Rochester, during the last ten years, has been twice as much as has taken place, in the same time, in any three of the southern States. Philadelphia has long been famous for her exotic gardens, and now even the little yard plats of the city dwellings, are filled with roses, jasmines, lagestrœmias, and the like. Such facts as these plainly prove to us, that only give our people a knowledge of the beauty of fine trees and plants, and the method of cultivating them, and there is no sluggishness or inaptitude on the subject in the public mind.

In looking about for the readiest method of diffusing a knowledge of beautiful trees and plants, and thereby bettering our homes and our country, several means suggest themselves, which are worthy of attention.

The first of these is, by *what private individuals may do.*

There is scarcely a single fine private garden in the country, which does not possess plants that are perhaps more or less coveted—or would at least be greatly prized by neighbors who do not possess, and perhaps cannot easily procure them. Many owners of such places, cheerfully give away to their neighbors, any spare plants that they may possess; but the majority decline, for the most part, to give away plants at all, because the indiscriminate practice subjects them to numerous and troublesome demands upon both the time and generosity of even the most liberally disposed. But every gentleman who employs a gardener, could well afford to allow that gardener to spend a couple of days in a season, in propagating some one or two really valuable trees, shrubs, or plants, that would be a decided acquisition to the gardens of his neighborhood. One or two specimens of such tree or plant, thus raised in abundance, might be distributed freely during the planting season, or during a given week of the same, to all who would engage to plant and take care of the same in their own grounds; and thus this tree or plant would soon become widely distributed about the whole adjacent country. Another season, still another desirable tree or plant might be taken in hand, and when ready for home planting, might be scattered broadcast among those who desire to possess it, and so the labor of love might go on as convenience dictated, till the greater part of the gardens, however small, within a considerable circumference, would contain at least several of the most valuable, useful, and ornamental trees and shrubs for the climate.

The second means is by *what the nurserymen may do.*

We are very well aware that the first thought which will cross the mind of a selfish and narrow-minded nurseryman, (if any such read the foregoing paragraph,) is that such a course of gratuitous distribution of good plants, on the part of private persons, will speedily ruin his business. But he was never more greatly mistaken, as both observation and reason will convince him. Who are the nurseryman's best customers? That class of men who have long owned a garden, whether it be half a rood or many acres, who have never planted trees—or, if any, have but those not worth planting? Not at all. His best customers are those who have formed a taste for trees by planting them, and who, having got a taste for improving, are seldom idle in the matter, and keep pretty regular accounts with the dealers in trees. If you cannot get a person who thinks he has but little time or taste for improving his place to buy trees, and he will accept a plant, or a fruit-tree, or a shade-tree, now and then, from a neighbor whom he knows to be "curious in such things"—by all means, we say to the nurseryman, encourage him to plant at any rate and all rates.

If that man's tree turns out to his satisfaction, he is an *amateur*, one only beginning to pick the shell, to be sure—but an amateur full fledged by-and-by. If he once gets a taste for gardening downright—if the flavor of his own rareripes touch his palate but once, as something quite different from what he has always, like a contented, ignorant donkey, bought in the market—if his Malmaison rose, radiant with the sentiment of the best of French women, and the loveliness of intrinsic bud-beauty once touches his hitherto dull eyes, so that the scales of his blindness to the fact that one rose "differs from another," fall off for ever—then we say, thereafter he is one of the nurseryman's best customers. Begging is both too slow and too dependent a position for him, and his garden soon fills up by ransacking the nurseryman's catalogues, and it is more likely to be swamped by the myriad of things which he would think very much alike, (if he had not bought them by different appellations,) than by any empty spaces waiting for the liberality of more enterprising cultivators.

And thus, if the nurseryman can satisfy himself with our reasoning that he ought not object to the amateur's becoming a gratuitous distributor of certain plants, we would persuade him for much the same reason, to follow the example himself. No person can propagate a tree or plant with so little cost, and so much ease, as one whose business it is to do so. And we may add, no one is more likely to know the really desirable varieties of trees or plants, than he is. No one so well knows as himself that the newest things—most zealously sought after at high prices—are by no means those which will give the most permanent satisfaction *in a family garden.* And accordingly, it is almost always the older and well-tried standard trees and plants—those that the nurseryman can best afford to spare, those that he can grow most cheaply, —that he would best serve the diffusion of popular taste by distributing gratis. We think it would be best for all parties if the variety were very limited—and we doubt whether the distribution of *two* valuable hardy trees or climbers for five years, or till they became so common all over the surroundings as to make a distinct feature of embellishment, would not be more serviceable than disseminating a larger number of species. It may appear to some of our commercial readers, an odd recommendation to urge them to give away precisely that which it is their business to sell—but we are not talking at random, when we say most confidently, that such a course, steadily pursued by amateurs and nurserymen throughout the country, for ten years, would increase the taste for planting, and the demand for trees, five hundred fold.

The third means is by *what the Horticultural Societies may do.*

We believe there are now about forty Horticultural Societies in North America. Hitherto they have contented themselves, year after year, with giving pretty much the same old schedule of premiums for the best cherries, cabbages, and carnations, all over the country—till the stimulus begins to wear out—somewhat like the effects of opium or tobacco, on confirmed *habitués*. Let them adopt our scheme of popularizing the taste for horticulture, by giving premiums of certain select small assortments of *standard* fruit trees, ornamental trees, shrubs, and vines, (purchased by the society of the nurserymen,) to the cultivators of such small gardens—suburban door-yards—or cottage inclosures, within a distance of ten miles round, as the inspecting committee shall decide to be best worthy, by their air of neatness, order, and attention, of such premiums. In this way, the valuable plants will fall into the right hands; the vendor of trees and plants will be directly the gainer, and the stimulus given to cottage gardens, and the spread of the popular taste, will be immediate and decided.

"Tall oaks from little acorns grow"—is a remarkably trite aphorism, but one, the truth of which no one who knows the aptitude of our people, or our intrinsic love of refinement and elegance, will underrate or gainsay. If, by such simple means as we have here pointed out, our great farm on this side of the Atlantic, with the water-privilege of both oceans, could be made to wear a little less the air of Canada-thistle-dom, and show a little more sign of blossoming like the rose, we should look upon it as a step so much nearer the millennium. In Saxony, the traveller beholds with no less surprise and delight, on the road between Wiessenfels and Halle, quantities of the most beautiful and rare shrubs and flowers, growing along the foot-paths, and by the sides of the hedges which line the public promenades. The custom prevails there, among private individuals who have beautiful gardens, of annually planting some of their surplus *materiel* along these public promenades, for the enjoyment of those who have no gardens. And the custom is met in the same beautiful spirit by the people at large; for in the main, those embellishments that turn the highway into pleasure grounds, are respected, and grow and bloom as if within the inclosures.

Does not this argue a civilization among these "down-trodden nations" of Central Europe, that would not be unwelcome in this. our land of equal rights and free schools?

III.

ON PLANTING SHADE-TREES.

November, 1847.

NOW that the season of the *present* is nearly over; now that spring with its freshness of promise, summer with its luxury of development, and autumn with its fulfilment of fruitfulness, have all laid their joys and benefits at our feet, we naturally pause for a moment to see what is to be done in the rural plans of the *future.*

The PLANTING SEASON is at hand. Our correspondence with all parts of the country informs us, that at no previous time has the improvement of private grounds been so active as at present. New and tasteful residences are every where being built. New gardens are being laid out. New orchards of large extent are rapidly being planted. In short, the horticultural zeal of the country is not only awake—it is brimfull of energy and activity.

Private enterprise being thus in a fair way to take care of itself, we feel that the most obvious duty is to endeavor to arouse a corresponding spirit in certain rural improvements of a more public nature.

We therefore return again to a subject which we dwelt upon at some length last spring—the planting of shade-trees in the streets of our rural towns and villages.

Pleasure and profit are certain, sooner or later, to awaken a large portion of our countrymen to the advantages of improving their own private grounds. But we find that it is only under two conditions that many public improvements are carried on. The first is, when nearly the whole of the population enjoy the advantages of education, as in New England. The second is, when a few of the more spirited and intelligent of the citizens move the rest by taking the burden in the beginning upon their own shoulders by setting the example themselves, and by most zealously urging all others to follow.

The villages of New England, looking at their sylvan charms, are as beautiful as any in the world. Their architecture is simple and unpretending—often, indeed, meagre and unworthy of notice. The houses are surrounded by inclosures full of trees and shrubs, with space enough to afford comfort, and ornament enough to denote taste. But the main street of the village is an avenue of elms, positively delightful to behold. Always wide, the overarching boughs form an aisle more grand and beautiful than that of any old Gothic cathedral. Not content, indeed, with one avenue, some of these villages have, in their wide, single street, three lines of trees, forming a double avenue, of which any grand old palace abroad might well be proud. Would that those of our readers, whose souls are callous to the charms of the lights and shadows that bedeck these bewitching rural towns and villages, would forthwith set out out on a pilgrimage to such places as Northampton, Springfield, New Haven, Pittsfield, Stockbridge, Woodbury, and the like.

When we contrast with these lovely resting places for the eye, embowered with avenues of elms, gracefully drooping like fountains of falling water, or sugar-maples swelling and towering up like finely formed antique vases—some of the uncared for towns and villages in our own State, we are almost forced to believe that the famous common schools of New England teach the æsthetics of art, and that the beauty of shade-trees is the care of especial professorships. Homer and Virgil, Cicero, Manlius, and Tully, shades of the great Greeks and Romans!—our citizens have named towns after you, but the places that bear your names scarcely hold leafy trees enough to renew the fading laurels round your heads!—while the direct descendants of stern Puritans, who had a holy horror of things ornamental, who cropped their hair, and made penalties for indulgences in fine linen, live in villages overshadowed by the very spirit of rural elegance!

It is neither from a want of means, or want of time, or any ignorance of what is essential to the beauty of body or of mind, that we see this neglect of the public becomingness. There are numbers of houses in all these villages, that boast their pianos, while the last Paris fashions are worn in the parlors, and the freshest periodical literature of both sides of the Atlantic fills the centre-tables. But while the comfort and good looks of the individual are sufficiently cared for, the comfort and good looks of the town are sadly neglected. Our education here stops short of New England. We are slow to feel that the character of the inhabitants is always, in some degree, indicated by the appearance of the town. It is, unluckily, no one's especial business to ornament the streets. No one feels it a reproach to himself, that verdure and beauty do not hang like rich curtains over the street in which he lives. And thus a whole village or town goes on from year to year, in a shameless state of public nudity and neglect, because no one feels it his particular duty to persuade his neighbors to join him in making the town in which he lives a gem of rural beauty, instead of a sorry collection of uninteresting houses.

It is the frequent apology of intelligent persons who live in such places, and are more alive to this glaring defect than the majority, that it is impossible for them to do any thing alone, and their neighbors care nothing about it.

One of the finest refutations of this kind of delusion exists in New Haven. All over the Union, this town is known as the "City of Elms." The stranger always pauses, and bears tribute to the taste of its inhabitants, while he walks beneath the grateful shade of its lofty rows of trees. Yet a large part of the finest of these trees were planted, and the whole of the spirit which they have inspired, was awakened by one person—Mr. Hillhouse. He lived long enough to see fair and lofty aisles of verdure, where, before, were only rows of brick or wooden houses; and, we doubt not, he enjoyed a purer satisfaction than many great conquerors who have died with the honors of capturing kingdoms, and demolishing a hundred cities.

Let no person, therefore, delay planting shade-trees himself, or persuading his neighbors to do the same. Wherever a village contains half a dozen persons zealous in this excellent work of adorning the country at large, let them form a society and make proselytes of those who are slow to be moved otherwise. A public spirited man in Boston does a great service to the community, and earns the thanks of his countrymen, by giving fifty thousand dollars to endow a professorship in a college; let the public spirited man of the more humble village in the interior, also establish his claim to public gratitude, by planting fifty trees annually, along its public streets, in quarters where there is the least ability or the least taste to be awakened in this way, or where the poverty of the houses most needs something to hide them, and give an aspect of shelter and beauty. Hundreds of public meetings are called, on subjects not half so important to the welfare of the place as this, whose object would be to direct the attention of all the householders to the nakedness of their estates, in the eyes of those who most love our country, and would see her rural towns and village homes made as attractive and pleasant as they are free and prosperous.

We pointed out, in a former article, the principle that should guide those who are about to select trees for streets of rural towns —that of choosing that tree which the soil of the place will bring to the highest perfection. There are two trees, however, which are so eminently adapted to this purpose in the Northern States, that they may be universally employed. These are the *American weeping elm* and the *silver maple.* They have, to recommend them, in the first place, great rapidity of growth; in the second place, the graceful forms which they assume; in the third place, abundance of fine foliage; and lastly, the capacity of adapting themselves to almost every soil where trees will thrive at all.

These two trees have broad and spreading heads, fit for wide streets and avenues. That fine tree, the *Dutch elm,* of exceedingly rapid growth and thick dark-green foliage, makes a narrower and more upright head than our native sort, and, as well as the sugar maple, may be planted in streets and avenues, where there is but little room for the expansion of wide spreading tops.

No town, where any of these trees are extensively planted, can be otherwise than agreeable to the eye, whatever may be its situation, or the style of its dwellings. To villages prettily built, they will give a character of positive beauty, that will both add to the value of property, and increase the comfort and patriotism of the inhabitants.

IV.

TREES IN TOWNS AND VILLAGES.

March, 1847.

"THE man who loves not trees, to look at them, to lie under them, to climb up them (once more a schoolboy,) would make no bones of murdering Mrs. Jeffs. In what one imaginable attribute, that it ought to possess, is a tree, pray, deficient? Light, shade, shelter, coolness, freshness, music,—all the colors of the rainbow, dew and dreams dropping through their soft twilight, at eve and morn,—dropping direct, soft, sweet, soothing, restorative from heaven. Without trees, how, in the name of wonder, could we have had houses, ships, bridges, easy chairs, or coffins, or almost any single one of the necessaries, comforts, or conveniences of life? Without trees, one man might have been born with a silver spoon in his mouth, but not another with a wooden ladle."

Every man, who has in his nature a spark of sympathy with the good and beautiful, must involuntarily respond to this rhapsody of Christopher North's, in behalf of trees—the noblest and proudest drapery that sets off the figure of our fair planet. Every man's better sentiments would involuntarily lead him to cherish, respect, and admire trees. And no one who has sense enough rightly to understand the wonderful system of life, order, and harmony, that is involved in one of our grand and majestic forest-trees, could ever destroy it, unnecessarily, without a painful feeling, we should say, akin at least to murder in the fourth degree.

Yet it must be confessed, that it is surprising, when, from the force of circumstances, what the phrenologists call the principle of *destructiveness*, gets excited, how sadly men's better feelings are warped and smothered. Thus, old soldiers sweep away ranks of men with as little compunction as the mower swings his harmless scythe in a meadow; and settlers, pioneers, and squatters, girdle and make a *clearing*, in a centennial forest, perhaps one of the grandest that ever God planted, with no more remorse than we have in brushing away dusty cobwebs. We are not now about to declaim against war, as a member of the peace society, or against planting colonies and extending the human family, as would a disciple of Dr. Malthus. These are probably both wise means of progress, in the hands of the Great Worker.

But it is properly our business to bring men back to their better feelings, when the fever of destruction is over. If our ancestors found it wise and necessary to cut down vast forests, it is all the more needful that their descendants should plant trees. We shall do our part, therefore, towards awakening again, that natural love of trees, which this long warfare against them—this continual laying the axe at their roots—so common in a new country, has, in so many places, well nigh extinguished. We ought not to cease, till every man feels it to be one of his moral duties to become a planter of trees; until every one feels, indeed, that, if it is the most patriotic thing that can be done to make the earth yield two blades of grass instead of one, it is far more so to cause trees to grow where no foliage has waved and fluttered before—trees, which are not only full of usefulness and beauty always, but to which old Time himself grants longer leases than he does to ourselves; so that he who plants them wisely, is more *certain* of receiving the thanks of posterity, than the most persuasive orator, or the most prolific writer of his day and generation.

The especial theme of our lamentation touching trees at the present moment, is the general neglect and inattention to their many charms, in country towns and villages. We say *general*, for our mind dwells with unfeigned delight upon exceptions—many beautiful towns and villages in New England, where the verdure of the loveliest elms waves like grand lines of giant and graceful plumes above the house tops, giving an air of rural beauty, that speaks louder for the good habits of the inhabitants, than the pleasant sound of a hundred church bells. We remember Northampton, Springfield, New Haven, Stockbridge, and others, whose long and pleasant avenues are refreshing and beautiful to look upon. We do not forget that large and sylan park, with undulating surface, the Boston Common, or that really admirable city *arboretum* of rare trees, Washington Square of Philadelphia.* Their groves are as beloved and sacred in our eyes, as those of the *Deo-dar* are to the devout Brahmins.

But these are, we are sorry to be obliged to say, only the exceptions to the average condition of our country towns. As an offset to them, how many towns, how many villages, could we name, where rude and uncouth streets bask in the summer heat, and revel in the noontide glare, with scarcely a leaf to shelter or break the painful monotony! Towns and villages, where there is no lack of trade, no apparent want of means, where houses are yearly built, and children weekly born, but where you might imagine, from their barrenness, that the soil had been cursed, and it refused to support the life of a single tree.

What must be done in such cases? There must be at least one right-feeling man in every such Sodom. Let him set vigorously at work, and if he cannot induce his neighbors to join him, he must not be disheartened—let him plant and cherish carefully a few trees, if only half a dozen. They must be such as will grow vigorously, and like the native elm, soon make themselves felt and seen wherever they may be placed. In a very few years they will preach more eloquent orations than "gray goose quills" can write. Their luxuriant leafy arms, swaying and waving to and fro, will make more convincing gestures than any member of congress or stump speaker; and if there is any love of nature dormant in the dusty hearts of the villagers, we prophesy that in a very short time there will be such a general yearning after green trees, that the whole place will become a bower of freshness and verdure.

In some parts of Germany, the government makes it a duty for every landholder to plant trees in the highways, before his property; and in a few towns that we have heard of, no young bachelor can

* Which probably contains more well grown specimens of different species of forest-trees, than any similar space of ground in America.

take a wife till he has planted a tree. We have not a word to say against either of these regulations. But Americans, it must be confessed, do not like to be over-governed, or compelled into doing even beautiful things. We therefore recommend, as an example to all country towns, that most praiseworthy and successful mode of achieving this result adopted by the citizens of Northampton, Massachusetts.

This, as we learn, is no less than an *Ornamental Tree Society.* An association, whose business and pleasure it is to turn dusty lanes and bald highways into alleys and avenues of coolness and verdure. Making a " wilderness blossom like the rose," is scarcely more of a rural miracle than may be wrought by this simple means. It is quite incredible how much spirit such a society, composed at first of a few really zealous *arboriculturists,* may beget in a country neighborhood. Some men there are, in every such place, who are too much occupied with what they consider more important matters, ever to plant a single tree, unsolicited. But these are readily acted upon by a society, who work for "the public good," and who move an individual of this kind much as a town meeting moves him, by the greater weight of numbers. Others there are, who can only be led into tasteful improvement, by the principle of *imitation,* and who consequently will not begin to plant trees, till it is the fashion to do so. And again, others who grudge the trifling cost of putting out a shade-tree, but who will be shamed into it by the example of every neighbor around them—neighbors who have been stimulated into action by the zeal of the society. And last of all, as we have learned, there is here and there an instance of some slovenly and dogged farmer, who positively refuses to take the trouble to plant a single twig by the road-side. Such an individual, the society commiserate, and beg him to let them plant the trees in front of his estate at their own cost!

In this way, little by little, the *Ornamental Tree Society* accomplishes its ends. In a few years it has the satisfaction of seeing its village the pride of the citizens—for even those who were the most tardy to catch the planting fever, are at last—such is the silent and irresistible influence of sylvan beauty—the loudest champions of green trees—and the delight of all travellers, who treasure it up in their hearts, as one does a picture drawn by poets, and colored by the light of some divine genius.

We heartily commend, therefore, this plan of *Social Planting Reform*, to every desolate, leafless, and repulsive town and village in the country. There can scarcely be one, where there are not *three* persons of taste and spirit enough to organize such a society; and once fairly in operation, its members will never cease to congratulate themselves on the beauty and comfort they have produced. Every tree which they plant, and which grows up in after years into a giant trunk and grand canopy of foliage, will be a better monument (though it may bear no lying inscription) than many an unmeaning obelisk of marble or granite.

Let us add a few words respecting the best trees for adorning the streets of rural towns and villages. With the great number and variety of fine trees which flourish in this country, there is abundant reason for asking, "where shall we choose?" And although we must not allow ourselves space at this moment, to dwell upon the subject in detail, we may venture two or three hints about it.

Nothing appears to be so captivating to the mass of human beings, as *novelty*. And there is a fashion in trees, which sometimes has a sway no less rigorous than that of a Parisian *modiste*. Hence, while we have the finest indigenous, ornamental trees in the world, growing in our native forests, it is not an unusual thing to see them blindly overlooked for foreign species, that have not half the real charms, and not a tenth part of the adaptation to our soil and climate.

Thirty years ago, there was a general *Lombardy poplar epidemic*. This tall and formal tree, striking and admirable enough, if very sparingly introduced in landscape planting, is, of all others, most abominable, in its serried stiffness and monotony, when planted in avenues, or straight lines. Yet nine-tenths of all the ornamental planting of that period, was made up of this now decrepit and condemned tree.

So too, we recall one or two of our villages, where the soil would have produced any of our finest forest trees, yet where the only trees thought worthy of attention by the inhabitants, are the ailanthus and the paper mulberry

The principle which would govern us, if we were planting the streets of rural towns, is this: *Select the finest indigenous tree or trees; such as the soil and climate of the place will bring to the highest perfection.* Thus, if it were a neighborhood where the elm flourished peculiarly well, or the maple, or the beech, we would directly adopt the tree indicated. We would then, in time, succeed in producing the finest possible specimens of the species selected: while, if we adopted, for the sake of fashion or novelty, a foreign tree, we should probably only succeed in getting poor and meagre specimens.

It is because this principle has been, perhaps accidentally, pursued, that the villages of New England are so celebrated for their sylvan charms. The elm is, we think, nowhere seen in more majesty, greater luxuriance, or richer beauty, than in the valley of the Connecticut; and it is because the soil is so truly congenial to it, that the elm-adorned streets of the villages there, elicit so much admiration. They are not only well planted with trees—but with a kind of tree which attains its greatest perfection there. Who can forget the fine lines of the sugar-maple, in Stockbridge, Massachusetts? They are in our eyes the rural glory of the place. The soil there is their own, and they have attained a beautiful symmetry and development. Yet if, instead of maples, poplars or willows had been planted, how marked would have been the difference of effect.

There are no grander or more superb trees, than our American oaks. Those who know them only as they grow in the midst, or on the skirts of a thick forest, have no proper notion of their dignity and beauty, when planted and grown in an avenue, or where they have full space to develop. Now, there are many districts where the native luxuriance of the oak woods, points out the perfect adaptation of the soil for this tree. If we mistake not, such is the case where that charming rural town in this State, Canandaigua, stands. Yet, we confess we were not a little pained, in walking through the streets of Canandaigua, the past season, to find them mainly lined with that comparatively meagre tree, the locust. How much finer and more imposing, for the long principal street of Canandaigua, would be an avenue of our finest and hardiest native oaks—rich in foliage and grand in every part of their trunks and branches.*

Though we think our native weeping elm, or sugar maple, and two or three of our oaks, the finest of street trees for country villages, yet there are a great many others which may be adopted, when the soil is their own, with the happiest effect. What could well be more beautiful, for example, for a village with a deep, mellow soil, than a long avenue of that tall and most elegant tree, the tulip-tree or whitewood? For a village in a mountainous district, like New Lebanon, in this State, we would perhaps choose the white pine, which would produce a grand and striking effect. In Ohio, the cucumber-tree would make one of the noblest and most admirable avenues, and at the south what could be conceived more captivating than a village whose streets were lined with rows of the magnolia grandiflora? We know how little common minds appreciate these natural treasures; how much the less because they are common in the woods about them. Still, such are the trees which should be planted; for fine forest trees are fast disappearing, and planted trees, grown in a soil fully congenial to them, will, as we have already said, assume a character of beauty and grandeur that will arrest the attention and elicit the admiration of every traveller.

The variety of trees for cities—densely crowded cities—is but small; and this, chiefly, because the warm brick walls are such hiding-places and nurseries for insects, that many fine trees—fine for the country and for rural towns—become absolute pests in the cities. Thus, in Philadelphia, we have seen, with regret, whole rows of the European linden cut down within the last ten years, because this tree, in cities, is so infested with odious worms, that it often becomes unendurable. On this account that foreign tree, the ailanthus, the strong scented foliage of which no insect will attack, is every day becoming a greater metropolitan favorite. The maples are among the thriftiest and most acceptable trees for large cities, and no one of them is more vigorous, cleaner, hardier, or more graceful than the silver maple (*Acer eriocarpum*).

* The oak is easily transplanted from the nurseries—though not from the woods, unless in the latter case, it has been prepared a year beforehand by shortening the roots and branches.

We must defer any further remarks for the present; but we must add, in conclusion, that the planting season is at hand. Let every man, whose soul is not a desert, plant trees; and that not alone for himself—within the bounds of his own demesne, but in the streets, and along the rural highways of his neighborhood. Thus he will not only lend grace and beauty to the neighborhood and county in which he lives, but earn, honestly and well, the thanks of his fellow-men.

V.

SHADE-TREES IN CITIES.

August, 1852.

"DOWN with the ailanthus!" is the cry we hear on all sides, town and country,—now that this "tree of heaven" (as the catalogues used alluringly to call it) has penetrated all parts of the Union, and begins to show its true character. Down with the ailanthus! "Its blossoms smell so disagreeably that my family are made ill by it," says an old resident on one of the squares in New-York, where it is the only shade for fifty contiguous houses. "We must positively go to Newport, papa, to escape these horrible ailanthuses," exclaim numberless young ladies, who find that even their best *Jean Maria Farina*, affords no permanent relief, since their front parlors have become so celestially embowered. "The vile tree comes up all over my garden," say fifty owners of suburban lots who have foolishly been tempted into bordering the outside of their "yards" with it—having been told that it grows so "surprising fast." "It has ruined my lawn for fifty feet all round each tree," say the country gentlemen, who, seduced by the oriental beauty of its foliage, have also been busy for years dotting it in open places, here and there, in their pleasure-grounds. In some of the cities southward, the authorities, taking the matter more seriously, have voted the entire downfall of the whole species, and the Herods who wield the besom of sylvan destruction, have probably made a clean sweep of the first born of celestials, in more towns than one south of Mason and Dixon's line this season.

Although we think there is picturesqueness in the free and luxuriant foliage of the ailanthus, we shall see its downfall without a word to save it. We look upon it as an usurper in rather bad *odor* at home, which has come over to this land of liberty, under the garb of utility,* to make foul the air, with its pestilent breath, and devour the soil, with its intermeddling roots—a tree that has the fair outside and the treacherous heart of the Asiatics, and that has played us so many tricks, that we find we have caught a Tartar which it requires something more than a Chinese wall to confine within limits.

Down with the ailanthus! therefore, we cry with the populace. But we have reasons beside theirs, and now that the favorite has fallen out of favor with the sovereigns, we may take the opportunity to preach a funeral sermon over its remains, that shall not, like so many funeral sermons, be a bath of oblivion-waters to wash out all memory of its vices. For if the Tartar is not laid violent hands upon, and kept under close watch, even after the spirit has gone out of the old trunk, and the coroner is satisfied that he has come to a violent end—lo, we shall have him upon us tenfold in the shape of suckers innumerable—little Tartars that will beget a new dynasty, and overrun our grounds and gardens again, without mercy.

The vices of the ailanthus—the incurable vices of the by-gone favorite—then, are twofold. In the first place, it *smells horribly*, both in leaf and flower—and instead of sweetening and purifying the air, fills it with a heavy, sickening odor; † in the second place, it *suckers* abominably, and thereby overruns, appropriates, and reduces to beggary, all the soil of every open piece of ground where it is planted. These are the mortifications which every body feels sooner or later, who has been seduced by the luxuriant outstretched welcome of its smooth round arms, and the waving and beckoning of its graceful plumes, into giving it a place in their home circle. For a few years, while the tree is growing, it has, to be sure, a fair

* The ailanthus, though originally from China, was first introduced into this country from Europe, as the "Tanner's sumac"—but the mistake was soon discovered, and its rapid growth made it a favorite with planters.

† Two acquaintances of ours, in a house in the upper part of the city of New-York, are regularly driven out by the ailanthus malaria every season.

and specious look. You feel almost, as you look at its round trunk shooting up as straight, and almost as fast as a rocket, crowned by such a luxuriant tuft of verdure, that you have got a young palm-tree before your door, that can whisper tales to you in the evening of that "Flowery Country" from whence you have borrowed it, and you swear to stand by it against all slanderous aspersions. But alas! you are greener in your experience than the Tartar in his leaves. A few years pass by; the sapling becomes a tree—its blossoms fill the air with something that looks like curry-powder, and smells like the plague. You shut down the windows to keep out the *unbalmy* June air, if you live in town, and invariably give a wide berth to the *heavenly* avenue, if you belong to the country.

But we confess openly, that our crowning objection to this petted Chinaman or Tartar, who has played us so falsely, is a patriotic objection. It is that he has drawn away our attention from our own more noble native American trees, to waste it on this miserable pig-tail of an Indiaman. What should we think of the Italians, if they should forswear their own orange-trees and figs, pomegranates and citrons, and plant their streets and gardens with the poison sumac-tree of our swamps? And what must a European arboriculturist think, who travels in America, delighted and astonished at the beauty of our varied and exhaustless forests—the richest in the temperate zone, to see that we neither value nor plant them, but fill our lawns and avenues with the cast-off nuisances of the gardens of Asia and Europe?

And while in the vein, we would include in the same category another less fashionable, but still much petted foreigner, that has settled among us with a good letter of credit, but who deserves not his success. We mean the abele or silver poplar. There is a pleasant flutter in his silver-lined leaves—but when the timber is a foot thick, you shall find the air unpleasantly filled, every spring, with the fine white down which flies from the blossom, while the suckers which are thrown up from the roots of old *abeles* are a pest to all grounds and gardens, even worse than those of the ailanthus. Down with the abeles!

Oh! that our tree-planters, and they are an army of hundreds of thousands in this country—ever increasing with the growth of good taste—oh! that they knew and could understand the surpassing beauty of our *native shade-trees.* More than forty species of oak are there in North America (Great Britain has only two species—France only five), and we are richer in maples, elms, and ashes, than any country in the old world. Tulip-trees and magnolias from America, are the exotic glories of the princely grounds of Europe. But (saving always the praiseworthy partiality in New England for our elms and maples), who plants an American tree—in America? And who, on the contrary, that has planted shade-trees at all in the United States, for the last fifteen years, has not planted either ailanthuses or abele poplars? We should like to see that discreet, sagacious individual, who has escaped the national ecstasy for foreign suckers. If he can be found, he is more deserving a gold medal from our horticultural societies, than the grower of the most mammoth pumpkin, or elephantine beet, that will garnish the cornucopia of Pomona for 1852.

In this confession of our sins of commission in planting filthy suckers, and omission in not planting clean natives—we must lay part of the burden at the door of the nurserymen. (It has been found a convenient practice—this shifting the responsibility—ever since the first trouble about trees in the Garden of Eden.)

"Well! then, if the nurserymen *will* raise ailanthuses and abeles by the thousands," reply the planting community, "and telling us nothing about pestilential odors and suckers, tell us a great deal about 'rapid growth, immediate effect—beauty of foliage—rare foreign trees,' and the like, it is not surprising that we plant what turn out, after twenty years' trial, to be nuisances instead of embellishments. It is the business of the nurserymen to supply planters with the best trees. If they supply us with the worst, who sins the most, the buyer or the seller of such stuff?"

Softly, good friends. It is the *business* of the nurserymen to make a profit by raising trees. If you will pay just as much for a poor tree, that can be raised in two years from a sucker, as a valuable tree that requires four or five years, do you wonder that the nurserymen will raise and sell you ailanthuses instead of oaks? It is the business (duty, at least) of the planter, to know what he is about to plant; and though there are many honest traders, it is a good maxim that the Turks have—"Ask no one in the bazaar to praise his own goods." To the eyes of the nurserymen a crop of ailanthuses and abeles is "a pasture in the valley of sweet waters." But go to an old homestead, where they have become naturalized, and you will find that there is a bitter aftertaste about the experience of the unfortunate possessor of these sylvan treasures of a far-off country.*

The planting intelligence must therefore increase, if we would fill our grounds and shade our streets with really valuable, ornamental trees. The nurserymen will naturally raise what is in demand, and if but ten customers offer in five years for the overcup oak, while fifty come of a day for the ailanthus, the latter will be cultivated as a matter of course.

The question immediately arises, what shall we use instead of the condemned trees? What, especially, shall we use in the streets of cities? Many—nay, the majority of shade-trees—clean and beautiful in the country—are so infested with worms and insects in towns as to be worse than useless. The sycamore has failed, the linden is devoured, the elm is preyed upon by insects. We have rushed into the arms of the Tartar, partly out of fright, to escape the armies of caterpillars and cankerworms that have taken possession of better trees!

Take refuge, friends, in the *American maples*. Clean, sweet, cool, and umbrageous, are the maples; and, much vaunted as ailanthuses and poplars are, for their lightning growth, take our word for it, that it is only a good go-off at the start. A maple at twenty years —or even at ten, if the soil is favorable, will be much the finer and larger tree. No tree transplants more readily—none adapts itself more easily to the soil, than the maple. For light soils, and the milder parts of the Union, say the Middle and Western States, the *silver maple*, with drooping branches, is at once the best and most graceful of street trees. For the North and East, the soft maple and

* We may as well add for the benefit of the novice, the advice to shun all trees that are universally propagated by *suckers*. It is a worse inheritance for a tree than drunkenness for a child, and more difficult to eradicate. Even ailanthuses and poplars *from seed* have tolerably respectable habits as regards *radical* things.

the sugar maple. If any one wishes to know the glory and beauty of the sugar maple as a street tree, let him make a pilgrimage to Stockbridge, in Massachusetts! If he desires to study the silver maple, there is no better school than Burlington, New Jersey. These are two towns almost wholly planted with these American trees—of the sylvan adornings of which any "native" may well be proud. The inhabitants neither have to abandon their front rooms from "the smell," nor lose the use of their back yards by "the suckers." And whoever plants either of these three maples, may feel sure that he is earning the thanks instead of the reproaches of posterity.

The most beautiful and stately of all trees for an avenue—and especially for an avenue street in town—is an American tree that one rarely sees planted in America*—never, that we remember, in any public street. We mean the *tulip-tree*, or liriodendron. What can be more beautiful than its trunk—finely proportioned, and smooth as a Grecian column? What more artistic than its leaf—cut like an arabesque in a Moorish palace? What more clean and lustrous than its tufts of foliage—dark-green, and rich as deepest emerald? What more lily-like and specious than its blossoms—golden and bronze-shaded? and what fairer and more queenly than its whole figure—stately and regal as that of Zenobia? For a park tree, to spread on every side, it is unrivalled, growing a hundred and thirty feet high, and spreading into the finest symmetry of outline.† For a street tree, its columnar stem, beautiful either with or without branches—with a low head or a high head—foliage over the second story or under it—is precisely what is most needed. A very spreading tree, like the elm, is always somewhat out of place in town, because its natural habit is to extend itself laterally. A tree with the habit of the tulip, lifts itself into the finest pyramids of foliage, exactly suited to the usual width of town streets—and thus embellishes and shades, without darkening and incumbering them. Be-

* Though there are grand avenues of it in the royal parks of Germany—raised from American seed.

† At Wakefield, the fine country-seat of the Fisher family, near Philadelphia, are several tulip-trees on the lawn, over one hundred feet high, and three to six feet in diameter.

sides this, the foliage of the tulip-tree is as clean and fresh at all times as the bonnet of a fair young quakeress, and no insect mars the purity of its rich foliage.

We know very well that the tulip-tree is considered difficult to transplant. It is, the gardeners will tell you, much easier to plant ailanthuses, or, if you prefer, maples. Exactly, so it is easier to walk than to dance—but as all people who wish to be graceful in their gait learn to dance (if they can get an opportunity), so all planters who wish a peculiarly elegant tree, will learn how to plant the liriodendron. In the first place the soil must be light and rich—better than is at all necessary for the maples—and if it *cannot* be made light and rich, then the planter must confine himself to maples. Next, the tree must be transplanted just about the time of commencing its growth in the spring, and the roots must be cut as little as possible, and *not suffered to get dry* till replanted.

There is one point which, if attended to as it is in nurseries abroad, would render the tulip-tree as easily transplanted as a maple or a poplar. We mean the practice of cutting round the tree every year in the nursery till it is removed. This developes a ball of fibres, and so prepares the tree for the removal that it feels no shock at all.* Nurserymen could well afford to grow tulip-trees to the size suitable for street planting, and have them twice cut or removed beforehand, so as to enable them to warrant their growth in any good soil, for a dollar apiece. (And we believe the average price at which the thousands of noisome ailanthuses that now infest our streets have been sold, is above a dollar.) No buyer pays so much and so willingly, as the citizen who has only one lot front, and five dollars each has been no uncommon price in New-York for "trees of heaven."

After our nurserymen have practised awhile this preparation of the tulip-trees for the streets by previous removals, they will gradually find a demand for the finer oaks, beeches, and other trees now considered difficult to transplant for the same cause—and about which there is no difficulty at all, if this precaution is taken. Any

* In many continental nurseries, this annual preparation in the nursery, takes place until fruit trees of bearing size can be removed without the slightest injury to the crop of the same year.

body can catch " suckers" in a still pond, but a trout must be tickled with dainty bait. Yet true sportsmen do not, for this reason, prefer angling with worms about the margin of stagnant pools, when they can whip the gold-spangled beauties out of swift streams with a little skill and preparation, and we trust that in future no true lover of trees will plant " suckers " to torment his future days and sight, when he may, with a little more pains, have the satisfaction of enjoying the shade of the freshest and comeliest of American forest trees.

The Cedar of Lebanon.

Full grown tree at Foxley, planted by Sir Uvedale Price

[*Scale* 1 *in. to* 12 *ft.*]

VI.

RARE EVERGREEN TREES.

June, 1847.

AN American may be allowed some honest pride in the beauty and profusion of fine forest trees, natives of our western hemisphere. North America is the land of oaks, pines, and magnolias, to say nothing of the lesser genera; and the parks and gardens of all Europe owe their choicest sylvan treasures to our native woods and hills.

But there is one tree, almost every where naturalized in Europe —an evergreen tree as pre-eminently grand and beautiful among evergreens, as a proud ship of the line among little coasting-vessels —a historical tree, as rich in sacred and poetic association as Mount Sinai itself—a hardy tree, from a region of mountain snows, which bears the winter of the middle States; and yet, notwithstanding all these unrivalled claims to attention, we believe there are not at this moment a dozen good specimens of it, twenty feet high, in the United States.

We mean, of course, that world-renowned tree, the Cedar of Lebanon: that tree which was the favorite of the wisest of kings; the wood of which kindled the burnt-offerings of the Israelites in the time of Moses; of which was built the temple of Solomon, and which the Prophet Ezekiel so finely used as a simile in describing a great empire;—"Behold, the Assyrian was a cedar in Lebanon, with fair branches, and with a shadowing shroud, and of a high stature; and his top was among the thick boughs. His boughs were multiplied, and his branches became long. The fir-trees were not like his boughs, nor the chestnut-trees like his branches, nor any tree in the garden of God like unto him in beauty."

The original forests of this tree upon Mount Lebanon, must have been truly vast, as Solomon's "forty thousand hewers" were employed there in cutting the timber used in building the temple. It is indeed most probable that they never recovered or were renewed afterwards, since modern travellers give accounts of their gradual disappearance. Such, however, is the great age and longevity of this tree, that it is highly credible that the few existing old specimens on Mount Lebanon, are remnants of the ancient forest. Lamartine, who made a voyage to the Holy Land, and visited these trees in 1832, gives the following account of them:

"We alighted and sat down under a rock to contemplate them. These trees are the most renowned natural monuments in the universe; religion, poetry, and history, have all equally celebrated them. The Arabs of all sects entertain a traditional veneration for these trees. They attribute to them not only a vegetative power, which enables them to live eternally, but also an intelligence, which causes them to manifest signs of wisdom and foresight, similar to those of instinct and reason in man. They are said to understand the changes of seasons; they stir their vast branches as if they were limbs; they spread out and contract their boughs, inclining them towards heaven, or towards earth, according as the snow prepares to fall or to melt. These trees diminish in every succeeding age. Travellers formerly counted 30 or 40; more recently 17; more recently still only 12; there are now but 7. These, however, from their size and general appearance, may be fairly presumed to have existed in biblical times. Around these ancient witnesses of ages long since past, there still remains a grove of yellower cedars, appearing to me to form a group of 400 or 500 trees or shrubs. Every year, in the month of June, the inhabitants of Beschieria, of Eden, of Kanobin, and the other neighboring valleys and villages, clamber up to these cedars, and celebrate mass at their feet. How many prayers have resounded under these branches; and what more beautiful canopy for worship can exist!"

The trunks of the largest of these venerable trees measure from 30 to 40 feet in circumference. The finest and most numerous

Cedars of Lebanon in the world, at the present moment, however, are in Great Britain. A people so fond of park scenery as the English, could not but be early impressed with the magnificence of this oriental cedar. It was accordingly introduced into England as early as 1683, and the two oldest trees on record there are said to have been planted by Queen Elizabeth. The Duke of Richmond of the year 1761, planted 1000 young Cedars of Lebanon; and nearly all the larger estates in England boast their noble specimens of this tree at the present day. The tallest specimen in England, is that at *Strathfieldsaye*, the seat of the Duke of Wellington, which is 108 feet high. Woburn Abbey boasts also many superb specimens varying from 60 to 90 feet high, *nine* of which measure from 4 to 6 feet each in the diameter of their trunks. But the largest, and, according to Loudon, unquestionably the handsomest cedar in England, is the magnificent specimen at *Syon House*, the seat of the Duke of Northumberland. This tree is 72 feet high, the diameter of its head 117 feet, and of the trunk 8 feet. We give a miniature engraving of this tree (Fig. 1) from the *Arboretum Britannicum*, and also of the tree at *Foxley*, planted by Sir Uvedale Price, which is 50 feet high, with a trunk measuring 4 feet in diameter.

Fig. 1. The Syon Cedar.

The finest specimen of this evergreen in the United States, is that upon the grounds of Thomas Ash, Esq., at *Throg's Neck*, Westchester county, N. Y. We made a hasty sketch of this tree in 1845, of which the annexed engraving is a miniature. (Fig. 2.) It is about 50 feet high, and has, we learn, been planted over 40 years. It is a striking and beautiful tree, but has as yet by no means attained the grandeur and dignity which a few more years will give it. Still, it is a very fine tree, and no one can look upon it without being inspired with a desire to plant Cedars of Lebanon.

The most remarkable peculiarity in the Cedar of Lebanon is the *horizontal* disposition of its wide spreading branches. This is not apparent in very young trees, but soon becomes so as they begin to develope large heads. Though in altitude this tree is exceeded by some of the pines lately discovered in Oregon, which reach truly gigantic heights, yet in *breadth* and *massiveness* it far exceeds all other evergreen trees, and when old and finely developed on every side, is not equalled in an ornamental point of view, by any sylvan tree of temperate regions.

Fig. 2. Cedar of Lebanon, at Mr. Ash's, near New-York.

Its character being essentially grand and magnificent, it therefore should only be planted where there is sufficient room for its development on every side. Crowded among other trees, all its fine breadth and massiveness is lost, and it is drawn up with a narrow head like any other of the pine family. But planted in the midst of a broad lawn, it will eventually form a sublime object, far more impressive and magnificent than most of the country houses which belong to the private life of a republic.

The Cedar of Lebanon grows in almost every soil, from the poorest gravel to the richest loam. It has been remarked in England that its growth is most rapid in localities where, though planted in a good dry soil, its roots can reach water—such as situations near the margins of ponds or springs. In general, its average growth in this country in favorable soils is about a foot in a year; and when the soil is very deeply trenched before planting, or when its roots are not stinted in the supply of moisture during the summer, it frequently advances with double that rapidity.

Although hardy here, we understand in New England it requires slight protection in winter, while the trees are yet small. The shelter afforded by sticking a few branches of evergreens in the ground around it, will fully answer this purpose. Wherever the Isabella grape matures fully in the open air, it may be cultivated successfully. The few plants that are offered for sale by the nurserymen in this country, are imported from England in pots, but there is no reason why they should not be raised here from seeds, and sold in larger quantities at a reduced price. The seeds vegetate freely, even when three or four years old, and the cones containing them may easily be obtained of London seedsmen.*

The *cone* of the Cedar of Lebanon (of which figure 3 is a reduced drawing) is about 4 inches long, and is beautifully formed.

Fig. 3. Branch and cone of the Cedar of Lebanon, one-sixth of the natural size.

The spring is the better time for planting the Cedar of Lebanon, in this climate. When the small trees are grown in pots, there is no difficulty in transporting them to any distance, and as the months of September and October are the best for importing them from England, we trust our leading nurserymen who are now importing thousands of fruit trees from London and Paris annually, will provide a sufficient stock of this most desirable evergreen for the spring sales of 1848. If the Cedar of Lebanon does not become a popular tree with all intelligent planters in this country, who have space enough to allow it to show its beauties, and a climate not too inclement for its growth, then we have greatly overrated the taste of those engaged in rural improvements at the present mo-

* Mr. Ash presented us with some cones from his tree in 1844, the seeds from which we planted and they vegetated very readily. They should be sown in the autumn, in light, rich soil, in broad flat boxes about four inches deep. These should be placed in a cellar till spring, and then kept during the summer following in a cool and rather shaded situation—the next winter in a cellar or cold pit, and the succeeding spring they may be transplanted into the nnrsery.

ment in the United States. The only reason why this grandest and most interesting of all evergreen trees, which may be grown in this country as easily as the hemlock, wherever the peach bears well, has not already been extensively planted, is owing to two causes. First: that its merits and its adaptation to our soil and climate, are not generally known; and, second, that it has as yet, without any sufficient reason, been difficult to procure it, even in our largest nurseies. We trust that our remarks may have the effect of inspiring many with an appreciation of its great charms, and that our energetic nurserymen, well knowing that there are thousands of young trees to be had in England, which may be imported *in autumn*, from one to three feet high, and in pots, in perfect condition, will be able in future to supply all orders for Cedars of Lebanon.

While we are upon the subject of evergreen trees, we will briefly call the attention of our readers to another rare coniferous species, which is likely to prove a very interesting addition to our hardy arboretums. This is the Chili Pine, *Araucaria imbricata*, a singular and noble evergreen from the Cordilleras mountains, in South America, where it attains the height of 150 feet.

This pine, commonly known as the *Araucaria* (from *Araucanos*, the name of the Chilian tribe in whose country it grows), is distinguished by its scale-like foliage, closely overlaid or imbricated, its horizontal branches springing out from the trunk in whorls or circles, and its immense globular cone, or fruit, as large as a man's head, containing numerous nutritious and excellent nuts. A single fruit contains between two hundred and three hundred of these kernels, which Dr. Pœppig informs us, supply the place of both the palm and corn to the Indians of the Chilian Andes. "As there are frequently twenty or thirty fruits on a stem, and as even a hearty eater among the Indians, except he should be wholly deprived of every other kind of sustenance, cannot consume more than two hundred nuts in a day, it is obvious that eighteen Araucaria trees will maintain a single person for a whole year." The kernel is of the shape of an almond, but twice as large, and is eaten either fresh, boiled, or roasted; and for winter's use, the women prepare a kind of pastry from them.*

* *Arboretum Britannicum*, p. 2438.

We borrow from the *Arboretum Britannicum*, an engraving *one-sixth* of the size of nature, showing the young branch and leaves (fig. 4), and also another (fig. 5), which is a portrait of a specimen growing at Kew Garden, England, taken in 1838, when it was only twelve feet high. We also add, from the London Horticultural Magazine, the following memorandum respecting a tree at *Dropmore*, taken last summer (1846).

Fig. 4.—Branch of the Araucaria, or Chili Pine, one-sixth of the natural size.

"The following is the height and dimensions of the finest specimen we have of this noble tree, and problably the largest in Europe: height 22 feet 6 inches; diameter of the spread of branches near the ground, 10 feet 6 inches; girth of the stem near the ground, 2 feet 10 inches; five feet above the ground, 2 feet. The tree has made a rapid growth this season, and promises to get a foot higher, or more, before autumn; it is about sixteen years old, and has never had the least protection; it stands in rather an exposed situation, on a raised mound, in which the tree delights. The soil is loam, with a small portion of poor peat, and the plant has never been watered, even in the hottest season we have had. A wet subsoil is certain death to the *araucaria* in very wet seasons. A plant here, from a cutting, made a leading shoot in the year 1833, and is now 19 feet 6 inches in height, and has every appearance of making a splendid plant."

In Scotland, also, it stands without the slightest protection, and we have before us, in the *Revue Horticole*, an account of a plantation of these trees at Brest, in the north of France, a climate very much like our own. The soil is a light sandy loam, poor and thin. Yet the trees, fully exposed, or sheltered only by a small belt of pines, have proved perfectly hardy, resisting without injury, even the rigorous winter of 1829-30, when the thermometer was several degrees below zero of Fahrenheit. "The largest now measures about twenty feet in height. Its circles or tiers of branches are five in number, disposed at perfectly equal distances, and closely resembling, in effect, a magnificent pyramid.—The stem, the branches, and their shoots, are all completely clothed with leaves of a fine deep green; these leaves are regularly and symmetrically disposed, and are remarkable in their being bent backwards at their extremities, giving the effect, as well as the form, of the antique girandole."

Fig. 5.—The Chili Pine, or Araucania-Tree.

Mr. Buist, the well known Philadelphia nurseryman, who has already distributed a good many specimens of this tree in the United States, informed us last season, that it is entirely hardy in Philadelphia; and our correspondent, Dr. Valk, of Flushing, who has in his garden a specimen three feet high, writes us that it has borne the past winter without protection, and apparently uninjured.

We may therefore reasonably hope that this unique South American tree, of most singular foliage, striking symmetry, and gigantic eatable fruit, will also take its place in our ornamental plantations, along with the cedar of Lebanon and the Deodar cedar, two of the grandest trees of the Asian world.

VII.

A WORD IN FAVOR OF EVERGREENS.

May, 1848.

"WHAT is the reason," said an intelligent European horticulturist to us lately, "that the Americans employ so few evergreens in their ornamental plantations? Abroad, they are the trees most sought after, most highly prized, and most valued in landscape-gardening; and that, too, in countries where the winters are comparatively mild and short. Here, in the northern United States, where this season is both long and severe, and where you have, in your forests, the finest evergreens, they are only sparingly introduced into lawns or pleasure-grounds."

Our friend is right. There is a lamentable poverty of evergreens in the grounds of many country places in this country. Our plantations are mostly deciduous; and while there are thousands of persons who plant, in this country, such trashy trees (chiefly fit for towns) as the ailanthus, there is not one planter in a hundred but contents himself with a few fir trees, as the sole representatives of the grand and rich foliaged family of evergreens.

They forget that, as summer dies, evergreens form the richest back-ground to the kaleidoscope coloring of the changing autumn leaves; that in winter, they rob the chilly frost-king of his sternest terrors; that in spring, they give a southern and verdant character to the landscape in the first sunny day, when not even the earliest poplar or willow has burst its buds.

More than this,—to look at the useful as well as the picturesque, they are the body guards—the grenadiers—the outworks and fortifications—which properly defend the house and grounds from the cold winds, and the driving storms, that sweep pitilessly over unprotected places in many parts of the country. Well grown belts of evergreens—pines and firs, which

> ——— "in conic forms arise,
> And with a pointed spear divide the skies,"

have, in their congregated strength, a power of shelter and protection that no inexperienced person can possibly understand, without actual experience and the evidence of his own senses. Many a place, almost uninhabitable from the rude blasts of wind that sweep over it, has been rendered comparatively calm and sheltered; many a garden, so exposed that the cultivation of tender trees and plants was almost impossible, has been rendered mild and genial in its climate by the growth of a close shelter, composed of masses and groups of evergreen trees.

Compared with England,—that country whose parks and pleasure grounds are almost wholly evergreen, because her climate is so wonderfully congenial to their culture that dozens of species grow with the greatest luxuriance there, which neither France, Germany, nor the northern United States will produce; we say, compared with England, the *variety* of evergreens which it is possible for us to cultivate is quite limited. Still, though the variety is less, the general effect that may be produced is the same; and there is no apology for our neglecting, at least, the treasures that lie at our very gates, and by our road-sides—the fine indigenous trees of our country. These are within every one's reach; and even these, if properly introduced, would give a perpetual richness and beauty to our ornamental grounds, of which they are at this time, with partial exceptions, almost destitute.

As we are addressing ourselves, now, chiefly to beginners, or those who have hitherto neglected this branch of arboriculture, we may commence by mentioning, at the outset, *four evergreen trees* worthy of attention—indeed, of almost universal attention, in our ornamental plantations. Those are the *Hemlock*, the *White Pine*, the *Norway Spruce*, and the *Balsam Fir*.

We place the hemlock (*Abies canadensis*) first, as we consider it, beyond all question, the most graceful and beautiful evergreen tree commonly grown in this country. In its wild haunts, by the side of some steep mountain, or on the dark wooded banks of some deep valley, it is most often a grand and picturesque tree; when, as in some parts of the northern States, it covers countless acres of wild forest land, it becomes gloomy and monotonous. Hence, there are few of our readers, unfamiliar as they are with it but in these phases, who have the least idea of its striking beauty when grown *alone*, in a smooth lawn, its branches extending freely on all sides, and sweeping the ground, its loose spray and full feathery foliage floating freely in the air, and its proportions full of the finest symmetry and harmony. For airy gracefulness, and the absence of that stiffness more or less prevalent in most evergreens, we must be allowed, therefore, to claim the first place for the hemlock, as a tree for the lawn or park.

Unfortunately, the hemlock has the reputation of being a difficult tree to transplant; and though we have seen a thousand of them removed with scarcely the loss of half a dozen plants, yet we are bound to confess, that, with the ordinary rude handling of the common gardener, it is often impatient of removal. The truth is, all evergreens are far more tender *in their roots* than deciduous trees. They will not bear that exposure to the sun and air, even for a short period, which seems to have little effect upon most deciduous trees. Once fairly dried and shrivelled, their roots are slow to regain their former vital power, and the plant in consequence dies.

This point well understood and guarded against, the hemlock is by no means a difficult tree to remove from the nurseries.* When taken from the woods, it is best done with a frozen ball of earth in the winter; or, if the soil is sufficiently tenacious, with a damp ball in the spring, as has lately been recommended by one of our correspondents.

Of all the well known pines, we give the preference to our native WHITE PINE (*Pinus strobus*) for ornamental purposes. The soft

* In the nurseries this, and other evergreens, over four feet, should be regularly root pruned; i. e., the longest roots shortened with a spade every year. Treated thus, there is no difficulty whatever in removing trees of ten or twelve feet high.

and agreeable hue of its pliant foliage, the excellent form of the tree, and its adaptation to a great variety of soils and sites, are all recommendations not easily overlooked.

Besides, it bears transplanting particularly well; and is, on this account also, more generally seen than any other species in our ornamental plantations. But its especial merit, as an ornamental tree, is the perpetually fine, rich, lively green of its foliage. In the northern States, many evergreens lose their bright color in midwinter, owing to the severity of the cold; and though they regain it quickly in the first mild days of spring, yet this temporary *dinginess*, at the season when verdure is rarest and most prized, is, undeniably, a great defect. Both the hemlock and the white pine are exceptions. Even in the greatest depression of the thermometer known to our neighbors on the "disputed boundary" line, we believe the verdure of these trees is the same fine unchanging green. Again, this thin summer growth is of such a soft and lively color, that they are (unlike some of the other pines, the red cedar, etc.) as pleasant to look upon, even in June, as any fresh and full foliaged deciduous tree, rejoicing in all its full breadth of new summer robes. We place the white pine, therefore, among the first in the regards of the ornamental planter.

Perhaps the most popular foreign evergreen in this country is the Norway Spruce (*Abies excelsa.*) In fact, it is so useful and valuable a tree, that it is destined to become much more popular still. So hardy, that it is used as a *nurse* plant, to break off the wind in exposed sites, and shelter more tender trees in young plantations; so readily adapting itself to any site, that it thrives upon all soils, from light sand, or dry gravel, to deep moist loam or clay; so accommodating in its habits, that it will grow under the shade of other trees, or in the most exposed positions; there is no planter of new places, or improver of old ones, who will not find it necessary to call it in to his assistance. Then, again, the variety of purposes for which this tree may be used is so indefinite. Certainly, there are few trees more strikingly picturesque than a fine Norway spruce, 40 or 50 years old, towering up from a base of thick branches which droop and fall to the very lawn, and hang off in those depending curves, which make it such a favorite with artists. Any one who wishes ocular demonstration of the truth of this, will do well to *daguerreotype* in his mind (for certainly, once seen, he can never forget them) the fine specimens on the lawn at the seat of Col. Perkins, near Boston; or two or three, still larger, and almost equally well developed, in the old Linnæan Garden of Mr. Winter, at Flushing, Long Island.

The Norway spruce, abroad, is thought to grow *rapidly* only on soils somewhat damp. But this is not the case in America. We saw, lately, a young plantation of them of 10 or 12 years growth, in the ground of Capt. Forbes, of Milton Hill, near Boston, on very high and dry gravelly soil, many of which made leading shoots, last season, of three or four feet. Their growth may be greatly promoted, as indeed may that of all evergreens, by a liberal top-dressing of ashes, applied early every spring or autumn.

Little seems to be known in the United States, as yet, of the great value of the Norway spruce, for *hedges.** We have no doubt whatever that it will soon become the favorite plant for *evergreen hedges*, as the buckthorn and Osage orange are already for deciduous hedges in this country. So hardy as to grow every where, so strong, and bearing the shears so well, as to form an almost impenetrable wall of foliage, it is precisely adapted to thousands of situations in the northern half of the Union, where an unfailing shelter, screen, and barrier, are wanted at *all seasons.*†

* This plant may be had from six inches to two feet high at the English nurseries, at such extremely low prices per 1000, that our nurserymen can well afford to import and grow it a year or two in their grounds, and sell it wholesale for hedges, at rates that will place it in the reach of all planters. Autumn is the safest season to import it from England; as, if packed dry and shipped at that season, not ten plants in a thousand will die on the passage. We hope in a couple of years it will be obtainable, in large quantities, in every large nursery in America. We also observe that Elwanger & Barry, at Rochester, advertise it at the present time as a hedge plant.

† "No tree," says the *Arboretum Britannicum*, "is better adapted than this for planting in narrow strips for *shelter* or *seclusion:* because, though the trees in the interior of the strip may become naked below, yet those from the outside will retain their branches from the ground upwards, and effectually prevent the eye from seeing through the screen. The tendency of the tree to preserve its lower branches renders it an excellent protection to

The Balsam Fir (*Picea balsamea*), or, as it is often called, the *Balm of Gilead* Fir, is a neat, dark green evergreen tree, perhaps more generally employed for small grounds and plantations than any other by our gardeners. In truth, it is better adapted to small gardens, yards, or narrow lawns, than for landscape gardening on a large scale, as its beauty is of a formal kind; and though the tree often grows to thirty or forty feet, its appearance is never more pleasing than when it is from ten to fifteen or twenty feet high. The dark green hue of its foliage, which is pretty constant at all seasons, and the comparative ease with which it is transplanted, will always commend it to the ornamental improver. But as a full grown tree, it is not to be compared for a moment, to any one of the three species of evergreens that we have already noticed; since it becomes stiff and formal as it grows old, instead of graceful or picturesque, like the hemlock, white pine, or Norway spruce. Its chief value is for shrubberies, small gardens, or courtyards, in a formal or regular style. The facility of obtaining it, added to the excellent color of its foliage, and the great hardiness of the plant, induce us to give it a place among the four evergreens worthy of the universal attention of our ornamental planters.

The *Arbor Vitæ*, so useful for hedges and screens, is, we find, so

game; and for this purpose, and also for the sake of its verdure during winter, when planted among deciduous trees and cut down to within five or six feet of the ground, it affords a very good and very beautiful undergrowth. The Norway spruce bears the shears; and as it is of rapid growth, it makes excellent hedges for shelter in nursery gardens. Such hedges are not unfrequent in Switzerland, and also in Carpathia, and some parts of Baden and Bavaria. In 1844, there were spruce hedges in some gentlemen's grounds in the neighborhood of Moscow, between 30 feet and 40 feet high. At the Whim (near Edinburgh), a Norway spruce hedge was planted in 1823 with plants 10 feet high, put in 3 feet apart. The whole were cut down 5 feet, and afterwards trimmed in a regular conical shape. The hedge, thus formed, was first cut on Jan. 25, the year after planting; and as the plants were found to sustain no injury, about the end of that month has been chosen for cutting it every year since. Every portion of this hedge is beautiful and green; and the annual growths are very short, giving the surface of this hedge a fine, healthy appearance." [This is an excellent illustration of the capacity of this tree for being sheared; but good hedges are more easily and better formed by using plants about 18 inches or 2 feet high.]

rapidly becoming popular among our planters, that it needs little further commendation.

Among the foreign evergreens worthy of attention, are the Chili pine (*Araucaria*), the Cedar of Lebanon, and the Deodar cedar,—three very noble trees, already described in previous pages, and worthy of attention in the highest degree. The two first have stood the past winter well, in our own grounds, and are likely to prove quite hardy here.

For a rapid growing, bold, and picturesque evergreen, the Austrian pine (*Pinus Austriaca*) is well deserving of attention. We find it remarkably hardy, adapting itself to all soils (though said to grow naturally in Austria on the lightest sands). A specimen here, grew nearly three feet last season; and its bold, stiff foliage, is sufficiently marked to arrest the attention among all other evergreens.

The Swiss stone pine (*Pinus cembra*) we find also perfectly hardy in this latitude. This tree produces an eatable kernel, and though of comparatively slow growth, is certainly one of the most interesting of the pine family. The Italian stone pine, and the pinaster, are also beautiful trees for the climate of Philadelphia. The grand and lofty pines of California, the largest and loftiest evergreen trees in the world, are not yet to be found, except as small specimens here and there in the gardens of curious collectors in the United States. But we hope, with our continually increasing intercourse with western America, fresh seeds will be procured by our nurserymen, and grown abundantly for sale. The great Californian silver fir (*Picea grandis*) grows 200 feet high, with cones 6 inches long, and fine silvery foliage; and the noble silver fir (*P. nobilis*) is scarcely less striking. "I spent three weeks," says Douglass, the botanical traveller, "in a forest composed of this tree, and, day by day, could not cease to admire it." Both these fine fir-trees grow in Northern California, where they cover vast tracts of land, and, along with other species of pine, form grand and majestic features in the landscape of that country. The English have been before us in introducing these natives of our western shores; for we find them, though at high prices, now offered for sale in most of the large nurseries in Great Britain.

The most *beautiful* evergreen-tree in America, and, perhaps,—

when foliage, flowers, and perfume are considered,—in the world, is the *Magnolia grandiflora* of our southern States. There, where it grows in the deep alluvial soil of some river valley, to the height of 70 or 80 feet, clothed with its large, thick, deep green, glossy leaves, like those of a gigantic laurel, covered in the season of its bloom with large, pure white blossoms, that perfume the whole woods about it with their delicious odor; certainly, it presents a spectacle of unrivalled sylvan beauty. Much to be deplored is it, that north of New-York it will not bear the rigor of the winters, and that we are denied the pleasure of seeing it grow freely in the open air. At Philadelphia, it is quite hardy; and in the Bartram Garden, at Landreth's, and in various private grounds near that city, there are fine specimens 20 or 30 feet high, growing without protection and blooming every year.

Wherever the climate will permit the culture of this superb evergreen, the ornamental planter would be unpardonable, in our eyes, not to possess it in considerable abundance. There is a variety of it, originated from seed by the English, called the Exmouth Magnolia (*M. g. exominsis*), which is rather hardier, and a much more abundant bloomer than the original species.

VIII.

THE CHINESE MAGNOLIAS.

January, 1850.

NATURE has bestowed that superb genus of trees, the *magnolia*, on the eastern sides of the two great continents—North America and Asia. The United States gives us eight of all the known species, and China and Japan four or five. Neither Europe, Africa, nor South America afford a single indigenous species of magnolia.

All the Chinese magnolias, excepting one (*M. fuscata*), are hardy in this latitude, and are certainly among the most striking and ornamental objects in our pleasure-grounds and shrubberies in the spring. Indeed, during the month of April, and the early part of May, two of them, the white or *conspicua*, and Soulange's purple or *soulangiana*, eclipse every other floral object, whether tree or shrub, that the garden contains. Their numerous branches, thickly studded with large flowers, most classically shaped, with thick kid-like petals, and rich spicy odor, wear an aspect of great novelty and beauty among the smaller blossoms of the more common trees and shrubs that blossom at that early time, and really fill the beholder with delight.

The Chinese white magnolia (*M. conspicua*) is, in the effect of its blossoms, the most charming of all magnolias. The flowers, in color a pure creamy white, are produced in such abundance, that the tree, when pretty large, may be seen a great distance. The Chinese name, GULAN, literally *lily-tree*, is an apt and expressive one, as the blossoms are not much unlike those of the white lily in size and shape, when fully expanded. Among the Chinese poets, they are considered the emblem of candor and beauty.

The engraving is a very correct portrait of a fine specimen of this tree, standing on the lawn in front of our house, as it appears now, April 25th. Its usual period of blooming here is from the 5th to the 15th of this month. Last year there were *three thousand*

Portrait of the Chinese White Magnolia in Mr. Downing's Grounds.

blossoms open upon it at once. The tree has been planted about fourteen years, and is now twenty feet high. The branches spread over a space of fifteen feet in diameter, and the stem, near the ground, is eight inches in diameter. Its growth is highly symmetrical. For the last ten years it has never, in a single season, failed to produce a fine display of blossoms, which are usually followed by a few seeds. Last year, however, it gave us quite a crop of large and fine seeds, from which we hope to raise many plants.*

This tree is perfectly hardy in this latitude, and we have never known one of its flower buds (which are quite large in autumn), or an inch of its wood, to be killed by the most severe winter. It is, however, grafted about a foot from the ground, on a stock of our western magnolia—sometimes called in Ohio the "cucumber-tree" (*M. acuminata*). This perhaps renders it a little more hardy, and rather more vigorous than when grown on its own root—as this native sort is the very best stock for all the Chinese sorts. It is so propagated by budding in August; and no doubt the *spring budding* recommended by Mr. Nelson, would be a highly successful mode.

The next most ornamental Chinese magnolia, is Soulange's purple (*M. soulangiana*). This is a hybrid seedling, raised by the late Chevalier Soulange Bodin, the distinguished French horticulturist. The habit of the tree is closely similar to that of the *conspicua;* its blossoms, equally numerous, are rather larger, but the outside of the petals is finely tinged with purple. It partakes of the character of both its parents—having the growth of *magnolia conspicua*, and the color of *magnolia purpurea* (or indeed a lighter shade of purple). Its term of blooming is also midway between that of these two species, being about a week later than that of the white or *Gulan* magnolia. It is also perfectly hardy in this latitude. The purple Chinese magnolia (*M. purpurea*) is a much dwarfer tree than the two preceding species. Indeed, it is properly a shrub, some six or eight feet in its growth in this latitude. Grafted on the "cucumber-tree," it would no doubt be more vigorous, and perhaps more hardy, for it is occasionally liable to have the ends of its branches slightly injured by severe winters here. Its flowers begin to open early in May, and on an old plant they continue blooming for six weeks, and indeed in a shaded situation, often for a considerable part of the summer. These blossoms are white within, of a fine dark lilac or purple on the outside, and quite fragrant like the others. This is the oldest Chinese magnolia known here, having been brought from

* There is, we learn, a fine large specimen of this tree in the garden of Mr. William Davidson, Brooklyn, N. Y.

China to Europe in 1790—and it is now quite frequently seen in our gardens.

There is another species (*M. gracilis*), the slender-growing magnolia, which very nearly resembles the purple flowering magnolia—and indeed only differs from it in its more slender growth, and narrower leaves and petals.

If these noble flowering trees have a defect, it is one which is inseparable from the early period at which they bloom, viz., that of having few or no leaves when the blossoms are in their full perfection. To remedy this, a very obvious mode is to plant them with *evergreen* trees, so that the latter may form a dark green background for the large and beautiful masses of magnolia flowers. The American arbor vitæ, and hemlock, seem to us best fitted for this purpose. To those of our readers who do not already possess the Chinese magnolia, and more especially the two first named sorts, it is impossible to recommend two trees, that may now be had at most of our large nurseries, which are in every respect so ornamental in their symmetrical growth, rich blossoms, and fine summer foliage, as the Chinese magnolias.

IX.

THE NEGLECTED AMERICAN PLANTS.

May, 1851.

IT is an old and familiar saying that a prophet is not without honor, except in his own country, and as we were making our way this spring through a dense forest in the State of New Jersey, we were tempted to apply this saying to things as well as people. How many grand and stately trees there are in our woodlands, that are never heeded by the arboriculturist in planting his lawns and pleasure-grounds; how many rich and beautiful shrubs, that might embellish our walks and add variety to our shrubberies, that are left to wave on the mountain crag, or overhang the steep side of some forest valley; how many rare and curious flowers that bloom unseen amid the depths of silent woods, or along the margin of wild water-courses. Yes, our hot-houses are full of the heaths of New Holland and the Cape, our parterres are gay with the verbenas and fuchsias of South America, our pleasure-grounds are studded with the trees of Europe and Northern Asia, while the rarest spectacle in an American country place, is to see above three or four native trees, rarer still to find any but foreign shrubs, and rarest of all, to find any of our native wild flowers.

Nothing strikes foreign horticulturists and amateurs so much, as this apathy and indifference of Americans, to the beautiful sylvan and floral products of their own country. An enthusiastic collector in Belgium first made us keenly sensible of this condition of our countrymen, but Summer, in describing the difficulty he had in procuring from any of his correspondents, here, American seeds or plants—even of well known and tolerably abundant species, by telling us that amateurs and nurserymen who annually import from him every new and rare exotic that the richest collections of Europe possessed, could scarcely be prevailed upon to make a search for native American plants, far more beautiful, which grow in the woods not ten miles from their own doors. Some of them were wholly ignorant of such plants, except so far as a familiarity with their names in the books may be called an acquaintance. Others knew them, but considered them "wild plants," and therefore, too little deserving of attention to be worth the trouble of collecting, even for curious foreigners. "And so," he continued, "in a country of azaleas, kalmias, rhododendrons, cypripediums, magnolias and nysas,—the loveliest flowers, shrubs, and trees of temperate climates,—you never put them in your gardens, but send over the water every year for thousands of dollars worth of English larches and Dutch hyacinths. *Voila le goût Republicain!*"

In truth, we felt that we quite deserved the sweeping sarcasm of our Belgian friend. We had always, indeed, excused ourselves for the well known neglect of the riches of our native Flora, by saying that what we can see any day in the woods, is not the thing by which to make a garden distinguished—and that since all mankind have a passion for novelty, where, as in a fine foreign tree or shrub, both beauty and novelty are combined, so much the greater is the pleasure experienced. But, indeed, one has only to go to England, where "American plants" are the fashion, (not undeservedly, too,) to learn that he knows very little about the beauty of American plants. The difference between a grand oak or magnolia, or tulip-tree, grown with all its graceful and majestic development of head, in a park where it has nothing to interfere with its expansion but sky and air, and the same tree shut up in a forest, a quarter of a mile high, with only a tall gigantic mast of a stem, and a tuft of foliage at the top, is the difference between the best bred and highly cultivated man of the day, and the best buffalo hunter of the Rocky Mountains, with his sinewy body tattooed and tanned till you scarcely know what is the natural color of the skin. A person accustomed to the wild Indian only, might think he knew perfectly well what a man is—and so indeed he does, if you mean a red man. But the "civilizee" is not more different from the aboriginal man of the forest, than the cultivated and perfect garden-tree or shrub (granting always that it *takes* to civilization—which some trees, like Indians, do not), than a tree of the pleasure-grounds differs from a tree of the woods.

Perhaps the finest revelation of this sort in England, is the clumps and masses of our mountain laurel, *Kalmia latifolia*, and our azaleas and rhododendrons, which embellish the English pleasure-grounds. In some of the great country-seats, whole acres of lawn, kept like velvet, are made the ground-work upon which these masses of the richest foliaged and the gayest flowering shrubs are embroidered. Each mass is planted in a round or oval bed of deep, rich, sandy mould, in which it attains a luxuriance and perfection of form and foliage, almost as new to an American as to a Sandwich Islander. The Germans make avenues of our tulip-trees, and in the South of France, one finds more planted magnolias in the gardens, than there are, out of the woods, in all the United States. It is thus, by seeing them away from home, where their merits are better appreciated, and more highly developed, that one learns for the first time what our gardens have lost, by our having none of these "American plants" in them.

The subject is one which should be pursued to much greater length than we are able to follow it in the present article. Our woods and swamps are full of the most exquisite plants, some of which would greatly embellish even the smallest garden. But it is rather to one single feature in the pleasure-grounds, that we would at this moment direct the attention, and that is, the introduction of two broad-leaved evergreen shrubs, that are abundant in every part of the middle States, and that are, nevertheless, seldom to be seen in any of our gardens or nurseries, from one end of the country to the other. The defect is the more to be deplored, because our ornamental plantations, so far as they are evergreen, consist almost entirely of pines and firs—all narrow-leaved evergreens—far inferior in richness of foliage, to those we have mentioned.

The *Native Holly* grows from Long Island to Florida, and is quite abundant in the woods of New Jersey, Maryland, and Virginia. It forms a shrub or small tree, varying from four to forty feet in height—clothed with foliage and berries of the same ornamental character as the European holly—except that the leaf is a shade lighter in its green. The plant too, is perfectly hardy, even in the climate of Boston—while the European holly is quite too tender for open air culture in the middle States—notwithstanding that peaches ripen here in orchards, and in England only on walls.

The *American Laurel*, or Kalmia, is too well known in all parts of the country to need any description. And what new shrub, we would ask, is there—whether from the Himmalayas or the Andes, whether hardy or tender—which surpasses the American laurel, when in perfection, as to the richness of its dark green foliage, or the exquisite delicacy and beauty of its gay masses of flowers? If it came from the highlands of Chili, and were recently introduced, it would bring a guinea a plant, and no grumbling!

Granting all this, let our readers who wish to decorate their grounds with something *new and beautiful*, undertake now, *in this month of May* (for these plants are best transplanted *after* they have commenced a new growth), to plant some laurels and hollies. If they would do this quite successfully, they must not stick them here and there among other shrubs in the common border—but prepare a bed or clump, in some cool, rather shaded aspect—a north slope is better than a southern one—where the subsoil is rather damp than dry. The soil should be sandy or gravelly, with a mixture of black earth well decomposed, or a cart-load or two of rotten leaves from an old wood, and it should be at least eighteen or twenty inches deep, to retain the moisture in a long drought. A bed of these fine evergreens, made in this way, will be a *feature* in the grounds, which, after it has been well established for a few years, will convince you far better than any words of ours, of the neglected beauty of our American plants.

X.

THE ART OF TRANSPLANTING TREES.

November, 1848.

WE must have a little familiar conversation, this month, on the subject of TRANSPLANTING TREES. Our remarks will be intended, of course, for the uninitiated; not for those who have grown wise with experience.

That there is a difficulty in transplanting trees, the multitude of complaints and inquiries which beset us, most abundantly prove. That it is, on the other hand, a very easy and simple process, the uniform success of skilful cultivators, as fully establishes.

The difficulty then, lies, of course, in a want of knowledge, on the part of the unsuccessful practitioner. This want of knowledge may be stated, broadly, under two heads, viz., ignorance of the *organization* of trees, and ignorance of the necessity of *feeding* them.

The first point is directly the most important, for the very process of transplanting is founded upon it. Since this art virtually consists in removing, by violence, a tree from one spot to another, it is absolutely necessary to know how much violence we may use without defeating the ends in view. A common soldier will, with his sword, cut off a man's limb, in such a manner that he takes his life away with it. A skilful surgeon, will do the same thing, in order to *preserve* life. There are, also, manifestly two ways of transplanting trees.

That the *vital principle* is a wonderful and mysterious power, even in plants, cannot be denied. But because certain trees, as poplars and willows, have enough of this power to enable pieces of them to grow, when stuck into the ground, like walking sticks, without roots, it does not follow that all other trees will do the same. There are some animals which swallow prussic acid with impunity; but it is a dangerous experiment for all other animals. What we mean to suggest, therefore, is, that he who would be a successful transplanter, must have an almost religious respect for the roots of trees. He must look upon them as the collectors of revenue, the wardens of the ports, the great viaducts of all solids and fluids that enter into the system of growth and verdure, which constitute the tree proper. Oh, if one could only teach hewers of "tap-roots" and drawers of "laterals," the value of the whole system of roots,—every thing, in short, that looks like, and is, a *radicle*,—then would nine tenths of the difficulty of transplanting be quite overcome, and the branches might be left pretty much to themselves!

Now a tree, to be perfectly transplanted, ought to be taken up with its whole system of roots *entire*. Thus removed and carefully replanted, at the proper dormant season, it need not suffer a loss of the smallest bough, and it would scarcely feel its removal. Such things are done every year, with this result, by really clever and experienced gardeners. We have seen apple-trees, large enough to bear a couple of bushels of fruit, which were removed a dozen miles, in the autumn, and made a luxuriant growth, and bore a fine crop the next season. But the workman who handled them had gone to the root of the business he undertook.

The fact, however, cannot be denied, that in common practice there are very few such perfect workmen. Trees (especially in the nurseries) are often taken up in haste, at a loss of a third, or even sometimes half of their roots, and when received by the transplanter, there is nothing to be done but *to make the best of it.*

In order to do this, we must look a little in advance, in order to understand the philosophy of growth. In a few words, then, it may be assumed that in a healthy tree, there is an exact "balance of power" between the roots and the branches. The first may be said to represent the stomach, and the second the lungs and perspiratory system. The first collects food for the tree; the other elaborates and prepares this food. You can, therefore, no more make a violent attack upon the roots, without the leaves and branches suffering harm by it, than you can greatly injure the stomach of an animal without disturbing the vital action of all the rest of its system.

In trees and plants, perhaps, this proportional dependence is still greater. For instance, the leaves, and even the bark of a tree, continually act as the perspiratory system of that tree. Every clear day, in a good sized tree, they give off *many pounds* weight of fluid matter,—being the more watery portion of the element absorbed by the roots. Now it is plain, that if you destroy, in transplanting, one-third of the roots of a tree, you have, as soon as the leaves expand, a third more lungs than you can keep in action. The perspiration is vastly beyond what the roots can make good; and unless the subject is one of unusual vitality, or the weather is such as to keep down perspiration by constant dampness, the leaves must flag, and the tree partly or wholly perish.

The remedy, in cases where you must plant a tree whose roots have been mutilated, is (after carefully paring off the ends of the wounded roots, to enable them to heal more speedily) to restore the "balance of power" by bringing down the perspiratory system—in other words, the branches, to a corresponding state; that is to say, in theory, if your tree has lost a fourth of its roots, take off an equal amount of its branches.

This is the correct *theory*. The *practice*, however, differs with the *climate* where the transplanting takes place. This is evident, if we remember that the perspiration is governed by the amount of sunshine and dry air. The more of these, the greater the demand made for moisture, on the roots. Hence, the reason why delicate cuttings strike root readily under a bell glass, and why transplanting is as easy as sleeping in rainy weather. In England, therefore, it is much easier to transplant large trees than on the continent, or in this country; so easy, that Sir Henry Stewart made parks of fifty feet trees with his transplanting machine, almost as easily and as quickly as Capt. Bragg makes a park of artillery. But he who tries this sort of fancy work in the bright sunshine of the United States, will find that it is like undertaking to besiege Gibraltar with cross-bows. The trees start into leaf, and all promises well; but unless under very favorable circumstances, the leaves beggar the roots, by their demands for more sap, before August is half over.

We mean to be understood, therefore, that we think it safest in practice, in this part of the world, when you are about to plant a tree deprived of part of its roots, to reduce the branches a little *below* this same proportion. To reduce them to precisely an equal proportion, would preserve the balance, if the ground about the roots could be kept uniformly moist. But, with the chances of its becoming partially dry at times, you must guard against the leaves flagging, by diminishing their number at the first start. As every leaf and branch, made after *growth* fairly commences, will be accompanied simultaneously by new roots, the same will then be provided for as a matter of course.

The neatest way of reducing the top of a tree, in order not to destroy its natural symmetry,* is to ***shorten-back*** the young growth of the previous season. We know a most successful planter who always, under all circumstances, shortens-back the previous year's wood, on transplanting, to *one bud;* that is, he cuts off the whole summer's growth down to a good plump bud, just above the previous year's wood. But this is not always necessary. A few inches (where the growth has been a foot or more) will usually be all that is necessary. It is only necessary to watch the growth of a transplanted tree, treated in this way, with one of the same kind unpruned; to compare the clean, vigorous new shoots, that will be made the first season by the former, with the slender and feeble ones of the latter, to be perfectly convinced of the value of the practice of shortening-in transplanted trees.

The necessity of a proper supply of food for trees, is a point that we should not have to insist upon, if starving trees had the power of crying out, like starving pigs. Unluckily, they have not; and, therefore, inhuman and ignorant cultivators will feed their cattle, and let their orchards starve to death. Now it is perfectly demonstrable, to a man who has the use of his eyes, that a tree can

* Cutting off large branches at random, often quite spoils the natural habit of a tree. *Shortening-back*, all over the head, does not affect it in the least.

be *fatted* to repletion, that it may be made to grow thriftily and well, or that it may be absolutely starved to death, as certainly as a Berkshire. It is *not* enough (unless a man has rich bottom lands) to *plant* a tree in order to have a satisfactory growth, and a speedy gratification in its fruit and foliage. You must provide a supply of food for it at the outset, and renew it as often as necessary during its lifetime. He who does this, will have five times the profit and ten times the satisfaction of the careless and sluggish man, who grudges the labor and expense of a little extra feeding for the roots. The cheapest and best food for fruit trees, with most farmers, is a mixture of swamp muck and stable manure, which has laid for some two or three months together. The best manure, perhaps, is the same muck, or black peat, reduced to an active state with wood ashes. A wheelbarrow load of this compost, mixed with the soil, for each small transplanted tree, will give it a supply of food that will produce a growth of leaf and young wood that will do one's heart good to look upon.

Any *well decomposed* animal manure may be freely used in planting trees; always thoroughly incorporating it with the *whole* of the soil that has been stirred, and not throwing it directly about the roots.

There are, however, some improvident men who will plant trees without having any food at hand, except manure in a crude state. "What shall we do," they ask, "when we have only fresh stable manure?" Perhaps we ought to answer—"wait till you have something better." But since they will do something at once, or not at all, we must give them a reply; and this is, make your hole twice as large and twice as deep as you would if you had suitable compost. Then bury part of the fresh manure *below* the depth where the roots will at first be, mixing it with the soil, treading the whole down well to prevent settling, and covering the whole with three inches of earth, upon which to plant the tree. Mix the rest with the soil, and put it at the *sides* of the hole, keeping the manure both at the sides and bottom, far enough away, that the roots of the tree shall not reach it for two months. Then plant the tree in some of the best good soil you can procure.

One of the safest and best general fertilizers that can be used in transplanting at all times, and in all soils, is *leached* wood ashes. A couple of shovelfuls of this may be used (intermixed with soil) about the roots of every tree, while replanting it, with great advantage. Lime and potash, the two largest inorganic constituents of all trees, are most abundantly supplied by wood ashes; and hence its utility in all our soils.

We have, previously, so largely insisted on the importance of *trenching* and *deepening the soil*, in all cases where trees are to be planted, that we trust our readers know that that is our *platform.* If any man wishes to know how to improve the growth of any tree in the climate of the United States, the first word that we have to say to him, is to " *trench* your soil." If your soil is exhausted, if your soil is thin and poor, if it is dry, and you suffer from drought, the remedy is the same; deepen it. If you have much to do, and economy must be considered, use the subsoil plough; if a few trees only are to be planted in the lawn or garden, use the spade. Always remember that the roots of trees will rarely go deeper than the " natural soil," (say from 10 to 20 inches on the average,) and that by trenching two or three feet deep you make a double soil, and therefore enlarge your " area of freedom " for the roots, and give them twice as much to feed upon. If you are a beginner, and are skeptical, make a trial of a few square yards, plant a tree in it, and then judge for yourself.

XI.

ON TRANSPLANTING LARGE TREES.

January, 1850.

IN a country where thousands of new rural homes are every year being made, how many times do the new proprietors sigh for LARGE TREES. "Ah, if one could only have half a dozen,—two or three,—nay, even a single one of the beautiful elms that waste their beauty by the roadside of some unfrequented lane, or stands unappreciated in some farmer's meadow, who grudges it ground room!"

"And is there no successful way of transplanting such trees?" inquires the impatient owner of a new site, who feels that there should be some special process—some patent regenerator of that forest growth, which his predecessors have so cruelly despoiled,—his predecessors, to whom cord-wood was of more consequence than the charms of sylvan landscape.

Though there is great delight in raising a tree from a liliputian specimen no higher than one's knee,—nay, even from the seed itself,—in feeling, as it grows upward and heavenward, year by year, till the little thing that had to be sheltered with rods, stuck about it, to prevent its being overlooked and trodden upon, has so far overtopped us that it now shelters and gratefully overshadows us; though, as we have said, there is great delight in this, yet it must be part and parcel of other delights. To a person who has just "settled" upon a bare field, where he has only a new house and a "view" of his neighborhood to look at, we must not be too eloquent about the pleasure of raising oaks from the acorn. He is too much in the condition of the hungry man, who is told to be resigned, for ther:

will be no hunger in heaven. It is the present state of affairs that, at this moment, lies nearest to him. How, in other words, shall a field, as bare as a desert, be at once enlivened with a few large trees?

Some ten or fifteen years ago, an ingenious Scotch baronet—Sir Henry Stuart—published a goodly octavo to the world, which apparently solved the whole mystery. And it was not all theory; for the baronet's own park was actually planted with forest trees of various kinds—oaks, ashes, elms, beeches, of all sizes, from twenty-five to sixty feet in height, and with fine heads. The thing was not only done, but the park was there, growing in the finest luxuriance; and half a dozen years after its creation, arboriculturists of every degree, from Sir Walter Scott down to humble ditchers, went to look at it, and pronounced it good, and the thing itself altogether satisfactory.

Sir Henry Stuart's process, though it fills a volume, may be compressed into a paragraph. First, the greatest *respect for the roots* of a tree, and some knowledge of the functions of the roots and branches; second, a pair of large wheels, with a strong axle and pole; third, practical skill and patience in executing the work.

A great many disciples had Sir Henry; and we, among the number, bore our share in the purchase of a pair of wheels, and the cost of moving some large trees, that for the most part *failed*. And now, that Sir Henry's mode has rather fallen into disrepute, and is looked upon as an impracticable thing for this country, it may be time well employed to look a little into the cause of its failure, and also to inquire if it is wholly and entirely a failure for us.

Undeniably, then, the main cause of the failure, here, of the Scotch mode of transplanting, lies in the difference of climate. He who knows how much the success of a newly planted tree, of small size, depends on the moist state of the atmosphere, when it begins to grow in its new position, can easily see that its importance is vastly greater to a large tree than a small one. It is the thirst of a giant and the sufferings of a giant, accustomed to a large supply of food, compared with that of a little child, which may be fed by the spoonful. And when we compare the moisture of that foggy and weeping climate of Scotia, with the hot, bright, dry atmosphere of the United States, we can easily see that a tree at all stubborn, moved by Sir Henry himself, and inclined to grow, would actually perish from the dryness of the air in mid-summer in our middle States. And such we have found by experiment is actually the case with trees of many kinds, when planted of large size.

We say of many kinds; for repeated experiment has proved that a few kinds of hardy native trees may be transplanted, even in this climate, with entire success by the Stuart method, or any other that will sufficiently preserve the entireness of the roots.

Fortunately, the two kinds of trees adapted for removal, when of large size, are the two most popular and most valuable for ornamental purposes. We mean the ELMS and the MAPLES. Few forest trees have more dignity and grace; none have more beauty of outline than our weeping elms and sugar maples, to say nothing of the other varieties of both these trees. And if the possessor of a new place can adorn it with a dozen or two fine specimens of these, of a size to give immediate shelter and effect to the neighborhood of his house, he can then afford to be patient, and enjoy the more gradual process of coaxing smaller specimens into luxuriant maturity.

The reason why oaks, nut trees, chestnuts, tulip trees, and the like, when transplanted of large size, do not succeed here, where elms and maples do, is that the former unluckily have a few strong, or *tap-roots*, running downwards, while the latter have great masses of fibrous roots, running near the surface of the ground.

Now a tap-rooted tree, even when small, has a much less *amiable* disposition when dug up, and asked to grow again, than a fibrous rooted tree; because, indeed, having fewer small roots, it has only one mouth to supply its hunger, and to gain strength to go on again, where the other has fifty. Hence, though it may, under very favorable circumstances, like the climate of Scotland, overcome all and succeed, yet it is nearly a death struggle to do so in our dry midsummer air.* It is not worth while to waste one's time, therefore, in transplanting large oaks, or hickories, in this hemisphere.

And now, having reduced our class of available subjects to elms

* We have found that large oaks, when transplanted, frequently live through the first year, but die the second, from their inability to contend against the climate and make new roots.

and maples, let us inquire what is the best method of transplanting them.

The first point regards the selection of the trees themselves. And here Sir Henry Stuart, or his book, would teach many planters a piece of real tree-craft which they are ignorant of; and that is, that there is as much difference, in point of hardiness and power of endurance, between a tree taken out of the woods, where it is sheltered by other trees, and one taken from the open field, where it stands alone, exposed to the fullest influences of wind and storm, light and sunshine, as there is between a languid drawing-room fop and a robust Green Mountain boy. For this good and sufficient reason, always choose a tree that grows alone, in an open site, and in a soil that will allow you to retain a considerable ball of roots entire.*

"How large an elm or maple may we transplant?" Our answer to this question might be, as large as you can afford—but for the great difficulty of managing a very large tree when out of the ground. That it may be done, is now a well-established fact; and hence, the only question is as to its expediency.† Trees from 20 to 30 feet in height, we conceive to be, on the whole, the most suitable size.

There are two modes now in considerable use for moving trees of this size; the first is the Stuart mode, to be performed in spring or autumn; the second, the frozen-ball mode, to be performed in winter.

The Stuart mode is the best for trees of the largest size. In this mode, the roots are laid bare with the greatest care; every root,

* The best *subjects*, when they can be had (as they frequently may in the neighborhood of towns), are trees planted some ten or fifteen years before, in some neighbor's grounds, where they require being taken out (if you can persuade him of it), because originally planted too thickly.

† One of the most successful instances of this kind of transplanting, in this country, is at the cottage residence of Thomas Perkins, Esq., at Brookline, near Boston. An *avenue* of considerable extent may be seen there, composed of elms thirty to forty feet high, beautifully shaped, and having the effect of full-grown trees. They were removed more than a fourth of a mile, from the seat of Col. Perkins, with perfect success, and we believe by the Stuart mode.

as far as possible, being preserved. The wheels are then brought up to the tree, the axle made fast to the body (with a stuffing between to prevent injury to the bark), and the pole is tied securely to the trunk and branches higher up. A long rope, or ropes, being now fixed to the pole and the branches, the pole serves as a lever, and the top is thus brought down, while the mass of roots is supported upon the axle. After the tree is properly balanced on the carriage, horses are attached, and it is transported to the hole prepared for it.

This mode is one which requires a good deal of practical skill in the management of roots, and in the whole art of transplanting, though great effects may be produced by it in the hands of skilful workmen.*

Transplanting with a frozen ball is a good deal practised in this country, and is much the cheapest and most perfect mode for trees of moderately large size; that is to say, trees from 20 to 30 feet high, and whose trunks measure from 6 inches to a foot in diameter. Trees of this proportion are indeed the most suitable for the embellishment of new places, since they unite immediate beauty of effect with comparative cheapness in removal, while it requires less mechanical skill to remove them.

The process of removing a tree with a frozen ball is a simple one, especially if performed in the early part of winter, while there is yet but little frost in the ground. In the first place, the hole should be made ready,† and a pile of suitable soil laid by the side of it and covered with straw, to prevent its being frozen when wanted.

Then a trench is dug all round the tree, in order to leave a ball

* We cannot but express our surprise that some of our exceedingly ingenious and clever Yankee teamsters have never taken up, as a business, the art of transplanting large trees. To a person competent to the task, with his machine, his oxen, and his trained set of hands, an abundance of occupation would be offered by wealthy improvers of new places, to whom the cost of a dozen elms, forty feet high, at a remunerating price, would be a matter of trifling moment.

† Especially should the soil, in the bottom of the hole, be well trenched and manured.

of earth from six to eight feet in diameter. The trench should be wide enough to allow the operator gradually to undermine the ball of roots, so that at last the tree just stands, as it were, upon one leg. In this condition let the ball be exposed to a sharp frosty night, that it may freeze quite firmly. The next day you approach the subject with a common low shed, or *stone boat*, drawn by a pair or two of oxen; (or if the tree measures only six inches, a pair of horses will do.) The tree with its ball is now thrown to one side; the sled is then placed under the ball on the opposite side; then the tree is righted, the ball placed upon the middle of the sled, and the whole drawn out of the hole. A teamster of very little practice will now see at a glance how to balance his load upon the sled; and once on level ground, it is no difficult matter to drag the whole for half a mile or more to its final location.

After the tree is placed in the hole previously prepared for it, the good soil must be closely pressed around the ball, and the trunk supported in its place, till after the equinoctial rains, by stakes or braces.*

There is no mode for the removal of trees in which they will suffer so little as this; partly because the roots are maintained more entire than in any other way, and partly because the soil is not even loosened or disturbed about a large portion of the fibres. Hence, though a slight reduction of the top is advisable, even in this case, to balance the loss of some of the long roots, it is not absolutely needful, and in no case is the symmetry of the head destroyed; and the possessor of the newly moved tree has the satisfaction of gazing upon a goodly show of foliage and shade as soon as June comes round again.

Those of our readers who are groaning for the want of trees, will see by these remarks that their case is by no means desperate; that, on the contrary, we think it a very hopeful one; and that, in short, if they can afford to expend from two to ten dollars per tree, and can get at the right kind of subjects in their neighborhood, they may,

* We may here add, that besides elms and maples, this mode is equally successful with *evergreens* of all kinds. We have seen white pines and firs, of twenty feet high, moved so perfectly in this manner, that they never showed the least mark of the change of place.

if they choose, transform their premises from a bleak meadow to a wood as thick as "Vallombrosa's shade," before the spring opens.

And now, one word more to those who, having trees, are impatient for luxuriant growth; who desire to see annual shoots of six feet instead of twenty inches; and who do not so much care what it costs to make a few trees in a favorite site advance rapidly, provided it is possible. What they wish to know is, can the thing be done?

We answer, yes. To make a hardy tree* grow three times as fast in a summer as it usually does (we speak now, of course, of trees in a common soil), it is only necessary that it should have three times the depth for the roots to grow in, and three times the amount of food for its consumption while growing.

And, first of all, for very rapid and luxuriant growth in our climate, the soil must be deep—deep—deep. Three feet of trenching or subsoiling is imperative; and we have seen astonishing results, where places for trees twelve feet broad and five feet deep have been prepared for them. If any one of our readers will take the trouble to watch an elm-tree making its growth next season, he will notice that, if the season is moist and cool, the shoots will continue to lengthen till past midsummer; but if, on the contrary, the season is a dry one, all growth will be over by the middle of June. Why does the growth cease so early in the season? Simply because the moment the moisture in the soil fails, and the roots feel the effects of the sun, the terminal buds form at the end of each shoot, and then all growth for the season is over. Deepen the soil, so that the roots go on growing in its cool, moist depths, and the tops will go on lengthening, despite the power of the sun; nay, so long as there is moisture, by the help of it. And hence, the length of time which a tree will continue to grow, depends mainly upon the depth of the soil in which it is planted.

If any skeptic wishes to be convinced of the effects of deep and

* We say a *hardy* tree, because every arboriculturist knows that to promote extra luxuriance, in a tree not perfectly hardy, increases its tenderness, because the wood will not ripen well, like short jointed growth; but there is no fear of this with elms, oaks, maples, or any perfectly hardy native trees.

rich soil upon the luxuriance of a plant, he has only to step into a vinery, like that in Clinton Point, and see, with his own eyes, the same sorts of grape, which in common soil, even under glass, usually grow but six or eight feet high in a season, and with stems like pipe-stems, growing twenty or thirty feet in a single season, with stems of the thickness of a man's thumb, and ripening delicious fruit in fourteen months after being planted. Now, exactly the same effect may be produced by deepening and enriching the soil, where the elm or any other hardy ornamental tree is to be planted · and we put it thus plainly to some of our readers, who are impatient of the growth of trees, that they may, if they choose, by a little extra pay, have more growth in three years than their neighbors do in ten.

XII.

A CHAPTER ON HEDGES.

February, 1847.

"THERE was a certain householder which planted a vineyard, and *hedged* it round about." What better proof can we give, than this sacred and familiar passage, of the antiquity, as well as the wisdom, of making hedges. But indeed the custom is older than the Christian era. Homer tells us that when Ulysses, after his great deeds, returned to seek his father Laërtes, he found the old king in his garden, preparing the ground for a hedge, while his servants were absent,

> "To search the woods for sets of flowery thorn,
> Their orchard bounds to strengthen and adorn."
>
> POPE'S ODYSSEY.

The lapse of 3000 years has not taught the husbandman or the owners of orchards and gardens, in modern times, any fairer or better mode of enclosing their lands, than this most natural and simple one of *hedging it round about.* Fences of iron or wood, carefully fashioned by art, are fitting and appropriate in their proper places —that is, in the midst of houses and great cities—but in the open, free expanse of country landscape, the most costly artificial barrier looks hard and incongruous beside the pleasant verdure of a live hedge.

Necessity, it is often said, knows no law, and the emigrant settler on new lands, where stone and timber are so abundant as to be the chief obstacles to the progress of his labors on the soil, must needs employ for a long time, rail fences, board fences, and stone walls. But in most of the Atlantic States these materials are already becoming so scarce, that hedges will soon be the most economical mode of enclosing grounds. In the prairie lands of the west, hedges must also, from the original and prospective scarcity of timber, soon be largely resorted to for all *permanently* divided grounds—such as gardens and orchards.

Touching the charms which a good hedge has for the eye, they are so striking, and so self-evident, that our readers hardly need any elaborate inventory from us. That clever and extraordinary man, William Cobbett, who wrote books on gardening, French grammar and political economy, with equal success, said, in his usual emphatic manner, "as to the beauty of a fine hedge, it is impossible for any one who has not seen it, to form an idea; contrasted with a wooden, or even a brick fence, *it is like the land of Canaan compared with the deserts of Arabia!*"

The advantages of a hedge over the common fence, besides its beauty, are its durability, its perfect protection against man and beast, and the additional value it confers upon the land which it encloses. A fence of wood, or stone, as commonly made, is, at the best, but a miserable and tottering affair; soon needing repairs, which are a constant drain upon the purse; often liable to be broken down by trespassing Philistines; and, before many years, decaying, or so far falling down, as to demand a complete renewal. Now a good hedge, made of two plants we shall recommend, will last *for ever;* it is an "everlasting fence," at least in any acceptation of the word known to our restless and changing countrymen. When once fully grown, the small trouble of annual trimming costs not a whit more than the average expense of repairs on a wooden fence, while its freshness and verdure are renewed with every vernal return of the "flower and the leaf."

As a protection to the choicer products of the soil, which tempt the spoiler of the orchard and the garden, nothing is so efficient as a good hedge. It is like an impregnable fortress, neither to be scaled, broken through, nor climbed over. Fowls will not fly over it, because they fear to alight upon its top; and men and beasts are not likely to make more than one attempt to force its green walls. It shows a fair and leafy shield to its antagonist, but it has thousands of concealed arrows ready at a moment of assault, and there are few creatures, however bold, who care to "come to the *scratch*" twice with such a foe. Indeed a well made and perfect thorn hedge is so thick that a bird cannot fly through it.

> "The hedge was thick as is a castle wall,
> So that who list without to stand or go,
> Though he would all the day pry to and fro,
> He could not see if there were any wight
> Within or no."—CHAUCER.

"This is all true," we hear some impatient reader say; "hedges are beautiful, excellent, good; but what an age they require—five, six, seven, years—to be cut down—the poor things—once or twice, to be kept back every year with shortening and shearing, and only to reach the height of one's head, with such an outlay of time and trouble. Ah! it is too tedious, I must build a paling—I shall never have patience to wait for a hedge!"

Build a paling, friend; nature does not get up hasty job-work, like journeymen carpenters. But at least be consistent. Fill your garden with annuals. Do not sow any thing more lasting, or asking longer leases of time than six weeks—beans and summer sun-flowers. Breed no stock, plant no orchards, drain no meadows and—set no hedges! Leave all these to wiser men, or rather be persuaded of the wisdom of doing in the best way, what tillers of the earth have not learned to do better after a lapse of centuries!

But there are also persons, readers of ours, who must be treated with more respect. They will tell us that they have more reason in their objections to hedges. They admire hedges—they have planted and raised them. But they have not succeeded, and they have great doubts of the possibility of making good hedges in the United States. We know all the difficulties which these cultivators have experienced, for we have made the same trials, and seen the same obstacles ourselves. But we are confident we can answer their objections in a few words. *The* HAWTHORN (*Cratægus*) *cannot be depended upon as a hedge plant in this country.*

Hundreds of emigrants from Great Britain, familiar all their lives with hawthorn hedges and their treatment, and deploring the unsightliness of "posts and rails" in America, have made hedges of their old favorite, the common English hawthorn, and given them every care and attention. Here and there we see an instance of success; but it cannot be denied that, in the main, there is no success. The English hawthorn is not adapted to our hot and bright summers, and can never be successfully used for farm hedges.*

Bnt there are many species of *native* hawthorn scattered through our woods. Will not these make good hedges? We answer, excellent ones—nothing can be much better. Almost any of them are superior to the foreign sort for our climate. We have seen hedges of the two species known in the nurseries as the Newcastle thorn (*Cratægus crus-galli*) and Washington thorn (*C. cordata*), that realized all we could desire of a beautiful and effective verdantless fence.

A few years ago, therefore, we strongly recommended these native thorns—we hoped to see them planted in all parts of the country. But we are forced to admit now that there is a reason why we fear they will never make permanent hedges for the country at large, and for farm purposes.

This is, their liability to be utterly destroyed by that insect, so multiplied in many parts of the country, the *apple borer*. Wherever there are old orchards, this insect sooner or later finds its way, and sooner or later it will attack all the hawthorns, whether native or foreign, for they all belong to the same family as the apple-tree, and are all its favorite food. Fifteen years ago, a person riding through the lower part of New Jersey and Delaware, would have been struck with the numerous and beautiful hedges of Newcastle and Washington thorns. Whole districts, in some parts, were

* We know there are exceptions. We have ourselves about 1000 feet of excellent hedge of this plant. And we saw, with great satisfaction, last summer, on the fine farm of Mr. Godfrey, near Geneva, N. Y., more than a mile of promising young hedge of the English thorn. But the soil and climate there, are peculiarly favorable. These are exceptions to thousands of instances of total failure.

fenced with them, and nurserymen could scarcely supply the demand for young plants. Now we learn that whole farms have lost their hedges by the *borer*, which in some places attacked them so suddenly, perforating and girdling the stems near the ground, that in two seasons, sometimes indeed in one, the hedge would be half killed. Of course the planting of thorn hedges is almost abandoned there, and we are assured by growers of the plant in those States, who frequently sold hundreds of thousands, that there is now no demand whatever for them.*

We do not doubt that there are many sections of the country where good hawthorn hedges of the best native species, may be grown. In some places this fatal foe to it may never appear—though it follows closely in the steps of every careless orchardist. In *gardens* where insects are closely watched, it is not very difficult to prevent their ravages upon the thorn plants. But what we mean now to point out as distinctly as possible, is this—that no species of hawthorn, or *Cratœgus*, is likely ever to become a hedge plant of general use and value to farmers in America.

What we want in a hedge plant for this country is, vigor, hardiness, longevity, and a sap and bark either offensive, or offering no temptations to any destructive insects. Are there such plants? We think we may now, after the matter has been pretty thoroughly tested, answer yes; and name the BUCKTHORN, and the OSAGE ORANGE; the former for the northern, and the latter for the southern portions of our country. These plants are both natives. As they may not be familiar to many of our readers, we shall, before entering upon the planting of hedges, briefly describe them, and give correct sketches of their leaves and growth, so that they may be identified by any person.

* We recall to mind an instance on the Hudson, where three years ago we saw a very beautiful hedge of the Newcastle thorn—almost as handsome in its glossy foliage as holly itself. During the past summer we again beheld it, nearly destroyed by the insidious attacks of the borer.

THE BEST HEDGE PLANTS.

I. THE BUCKTHORN.

Rhamnus catharticus.—L.

Fig. 1. The Buckthorn.

The buckthorn is a deciduous shrub growing from ten to fifteen feet high, bushy, or with numerous branches. The bark is grayish brown; the leaves are about an inch or an inch and a half long, dark green, smooth, ovate, and notched or serrated on the edges, and are placed nearly opposite each other on the branches. There are no independent thorns, properly speaking, but the end of each year's shoots terminates in a sharp point or thorn. (See fig. 1.) The blossoms are small and yellowish green. They are succeeded by numerous round, black berries, which ripen in autumn, and hang till frost, and give the plant something of an ornamental appearance. The roots are unusually *black* in color, and are very numerous.

The buckthorn is a native of the north of Europe, Asia, and North America. It is not a common shrub in the woods in this country, but we find it very frequently in this neighborhood and in various parts of Dutchess county, N. Y., as well as on the borders of woods in Massachusetts.*

The bark and berries of the buckthorn are powerful cathartics. The sap of the berries, mixed with alum, makes the color known to painters as sap-green, and the bark yields a fine yellow dye.

As a hedge plant, the buckthorn possesses three or four points of great merit. In the first place, its bark and leaf are offensive to insects, and the borer, the aphis, and others, which are so destructive to all hawthorns in many parts of our country, will not touch it.

In the second place, it is remarkable for its hardiness, its robustness, and its power of adapting itself to any soil. It will bear any climate, however cold, for it grows wild in Siberia; hence it will never suffer, as the English thorn has been known to do, with an occasional winter of unusual severity. We have seen it growing under the shade of trees, and in dry and poor soil, as well as thriving in moist and springy soil; and in this respect, and in its natural rigid *thicket-like* habit, it seems more admirably fitted by nature for the northern hedge plant than almost any other. In the third place, it bears the earliest transplanting, has great longevity, and is very thrifty in its growth. We have already remarked that it is well supplied with roots. Indeed its fibres are unusually numerous even in seedlings of one year's growth. Hence it is transplanted with remarkable facility, and when treated with any thing like proper care, not one in five thousand of the plants will fail to grow. It is scarcely at all liable to diseases, and no plant bears the shears better, or gives a denser and thicker hedge, or is longer lived in a hedge. Its growth is at least one-third more rapid than that of the hawthorn, and the facility of raising it, at least half greater.

* Some botanists consider it a foreign plant, introduced and naturalized in this country. But we have found it in solitary and almost inaccessible parts of the Hudson Highlands, which forbids such a belief on our part.

Lastly, it is one of the easiest plants to propagate. It bears berries in abundance. These, if planted in autumn as soon as they are ripe (or even in the ensuing spring), will germinate in the spring, and if the soil is good, give plants from a foot to twenty inches high the first year—which are large enough for transplanting the next spring following. The seeds of the hawthorn do not vegetate till the second year, and the plants properly require to be transplanted once in the nurseries, and to be three years old, before they are fit for making hedges. Here is at once a most obvious and important saving of time and labor.

It is but a simple matter to raise buckthorn plants. You begin by gathering the seeds as soon as they are ripe, say by the middle of October.* Each berry contains four seeds, covered with a thin black pulp. Place them in a box or tub; mash the pulp by beating the berries moderately with a light wooden pounder. Then put them in a sieve, pour some water over them, rub the seeds through, and throw away the skin and pulp. Two or three rubbings and washings will give you clean seed. Let it then be dried, and it is ready for sowing.

Next, choose a good bit of deep garden soil. Dig it thoroughly, and give it a good dressing of manure. Open a drill with the hoe, exactly as you would for planting peas, and scatter the seed of the buckthorn in it, at an average of two or three inches apart. Cover them about an inch and a half deep. The rows or drills may, if you are about to raise a large crop, be put three feet apart, so that the horse cultivator may be used to keep the ground in order.

In the spring the young plants will make their appearance plentifully. All that they afterwards require is a thorough weeding, and a dressing with a hoe as soon as they are all a couple of inches high, and a little attention afterwards to keep the ground mellow and free from weeds. One year's growth in strong land, or two in that of tolerable quality, will render them fit for being transplanted into the hedge-rows.

* The buckthorn is pretty largely cultivated for its berries at the various Shaking Quaker settlements in this State and New England: and seeds may usually be procured from them in abundance, and at reasonable prices.

If the buckthorn has any defect as a hedge plant it is this; while young it is not provided with strong and stout roots like the hawthorn. Its thorns, as we have already said, stand at the point of each shoot of the old wood. Hence it is that a buckthorn hedge does not appear, and is not, really well armed with thorns till it has attained its full shape, and has had a couple of seasons' shearing. After that, the hedge being well furnished with the ends of the shoots, it presents thorns on every face, and is a thorough defence. Besides this, it is a stronger and stouter plant than the thorn, and offers more absolute resistance than the latter plant. Though it may be kept low, yet it makes a most efficient shelter if allowed to form a high hedge. One of the largest and oldest specimens in New England is that at Roxbury, planted by the late Hon. John Lowell, and still growing on the estate of his son. It is very strong, and if we remember right, twelve or fifteen feet high.*

II. THE MACLURA, OR OSAGE ORANGE.

Maclura aurantiaca.

The osage orange, or maclura, grows wild in abundance in the State of Arkansas, and as far north as the Red River.

It is one of the most striking and beautiful of American trees. Its foliage is not unlike that of the orange, but more glossy, and

* Mr. Derby, of Salem, was one of the first persons to employ the buckthorn, and to urge its value upon the public. From the *Transactions of the Essex Agricultural Society* for 1842, we extract some of his remarks relating to it: "I do not hesitate to pronounce the buckthorn the most suitable plant for hedges I have ever met with. It vegetates early in the spring, and retains its verdure late in autumn. Being a native plant, it is never injured by the most intense cold, and its vitality is so great that the young plants may be kept out of ground for a long time, or transported to a great distance without injury. It never sends up any suckers, nor is disfigured by any dead wood. It can be clipped into any shape which the caprice or ingenuity of the gardener may devise, and it needs no plashing or interlacing, the natural growth of the plants being sufficiently interwoven. It is never cankered by unskilful clipping, but will bear the knife to any degree."

polished; indeed it is of a bright varnished green. It grows luxuriantly, about thirty or forty feet high, with a wide and spreading head. The flowers are small and inconspicuous, pale green in color, those preceding the fruit resembling a little ball, (*see figure*.)* The fruit itself is very near the size and shape of an orange, yellow at full maturity, and rough on the outside, not unlike the seed of the buttonwood or sycamore. It hangs till October, is not eatable, but is striking and ornamental on a large tree. This tree was first introduced into our gardens, where it is now well known, from a village of the Osage Indians, which, coupled with its general appearance, gave rise to its popular name. The wood is full of milky sap, and we have never seen it attacked by any insects.

Fig. 2. The Osage Orange.

A great many trials have been made within the last ten years,

* The male and female flowers are borne on separate trees.

in various parts of the country, with the Osage orange, as a hedge plant. The general result, south of this, has been in the highest degree favorable. Many who have failed with all species of hawthorn, have entire faith in the value of this plant, and we have no longer a doubt that it is destined to become the favorite hedge plant of all that part of the Union lying south and west of the State of New-York.*

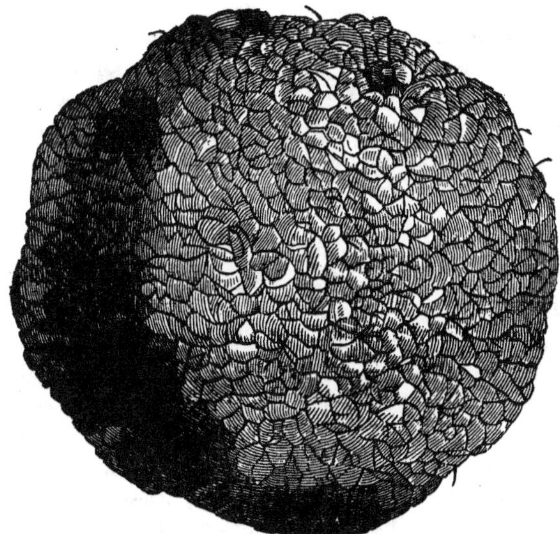

Fig. 8. Fruit of the Osage Orange Tree.

The Osage orange, when treated as a hedge plant, has many ex-

* The Osage orange is hardy in our own grounds, where we have cultivated it for many years. In New England it will probably be found too tender in winter, though there is an excellent young hedge of it at Belmont Place, the residence of J. P. Cushing, Esq., near Boston, which we were told the past season, has proved quite hardy. Pruning in hedge form, by checking its luxuriance, will render any partially tender shrubs more hardy. It may be safely laid down as a rule, judging from our own observations, that the Osage orange will succeed perfectly as a hedge, wherever the Isabella grape will ripen in the open air without shelter or protection. This is a better and safer guide than a reference to parallels of latitude.

cellent characteristics. It is robust, vigorous, and long-lived. It sends out a great abundance of branches, bears trimming perfectly well, is most amply provided at all times with stout thorns, and its bright and glossy foliage gives it a very rich and beautiful appearance. It grows well on almost any soil, and makes a powerful and impenetrable fence in a very short time. Though it will bear rough and severe pruning, and is therefore well adapted for farm fences, yet it must be regularly trimmed twice every year, and requires it even more imperatively than other hedge plants, to prevent its sending out strong shoots to disfigure the symmetry of the hedge.

The Osage orange is not yet sufficiently well known to be a cheap plant in the nurseries.* But this is because it is not yet sufficiently in demand. It is easily propagated, and will, no doubt, soon be offered at very moderate rates.

This propagation is done in two ways; by the seed, and by the cuttings of the roots.

The seed is produced plentifully by the female trees. There are large bearing trees in the old Landreth and McMahon gardens, near Philadelphia. But it is not difficult now to have resort to those of native growth. We learn that this tree is so common in the neighborhood of Columbus, Hempstead Co., Arkansas, that the seeds may be had there for the expense of gathering them. They should be gathered at the latter part of September, and the clean seed, packed in an equal quantity of dry sand, may be sent to any part of the Union before planting time. A quart will produce at least 5000 plants. The seed may be planted in broad drills, and treated just as we have already recommended for that of the buckthorn. But the plants are seldom fit for hedge planting till the second year.

The other mode of propagation is by the roots. Pieces of the roots, of the thickness of one's little finger, made into cuttings three or four inches long, and planted in lines, in mellow soil, with the top of the root just below the surface, will soon push out shoots, and become plants. The trimmings of a hundred young plants, when

* Messrs. Landreth and Fulton, of Philadelphia, have a stock of it for sale at $12 per 1000. The usual price of hawthorns and buckthorns is $6 per 1000; but the latter may be raised at a cost of not more than $3.

taken up from the nursery for transplanting, will thus give nearly a thousand new plants.

PLANTING AND REARING THE HEDGE.

Having secured the plants, the next step necessary is to prepare the ground where the future hedge is to be formed.

For this purpose a strip must be marked out, three or four feet in width, along the whole line where the hedge is to grow. This must be thoroughly trenched with a spade, eighteen inches deep, if it is to be a garden hedge; or sub-soil ploughed to that depth, if it is to be a farm hedge. We know many persons content themselves with simply digging the ground in the common way, one spade deep; but we take it for granted no readers of ours will hesitate about the little additional trouble of properly trenching or deepening the soil,* when they may be assured that they will gain just one-half in the future growth and luxuriance of the hedge.

It is the custom in England to plant hedges on a bank with a ditch at one side, to carry off the water—and some persons have, from mere imitation, attempted the same thing here. It is worse than useless in our hot and dry climate. The hedge thrives better when planted on the level strip, simply because it is more naturally placed and has more moisture. If the bank and ditch is used, they are continually liable to be torn away by the violence of our winter frosts.

As regards the season, the spring is the best time for the northern States—the autumn for the southern. Autumn planting at the north often succeeds perfectly well, but the plants must be examined in the spring; such as are thrown out of place by the frosts require to be fixed again, and this often involves a good deal of trouble in strong soil. Early spring planting, therefore, for this latitude, is much preferable on the whole.

A good dressing of any convenient manure that is not so coarse as to be unmanageable in planting, should be put upon the soil and

* Those who may be fortunate enough to possess rich deep bottom or alluvial lands, are the only persons who need not be at the trouble of trenching their soil.

turned under while the trenching is going on. The soil must be thoroughly pulverized and freed from stones, lumps, and rubbish, before the planting begins.

The plants are now to be made ready. This is done in the first place, by assorting them into two parcels—those of *large* and those of *small size.* Lay aside the smaller ones for the richest part of your ground, and plant the larger ones on the poorest of the soil. This will prevent that inequality which there would be in the hedge if strong and weak plants were mixed together, and it will equalize the growth of the whole plantation by dividing the advantages.

The plants should then be trimmed. This is speedily done by cutting down the top or stem to within about an inch of what was the ground line, (so that it will, when planted again, have but an inch of stem above the soil,) and by correspondingly shortening all the larger roots about one-third.

If you have a good deal of planting to do, it is better to bury the plants in a trench close at hand, or *lay-them-in-by-the-heels*, as it is technically called, to keep them in good order till the moment they are wanted.

The hedge should be planted in a double row, with the plants placed, not opposite to each other, but alternate—thus:

  *   *   *   *   *   *   *
    *   *   *   *   *   *

The rows should be six inches apart, and the plants one foot apart in the rows. This will require about 32 plants to a rod, or 2000 plants to 1000 feet.

Fig. 4. Manner of Planting Hedges.

Having well pulverized the soil, set down the line firmly for the first row, and with a spade throw out a trench about eight or ten inches deep, keeping its upright or firm bank next to the line. Drop the plants along the line at about the distance they will be needed, and then plant them twelve inches apart, keeping them as nearly as possible in a perfectly straight line; for it is worth bearing in mind, that you are performing an act, the unimpeachable *straightforwardness* of which will no doubt be criticized for a great many years afterwards. Press the earth moderately round the stem of the plant with the foot, when the filling-in of the pulverized soil is nearly completed. And, finally, level the whole nicely with the hoe.

Having finished this row, take up the line and fix it again, six inches distant; open the trench in the opposite direction, and set the plants in the same manner. This completes the planting. The next point, and it is one of great importance, is the *cultivation* which the young plants require until they become a hedge. It is indeed quite useless to plant a hedge, as some persons do, and leave it afterwards to be smothered by the evil genius of docks and thistles. A young hedge requires about the same amount of cultivation as a row of Indian corn. The whole of the prepared strip of ground must be kept loose with the hoe, and free from weeds. Then light dressings for the first two or three summers will be required to effect this, and the thrifty and luxuriant state in which the plants are thereby kept, will well repay it, to the eye alone. After that, the branches of the hedge will have extended so, as in a good degree to shade and occupy the ground, and little more than a slight occasional attention to the soil will be required.

A few words must be given to the trimming and clipping of our now established hedge.

The plants having, before they were planted, been cut off nearly even with the surface of the ground, it follows, that, in the ensuing spring, or one year from the time of planting, they have made many shoots from each stem. Let the whole of this growth then be cut down to within *six inches* of the ground.

The following spring, which will be two years of growth, cut back the last season's shoots, leaving only one foot of the current season's growth. This will leave our hedge, altogether, eighteen inches high.

The third year shorten back the tops so as to leave again one foot of the year's growth. The hedge will now be two and a half feet high.

This course must be pursued every spring until the hedge is of the desired height and form, which will take place in five or six years. The latter time is usually required to make a perfect hedge—though the buckthorn will make a pretty good hedge in five years.

This severe process of cutting off all the top at first, and annually shortening back half the thrifty growth of a young hedge, seems to the novice like an unnecessary cruelty to the plant, and trial of one's own patience. We well remember as a boy, how all our indignation was roused at the idea of thus seeing a favorite hedge "*put back*" so barbarously every year. But it is the "*inexorable must*," in hedge growing. Raising a hedge is like raising a good name; if there is no base or foundation for the structure, it is very likely to betray dreadful gaps at the bottom before it is well established. In a hedge, the great and all important point is to make a broad and thick base. Once this is accomplished, the task is more than half over. The top will speedily grow into any shape we desire, and the sides are pliant enough to the will of him who holds the shears. But no necromancy, short of cutting the whole down again, will fill up the base of a hedge that is lean and open at the bottom.* Hence the imperative necessity of cutting back the shoots till the base becomes a perfect thicket.

The hedge of the buckthorn, or Osage orange, that has been treated in this way, and has arrived at its sixth year, should be about six feet high, tapering to the top, and three feet wide at the base. This is high enough for all common purposes; but when shelter, or extra protection is needed, it may be allowed to grow eight or ten feet high, and four feet wide at the base.

In trimming the hedge, a pair of large shears, called hedge shears, are commonly used. But we have found that English laborers in our service, will trim with double the rapidity with the instrument they call a "hook." It may be had at our agricultural warehouses, and is precisely like a sickle, except that it has a sharp edge.

When the hedge has attained the size and shape which is finally

* *Plashing* is a mode of interlacing the branches of hedges that are thin and badly grown, so as to obviate the defect as far as possible. It need never be resorted to with the buckthorn, when a hedge is properly trimmed from the first.

desired, it is not allowed to grow any larger. Two shearings or clippings are necessary, every season, to keep it in neat order—one in June, and the other at the end of September.

Counting the value of the plants at the commencement at five dollars per thousand, the entire cost of the hedge, at the end of the sixth year,—including planting, cultivating, and shearing in the best manner,—would here be about seventy-five cents a rod; which, for an everlasting fence, and one of so much beauty, we think a very moderate sum.

We have said nothing about the temporary fencing which our hedge will need, till it is at least five years old—that is, if it is a boundary hedge, or is bordered on one or both sides by fields where animals run. It is evident enough that for this purpose, in most cases, the cheaper the fence the better. A very indifferent wooden fence will last five years, and a light barrier of posts and rails will best suit the taste of most farmers. A much more convenient, and very excellent one for the purpose, is the movable *hurdle fence*, made of light chestnut rails, which costs but little, and may be readily removed from one place or field to another, as the case requires.

No better *tail piece* can be given to this long article, than the following sketch, representing the remarkably fine specimen of the buckthorn hedge in the grounds of John C. Lee, Esq. of Salem, Mass.

Fig. 5. Mr. Lee's Hedge.

XIII.

ON THE EMPLOYMENT OF ORNAMENTAL TREES AND SHRUBS IN NORTH AMERICA.

[From Hovey's Mag. of Horticulture.]

December, 1835.

IT is remarkable, that notwithstanding the rapid progress which horticulture is making in the United States, so little attention is paid to the planting of ornamental trees, with a view to the embellishment of our country residences. The magnificent parks of England have been long and justly admired, as constituting one of the most beautiful features of that highly cultivated country; and although the horticultural creations of our more limited means, may never equal in extent and grandeur some of those of the aristocracy of Europe, yet every person of cultivated mind, is aware how beautiful the hand of taste can render even very limited scenes, by the proper application of the principles and materials necessary to mental pleasure and gratification.

Considered in a single point of view, what an infinite variety of beauty there is in a tree itself! Every part is admirable, from the individual beauty of its leaves, to its grand effect as a whole. Who has not witnessed in some favorite landscape the indescribable charm thrown over the whole scene by a single tree? Perhaps a huge giant, whose massy trunk and wide out-stretched arms have been the production of ages; or the more graceful form of another whose delicate foliage reflects the sunbeam, and trembles with the slightest breeze that passes over it. There is no monotony in nature—even in trees, every season has its own charms. Spring, the season of renewed life, witnesses the rush of the newly imbibed sap—the buds swell—the tender leaves unfold, and the admirer of nature is delighted by the freshness and vividness of the young foliage. Summer comes—he is refreshed by the fragrance of their blossoms—their shade is a welcome luxury in the noontide sun—perchance their fruit may be an acceptable offering to the palate—and who in this country has not witnessed the autumnal glories of an American forest?

There is no country of the globe which produces a greater variety of fine forest trees, whether considered for the purposes of ornament or timber, than North America. Yet it is a fact that for both these purposes, more particularly the first, they are horticulturally better known in many parts of Europe, than they are now at home. Those governments have imported the seeds of all our most valuable forest trees, annually, for more than a century. Instead of planting, our agriculturists have hitherto been engaged in destroying. In the Atlantic States, this period is now past; and we would, therefore, first direct the attention of the arboriculturist to our own trees.

There is not in the whole catalogue, scarcely a more interesting object than an immense oak tree, when placed so as to be considered in relation to the large mansion of a wealthy proprietor. Its broad ample limbs and aged form, give a very impressive air of dignity to the whole scene. It is a very common inhabitant of our woods, there being forty-four species of indigenous growth between the 20th and 48th degrees of north latitude.* The pendulous branches of the American elm—the light foliage of the birch—the cheerful vernal appearance of some of the species of maple—the delicate leaf of the locust, and the heavy masses of verdure produced by the beech, are sufficient to render them all ornamental in park scenery, and they should ever find a proper situation in an extensive lawn. Our American poplars should be recollected, when a rapid growth and immediate effect is required. Gledítschia triacánthos, or the sweet locust, is interesting from its long masses of thorns. The plane or sycamore (Plátanus occidentàlis) is too much neglected because it is so common; but in favorable situations, in deep

* Michaux.

soils, and where ample room is afforded, it produces a noble tree of immense size. Several have been measured on the banks of the Ohio from forty to fifty feet in circumference.

A native tree, but little known in our ornamental plantations, is the Kentucky coffee (Gymnócladus canadénsis). It is a native of Kentucky and Tennessee, grows to the height of forty feet, and its doubly compound foliage, and very singular appearance when defoliated in the winter months, are well calculated to render it an interesting feature in the landscape. Cupréssus dístichum (Taxòdium *Rich.*), the deciduous cypress, flourishing in vast quantities in the southern parts of the Union, is, though perfectly hardy, and of easy cultivation, but little known in the northern States.* Its beautiful light green foliage contrasts elegantly with the denser hue of other deciduous trees, and we are hardly aware of an upright growing tree, better calculated to give variety of color to groups and masses, than this. *Catálpa* syringæfòlia is a most striking ornament to a lawn, when in the summer months it is loaded with its large clusters of parti-colored flowers.

But the most splendid, most fragrant, and most celebrated ornamental production of the woods and forests of our country, is yet to be mentioned. It is the unrivalled Magnòlia grandiflòra: the most magnificent of the genus, a beautiful tree of seventy feet in its native soil, only attains the size of a large shrub in the middle States, and will scarcely withstand the winters of the northern. But M. acuminàta, though not so beautiful, is a fine large tree, sometimes attaining the height of ninety feet. It is abundant in western New-York and Ohio. M. macrophylla is not only remarkable for the beauty of its flowers, but also for the extraordinary size of its leaves; they having been measured so long as three feet. M. tripétela, the umbrella tree, is also a fine species growing in districts from Georgia to New-York; its large, cream-colored flowers measuring seven or eight inches in diameter. Still more rare, though highly ornamental, are M. cordàta and M. auriculàta; small trees which ought to be indispensable to every collection. The species of smallest stature

* We have seen a celebrated specimen in Col. Carr's garden, Philadelphia, 180 feet high, 25 feet in circumference, and 91 years old.

and most frequent occurrence in the middle States, is M. glaúca, the flowers of which are highly odoriferous. It succeeds best in damp soils, and is found very plentifully in situations of this kind in New Jersey.

Ornamental trees from other countries should find a prominent place in the plantations of our horticulturists. They not only have an intrinsic value in themselves, but, to a refined taste, they offer gratifications from the associations connected with them. Thus the proprietor may view, in the walks over his grounds, not only productions of his *own* country, but their fellows from many other climes. We may witness flourishing upon the same soil, many of the productions of southern Europe and Asia; individuals from the frigid regions of Siberia, and the almost unknown forests of Patagonia; vegetables which perseverance has abstracted from the jealous Chinese, and which the botanical traveller has discovered among the haunts of the savage Indian.

Among the foreign trees which are most generally cultivated for ornament in this country, we may mention the two genera of Tilia and Æsculus. The European lime or linden-tree, with its fine stately form and fragrant blossoms, is a most pleasing object as an ornamental tree. The horse chestnut (Æ. hippocástanum) is perhaps better known than any foreign tree in the country; its compact growth, fine digitate leaves, and above all, its superb, showy flowers, distributed in huge bouquets over the foliage, have rendered it here, as in Europe, an object of universal admiration. We would here beg leave to direct the attention of planters to the less known, but no less interesting species of this tree, natives of our own soil. Æ. pavìa, producing red, and Æ. flàva, yellow flowers, form very beautiful trees of moderate size. The other species are rather large shrubs than trees, and are very pretty ornaments to the garden.

The brilliant appearance of the European mountain ash (Sorbus aucupària), when in autumn it is densely clad with its rich crimson fruit, is a circumstance sufficient to give it strong claims to the care of the arboriculturist, independently of the beauty of its foliage.

We must not forget, in this brief notice, the larches both of Europe and our country. Pínus làrix has long been considered among the first timber trees of the other continent. The singularity of its foliage, as a deciduous tree, its long declining branches and drooping spray, are well calculated to give variety to the landscape, and we are happy to see, that both this and our two American species, P. microcárpa and P. péndula, are becoming more generally objects of attention and cultivation.

Among the interesting trees of more recent introduction, and which are yet rare in this country, we may mention Salisbùria adiantifòlia, the Japanese maiden-hair tree. The foliage is strikingly singular and beautiful, resembling that well known fern, Adiántum pedàtum, and the tree appears to be very hardy. The purple beech, a variety of Fàgus sylvática, is a very unique object, with its strangely colored leaves, and a splendid tree lately introduced from the banks of the Missouri and Arkansas, is the Osage orange (Maclùra aurantiàca). Its vivid green leaves and rapid growth are already known to us; but it is described to us as being a tree, in its native soil, of thirty or forty feet in height, and bearing abundance of beautiful fruit, of the size and appearance of an orange. The weeping ash is also a very unique and desirable object, and its long, seemingly inverted shoots may be introduced in some situations with an excellent effect.

We have often regretted that, in decorating the grounds of country residences, so little attention is paid by the proprietors, to hardy evergreen trees. Ornamental at any season, they are eminently so in winter—a period, in this latitude, when every other portion of vegetable matter yields to the severity of our northern climate, and when those retaining their coats of verdure uninjured are beautiful and cheerful memorials of the unceasing vitality of the vegetable world. Deciduous trees at this season present but a bleak and desolate aspect—a few evergreens, therefore, interspersed singly over the lawn, or tastefully disposed in a few groups, so as to be seen from the windows of the mansion, will give a pleasing liveliness to the scene, which cannot fail to charm every person. We would earnestly advise every person engaged in ornamental planting, to transfer some of our fine native evergreen trees to their lawn, park, or terrace. We are aware that many think that there is great difficulty in transplanting them with success, but experience has taught us that, with the following precautions, no more difficulty is found than with deciduous trees. In transplanting, choose the spring of the year, at the time the *buds are swelling: cut as few of the roots as possible, and do not suffer them to become dry before you replace them in the soil.* Among our most ornamental evergreen trees may be mentioned the different species of pine, natives of North America. Several of them are fine stately trees, and one which is particularly ornamental as a park tree, is the white or Weymouth pine, Pínus stròbus. Pínus rígida, when old and large, is a very picturesque tree; and Pínus álba, rùbra et frasèri, the white, red, and double spruce firs, are trees of moderate size, very generally diffused in the middle States, and easily obtained. The well known balsam fir, Pínus balsámea, is such a beautiful evergreen, and succeeds so well in this climate, that it should find a place in the smallest plantations. We have observed it thriving well even in confined spaces in cities. Thùja occidentàlis, the arborvitæ, is a very interesting tree, and, as well as the exotic T. orientàlis, will be considered very ornamental in districts where it is not common.

Among the most ornamental foreign coniferous trees we will notice the Norway spruce, the drooping branches of which, in a large specimen, are so highly admired; the well known Scotch fir, the finest timber tree of Europe, celebrated for growing on thin soils; and the beautiful silver fir, Pínus pícea; all of them are noble trees, and as they can be readily procured at the nurseries, should be found in the grounds of every country residence.

Several other species of this genus which are thought the most beautiful trees of Europe, unfortunately are yet scarce in this country. The stone pine, whose seeds are a delicious fruit, and whose "vast canopy, supported on a naked column of immense height, forms one of the chief and peculiar beauties in Italian scenery and in the living landscapes of Claude," and the not less interesting Pínus Pínáster and P. Cémbra of the mountains of Switzerland. But the most desirable evergreen tree which flourishes in temperate climates, is the classic cedar of Lebanon, Pínus cèdrus. Its singular ramose branches and wild picturesque appearance in a large specimen, give a more majestic and decided character to a fine building and its adjacent scenery, than any other tree whatever. It is a native of the coldest parts of Mt. Libanus, but according to Professor Martyn, more trees are to be found in England at the present time than on its original site. As it is scarcely yet known as an ornamental tree in this country, we certainly do not know of an object better worth the attention of the arboriculturist.

We observe in foreign periodicals that several magnificent hardy individuals belonging to this section of trees, have been lately introduced into Europe, and we hope before long they will find their way to the hands of *our* cultivators. Among the most remarkable, we may mention a splendid new genus of pine (Pínus Lambertiàna) lately found in northern California. The discoverer, Mr. D. Douglas, botanical collector to the London Horticultural Society, describes it as growing from one hundred and fifty to two hundred feet in height, producing cones sixteen inches in length. He measured a specimen two hundred and fifteen feet long and fifty-seven in circumference.* Several other specimens of this genus, of much grandeur and beauty, are but lately introduced into cultivation, and which our present limits will barely permit us to enumerate. Pínus Douglásii, P. montícola, P. grándis, are immense trees from the northwest coast of America; Pínus deodàra [Cèdrus *deodàra*, Rox.], from Himalaya, P. taúrica, from Asiatic Turkey, and P. Láricio, from the mountains of Corsica, are spoken of as being highly ornamental; Araucària imbricàta, a beautiful evergreen tree of South America, and Cupréssus péndula, the weeping cypress of the Chinese, are extremely elegant—are found to withstand the climate of Britain, and would probably also endure that of this country.

We cannot close these remarks without again adverting to the infinite beauty which may be produced by a proper use of this fine material of nature. Many a dreary and barren prospect may be rendered interesting—many a natural or artificial deformity hidden, and the effect of almost every landscape may be improved, simply by the judicious employment of trees. The most fertile countries would appear but a desert without them, and the most picturesque scenery in every part of the globe has owed to them its highest charms. Added to this, by recent improvements in the art of transplanting,†

* Trans. Linnæan Soc., vol. 15, p. 497.

† Vide Sir Henry Stuart on Planting.

the ornamental planter of the present day may realize almost immediately what was formerly the slow and regular production of years.

Additional Note.—The beauty of our autumnal foliage is well known to the whole world: it has long been the theme of admiration with the poet and the painter, and, to a foreigner, it appears to be one of the most superb features of this fresh "green forest land." Yet, every year, the axe of the woodsman erases wide masses of the rich coloring from the panorama. Will it not be worth the consideration of persons who are now making, or who, in many parts of the country, before much time has elapsed, will make extensive plantations of forest trees for ornament, shelter and profit, to consider how splendid an effect may be produced, by a disposition of the most brilliantly colored of our indigenous trees in separate groups and masses, on the parks and lawns of extensive country residences? It is true, that autumn's gay colors remain with us but for a short time, but is this not also true with respect to the vivid greenness of vernal foliage, and the still more fugitive beauty of blossom which constitutes one of the chief points of attraction in ornamental trees? We feel confident that, when landscape-gardening shall arrive at that perfection which it is yet destined to attain in this country, this will be a subject of important consideration. The high beauty with which the richness of our autumnal tints may invest even the tamest scene, we were never more deeply impressed with, than in travelling through New Jersey, during the months of September and October of the present year. Every one is aware of the tame, monotonous appearance of a great portion of the interior of that State; but only those who have seen the same landscapes in autumn, can imagine with what a magic glow even they are enshrined in that season. The following are some of the trees we noticed, as assuming the richest hues in their foliage. Scarlet oak (Quércus coccínea) bright scarlet, dogwood (Córnus flórida), and the tupelo and sour gum (Nyssa villòsa, etc.) deep crimson, different species of Acer or maple, various shades of yellow and deep orange; the sweet-gum (Liquidámber) reddish purple, and our American ash, a distinct sombre purple. These are but a few of the most striking colors; and all the intermediate shades were filled up by the birches, sycamores, elms, chesnuts, and beeches, of which we have so many numerous species in our forests, and the whole was thrown into lively contrast by a rich intermingling of the deep green in the thick foliage of the pines, spruces, and hemlocks.

AGRICULTURE.

I.

CULTIVATORS,—THE GREAT INDUSTRIAL CLASS OF AMERICA.

June, 1848.

AT this moment, when the old world's monarchical institutions are fast falling to pieces, it is interesting to look at home, at the prosperous and happy condition of our new-world republic.

Abroad, the sovereign springs from a privileged class, and holds his position by the force of the army. His state and government are supported by heavy taxes, wrung from the laboring classes, often entirely without their consent. At home, the people are the sovereign power. The safety of their government lies in their own intelligence; and the taxes paid for the maintenance of public order, or to create public works, fall with no heavy or unequal pressure, but are wisely and justly distributed throughout all classes of society.

In the United States, the *industrial classes* are the true sovereigns. *Idleness* is a condition so unrecognized and unrespected with us, that the few professing it find themselves immediately thrown out of the great machine of active life which constitutes American society. Hence, an idle man is a cipher. Work he must, either with his head, his hands, or his capital; work in some mode or other, or he is a *dethroned sovereign.* The practical and busy spirit of our people repudiates him, and he is of no more absolute consequence than the poor fugitive king,—denied and driven out by his subjects.

The CULTIVATORS OF THE SOIL constitute the great industrial class in this country. They may well be called its "bone and sinew;" for, at this moment they do not only feed all other classes, but also no insignificant portion of needy Europe, furnish the raw material for manufactures, and raise the great staples which figure so largely in the accounts of the merchant, the ship owner and manufacturer, in every village, town, and sea-port in the Union.

The *sovereign people* has a better right to look over its "*rent roll*"—to examine the annual sum total of the products of its industry, than any other sovereign whatever; and it has accordingly employed Mr. Burke, the excellent commissioner of patents, to collect statistical facts, and publish them in the annual report of his office.

An examination of the condition of this country, as exhibited in Mr. Burke's report of its industrial resources, will, we think, afford the best proof ever exhibited of the value of the American Union, and the extraordinary wealth of our territory. The total value of the *products of the soil*, alone, for the past year, he estimates at more than *one thousand five hundred millions* of dollars.*

The value of the grain crops and great agricultural staples of the country, for 1847, amounts to $815,863,688.

The value of all horticultural products (gardens, orchards, and nurseries), is estimated at $459,577,533.

The value of the live stock, wool, and dairy products, amounts to $246,054,579.

The value of the products of the woods and forests, amounts to $59,099,628.

It is also estimated that there were produced last year 224,384,502 bushels of *surplus* grains of various kinds, over and above what was amply sufficient for home consumption. This is much more than enough to meet the ordinary demand of all the corn-buying countries of Europe.

Over *one thousand five hundred millions* of dollars, in the products of the soil, for a single year! Does not this fully justify us in

* $1,579,595,428.

holding up the cultivators of the American soil as the great industrial class? But let us compare them a little, by Mr. Burke's aid, with the other industrial classes.

The annual product of all the *manufactures* in the Union, for 1847, is estimated at $500,000,000. The profits of trade and commerce at $23,458,345. The profits of fisheries $17,069,262; and of banks, money institutions, rents, and professions, $145,000,000. Total, $809,697,407.

Here we have the facts, or something, at least, like an approximation to the facts, of the results of the yearly industrial labor of the republic. The average amount is the enormous sum of over *two thousand three hundred and eighty-nine millions of dollars.*

Of this, the agricultural class produces *nearly double that of all other classes*, or over one thousand five hundred and seventy-nine millions; while all other classes, merchants, manufacturers, professional men, etc., produce but little more than *eight hundred and nine millions.*

There are a few, among the great traders and "merchant princes," who do not sufficiently estimate the dignity or importance of any class but their own. To them we commend a study of Mr. Burke's statistical tables. There are some few farmers who think their occupation one of narrow compass and resources; we beg them to look over the aggregate annual products of their country, and take shame to themselves.

It is no less our duty to call the attention of our own readers to the great importance of the *horticultural interest* of the country. Why, its products ($459,000,000) are more than half as great in value as those strictly agricultural; they are almost as large as the whole manufacturing products of the country; and half as large as the manufacturing and all other interests, excepting the agricultural, combined.

In truth, the profits of the gardens and orchards of the country, are destined to be enormous. Mr. Burke's estimate appears to us very moderate; and from the unparalleled increase in this interest very recently, and the peculiar adaptation of our soil and climate to the finest fruits and vegetables, the next ten years must exhibit an amount of horticultural products which will almost challenge belief.

The markets of this country will not only be supplied with fruit in great abundance and excellence, but thousands of orchards will be cultivated solely for foreign consumption.

The system of railroads and cheap transportation already begins to supply the seaboard cities with some of the fair and beautiful fruits of the fertile west. When the orchards of Massachusetts fail, the orchards of western New-York will supply the Boston market with apples; and thus, wherever the finest transportable products of the soil are in demand, there they will find their way.

There are, however, many of the finer and more perishable products of the garden and orchard which will not bear a long journey. These, it should be the peculiar business of the cultivator of the older and less fertile soil in the seaboard States to grow. He may not, as an agriculturist, be able to compete with the fertile soils of the west; but he may still do so as a horticulturist, by devoting his attention and his land to orchards and gardens. If it is too difficult and expensive to renovate an old soil that is worn out, or bring up a new one naturally poor, for farm crops, in the teeth of western grain prices, he may well afford to do so for the larger profit derived from orchard and garden culture, where those products are raised for which a market must be found without long transportation. He who will do this most successfully must not waste his time, labor, and capital, by working in the dark. He must learn gardening and orcharding as a practical art, and a science. He must collect the lost elements of the soil from the animal and mineral kingdoms, and bring them back again to their starting point. He must seek out the food of plants in towns and villages, where it is wasted and thrown away. He must plant and prune so as to aid and direct nature, that neither time nor space are idly squandered.

Certainly, we have just pride and pleasure in looking upon the great agricultural class of America. Landholders and proprietors of the soil, as they are, governing themselves, and developing the resources of a great nation—how different is their position from that of the farmers of England,—hundreds of thousands of men, working, generation after generation, upon lands *leased* by a small privileged body, which alone owns and entails the soil; or even from that of France, where there are millions of proprietors, but proprietors of a soil so subdivided that the majority have half a dozen acres, or perhaps, even a half or fourth of an acre in extent,—often scarcely sufficient to raise a supply of a single crop for a small family.

If we have said any thing calculated to inspire self-respect in the agricultural class of this country, it is not with a view to lessen that for any other of its industrial classes. Far from it. Indeed, with the versatility of power and pursuits which characterize our people, no class can be said to be fixed. The farming class is the great nursery of all the professions, and the industrial arts of the country. From its bosom go out the shrewdest lawyers and the most successful merchants of the towns; and back to the country return these classes again, however successful, to be regenerated in the primitive life and occupation of the race.

But the agricultural class perhaps is still wanting in a just appreciation of its importance, its rights, and its duties. It has so long listened to sermons, lectures and orations, from those who live in cities and look upon country life as "*something for dull wits*," that it still needs apostles who draw their daily breath in green fields, and are untrammelled by the schools of politics and trade.

The agricultural journals, over the whole country, have done much to raise the dignity of the calling. They have much still to do. The importance of agricultural schools, of a high grade, should be continually insisted upon, until every State Legislature in the Union comes forward with liberal endowments; and if pledges ought ever to be demanded of politicians, then farmers should not be slow to require them of their representatives, for legislation favorable to every sound means of increasing the intelligence of this great bulwark of the country's safety and prosperity—the *cultivators of the soil.*

II.

THE NATIONAL IGNORANCE OF THE AGRICULTURAL INTEREST.

September, 1851.

TO general observers, the prosperity of the United States in the great interests of trade, commerce, manufactures, and agriculture, is a matter of every-day remark and general assent. The country extends itself from one zone to another, and from one ocean to another. New States are settled, our own population increases, emigration pours its vast tide upon our shores, new soils give abundant harvests, new settlements create a demand for the necessaries and luxuries of life provided by the older cities, and the nation exhibits at every census, so unparalleled a growth, and such magnificent resources, that common sense is startled, and only the imagination can keep pace with the probable destinies of the one hundred millions of Americans that will speak one language, and, we trust, be governed by one constitution, half a century hence.

As a wise man, who finds his family increasing after the manner of the ancient patriarchs, looks about him somewhat anxiously, to find out if there is likely to be bread enough for their subsistence, so a wise statesman, looking at this extraordinary growth of population, and this prospective wealth of the country, will inquire, narrowly, into its productive powers. He will desire to know whether the national domain is so managed that it will be likely to support the great people that will be ready to live upon it in the next century He will seek to look into the present and the future sufficiently to ascertain whether our rapid growth and material abundance do not arise almost as much from the migratory habits of our people, and the constant taking-up of rich prairies, yielding their virgin harvests of breadstuffs, as from the institutions peculiar to our favored country.

We regret to say, that it does not require much scrutiny on the part of a serious inquirer, to discover that we are in some respects like a large and increasing family, running over and devouring a great estate to which they have fallen heirs, with little or no care to preserve or maintain it, rather than a wise and prudent one, seeking to maintain that estate in its best and most productive condition.

To be sure, our trade and commerce are pursued with a thrift and sagacity likely to add largely to our substantial wealth, and to develope the collateral resources of the country. But, after all, trade and commerce are not the great interests of the country. That interest is, as every one admits, agriculture. By the latter, the great bulk of the people live, and by it all are fed. It is clear, therefore, if that interest is neglected or misunderstood, the population of the country may steadily increase, but the means of supporting that population (which can never be largely a manufacturing population) must necessarily lessen, proportionately, every year.

Now, there are two undeniable facts at present staring us Americans in the face—amid all this prosperity: the first is, that the productive power of nearly all the land in the United States, which has been ten years in cultivation, is fearfully lessening every season, from the desolating effects of a ruinous system of husbandry; and the second is, that in consequence of this, the rural population of the older States is either at a stand-still, or it is falling off, or it increases very slowly in proportion to the population of those cities and towns largely engaged in commercial pursuits.

Our census returns show, for instance, that in some of the States (such as Rhode Island, Connecticut, Delaware, and Maryland), the only increase of population is in the *towns*—for in the rural population there is no growth at all. In the great agricultural State of New-York, the gain in the fourteen largest towns is sixty-four per cent., while in the rest of the State it is but nineteen per cent. In Pennsylvania, thirty-nine and a quarter per cent. in the large towns, and but twenty-one per cent. in the rural districts. The politicians in this State, finding themselves losing a representative in the new ratio, while Pennsylvania gains two, have, in alarm, actually deigned to inquire into the growth of the agricultural class, with some little attention. They have not generally arrived at the truth, however, which is, that Pennsylvania is, as a State, much better farmed than New-York, and hence the agricultural population increases much faster.

It is a painful truth, that both the press and the more active minds of the country at large are strikingly ignorant of the condition of agriculture in all the older States, and one no less painful, that the farmers, who are not ignorant of it, are, as a body, not intelligent enough to know how to remedy the evil.

"And what is that evil?" many of our readers will doubtless inquire. We answer, the miserable system of farming steadily pursued by eight-tenths of all the farmers of this country, since its first settlement; a system which proceeds upon the principle of taking as many crops from the land with as little manure as possible—until its productive powers are exhausted, and then —— emigrating to some part of the country where they can apply the same practice to a new soil. It requires far less knowledge and capital to wear out one good soil and abandon it for another, than to cultivate a good soil so as to maintain its productive powers from year to year, unimpaired. Accordingly, the emigration is always "to THE WEST." There, is ever the Arcadia of the American farmer; there are the acres which need but to be broken up by the plough, to yield their thirty or forty bushels of wheat to the acre. Hence, the ever full tide of farmers or farmers' sons, always sets westward, and the lands at home are left in a comparatively exhausted and barren state, and hence, too, the slow progress of farming as an honest art, where every body practises it like a highway robber.

There are, doubtless, many superficial thinkers, who consider these western soils *exhaustless*—"prairies where crop after crop can be taken, by generation after generation." There was never a greater fallacy. There are acres and acres of land in the counties bordering the Hudson—such counties as Dutchess and Albany—from which the early settlers reaped their thirty to forty bushels of wheat to the acre, as easily as their great-grandchildren do now in the most fertile fields of the valley of the Mississippi. Yet these very acres now yield only twelve or fourteen bushels each, and the average yield of the county of Dutchess—one of the most fertile and best managed on the Hudson, is at the present moment only six bushels of wheat to the acre! One of our cleverest agricultural writers has made the estimate, that of the twelve millions of acres of cultivated land in the State of New-York, eight millions are in the hands of the "skinners," who take away every thing from the soil, and put nothing back; three millions in the hand of farmers who manage them so as to make the lands barely hold their own, while one million of acres are well farmed, so as to maintain a high and productive state of fertility. And as New-York is confessedly one of the most substantial of all the older States, in point of agriculture, this estimate is too flattering to be applied to the older States. Even Ohio—newly settled as she is, begins to fall off per acre, in her annual wheat crop, and before fifty years will, if the present system continues, be considered a worn out soil.

The evil at the bottom of all this false system of husbandry, is no mystery. A rich soil contains only a given quantity of vegetable and mineral food for plants. Every crop grown upon a fertile soil, takes from it a certain amount of these substances, so essential to the growth of another crop. If these crops, like most of our grain crops, are sent away and consumed in other counties, or other parts of the counties—as in the great cities, and *none of their essential elements* in the way of vegetable matter, lime, potash, etc., *restored to the soil*, it follows as a matter of course, that eventually the soil *must* become barren or miserably unprofitable. And such is, unfortunately, the fact. Instead of maintaining as many animals as possible upon the farm, and carefully restoring to the soil in the shape of animal and mineral manure, all those elements needful to the growth of future vegetables, our farmers send nearly all their crops for sale in cities—and allow all the valuable animal and mineral products of these crops to go to waste in those cities.*

"Oh! but," the farmer upon worn out land will say, "we cannot

* In Belgium—the most productive country in the world,—the urinary excrements of each cow are sold for $10 a year, and are regularly applied to the land, and poudrette is valued as gold itself.

afford to pay for all the labor necessary for the high farming you advocate." Are you quite sure of that assertion? We suspect if you were to enter carefully into the calculation, as your neighbor, the merchant, enters into the calculation of his profit and loss in his system of trade, you would find that the difference in value between one crop of 12 bushels and another of 30 bushels of wheat to the acre, would leave a handsome profit to that farmer who would pursue with method and energy, the practice of never taking an atom of food for plants from the soil in the shape of a crop, without, in some natural way, replacing it again. For, it must be remembered, that needful as the soil is, every plant gathers a large part of its food from the air, and the excrement of animals fed upon crops, will restore to the soil all the needful elements taken from it by those crops.

The principle has been demonstrated over and over again, but the difficulty is to get the farmers to *believe* it. Because they can get crops, such as they are, from a given soil, year after year, without manure, they think it is only necessary for them to *plant*—Providence will take care of the harvest. But it is in the pursuit of this very system, that vast plains of the old world, once as fertile as Michigan or Ohio, have become desert wastes, and it is perfectly certain, that when we reach the goal of a hundred millions of people, we shall reach a famine soon afterwards, if some new and more enlightened system of agriculture than our national "skinning" system, does not beforehand spring up and extend itself over the country.

And such a system can only be extensively disseminated and put in practice by raising the *intelligence* of farmers generally. We have, in common with the Agricultural Journals, again and again pointed out that this is mainly to be hoped for through a *practical* agricultural education. And yet the legislatures of our great agricultural States vote down, year after year, every bill reported by the friends of agriculture to establish schools. Not one such school, efficient and useful as it might be, if started with sufficient aid from the State, exists in a nation of more than twenty millions of farmers. "What matters it," say the wise men of our State legislatures, "if the lands of the Atlantic States are worn out by bad farming? Is not the GREAT WEST the granary of the world?" And so they build canals and railroads, and bring from the west millions of bushels of grain, and send not one fertilizing atom back to restore the land. And in this way we shall by-and-by make the fertile prairies as barren as some of the worn out farms of Virginia. And thus "the sins of the fathers are visited upon the children, even to the fourth generation!"

III.

THE HOME EDUCATION OF THE RURAL DISTRICTS.

January, 1852.

WHILE the great question of Agricultural Schools is continually urged upon our legislatures, and, as yet, continually put off with fair words, let us see if there is not room for great improvement in another way—for the accomplishment of which the farming community need ask no assistance.

Our thoughts are turned to the subject of *home education*. It is, perhaps, the peculiar misfortune of the United States, that the idea of education is always affixed to something *away* from home. The boarding-school, the academy, the college—it is there alone we suppose it possible to educate the young man or the young woman. *Home* is only a place to eat, drink, and sleep. The parents, for the most part, gladly shuffle off the whole duties and responsibilities of training the heart, and the social nature of their children—believing that if the intellect is properly developed in the schools, the whole man is educated. Hence the miserably one-sided and incomplete character of so many even of our most able and talented men—their heads have been educated, but their social nature almost utterly neglected. Awkward manners and a rude address, are not the only evidences that many a clever lawyer, professional man, or merchant, offers to us continually, that his education has been wholly picked up away from home, or that home was never raised to a level calculated to give instruction. A want of taste for all the more genial and kindly topics of conversation, and a want of relish for refined and innocent social pleasures, mark such a man as an ill-balanced or one-sided man in his inner growth and culture. Such a man is often successful at the bar or in trade, but he is uneasy and out of his element in the social circle, because he misunderstands it and despises it. His only idea of society is display, and he loses more than three-fourths of the delights of life by never having been educated to use his best social qualities—the qualities which teach a man how to love his neighbor as himself, and to throw the sunshine of a cultivated understanding and heart upon the little trifling events and enjoyments of everyday life.

If this is true of what may be called the wealthier classes of the community, it is, we are sorry to say, still more true of the agricultural class. The agricultural class is continually complimented by the press and public debaters,—nay, it even compliments itself with being the "bone and sinew of the country"—the "substantial yeomanry"—the followers of the most natural and "noblest occupation," &c. &c. But the truth is, that in a country like this, knowledge is not only power; it is also influence and position; and the farmers, as a class, are the least educated, and therefore the least powerful, the least influential, the least respected class in the community.

This state of things is all wrong, and we deplore it—but the way to mend it is not by feeding farmers with compliments, but with plain truths. As a natural consequence of belonging to the least powerful and least influential class, the sons and daughters of farmers—we mean the *smartest* sons and daughters—those who might raise up and elevate the condition of the whole class, if they would recognize the dignity and value of their calling, and put their talents into it—are no sooner able to look around and choose for themselves, than they bid good bye to farming. It is too *slow* for the boys, and not *genteel* enough for the girls.

All the education of the schools they go to, has nothing to do with making a farmer of a talented boy, or a farmer's wife of a bright and clever girl—but a great deal to do with unmaking them, by pointing out the superior advantages of merchandise, and the "honorable" professions. At home, it is the same thing. The farmer's son and daughter find less of the agreeable and attractive, and more of the hard and sordid at their fireside, than in the houses of any other class of equal means. This helps to decide them to leave "dull care" to dull spirits, and choose some field of life which has more attractions, as well as more risks, than their own.

We have stated all this frankly, because we believe it to be a false and bad state of things which cannot last. The farming class of America is not a rich class—but neither is it a poor one—while it is an independent class. It may and should wield the largest influence in the state, and it might and should enjoy the most happiness—the happiness belonging to intelligent minds, peaceful homes, a natural and independent position, and high social and moral virtues. We have said much, already, of the special schools which the farmer should have to teach him agriculture as a practical art, so that he might make it compare in profit, and in the daily application of knowledge which it demands, with any other pursuit. But we have said little or nothing of the farmer's *home education* and social influences—though these perhaps lie at the very root of the whole matter.

We are not ignorant of the powerful influence of *woman*, in any question touching the improvement of our social and home education. In fact, it is she who holds all the power in this sphere; it is she, who really, but silently, directs, controls, leads and governs the whole social machine—whether among farmers or others, in this country. To the women of the rural districts—the more intelligent and sensible of the farmers' wives and daughters, we appeal then, for a better understanding and a more correct appreciation of their true position. If they will but study to raise the character of the farmer's social life, the whole matter is accomplished. But this must be done truthfully and earnestly, and with a profound faith in the true nobility and dignity of the farmer's calling. It must not be done by taking for social growth the finery and gloss of mere city customs and observances. It is an improvement that can never come from the atmosphere of boarding-schools and colleges as they are now constituted, for boarding-schools and colleges pity the farmer's ignorance, and despise him for it. It must, on the contrary, come from an intelligent conviction of the honesty and dignity of rural life; a conviction that as agriculture embraces the sphere of God's most natural and beautiful operations, it is the best calculated, when rightly understood, to elevate and engage man's faculties; that, as it feeds and sustains the nation, it is the basis of all material wealth; and as it supports all other professions and callings, it is intrinsically the parent and superior of them all. Let the American farmer's wife never cease to teach her sons, that though other callings may be more lucrative, yet there is none so true and so safe as that of the farmer,—let her teach her daughters that, fascinating and brilliant as many other positions appear outwardly, there is none with so much intrinsic satisfaction as the life of a really intelligent proprietor of the soil, and above all, let her show by the spirit of intelligence, order, neatness, taste, and that *beauty of propriety*, which is the highest beauty *in her home*, that she really knows, understands, and enjoys her position as a wife and mother of a farmer's family—let us have but a few earnest apostles of this kind, and the condition and prosperity of the agricultural class, intellectually and socially, will brighten, as the day brightens after the first few bars of golden light tinge the eastern horizon.

We are glad to see and record such signs of daybreak—in the shape of a recognition of the low social state which we deplore, and a cry for reform—which now and then make themselves heard, here and there in the country. Major Patrick—a gentleman whom we have not the pleasure of knowing, though we most cordially shake hands with him mentally, has delivered an address before the Jefferson County Agricultural Society in the State of New-York, in which he has touched with no ordinary skill upon this very topic. The two pictures which follow are as faithful as those of a Dutch master, and we hang them up here, conspicuously, in our columns, as being more worthy of study by our farmers' families, than any pictures that the Art-Union will distribute this year, among all those that will be scattered from Maine to Missouri.

"An industrious pair, some twenty or thirty years ago, commenced the world with strong hands, stout hearts, robust health, and steady habits. By the blessing of Heaven their industry has been rewarded with plenty, and their labors have been crowned with success. The dense forest has given place to stately orchards of fruits, and fertile fields, and waving meadows, and verdant pastures, covered with evidences of worldly prosperity. The log cabin is gone, and in its stead a fair white house, two stories, and a wing with kitchen in the rear, flanked by barns, and cribs, and granaries, and dairy houses.

"But take a nearer view. Ha! what means this mighty crop of unmown thistles bordering the road? For what market is that still mightier crop of pigweed, dock and nettles destined, that fills up the space *they call* the 'garden?' And look at those wide, unsightly thickets of elm, and sumac, and briers, and choke-cherry, that mark the lines of every fence!

"Approach the house, built in the road to be *convenient*, and save land! Two stories and a wing, and every blind shut close as a miser's fist, without a tree, or shrub, or flower to break the air of barrenness and desolation around it. There it stands, white, glaring and ghastly as a pyramid of bones in the desert. Mount the unfrequented door stone, grown over with vile weeds, and knock till your knuckles are sore. It is a beautiful moonlight October evening; and as you stand upon that stone, a ringing laugh comes from the *rear*, and satisfies you that somebody lives *there*. Pass now around to the rear: but hold your nose when you come within range of the piggery, and have a care that you don't get swamped in the neighborhood of the sink-spout. Enter the kitchen. Ha! here they are all alive, and here they *live* all together. The kitchen is the kitchen, the dining-room, the sitting-room, the room of all work. Here father sits with his hat on and in his shirt-sleeves. Around him are his boys and his hired men, some with hats and some with coats, and some with neither. The boys are busy shelling corn for samp; the hired men are scraping whip-stocks and whittling bow-pins, throwing every now and then a sheep's eye and a jest at the girls, who, with their mother, are *doing-up* the house-work. The younger fry are building cob-houses, parching corn, and burning their fingers. Not a book is to be seen, though the winter school has commenced, and the master is going to board there. Privacy is a word of unknown meaning in that family; and if a son or daughter should borrow a book, it would be almost impossible to read it in that room, and on no occasion is the front house opened, except when 'company come to spend the afternoon,' or when things are brushed and dusted, and 'set to rights.'

"Yet these are as honest, as worthy, and kind-hearted people as you will find anywhere, and are *studying out* some way of getting their younger children into a better position than they themselves occupy. They are in easy circumstances, owe nothing, and have money loaned on bond and mortgage. After much consultation, a son is placed at school that he may be fitted to go into a store, or possibly an office, to study a *profession;* and a daughter is sent away to learn books, and manners, and *gentility*. On this son or daughter, or both, the hard earnings of years are lavished; and they are reared up in the belief that whatever smacks of the country is vulgar—that the farmer is *necessarily* ill-bred and his calling ignoble.

"Now, will any one say that this picture is overdrawn? I think not. But let us see if there is not a ready way to change the whole expression and character of the picture, almost without cost or trouble. I would point out an easier, happier, and more economical way of educating those children, far more thoroughly, while at the same time the minds of the parents are expanded, and they are prepared to enjoy, in the society of their educated children, the fruits of their own early industry.

"And first, let the *front* part of that house be thrown open, and the most convenient, agreeable, and pleasant room in it, be selected as the *family room*. Let its doors be ever open, and when the work of the kitchen is completed, let mothers and daughters be found *there*, with their appropriate work. Let it be the room where the family altar is erected, on which the father offers the morning and the evening sacrifice. Let it be consecrated to Neatness, and Purity, and Truth. Let no *hat* ever be seen in that room on the head of its owner [unless he be a Quaker friend]; let no *coatless* individual be permitted to enter it. If father's head is bald (and some there are in that predicament), his daughter will be proud to see his temples covered by the neat and graceful silken cap that her own hands have fashioned for him. If the coat he wears by day is too heavy for the evening, calicoes are cheap, and so is cotton wadding. A few shillings placed in that daughter's hand, insures him the most comfortable wrapper in the world; and if his boots are hard, and the nails cut mother's carpet, a bushel of wheat once in three years, will keep him in slippers of the easiest kind. Let the table, which has always stood under the looking-glass, *against the wall*, be wheeled into the room, and plenty of useful (not ornamental) books and periodicals be laid upon it. When evening comes, bring on the lights—and plenty of them—for sons and daughters—all who can—will be most willing students. They will read, they will learn, they will discuss the subjects of their studies with each other; and parents will often be quite as much instructed as their children. The well conducted agricultural journals of our day throw a flood of light upon the *science* and *practice* of agriculture; while such a work as Downing's Landscape Gardening [or the *Horticulturist*], laid one year upon that centre-table, will show its effects to every passer-by, for with books and studies like these, a purer taste is born, and grows more vigorously.

"Pass along that road after five years working of this system in the family, and what a change! The thistles by the roadside enriched the manure heap for a year or two, and then they died. These beautiful maples and those graceful elms, that beautify the grounds around that renovated home, were grubbed from the wide hedge-rows of five years ago; and so were those prolific rows of blackberries and raspberries, and bush cranberries that show so richly in that *neat garden*, yielding abundance of small fruit in their season. The unsightly out-houses are screened from observation by dense masses of foliage; and the many climbing plants that now hang in graceful festoons from tree, and porch, and column, once clambered along that same *hedge-row*. From the meadow, from the wood, and from the gurgling stream, many a native wild flower has been transplanted to a genial soil, beneath the homestead's sheltering wing, and yields a daily offering to the household gods, by the hands of those fair priestesses who have now become their ministers. By the planting of a few trees, and shrubs, and flowers, and climbing plants, around that once bare and uninviting house, it has become a tasteful residence, and its money value is more than doubled. A cultivated taste displays itself in a thousand forms, and at every touch of its hand gives beauty and value to property. A judicious taste, so far from plunging its possessor into expense, makes money for him. The *land* on which that *hedge-row* grew five years ago, for instance, has produced enough since to *doubly pay* the expense of grubbing it, and of transferring its fruit briers to the garden, where they have not only supplied the family with berries in their season, but have yielded many a surplus quart, to purchase that long row of red and yellow Antwerps, and English gooseberries; to say nothing of the scions bought with their money, to form new heads for the trees in the old orchard.

"These sons and daughters sigh no more for city life, but love with intense affection every foot of ground they tread upon, every tree, and every vine, and every shrub their hands have planted, or their taste has trained. But stronger still do their affections cling to that *family room*, where their minds first began to be developed, and to that centre-table around which they still gather with the shades of evening, to drink in knowledge, and wisdom, and understanding.

"The stout farmer, who once looked upon his acres only as a laboratory for transmuting labor into gold, now takes a widely different view of his possessions. His eyes are opened to the *beautiful* in nature, and he looks with reverence upon every giant remnant of the forest, that by good luck escaped his murderous axe in former days. No leafy monarch is now laid low without a stern necessity demands it; but many a vigorous tree is planted in the hope that the children of *his* children may gather beneath the spreading branches, and talk with pious gratitude of him who planted them. No longer feeling the need of taxing his physical powers to the utmost, his eye takes the place of his hand, when latter grows weary, and *mind* directs the operations of labor. See him stand and look with delighted admiration at his sons, *his educated sons*, as they take hold of every kind of work, and roll it off with easy motion, but with the power of mind in every stroke.

"But it is the proud mother who takes the solid comfort, and wonders that it is so easy after all, *when one knows how*, to live at ease, enjoy the society of happy daughters and contented sons, to whom the *city folks* make most respectful bows, and treat with special deference, as truly *well-bred ladies and gentlemen.*

"Now, this is no more a fancy picture than the other. It is a process that I have watched in many families, and in different States. The results are everywhere alike, because they are natural. The same causes will always produce the same effects, varying circumstances only modifying the intensity."

IV.

HOW TO ENRICH THE SOIL.

November, 1849.

GOOD cultivation depends on nothing so much as the supply of an *abundance of food.* And yet there are hundreds and thousands of cultivators who do not recognize this fact in their practice. They feed their horses and cows regularly, because it is undeniable that they have mouths and stomachs; and experience has demonstrated, that not to keep these sufficiently supplied amounts at last to starvation. But, because a plant has a thousand little concealed mouths, instead of one wide, gaping one,—because it finds enough even in poor soils to keep it from actually starving to death, ignorant cultivators appear to consider that they deserve well of their trees and plants, if they barely keep their roots covered with earth. They make plantations in thin soil, or upon lands exhausted of all inorganic food by numberless croppings, and then wonder why they succeed so poorly in obtaining heavy products.

Too much, therefore, can never be written about manures. After all that has been said about them, they are yet but little understood; and there is not one person in ten thousand, among all those owning gardens in this country, who does not annually throw away, or neglect to make use of, some of the most valuable manures for trees and plants,—manures constantly within his reach, and yet entirely neglected.

We must therefore throw out a few seasonable hints, on the preparation and use of manures, which we hope may aid such of our readers as are anxious to feed their trees and plants in such a generous manner as to deserve a grateful return.

Among the first and best of wasted manures, constantly before our eyes in the autumn, are the *falling leaves* of all deciduous trees. When we remember that these leaves contain not only *all the substances* necessary to the growth of the plants from which they fall; but those substances in the proportions actually needed for new growth, it is surprising that we can ever allow a barrowful to be lost. The whole riddle of the wonderful growth of giant forests, on land not naturally rich, and to which nature scarce allows a particle of what is commonly called manure, lies hidden in the deep beds of fallen leaves which accumulate over the roots, and, by their gradual decay, furnish a plentiful supply of the most suitable food for the trees above them. Gather and take away from the trees in a wood this annual coat of leaves, and in a few seasons (unless manure is artificially given), the wood will begin to decline and go to decay. Hence, we must beseech all our good orchardists and fruit-growers not to forget that dead leaves are worth looking after. They should be held fast in some way, either by burying them about the roots of the trees from which they fall, or by gathering them into the compost heap, to be applied when duly decomposed in the spring.

And this leads us to say that an excellent, and perhaps the best mode of using leaves for the orchard, fruit-garden, or any plantations of trees or shrubs, is the following: Take fresh lime and slake it with *brine* (or water saturated with salt), till it falls to a powder. This powder is not common lime, but muriate of lime. Gather the leaves and lay them up in heaps, sprinkling over every layer with this new compound of lime, at the rate of about four bushels to a cord of leaves. This will be ready for use in about a month if the weather is mild, or it may lie all winter, to be used in the spring; but in either case, the heap should be turned over once or twice. The lime decomposes the leaves thoroughly; and the manure thus formed is one of the most perfect composts known for *trees* of all kinds. We need not add that its value to any given kind of tree, as, for example, the pear, the apple, or the oak, is increased by using the leaves of that tree only; though a mass of mixed leaves gives a compost of great value for trees and shrubs generally. The practice in the best vineyards, of burying the leaves of each vine at its root, every autumn, is not only one of the most successful modes of manuring that plant, but one founded in the latest discoveries in science.

The most economical mode of making manure, in most parts of the country, is that of using muck or peat from swamps. Though worth little or nothing in its crude state, it contains large quantities of the best food for trees and plants. No cultivator, who has it at command, should complain of the difficulty of getting manure, since he can so easily turn it into a compost, equal in bulk to farm-yard manure.

The cheapest mode of doing this, is, undoubtedly, to place it in the stalls underneath the cattle for a few days, and then lay it up with the barn-yard manure, in the proportion of one part muck to six or eight parts manure. The whole will then ferment, and become equal in value to the ordinary product of the barn-yard. But a much more practicable mode for horticulturists—who are not all farmers with cattle yards—is that of reducing it by means of ashes, or lime slaked with brine.

As we have already pointed out how to use ashes, and as we think, after what we have observed the past season, the latter mode gives a compost still more valuable for many trees than ashes and muck, we recommend it to the trial of all those forming composts for their orchards and gardens. The better mode is to throw out the peat from the swamps now, or in winter, expose it to the action of the frost, and, early in the spring, to mix it with the brine-slaked lime, at the rate of four bushels to the cord. It should be allowed to lie about six weeks. The good effects of this compost, when applied as a manure to the kitchen garden, or mixed with the soil in planting trees, are equally striking and permanent.

We cannot let the opportunity pass by without saying a word or two about that much lauded and much abused substance—guano. Nothing is more certain than that, in Peru and England, this is the best of all manures; or that in the United States, as it has hitherto been used, it is one of the worst. Now, as a substance cannot thus wholly change its nature in these different countries without some good reason, we are naturally led to inquire, what is the secret of its success?

If we recall to mind the facts, that in Peru, guano is no sooner applied than the land is irrigated, and that in England no sooner is it spread over the land than a shower commences; and that this shower, or something very near akin to it, keeps itself up all summer long, in the latter country; and if we then recollect, that in the middle States, five summers out of six, any substance applied near the surface of the ground is as dry as a snuff-box, for the most part of the time, from June to September, we shall not be greatly at a loss to know why so many persons, in this country, believe guano to be nothing more or less than a "humbug."

If any very good proof of this were wanted, we need go no further than to the exotic florists in our cities, who cultivate their plants in pots, for their experience. They are nearly the only class of cultivators among us who are sturdy champions for the use of guano. The reason is plain. They use it only in the liquid state, and apply it so as to give the plants under their care every now and then a good wholesome drink,—a thorough soaking of a sort of soup more relishing to them than any in M. Soyer's new cookery book, to an epicure in a London club-house.

Now it is quite impossible for an American cultivator to do any thing worth mentioning, in the way of watering his trees or crops with liquid guano; partly because labor is too dear, but mainly because the air is so dry and hot, that in a few hours the earth is drier than before; and so all good effects are at an end. What then is to be done, to enable us to use guano with success?

We answer in a few words. Use it in the autumn.

We know this is quite contrary to the advice of previous writers, and that it will be considered by many a great waste of riches. But our advice is founded on experience,—an ounce of which, in such a matter as this, is worth a ton of theory drawn from observation in other climates.

After having tried guano in various ordinary modes, at the usual season, and with so little satisfaction as to find ourselves among the skeptics as to its merits for this country, we at last made trial of it in the autumn. We spread it over the soil of the kitchen garden, before digging it up at the approach of winter, and, to our astonishment, found our soil so treated more productive, even in very dry seasons, than we had ever known it before. We have also recommended it as an autumnal manure for enfeebled fruit trees (turning it under the surface at once with a spade), and find it wonderfully improved in luxuriance and vigor. In short, our observations for the past two years have firmly convinced us, that in all parts of the country, where the climate is hot and dry from June to October, guano should be used in the autumn. Applied at that season, and turned under the surface by the plough or spade, so as not to waste its virtues in the air, or by surface rains, its active qualities are gradually absorbed by the soil, and, so far from being lost, are only rendered more completely soluble, and ready for feeding the plants when the spring opens.

Guano, applied as a top-dressing, or near the surface, in the spring, is undoubtedly a manure of little permanence,—generally lasting only one season; for it always loses much of its virtue in the atmosphere. But when buried beneath the surface, it becomes incorporated with the soil, and its good effects last several seasons.

The common rate of manuring farm lands is three hundred pounds of guano to the acre. But when old gardens are to be manured, or worn-out orchards or fruit-yards renovated, we find six hundred pounds a better dressing. We would recommend its use at any time between the present moment and the frosts of winter. It should be spread evenly over the surface, and immediately turned at least three inches below it.

At the present price of guano, it is certainly the cheapest of all manures to be bought in the market; and as it is undeniably richer in all the elements necessary for most crops than any other single substance, it deserves to have a more thorough trial at the hands of the American public. We commend it anew to all those who have once failed, and beg them to try it once more, using it in the autumn.

The large proportion of phosphate of lime which exists in Peruvian guano, makes it very valuable for fruit-growers; and a good dressing of guano—so that it visibly covers the surface under each tree—dug under during the month of November, will certainly give a most thrifty and healthy start to the next season's growth, as well as prepare the tree for the highest state of productiveness. The concentrated form of guano, saving, as it does, so much labor in carriage and spreading over the soil, is no small recommendation in its favor to those whose finances admonish them to practise economy of means and time.

We might enlarge upon manures, so as to occupy volumes. But it will suffice for the present, if we have drawn the attention of our readers to the fact, that food *must* be supplied, and that the present is the time to set about it.

V.

A CHAPTER ON AGRICULTURAL SCHOOLS.

December, 1849.

"MOVABLE property, or capital, may procure a man all the advantages of wealth; but PROPERTY IN LAND gives him much more than this. It gives him a place in the domain of the world; it unites his life to the life which animates all creation. Money is an instrument by which man can procure the satisfaction of his wants and his wishes. Landed property is the establishment of man as sovereign in the midst of nature. It satisfies not only his wants and his desires, but tastes deeply implanted in his nature. For his family, it creates that domestic country called *home*, with all the loving sympathies and all the future hopes and projects which people it. And whilst property in land is more consonant than any other to the nature of man, it also affords a field of activity the most favorable to his moral development, the most suited to inspire a just sentiment of his nature and his powers. In almost all the other trades and professions, whether commercial or scientific, success appears to depend solely on himself—on his talents, address, prudence and vigilance. In agricultural life, man is constantly in the presence of God, and of his power. Activity, talents, prudence and vigilance, are as necessary here as elsewhere to the success of his labors; but they are evidently no less insufficient than they are necessary. It is God who rules the seasons and the temperature, the sun and the rain, and all those phenomena of nature which determine the success or the failure of the labors of man on the soil which he cultivates. There is no pride which can resist this dependence, no address which can escape it. Nor is it only a senti ment of humanity, as to his power over his own destiny, which is thus inculcated upon man; he learns also tranquillity and patience. He cannot flatter himself that the most ingenious inventions, or the most restless activity, will secure his success; when he has done all that depends upon himself for the cultivation and fertilization of the soil, he must wait with resignation. The more profoundly we examine the situation in which man is placed, by the possession and cultivation of the soil, the more do we discover how rich it is in salutary lessons to his reason, and benign influences on his character. Men do not analyze these facts; but they have an instinctive sentiment of them, which powerfully contributes to the peculiar respect in which they hold property in land, and to the preponderance which that kind of property enjoys over every other. This preponderance is a natural, legitimate, and salutary fact, which, especially in a great country, society at large has a strong interest in recognizing and respecting."

We have quoted this sound and excellent exposé, of the importance and dignity of the landed interest, from a late pamphlet by a great continental statesman, only to draw the attention of our agricultural class to their position in all countries—whether monarchical or republican—and especially to the fact, that upon the intelligence and prosperity of the owners of the soil, here, depend largely the strength and security of our government, and the well working of most of its best institutions.

Where, then, must we look for the explanation of the fact, that in every country the cultivators of the soil are the last to avail themselves of the advantages of skill and science? That every where they are the last to demand of government a share of those benefits which are continually heaped upon less important, but more sagacious and more clamorous branches of the body politic?

Is it because, obliged to trust largely to nature and Providence, they are less active in seizing the advantages of education than those whose intellect, or whose inventive powers, are daily tasked for their support, and who cultivate their powers of mind in order to live by their exercise?

These are pertinent questions at this moment; for it is evident that we are on the eve of a great change in the future position and influence of the agricultural class in this country. The giant that tills the soil is gradually wakening into conscious activity; he perceives his own resources; he begins to feel that upon his shoulders rests the state; that from his labor come the material forces that feed the national strength; that from his loins are largely drawn the strong men that give force and stability to great impulses and sound institutions in republican America.

Is it to be supposed that with this newly awakening consciousness of the meaning and value of his life, the farmer—the owner of the soil in America—is not to seize any advantages to develope his best faculties? Does any thinking man believe that such a class will continue to plough and delve in an ignorant routine, in an age when men force steam to almost annihilate space and lightning to outrun time?

And this brings us at once to the great topic of the day, with the farmer—AGRICULTURAL SCHOOLS.

Now, that it is confidently believed that we are to have a great agricultural school in the State of New-York—a school which will probably be the prototype of many in the other States—some diversity of opinion exists as to the character of that school.

"Let it be a school for practical farming—a school in which farmers' sons shall be taught how to plough and mow, and 'make both ends meet,' and show farmers how they can make money," says one.

"Give us a school in which the science of agriculture shall be taught, where the farmer's son shall be made a good chemist, a good mathematician, a good naturalist,—yes, and even taught Greek and Latin, etc., so that he shall be as well educated as any gentleman's son," says the second.

"A farm school ought to be able to support itself, or it is worth nothing," says a third.

"It should be liberally endowed by the State, so as to secure the best talent in the country, or it will be the nest of charlatans," says a fourth.

"It should be a model farm, where only the best practice and the most profitable modes of cultivation should be seen," says a fifth.

"It should be an experimental farm, where all the new theories could be tested, in order to find out what is of real value," says a sixth.

And thus, there is no end to the variety of projects for an agricultural school,—each man building on a different platform.

Yet there must be some real and solid foundation on which to erect the edifice of a great educational institution for farmers. And we imagine these supposed differences of opinion may all be reconciled, if we examine a little the sources from whence they originate.

Agriculture is both a science and an art. It may be studied in the closet, the laboratory, the lecture-room; so that a man may have a perfect knowledge of it in his head, and not know how to perform well a single one of its labors in the field; or it may be gained by rote in the fields, by one who cannot give you the reason for the operation of a single law of nature which it involves. The first is mere theory—the second, mere practice.

It is easy to see, that he who is only a theorist is no more likely to raise good crops profitably, than a theoretical swimmer is to cross the Hellespont like Leander; and that the mere practical farmer is as little likely to improve on what he has learned by imitation, as his horse is to invent a new mode of locomotion.

The difference of opinion, regarding the nature or the province of an agricultural school, seems mainly to grow out of the different sides from which the matter is viewed—whether the advocate favors science or practice most,—forgetting that the well-educated agriculturist should combine in himself both the science and the art which he professes.

The difference between *knowledge* and *wisdom* is nowhere better illustrated than in a mixed study, like agriculture. Knowledge may be either theoretical or practical; but wisdom is "*knowledge put in action.*" What the agricultural school, which this age and country now demands, must do to satisfy us, is to teach—not alone the knowledge of the books—not alone the practice of the fields, but that *agricultural wisdom* which involves both, and which can never be attained without a large development of the powers of the pupil in both directions. His head and hands must work together. He must try all things that promise well, and know the reason of his failure as well as his success. To this end, he must not be in the hands of quack chemists and quack physiologists in the lecture halls, or those of chimerical farmers or dull teamsters in the fields. Hence, the State must insist upon having, for teachers, only the ablest men; men who will teach wisely, whether it be chemistry or ploughing,—teach it in the best and most thorough manner, so that it may become wisdom for the pupil. Such men are always successful in their own sphere and calling, and can no more be had for the asking than one can have the sun and stars. They must be sought for and carried off by violence, and made to understand that the State has a noble work for them, which she means to have rightly and well done.

To achieve this, an agricultural school must be planned, neither with a lavish nor a niggardly spirit. As agriculture is especially an industrial art, the manual labor practice of that art should be an inevitable part of the education and discipline of the pupils. But to base the operation of the school upon the plan of immediate profit, in all its branches, solely, would, we conceive, cut off in a great degree the largest source of profit to the country at large. The pupils would leave the school either as practical farmers after a single model, or they would leave it with their heads full of unsatisfied longings after theories which they had not been permitted to work out. They would be destitute of that *wisdom* which comes only from knowledge and experience combined, and would go home only to fail in applying a practice suited to a different soil from their own, or to indulge (at a large personal loss) theories which might have been for ever settled in company with a hundred others, at the smallest possible cost to the State.

We rejoice to see the awakened zeal of the farmers of the State of New-York, in this subject of agricultural education. We rejoice to find a large majority of our legislature warmly seconding and supporting their wishes; and most of all, we rejoice to see a governor who unceasingly urges upon our law-makers the value and necessity of a great agricultural school. One of our contemporaries —the editor of the *Working Farmer*—has aptly remarked that WASHINGTON was our only great statesman who had "the moral courage to advocate the rights of farmers. Statesmen mistake the more apparent praise of other classes for the praise of the majority." If, however, the views of Hamilton Fish, regarding this subject, are carried out by the legislature of this State, the people will owe him a great debt of gratitude, for urging the formation of an educational institution, which will, both directly and indirectly, do more to elevate the character of the great industrial class of the nation, and develope the agricultural wealth of the country at large, than any step which has been taken since the foundation of the republic.

An agricultural college, for the complete education of farmers, where the *wisest general economy of farming*, involving all its main scientific and practical details, successfully established in the State of New-York, will be the model and type of a similar institution in every State in the Union. Its influence will be speedily felt in all parts of the country; and it is therefore of no little importance that the plan adopted by the legislature should be one worthy of the object in view, and the ripeness of the times.

Above all, when a good plan is adopted, let it not be rendered of little value by being intrusted for execution to the hands of those who stand ready to devour the loaves and fishes of State patronage. It is easy to devise, but it is hard to execute wisely; and we warn the farmers in our legislature, the State Agricultural Society (which has already done such earnest service in this good cause), and the Executive, to guard against a failure in a great and wise scheme, by intrusting its execution to any but those whose competence to the task is beyond the shadow of a doubt.

VI.

A FEW WORDS ON THE KITCHEN GARDEN.

April, 1848.

THE Kitchen Garden is at once the most humble and the most useful department of horticulture. It can no more be allowed to stand still than the sun himself. Luckily (or unluckily), man must eat; and, omnivorous as he is, he must gather food from both the animal and the vegetable kingdom.

Now there are, we trust, few of our readers who need an argument to prove what a wide difference is very often found between vegetables grown in different gardens; how truly the products of one shall be small, tough, and fibrous, and those of another, large, tender, and succulent. Sometimes the former defects are owing to bad culture, but more frequently to *unsuitable soil*. It is to this latter condition of things that we turn, with the hope of saying something which, if not new, shall at least be somewhat useful, and to the point.

Nothing, in any temperate climate, is easier than the general cultivation of vegetables in most parts of the United States. With our summer sun, equal in heat and brilliancy to that of the equator, we can grow the beans of Lima, the melons of the Mediterranean, the tomatoes and egg-plants of South America, without hot-beds; and with such ease and profusion that it fills a newly arrived English or French gardener with the most unqualified astonishment. Hence, in all good soils, with a smaller amount of labor than is elsewhere bestowed in the same latitudes, our vegetables are produced in the most prodigal abundance.

But now for the exceptions. Every man cannot "locate" himself in precisely that position where the best soil is to be found. Circumstances, on the contrary, often force us to build houses, and make kitchen gardens, where Dame Nature evidently never contemplated such a thing; where, in fact, instead of the rich, deep accumulations of fertile soil, that she frequently offers us in this country, she has only given us the "short commons" allowance of *sand* or *clay*.

The two kinds of kitchen gardens among us, which most demand skill and intelligent labor, are those which are naturally too sandy or too clayey. It is not difficult, at a glance, to see how these might be, and ought to be treated to improve them greatly. But we have observed—such is the foree of habit—that nine-tenths of those who have gardens of this description, go on in the same manner as their neighbors who have the best soil,—manuring and cultivating precisely in the ordinary way, and then grumbling in quite a different mode about short crops, and poor vegetables, instead of setting about remedying the evil in good earnest.

The natural remedy for a heavy clay soil in a kitchen garden, is to mix sand with it. This acts like a charm upon the stubborn alumina, and, allowing the atmospheric influences to penetrate where they were formerly shut out, gives a stimulus, or rather an *opportunity*, to vegetable growth, which quickly produces its result in the quantity and quality of the crops.

But it not unfrequently happens that sand is not to be had abundantly and cheaply enough to enable the proprietor of moderate means to effect this beneficial change. In this case, we propose to the kitchen gardener to achieve his object by another mode, equally efficient, and so easy and cheap as to be within the reach of almost every one.

This is, to alter the texture of too heavy soils, by *burning* a portion of the *clay*.

Very few of our practical gardeners seem to be aware of two important facts. First, that clay, when once burnt, never regains its power of cohesion, but always remains in a pulverized state; and therefore is just as useful, mechanically, in making a heavy soil light, as sand itself. Second, that burnt clay, by its power of attracting from the atmosphere those gases which are the food of vegetables, is really a most excellent manure itself. Hence, in any clayey kitchen garden, where brush, faggots, or refuse fuel of any description can be had, there is no reason why its cold compact soil should not be turned at once, by this process of burning the clay, into one comparatively light, warm, and productive.*

The difficulty which stands in the way of the kitchen gardener, who has to contend with a very light and too sandy soil, is its want of capacity for retaining moisture, and the consequent failure of the summer crops.

In some instances, this is very easily remedied. We mean in those cases where a loam or heavier subsoil lies *below* the surface. Trenching, or subsoil-ploughing, by bringing up a part of the alumina from below, and mixing it with the sand of the surface soil, remedies the defect very speedily. But, where the subsoil is no better than the top, or perhaps even worse, there are but two modes of overcoming this bad constitution of the soil. One of those, is to grasp the difficulty at once, by applying a coat of clay to the surface

* A simple mode of burning clay in the kitchen garden is the following: Make a circle of eight or ten feet in diameter, by raising a wall of sods a couple of feet high. Place a few large sticks loosely crosswise in the bottom, and upon those pile faggots or brush, and set fire to the whole. As soon as it is well lighted, commence throwing on lumps of clay, putting on as much at a time as may be without quite smothering the fire. As soon as the fire breaks through a little, add more brush, and then cover with more clay, till the heap is raised as high as it can be conveniently managed. After lying till the whole is cold, or nearly so, the heap should be broken down, and any remaining lumps pulverized, and the whole spread over the surface and well dug in.

"As an example," says Loudon, "of the strong clayey soil of a garden having been improved by burning, we may refer to that of Willersly Castle, near Mattock, which the gardener there, Mr. Stafford, has rendered equal in friability and fertility to any garden soil in the country. "When I first came to this place," says Mr. Stafford, "the garden was for the most part a strong clay, and that within nine inches of the surface; even the most common article would not live on it; no weather appeared to suit it; at one time being covered by water, at another time rendered impenetrable by being too dry. Having previously witnessed the good effects of burning clods, I commenced the process, and produced, in a few days, a composition three feet deep, and equal, if not superior, to any soil in the country.'"—*Suburban Horticulturist.*

of the soil, and mixing it with the soil as you would manure; the other (a less expensive and more gradual process), is to manure the kitchen garden every year with compost, in which clay or strong loam forms a large proportion.

It may seem, to many persons, quite out of the question to attempt to ameliorate sandy soils by adding clay. But it is surprising how small a quantity of clay, thoroughly intermingled with the loosest sandy soil, will give it a different texture, and convert it into a good loam. And even in sandy districts, there are often valleys and low places, quite near the kitchen garden, where a good stock of clay lies (perhaps quite unsuspected), ready for uses of this kind.

In the *Journal of the Agricultural Society of England*, a case is quoted (vol ii., p. 67), where the soil was a *white sand*, varying in depth from one to four feet; it was so sterile that no crops could ever be grown upon it to profit. By giving it a top-dressing of clay, at the rate of 150 cubic yards to the acre, the whole surface of the farm so treated was improved to the depth of ten or twelve inches, so as to give excellent crops.

Since a soil, once rendered more tenacious in this way, never loses this tenacity, the improvement of the kitchen garden, where economy is necessary, might be carried on *gradually*, by taking one or two compartments in hand every year; thus, in a gradual manner, bringing the whole surface to the desired condition.

A great deal may also be done, as we have just suggested, by a judicious system of manuring very sandy soils. It is the common practice to enrich these soils precisely like all others; that is, with the lighter and more heating kinds of manures; stable-dung for example. Nothing could be more injudicious. Every particle of animal manure used in too light a soil ought, for the kitchen garden, to be composted, for some time previously, with eight or ten times its bulk of strong loam or clay. In this way, that change in the soil, so much to be desired, is brought about; and the whole mass of clay-compost, made in this way, is really equal in value, for such sandy soils, to the same bulk of common stable manure.

Whatever the soil of a kitchen-garden, our experience has taught us that it should be *deep*. It is impossible that the steady and uniform moisture at the roots, indispensable to the continuous growth of many crops, during the summer months, can be maintained in a soil which is only one *spade* deep. Hence, we would *trench* or *subsoil-plough* all kitchen-gardens (taking care, first, that they are well drained), whether sandy or clayey in texture. We know that many persons, judging from theory rather than practice, cannot see the value of deepening soils already too porous. But we have seen its advantages strongly marked in more than one instance, and therefore recommend it with confidence. It is only necessary to examine light soils, trenched and untrenched, to be convinced of this. The roots in the former penetrate and gather nourishment from twice the cubic area that they do in the former; and they are not half so easily affected by the atmospheric changes of temperature.

Old gardens, that have been long cultivated, are greatly improved by trenching and reversing the strata of soil. The inorganic elements, or mineral food of plants, often become so much exhausted in long cultivated kitchen gardens, that only inferior crops can be raised, even with abundant supplies of animal manure. By turning up the virgin loam of the subsoil, and exposing it to the action of the atmosphere, its gradual decomposition takes place, and fresh supplies of lime, potash, etc., are afforded for the vigorous growth of plants.

We have only room for a single hint more, touching the kitchen garden. This is, to recommend the annual use of *salt*, in moderate quantities, sown broadcast over the whole garden early in the spring, and more especially on those quarters of it where vegetables are to be planted which are most liable to the attacks of insects that harbor in the earth. We are satisfied that salt, spread in this way, before vegetation has commenced, or the earth is broken up for sowing seeds, at the rate of ten bushels per acre, is one of the best possible applications to the soil.

It destroys insects, acts specifically on the strength of the stems, and healthy color of the foliage of plants, assists porous soils in collecting and retaining moisture, and is an admirable stimulant to the growth of many vegetables. In all the Atlantic States, where it is easily and cheaply procured, it ought, therefore, to form an annual top-dressing for the whole kitchen garden.

VII.

A CHAT IN THE KITCHEN GARDEN.

October, 1849.

EDITOR. We find you, as usual, in your kitchen garden. Admirable as all the rest of your place is, your own fancy seems to centre here. Do you find the esculents the most satisfactory of your various departments of culture?

Subscriber. Not exactly that; but I find while the shrubbery, the lawn, the flowers, and even the fruit-trees, are well cared for and made much of by my family and my gardener, the kitchen garden is treated merely as a necessity. Now, as I estimate very highly the value of variety and excellence in our culinary vegetables, I take no little interest in my kitchen garden, so that at last it has become a sort of hobby with me.

Ed. We see evidences of that all around us. Indeed, we scarcely remember any place where so large a variety of excellent vegetables are grown as here. Artichokes, endive, sea-kale, celeriac, winter melons and mushrooms, and many other good and rare things, in addition to what we usually find in country gardens.

Sub. And what a climate ours is for growing fine vegetables. From common cabbages, that will thrive in the coldest climate, to egg-plants, melons and tomatoes, that need a tropical sun,—all may be so easily had for the trouble of easy culture in the open air; and yet, strange to say, three-fourths of all country folks, blessed with land in fee simple, are actually ignorant of the luxury of good vegetables, and content themselves with potatoes, peas, beans and corn; and those, perhaps, of the poorest and least improved va rieties.

Ed. Still, you cannot say we stand still in these matters. Almost every year, on the contrary, some new species or variety is brought forward, and, if it prove good, is gradually introduced into general cultivation. Look at the tomato, for instance. Twenty years ago, a few curious amateurs cultivated a specimen or two of this plant in their gardens, as a vegetable curiosity; and the visitor was shown the "love apples" as an extraordinary proof of the odd taste of "French people," who outraged all natural appetites by eating such odious and repulsive smelling berries. And yet, at the present moment, the plant is grown in almost every garden from Boston to New Orleans; may be found in constant use for three months of the year in all parts of the country; and is cultivated by the acre by all our market gardeners. In fact, it is so popular, that it would be missed next to bread and potatoes.

Sub. Quite right; and a most excellent and wholesome vegetable it is. It is almost unknown in England, even now; and, indeed, could only be raised by the aid of glass in that country,—a proof of how much better the sun shines for us than for the subjects of her majesty, across the Channel. But there is another vegetable which you see here, really quite as deserving as the tomato, and which is very little known yet to the cultivators in the country generally. I mean the okra.

Ed. Yes. It is truly a delicious vegetable. Whoever has once tasted the "gumbo soup," of the South, of which the okra is the indispensable *material*, has a recollection of a good thing, which will not easily slip from his memory. All over the southern States okra is cultivated, and held in the highest esteem.

Sub. And there is no reason why it should not be equally so here. Except to the north of Albany, it will thrive perfectly well, and mature an abundance of its pods, with no trouble but that of planting it in a warm rich soil. See what a handsome sight is this plat, filled with it, though only ten yards square,—rich, luxuriant leaves, blossoms nearly as pretty as an African hibiscus, and pods almost as delicate and delicious as an East India bird's nest. It has kept my family in materials for soups and stews all the season, to say nothing of our stock for winter use. And besides being so excellent, it is, do you know, the most *wholesome* of all vegetables in summer.

Ed. We know its mucilaginous qualities seem intended by nature to guard the stomach against all ill effects of summer temperature in a hot climate. How do you account for its being so little known, though it has been in partial cultivation nearly as long as the tomato?

Sub. From the fact that inexperienced cooks always blunder about the proper time to use it. They pluck it when the pod is two-thirds grown and quite firm, so that it colors the soup dark, and all its peculiar excellence is lost. Whoever gathers okra should know that, like sweet-corn, it must be in its tender, "milky state," or it is not fit for use. A day too old, and it is worthless.

Ed. You spoke just now of okra for winter use. As your *ménage* is rather famous for winter vegetables, we must beg you to make a clean breast of it to-day, since you are fairly in the talking mood, and tell us something about them. Begin with okra, if you please.

Sub. Nothing so simple. To prepare most vegetables is, by the aid of our plentiful hot, dry weather, as easy as making raisins in Calabria. You have, for instance, only to cut the okra pods into slices or cross cuts, half an inch thick, spread them out on a board, or string them, and hang them up in an airy place to dry, and in a few days they will be ready to put away in clean paper bags for winter use; when, for soups, they are as good as when fresh in summer.

Ed. At what age do you take the pods for drying?

Sub. Exactly in the same tender state as for use when fresh.

Ed. And the delicious Lima beans which you gave us—when we dined with you last Christmas Day—as green, plump, fresh and excellent as if just taken from the vines?

Sub. That is still easier. You have only to take the green beans and spread them thinly on the floor of the garret, or an airy loft; they will dry without farther trouble, than turning them over once or twice. To have them in the best condition, they should be gathered a little younger than they are usually for boiling in summer. Lima beans are so easily grown and prepared for winter use, and are so truly excellent, that my family usually dry enough for use every other day all winter; and they are so fresh and tender (being soaked in warm water for twelve hours before cooking), that I have frequently some little difficulty in persuading my guests at a dinner in the holidays, that I have not a forcing house for beans, with the temperature of Lima all winter.

Ed. That is an easy and simple process, and its excellence we well know from experience. But, best of all, and most rare of all, is the tomato, as we have eaten it here, in mid-winter. As we have seen many trials in preserving this capital vegetable for winter use, nearly all of which were partly or wholly failures, pray let us into the secret of your tomato formula, which we promise not to repeat to more than eight or ten thousand of our particular friends and readers.

Sub. You are heartily welcome to tell it to twenty thousand. It *is* a real discovery for the gourmand in winter, who loves the pure, genuine, unalloyed and delicious acid flavor of the *Solanum Lycopersicum*, and knows how greatly it adds to the piquancy of a beef-steak, done to a second, and reposing, as CHRISTOPHER NORTH would say, in the mellow richness of its own brown juices.

Ed. Don't grow so eloquent over the remembrance as to forget the *modus operandi* of drying. Remember we must stake our reputation on its being equal to the genuine natural berry, when it is of the color of cornelian, and plucked in the dew of a July morning.

Sub. I remember. First,—gather the tomatoes.

Ed. When?

Sub. When they are quite ripe, least full of water, and most full of the tomato *principle;* that is to say, in sunny weather in July or August. If you wait till September, or, rather, till the weather is so cold that the fruit is watery, you will fail in the process for want of flavor.

Ed. Go on.

Sub. Choose tomatoes of small or only moderate size. Scald them in boiling water. Next,—peel them, and squeeze them slightly. Spread them on earthen dishes, and place the dishes in a brick oven, after taking the bread out. Let them remain there till the next morning. Then put them in bags, and hang them in a dry place.

Ed. That is certainly not a difficult process, and may be put in practice every baking day by the most time-saving farmer's wife in the country. And the cooking?

Sub. Is precisely like that of the fresh tomato, except that the dried tomato is soaked in warm water a few hours beforehand. For soups, it may be used without preparation; and a dish of this vegetable, dried in this way and stewed, is so exactly like the fresh tomatoes in appearance and flavor, that he must be a nice connoisseur in such matters who could tell in what the difference consists.

Ed. We can vouch most entirely for that; and after thanking you for the detail, have only to regret that we could not have published it in midsummer, so that all our readers could have had a fine dish of tomatoes when the thermometer is down below zero.

Sub. By steadily pursuing the tomato drying every baking day in July and August, we get enough to enable us to use it freely, and even profusely, as a winter vegetable; not as an occasional variety, but a good heaping dishful very often.

Ed. What is to be done with these small green melons which I see your man gathering in his basket? It is so late now that they will not ripen, and they are the perquisites of the pigs, doubtless.

Sub. You never made a greater mistake. For the pigs! Not if they were Westphalia all over. Why, that is the most delicious vegetable we have, at this season of the year. "Butter would not melt in your mouth" more quickly than that vegetable, as you shall have it served up on my table to-day.

Ed. Pray, what do you mean?

Sub. That these tardy after-crop musk-melons, trampled under foot and fed to the pigs, are the greatest delicacy of the season.

Ed. *Fricaseed,* I suppose; or "cut and dried," for winter use!

Sub. By no means; but simply cut in slices, about the fourth of an inch thick, and fried exactly in the same manner as egg plants. Whoever tastes them so prepared, will immediately make a memorandum that egg plants are thenceforward *tabooed,* and that melons, "rightly understood," are as melting and savory in their tender infancy, as they are luscious and sugary in their ripe maturity.

Ed. We shall be glad to put it to the immediate proof. But we must bring this talk to a close, or we shall be suspected of having lost all taste but the taste for the flesh-pots of Egypt.

Sub. But not till I have shown you my plat of "German greens," all growing for use next March, and my fine Walcheren cauliflowers, planted late, and which I shall "lift" at the first smart frost, and carry them into the cellar of my outbuildings, where they will flower and give me the finest and most succulent of vegetables all winter long, when my neighbors have only turnips and Irish potatoes. But you have taught the public how to manage all this in the previous number of your journal, so that I find every one begins to understand that it is as easy to have fine cauliflowers at Easter as Newtown Pippins. And now let us end this gossip and take a turn in the orchard, where I must show you my Beurrés and Bergamots.

VIII.

WASHINGTON, THE FARMER.

A REVIEW.

LETTERS ON AGRICULTURE, *from His Excellency* GEORGE WASHINGTON, *to* ARTHUR YOUNG *and* Sir JOHN SINCLAIR, *etc.* *Edited by* FRANKLIN KNIGHT. Washington, 1847. Published by the Editor. New-York, Baker & Scribner. 1 vol. quarto, with plates, 198 pp.

FOR a long time, the halo of Washington's civil and military glory has kept out of view his extraordinary talent in other directions. Mankind, too, are so reluctant to allow great men the meed of greatness in more than one sphere of action, that there has, we think, always been a national want of faith regarding the pre-eminence as an agriculturist, to which Washington is most undeniably entitled.

We are inclined to think that, considering the great disadvantages of the time in which he lived, he was one of the wisest, most successful, and most scientific farmers that America has ever yet produced.

Washington, as it is well known, was a very large landed proprietor. Before the Revolution, he was one of the most extensive tobacco planters in Virginia. His crops of this staple, he shipped in his own name, to Liverpool or Bristol, loading the vessels that came up the Potomac, either at Mount Vernon, or some other convenient point. In return, he imported from his agents abroad, improved agricultural implements, and all the better kinds of clothing, implements, and stores, needed in the domestic economy of his estate. During the Revolution, although necessarily absent from Mount Vernon, he endeavored to carry out his plans by frequent and minute directions to his manager there.

No sooner had the war closed, than Washington immediately retired to his beloved Mount Vernon, and was soon deeply immersed in the cares and pleasures of the life of an extensive landed proprietor. But it was by no means a life of indolent repose, though upon an estate large enough to secure him in the possession of every comfort. The very first year after the war, he directed his attention and his energies to the improvement of the mode of farming then in vogue in the whole of that part of the country.

He quickly remarked, that the system of the tobacco planters was fast exhausting the lands, and rendering them of little or no value. He entered into correspondence with the most distinguished scientific agriculturists in Great Britain, studied the ablest treatises then extant abroad on that subject, and immediately carried into practice the most valuable principles which he could draw from the soundest theory and practice then known. At a time when the planters were thinking of abandoning their worn-out lands, Washington began a new and most excellent system of *rotation of crops*, based on a careful examination of the qualities of the soils, on his estate, and by substituting grains, grass, and root crops, for tobacco, he soon restored the soil to good condition, and found his income materially increasing, while his neighbors, who pursued the old system, were daily growing poorer.

Nothing was more remarkable, among the trials of this great man's character, and nothing contributed more to his success in all he undertook, than the complete manner in which he first mastered his subject, and the exact method in which he afterwards marked out and pursued his plans.

In farming, this was evinced in the thoroughly systematic course of culture which he adopted on his Mount Vernon estate. This estate consisted of about 8000 acres, of which over 2000 acres, divided into five farms, were under cultivation. On his map of this estate, every field was numbered, and in his accompanying agricultural field-book, the crops were assigned to each field for several years in advance. So well had he studied the nature of the soils, that with slight subdivisions and experimental deviations, this scientific system of rotation was pursued with great success, from about 1785 to the close of his life.

After about four years—the most agreeable, doubtless, of his whole life—passed at Mount Vernon, in its improved condition, he was again called, by the spontaneous voice of one people to the Presidency. Much has been said and written about the reluctance of Cincinnatus to leave his farm, and return to the service of the Roman Republic; but the sources for regret in his position must have been small, compared to those which Washington felt, when he left Mount Vernon on this occasion. The farm of Cincinnatus, which has been rendered famous in classical history; was an hereditary allotment of *four acres*, and its cultivation was part of the daily toil of his own hands. Mount Vernon, on the other hand, was one of the largest and loveliest estates in America; it stood amid the rich landscape beauty of the Potomac, its beautiful lawns running down to the river, its serpentine walks of shrubbery, its fruit and flower-garden, planted by its master's own hands,* and its broad acres rendered productive by an intelligent and comprehensive system of agriculture of his own construction—think, oh ye who have never thus taken root in the soil, how hard it must have been for Washington *the Farmer*, to surrender again, even to the flattering wish of a whole nation, the life that he so much loved, for the hard yoke of what he felt to be the most difficult public service.

It is the best proof of how thoroughly devoted by natural taste was Washington to agriculture, that instead of leaving Mount Vernon to the charge of the excellent agent whom he had well grounded in his own system of practice, and who could no doubt have continued that practice with success, he never lost sight for a

* Washington's residence exhibited every mark of the cultivated and refined country gentleman. He appears to have had considerable taste in ornamental gardening; he decorated his pleasure-grounds with much effect: and his diary shows that he collected and planted a variety of rare trees and shrubs with his own hands, and watched their growth with the greatest interest. He employed skilful gardeners, and pruning was one of his favorite exercises.

moment, amid all the pressing cares of public life, of his rural home, or his favorite occupation. We can scarcely give a better idea of the man and his system, than by the following extract, touching this very portion of his life, from Sparks' admirable biography:

"With his chief manager at Mount Vernon, he left full and minute directions in writing, and exacted from him a weekly report, in which were registered the transactions of each day on all the farms, such as the number of laborers employed, their health or sickness, the kind and quantity of work executed, the progress in planting, sowing or harvesting the fields, the appearance of the crops at various stages of their growth, the effects of the weather on them, and the condition of the horses, cattle and other live stock. By these details, he was made perfectly acquainted with all that was done, and could give his orders with almost as much precision as if he had been on the spot. Once a week, regularly, and sometimes twice, he wrote to the manager, remarking on his report of the preceding week, and giving new directions. These letters frequently extended to two or three sheets, and were always written with his own hand. Such was his laborious exactness, that the letter he sent away was usually transcribed from a rough draft, and a press copy was taken of the transcript, which was carefully filed away with the manager's report, for his future inspection. In this habit, he persevered with unabated diligence, through the whole eight years of his Presidency, except during the short visits he occasionally made to Mount Vernon, at the close of the sessions of Congress, when his presence could be dispensed with at the seat of government. He, moreover, maintained a large correspondence on Agriculture with gentlemen in Europe and America. His letters to Sir John Sinclair, Arthur Young and Dr. Anderson, have been published, and are well known. *Indeed his thoughts never seemed to flow more freely, nor his pen move more easily, than when he was writing on Agriculture, extolling it as a most attractive pursuit, and describing the pleasure derived from it, and its superior claims, not only on the practical economist, but on the statesman and philanthropist.*"

The volume before us, which Mr. Knight has given to the public, in a very handsome quarto form, consists mainly of the correspondence referred to in the preceding quotation. The letters to Sir John Sinclair are rendered more interesting by their being facsimiles, showing the fine bold handwriting of their illustrious author. Besides, there is some very interesting collateral correspondence by Jefferson, Peters, and others, throwing additional light on the husbandry of that period. Engraved portraits of General and Mrs. Washington, views of the mansion at Mount Vernon, a map of the farms, etc., render the volume more complete and elegant.

It is not as conveying instruction to the intelligent agriculturist of the present day, that we commend this work; for the art and science of farming have made extraordinary progress since this early era in the history of our country. But it is as revealing a most interesting and little known portion of Washington's life and character, in which his own tastes were more peculiarly gratified, and in which he was no less successful, than in any other phase of his wonderfully great and pure life.

FRUIT.

28

FRUIT.

I.

A FEW WORDS ON FRUIT CULTURE.

July, 1851.

BY far the most important branch of horticulture at the present moment in this country, is the cultivation of Fruit. The soil and climate of the United States are, on the whole, as favorable to the production of hardy fruits as those of any other country—and our northern States, owing to the warmth of the summer and the clearness of the atmosphere, are far more prolific of fine fruits than the north of Europe. The American farmer south of the Mohawk, has the finest peaches for the trouble of planting and gathering—while in England they are luxuries only within the reach of men of fortune, and even in Paris, they can only be ripened upon walls. By late reports of the markets of London, Paris, and New-York, we find that the latter city is far more abundantly supplied with fruit than either of the former—though finer specimens of almost any fruit may be found *at very high prices*, at all times, in London and Paris, than in New-York. The fruit-grower abroad, depends upon extra size, beauty, and scarcity for his remuneration, and asks, sometimes, a guinea a dozen for peaches, while the orchardist of New-York will sell you a dozen *baskets* for the same money. The result is, that while you may more easily find superb fruit in London and Paris than in New-York—if you can afford to pay for it—you know that not one man in a hundred tastes peaches in a season, on the other side of the water, while during the month of September, they are the daily food of our whole population.

Within the last five years, the planting of orchards has, in the United States, been carried to an extent never known before. In the northern half of the Union, apple-trees, in orchards, have been planted by thousands and hundreds of thousands, in almost every State. The rapid communication established by means of railroads and steamboats in all parts of the country, has operated most favorably on all the lighter branches of agriculture, and so many farmers have found their orchards the most profitable, because least expensive part of their farms, that orcharding has become in some parts of the West, almost an absolute distinct species of husbandry. Dried apples are a large article of export from one part of the country to another, and the shipment of American apples of the finest quality to England, is now a regular and profitable branch of commerce. No apple that is sent from any part of the Continent will command more than half the price in Covent Garden market, that is readily paid for the Newtown pippin.

The pear succeeds admirably in many parts of the United States—but it also fails as a market fruit in many others—and, though large orchards have been planted in various parts of the country, we do not think the result, as yet, warrants the belief that the orchard culture of pears will be profitable generally. In certain deep soils—abounding with lime, potash, and phosphates, naturally, as in central New-York, the finest pears grow and bear like apples, and produce very large profits to their cultivators. Mr. Pardee's communication on this subject, in a former number, shows how largely the pear is grown as an orchard fruit in the State of New-York, and how profitable a branch of culture it has already become.

In the main, however, we believe the experience of the last five years has led most cultivators—particularly those not in a region naturally favorable in its soil—to look upon a pear as a tree rather to be confined to the fruit-garden than the orchard; as a tree not so hardy as the apple, but sufficiently hardy to give its finest fruit, provided the soil is deep, and the aspect one not too much exposed to violent changes of temperature. As the pear-tree (in its finer varieties) is more delicate in its bark than any other fruit-tree excepting the apricot, the best cultivators now agree as to the utility of sheathing the stem from the action of the sun all the year round—either by keeping the branches low and thick, so as to shade the trunk and principal limbs—the best mode—or by sheathing the stems with straw—thus preserving a uniform temperature. In all soils and climates naturally unfavorable to the pear, the culture of this tree is far easier upon the quince stock than upon the pear stock; and this, added to compactness and economy of space for small gardens, has trebled the demand for dwarf pears within the last half-dozen years. The finest pears that make their appearance in our markets, are still the White Doyenne (or Virgalieu), and the Bartlett. In Philadelphia the Seckel is abundant, but of late years the fruit is small and inferior, for want of the high culture and manuring which this pear demands.

If we except the neighborhood of Rochester and a part of central New-York (probably the future Belgium of America, as regards the production of pears), the best fruit of this kind yet produced in the United States is still to be found in the neighborhood of Boston. Neither climate nor soil are naturally favorable there, but the great pomological knowledge and skill of the amateur and professional cultivators of Massachusetts, have enabled them to make finer shows of pears, both as regards quality and variety, than have been seen in any part of the world. And this leads us to observe that the very facility with which fruit is cultivated in America—consisting for the most part only in planting the trees, and gathering the crop—leads us into an error as to the standard of size and flavor attainable generally. One half the number of trees well cultivated, manured, pruned, and properly cared for, annually, would give a larger product of really delicious and handsome fruit, than is now obtained from double the number of trees, and thrice the area of ground. The difficulty usually lies in the want of knowledge, and the high price of labor. But the horticultural societies in all parts of the country, are gradually raising the criterion of excellence among amateurs, and the double and treble prices paid lately by confectioners for finely-grown specimens, over the market value of ordinary fruit, are opening the eyes of market growers to the pecu niary advantages of high cultivation.

Perhaps the greatest advance in fruit-growing of the last half-dozen years, is in the culture of foreign grapes. So long as it was believed that our climate, which is warm enough to give us the finest melons in abundance, is also sufficient to produce the foreign grape in perfection, endless experiments were tried in the open garden. But as all these experiments were unsatisfactory or fruitless, not only at the North but at the South—it has finally come to be admitted that the difficulty lies in the variableness, rather than the want of heat, in the United States. This once conceded, our horticulturists have turned their attention to vineries for raising this delicious fruit under glass—and at the present time, so much have both private and market vineries increased, the finest Hamburgh, Chasselas, and Muscat grapes, may be had in abundance at moderate prices, in the markets of Boston, New-York, and Philadelphia. For a September crop of the finest foreign grapes, the heat of the sun accumulated in one of the so-called cold vineries (i. e. a vinery without artificial heat, and the regular temperature insured by the vinery itself) is amply sufficient. A cold vinery is constructed at so moderate a cost, that it is now fast becoming the appendage of every good garden, and some of our wealthiest amateurs, taking advantage of our bright and sunny climate, have grapes on their tables from April to Christmas—the earlier crops forced—the late ones slightly retarded in cold vineries. From all that we saw of the best private gardens in England, last summer, we are confident that we raise foreign grapes under glass in the United States, of higher flavor, and at far less trouble, than they are usually produced in England. Indeed, we have seen excellent Black Hamburghs grown in a large pit made by covering the vines trained on a high board fence, with the common sash of a large hot-bed.

On the Ohio, the native grapes—especially the Catawba—have risen to a kind of national importance. The numerous vineries which border that river, particularly about Cincinnati, have begun to yield abundant vintages of pure light wine, which takes rank with foreign wine of established reputation, and commands a high price in the market. Now that the Ohio is certain to give us Hock and

Claret, what we hear of the grapes and wine of Texas and New Mexico, leads us to believe that the future vineyards of New World Sherry and Madeira may spring up in that quarter of our widely extended country.

New Jersey, so long famous for her prolific peach orchards, begins to show the effects of a careless system of culture. Every year, the natural elements of the soil needful to the production of the finest peaches, are becoming scarcer and scarcer, and nothing but deeper cultivation, and a closer attention to the inorganic necessities of vegetable growth, will enable the orchardists of that State long to hold their ground in the production of good fruit. At the present moment, the peaches of Cincinnati and Rochester are far superior, both in beauty and flavor, to those of the New-York market—though in quantity the latter beats the world. The consequence is, that we shall soon find the peaches of Lake Ontario outselling those of Long Island and New Jersey in the same market, unless the orchardists of the latter State abandon *Malagatunes* and the *yellows*, and shallow ploughing.

The fruit that most completely baffles general cultivation in the United States, is the plum. It is a tree that grows and blossoms well enough in all parts of the country, but almost every where it has for its companion the curculio, the most destructive and the least vulnerable of all enemies to fruit. In certain parts of the Hudson, of central New-York, and at the West, where the soil is a stiff, fat clay, the curculio finds such poor quarters in the soil, and the tree thrives so well, that the fruit is most delicious. But in light, sandy soils, its culture is only an aggravation to the gardener. In such sites, here and there only a tree escapes, which stands in some pavement or some walk for ever hard by the pressure of constant passing. No method has proved effectual but placing the trees in the midst of the pig and poultry yard; and notwithstanding the numerous remedies that have been proposed in our pages since the commencement of this work, this proves the only one that has not failed more frequently than it has succeeded.

The multiplication of insects seems more rapid, if possible, than that of gardens and orchards in this country. Every where the culture of fruit appears, at first sight, the easiest possible matter, and really would be, were it not for some insect pest that stands ready to devour and destroy. In countries where the labor of women and children is applied, at the rate of a few cents a day, to the extermination of insects, it is comparatively easy to keep the latter under control. But nobody can afford to catch the curculios and other beetles at the price of a dollar a day for labor. The entomologists ought, therefore, to explain to us some natural laws which have been violated to bring upon us such an insect scourge; or at least point out to us some cheap way of calling in nature to our aid, in getting rid of the vagrants. For our own part, we fully believe that it is to the gradual decrease of small birds—partly from the destruction of our forests, but mainly from the absence of laws against that vagabond race of unfledged sportsmen who shoot sparrows when they ought to be planting corn—that this inordinate increase of insects is to be attributed. Nature intended the small birds to be maintained by the destruction of insects, and if the former are wantonly destroyed, our crops, both of the field and gardens, must pay the penalty. If the boys must indulge their spirit of liberty by shooting *something* innocent, it would be better for us husbandmen and gardeners to subscribe and get some French masters of the arts of domestic sports, to teach them how to bring their light artillery to bear upon bull-frogs. It would be a gain to the whole agricultural community, of more national importance than the preservation of the larger birds by the game laws.

We may be expected to say a word or two here respecting the result of the last five years on pomology in the United States. The facts are so well known that it seems hardly necessary. There has never been a period on either side of the Atlantic, when so much attention has been paid to fruit and fruit culture. The rapid increase of nurseries, the enormous sales of fruit-trees, the publication and dissemination of work after work upon fruits and fruit culture, abundantly prove this assertion. The Pomological Congress which held its third session last year in Cincinnati, and which meets again this autumn in Philadelphia, has done much, and will do more towards generalizing our pomological knowledge for the country generally. During the last ten years, almost every fine fruit known in Europe has been introduced, and most of them have been proved in this country. The result, on the whole, has been below the expectation; a few very fine sorts admirably adapted to the country; a great number of indifferent quality; many absolutely worthless. This, naturally, makes pomologists and fruit-growers less anxious about the novelties of the nurseries abroad, and more desirous of originating first-rate varieties at home. The best lessons learned from the discussions in the Pomological Congress—where the experience of the most practical fruit-growers of the country is brought out—is, that for every State, or every distinct district of country, there must be found or produced its improved indigenous varieties of fruit—varieties born on the soil, inured to the climate, and therefore best adapted to that given locality. So that after gathering a few kernels of wheat out of bushels of chaff, American horticulturists feel, at the present moment, as if the best promise of future excellence, either in fruits or practical skill, lay in applying all our knowledge and power to the study of our own soil and climate, and in helping nature to perform the problem of successful cultivation, by hints drawn from the facts immediately around us.

II.

THE FRUITS IN CONVENTION.

February, 1850.

WHAT an extraordinary age is this for conventions! Now-a-days, if people only imagine something is the matter, they directly hold a convention, and resolve that the world shall be amended. We should not be surprised to hear next, of a convention of crows, resolving that the wicked practice of setting scare-crows in cornfields be henceforth abolished.

Sitting in our easy chair a few evenings since, we were quite surprised to see the door of our library open, and a small boy—dressed in dark green, who had something of the air of a locust or a grass-hopper—walk in with a note.

It was an invitation to attend a mass meeting of all the fruits of America, ass embled to discuss the propriety of *changing their names.* Horrified at the revolutionary spirit, we seized our hat directly, and bade the messenger lead the way.

He lost no time in conducting us at once to a large building, where we entered a lofty hall, whose dome, ribbed like a melon, was lighted by a gigantic chandelier, in the form of a Christmas tree, the lights of which gleamed through golden and emerald drops of all manner of crystal fruits.

In the hall itself were assembled all our familiar acquaintances, and many that were scarcely known to us by sight. We mean our acquaintances—the fruits. On the right of the speaker sat the Pears; rather a tall, aristocratic set of gentlemen and ladies,—many of them foreigners, and most of them of French origin. One could see by the gossiping and low conversation going on in knots among them, that they were full of little schemes of finesse. On the left, sat the numerous Apple family, with honest, ruddy faces; and whether Yankee, English, or German, evidently all of the Teutonic race. They had a resolute, determined air, as if they had business of importance on hand. Directly behind the Pears sat the Peaches, mostly ladies, with such soft complexions and finely turned figures as it did one's eyes good to contemplate; or youths, with the soft down of early manhood on their chins. Apricots and Nectarines were mingled among them, full of sweet smiles and a honeyed expression about their mouths. The Plums were there, too, dressed in purple and gold,—many of them in velvet coats, with a fine downy bloom upon them; and near them were the Cherries, an arrant, coquettish set of lasses and lads,—the light in their eyes as bright as rubies. The Strawberries sat on low stools in the aisles, overhung and backed by the Grapes,—tall fellows, twisting their moustaches (tendrils), and leaning about idly, as if they took but little interest in the proceedings. The only sour faces in the crowd were those of a knot of Morello Cherries and Dutch Currants, who took every occasion to hiss any speaker not in favor.

We said this was a convention of fruits; but we ought also to add that the fruits looked extremely like human beings. On remarking this to our guide, he quietly said,—"Of course, you know you see them now in their spiritual forms. If you half close your eyes, you will find you recognize them all in their everyday, familiar shapes." And so indeed we did, and were shaking hands warmly with our neighbors and friends—the Beurrés, and Pippins, and Pearmains, when we were interrupted by the speaker, calling the meeting to order.

The Speaker (on giving him the *blink*), we found to be a fine large specimen of the *Boston Russet*, with a dignified expression, and a certain bland air of one accustomed to preside. He returned thanks very handsomely to the convention for the honor of the chair; assuring them that having been bred in the land of steady habits, he would do all in his power to maintain order and expedite the business of the convention. We noticed, as he sat down, that there were vice-presidents from every State,—many of them old and well-known fruits; and that the Le Clerc Pear and an Honest John Peach were the secretaries; and a pair of very astringent looking fellows—one a Crab Apple, and the other a Choke Pear—were sergeants-at-arms, or door-keepers. Their duties seemed to be chiefly that of preventing some brambles from clambering up the walls and looking in the windows, and a knot of saucy looking blackamoors, whom we discovered to be only Black Currants, from crowding up the lobbies; the latter in particular, being in bad odor with many of the members.

There was a little stir on the left, and a solid, substantial, well-to-do personage rose, who we recognized immediately as the Newtown Pippin. He had the air of a man about sixty; but there was a look of sound health about him which made you feel sure of his hundredth year.

The Newtown Pippin said it was needless for him to remark that this was no common meeting. The members were all aware that no ordinary motives had called together this great convention of fruits. He was proud and happy to welcome so many natives and naturalized citizens,—all bearing evidence of having taken kindly to the soil of this great and happy country. Every one present knows, the world begins to know, he remarked, that North America is the greatest of fruit-growing countries (hear, hear), that the United States was fast becoming the favored land of Pomona, who, indeed, was always rather republican in her taste, and hated, above all things, the fashion in aristocratic countries of tying her up to walls, and confining her under glass. He preferred the open air, and the free breath of orchards.

But, he said, it was necessary to come to business. This convention had met to discuss the propriety and necessity of passing an alien law, by which all foreigners, on settling in this country, should be obliged to drop their foreign names, or, rather, have them translated into plain English. The cultivators of fruit were, take them altogether, a body of plain, honest countrymen, who, however they might relish foreign fruits, did not get on well with foreign names. They found them to stick in their throats to such a degree that they could not make good bargains over such gibberish. The question to be brought before this meeting, therefore, was nothing more nor less than whether things should be called by names that sounded real, or names that had a foreign, fictitious and romantic air; whether an honest man might be called in plain English a "good Christian," or whether he should forever be doomed to be misrepresented and misunderstood as a "*Bon Chrétien.*" For his own part, he said, he thought it was time to assert our nationality; and while he was the last man to say or do any thing to prevent foreigners from settling among us, he did think that they should have the courtesy to drop foreign airs and come down to plain English, or plain Yankee comprehension. He was himself a "native American," and he gloried in it. He considered himself, though a plain republican, as good as any foreigners, however high-sounding their titles; and he believed that if fruits would be more careful about their intrinsic flavor, and study, as he did, how to maintain their credit perfect and unimpaired for the longest possible period, it would in the end be found more to their advantage than this stickling for foreign titles. His ancestors, he said, were born in the State of New-York; and he was himself raised in a great and well-known orchard on the Hudson. (Hear, hear.) If any gentleman present wished to know the value of a plain American name, he would be glad to show him, in dollars and cents, the income of that orchard. He was in greater favor in Covent Garden market than any English or continental fruit; and such sums had been realized from the sales of that orchard, that it was seriously proposed in the English parliament to impose a duty on Newtown Pippins, to pay off the national debt. (*Great applause, and a hiss from a string of Currants.*) He concluded, by trusting the chairman would pardon this allusion to his own affairs, which he only gave to show that a Pippin, in plain English, was worth as much in the market and the world's estimation, as the finest French title that was ever lisped in the Faubourg St. Germain. He moved that all foreign names of fruits be done into plain English.

This speech produced a great commotion among the Pears on the right, who had evidently not expected such a straightforward way of treating the matter. For a moment all was confusion. That little fellow, the *Petit Muscat*,—always the first on the carpet,—ran hither and thither gathering little clusters about him. The

Sans-peau, or Skinless, was evidently touched to the quick. The *Pomme glacé* gave all the Pippins a freezing look; and the *Fondante d'Automne*, a very tender creature, was so overcome that she melted into tears at such a monstrous proposition. The *Belle de Bruxelles* muttered that *she* had seen Newtown Pippins that were false-hearted; and the *Poire Episcopal* declared that the man who could utter such sentiments was a radical, and dangerous to the peace of established institutions.

Just as we were wondering who would rise on the opposition, a tall, well proportioned Pear got up, with a pleasant Flemish aspect. It was *Van Mons' Léon le Clerc.* He said he was sorry to see this violent feeling manifested against foreign names; and being a foreigner, and having had a pretty long acquaintance with foreign Pears abroad, he felt called upon to say something in their defence. He thought the remarks of the gentleman who had preceded him, both uncourteous to foreigners and unreasonable. He could not understand why people should not be allowed to retain their *names*, at least such as had any worth retaining, even if they did become rooted to the soil of this country. Especially when those names were in the most polite language in the world,—a language which every educated person was bound to understand,—a language spoken by Duhamel and Van Mons, the greatest of pomologists,—a language more universal than the English,—spoken, in short, in all civilized countries, and especially spoken by fine ladies over a dish of fine pears at the dessert. (*Great applause.*)

Here, a stranger to us, the *Bezi des Vétérans*, rose and said :—Sare, I have de honor to just arrive in dis country. I am very much *chagrineé* at dis proposition to take away my name. I have run away from de revolutions, what take away my property, and here I hope to find *la liberté—la paix;* and I only find *les voleurs*—robbers—vat vish to take away my name. Yes, sare; and what they will call me den ?—" wild old mans," or " old sojair ? " Bah! Me no like to be so, Moi, who belong to de *grand bataillon—le garde Napoléon!*

Here a pleasant and amiable lady rose, evidently a little embarrassed. It was *Louise Bonne de Jersey*. She said she loved America. True, she had found the climate not to agree with her at first, and her children seemed to pine away; but since she had taken that hardy creature, the Quince, for a partner, they had done wonderfully well. For her own part, she had no objection whatever to being called "Good Louise," or even "Dear Louisa," if her American friends and cousins liked it better. All she asked was to be allowed to live in the closest intimacy with the Quince, and not to have any *cutting* remarks made at her roots. She could not bear that.

A very superb and stately lady next rose, giving a shake to her broad skirts of yellow satin, and looking about her with the air of a duchess. In fact, it was the *Duchesse d'Angoulême;* and though she was a little high shouldered, and her features somewhat irregular, she had still a very noble air. She remarked, in a simple and dignified voice, that she had been many years in this country, and had become very partial to the people and institutions. Naturally, she had strong attachments to old names and associations, especially where, as in her case, they were names that were names. But, she added, it was impossible to live in America without mixing with the people, if one's very name could not be understood. It was very distressing to her feelings to find, as she did, that French was not taught in the common schools; and she hoped if an agricultural college was established, the scholars would be taught that language which was synonymous with every thing elegant and refined. She trusted, in conclusion, that though names should be anglicized, the dignity would be preserved. A duchess, in name at least, she must always be; but if republicans preferred to call her simply the Duchess of Angouleme, she saw nothing amiss in it. Especially,—she remarked, with a slight toss of the head,—especially, since she had heard an ignorant man, at the country-seat where she resided call her repeatedly "Duchy-Dan goes-lame;" and another, who visits him, speak of her, as "Dutch Dangle-um," forgetting that she abhorred Holland.

She was followed by the *Red Streak Apple*, from New Jersey, a very blunt, sturdy fellow, who spoke his mind plainly. He said he liked the good sense of the lady who had just spoken; she was a woman he should have no objection to call a Duchess himself. About this matter he had but few words to say. Some folks were all talk and no *cider;* that, thank God! was not his fashion. What he had to say he said; and that was, that he was sick of this tom-foolery about foreign names. A name either meant something or it did not. Any body who looked at him could see that he was a Red-Streak, and that was all that his father expected when he named him. Any body could believe that the last speaker was a Duchess. But what, he should like to know, did the man mean who named a Peach "*Sanguinole a chair adherent!*" He should like to meet that chap. It would be a regular raw-head and bloody-bones piece of business for him. And "*Fondante du Bois;*" he supposed that was the fond aunt of some b'hoys,—it might be the "old boy," for all he knew. And "*Beurré Gris d'Hiver nouveau.*" Could any thing be more ridiculous! He should like to know how those clever people, the pomologists, would translate that? They told him, "new gray winter butter," (*laughter;*) and what sort of winter butter, pray, was that? "*Reine de Pays bas;*" what this meant, he did not exactly know,—something, he supposed, about "rainy weather pays bad," which would not go down, he could tell the gentleman, in our dry climate. There was no end to this stuff, he said. He seconded the Pippin. Clear it all away; boil it down to a little pure, plain English essence, if there was any substance in it; if not, throw the lingo to the dogs. He hoped the Pears would excuse him. He meant no offence to them personally. But he didn't like their names, and he told them so to their faces.

The *Minister* Apple here observed that he had some moral scruples about changing the names of all the fruits. It might have a bad effect on the hearts and minds of the community. He begged leave to present to the speaker's consideration such names, for example, as the "*Ah mon Dieu,*" and the "*Cuisse Madame*" Pears! There were many who grew those Pears, and, like our first parents, did not *know* the real nature of the fruits in the garden. Happy ignorance! Translate them, and they would, he feared, become fruits of the tree of knowledge.

A tall *Mazzard* Cherry hereupon remarked (wiping his spectacles), that a very easy way of avoiding the danger which his worthy friend, who had just sat down, had pointed out, would be to reject both the Pears and the names, when they were no better than the last. He was a warm friend to progress in horticulture, and he was fully of the opinion of the Jersey Red-Streak, that things should not come among us, plain republicans, in disguise. How, indeed, did we know that these Pears of France were not sent out here under these queer names for the very purpose of corrupting our morals; or, at least, imposing on us in some way? He had been settled in a garden for some years, among a pleasant society of trees, when last spring the owner introduced a new Pear from abroad, under the fine name of "*Chat brulé.*" For some time the thing put on airs, and talked about its estate and chateau having been destroyed by incendiaries; and it showed a petition for charity. What was his amazement, one day, when the daughter of the proprietor came in the garden, to see the contempt with which she turned away from this Pear, and exclaimed, "what could have induced pa to have brought this 'singed cat' here?" *Chat brulé,* indeed! He bent over the creature and switched her finely the first stormy day. He was for translating all good fruits and damning all bad ones. (At hearing this, certain second-rate Strawberries commenced *running*.)

The convention grew very excited as the Mazzard sat down. The *Muscat Noir* Grape looked black in the face; the Crown Bob Gooseberry threw up his hat; and the Blood Peach, who had been flirting with a very worthless fellow—the French soft-shelled Almond—turned quite crimson all over. Cries of "order, order," were heard from all sides; and it was only restored when a little, plump, Dolly-Varden-looking young girl, who was a great favorite in good society, sprang upon a chair in order to be seen and heard.

This was the Lady Apple. Her eyes sparkled, and set off her brilliant complexion, which was quite dazzlingly fair. It was easy to see that she was a sort of spoiled child among the fruits.

Mr. Speaker, she said in a very sweet voice, you will indulge me, I am sure, with a very little speech—my maiden speech. I should not have ventured here, but I positively thought it was to have been a private party, and not one of these odious mass meetings. I am accustomed to the society of well-bred people, and know something of the polite language of both hemispheres. Indeed, my ancestors still live in France, though I am myself a real American. What I have to tell is only a little of my own experience; which is, that one may, if one has good looks, and is a person of taste, have her name changed without suffering the least loss of character or reputation. Indeed, I am convinced it may often add to her circle of admirers, by making her better understood and appreciated. I am almost ashamed, ladies and gentlemen, to refer to my own life, illustrative of this remark. (*Cheers*). [Here she blushed, and looked around her very sweetly.] At home, there in *la belle France*, I belong to the old and very respectable family of the Api's. There was not much in that; but mostly shut up in an old dingy chateau,—no society—no evening parties—no excitement. I assure you it was very dull. In this country, where I am known every where as the "Lady Apple," I am invited every where among the most fashionable people. Yes, Mr. Speaker, this country has charmingly been called the paradise of ladies; and I would advise all deserving and modest girls in *jeune France*, to come over to younger America, and *change their names* as quickly as they can. (*Hear, hear*, especially from the *Jonathan* Apple.) If they will take *my* advice, they will put off all foolish pride and fine names that mean nothing, and try to speak plain English, and dress in the latest republican style; (especially,—she added, *aside*, turning to the foreign Pears,—especially as the fashions always come from Paris.)

This lively little sally evidently made a favorable impression. The Bartlett Pear said he was nobody in France as the *Poire Guillame*, while here, where the climate agreed so much better with his constitution, he was a favorite with high and low. The *Duchesse d'Orleans* thought it best for ladies like herself, who did not expect to associate with any but the educated class, to retain their foreign names. The *Jargonell* Pear said he had heard a great deal of talk, which to him was a mere babel of tongues. His name was the same on both sides of the water. The Flemish Beauty said, on the other hand, that she was a great deal more loved in this country now, than when she first came here as the *Belle de Flandres*. The *Bellefleur* Apple observed, she had tried to maintain her foreign etymology in this country without success, and meant to be henceforth plain Bellflower: and the *Surprise* Apple turned red, as he attempted to say something (the Morello trying to hiss him down); but he was only able to stammer out his astonishment that any one could doubt the policy of so wise a movement.

There was here a tumult among some of the foreign Grapes, accustomed to live in glass-houses, who had been caught by the Crab Apples *stoning* the windows, and sticking their spurs (they were short-pruned vines) into some patient-looking old *Horse* Apples from the western States. A free-soiler, who was known as the *Northern Spy*, was about to sow the seeds of the apple of discord in the convention, by bringing forward an amendment, that no foreign fruits, and especially none which were not "on their own bottoms," should be allowed to settle in any of the new States or territories, when that old favorite, the Vergal Pear, made a soothing speech, in his usual melting and *buttery* manner, which brought all the meeting to a feeling of unanimity again; when they resolved to postpone further action, but to prepare a memorial on the subject, to be laid before the Congress of Fruit-growers, at its meeting next fall in Cincinnati.

III.

THE PHILOSOPHY OF MANURING ORCHARDS

January, 1848.

THE culture of the soil may be viewed in two very different aspects. In one, it is a mean and ignorant employment. It is a moral servitude, which man is condemned to pay to fields perpetually doomed to bear thorns and thistles. It is an unmeaning routine of planting and sowing, to earn bread enough to satisfy the hunger and cover the nakedness of the race. And it is performed in this light, by the servants of the soil, in a routine as simple, and with a spirit scarcely more intelligent than that of the beasts which draw the plough that tears open the bosom of a hard and ungenial earth!

What is the other aspect in which agriculture may be viewed? Very different indeed. It is an employment at once the most natural, noble, and independent that can engage the energies of man. It brings the whole earth into subjection. It transforms unproductive tracts into fruitful fields and gardens. It raises man out of the uncertain and wild life of the fisher and hunter, into that where all the best institutions of society have their birth. It is the mother of all the arts, all the commerce, and all the industrial employments that maintain the civilization of the world. It is full of the most profound physical wonders, and involves an insight into the whole history of the planet, and the hidden laws that govern that most common and palpable, and yet most wonderful and incomprehensible substance—matter! There has never yet lived one who has been philosopher enough to penetrate farther than the outer vestibules of its great temples of truth; and there are mysteries enough yet unexplained in that every-day miracle, the growth of an acorn, to excite for ages the attention and admiration of the most profound worshipper of God's works.

Fortunately for us and for our age, too much light has already dawned upon us to allow intelligent men ever to relapse into any such degrading view of the aim and rights of the cultivator as that first presented. We have too generally ascertained the value of science, imperfect as it still is, applied to farming and gardening, to be contented any more to go back to that condition of things when a crooked tree was used for a plough, and nuts and wild berries were sufficient to satisfy the rude appetite of man. The natural sciences have lately opened new revelations to us of the hidden problems of growth, nutrition, and decay, in the vegetable and animal kingdoms. Secrets have been laid bare that give us a new key to power, in our attempts to gain the mastery over matter, and we are continually on the alert to verify and put in practice our newly acquired knowledge, or to add in every possible way to the old stock. Men are no longer contented to reap short crops from worn-out soil. They look for scientific means of renovating it. They would make the earth do its utmost. Agriculture is thus losing its old character of being merely physical drudgery, and is rapidly becoming a science, full of profound interest, as well as a grand practical art, which, Atlas-like, bears the burden of the world on its back.

It is not to be denied that CHEMISTRY is the great railroad which has lately been opened, graded, and partially set in operation, to facilitate progress through that wide and comparatively unexplored territory—*scientific cultivation:* chemistry, which has scrutinized and analyzed till she has made many things, formerly doubtful and hidden, as clear as noonday. And it is by watching her movements closely, by testing her theories by practice, by seizing every valuable suggestion, and working out her problems patiently and fairly, that the cultivator is mainly to hope for progress in the future.

No one who applies his reasoning powers to the subject will fail to see, also, how many interesting points are yet in obscurity; how many important facts are only just beginning to dawn upon the patient investigator; how much is yet to be learned only by repeated experiments; and how many fail who expect to get *immediate* replies from nature, to questions whose satisfactory solution must depend upon a variety of preliminary knowledge, only to be gathered slowly and patiently, by those who are unceasing in their devotion to her teachings.

There are no means of calculating how much chemistry has done for agriculture within the last ten years. We say this, not in the sanguine spirit of one who reads a volume on agricultural chemistry for the first time, and imagines that by the application of a few salts he can directly change barren fields into fertile bottoms, and raise one hundred bushels of corn where twenty grew before. But we say it after no little observation of the results of experimental farming—full of failures and errors, with only occasional examples of brilliant success—as it is.

There are numbers of readers who, seeing the partial operations of nature laid bare, imagine that the whole secret of assimilation is discovered, and by taking too short a route to the end in view, they destroy all. They may be likened to those intellectual sluggards who are captivated by certain *easy roads to learning*, the gates of which are kept by those who teach every branch of human wisdom in *six lessons!* This gallop into the futurity of laborious effort, generally produces a giddiness that is almost equivalent to the obliteration of all one's power of discernment. And though one may, now, by the aid of magnetism, "put a girdle round the earth" in *less* than "forty minutes," there are still conditions of nature that imperiously demand time and space.

Granting, therefore, that there are hundreds who have failed in their experiments with agricultural chemistry, still we contend that there are a few of the more skilful and thorough experimenters who have been eminently successful; and *whose success will gradually form the basis of a new and improved system of agriculture.*

More than this, the attention which has been drawn to the value of careful and intelligent culture, is producing indirectly the most valuable results. Twenty years ago not one person in ten thousand, cultivating the land, among us, thought of any other means of enriching it than that of supplying it with barn-yard manure. At the present moment there is not an intelligent farmer in the country who is not conversant with the economy and value of muck, ashes, lime, marl, bones, and a number of less important fertilizers. In all the older and less fertile parts of the country, where manure is no longer cheap, the use of these fertilizers has enabled agriculturists of limited means to keep their land in high condition, and add thirty per cent. to their crops. And any one who will take the trouble to examine into the matter in our principal cities, will find that fifty articles, in the aggregate of enormous value for manure to the farmer and gardener, which were until lately entirely thrown away, are now preserved, are articles of commerce, and are all turned to the utmost account as food for the crops.

We have been led into this train of thought by observing that after the great staples of the agriculturist—bread-stuffs and the grasses—have had that first attention at the hands of the chemist which they so eminently deserve, some investigation is now going on for the benefit of the horticulturist and the orchardist, of which it is our duty to keep our readers informed. We allude to the analyses which have been made of the composition of the inorganic parts of vegetables, and more especially of some of the *fruit-trees* whose culture is becoming an object of so much importance to this country.

We think no one at all familiar with modern chemistry or scientific agriculture, can for a moment deny the value of *specific manures*. It is the great platform upon which the scientific culture of the present day stands, and which raises it so high above the old empirical routine of the last century. But in order to be able to make practical application, with any tolerable chance of success, of the doctrine of special manures, we must have before us careful analyses of the composition of the plants we propose to cultivate. Science has proved to us that there are substances which are of universal value as food for plants; but it is now no less certain that, as the composition of different plants, and even different species of plants, differs very widely, so must certain substances, essential to the growth of the plant, be present in the soil, or that growth is feeble and imperfect.

A little observation will satisfy any careful inquirer, that but little is yet practically known of the proper mode of *manuring orchards*, and rendering them uniformly productive. To say that in almost every neighborhood, orchards will be found which bear large crops of fine fruit, while others, not half a mile off, produce only small crops; that in one part of the country a given kind of fruit is always large and fair, and in another it is always spotted and defective; that barn-yard manure seems to produce but little effect in remedying these evils; that orchards often nearly cease bearing while yet the trees are in full maturity, and by no means in a worn-out or dying condition: to say all this, is only to repeat what every experienced cultivator of orchards is familiar with, but for which few or no practical cultivators have the explanation ready.

We have seen a heavy application of common manure made to apple-trees, which were in this inexplicable condition of bearing no sound fruit, without producing any good effects. The trees grew more luxuriantly, but the fruit was still knotty and inferior. In this state of things, the baffled practical man very properly attributes it to some inherent defect in the soil, and looks to the chemist for aid.

We are glad to be able to say, this aid is forthcoming. Many valuable analyses of the *ashes* of trees and plants, have been made lately at *Giessen*, and may be found in the appendix to the *last edition* of Liebig's *Agricultural Chemistry.** And still more recently, Dr. Emmons, of Albany, well known by his labors in the cause of scientific agriculture,† has devoted considerable time and attention to ascertaining the elements which enter into the composition of the *inorganic parts of trees.*

The result of this investigation we consider of the highest importance to the fruit cultivator and the orchardist. In fact, though still imperfect, it clears up many difficult points, and gives us some basis for a more philosophical system of manuring orchards than has yet prevailed.

The importance of the gaseous and more soluble manures—ammonia, nitrogen, etc., to the whole vegetable kingdom, has long been pretty thoroughly appreciated. The old-fashioned, practical man, dating from Noah's time, who stands by his well-rotted barn-yard

* Published by Wiley & Putnam, New-York.

† See his quarto vol. on the *Agriculture of New-York*, lately published, and forming part of the State survey.

compost, and the new-school disciple, who uses guano and liquid manures, are both ready witnesses to prove the universal and vital importance of these animal fertilizers,—manures that accelerate the growth, and give volume and bulk to every part of a tree or plant.

But the value and importance of the heavier and more insoluble earthy elements have often been disputed, and, though ably demonstrated of late, there are still comparatively few who understand their application, or who have any clear and definite ideas of their value in the economy of vegetable structure.

To get at the exact quantities of these ingredients, which enter into the composition of plants, it is necessary to analyze their *ashes.*

It is not our purpose, at the present moment, to go beyond the limits of the orchard. We shall therefore confine ourselves to the most important elements which make up the wood and bark of the *apple*, the *pear*, and the *grape-vine.*

According to Dr. Emmons's analysis, in 100 parts of the ashes of the *sap-wood* of the apple-tree, there are three elements that greatly preponderate, as follows: 16 parts *potash*, 17 parts *phosphate of lime*, and 18 parts *lime.* In the *bark* of this tree, there are 4 parts *potash* and 51 parts *lime.*

100 parts of the ashes of the sap-wood of the *pear*-tree, show 22 parts *potash*, 27 parts *phosphate of lime*, and 12 parts *lime;* the bark giving 6 parts *potash*, 6 parts *phosphate*, and 30 parts *lime.*

The analysis of the common wild *grape-vine*, shows 20 parts *potash*, 15 parts *phosphate of lime*, and 17 parts *lime*, to every 100 parts; the bark giving 1 part *potash*, 5 parts *phosphate of lime*, and 39 parts *lime.*

Now, no intelligent cultivator can examine these results (which we have given thus in the rough* to simplify the matter) without

* The following are Dr. Emmons's exact analyses:

ASH OF THE PEAR.

	Sap-wood.	*Bark.*
Potash,	22·25	6·20
Soda,	1·84	
Chlorine,	0·31	1·70
Sulphuric acid,	0·50	1·80
Phosphate of lime,	27·22	6·50

being conscious at a glance, that this large necessity existing i[n] these fruit-trees for *potash*, *phosphate of lime*, and *lime*, is not at a[ll]

	Sap-wood.	Bark.
Phosphate of peroxide of iron,	0·31	
Carbonic acid,	27·69	37·29
Lime,	12·64	30·36
Magnesia,	3·00	9·40
Silex,	0·30	0·40
Coal,	0·17	0·65
Organic matter,	4·02	4·20
	100·25	98·30

ASH OF THE APPLE.

	Sap-wood.	Bark.
Potash,	16·19	4·930
Soda,	3·11	3·285
Chloride of sodium,	0·42	0·540
Sulphate of lime,	0·05	0·637
Phosphate of peroxide of iron,	0·80	0·375
Phosphate of lime,	17·50	2·425
Phosphate of magnesia,	0·20	
Carbonic acid,	29·10	44·830
Lime,	18·63	51·578
Magnesia,	8·40	0·150
Silica,	0·85	0·200
Soluble silica,	0·80	0·400
Organic matter,	4·60	2·100
	100·65	109·450

COMMON WILD GRAPE-VINE.

	Wood.	Bark.
Potash,	20·84	1·77
Soda,	2·06	0·27
Chlorine,	0·02	0·40
Sulphuric acid,	0·23	trace.
Phosphate of lime,	15·40	5·04
Phosphate of peroxide of iron,	1·20	5·04
Carbonic acid,	34·83	32·22
Lime,	17·33	39·32
Magnesia,	4·40	0·80
Silex,	2·80	14·00
Soluble silica,	0·00	0·30
Coal and organic matter,	2·20	1·70
	100·21	100·86

provided for by the common system of manuring orchards. Hence, in certain soils, where a part or all of these elements naturally exist, we see both the finest fruit and extraordinary productiveness in the orchards. In other soils, well suited perhaps for many other crops, orchards languish and are found unprofitable.

More than this, Dr. EMMONS has pointed out what is perhaps known to few of our readers, that these inorganic substances form, as it were, the skeleton or bones of all vegetables as they do more tangibly in animals. The bones of animals are lime—in the form of phosphate and carbonate—and the frailer net-work skeleton of trunk, leaves and fibres in plants, is formed of precisely the same substance. The bark, the veins and nerves of the leaves, the skin of fruit, are all formed upon a framework of this organized salt of lime, which, in the growth of the plant, is taken up from the soil, and circulates freely to the outer extremities of the tree or plant in all directions.

As these elements, which we have named as forming so large a part of the ashes of plants, are found in animal manures, the latter are quite sufficient in soils where they are not naturally deficient. But, on the other hand, where the soil is wanting in lime, potash and phosphate of lime, common manures will not and do not answer the purpose. Experience has abundantly proved the latter position; and science has at length pointed out the cause of the failure.

The remedy is simple enough. Lime, potash and bones (which latter abound in the phosphate) are cheap materials, easily obtained in any part of the country. If they are not at hand, common *wood ashes*, which contains all of them, is an easy substitute, and one which may be used in much larger quantities than it is commonly applied, with the most decided benefit to all fruit-trees.

The more scientific cultivator of fruit will not fail, however, to observe that there is a very marked difference in the proportion of these inorganic matters in the ashes of the trees under our notice. Thus, potash and phosphate of lime enter much more largely into the composition of the pear than they do in that of the apple tree; while lime is much more abundant in the apple than in the pear; the ashes of the bark of the apple-tree being more *than half lime.*

Potash and lime are also found to be the predominant elements of the inorganic structure of the grape-vine.

Hence *potash* and *bone dust* will be the principal substances to nourish the structure of the pear-tree; *lime*, the principal substance for the apple; and *potash* for the grape-vine; though each of the others are also highly essential.

Since these salts of lime penetrate to the remotest extremities of the tree; since, indeed, they are the foundation upon which a healthy structure of all the other parts must rest, it appears to us a rational deduction that upon their presence, in sufficient quantity, must depend largely the general healthy condition of the leaves and fruit. Hence, it is not unlikely that certain diseases of fruit, known as the bitter rot in apples, the mildew in grapes, and "cracking" in pears, known and confined to certain districts of the country, may arise from a deficiency of these inorganic elements in the soil of those districts, (not overlooking *sulphate of iron*, so marked in its effect on the health of foliage.) Careful experiment will determine this; and if such should prove to be the case, one of the greatest obstacles to universal orchard culture will be easily removed.*

What we have here endeavored to convey of the importance of certain specific manures for fruit-trees, is by no means all theory. We could already give numerous practical illustrations to fortify it. Two will perhaps suffice for the present.

The greatest orchard in America, most undeniably, is that at Pelham farm, on the Hudson. How many barrels of apples are raised

* It will be remembered that, in our work on Fruits, we opposed the theory that all the old pears, liable to *crack* along the sea-coast, and in some other sections of the country, were "worn out." We attributed their apparent decline to unfavorable soil, injudicious culture and ungenial climate. A good deal of observation since those views were published, has convinced us that "cracking" in the pear is to be attributed more to an exhaustion, or a want of certain necessary elements in the soil, than to any other cause. Age has little or nothing to do with it, since *Van Mon's Leon Le Clerc*, one of the newest and most vigorous of pears, has cracked in some soils for the past two years around Boston, though perfectly fair in other soils there, and in the interior.

there annually, we are not informed. But we do know, first, that the crop this season, numbered *several thousand barrels* of Newtown pippins, of a size, flavor and beauty that we never saw surpassed; and second, that the Pelham Newtown pippins are as well known in Covent Garden market, London, as a Bank of England note, and can as readily be turned into cash, with the highest premium over any other goods and chattels of the like description. Now the great secret of the orchard culture at the Pelham farm, is the *abundant use of lime.* Not that high culture and plenty of other necessary food are wanting; but that lime is the great basis of large crops and smooth, high-flavored fruit.

Again, the greatest difficulty in fruit culture in America, is to grow the foreign grape in the open air. It is not heat nor fertility that is wanting, for one section or another of the country can give both these in perfection; but in all sections the fruit mildews, and is, on the whole, nearly worthless. An intelligent cultivator, living in a warm and genial corner of Canada West, (bordering on the western part of Lake Erie,) had been more than usually successful for several seasons in maturing several varieties of foreign grapes in the open air. At length they began to fail—even upon the young vines, and the mildew made its appearance to render nearly the whole crop worthless. Last season, this gentleman, following a hint in this journal, gave one of his grape borders a *heavy dressing of wood ashes.* These ashes contained, of course, both the potash and the lime so necessary to the grape. He had the satisfaction of raising, this season, a crop of fair and excellent grapes, (of which we had occular proof,) from this border, while the other vines of the same age (and treated, otherwise, in the same way) bore only mildewed and worthless fruit. We consider both these instances excellent illustrations of the value of specific manures.

We promise to return to this subject again. In the mean time it may not be useless to caution some of our readers against pursuing the *wholesale* course with specifics which all quack doctors are so fond of recommending—i. e., "if a thing is good, you cannot give too much." A tree is not all *bones*, and therefore something must be considered besides its anatomical structure—important as that may be. The good, old-fashioned, substantial nourishment must not be withheld, and a suitable ration from the compost or manure heap, as usual, will by no means prevent our orchards being benefited all the more by the substances of which they have especial need, in certain portions of their organization.

IV.

THE VINEYARDS OF THE WEST.

August, 1850.

TO sit under our own vine and fig-tree, with no one to make us afraid, is the most ancient and sacred idea of a life of security, contentment, and peace. In a national sense, we think we may begin to lay claim to this species of comfort, so largely prized by our ancestors of the patriarchal ages. The southern States have long boasted their groves and gardens of fig-trees; and there is no longer any doubt regarding the fact, that the valley of the Ohio, with its vine-clad hills, will soon afford a resting-place for millions of cultivators, who may sit down beneath the shadow of their own vines, with none to make them afraid.

There has been so much "stuff," of all descriptions, made in various parts of the country under the name of domestic wine—ninety-nine hundredths of which is not half so good or so wholesome as poor cider—that most persons whose palates are accustomed to the fine products of France, Spain, or Madeira, have, after tasting of the compounds alluded to, concluded that it was either a poor piece of patriotism, or a bad joke,—this trying to swallow American wine.

On the other hand, various enterprising Frenchmen, observing that the climate of a large part of the Union ripened peaches and other fruits better than their own country, naturally concluded that if they brought over the right kinds of French wine grapes, wine must be produced here as good as that made at home. Yet, though the experiment has been tried again and again by practical vignerons, who know the mysteries of cultivation, and wine merchants who had an abundance of capital at their command, there is no record of one single case of even tolerable success. In no part of the United States is the climate adapted to the vineyard culture of the foreign grape.

So much as this was learned, indeed, twenty years ago. But was the matter to be given up in this manner? Could it be possible that a vast continent, over which, from one end to the other, the wild grape grows in such abundance that the Northmen, who were perhaps the first discoverers, gave it the beautiful name of VINLAND, should never be the land of vineyards? There were at least two men who still believed wine-making possible; and who, twenty years or more ago, noticing that the foreign grape proved worthless in this country, had faith in the good qualities of the indigenous stock.

We mean, of course, Major Adlum, of the District of Columbia, and Nicholas Longworth, Esq., of Ohio. Both these gentlemen, after testing the foreign grape, abandoned it, and took up the most promising native sorts; and both at last settled upon the *Catawba*, as the only wine grape, yet known, worthy of cultivation in America.

Major Adlum planted a vineyard, and made some wine, which we tasted. It was of only tolerable quality; but it proved that good wine can be made of native grapes, the growth of our own soil. And though Adlum was not a thorough cultivator, he published a volume on the culture of native grapes, which roused public attention to the subject. He made the assertion before he died, that in introducing the Cawtaba grape to public attention, he had done more for the benefit of the country than if he had paid off our then existing national debt. And to this sentiment there are many in the western States who are ready now to subscribe heartily.

Mr. Longworth is a man of different stamp. With abundant capital, a great deal of patriotism, and a large love of the culture of the soil, he adds an especial talent for overcoming obstacles, and great pertinacity in carrying his point. What he cannot do himself, he very well knows how to find other persons capable of doing. Hence he pursued quite the opposite system from those who undertook the naturalization of the foreign grape. He advertised for native grapes of any and every sort, planted all and tested all; and at last, he too has come to the conclusion that the Catawba is the wine grape of America.

"What sort of wine does the Catawba make?" inquires some of our readers, who like nothing but Madeira and Sherry; "and what do you think will be the moral effect of making an abundance of cheap wine?" asks some ultra temperance friend and reader. We will try to answer both these questions.

The natural wine which the Cawtaba makes is a genuine hock—a wine so much like the ordinary wines of the Rhine, that we could put three of the former bottles among a dozen of the latter, and it would puzzle the nicest connoisseur to select them by either color or flavor. In other words, the Catawba wine (made as it is on the Ohio, made without adding either alcohol or sugar) is a pleasant light hock,—a little stronger than Rhine wine, but still far lighter and purer than nineteen-twentieths of the wines that find their way to this country. Its subacid flavor renders it especially grateful, as a summer drink, in so hot a climate as ours; and the wholesomeness of the Rhine wine no one will deny.* Indeed, certain maladies, troublesome enough in other lands, are never known in hock countries; and though the taste for hock—like that for tomatoes—is an acquired one, it is none the less natural for that; any more than *walking* is, which, so far as our observation goes, is not one of the things we come into the world with, like seeing and hearing.

As to the temperance view of this matter of wine-making, we think a very little familiarity with the state of the case will settle this point. Indeed, we are inclined to adopt the views of Dr. Flagg, of Cincinnati. "The temperance cause is rapidly preparing public sentiment for the introduction of pure American wine. So long as public taste remains vitiated by the use of malt and alcoholic drinks, it will be impossible to introduce light pleasant wine, except to a very limited extent; but just in proportion as strong drinks are abandoned, a more wholesome one will be substituted. Instead of

* Mr. Longworth is now making large quantities of sparkling Catawba wine, of excellent quality—perhaps more nearly resembling sparkling hock than Champagne.

30

paying millions to foreigners for deleterious drinks, let us produce from our own hillsides a wholesome beverage, that will be within reach of us all—the poor as well as the rich."

Very few of the friends of temperance are perhaps aware of two facts. First, that *pure* light wines, such as the Catawba of this country, and the Hock and Clarets of Europe, contain so little alcohol (only 7 or 8 per cent.) that they are not intoxicating unless drank in a most inordinate manner, to which, from the quantity required, there is no temptation. On the other hand, they exhilarate the spirits, and act in a salutary manner on the respiratory organs. We do not mean to say that men could not live and breathe just as well, if there were no such thing as wine known; but that since the time of Noah, men will not be contented with merely living and breathing; and it is therefore better to provide them with proper and wholesome food and drink, than to put improper aliments within their reach.

Second, that it is universally admitted that in all countries where light wines so abound that the peasant or working-man may have his pint of light wine per day, drunkenness is a thing unknown. On the other hand, in all countries which do not produce claret, hock, or some other wholesome light wine, ardent spirits are used, and drunkenness is the invariable result. As there is no nation in the world where only cold water is drank, (unless opium is used,) and since large bodies of men will live in cities, instead of forests and pastures, there is not likely to be such a nation, let us choose whether it is better to have national temperance with light wines, or national intemperance with ardent spirits. The question resolves itself into that narrow compass, at last.

As we think there are few who will hesitate which horn of the dilemma to choose, (especially, as an Irishman would say, "where one is no horn at all,") it is, we think, worth while to glance for a moment at the state of the vine culture in the valley of the Ohio.

We have before us a very interesting little pamphlet, full of practical details and suggestions on the subject.* It is understood

* *A Treatise on Grape Culture in Vineyards in the vicinity of Cincinnati:* By a member of the Cincinnati Horticultural Society. Sold by I. F. De Silver, Main-street, Cincinnati.

to be from the pen of R. Buchanan, Esq., president of the Cincinnati Horticultural Society. It deals more with facts, actual experience, and observation, and less with speculation, supposition, and belief, than any thing on this topic that has yet appeared in the United States. In other words, a man may take it, and plant a vineyard, and raise grapes with success. He may even make good wine; but no book can wholly teach this latter art, which must come by the use of one's eyes and hands in the business itself.

Among other interesting facts, which we glean from this pamphlet, are the following: The number of acres of vineyard culture, within twenty miles of Cincinnati, is *seven hundred and forty-three.* Those belong to 264 proprietors and tenants. Mr. Longworth owns 122 acres, cultivated by 27 tenants.

The average product per acre in 1848 (a good season) was 300 gallons to the acre. In 1849 (the worst year ever known) it was 100 gallons. One vineyard of two acres (that of Mr. Rentz) has yielded 1300 gallons in a season. New Catawba wine, *at the press*, brings 75 cents a gallon. When ready for sale, it readily commands about $1.25 per gallon.

The best vineyard soil on the Ohio, as in the old world, is one abounding with *lime.* A "dry calcareous loam" is the favorite soil near Cincinnati. This is well drained and trenched, two or three feet deep, before planting the vines; trenching being considered indispensable, and being an important part of the expense. The vines, one year old, may be had for $6 per 100, and are usually planted three by six feet apart—about 2,420 vines to the acre. They are trained to single poles or stakes, in the simple mode common in most wine countries; and the product of the Catawba per acre is considerably more than that of the wine-grape in France.

V.

ON THE IMPROVEMENT OF VEGETABLE RACES.

April, 1852.

NOTWITHSTANDING all the drawbacks of the violent extremes of climate, the United States, and especially all that belt of country lying between the Mohawk and the James Rivers, is probably as good a fruit country as can be found in the world. Whilst every American, travelling in the north of Europe, observes that very choice fruit, grown at great cost, and with the utmost care, is more certainly to be found in the gardens of the wealthy than with us, he also notices that the broad-cast production of tolerably good fruit in orchards and gardens, is almost nothing in Europe, when compared to what is seen in America. As we have already stated, one-fourth of the skill and care expended on fruit culture in the north of Europe, bestowed in America, would absolutely load every table with the finest fruits of temperate climates.

As yet, however, we have not made any progress beyond common orchard culture. In the majority of cases, the orchard is planted, cultivated two or three years with the plough, pruned badly three or four times, and then left to itself. It is very true, that in the *fruit gardens*, which begin to surround some of our older cities, the well-prepared soil, careful selections of varieties, judicious culture and pruning, have begun to awaken in the minds of the old fashioned cultivators a sense of astonishment as to the size and perfection to which certain fruits can be brought, which begins to react on the country at large. Little by little, the orchardists are beginning to be aware that it is better to plant fifty trees carefully, in well-prepared soil, than to stick in five hundred, by thrusting the roots in narrow holes, to struggle out an imperfect existence; little by little, the horticultural shows and the markets have proved, that while fruit-trees of the best standard sorts cost no more than those of indifferent quality—the fruit they bear is worth ten times as much; and thus by degrees, the indifferent orchards are being renovated by grafting, manuring, or altogether displaced by new ones of superior quality.

Still, there are some important points in fruit culture overlooked. One of the most conspicuous of these is, that varieties may be found, or, if not existing, may be originated to suit every portion of the United States. Because a fruit-grower in the State of Maine, or the State of Louisiana, does not find, after making a trial of the fruits that are of the highest quality in New-York or Pensylvannia, that they are equally first rate with him, it by no means follows that such wished-for varieties may not be produced. Although there are a few sorts of fruits, like the Bartlett Pear, and the Roxbury Russet Apple, that seem to have a kind of cosmopolitan constitution, by which they are almost equally at home in a cool or a hot country, they are the exceptions, and not the rule. The English Gooseberries may be said not to be at home any where in our country, except in the cool, northern parts of New England—Maine, for example. The foreign grape is fit for out-of-door culture nowhere in the United States, and even the Newtown Pippin and the Spitzenberg apples, so unsurpassed on the Hudson, are worth little or nothing on the Delaware. On the other hand, in every part of the country, we see fruits constantly being originated—chance seedlings in the orchards, perfectly adapted to the climate and the soil, and occasionally of very fine quality.

An apple-tree which pleased the emigrant on his homestead on the Connecticut, is carried, by means of grafts, to his new land in Missouri, and it fails to produce the same fine pippins that it did at home. But he sows the *seeds* of that tree, and from among many of indifferent quality, he will often find one or more that shall not only equal or surpass its parent in all its ancient New England flavor, but shall have a western constitution, to make that flavor permanent in the land of its birth.

In this way, and for the most part by the ordinary chances and results of culture, and without a direct application of a scientific system, what may be called the natural limits of any fruit-tree or plant, may be largely *extended.* We say largely, because there are certain boundaries beyond which the plants of the tropics cannot be acclimated. The sugar cane cannot, by any process yet known, be naturalized on Lake Superior, or the Indian corn on Hudson's Bay. But every body at the South knows that the range of the sugar cane has been gradually extended northward, more than one hundred miles; and the Indian corn is cultivated now, even far north in Canada.

It is by watching these natural laws, as seen here and there in irregular examples, and reducing them to something like a system, and acting upon the principles which may be deduced from them, that we may labor diligently towards a certain result, and not trust to chance, groping about in the dark, blindly.

Although the two modes by which the production of a new variety of a fruit or flower—the first by saving the seeds of the very fruit only, and the other by *cross-breeding* when the flowers are about expanding—are very well known, and have been largely practised by the florists and gardeners of Europe for many years, in bringing into existence most of the fine vegetables and flowers, and many of the fruits that we now possess, it is remarkable that little attention has been paid in all these efforts to *acclimating* the new sorts by scientific reproduction from seed. Thus, in the case of flowers—while the catalogues are filled with new verbenas every year, no one, as we can learn, has endeavored to originate a *hardy* verbena, though one of the trailing purple species is a hardy herbaceous border flower—and perhaps hybrids might be raised between it and the scarlet sorts, that would be lasting and invaluable ornaments to the garden. So with the gooseberry. This fruit shrub, so fine in the damp climate of England, is so unsuited to the United States generally—or at least most of the English sorts are—that not one bush in twenty, bears fruit free from mildew. And yet, so far as we know, no horticulturist has attempted to naturalize the cultivated gooseberry in the only way it is likely to become naturalized, viz.—by raising new varieties from seed in this country, so that they may have *American constitutions*, adapted to the American climate--and therefore not likely to mildew. The same thing is true of the foreign grape. Millions of roots of the foreign grape have, first and last, been planted in the United States. Hardly one can be pointed to that actually "succeeds" in the open-air culture—not from want of heat or light—for we have the greatest abundance of both; but from the want of constitutional adaptation. And still the foreign grape is abandoned, except for vineries, without a fair trial of the only modes by which it would naturally be hoped to acclimate it, viz.—raising seedlings here, and crossing it with our best native sorts.

Every person interested in horticulture, must stumble upon facts almost daily, that teach us how much may be done by a new race or generation, in plants as well as men, that it is utterly out of the question for the old race to accomplish. Compare, in the Western States, the success of a colony of foreign emigrants in subduing the wilderness and mastering the land, with that of another company of our own race—say of New Englanders. The one has to contend with all his old-world prejudices, habits of labor, modes of working; the other being "to the manor born," &c., seizes the Yankee axe, and the forest, for the first time, acknowledges its master. While the old-countryman is endeavoring to settle himself snugly, and make a little neighborhood comfortable, the American husbandman has cleared and harvested a whole state.

As in the man so in the plant. A race should be adapted to the soil by being produced upon it, of the best possible materials. The latter is as indispensable as the first—as it will not wholly suffice that a man or a tree should be indigenous—or our American Indians, or our Chickasaw Plums, would never have given place to either the Caucasian race, or the luscious "Jefferson;"—but the best race being taken at the starting point, the highest utility and beauty will be found to spring from individuals adapted by birth, constitution, and education, to the country. Among a thousand native Americans, there may be nine hundred no better suited to labor of the body or brains, than so many Europeans—but there will be five or ten that will reach a higher level of adaptation, or to use a western phrase, "climb higher and dive deeper," than any man out of America.

We are not going to be led into a physiological digression on the subject of the inextinguishable rights of a superior organization in certain men and races of men, which nature every day reaffirms, notwithstanding the socialistic and democratic theories of our politicians. But we will undertake to say, that if the races or plants were as much improved as they might be, and as much adapted to the various soils and climates of the Union, as they ought to be, there is not a single square mile in the United States, that might not boast its peaches, melons, apples, grapes, and all the other luxuries of the garden now confined to a comparatively limited range.

And this is not only the most interesting of all fields for the lover of the country and the garden, but it is that one precisely ready to be put in operation at *this season.* The month of April is the *blossoming season* over a large part of the country, and the blossom governs and fixes the character of the new race, by giving a character to the seed. Let those who are not already familiar with *hybridizing* and *cross-breeding* of plants—always effected when they are in bloom—read the chapter on this subject in our "Fruit Trees," or any other work which treats of this subject. Let them ascertain what are the desiderata for their soil and climate, which have not yet been supplied, and set about giving that character to the new seedlings, which a careful selection from the materials at hand, and a few moments light and pleasant occupation will afford. If the man who only made two blades of grass grow where one grew before, has been pronounced a benefactor to mankind, certainly he is far more so who originates a new variety of grain, vegetable, or fruit, adapted to a soil and climate where it before refused to grow—since thousands may continue to reap the benefit of the labors of the latter for an indefinite length of time, while the former has only the merit of being a good farmer for the time being.

LETTERS FROM ENGLAND.

LETTERS FROM ENGLAND.

I.

WARWICK CASTLE: KENILWORTH: STRATFORD-ON-AVON.

July, 1850.

MY DEAR SIR:—As, after looking at some constellation in a summer night, one remembers most vividly its largest and most potent star, so, from amid a constellation of fine country-seats, I can write you to-day only of my visit to one, but that one which, for its *peculiar* extent, overtops all the rest—WARWICK CASTLE.

Warwick Castle, indeed, combines in itself perhaps more of romantic and feudal interest than any actual residence in Europe, and for this very reason, because it unites in itself the miracle of exhibiting at the same moment hoar antiquity, and the actual vivid present, having been held and maintained from first to last by the same family. In most of the magnificent country-seats of England, it is rather vast extent and enormous expense which impresses one. If they are new, they are sometimes overloaded with elaborate details;*

* Like Eton Hall, near Liverpool, perhaps visited by more Americans than any other seat—though the architecture is meretricious, and the whole place as wanting in genuine taste as it is abounding in evidences of immense wealth. Warwick Castle bears, to an American, the same relation to all modern castles that the veritable Noah's ark, if it could be found still in full preservation, would to a model made by an ingenious antiquarian.

if old, they are often modernized in so tasteless a manner as to destroy all sentiment of antiquity. Plate glass windows ill accord with antique casements, and Paris furniture and upholstery are not in keeping with apartments of the time of Elizabeth.

In Warwick Castle and all that belongs to it, I found none of this. AL was entire harmony, and I lingered within and about it, enjoying its absolue perfection, as if the whole were only conjured up by an enchanter's spell, and would soon dissolve into thin air. And yet, on the contrary, I knew that here was a building which is more than nine hundred years old; which has been the residence of successive generations of the same family for centuries; which was the fortress of that mightiest of English subjects, WARWICK, "the great king-maker," (who boasted that he had deposed three English sovereigns and placed three in their vacant throne,) which, long before the discovery of America, was the scene of wild jarring and haughty chivalry, bloody prowess—yes, and of gentle love and sweet affections, but which, as if defying time, is still a castle, as real in its character as a feudal stronghold, and yet as complete a baronial residence, as the imagination can conceive. To an American, whose country is but two hundred years old, the bridging over such a vast chasm of time by the domestic memorials of a single family, when, as in this case, that family has so made its mark upon the early annals of his own race, there is something that approaches the sublime.

The small town of Warwick, a quaint old place, which still bears abundant traces of its Saxon origin, is situated nearly in the centre of England, and lies on one side of the castle, to which it is a mere dependency. It is placed on a rising hill or knoll, the castle occupying the highest part, though mostly concealed from the town by thick plantations. Around the other sides of the castle flows the Avon, a lovely stream, whose poetical fame has not belied its native charms; and beyond it stretch away the broad lands which belong to the castle.

The finest approach for the stranger is from the pretty town of Leamington, about two miles east of Warwick. At a turn, a few hundred rods distant from the castle, the road crosses the Avon by a wide bridge with a mossy stone balustrade, and here, looking upward,

> "Bosomed high in tufted trees,
> Towers and battlements he sees."

The banks of the stream are finely fringed with foliage; beyond them are larger trees; upon the rising ground in the rear grow lofty and venerable chestnuts, oaks, and elms; and over this superb foreground, rises up, grand and colossal, the huge pile of gray stone, softened by the effects of time, and the rich masses of climbers that hang like floating drapery about it. For a few moments you lose sight of it, and the carriage suddenly stops before a high embattled wall, where the porter answers the knock by slowly unfolding the massive iron gates of the portal. Driving through this gateway you wind through a deep cut in the solid rock, almost hidden by the masses of ivy that hang along its sides, and in a few moments find yourself directly before the entrance front of the castle. Whoever designed this front, made up as it is of lofty towers and irregular wall, must have been a poet as well as architect, for its composition and details struck me as having the proportions and congruity of a fine scene in nature, which we feel is not to be measured and defined by the ordinary rules of art. And as it rose up before me, hoary and venerable, yet solid and complete, I could have believed that it was rather a magnificent effort of nature than any work of mere tools and masonry.

In the central tower opened another iron gate, and driving through a deep stone archway, I found myself in the midst of a large open space of nearly a couple of acres, carpeted with the finest turf, dotted with groups of aged trees and shrubs, and surrounded on all sides by the castle walls. This is the inner court-yard of the castle. Around it, forming four sides, are grouped in the most picturesque and majestic manner, the varied forms and outlines of the vast pile, partly hidden by the rich drapery of ivy and old mossy trees. On the most sheltered side of the circular walk which surrounds this court-yard, among many fine evergreens, I noticed two giant *Arbutuses* (a shrub which I have vainly attempted to acclimatize in the northern States,) more than thirty feet high, with trunks a couple of feet in diameter, the growth of more than 200 years.

On the south side of this court lies the principal mass of the castle, affording an unbroken suite of rooms 333 feet long. At the northeast, Cæsar's tower, built in Saxon times,—the oldest part of the whole edifice, whose exact date is unknown—which rises dark, gloomy and venerable, above all the rest; while at the southeast stands the tower built by the great WARWICK—broader and more massive, and partly hidden by huge chestnuts. The other sides are not inhabited, but still remain as originally built,—a vast mass of walls, with embattled parapets broken by towers with loopholes and positions for defence—but with their sternness and severity broken by the tender drapery of vines and shrubs, and the luxuriant beauty of the richest verdure.

In the centre of the south side of this noble court-yard, you enter the castle by a few steps. Passing through the entrance hall, you reach the great hall, vast, baronial and magnificent—the floor paved with marble—and the roof carved in oak. Along the sides, which are panelled in dark cedar, are hung the armor and the weapons of every age since the first erection of the castle. I was shown the leather shirt, with its blood-stains blackened by time, worn by an ancestor of the present earl, who was slain at the battle of Litchfield, and many other curious and powerful weapons used by the great warriors of the family through a course of centuries.

On either side of this hall, to the right and left, in a straight line, extend the continuous suite of apartments. The first on the right is the ante-drawing-room, the walls crimson and gold; next, the cedar drawing-room—the walls richly wainscoted with wood of the cedar of Lebanon; third, the great drawing-room, finely proportioned and quite perfect in tone—its walls delicate apple-green, relieved by a little pure white, and enriched with gilding; next, Queen Anne's state bedroom, with a superb state bed presented to the then Earl of Warwick, by that queen, being antique, with tapestry, and decorated with a fine full-length picture of Queen Anne; and beyond this a cabinet filled with the choicest specimens of ancient Venetian art and workmanship. Behind the hall is the chapel, and on the left the suite is continued in the same manner as on the right. Of course a good deal of the furniture has been removed from time to time, and large portions of the interior have been restored by the present earl. But this has been done with such admirable taste that there is nothing which disturbs the unity of the whole. The furniture is all of dark wood, old cabinets richly inlaid with brass, old carved oaken couches, or those rich mosaic tables which were brought to England in the palmy days of the Italian states. Every thing looks old, genuine and original. The apartments were hung with very choice pictures by Van Dyck, Titian and Rubens—among which I noticed a magnificent head of Cromwell, and another of Queen Mary, that riveted my attention—the former by its expression of the powerful self-centred soul, and the latter by the crushed and broken-hearted pensiveness of the countenance—for it was Mary at 40, just before her death—still beautiful and noble, but with the marks in her features of that suffering which alone reveals to us the depth of the soul.

Not to weary you with the interior of what is only the first floor of the castle, let me take you to one of the range of large, deep, sunny windows which lights the whole of this suite of apartments on their southern side. Each window is arched overhead and wainscoted on the side, and as the walls of the castle are 10 to 12 feet thick, and each window above 8 feet wide, it forms almost a little room or closet by itself. And from these windows how beautiful the landscape! Although we entered these apartments by only a few steps from the level of the court-yard, yet on looking from these windows I found myself more than 60 feet above the Avon, which almost washes the base of the castle walls on this side, winding about in the most graceful curve, and losing itself in the distance among groups of aged elms. On this side of the castle, beyond the Avon, stretches away the park of about a thousand acres. As far as the eye reaches it is a beautiful English landscape, of fresh turf and fine groups of trees—and beyond it, for several miles, lie the rich farm lands of the Warwick estate. There are few pictures more lovely than such a rural scene, and perhaps its quietness and serenity were enhanced by contrast with the sombre grandeur of the feudal court-yard where I first entered.

Passing through a gate in the castle wall, I entered the pleasure grounds, and saw in the orangery or green-house, the celebrated Warwick vase—the giant among vases. It is a magnificent mass of marble, weighing 8 tons, of beautiful proportions, of which reduced copies are now familiar to us all over the world. It was brought from the temple of Vesta, and is larger than I had been led to believe, holding nearly two hogsheads. It is also rather more globular in form, and more delicate in detail than one would suppose from the copies.

In the pleasure grounds my admiration was riveted by the "cedar walk"—a fine avenue of cedars of Lebanon—that noblest of evergreens—some sixty feet high, a tree which in its stately symmetry and great longevity, seemed a worthy companion of this princely castle. But even the cedar of Lebanon is too short-lived, for the two oldest trees which stand almost close to the southern walls of the castle, and which are computed to be about five hundred years old—gigantic and venerable in appearance—have lately lost several of their finest branches, and are evidently fast going to decay. It was striking to me to see, on the other hand, how much the hoary aspect of the outer walls of the castle were heightened by the various beautiful vines and climbers intermingled with harebells, daisies and the like, which had sprung up of themselves on the crevices of the mighty walls that overhang the Avon, and, sustained by the moisture of its perennial waters, were allowed to grow and flower without molestation, though every thing else that hastens the decay of the building is jealously guarded against.

If any thing more were wanting to heighten the romantic interest of this place, it would be found in the relics which are kept, partly in the castle, and partly in the apartments at the outer portal, of the famous Guy, Earl of Warwick, who lived in Saxon times, and whose history and exploits heretofore always seemed as fabulous to me as those of Blue-Beard himself. Still, here is his sword, an enormous weapon six feet long, which it requires both hands to lift, his breastplate weighing fifty-two pounds, and his helmet seven pounds. The size of these (and their genuineness is beyond dispute,) shows that he must have been a man whose gigantic stature almost warrants the belief in the miracles of valor which he performed in battle—as an enormous iron "porridge pot" of singular clumsy antique form, which holds 102 gallons, does any amount of credulity as to the digestive powers necessary to sustain the Colossus who slew all the dragons of his day.

While I was at Warwick, I ascended on a fine moonlight evening, the top of the highest tower, commanding the whole panorama of feudal castle, tributary town, and lovely landscape. It would be vain to attempt to describe the powerful emotions that such a scene and its many associations, under such circumstances, awakened within me; but I turned my face at last, westward, toward my native land, and with uplifted eyes thanked the good God, that, though to England, the country of my ancestors, it had been given to show the growth of man in his highest development of class or noble, to America has been reserved the greater blessing of solving for the world the true problem of all humanity—that of the abolition of all castes, and the recognition of the divine rights of every human soul.

This neighborhood is equally beautiful to the eye of the picturesque or the agricultural tourist. I was shown farms on the Warwick estate which are let out to tenants at over £2 per acre—and everywhere the richness of the grain-fields gave evidence both of high cultivation and excellent soil. The chief difference, after all, between an English rural landscape and one in the older and better cultivated parts of the United States, is almost wholly in the universality of verdant hedges, and the total absence of all other fences. The hedges (for the most part of hawthorn) divide all the farm-fields, and line all the roadsides—and even the borders of the railways, in all parts of the country. I was quite satisfied with the truth of this conjecture, when I came accidentally, in my drive yesterday, upon a little spot of a few rods—where the hedges had been destroyed, and a temporary post and rail fence, like those at home, put in their place. The whole thing was lowered at once to the harshness and rickety aspect of a farm at home. The majority of the farm hedges are only trimmed once a year—in winter—and therefore have, perhaps, a more natural and picturesque look than the more carefully trimmed hedges of the gardens. Hence, for a farm hedge, a plant should be chosen that will grow thick of itself with only this single annual clipping, and which will adapt itself to all soils. I am, therefore, confirmed in my belief, that the buckthorn is the farmer's hedge plant for America, and I am also satisfied that it will make a better and far more durable hedge than the hawthorn does, even here.

Though England is beautifully wooded, yet the great preponderance of the English elm—a tree wanting in grace, and only grand when very old, renders an English roadside landscape in this respect, one of less sylvan beauty than our finest scenery of like character at home. The American elm, with its fine drooping branches, is rarely or never seen here, and there is none of that *variety* of foliage which we have in the United States. For this reason (leaving out of sight rail fences), I do not think even the drives through Warwickshire so full of rural beauty as those in the valley of the Connecticut—which they most resemble. In June our meadows there are as verdant, and our trees incomparably more varied and beautiful. On the other hand, you must remember that here, wealth and long civilization have so refined and perfected the details, that in this respect there is no comparison—nothing in short to be done but to admire and enjoy. For instance, for a circuit of eight or ten miles or more here, between Leamington and Warwick and Stratford-on-Avon, the roads, which are admirable, are regularly sprinkled every dry day in summer, while along the railroads the sides are cultivated with grass, or farm crops or flowers, almost to the very rails.

The ruins of Kenilworth, only five miles from Warwick, have been so often visited and described that they are almost familiar to you. Though built long after Warwick castle, this vast palace, which covered (including the garden walls) six or seven acres, is entirely in ruins—like most of the very old castles in England. The magnificent suites of apartments where the celebrated Earl of Leicester, the favorite of Elizabeth, entertained his sovereign with such regal magnificence, are roofless and desolate—only here and there a fragment of a stately window or a splendid hall, attesting the beauty of the noble architecture. Over such of the walls and towers as are yet standing, grows, however, the most gigantic *trees* of ivy—absolutely *trees*—with trunks more than two feet in diameter, and rich masses of foliage, that covered the hoary and crumbling walls with a drapery so thick that I could not fathom it with an arm's length. When the ivy gets to be a couple of hundred years old, it loses something of its vine-like character, and more resembles a gigantic laurel tree, growing against and partly hiding the venerable walls.

In the ancient pleasure-grounds of Kenilworth—those very pleasure-grounds whose alleys, doubtless Elizabeth and Leicester had trodden together, I saw remaining the most beautiful hedges of old, gold and silver holly—almost (to one fond of gardening) of themselves worth coming across the Atlantic to see—so rich were they in their variegated glossy foliage, and so large and massive in their growth. As these ruins are open to the public, and are visited by thousands, the keepers find it to their account to preserve, as much as possible, the relics of the old garden in good order, though the palace itself is past all renovation.

In this neighborhood, at a distance of eight miles, is also that spot dearest to all who speak the English language, and all who respect human genius, Stratford-on-Avon. The coachman who drove me thither from Warwick Castle, and whose mind probably measures greatness by the size of the dwelling it inhabits—volunteered the information to me on the way there that it was "a very smallish poor sort of a house," that I was going to see. As I stood within the walls of the humble room, little more than seven feet high, and half a dozen yards long, where the greatest of poets was born and passed so many days of his life, I involuntarily uncovered my head and felt how much more sublime is the power of genius, which causes this simplest of birth-places to move a deeper chord in the heart than all the pomp and external circumstance of high birth or heroic achievements, based as they mostly are, upon the more selfish side of man's nature. It was, indeed, a very "smallish" house, but it was large enough to be the home of the mightiest soul that England's sky ever covered.

Not far distant is the parish church, where Shakspeare lies buried. An avenue of lime-trees, singularly clipped so as to form an arbor, leads across the churchyard to the porch. Under a large slab of coarse stone, lies the remains of the great dramatist, bearing the simple and terse epitaph composed by himself; and above it, upon the walls, is the monumental bust which is looked upon as the most authentic likeness. It has, to my eye, a wooden and unmeaning expression, with no merit as a work of art—and if there is any truth in physiognomy could *not* have been a likeness—for the upper lip is that of a man wholly occupied with self-conceit. I prefer greatly, the portrait in Warwick Castle—which shows a face paler and strongly marked with traces of thought, and an eye radiant with the fire of genius—but ready with a warm, lightning glance, to read the souls of others.

I write you from London, where I have promised to make a visit to Sir William Hooker, who is the director of the Royal Botanic Garden at Kew, and have accepted an invitation from the Duke of Northumberland to see the fine trees at Sion House.

II.

KEW-GARDENS: NEW HOUSES OF PARLIAMENT: A NOBLEMAN'S SEAT.

August, 1850.

MY DEAR SIR:—I intended to say something to you in this letter of the enormous parks of London—absolute woods and prairies, in the midst of a vast and populous city; but the subject is one that demands more space than I have at my disposal to-day, and I shall therefore reserve it for the future. I will merely say, *en passant*, that every American who visits London, whether for the first or the fiftieth time, feels mortified that no city in the United States has a public *park*—here so justly considered both the highest luxury and necessity in a great city. What are called parks in New-York, are not even apologies for the thing; they are only squares, or paddocks. In the parks of London, you may imagine yourself in the depths of the country, with, apparently, its boundless space on all sides; its green turf, fresh air, and, at certain times of the day, almost its solitude and repose. And at other times, they are the healthful breathing zone of hundreds of thousands of citizens!

THE NATIONAL GARDEN AT KEW.—I have just come from a visit to Sir William Hooker's, at Kew Park. He is the director of the Royal Gardens at Kew,—a short distance from his house,—where we spent almost the entire day together, exploring in detail the many intersting features of this place, now admitted to be the finest public botanic garden in Europe.

It is only within a few years that Kew Gardens have been given up to the public; and it is wholly owing to the spirited administration of Sir William Hooker—so well known in both hemispheres for his botanical science—that it has lately reached so high a rank among botanical collections. Originally, the place is interesting, as having been the favorite suburban residence of various branches of the royal family. George III. lived here; and here Queen Charotte died. The botanical taste of the latter is well known, and has been commemorated in that striking and beautiful plant, the *Strelitzia*, named in her honor* by Sir Joseph Banks. For a long time the garden was the receptacle of all the rare plants collected by English travellers—Capt. Cook, Sir Joseph Banks, Cunningham, and others. What was formerly of little value has, however, lately become a matter of national pride; and this is owing to the fact, that the present queen has wholly given Kew up to the public, even adding a considerable sum annually from her private purse towards maintaining it. The old "Kew Palace," which stands in the grounds, is a small, simple, brick mansion, without the least pretension to state, and shows very conclusively that those of the Hanover family who lived here did it from real attachment to the place—like Queen Charlotte, from love of botany; as there is nothing about it to please the tastes of an ambitious mind.

As Kew has been already described by one of the correspondents of this journal, I shall not go into those details which might otherwise be looked for. I shall rather prefer to give you a comprehensive idea of the attractions of the place, which, though about eight miles from London, was visited last year by one hundred and thirty-seven thousand persons. The only requisite for admission is to be decently dressed.

When you hear of a *garden*, in America, you fancy some little place, filled with borders and beds of shrubs and flowers, and laid out with walks in various styles. Dispossess your mind at once, however, of any such notions as applied to Kew. Fancy, on the other hand, a surface of about two hundred acres; about sixty of which is the botanic garden proper, and the rest open park or pleasure-grounds. The groundwork of the whole is turf; that is,

* She was Princess of the house of Mecklenberg Strelitz.

smoothly-mown lawn in the sixty acres of botanic garden, and park-like lawn, occasionally mown, in the remainder. Over this, is picturesquely disposed a large growth of fine trees—in the botanic garden, of all manner of rare species, every exotic that will thrive in England—growing to their natural size without being in the least crowded—tall pines, grand old Cedars of Lebanon, and all sorts of rare deciduous trees. Between the avenues and groups are large open glades of smooth lawn, in which are distributed hot-houses, ornamental cottages, a large lake of water, parterres of brilliant flowers for show, and a botanical arrangement of plants, shrubs, and trees for scientific study.

In the centre of a wide glade of turf rises up the new palm-house, built in 1848. It is a palace of glass—362 feet in length, and 66 feet high—and fairy-like and elegant in its proportions, though of great strength; for the whole, framework and sashes, is of cast iron, glazed with 45,000 feet of glass. You open the door, and, but for the glass roof that you see instead of sky above your head, you might believe yourself in the West Indies. Lofty palm trees, thirty or forty feet high, are growing, rooted in the deep soil beneath your feet, with the same vigor and luxuriance as in the West Indies. Huge clusters of golden bananas hang across the walks, and cocoa-nut trees, forty-two feet high, wave their tufts of leaves over your head. The foliage of the cinnamon and camphor scents the atmosphere, and rich air-plants of South America dazzle the eye with their strange and fanciful blossoms. Most beautiful of all are the *tree ferns*, with trunks eight or ten inches in diameter, and lofty heads, crowned with plume-like tufts of the most delicate and graceful of all foliage. From the light iron gallery, which runs round the inside of this tropical forest-conservatory, you look down on the richest assemblage of vegetable forms that can be conceived; while over your head clamber, under the iron rafters, in charming luxuriance, the richest passion flowers and other vines of the East Indian islands.

If you are interested in exotic botany, you may leave this palm house, and pass the entire day in only a casual inspection of the treasures of other climates, collected here from all parts of the world. Green-houses, the stoves, the orchidaceous house, the Australian house, the New-Zealand house, and a dozen other glass structures, contain all the riches of the vegetable kingdom which will not bear the open air,—and each in the highest state of cultivation. Giant cactuses from Mexico, fourteen feet high, and estimated to be four hundred years old, and rock gardens under glass, filled with all the ferns and epiphytes of South America, detain and almost satiate the eye with their wonderful variety, and grotesqueness of forms and colors.

In the open grounds are many noble specimens of hardy trees, of great beauty, which I must pass by without even naming them. I saw here the old Deodar cedar and araucaria imbricata in England, each about twenty-five feet high, and justifying all the praises that have been lavished upon them; the former as the most graceful, and the latter the boldest and most picturesque of all evergreens. The trunk of the largest araucaria, or Chili pine, here, is of the thickness of a man's leg; and the tree looks, at a distance, like a gigantic specimen of deep green *coral* from the depths of the ocean. I was glad to know, from experience, that those two noble evergreens are quite hardy in the northern States. You may judge of the scale on which things are planned in Kew, when I mention that there is a wide avenue of Deodars, newly planted (extending along one of the vistas from the palm-house), 2,800 feet long. A steam engine occupying the lower part, and a great reservoir the upper part of a lofty tower, supplies, by the aid of concealed pipes, the whole of the botanic garden with water.

I should not omit the museum—a department lately commenced, and upon which Sir William Hooker is expending much time. It is in some respects, perhaps, the most useful and valuable feature in the establishment. Here are collected, in a dried state, all the curious and valuable vegetable products—especially those useful in the arts, medicine, and domestic economy—all the raw vegetable materials—the fibre—the manufactured products, etc. Here, one may see the gutta percha, of the East Indies, in all its states—the maple sugar of America—the lace-bark of Jamaica—the teas of China, and a thousand other like useful vegetable products, arranged so as to show the stages of growth and manufacture. Collections of all the fine woods, and specimens of interesting seeds, are also kept in glass cases duly labelled.

Now that I have perhaps feebly given you a *coup d'œil* of the whole (omitting numberless leading features for want of time and space), you must, in order to give the scene its highest interest, imagine the grounds, say at 2 o'clock, filled with a thousand or twelve hundred men, women and children, of all ages,—well dressed, orderly and neat, and examining all with interest and delight. You see that they have access, not only to the open grounds, but all the hot-houses, full of rare plants and flower-gardens, gay with the most tempting materials for a nosegay. Yet, not a plant is injured—not the least harm is done to the rarest blossom. Sir William assured me that when he first proposed to try the experiment of throwing the whole collection open to the public, many persons believed it would prove a fatal one; that, in short, Anglo-Saxons could not be trusted to run at large in public gardens, full of rarities. It has, however, turned out quite the contrary, as he wisely believed; and I learned with pleasure (for the fact has a bearing at home), that on days when there had been three thousand persons in the garden at a time, the destruction did not amount to the value of fourpence! On the other hand, the benefits are not only felt indirectly, in educating, refining, and elevating the people, but directly in the application of knowledge to the arts of life. I saw, for example, artists busy in the garden, who had come miles to get an accurate drawing of some plant necessary to their studies; and artisans and manufacturers in the museum, who had been attracted there solely to investigate some matter connected with their business, in the productions of the loom or the workshop.

In short, I left Kew with the feeling, that a national garden in America might not only be a beautiful, but a most useful and popular establishment; one not too dearly bought, even at the expense bestowed annually upon Kew.

The New Houses of Parliament.—I spent a whole morning with Mr. Barry, the distinguished architect of the new houses of Parliament, in examining every part in detail. It is a common feeling that the age for such gigantic works in architecture as the Gothic cathedrals, has gone by. Perhaps this may be the case, with religious edifices; though I doubt even that, with such a great church and state empire as Russia growing up, and already casting a gigantic, though yet vague shadow over Europe. But here is certainly a flat denial of the opinion, in this new legislative hall of Great Britain—quite the masterpiece of modern Gothic architecture (excepting perhaps the cathedral of Strasbourg). Concisely, this vast pile, not yet finished, covers, with its courts, about eight acres of ground. Ten years have been consumed in its erection; and as many more will probably be required for its completion. You must remember, too, that not only have as many as 3000 men been employed on it at a time, but all appliances of steam-lifting and other machinery are used besides, which were not known in the days of cathedrals.

The style chosen by Mr. Barry is the perpendicular, or latest decorated Gothic—the exterior, rather very nearly akin to that of the beautiful town halls of the Low Countries, than that of any English examples. The stone is a hard limestone from Yorkshire, of a drab color; and the decorative sculpture is elaborate and beautiful in the highest degree. What particularly charmed me, was the elegance, resulting from the union of fine proportions and select forms of modern cultivated tastes, with the peculiarly grand and venerable character of Gothic architecture. One is so accustomed to see only strength and picturesqueness in middle-age examples, that one almost limits the pointed style to this compass. But Mr. Barry has conclusively shown that that *elegance*—which is always and only the result of fine proportions—is a beauty of which Gothic architecture is fully capable. Of the splendor of the House of Lords, and the richness and chasteness of many other portions of the building, you have already had many accounts. I will therefore only say, at present, that so carefully has the artistic effect of every portion of this vast building been studied, that not a hinge, the key of a door, or even the candlesticks on the tables, has been *bought* at the dealer's; but every detail that meets the eye has been especially designed for the building. The result, as you may suppose, is a unity and harmony throughout, which must be seen to be thoroughly appreciated.

The profession has often found fault with the employment of a florid Gothic architecture for this building. Certainly it looks like throwing away such delicate details,—to pile them up amid the smoke of London, which is, indeed, already beginning to blacken and deface them. But, on the other hand, the beauty and fitness of the style for the interior seem to me unquestionable. The very complexity appears in keeping with the intricate machinery of a government, that rules an empire almost extending over half the globe.

PICTURE OF A NOBLEMAN'S SEAT.—I shall finish this letter with a sketch of a nobleman's seat, where I am just now making a visit; and can therefore give you the outlines in a better light than travellers generally can do. The seat is called Wimpole—the property of the Earl of H——, and is situated in the fine agricultural district of Cambridgeshire. It is not a "show place;" and though a residence of the first class, especially in extent, it is only a fair specimen of what you may find, with certain variations, in many counties in England.

The landed estate, then, amounts to more than thirty-seven thousand acres—a large part admirably cultivated. The mansion, which stands in the midst of one of those immense and beautiful parks which one only finds in England, is a spacious pile in the Roman style, four hundred and fifty feet front; rather plain and antique without, but internally beautiful, and in the highest degree complete —both as regards arrangement and decoration. The library, for example, is sixty feet long, quite filled with a rich collection of books. The suite of drawing-rooms abounds with pictures by Van Dyck, Rubens, and other great masters; and there is a private chapel, in which prayers are read every morning, capable of containing a couple of hundred persons.

In front of the house, a broad level surface of park stretches before the eye, and is finely taken advantage of as a position for one of the noblest avenues of grand old elms that I have seen in England; an avenue three miles long, and very wide—not cut in two by a road,* but carpeted with grass, like a broad aisle of verdure. Place at the end of this a distant hill, and let the avenue be the

* The approach is at the side.

central feature to a wide park, that rises into hills and flows into graceful swells behind the house, and fill it with herds of deer and groups of fine cattle, and you have a general idea of the sylvan features of Wimpole.

But it is not yet complete. Behind the house, and separated from the park by a terrace walk, is a parterre flower-garden, lying directly under the windows of the drawing-rooms. Like all English flower-gardens, it is set in velvet lawn—each bed composed of a single species—the most brilliant and the most perpetual bloomers that can be found. Something in the soil or culture here seems admirably adapted to perfect them, too; for nowhere have I seen the beds so closely covered with foliage, and so thickly sprinkled with bloom. Some of them are made of two new varieties of scarlet geraniums, with *variegated* leaves, that have precisely the effect of a mottled pattern in worsted embroidery.

Beyond this lie the pleasure-grounds,—picturesque, winding walks, leading a long way, admirably planted with groups and masses of the finest evergreens and deciduous trees. Here is a weeping ash, the branches of which fall over an arbor in the form of half a globe, fifty feet in diameter; and a Portugal laurel, the trunk of which measures three feet in circumference. A fine American black-walnut tree was pointed out to me as something rare in England. And the underwood is made up of rich belts and masses of rhododendrons and English laurels.

I must beg you to tell my lady friends at home, that many of them would be quite ashamed were they in England, at their ignorance of gardening, and their want of interest in country life. Here, for instance, I have been walking for several hours to-day through these beautiful grounds with the Countess of H., who, though a most accomplished person in all other matters, has a knowledge of every thing relating to rural life, that would be incomprehensible to most American ladies. Every improvement or embellishment is planned under her special direction. Every plant and its culture are familiar to her; and there is no shrinking at barn-yards—no affected fear of cows—no ignorance of the dairy and poultry-yard. On the contrary, one is delighted with the genuine enthusiasm and knowledge that the highest class (and indeed all classes) show in the country life here, and the great amount of health and happiness it gives rise to. The life of an English woman of rank, in the country, is not the drawing-room languor which many of my charming country-women fancy it. Far from it. On the contrary, it is full of the most active duties and enjoyments. But it must be admitted that the cool and equal temperature of the summers here, is greatly more inviting to exercise than our more sultry atmosphere at home.

We measured, in the course of the morning's ramble, several English elms, with which the park here abounds, from fifteen to eighteen feet in circumference.* I was not so much surprised at this, as at the grandeur of the horse chestnuts, which are truly majestic—many measuring not less in girth, with a much greater spread of branches; each lower branch of the dimensions of an ordinary trunk, and, after stretching far out from the parent stem, drooping down and resting upon the turf, like a giant's elbow, and then turning up again in the most picturesque manner. The trees in England have a more uniform deep green tint than with us, which I think rather lessens the richness and variety of the landscape.

The queen made a visit here in 1844; and as every thing which royalty does in a monarchy is commemorated—and especially when, as in the present case, the character of the sovereign is a really good one—I was shown a handsome new gate at the side of the park, opposite to that which I entered, with a striking lodge in the Italian taste, bearing the royal arms, and called the "Victoria gate." What interested me much more, was an alms-house, built and managed wholly by Lady H., as a refuge for deserving persons, grown old or infirm in the service of the family, and unable, through ill health or incapacity, to take care of themselves. The building—cottage-like—is not only quite an ornamental structure in the old English manner, but the interior is planned so as to secure the greatest comfort and convenience of the inmates. Nothing could be more delightful than the kind interest felt and acknowledged between the benevolent originator of this charity and those who were its recipients. The eyes of an infirm old woman, to whom my hav-

* But, after all, not so noble or beautiful as, in their heads, the American elms in the Connecticut valley.

ing come from America was mentioned, and who had sons in the new world, brightened up with a strange joy at seeing one from a land where her heart had evidently been of late more busy than at home. "It was a good country," she said; "her sons had *bought land*, and were doing famous." For a working man to own land, in a country like this, where the farmers are almost all only tenants of the few great proprietors, is to their minds something like holding a fee-simple to part of paradise.

The morning yesterday was spent on horseback in examining the agriculture of the estate. The rich harvest-fields, extending over the broad Cambridgeshire plains, afford, at this season, a fine picture of the great productiveness of England. About a thousand acres are farmed by Lord H., and the rest let to tenants. I was glad to hear from him that he has endeavored, with great success, to abolish the enormous consumption of malt liquor among laborers of all classes here, by giving them only a very small allowance joined to a sum equal to the largest allowance on other estates, in the shape of an addition to their wages. He confirmed my previous impressions of the bad effects produced by this monstrous guzzling of beer by the working men of England; a consumption actually astounding to one accustomed to the abstinent and equally hard working farmers of the United States.*

Farming, here, is a vastly more scientific and carefully studied occupation than with us; and the attention bestowed upon landed estates, (many of which yield a revenue of $50,000 or $60,000 a year, and some much more,) is, as you may suppose, one of no trifling moment. Hence the knowledge of practical agriculture, by the owners of many of these vast English estates, is of a very high order; and I am glad, from considerable observation, to say that the relations between owner and tenant are often of the most considerate and liberal kind. No doubt the present free trade prices

* At the celebrated farm of Mr. W., in this county, his cellar contained, at the commencement of harvest, twenty-four *hogsheads of beer;* barely enough, as I was told, for the harvest labor—about nine pints per day to each man. There was nearly a strike among the workmen for ten pints; indeed, a gallon per day is no very uncommon thing for a beer drinker in England!

[illegible] make a hard market for many of the tenant farmers of England. Yet, as the interests of the landlord and tenant run in parallel lines, it is clear that rents must be modified accordingly. Upon this estate, this has been done most wisely and judiciously. The good understanding that exists between both parties is therefore very great; as a proof of which, I will mention that the Earl gives a dinner twice a year, to which all his tenants are invited. At the last festival of this sort, he took occasion to speak publicly of the low prices of bread-stuffs, and the complaint so frequently made of the high rents at which farms are still held. To meet the state of the times, he added, that he had, from time to time, altered the scale of his rents; and had now resolved to make a still further reduction of a certain number of shillings per acre to all who would apply for the same after that day. He now mentioned to me, that although nearly two months had now elapsed, not a single application had been made; and this, perhaps, solely because the tenants appreciated the justice and liberality with which the estate had been managed, and knew the free trade policy, where this is the case, falls as heavily on the landlords as on themselves.

Nothing can well be more complete, of its kind, than this highest kind of country life in England. I leave out of the question now, of course, all republican reflections touching the social or political bearing upon other classes. Taken by itself, it has been perfected here by the long enjoyment of hereditary right, united to high cultivation and great natural taste for rural and home pleasures, till it is difficult to imagine any thing (except, perhaps, a little more sunshine out of doors) that would add to the picture. In the first place, an Englishman's park, on one of these great estates, is a species of kingdom by itself—a vast territorial domain, created solely for his own enjoyment, and within the bounds of which his family and guests may ride, drive, walk, or indulge their tastes, without in the least interfering with any one, or being interfered with, by the presence of any of the rest of the world. In the next place, the climate not only favors the production of the finest lawns and pleasure-grounds in the world, but promotes the out-of-door interest in, and enjoyment of them. Next, these great domestic establishments (so immense and complete that we have nothing in America with which to compare them) are still managed (owing to the exercise of the service and the division of labor) with an ease and simplicity quite incomprehensible to an American, who knows from experience how difficult it is to keep a household of half a dozen domestics together, even in the older parts of the Union. Here, there are sixty servants, and I have been in houses in England where there are above a hundred, and yet all moving with the quiet precision of a chronometer. There are few people in England, I think, who seem inclined to say amen, to the doctrine that

"Man wants but little here below."

I would however be quite willing to subscribe to it, so far as regards one's domestic establishment in America, if, alas! we could have "that little"—*good!*

I must close my letter here, with a promise to give you some account of Chatsworth in my next, which stands, in some respects, at the head of all English places.

III.

CHATSWORTH.

[Mr. Downing's remarks upon introducing a friend's "Impressions of Chatsworth," in the Horticulturist for January, 1847, will well precede his own letters from that place.]

WHAT one would do if he were a Duke, and had half a million a year? is a question which, if it could be audibly put by a magician or a fairy, as in the bygone days of wands and enchantments, would set all the restless and ambitious directly to air-castle-building. Visions of the enjoyment of great estates, grand palaces, galleries of pictures, richly stored libraries, stately gardens, and superb equipages, would no doubt quickly crowd upon the flushed imaginations of many even of our soberest readers. Each person would give an unlimited scope, in the ideal race of happiness, to his favorite hobby, which nothing but the actual trial would convince him that he could not ride better and more wisely than all the rest of his fellow-men.

We have had placed in our hands some clever and graphic notes of a visit to *Chatsworth*, the celebrated seat of the Duke of Devonshire. This place, as a highly artistical country residence, is admitted to stand alone even in England, and therefore in the world. To save our readers the trouble of perplexing their own wits to conjecture what they would do, if they were burdened or blessed with the expenditure of the best ducal revenue in Great Britain, we beg leave to refer them to the notes that follow.

We may give a personal relish to the account, by observing that the Duke of Devonshire is a bachelor; that it is a principle with him to expend the most of his enormous income on his estate, and that gardening is his passion. He is the President of the London Horticultural Society, where he is, among enthusiastic amateurs, the most enthusiastic among them all. He sends botanical collectors to the most distant and unexplored countries, in search of new plants at his own cost. He travels, with his head gardener, all over Europe, to examine the finest conservatories, and returns home to build one larger and loftier than them all. He goes to Italy, to study the effect of a ruined aqueduct, that he may copy it on a grand scale in the waterworks at his private country-place; and he takes down a whole village near the borders of his park, in order to improve and rebuild it in the most tasteful, comfortable, and picturesque manner.

But it is not only in gardening, that the Duke of Devonshire displays his admirable taste. Chatsworth is not less remarkable for the treasures of art collected within its walls. Its picture galleries, its library, its hall of sculpture, its Egyptian antiquities, its stores of plate, each is so remarkable in its way, that it would make a reputation for any place of less note. In his equipage, though often simple enough, the Duke has an individuality of his own, and we remember reading a description by that excellent judge of such matters, Prince Puckler Muskau, of the Duke's turn-out at Doncaster races—a coach with six horses and twelve outriders, which in point of taste and effect, eclipsed all competitors, even there.

But this is of little moment to our readers, most of whom, doubtless, relish more their *Maydukes*, than anecdotes of even the *Royal Dukes* themselves. But there is a certain satisfaction, even to the humble cultivator of a dozen trees or plants, or a little plat of ground, in feeling that his dearest hobby—gardening is also the favorite resource of one of the wealthiest and most cultivated English nobles. It is, perhaps, doubtful whether the former does not gather with a stronger satisfaction, the few fruits and flowers so carefully watched and reared by his own hands, than the latter experiences in beholding the superb desserts of hot-house growth, which every day adorn his table, but which he does *not* know individually and by heart—which others have reared for him—thinned, watered, and shaded—watched the sunny cheek redden, and the bloom deepen—without any of that strong personal interest which glads the heart of the possessor of a small, dearly-prized garden. He gains by the possession of the mighty whole, but he loses as much by losing the familiar interest in the inexhaustible little. Such is the divine nature of the principle of *compensation!*

August, 1850.

Chatsworth, the magnificent seat of the Duke of Devonshire, has the unquestionable reputation of being the finest private country residence in the world. You will pardon me, then, if I bestow a few more words on it, than the passing tourist is accustomed to do.

I ought to preface my account of it by telling you that the present Duke, now about sixty, with an income equal to what passes for a very large fortune in America, has all his lifetime been remarkable for his fine taste, especially in gardening: and that this residence has an immense advantage over most other English places, in being set down in the midst of picturesque Derbyshire, instead of an ordinary park level. In consequence of the latter circumstance, the highest art is contrasted and heightened by the fine setting of a higher nature.

If you enter Chatsworth, as most visitors do, by the Edensor gate, you will be arrested by a little village—Edensor itself; a lovely lane, bordered by cottages, just within the gate, that has been wholly built by the present Duke. It is quite a study, and is precisely what everybody imagines the possibility of doing, and what no one but a king or a subject with a princely fortune, and a taste not always born with princes, could do. In short, it is such a village as a poet-architect would design, if it were as easy to make houses of solid materials as it is to draw them on paper. There may be thirty or forty cottages in all, and every one most tasteful in form and proportions, most admirably built, and set in its appropriate framework of trees and shrubbery,—making an *ensemble* such as I saw nowhere else in England. There are dwellings in the Italian, Gothic, Norman, Swiss, and two or three more styles; each as capital a study as you will find in any of the architectural works, with the advantage which the reality always has over its counterfeit.

From this little village to Chatsworth House, or palace, is about two miles, through a park, which is a broad valley, say a couple of miles wide by half a dozen long. It is indeed just one of those valleys which our own Durand loves to paint in his ideal landscapes, backed by wooded hills and sylvan slopes, some three hundred or four hundred feet high, with a lovely English river—the Derwent—running like a silver cord through the emerald park, and grouped with noble drooping limes, oaks, and elms, that are scattered over its broad surface. After driving about a mile, the palace bursts upon your view—the broad valley park spread out below and before it—the richly wooded hill rising behind it—the superb Italian gardens lying around it—the whole, a palace in Arcadia. On the crest of the hill, from the top of a picturesque tower, floats the flag which apprises you that the owner of all that you see on every side—the park of twelve miles circuit (filled with herds of the largest and most beautiful deer I have yet seen), valley, hills, and the little world which the horizon shuts in—is at home in his castle.

The palace is a superb pile, extending in all some eight hundred feet. It is designed in the classical style, and is built of the finest material,—a stone of a rich golden brown tint, which harmonizes well with the rich setting of foliage, out of which it rises.

Cavendish is the family name of the Duke of Devonshire, and this estate became the property of Sir W. Cavendish, in the time of Elizabeth. The main building was erected by the first Duke in 1702, and the stately wings, containing the picture and sculpture galleries, by the present Duke. Every portion, however, is in the finest possible order and preservation; and it would be difficult for the stranger to point out which part of the palace belongs to the eighteenth, and which to the nineteenth centuries.

You enter the gilded gates at the fine portal at one end of the range, and drive along a court some distance, till you are set down at the main entrance door of the palace. The middle of the court is occupied by a marble statue of Orion, seated on the back of a dolphin, about which the waters of a fountain are constantly playing. From the chaste and beautiful entrance hall rises a broad flight of stairs, which leads to the suite of state rooms, sculpture gallery, collection of pictures, etc.

The state rooms—a magnificent suite of apartments, with windows composed each of one single plate of glass, and commanding the most exquisite views—are hung with tapestry, or the walls are covered with stamped leather, enriched with gilding. In these rooms are the matchless carvings in wood, by Gibbons, of which, like everybody else curious in such matters, I had heard much, but which fairly beggar all praise. No one can conceive carving so wonderfully beautiful and true as this. The groups of dead game hang from the walls with the death flutter in the wings of the birds, and a bit of lace ribbon, which ties one of the festoons, is—more delicate than lace itself. The finest pictures of Raphael could not have *astonished* me so much as these matchless artistic carvings in wood.

A very noble library, a fine collection of pictures, and the choicest sculpture gallery in England (over one hundred feet long, especially rich in the works of Canova, Thorwalsden, and Chantrey), a long corridor, completely lined with original *sketches* by the great masters, and a very richly decorated private chapel, are among the show apartments of Chatsworth.

So much of the palace as I have enumerated, along with all the out-of-door treasures of the domain, is generously thrown open to the public by the Duke; and you may believe that the opportunity of gratifying their curiosity is not thrown away, when I tell you that upwards of 80,000 persons visited Chatsworth last year. Having heard this before I went there, I fancied the annoyance which all this publicity must give to the possessor and his guests. But when I saw the vast size of the house, and how completely distinct the rooms of the guests and the private apartments of the Duke are, from the portion seen by the public, I became aware how little inconvenience the proper inmates of the palace suffered by the relinquishment of the show rooms. The private suite of drawing-rooms, appropriated to the guests at Chatsworth, is decorated and furnished in a far more chaste and simple style than the state rooms, though with the greatest refinement and elegance. Among these adornings, I observed a superb clock, and some very large vases of green malachite, presented by the Emperor of Russia; Landseer's original picture of Bolton Abbey, and that touching story of Belisarius—old, blind, and asking alms—told upon canvass by Murillo, so powerfully as to send a thrill through the dullest observer.

In the ground floor, opening on a level with the Italian gardens, is the charming suite of apartments, occupied chiefly by the Duke when his guests are not numerous. Nothing can well be imagined more tasteful than these rooms,—a complete suite, beginning with a breakfast-room, and ending with the most select and beautiful of small libraries, and including cabinets of minerals, gems, pictures, etc. The whole had all that snugness and cosiness which is so exactly opposite to what one expects to find in a palace, and which gave me the index to a mind capable of seizing and enjoying the delights of both extremes of refined life. The completeness of Chatsworth House, as you will gather from what I have said, is that it contains under one roof suites of apartments for living in three different styles—that of the palace, the great country house, and the cottage orneé. With such a prodigality of space, you can easily see that the Duke can afford, for the greater part of the year, to throw the palace proper, i. e., the state rooms, open to the enjoyment of the public.

The next morning after my arrival at Chatsworth, was one of unusual brilliancy. The air was soft, but the sunshine was that of our side of the Atlantic, rather than the mild and tempered gray of England. After breakfast, and before making our exploration of the gardens and pleasure-grounds, the Duke had the kindness to direct the whole wealth of fountains and *grandes eaux* to be put in full play for the day,—a spectacle not usually seen; as indeed the Emperor fountain is so powerful and so high that it is dangerous to play it, except when the atmosphere is calm.

We enter the Italian gardens. And what are the Italian gardens? you are ready to inquire. I will tell you. They are the series of broad terraces, on two or three levels, which surround the palace, and which, containing half a dozen acres or more of highly dressed garden scenery, separate the pleasure-grounds and the house from the more sylvan and rural park. As the house is on a higher level than most of the valley, you lean over the massive Italian balustrade of the terrace (all of that rich golden stone), and catch fine vistas of the park scenery below and beyond you. Of course, the Italian gardens are laid out in that symmetrical style which best accords with a grand mass of architecture, and are decorated with fine vases, statues, and fountains. A pretty effect is produced by avenues of Portugal laurels, grown with single stems and round heads, like the orange-trees that always border the walks of the gardens of the continent; and the Duke mentioned, in passing, that the Prince and Princess Borghese, who had been guests at Chatsworth but a few days before, had really mistaken them for orange-trees. But one point where the Italian gardens of Chatsworth must always be finer than any in Italy, is in the carpet of turf which forms their groundwork. The "velvet turf" of England is world-wide in its reputation; but no one, till he sees it as it is here—short, tufted, elastic to the tread—can realize that the phrase is *not* a metaphor. A surface of real dark green velvet of a dozen acres, would scarcely soothe the eye more, by its look of softness and smoothness, than the turf in the Italian gardens at Chatsworth.

But the crowning glory in Chatsworth, is its fountains. In a country where water is always scarce, a situation that affords a pretty stream, or a small artificial lake, is a rarity. But the whole of the hill, or mountain, that rises behind the house and pleasure-grounds, is full of springs, and has been made a vast reservoir, which is perfectly under command, and fulfils its purposes of beauty as if it were under the spell of some enchanter. If you will suppose yourself standing with me on the upper terrace of the Italian gardens that morning, behind you rises up the palace, stately and magnificent; all along its front of eight hundred feet, those gardens extend —a carpet of velvet, divided by broad alleys, enriched by masses of the richest flowers, and enlivened by fountains of various form, sparkling in the sunshine like silver. Before you, also, stretches part of these gardens—a part in which the principal feature is a mirror-like lake, set in turf, and overhung by a noble avenue of drooping lime trees—beyond which you catch a vista of the distant hills.

Out of this limpid sheet springs up a fountain, so high that, as you look upward and fairly hold your breath with astonishment you almost expect it, with its next leap, to reach the sky; and yet, with all this vast power and volume, it is so light, and airy, and beautiful, and it bursts at the top, and falls in such a superb storm of diamonds, that you will not be convinced that it is not a production of nature, like Niagara. This is the Emperor Fountain—the highest in the world; about the height, I should say, of Trinity Church spire.* It is only suffered to play on calm days, as the weight of the falling water, if blown aside by a high wind, would seriously damage the pleasure-grounds.

As the eye turns to the left, the wooded hill, which forms the rich forest back-ground to this scene, seems to have run mad with cataracts. Far off among the precipices, near its top, you see waterfalls bursting out among the rocks,—now disappearing amid the thick foliage of the wood, and then reappearing lower down, foaming with velocity, and plunging again into the dark woods. Towards the base of the hill stands a circular water-temple, out of which the water rises. It gushes out as if from the hydrant of the water gods, and, running down a slope, falls at the back of the gardens down a long flight of very broad marble steps, that lead from the water-temple to the edge of the pleasure-grounds, so as to give the effect of a waterfall of a hundred or more feet high. This wealth of water, as if some river at the back of the mountain had broke loose, and, after wild pranks in the hills, had been forced into order and symmetry in the pleasure-grounds, gives almost the tumult and excitement of a freshet in the wilderness to this most exquisite combination of garden and natural scenery.

Leaving the point—where you take in, without moving, all this magical landscape—you wander through flower gardens, and amid pleasure-grounds, till you reach a more wooded and natural looking *paysage*. The fountains, the carefully polished Italian gardens, are no longer in view. The path becomes wild, and, after a turn, you enter upon a scene the very opposite to all that I have been describing. You take it for a rocky wilderness. The rocks are of vast size, and indeed of all sizes; with thickets of laurels, rhododen-

* The height of the Emperor Fountain is 267 feet. The next highest fountains in the world, are one at Hesse Cassel, 190 feet; one at St. Cloud, 160 feet; and the great jet at Versailles, 90 feet.

drons and azaleas growing among them, ivy and other vines climbing over them, and foot-paths winding through them. From the top of a rocky precipice, some thirty feet high, dashes down a waterfall, which loses itself in a pretty meandering stream that steals away from the foot of the rock. Nothing can well look wilder or more natural than this spot; and yet this spot, the "rock-garden," of six acres, has all been created. Every one of these rocks has been brought here—some of them from two or three miles away. It is just as wild a scene as one finds on the skirts of some wooded limestone ridge in America. Though it was all made a few years ago, yet now that the trees and shrubs have had time to take forms of wild luxuriance, all traces of art are obliterated. The eye of the botanist only, detects that the masses of laurels are rare rhododendrons, and that beautiful azaleas of the Alps * make the underwood to the forest that surrounds it.

You wish to go onward. We will leave the rock garden by this path, on the side opposite to that which we entered. No, that, you see, is impossible; a huge rock, weighing fifty or sixty tons, exactly stops up the path and lies across it. Your companion smiles at your perplexity, and with a single touch of his hand, the rock slowly turns on its centre, and the path is unobstructed! There is no noise, and nothing visible to explain the mystery; and when the rock has been as quietly turned back to its place, it looks so firm and solid upon its base, that you feel almost certain that either your muscles or the rocks themselves obey the spell of some unseen and supernatural wood-spirit.

One of the greatest beauties at Chatsworth lies in the diversity of surface—the succession of hill and dale, which, especially in the pleasure-grounds, continually occurs. This variation offers excellent opportunities for the production of a succession of scenes, now highly ornate and artistic, like the flower gardens, now romantic and picturesque, like the rocky valley. And as we continue our ramble, after entirely losing sight of the wild scene I have just described, we enter upon another still different,—a wide glade or

* *Azalea*, or, rather, *Rhododendron hirsutum* and *ferrugineum;* two beautiful sorts, perfectly hardy.

opening, like an amphitheatre, in the midst of a fine grove of trees. An immense palace of glass rises before us. Its curved roof, springing seventy feet high, gleams in the morning sun; and you would be at a loss to conceive for what purpose this vast structure was intended, did you not see as you approached, by the indistinct forms of the foliage, that it incloses another garden. This is the great conservatory, which is three hundred feet long, and covers rather more than an acre of ground. Through its midst runs a broad road, over which the Duke and his guests occasionally drive in a carriage and four. All the riches of the tropics are grown here, planted in the soil, as if in their native climate; and a series of hot-water pipes maintain, perpetually, the temperature of Cuba in the heart of Derbyshire. The surface is not entirely level, but there are rocky hills and steep walks winding over them; and lofty as the roof is, some of the palms of South America have already nearly reached the glass. From the branches and trunks of many of the largest, hang curious air plants, brilliant, and apparently as little fixed to one spot as summer butterflies.

But I shall never bring this letter to a close, if I dwell even slightly upon any interesting scene in detail. I must mention, however, in passing, the *arboretum*—perhaps a mile long—planted with the rarest trees, and every day becoming richer and more interesting to the botanist and the landscape gardener. The trees are neither set in formal lines, nor grouped in a single scene, but are scattered along a picturesque drive, with space enough for each to develope its natural habit of growth. There are some very graceful Deodar cedars here, and a great many araucarias. But the two most striking and superb trees, which I nowhere else saw half so large and in such perfection, were Douglass' fir (*Abies Douglassi*), and the noble fir (*Abies nobilis*). They are two of the magnificent evergreens of California and Oregon, discovered by Douglass, and brought to England about eighteen years ago. These two specimens are now about thirty-five feet high, extremely elegant in their proportions, as well as beautiful in shape and color. I cannot describe them, briefly, so well as by comparing the first to a gigantic and superb balsam fir, with far larger leaves, a luxuriance and freedom always wanting in the balsam, together with the richest dark bronze-green foliage; and the latter to the finest drooping Norway spruce, equally multiplied in the scale of luxuriance and grace. They grow upon a rocky bank, overhanging a pool of clear water, and look as if thoroughly at home, on the slope of a hill-side in Oregon.

The arboretum walk forms a complete collection of all the hardy trees that will grow out of doors at Chatsworth, with space for planting every new species as it may be introduced into Great Britain. A fine effect is produced by grafting the weeping ash into the top of a common ash tree with a tall trunk thirty feet high, whence it falls on all sides more gracefully and prettily than when grafted low; a hint that I laid up for easy practice at home.

A mile further on, and you reach the tower, on the hill top, where the eye commands the whole of Chatsworth valley,—such a picture of palace and pleasure-ground, park and forest scenery as can be found, perhaps, nowhere else in the circle of the planet.

After a long exploration—after exhausting all the well-bred expressions of enthusiasm in my vocabulary, and imagining that it was impossible that landscape gardening, and embellishment, and park scenery, and pleasure-ground decoration, could farther go—the Duke reminded me that I had neither seen the kitchen gardens, the great peach-tree, nor the famous new water lily—the *Victoria Regia;* and that Mr. Paxton, his able *chef*, would never forgive a neglect of so important a feature in a place. As the gardens where all these new wonders lay, were quite on the opposite side of the park, we gladly took to the carriage after our industrious morning's ramble.

I shall not attempt to describe these large and complete fruit and forcing gardens. But the peach-tree of Chatsworth has not, to my recollection, been described, though it deserves to be as famous as the grape-vine of Hampton Court. It is the more wonderful, because, as you know, peach-trees do not grow in England in orchards of five hundred acres, like those of the Reybolds, in Delaware; but are only seen upon walls, or under glass. Yet I assure you, our friend R.'s eyes, accustomed as they are to peach blossoms by the mile, would have dilated at the sight of this monster tree, occupying a glass house by itself, and extending over a trellis—I should say a hundred feet long. I inquired about the product of this tree, and when the number was mentioned, I imagined His Grace detected a slight smile of incredulity; for he begged Mr. Paxton to copy for me, and subscribe his name to, the accurate statistics of the present crop. I send it to you in a note,* with the addition, that the fruit was of the variety known as the Royal George, very large, and finer flavored than I had before tasted from trees grown under glass. The whole trellis from one end to the other, was most admirably clothed—not a vacant place to be found.

Of the superb water lily, lately discovered in Brazil, and named *Victoria Regia*, in honor of the Queen, you have already published an account. It has grown and bloomed here more perfectly than elsewhere; though there are, also, good specimens at the Duke of Northumberland's, and at Kew. The finest plant here occupies a house built specially for it, 60 by 45 feet, inclosing a small pond 33 feet in diameter for it to grow in. The plant is, unquestionably, the most magnificent aquatic known. The huge circular leaves, 4 to 5 feet across, are like great umbrellas in size; and the blossoms, as large as a man's hat—pure white, tipped with crimson—float upon the surface with a very queenly dignity, as if ready to command admiration. A small frame or board was placed on one of the leaves, merely in order to divide the weight equally as it floated; and it upheld the weight of a man readily. Some seeds were presented to me of this beautiful floral amazon before I left Chatsworth; but as it requires the tank to be heated to a temperature of 85°, and the water kept constantly in motion by a small wheel, I fear I shall not readily find an amateur in the United States who will be inclined to indulge a taste for so expensive a floral fancy.

The kitchen and forcing grounds are on an immense scale, and some handsome fruit was being packed to go as a present to the Queen. The pines were usually large and fine; and the Duke remarked that Mr. Paxton has reduced the cost of producing them two-thirds, since he has had charge of that department,—some ten or twelve years.

* "*Memorandum of Peaches, borne by the Great Peach Tree at Chatsworth, in* 1850.—Fruit thinned out at various times before maturity, 7,801; do. left to ripen, 926; total crop, 8,727.

JOS. PAXTON."

If, after this lengthy description, I have almost wholly failed to give you an idea of Chatsworth, it is not wholly because my pen is not equal to the task. Something must be allowed for the difficulty of presenting to you any adequate notion of the variety, richness, and completeness of an estate, where you may spend many days with new objects of interest and beauty constantly before you; objects which, only to enumerate, would be presenting you with dry catalogues, instead of living pictures, brilliant and varying as those of the kaleidoscope.

And, I think I hear you say, this is all for the pride and pleasure of a single individual! All this is done to minister to his happiness. Not entirely. The Duke of Devonshire has the reputation, very deservedly, I should think, of being second to no man in England for his benevolence, kind-heartedness and liberality. Certainly, I think I may safely say, that Chatsworth shows more *refined taste*, joined to magnificence, both externally and internally, than any place I have ever seen. When one sees how many persons are constantly employed in the various works of improvement on this single estate, and how cheerfully the whole is thrown open to the study and enjoyment of thousands and tens of thousands annually, one cannot but concede a liberal share of admiration and thanks to a nobleman who might follow the example of many others, and make his home his closed castle; but who prefers, on the other hand, to open, like a national picture gallery, this magnificent specimen of landscape gardening and architecture, on which his fine taste and ample fortune have been lavished for half a century. One has only to visit Windsor and Buckingham Palace *after* Chatsworth, to see the difference between a noble and pure taste, and a royal want of it. The one may serve to educate and reform the world. The utmost that the other can do, is to dazzle and astonish those who cannot recognize real beauty or excellence in art.

IV.

ENGLISH TRAVELLING: HADDON HALL: MATLOCK: THE DERBY ARBORETUM: BOTANIC GARDEN IN REGENT'S PARK.

August, 1850.

DERBYSHIRE (you remember you left me at Chatsworth), is so picturesque a country, that I drove about among its hills and valleys with the luxury of good roads and the easiest of private carriages. It is, indeed, only in this way that England can be seen or understood. To dash through such a country as this, where the details are all worked up into such perfect finish, is like going through a gallery of cabinet pictures at the speed of Capt. Barclay, or some "crack pedestrian," who performs a thousand miles in a thousand hours. Here is indeed a hilly country, where you get a glimpse of something new and interesting at every turn: and yet the roads are by no means those we are accustomed to see in such a district, but smooth and hard as a Macadam can make them. It would, however, amuse one of our expert Alleghany stage-drivers, who goes down a five mile mountain on a *full run*, to see an English coachman lock his wheels on such smooth and easy grades as these, among the Derbyshire hills. A proposal of such feats to an English driver as are performed daily in the Alleghanies, with the most perfect success and nonchalance, would be received by him with the same belief in your sanity, as if you should ask him to oblige you by swallowing the cupola of St. Paul's. On the other hand, the perfect neatness of dress (especially in snowy linen, and spotless white-top boots), the obliging manners, and the careful and rapid driving (on those level roads) of a John Bull who is bred to hold the reins, would be a stranger revelation to one of our uncouth looking drivers, than an explanation of the whole art of governing a monarchy.

These Derbyshire hills are, in some parts, covered with wood, and in others entirely bare, or rather only covered with grass,—affording pasture to large flocks of sheep. As I drove amid long slopes and rounded summits, some 200 or 300 feet high, I was struck with the exquisite purple hue, like the bloom on a plum, with which some of the hill-sides were suffused in the soft afternoon light. A little nearer approach enables one to solve the riddle of the mysterious color. The whole hill-side was thickly covered with purple heather, in full bloom, which, at a distance, gave it the seeming of having been dipped in some delicate dye. I cannot tell you how these hills, and the wild wastes and downs of England, covered with the delicate bells of the heath, affected me when I first saw them. When you remember, that with all the forest and meadow richness of America, not a single *heath* grows wild from one end of the country to the other, and that we scarcely know the plant, except as a delicate and cherished green-house exotic—a plant which every English poet has embalmed in his verse, and which is the very emblem of wild, airy freshness—you may believe me, when I tell you that a million, spent in gardens under glass, could not have given me the same exquisite delight, which I experienced in running over, plucking, and feasting my eyes upon these acres of wild heather. There are half a dozen species, with different shades of color—white, pink, pale and deep purple; but the latter is the most beautiful, as well as the most common.

Haddon Hall.—Next to Chatsworth, Haddon Hall is the most noted locality in Derbyshire. As the two places are but a few miles apart, they form the best possible contrast,—Chatsworth being one of the most finished specimens of the luxury, refinement, and grandeur of modern England, as Haddon is of the domestic abodes and habits of an English nobleman two hundred years ago.

Haddon Hall gives, perhaps, the best idea that may be gathered any where in this country, of the ancient baronial residence, *exactly as it was.* No part of this large castellated pile (which is finely situated on the slope of a wooded hill), is of later date than the sixteenth century. Its history is that of the Vernon family, who built and inhabited it for more than three centuries. Sir George Vernon, the last male heir, lived here in the time of Elizabeth; and his magnificent hospitality and great establishment gave him he name of the "king of the Peak."

What struck me at Haddon was the *realness* and the *rudeness* of those halls of ancient grandeur. There is not one alteration to suit more modern tastes—not a single latter-day piece of furniture—nothing, in short, that does not remind you of the solidly *material* difference between ancient and modern times. Vast chimney-pieces, with huge fire-dogs in them, for burning wood, large halls, with open timber roofs, instead of ceilings, wainscot covered with tattered arras, which hung loosely over secret panelled doors in the walls, rude and massive steps to the staircases, and clumsy, though strong bolts and hasps to the doors,—all these, with many rude utensils, show that strength, and not elegance, stamped its character upon the domestic life, even of the great nobles in those days. Here is a house which held accommodation for upwards of four-score servants, in all the luxury of the time; and yet, so great has been the progress of civilization, that many of our working men would doubtless think the best accommodation of those days but rough apartments to live in. The seats in the kitchen are of stone; and there must have been cold draughts in these great barn-like halls, that would make modern effeminacy's teeth chatter.

There is a singular charm about such a veritable antique castle as this, which perhaps an American feels more strongly than an Englishman. It gives one the feeling of a conversation with the *spirits* of antiquity; and it has for us the additional piquancy, growing out of the fact, that we come from a land where such spirits are wholly unrecognized and unknown. To feel that in this rude dining-hall the best civilization of the time flourished, and mighty barons, ladies, and vassals feasted and revelled, long before the first settlement was made at Jamestown, is very much like being invited to smoke a cigar with Sir Walter Raleigh, or go to the Globe playhouse with Manager Shakspeare.

The terraced garden, too, is quaint and "old-timey." The special point of interest is "Dorothy Vernon's Walk;" for it has both romance and reality about it. Dorothy was the beautiful daughter and heiress of the last Vernon. The son of the first Duke of Rutland fell so violently in love with her, when she was but eighteen, that (his suit not being favored by her father) he lived some time in the woods of Haddon, disguised as a gamekeeper; and finally (during a masked ball), eloped with the fair Dorothy, heiress of Haddon, through the door from the long gallery, which leads down to this walk.

And this gives me the opportunity to say, that this marriage, of course, brought Haddon Hall into the family of the Dukes of Rutland, who, for a time, inhabited it in great state; but about a hundred years ago abandoned it for their more modern residence—Belvoir Castle. Haddon Hall is, however, though uninhabited, wisely prevented from falling into complete decay by the present Duke of Rutland, and is open to the inspection of visitors at all times.

Matlock, considered the most picturesque spot in Derbyshire, is in the ordinary route of travellers, but would, I think, disappoint any one accustomed to the Hudson; as would, indeed, any scenery in England (I will except Wales) in point of picturesqueness. The village of Matlock Bath is a watering-place, nestled in a pretty, quiet dale, surrounded by rocky cliffs some 200 or 300 feet high. Excellent walks, charmingly laid out and well kept, sparry caverns, petrifying wells, with mineral springs, make up the attractions of this rural neighborhood. The real beauty of Matlock, to my eyes—and it is the essentially English feature—is in the luxuriance of the vines and shrubbery that clamber over and enwreath every object—natural, artificial, and picturesque. A bare, rocky bank, unless it has great magnitude or grandeur of outline, is hard and repulsive. But let that same bank be covered with rich masses of ivy, and overhung with verdure of luxuriant shrubs and trees, and what was ugly and harsh is transformed into something exceedingly beautiful. In this respect, both climate and culture conspire to make English scenery of this character very captivating. The ivy springs up and grows readily any where; and the people, with an instinctive feeling for rural expression, encourage this and other drapery, wherever

33

it is becoming. Strip away from the English cottages, that are so much admired, the vines that cover, and the shrubbery that embowers them, and they would look as bald and commonplace as the most ordinary rural dwellings in America. The only difference would be, that an English cottage, stripped of *drapery*, would show plain brick walls, and tile or thatch roof—ours, wooden clap-boarding and shingles. Architecturally, however, the English cottages—four-fifths of them—are no better than our own; but they are so *affectionately* embosomed in foliage, that they touch the heart of the traveller more than the designs of Palladio would, if they bordered the lanes and road-sides.

As no decoration is so cheap as vines, I was one day expressing my regret to an English landscape-gardener, that the ivy was neither a native of America, nor would it thrive in the northern States, without considerable care. "You Americans are an ungrateful people," said he; "look at that vine, clambering over yonder building, by the side of the ivy. It is, as you see, more luxuriant, more rapid in growth, and a livelier green than our ivy. It is true, it has neither the associations nor the evergreen habit of the ivy; but we think it quite as beautiful for the purpose of covering walls and draping cottages." The plant he eulogized was the Virginia Creeper (*Ampelopsis quinquefolia*), an old favorite of mine, and which we are just beginning rightly to estimate at home as it deserves.*

THE DERBY ARBORETUM.—Derby is an interesting old town, and I passed a day there with much satisfaction. What I particularly wished to see, however, was the public garden or pleasure-

* Nothing can be more brilliant, as your readers well know, than the Virginia Creeper in the autumn woods at home, where it frequently climbs up the leading stem of some evergreen, and shines, in its autumnal glory, like foliage of fire, through the dark foliage of a cedar or a hemlock. It grows in almost every part of the country, and will cling to walls or woodwork, like the ivy, without any artificial aid. We believe this vine is less frequently planted than it would be, from many persons confounding it with the poison sumac vine, which a little resembles it. The Virginia Creeper is, however, perfectly harmless, and may be easily known from the poison vine, by the latter bearing only three leaflets to a leaf, while the Virginia Creeper has five leaflets.

grounds, called the Derby Arboretum. It interested me in three ways: first, as having been especially formed for, and presented to the inhabitants of the town by their member of Parliament, Joseph Strutt, Esq., a wealthy silk manufacturer here; then, as containing a specimen of most of the hardy trees that will grow in Britain; and lastly, as having been laid out by the late Mr. Loudon.

As a public garden—the gift of a single individual—it is certainly a most noble bequest. The area is about eleven acres, and is laid out so as to appear much larger,—the boundaries concealed by plantations, etc. There are neat and tasteful entrance lodges, with public rooms for the use of visitors (where a lunch is provided, at the bare cost of the provisions), and where books of reference are kept; so that any person who wishes to pursue the study of trees, can, with the aid of the specimens in the garden, quickly become familiar with the whole history of every known species. During five days in the week, these grounds are open to all persons without charge; and on the other two days, the admission fee is sixpence —merely enough to keep the place in good condition.

The grounds were in beautiful order, and are evidently much enjoyed, not only by the good people of Derby, but by strangers, and visitors from the neighborhood. I met numbers of young people strolling about and enjoying the promenade, plenty of nurses and children gathering health and strength in the fresh air, and, now and then, saw an amateur carefully reading the labels of the various trees and shrubs, and making notes in his memorandum-book—doubtless, with a view to the improvement of his own grounds. Every tree or plant is conspicuously marked with a printed label (a kind of brick set in the ground at the foot of the tree or shrub, with the name under a piece of glass, sunk in a panel upon the top of the brick); and this label contains the common name of the plant, the botanical name, its native country, the year of its introduction (if not a native), and the height to which it grows. The most perfect novice in trees, can thus, by walking round the arboretum, obtain in a short time a very considerable knowledge of the hardy Sylva, while the arboriculturist can solve many a knotty point, by looking at the trees and plants themselves, which no amount of study, without the living specimen, would settle. Then the whole collection, consisting of about a thousand different species and varieties, is arranged according to the natural system, so that the botanist may study classification, as well as structure and growth, with the whole clearly before his eyes. As the great point is to show the natural character of the different trees and shrubs, they are all planted quite separately, and allowed room to grow on all sides; and no pruning which would prevent the natural development of the habits of the tree or shrub, is permitted.

The whole arboretum was laid out and planted ten years ago—in 1840; so that, of course, one can, now, very well judge of its value and its effects.

That it is, and will be, one of the most useful and instructive public gardens in the world, there can be no doubt; for it certainly combines the greatest possible amount of instruction, with a great deal of pleasure for all classes, and especially the working classes. That it may appeal largely to the sympathies of the latter, even to those to whom all trees are alike, there is a fine piece of smooth lawn (added, I think, to the original eleven acres), expressly used as a *skittle ground*,—a favorite English game with ball; at which numbers of men and boys were playing while I was there.

As regards *taste*, I do not hesitate to confess my disappointment. There is no other beauty in these grounds, than what grows out of the entire surface being covered with grass, neatly mown, with broad straight walks through the central portions, and a series of narrower covered walks, making a connected circuit of the whole. The peculiarity of the design belongs to the *surface* of the ground. This was naturally a level; but in order to produce the greatest possible intricacy and variety, in a limited space, it was thrown up, here and there, into ridges from six to ten feet high. These ridges are not abrupt, but gentle; and the walks are led between them, so that even when there are no intervening trees and shrubs, you could not easily see a person in one walk from another one parallel to it, though only twenty or thirty feet off. If these ridges, or undulations in the surface, had been cleverly planted with groups and masses of trees and shrubs, the effect would have been very good; but dotted as they are with *scattered* single trees and shrubs, the result is a little harsh, with neither the ease of nature nor the symmetry of art. If one looks at the Derby arboretum, therefore, as an example of Mr. Loudon's landscape-gardening, one would not get a high idea of his taste. But I believe this would not be judging him fairly, as I think he intended this place as a garden for instructing the British public in arboriculture, even more than as a specimen of public pleasure-grounds. And every one who is familiar with botanical gardens, knows how ugly they generally are, from the very plain reason, that instead of planting only beautiful objects, they must necessarily contain a great mass of species, very uninteresting except to the scientific student.

I noticed one tree that was entirely new to me, and which I am sure will be a valuable acquisition to our pleasure-grounds at home. It is the "hoary Pyrus," from Nepaul, *Pyrus vestita*,—a very striking tree, in its large foliage, which is dark green above, and hoary white below. It is very vigorous and hardy; the specimen about thirty feet high.

The Derby arboretum, altogether, as I learned there, cost above $50,000. Considered as the creation and bequest of a private citizen to his townsmen (and to the country at large), it is certainly a magnificent donation. When one remembers what a gratification is afforded to the numerous inhabitants of a large town, *for all time to come*, by this arboretum, what a refreshment after a day's labor for those who have no garden of their own, what an instructive walk—every year increasing in extent—even for those who have, what an attraction to strangers, and what a source of pride to the citizens to whom it especially belongs, one cannot but look upon Mr. Strutt's gift, as something done in the largest spirit of philanthropy. Quite as considerable sums have often been given by merchants in my own country, to found hospitals and asylums for the diseased in mind and body. Perhaps it may not be long before some one of them will follow the example of Mr. Strutt, and form a public garden or park, as such places should be formed, and present it to one of our large cities or towns, now so much in need of it. Would it not keep his memory more lovingly fresh in the minds of his fellow-men, and their descendants, than any other bequest it is possible to conceive?

THE BOTANIC GARDEN IN REGENT'S PARK.—As a *pendant* to

this sketch of the arboretum at Derby, let me give you an outline of another garden in the midst of the Regent's Park, at the west end of London. It cannot, perhaps, be strictly called a public garden; it is, more properly, a *subscription garden*, as it was made, and is maintained, by about sixteen hundred members, who either pay twenty guineas at the outset, or two guineas a year. The privileges they have, are the free enjoyment of the grounds, conservatories, etc., at all times, and the admission of their friends (not more than two per day) by tickets. As there is no other way of getting admission (even the *fee*, that is so all-potent in most cases, does not prevail here), of course, very few strangers ever see this garden—the best worth seeing, of its kind, perhaps, in all Europe. As I had, fortunately, been one of the honorary members for some years, I was glad to claim my rights, soon after my arrival in London.

The scene, as you enter the grounds, is extremely beautiful and striking, especially when you recall (what, without an effort, you would certainly forget) that you are in the midst of a vast city; or, at the most, barely on the borders of it. Here is a large velvet lawn, admirably kept, the surface gently undulating, and stretching away indefinitely (to all appearance) on either side, losing itself amid belts and groups and masses of shrubs and trees, with winding walks stealing off, here and there, in the most inviting manner, to the right and left. At the end of the broad walk, at the farther side of the great lawn, which forms the central feature to the garden, stands a noble conservatory of immense size, with lofty curved roof; and on either side of it are small hot-houses, full of all the novelties of the day, and all the treasures of the exotic Flora.

There cannot be a finer contrast, in point of tasteful arrangement and beauty of effect, than that which this garden presents to the arboretum at Derby. They were both formed about the same time, and the extent is not greatly different; the whole area of this place being only eighteen acres.* Here, the utmost beauty, variety, and interest are concentrated within these moderate limits. As you enter, you are struck by the breadth and extent of the broad velvet

* It gains greatly by being in the midst of the Regent's Park, with its boundaries concealed by thickets, over which the trees in the park make a pleasingly indefinite background.

lawn. As you ramble about the finely planted and well grown walks, which form the border to this lawn—now quite concealed from all observation in a thicket of foliage—now emerging upon some pretty garden vista, and again opening upon a little separate nook, devoted to some single kind of culture, as groups of rhododendrons, or American plants, or a flower garden set in turf, or a rock-work filled with curious alpines—you imagine you have been introduced into some pleasure-grounds of fifty acres, instead of the moderate compass of less than twenty. The surface is most gracefully undulating, so as to give that play of light and shade—those *sunny smiles*, so pleasant in a lawn, and to prevent your eye from ranging over too large a sweep at one time; and though this variation of surface was, as I was told, wholly the work of art when the grounds were laid out, it has none of the stiff and hard look of the surface in the arboretum at Derby, but is charmingly like the most pleasing bits of natural flowing surface. I cannot, therefore, but believe that Mr. Marnock, the able landscape gardener who laid out this place, convinced me by this single specimen, that he is a man of great skill and refined taste in his art. I saw no *new* place abroad laid out in a more entirely satisfactory manner.

In order to give the garden a character and purpose, beyond that of mere pleasure-grounds (although enjoyment of it in the latter sense is the main object), a botanical arrangement and a medical arrangement of plants, are both very well carried out here—I believe for the use of the students of the London University. But instead of bringing these scientific arrangements into the pleasure-ground portion, which meets the eye of the ordinary visitor of the garden, they are kept in one of the *side scenes*—quite in the background; so that though they add greatly to the interest, and general extent of the garden when sought for, they do not mar the beauty or elegance of its conspicuous outlines.

In the great conservatory, though the larger number of the plants were out in their summer quarters, the whole effect was still extremely pleasing, from the noble specimens of certain showy summer-blooming plants, growing here and there throughout the open space, which was elsewhere turned into a broad gravel walk. These were either gigantic specimens of *brugmansias*, loaded with their great white trumpet flowers—enormous scarlet geraniums, trained as *pyramids*, ten feet high, and brilliant with bloom—rich passifloras, and other vines, climbing up the rafters, or very finely grown exotics, in tubs or large pots.

Among the latter, I noticed with astonishment, *fuchsias*, grown like standard roses to a wonderful size, running up with a perfectly straight stem *sixteen feet high*, and branching into a fine spreading or depending head of foliage, studded at every point with their graceful ear-drops. *Fuchsia corrallina*, among several species, was much the finest, treated in this way,—its luxuriant dark foliage, and deep crimson-purple flowers being quite beautiful.

I saw here two rare plants, which will, I think, be very fine decorations to our gardens in summer. The first is *Habrothamnus elegans;* a plant from Mexico, which, it is thought, may stand the winter here.* It was planted in the ground here, and trained to a pillar some ten or twelve feet high. The end of every branch was loaded with clusters of fine dark pink flowers (of the tint of a ripe Antwerp raspberry); and I was told it blooms without interruption from spring to winter. The size, color, and profusion of the blossoms are striking, and the whole plant is extremely showy. The second favorite is the *Cestrum aurantiacum;* a greenhouse shrub, lately introduced from Guatemala. It grows six or eight feet high, with fine luxuriant shoots, and is loaded all summer with rich clusters of *golden buff* blossoms—very ornamental. Both these plants made a grand display here in the conservatory, planted in the ground and trained to the columns; but if I am not greatly mistaken, both will thrive equally well in the United States, if turned out in the open border, and trained up to stakes like the dahlia,—the roots being taken up and housed in winter.

The society of subscribers to whom this garden belongs, have two or three horticultural shows in the grounds, every year, which are among the most brilliant things of the kind on this side of the Atlantic. On these occasions, the grounds are open to any one who chooses to purchase tickets, and are thronged by thousands of visit-

* I think Mr. Buist has introduced this fine plant, and has it in his nursery.

ors. The display of fruits and flowers takes place in large tents and marquées, pitched on the lawn, and bands of music perform in the gardens. All the *élite* of the West End of London are here; for in London, horticultural shows are even more *fashionable* than the opera; and a gayer or more beautiful sight is not easily found. At the last festival of this sort, the great novelty was a magnificent plat, or garden of rhododendrons, of all colors; the plants, in full bloom, were large and finely-grown specimens, sent beforehand from various nursery gardens fifty or one hundred miles off, planted here in a scene by themselves, where they bloomed in the same perfection as if they had grown here for a dozen years.

I was exceedingly gratified with this subscription garden, and examined it in all its details with great attention. In its tasteful arrangement, its moderate extent, its management and its position, it afforded the finest possible type for a similar establishment near one of our largest cities. Here are eighteen acres of the most exquisite lawn, pleasure-grounds, and conservatory, wholly created and maintained by sixteen hundred individuals, and enjoyed by, perhaps, five or six thousand persons more—their friends at all times. Here is a fine example of the art of landscape-gardening, which, if it were near New-York, Philadelphia, or Boston, so that it could be seen by those who are anxious to learn, would have a great influence on the taste of the country in ornamentel gardening; here is the most perfect exhibition ground, for the shows of a horticultural society, that can be imagined or devised; and here is a scientific arrangement of plants, for the study of botanical and medical classes,—the living plants arranged according to the best system. Half the money which has been paid annually into the credit account of the cemeteries of Greenwood, Mount Auburn, or Laurel Hill, would keep up in the very highest condition (as this garden is kept), one like it in the neighborhood of any of our cities. And the precincts of the Elysian fields, near New-York—Brookline, near Boston—on the banks of the Wissahicon, near Philadelphia, would be as fine localities for such subscription gardens as Regent's Park is for London. If our citizens, who have the money, could come here and see what it will do, expended in this way, I am sure they would not hesitate to subscribe the "needful."

V.

THE ISLE OF WIGHT.

August, 1850.

FOUR days in the Isle of Wight:—the weather, the climate, and the scenery, all delightful. The Island itself, about fifteen miles long, is England in miniature—with its hedges, green lawns, soft-tufted verdure—now and then a great house, and plenty of *ornée* cottages. In some respects it fell below, but in many, fully equalled my expectations. If you think of it as the "Garden of England," it will disappoint you, for there are counties in England —for example, Warwickshire—better cultivated, and more *soignée*, than this spot. A considerable portion of the Island—especially the western end, is neither cultivated fields nor gardens, but broad downs and high bluffs. I should say that you would get the best idea of the Isle of Wight, without seeing it, by imagining it composed partly of Nahant, and partly of Brookline—near Boston— the prettiest rural nest of cottage villas in America. The bare grass slopes and bluffs of Nahant, will correspond to the western part of the Isle of Wight, while the suburbs of Boston, that I have mentioned, are a very fair offset to the more decorated and cultivated cottages and grounds of the eastern and southern portions.

You cross from Southampton to the Island, in rather less than an hour, by one of the small mail steamers plying here. The towns of East and West Cowes, where you land, as well as Ryde, which is a few miles further, have quite a gay appearance at this season of the year, from the harbors being filled with the pretty vessels of the various yacht clubs, that hold their regattas here—

and the accommodation at the hotels is, for the time at least, brought up to the style and prices which the titled yachtmen naturally beget. The flag of the admiral of this fancy fleet, the Earl of Yarborough, floated from the mast of his fast-looking vessel, and a variety of craft, of all sizes, lying about her, gave the whole neighborhood an air of great life and animation.

Our party, three in number, took one of the light, open carriages, with which the Island abounds, and started, the next morning after our arrival, to explore it pretty thoroughly.

The neighborhood of East Cowes, abounds with pretty seats, and, on the opposite shore, are numberless little cottages, by the side of the water, "to let," with all the cosy furniture in-doors, of English domestic life, and out-of-door accompaniments of trees and shrubs, and overhanging vines, that gave them a very inviting appearance. Although I had never lived under the authority of a landlord, I could find nothing but temptations to become a lessee of such pretty domicils as these. They look so truly home-ish, and tell you at a glance, such a story of years of the tenderest care and attention, in all that makes a cottage charming, that they make one long to stop acting the traveller, and nestle down in the bosom of that peaceful domestic life, which they suggest.

A short distance, perhaps a mile, from Cowes, is Osborne House —the marine residence of Victoria. This place is her private property, and having been almost wholly erected within a few years past, may be said to afford a tolerable index to the taste of her Majesty. The residence is an extensive villa, in the modern Italian style, with a front of perhaps two hundred feet, and the outlines picturesquely broken by tower or campanile. It stands in the midst of a sandy plain, which is level around the house and towards the road, and undulating and broken towards the sea—of which it commands fine views.

It is fenced off from the highway by a close, rough board "park paling," some seven or eight feet high. Within this fence is a belt of young trees, and scattered here and there, over the surface of most of the inclosure, are groups and patches of small trees and shrubs, newly planted. The whole place has, most completely, the look of the pretentious place of some of our wealthy men at home, who, turning their backs upon the numberless fine natural sites, with which our country abounds, choose the barest and baldest situation, in order that they may dig, delve, level and grade, and spend half their fortunes, in doing what nature has, not a mile distant, offered to them ready made, and a thousand times more beautifully done. Osborne House may be a tolerable residence (we mean respecting its out-of-door pleasure) fifty years hence; but it is almost the only country-seat that we saw in England, that looked thoroughly raw and uncomfortable. I suppose, in a country where every thing seems finished, there is a singular pleasure in taking a place in the rough, and working beauties out of tameness and insipidity. The Queen lives here, and walks and drives about the neighborhood, in a comparatively simple and unostentatious manner, and attracts very little attention, and her husband practises farming and planting, quite in good earnest.

A country-seat, only a mile distant, in a thoroughly English taste, was a complete contrast to the foregoing, and gave us great pleasure. This is Norris Castle, built by Lord Seymour, but now the property of Mr. Bell, who resides here. Neither the place, nor the house, is larger than several on the Hudson, and the grounds reminded me, in the simple lawn or park, sprinkled with fine groups of trees, of Livingston Manor and Ellerslie. The house gave me greater pleasure, than any modern castellated building that I have seen; partly because it was simple, and essentially domestic-looking, and yet, with a fine relish of antiquity about it. The façade may, perhaps, be one hundred and thirty feet, and I was never more surprised than when I learned that the whole was erected quite lately. The walls are of gray stone, rather rough, and they get a large part of their beauty from the luxuriant vines that festoon every part of the castle. The vines are the Ivy, and our Virginia creeper, intermingled, and as both cling to the stone, they form the most picturesque drapery, which has, in a few years, reached to the top of the battlemented tower, and given a mellow and venerable character to the whole edifice.

We dined at Newport, the substantial little town, which, lying nearly in the centre of the Island, serves as its capital and principal market. The Isle of Wight, enjoying, as it does, a wholly insulated position, is almost the only English ground not interlaced by railroads. For this season, the genuine stage-coach, now comparatively obsolete elsewhere, still flourishes here, and still carries a number of passengers outside, quite at variance with all our ideas of safety and speed. The guard, who accompanies these coaches, usually performs an *obligato* on the French horn or key bugle, just before the coach starts—and performs it too, with so much spirit and taste, that it was not without some difficulty I could resist the temptation to join his party. Progress, and the spirit of the times, though they give us most substantial benefits, in the shape of railroads, etc., certainly do not add to the poetry of life—as I thought when I compared the delicious air of Bellini, played by the coach guard, with the horrible screams of the steam-whistle of the locomotive—now associated with the travel of all christendom.

It is but a mile from Newport to Carisbrook Castle—one of the most interesting old ruins in England. It crowns a fine hill, and from the top of its ruined towers, you look over a lovely landscape of hill and vale, picturesque villages, and green meadows. The castle, itself, with its fortifications, covers perhaps half a dozen acres, and is just in that state of ruin and decay, best calculated to excite the imagination, and send one upon a voyage into dream-land. You clamber over the parapets, and look out from amid the mouldering battlements, mantled with the richest masses of ivy, and see wild trees growing in the very centre of what were once stately apartments. Here is the very window from which Charles I. vainly endeavored to make his escape, when he was a prisoner within these walls, two hundred years ago (1647). I felt tempted to question the stone walls around me, of the sad soliloquies which they had heard uttered by that royal prisoner and his children, confined here after him. But the stone looked silent and cold; the ivy, however, so full of mingled life and health and antiquity, seemed full of the mysterious secrets of the place, and would, doubtless, have unburdened itself to a willing ear, if any such would linger here long enough to get into its confidence. I looked down into the vast well, in the centre of the castle, three hundred feet deep, and still in excellent order—from which water is drawn by an ass, walking his slow rounds inside a large windlass wheel. I clambered up the seventy-two stone steps that led into the high old ruined *keep*, and found one of my companions (who is a military man) discoursing to a little group of tourists, who had made a picnic on the ramparts, about the nature of the fortifications—breastworks—and bastions, which cover some fifteen or twenty acres under the castle walls. While he was demonstrating how easily this ancient stronghold could be taken by a modern besieger, I speculated on the quiet way in which a few types and a printing press are, at the present moment, far more powerful restrainers of wayward sovereigns, and more able protectors of the rights of the people, than the fierce battlements, and standing war dogs, of the old castles of two centuries ago. The imagination is so excited by these strong old castles, now fast crumbling into dust, that we wonder what the people of two hundred years hence will have, to be romantic and picturesque about, as emblems of power in a by-gone age. An old printing-press, or galvanic battery, perhaps! No—even they will be melted up for their value, as old metal.

We drove from Carisbrook, to the extreme end of the Island—saw the Needles, the colored sands, and the white cliffs of Albion, and returned by the south side. What pleased me more than even the sea views, and the bold bays, and snowy cliffs (perhaps from novelty), were the *Downs*—those long reaches of gently sloping surface, covered with very short grass—as close and fine as the finest lawn. They are so smooth and hard, and the air is so pure and exhilarating, the temperature so bracing and delightful, that one is tempted into walking—or even running—miles and miles, upon them. Here and there, mingled with the grass, on the breeziest parts of the Downs, I saw tufts of heather, in full bloom, only two or three inches high—their purple bells embroidering, as with the most delicate pattern, the fragrant turf. Herds of sheep graze upon these Downs, and the flavor of the mutton, as you may suppose, is not despised by those who cannot live upon air, however elastic and exhilarating.

All over the Island, the roads, sometimes broad—but often mere narrow lanes—are bordered by high hawthorn hedges—so that frequently you drive for a mile or more, without getting a peep beyond these leafy walls of verdure. I could imagine that in May, when these hedges are all white with blossoms, the whole Island must be a very gay landscape—but just now, they only served to confirm me in my opinion of the Englishman's fondness for seclusion and privacy, in his own demesne. Just in proportion to the smallness of his place, his desire to shut out all the rest of the world increases—so that if he only owns half an acre, his hedge shall be eight feet high, and the sanctity of the paradise within remains inviolate. The solid, high, well-built stone wall around some of the little cottage and villa places, of half an acre, on the south side of the Island, astonished me, and gave me a new understanding of the saying, that "every man's house is his castle." Here, at least, I thought, it is clear that people understand what is meant by private rights, and intend to have them respected.

It was not until I reached the pretty villages of Bowchurch, Shanklin, and Ventnor, that my ideal of the Isle of Wight was realized. These villages lie on the south side of the Island, backed by steep hills, and sloping to the sea. The climate is almost perfection. It is neither hot in summer nor cold in winter, and though open to all the sea-breezes, the latter seem shorn of all their violence here. The consequence is, they enjoy that perfect marriage of the land and sea so rarely witnessed in northern climates. The finest groves and woods, the richest shrubbery and flower-gardens, the most emerald-like glades of turf, here run down almost to the beach, and you have all the luxuriant beauty of vegetation, in its loveliest forms, joined to all the sublimity, life and excitement of the ocean views. As to the climate, you may judge of its mildness and uniformity, when I tell you that the bay trees of the Mediterranean grow here on the lawns, as luxuriantly as snow-balls do at home, and fuchsias, as tall as your head, make rich masses in almost every garden, and stand the winter as well here, as lilacs or syringoes do with us. In the neighborhood of Shanklin, I saw a charming old parsonage house—the very picture of spacious ease and comfort—with its great bay windows, its picturesque gables, and its thatched roof—quite embowered in tall *myrtles*—Roman myrtles—one of our cherished green-house plants, that here have grown thirty or forty feet high, quite above the eaves! Bays, Portugal laurels, hollies and China roses, surround this parsonage, and never lose their freshness and verdure (the owner assured me that the roses bloomed all winter long), cheating the inhabitants into the belief that winter is an allegory, or if not, has only a substantial existence in Iceland or Spitzbergen.

Then the hotels here—especially in Shanklin—are absolutely ro mantic in their rural beauty. Designed like the prettiest cottages, or rather in a quaint and rambling style, half cottage and half villa, the roof covered with thatch, and the walls with ivy, jessamines, and perpetual roses, and set down in the midst of a charming lawn, and surrounded by shrubbery, you feel the same reluctance to take the room which the chambermaid—with the freshest of roses in her cheeks, and the cleanest of caps upon her head—shows you, as you would in hiring the apartments of some tasteful friend in reduced circumstances. When you rise from your dinner (admirably served), always in a private parlor, the casement windows open upon a velvety lawn, bright with masses of scarlet geraniums, verbenas, and tea roses set in the turf, and you give yourself up to the profound conviction that for snugness, and cosiness, and perfection at a rural inn, the world can contain nothing better than may be found in the Isle of Wight.

Bonchurch disputes the palm with Shanklin, for picturesque and sylvan beauty. We made a visit here to Capt. S—— of the Royal Navy, whose beautiful villa in the Elizabethan style, gave me an opportunity for indulging my architectural and antiquarian taste to the utmost. Imagine an entrance through a rocky dell, the steep sides of which are clothed with the richest climbing plants, between which your carriage winds for some distance, passing under a light airy bridge, with festoons of ivy and clusters of blooming creepers waving over your head. You soon emerge upon the prettiest of little lawns, studded with fine oaks, and running down to the very shore of the sea. On the left are shrubberies, pleasure-grounds, kitchen and flower gardens, all in their place, and though you think the place one of sixty or eighty acres, there are not above twenty.

The house itself is one of the most picturesque and agreeable residences of moderate size that I have ever seen. Its interior, especially, unites architectural beauty, antique character, and modern comfort, to a surprising degree. Every room seemed to have been studied, so that not a feature was omitted, or an effect lost, that could add to the pleasure or increase the beauty of a home of this kind.

If I was delighted with the house, I was astonished with the furniture. It was all in the antique Elizabethan style — richly carved in dark oak or ebony. This is not very rare in England, and I had seen a good deal of the same style in many of the great country mansions before. But almost every piece here, was either a masterpiece of workmanship, or marked by singular beauty of design, or of great historical interest. Yet the effect of the whole, and the adaptation to the uses of each separate room, had been considered, so that the *ensemble* gave the impression of the finest unity of taste. Among the fine specimens which Lady S—— had the goodness especially to make us acquainted with, I remember an exquisitely carved work-box once presented by Essex to Elizabeth, a curious silver clock that belonged to Charles I. (and was carried about with him in his carriage on his journeys); and a superbly carved, high bedstead, once Sir Walter Raleigh's, and the couch of Cardinal Wolsey. There was an old Dutch organ, bearing the date 1592, of singularly beautiful workmanship, and still in perfect tone. Some rare and unique carved oak cabinets, of flemish origin one of them with the history of John the Baptist carved in the different panels, challenged the most elaborate investigation. Of beautiful chairs, seats, and carved wainscot, there was the greatest variety, and in short the house was at once a museum for an antiquarian— and the most agreeable home to live in.

This villa was built by a wealthy eccentric—I think a bachelor —who wholly finished the collection only a few years ago. He carried his passion for collecting very choice and rare antique furniture—especially that of undoubted historical interest—to such an extent, that it became a species of madness, and at last led him through a very large fortune, and forced him to surrender the whole to his creditors. You may judge something of the cost of the furniture—every room in the house being well filled—when I tell you that for a single Flemish cabinet, only remarkable for its superb carving, not for any history attached to it, he paid £900 (about $4,500). The property, when brought into market in the gross was of course bought by the present owner at a merely nominal sum, compared with its original cost.

England, though in the main remarkable for its common sense, abounds with instances like this, of large wealth applied to the indulgence of personal taste—to the building of a great mansion, the collection of books, pictures, or to the indulgence of personal whims or fancies. Thus the Earl of Harrington has in his seat near Derby, a peculiar spot of twenty or thirty acres, wholly filled with the rarest and most beautiful *evergreens* in the world—where araucarias and deodars, bought when they were worth five or ten guineas apiece, are as plentiful now as hemlocks in Western New-York; where dark-green Irish yews stand along the walks like sable sentinels, and gold and silver hollies and yews are cut into peacocks, shepherds, and shepherdesses, and all manner of strange and fantastical whimsies. The conceit, though odd (I had a glimpse of it), is the finest specimen of its kind in the world—yet the owner—an old man now —who has amused himself and spent vast sums on this garden for twenty years past, will not let a soul enter it—unless it may be some gardener whom it is impossible to imagine a critic. Even the Duke of Devonshire—so the story goes—in order to get a sight of it went *incog.* as a kitchen gardener. The Duke of Marlborough, a few years ago, had a private garden at Blenheim, surrounded by a high wall, into which even his own brother had not been admitted. You see even the most amiable qualities of the heart—those which lead us to make our homes happy—occasionally run into a monomania.

I left the Isle of Wight with the feeling that if I should ever need the nursing of soft airs and kindly influences in a foreign land, I should try to find my way back to it again. Even one, blest with excellent health, and usually insensible to the magical influence which most persons find in a change of air, finds something added to the pleasurable sensation of breathing and taking exercise, in the delicious summer freshness of this spot.

There is another memorandum which I made here and which is worth relating. In England at large, the great wealth of the landed aristocracy, and the enormous size of their establishments, raises the houses and gardens to a scale so far above ours, that they are not directly or practically instructive to Americans. In the Isle of Wight, on the other hand, are numerous pretty cottages, villas and country houses, almost precisely on a transatlantic scale as to the first cost and the style of living. For this reason, one who can only learn by seeing the thing done to a scale that he can easily measure, should come to the Isle of Wight to study how to get the most for his money—rather than to Chatsworth or Eaton Hall. And it is this kind of rural beauty, the tasteful embellishment of small places, for which the United States will, I am confident, become celebrated in fifty years more.

VI.

WOBURN ABBEY.

September, 1850.

I RECEIVED in London, a note from the Duke of Bedford, which led me, while I was in Bedfordshire, to make a visit to Woburn Abbey.

This is considered one of the most complete estates and establishments in the kingdom. It is fully equal to Chatsworth, but quite in another way. Chatsworth is semi-continental, or rather it is the concentration of every thing that European art can do to embellish and render beautiful a great country residence. Woburn Abbey is thoroughly English; that is, it does not aim at beauty, so much as grandeur of extent and substantial completeness, united with the most systematic and thorough administration of the whole. Besides this, it interested me much as the home, for exactly *three centuries*, of a family which has adorned its high station by the highest virtues, and by an especial devotion to the interests of the soil.* The present Duke of Bedford is one of the largest and most scientific farmers in England, and his father, the late Duke, was not only an enthusiastic agriculturist, but the greatest arboriculturist and botanist of his day, whose works, both practical and literary, made their mark upon the age.

The Woburn estate consists of about thirty thousand acres of

* The first John Russell, Duke of Bedford, came into possession of this estate, in 1549, and it has descended in the family ever since. In one of the apartments of the palace is a series of miniature portraits of the heads of the family in an unbroken line, for 300 years.

land. There is a fine park of three thousand acres. You enter the approach through a singularly rich avenue of evergreens, composed of a belt perhaps one hundred feet broad, sloping down like an amphitheatre of foliage, from tall Norway spruces and pines in the background, to rich hollies and Portugal laurels in front. This continues, perhaps, half a mile, and then you leave it and wind through an open park, spacious and grand—for a couple of miles—till you reach the Abbey. This is not a building in an antique style, but a grand and massive pile in the classical manner, built about the middle of the last century on the site of the old Abbey. I have said this place seemed to me essentially English. The first sight of the house is peculiarly so. It is built of Portland stone, and has that mossy, discolored look which gathers about even modern buildings in this damp climate, and which we in America know nothing of, under our pure and bright skies—where the freshness of stone remains unsullied almost any length of time.

Woburn Abbey is a large palace, and containing as it does the accumulated luxuries, treasures of art, refinements, and comforts of so old and wealthy a family (with an income of nearly a million of our money), you will not be surprised when I say that we have nothing with which to compare it. Indeed, I believe Woburn is considered the most complete house in England, and that is saying a good deal, when you remember that there are 20,000 private houses in Great Britain, larger than our President's House. To get an idea of it, you must imagine a square mass, about which, externally—especially on the side fronting the park—there is little to impress you; only the appearance of large size and an air of simple dignity. Imagine this quadrangular pile three stories high on the park or entrance front, and two stories high on the garden or rear, and over two hundred feet in length, on each side. The drawing-room floor, though in the second story, is therefore exactly on a level with the gardens and pleasure-grounds in the rear, and the whole of this large floor is occupied with an unbroken suite of superb apartments—drawing-rooms, picture galleries, music-rooms, library, etc.—projecting and receding, and stealing out and in among the delicious scenery of the pleasure-grounds, in the most agreeable manner. There is a noble library with 20,000 volumes; a gallery, one hundred and forty feet long, filled with fine sculpture (among other things the original group of the three graces, by Canova), and a sort of wide corridor running all around the quadrangle, filled with cabinets of natural history, works of art, &c., and forming the most interesting in-door walk in dull weather. Pictures by the great masters, especially portraits, these rooms are very rich in, and among other things I noticed casts in plaster, of all the celebrated animals that were reared here by the late Duke.

Now, imagine the quadrangle continued in the rear on one side next the sculpture gallery, through a colonnade-like side series of buildings, including riding-house, tennis court, etc., a quarter of a mile, to the stables, which are of themselves larger than most country houses; imagine hot-houses and conservatories almost without number, connected with the house by covered passages, so as to combine the utmost comfort and beauty; imagine an aviary consisting of a cottage and the grounds about it fenced in and filled with all manner of birds of brilliant and beautiful plumage; imagine a large dairy, fitted up in the Chinese style with a fountain in the middle, and the richest porcelain vessels for milk and butter; imagine a private garden of bowers and trellis work, embosomed in creepers, which belongs especially to the Duchess, and you have a kind of sketchy outline of the immediate accessories of Woburn Abbey. They occupy the space of a little village in themselves; but you would gather no idea of the luxury and comfort they afford, did you for a moment forget that the whole is managed with that order and system which are nowhere to be found so perfect as in England. I must add, to give you another idea of the establishment, that a hundred beds are made up daily for the family and household alone, exclusive of guests. The pleasure-grounds, which surround three sides of the house, and upon which these rooms open, are so beautiful and complete that you must allow me to dwell upon them a little. They consist of a series of different gardens merging one into the other, so as to produce a delightful variety, and covering a space of many acres—about which I walked in so bewildered a state of delight that I am quite unable to say how large they are. I know, however, that they contain an avenue of araucarias backed by another of Deodar cedars in the most luxuriant growth—each line upwards of 1,000 feet long. A fine specimen of the latter tree, twenty-five or thirty feet high, attracted my attention, and there was another, twenty-five feet, of the beautiful Norfolk Island pine, growing in the open ground, with the shelter of a glazed frame in winter. These pleasure-grounds, however, interested me most in that portion called the American garden—several acres of sloping velvety turf, thickly dotted with groups of rhododendrons, azaleas, &c., forming the richest masses of dark green foliage that it is possible to conceive. In the months of May and June, when these are in full bloom, this must be a scene of almost dazzling brilliancy. The soil for them had all been formed artificially, and consisted of a mixture of peat and white sand, in which the rhododendrons and kalmias seemed to thrive admirably.

Besides this scene, there is a garden composed wholly of heaths, the beds cut in the turf, one species in each bed, and full of delicate bells; a parterre flower-garden in which a striking effect was produced by contrasting vases colored quite black, with rich masses (growing in the vases) of scarlet geraniums. I also saw a garden devoted wholly to willows, and another to grasses—both the most complete collections of these two genera in the world—the taste of the former Duke—and with which I was familiar beforehand, through the "*Salictum Woburnense*," and Mr. Sinclair's work on the "*Grasses of Woburn*."

The park is the richest in large evergreens of any that I have ever seen. The planting taste of the former Duke has produced at the present moment, after a growth of fifty or sixty years, the most superb results. The Cedars of Lebanon—the most *sublime* and venerable of all trees, and the grandest of all evergreens, bore off the palm—though all the rare pines and firs that were known to arboriculturists half a century ago are here in the greatest perfection—including hollies and Portugal laurels which one is accustomed to think of as shrubs, with great trunks like timber trees and magnificent heads of glossy foliage. A grand old silver fir has a straight trunk eighty feet high, and a lover of trees could spend weeks here without exhausting the arboricultural interest of the park alone—which is, to be sure, some ten or twelve miles round.

A very picturesque *morceau* in the park, inclosed and forming a little scene by itself, is called the *Thornery*. It is an abrupt piece of ground covered with a wild looking copse of old thorns, hazels, dog-woods and fantastic old oaks, and threaded by walks in various directions. In the centre is a most complete little cottage, with the neatest Scotch kitchen, little parlor and furniture inside, and a sort of fairy flower garden outside.

All this may be considered the ornamental portion of Woburn, and I have endeavored to raise such a picture of it in your mind as would most interest your readers. But you must remember that *farming* is the pride of Woburn, and that farming is here a matter of immense importance, involving the outlay of immense capital, and a personal interest and systematic attention which seems almost like managing the affairs of state. About half a mile from the house is the farmery—the most complete group of farm buildings, perhaps, in the world, where the incoming harvest make a figure only equalled by the accommodations to receive it. Besides these there are mills and workshops of all kinds, and on the outskirts of the park a whole settlement of farm cottages. I can only give you an idea of the attention bestowed on details, and the interest taken in the comforts of the immediate tenants by resorting to figures, and telling you that the present Duke has expended £70,000 (£350,000), within the past five years, in the farm cottages on this estate, which are model cottages—combining the utmost convenience and comfort for dwellings of this class, with so much of architectural taste as is befitting to dwellings of this size. Of course, a large part of this estate is let out to tenants, but still a large tract is managed by the Duke himself, who pays more than 400 laborers weekly throughout the year. The farming is very thorough, and the effects of draining in improving the land have been very striking. Above fifty miles of drain have been laid, in this estate alone, *annually*, for several years past.

You will gather from this, that English agriculture is not made a mere recreation, and that even with the assistance of the most competent and skilful agents, the life of a nobleman, with the immense estate and the agricultural tastes of the Duke of Bedford, is one of constant occupation and active employment. Besides this estate, he has another in Cambridgeshire, called the "Bedford Level"—a vast prairie of some 18,000 acres reclaimed from the sea, and kept dry by the constant action of steam engines, but which is very productive, and is, perhaps, the most profitable farm land in the kingdom.

VII.

DROPMORE.—ENGLISH RAILWAYS.—SOCIETY.

September, 1850.

DROPMORE is the seat of Lady Grenville, and has been celebrated, for some time, for its collection of rare trees—especially evergreens. It is in the neighborhood of Windsor, and I passed a morning there with a good deal of interest.

In point of taste and beauty, Dropmore disappointed me. The site is flat, the soil sandy and thin, and the arrangement, in no way remarkable. The mansion is not so fine as some upon the Hudson, and the scenery about it, does not rise above the dead level of a uniformity rendered less insipid by abundant plantations. There is, however, a wilderness of flower-garden about the house, in which I saw scarlet geraniums and garden vases enough to embellish a whole village. The effect, however, was *riant* and gay without the sentiment of real beauty.

But one does not go to Norway to drink sherbet, and Dropmore is only a show place by virtue of its *Pinetum.* This is its collection of evergreen trees, and particularly of the *pine* tribe—every species that will grow in England being collected in this one place.

Of course, in a scientific collection of evergreen trees, there are many that are only curious to the botanist—many that are only valuable for timber, and many that are almost ugly in their growth—or at least present no attractive feature to the general eye. But there are also, in this Pinetum, some evergreens of such rare and wonderful beauty, growing in such exquisite perfection of development, that they effect a tree-lover like those few finest Raphaels and Vandykes in the great galleries, which irradiate whole acres of common art.

The oldest and finest portion of the Pinetum occupies a lawn of several acres near the house, upon which are assembled, like belles at a levee, many of those loveliest of evergreens—the araucaria or pine of Chili, the Douglass' fir of California, the sacred cedar of India, the funcebral cypress of Japan, and many others.

Perhaps the finest tree in this scene is the Douglass' fir (*Abies Douglassii*). It is sixty-two feet high, and has grown to this altitude in twenty-one years from the seed. It resembles most the Norway spruce, as one occasionally sees the finest form of that tree, having that graceful downward sweep of the branches and *feathering* out quite down to the turf—but it is altogether more airy in form and of a richer and darker green in color. At this size it is the symbol of stately elegance. Here is also a specimen, thirty feet high, of *Pinus insignis*, the richest and darkest of all pines, as well as *Pinus excelsa*, one of the most *affectedly* pretty evergreens—its silvery leaves resembling those of the white pine, but drooping languidly—and *Pinus macrocarpa* with longer leaves than those of the pinaster.*

But the gem of the collection is the superb Chili pine or araucaria—the oldest, I think, in England, or, at all events, the finest. The seed was presented to the late Lord Grenville by William IVth —who had some of the first gigantic cones of this tree that were imported. This specimen is now thirty feet high, perfectly symmetrical, the stem as straight as a column—the branches disposed with the utmost regularity, and the lower ones drooping and touching the ground like those of a larch. If you will not smile, I will tell you that it struck me that the expression of this tree is *heroic*—that is, it looks the very Mars of evergreens. There are no slender twigs, no small branches—but a great stem with branches like a colossal bronze candelabrum, or perhaps the whole reminds one more of some gigantic, dark green coral than a living, flexible

* *Taxodium sempervirens* is here seventeen feet high—rich dark green in foliage and very ornamental. *Cryptomeria japonica*, nearly as large, rather disappointed me—keeping its brown leaves so long as to disfigure the plant somewhat. *Picea nobilis* is a truly beautiful fir tree.

tree. Yet it is a grand object—in its richest of dark green, its noble aspect, and its powerful, defiant attitude. This is quite the best specimen that I have seen, and stands in a light, sandy soil on a gravelly bottom—on which soil, I was told, it only grows luxuriantly. I do not know how well this fine evergreen will succeed at home. It is now on tria'—but I would hint to those who may fail from planting it in *rich* damp soil, that even here, it completely fails in such situations.

After leaving what I should call the Pinetum in full dress—i. e. in the highly-kept part of the grounds near the house, you emerge gradually into a tract of many acres of nearly level surface, which reminded me so strongly of a scattered Jersey pine barren, that had it not been for tufts and patches of that charming little plant the *heather* in full bloom, growing wild on all sides, I might have fancied myself in the neighborhood of Amboy. The whole looked, and much of it was, essentially wild, with the exception of carriage-drives and foot-paths running through the mingled copse, heath and woodland. But I was soon convinced of the fact that it was not entirely a wild growth, by being shown, here and there, looking quite as if they had come up by chance, rare specimens of pines, firs, cedars, etc., from all parts of the world, and presently I came upon a noble avenue, half a mile long, of cedars of Lebanon (a tree to which I always feel inclined to take off my hat as I would do to an old cathedral). The latter have been planted about twenty-five years, and are just beginning to merge the beautiful in the grand. Every thing in the shape of an evergreen seems to thrive in this light sandy soil, and I suggest to the owners of similar waste land in the middle and southern States, to take the hint from this part of Dropmore—plant here and there in the openings the same evergreen trees, protecting them by slight paling at first, and gradually clearing away all the common growth as they advance into beauty. In this way they may get a wonderfully interesting park—in soil where oaks and elms would never grow—at a very trifling outlay.

I cannot dismiss Dropmore without mentioning a superb hedge of Portugal laurel, thirty-one feet high—and the beautiful "Burnam beeches," almost as fine as one ever sees in America, that I passed on the way back tc the railway station.

The last word reminds me that I must say a word or two here, about the English railways. In point of speed I think their reputation outruns the fact. I did not find their average (with the exception of the road between Liverpool and London) much above that of our best northern and eastern roads. They make, for instance, hardly twenty miles an hour with the ordinary trains, and about thirty-six miles an hour with the express trains. But the perfect order and system with which they are managed; the obliging civility of all persons in the employment of the companies to travellers, and the quietness with which the business of the road is carried on, strikes an American very strongly. For example, suppose you are on a railroad at home. You are about to approach a small town, where you may leave and take up, perhaps, twenty passengers. As soon as the town is in sight, the engine or its whistle begins to scream out—the bell rings—the steam whizzes—and the train stops. Out hurry the way passengers, in rush the new comers. Again the bell rings, the steam whizzes, and with a noise something between a screech and a yell, but more infernal than either—a noise that deafens the old ladies, delights the boys, and frightens all the horses, off rushes the train—whizzing and yelling over a mile or two more of the country, before it takes breath for the like process at the next station.

In an English railway you seldom hear the scream of the steam whistle at all. It is not considered part of the business of the engineer to disturb the peace of the whole neighborhood, and inform them that he and the train are coming. The guard at the station notices the train when it first comes in sight. He immediately rings a *hand-bell*, just loud enough to warn the passengers in the station, to get ready. The train arrives—no yelling, screaming—or whizzing—possibly a gentle letting off of the steam—quite a necessary thing—not at all for effect. The passengers get out, and others get in, and are all carefully seated by the aforesaid guard or guards. When this is all done, the guard of the station gives a tinkle or two with his hand-bell again, to signify to the conductor that all is ready, and off the train darts, as quietly as if it knew screaming to be a thing not tolerated in good society. But the difference is national after all. John Bull says in his railroads, as in every thing else, " steady—all right." Brother Jonathan, " clear the coast—go ahead!" Still, as our most philosophical writer has said, it is only boys and savages who scream—men learn to control themselves—we hope to see the time when our people shall find out the advantages of possessing power without making a noise about it.

If we may take a lesson from the English in the management of railways, they might learn vastly more from us in the accommodation of passengers. What are called " first-class carriages" on the English rails, are thoroughly comfortable, in the English sense of the word. They have seats for six—each double-cushioned, padded, and set-off from the rest, like the easy chair of an alderman, in which you can intrench yourself and imagine that the world was made for you alone. But only a small part of the travel in England is in first-class cars, for it is a luxury that must be paid for in hard gold —costing four or five times as much as the most comfortable travelling by railroad in the United States. And the second-class cars—in which the great majority of the British people really travel—what are they? Neat boxes, in which you may sit down on a perfectly smooth board, and find out all the softness that lies in the grain of deal or good English oak—for they are guiltless of all cushions. Our neighbors of this side of the Atlantic have been so long accustomed to catering for the upper class in this country, that the fact that the railroad is the most democratic institution of the day, has not yet dawned upon them in all its breadth. An American rail-car, built to carry a large number in luxurious comfort, at a price that seems fabulous in England, pays better profits by the immense travel it begets, than the ill-devised first and second-class carriages of the English railways.

But what finish and nicety in these English roads! The grades all covered with turf, kept as nice as a lawn, quite down to the rails, and the divisions between the road and the lands adjoining, made by nicely trimmed hedges. The larger stations are erected in so expensive and solid a manner as to have greatly impaired the profits of some of the roads. But the smaller ones are almost always built in the style of the *cottage ornée*—and, indeed, are some of the prettiest and most picturesque rural buildings that I have seen in England. They all have their little flower-gardens, generally a parterre lying open quite to the edge of the rail, and looking like a gay carpet thrown on the green sward. If the English are an essentially common sense people, they, at least, have a love of flowers in all places, that has something quite romantic in it.

I reached London only to leave it again in another direction, to accept a kind invitation to the country house of Mrs. ——, the distinguished authoress of some charming works of fiction—which are widely known in my country, though I shall not transgress English propriety by giving you a clew to her real name.

This place reminded me of home more than any that I have seen in England; not, indeed, of my own home in the Hudson highlands, with its bold river and mountain scenery, but of the general features of American cultivated landscape. The house, which is not unlike a country house of good size with us, is situated on a hill which rises gently, but so high above the surrounding country, as to give a wide panorama of field and woodland, such as one sees from a height about Boston and Philadelphia. The approach, and part of the grounds, are bordered with plantations of forest-trees, which, though all planted, have been left to themselves so much as to look quite like our native after-growth at home. The place, too, has not the thorough *full-dress* air of the great English country places where I have been staying lately, and, both in extent and keeping, is more like a residence on the Hudson. The house sits down quite on a level with the ground, however, so that you can step out of the drawing-room on the soft grass, and stroll to yonder bright flower-garden, grouped round the fountain dancing in the sunshine, as if you were only going out of one room into another. In the library is a great bay-window, and a spacious fire-place set in a deep recess lined with books, suggesting warmth and comfort at once, to both mind and body; and the air of the whole place, joined to the unaffected and cordial welcome from many kind voices, gave me a feeling of *maladie du pays* that I had not felt before in England.

There are no especial wonders of park or palace here, though there is a great deal of quiet beauty, and as I have, perhaps, given you almost a surfeit of great places lately, you will not regret it. I look out of the windows, however, and see in abundance here, as every where, those two evergreens that enrich with their broad glossy leaves all English gardens and pleasure-grounds, and which I never cease to reproach for their monarchical habits—since they so obstinately refuse to be naturalized in our republic—I mean the English and Portugal laurels. I would give all the hot-house plants that Yankee glass covers, to have these two evergreens as much at home in our pleasure-grounds as they are every where in England.

There are other guests in the house—Sir Charles M——, Lady P., some Irish ladies without titles (but so rich in natural gifts as to make one feel the poverty of mere rank), and a charming family of grown up daughters. It would be difficult, perhaps, to have a better opportunity to judge of the life of the educated middle class of this country, than in such homes as this. And what impressions do such examples make upon my mind, you will ask? I will tell you (not without remembering how many fair young readers you have at home). The young English woman is less conspicuously *accomplished* than our young women of the same position in America. There is, perhaps, a little less of that *je ne sais quoi*—that nameless grace which captivates at first sight—than with us, but a better and more solid education, more disciplined minds, and above all, more common sense. In the whole art of conversation, including all the topics of the day, with so much of politics as makes a woman really a companion for an intelligent man in his serious thoughts, in history, language, and practical knowledge of the duties of social and domestic life, the English women have, I imagine, few superiors. But what, perhaps, would strike one of our young women most, in English society, would be the thorough cultivation and refinement that exist here, along with the absence of all false delicacy. The fondness of English women (even in the highest rank) for out-of-door life, horses, dogs, fine cattle, animals of all kinds,—for their grounds, and in short every thing that belongs to their homes—their real, unaffected knowledge of, and pleasure in these things, and the unreserved way in which they talk about them, would startle some of my young friends at home, who are educated in the fashionable boarding-school of Madame —— to consider all such things "vulgar," and "unlady-like." I accompanied the younger members of the family here this morning, in an exploration of the mysteries of the place. No sooner did we make our appearance out of doors, than we were saluted by dogs of all degrees, and each had the honor of an interview and personal reception, which seemed to be productive of pleasure on both sides. Then some of the horses were brought out of the stable, and a parley took place between them and their fair mistresses; some favorite cows were to be petted and looked after, and their good points were descanted on with knowledge and discrimination; and there was the *basse cour*, with its various population, all discussed and shown with such lively, unaffected interest, that I soon saw my fair companions were "born to love pigs and chickens." I have said nothing about the garden, because you know that it is especially the lady's province here. An English woman with no taste for gardening, would be as great a marvel as an angel without wings. And now, were these fresh looking girls, who have so thoroughly entered into these rustic enjoyments, mere country lasses and dairy maids? By no means. They will converse with you in three or four languages; are thoroughly well-grounded in modern literature; sketch from nature with the ease of professional artists, and will sit down to the piano-forte and give you an old ballad, or the finest German or Italian music, as your taste may dictate. And yet many of my young countrywomen of their age, whose education—wholly intended for the drawing-room—is far below what I have described, would have half fainted with terror, and half blushed with false delicacy, twenty times in the course of the morning, with the discussions of the farm-yard, meadow and stables, which properly belong to a wholesome country life, and are not in the slightest degree at variance with real delicacy and refinement. I very well know that there are many sensibly educated young women at home, who have the same breadth of cultivation, and the same variety of resources, that make the English women such truly agreeable companions; but alas, I also know that there are many whose beau ideal is bounded by a circle that contains the latest fashionable dance for the feet, the latest fashionable novel for the head, and the latest fashionable fancy-work for the fingers.

If I have unconsciously run into something like a sermon, it is from the feeling that among my own lovely countrywomen is to be found the ground-work of the most perfectly attractive feminine character in the world. But of late, their education has been a little vitiated by the introduction of the flimsiest points of French social requirements—rather than the more solid and estimable qualities which belong to English domestic life. The best social development in America will, doubtless, finally result from an internal movement springing from the very bosom of our institutions; but before that can happen, a great many traits and refinements will necessarily be borrowed from the old world—and the larger interests, healthier home tastes, and more thorough education of English women, seem to me hardly rated so highly by us as they deserve. Go to Paris, if you will, to see the most perfect taste in dress, and the finest charm of merely external manners, but make the acquaintance of English women if you wish to get a high idea of feminine character as it should be, to command your sincerest and most lasting admiration and respect.

VIII.

THE LONDON PARKS.

September, 1850.

MY DEAR SIR:—If my English letters have told you mostly of country places, and country life, it is not that I have been insensible to sight-seeing in town. London is a great world in itself. Ink enough has, however, already been expended upon it to fill the Grand Canal, and still it is a city which no one can understand without seeing it. Its vastness, its grave aspect of business, the grandeur of some parts, the poverty of others, the air of order, and the taint of smoke, that pervade it every where, are its great features. To an American eye, accustomed to the clear, pure, transatlantic atmosphere, there is, at first, something really repulsive in the black and dingy look of almost all buildings, whether new or old (not painted within the last month). In some of the oldest, like Westminster Abbey, it is an absolute covering of dirty soot. That hoary look of age which belongs to a time-honored building, and which mellows and softens all its lines and forms, is as delicious to the sense of sight as the tone of old pictures, or the hue of old wine. But there is none of this in the antiquity of London. You are repelled by the sooty exterior of all the old façades, as you would be by that of a chimney-sweep who has made the circuit of fifty flues in a morning, and whose outer man would almost defy an entire hydropathic institution.

If I have shown you the dark side of the picture of the great Metropolis, first, let me hasten to present you with some of its lights, which made a much stronger impression upon me. I mean the grand and beautiful parks of London.

If every thing one sees in England leads one to the conviction that the English do not, like the French and Germans, possess the genius of high art, there is no denying that they far surpass all other nations in a profound sentiment of nature. Take, for example, the West end of London, and what do you see there? Magnificent palaces, enormous piles of dwellings, in the shape of "terraces," "squares," and "places"—the same costly town architecture that you find every where in the better portions of populous and wealthy capitals. But if you ask me what is the peculiar and distinguishing *luxury* of this part of London, I answer, in its holding the country in its lap. In the midst of London lie, in an almost connected series, the great parks. Hyde Park, Regent's Park, St. James's and Green Parks. These names are almost as familiar to you as the Battery and Washington Square, and I fear you labor under the delusion that the former are only an enlarged edition of the latter. Believe me, you have fallen into as great an error as if you took the "Brick meeting-house" for a suggestion of St. Peter's. The London parks are actually like districts of open country—meadows and fields, country estates, lakes and streams, gardens and shrubberies, with as much variety as if you were in the heart of Cambridgeshire, and as much seclusion in some parts, at certain hours, as if you were on a farm in the interior of Pennsylvania. And the whole is laid out and treated, in the main, with a broad and noble feeling of natural beauty, quite the reverse of what you see in the public parks of the continental cities. This makes these parks doubly refreshing to citizens tired of straight lines and formal streets, while the contrast heightens the natural charm. Unaccustomed to this breadth of imitation of nature—this creating a piece of wide-spread country large enough to shut out for the time all trace of the houses, though actually in the midst of a city, an American is always inclined to believe (notwithstanding the abundance of evidence to the contrary) that the London parks are a bit of the *native* country, surprised and fairly taken prisoner by the outstretched arms of this giant of modern cities.

St. James's Park and Green Park are enormous pieces of real

pleasure-ground scenery—with broad glades of turf, noble trees, rich masses of shrubbery and flowering plants—lakes filled with rare water-fowl, and the proper surroundings, in fact, to two royal palaces and the finest private houses in London ; but still, all open to the enjoyment of hundreds of thousands daily. You look out upon the forest of verdure in Green Park, as you sit in the windows of our present minister's fine mansion in Piccadilly, astonished at the breadth and beauty of the green landscape, which seems to you more like a glimpse into one of the loveliest pleasure-grounds on the Hudson, than the belongings of the great Metropolis.

But the pride of London is in Hyde Park and Kensington Gardens, which, together, contain nearly eight hundred acres, so that you have to make a circuit of nearly *seven miles* to go over the entire circumference. If you enter Hyde Park between seven and eight in the morning, when all the world of fashion is asleep, you will fancy, after you have left the great gateways and the fine collosal statue of Achilles far enough behind you to be quite out of sight, that you have made a mistake and strolled out into the country unawares. Scarcely a person is to be seen at this time of day, unless it be some lonely foot-passenger, who looks as if he had lost his way, or his wits, at this early hour. But you see broad grass meadows with scattered groups of trees, not at all unlike what you remember on the smooth banks of the Connecticut, and your impression that you have got astray and quite out of the reach of the Metropolis, is confirmed by hearing the tinkle of sheep-bells and seeing flocks of these and other pastoral creatures, feeding quietly on the short turf of the secluded portions of the park. You walk on till you are quite weary, without finding the end of the matter —for Kensington Gardens, which is only another and a larger park, is but the continuation of Hyde Park—and you turn back in a sort of bewildered astonishment at the vastness and wealth of a city which can afford such an illimitable space for the pleasure of air and exercise of its inhabitants.

That is Hyde Park in dishabille. Now go in again with me in the afternoon, any time during the London season, and you shall see the same place in full dress, and so altered and animated by the *dramatis personæ*, that you will hardly identify it as the locale of the solitary country ramble you took in the morning.

It is half past four in the afternoon, and the fashionable world (who dine at seven all over England) is now taking its morning airing. If you will sit down on one of these solid-looking seats under the shadow of this large elm, you will see such a display of equipage, pass you in the cousre of a single hour, as no other part of the world can parallel. This broad, well-macadamized carriage-drive, which makes a circuit of some four or five miles in Hyde Park, is, at this moment, fairly filled with private carriages of all degrees. Here are heavy coaches and four, with postilions and footmen, and massive carriages emblazoned with family crests and gay with all the brilliancy of gold and crimson liveries; yonder superb barouche with eight spirited horses and numerous outriders, is the royal equipage, and as you lean forward to catch a glimpse of the sovereign, the close coach of the hero of Waterloo, the servants with cockades in their hats, dashes past you the other way at a rate so rapid that you doubt if he who rides within, is out merely for an airing. Yonder tasteful turn-out with liveries of a peculiar delicate mulberry, with only a single tall figure in the coach, is the Duke of Devonshire's. Here is the carriage of one of the foreign ambassadors, less showy and lighter than the English vehicles, and that pretty phaeton drawn by two beautiful blood horses, is, you see, driven by a woman of extraordinary beauty, with extraordinary skill. She is quite alone, and behind her sits a footman with his arms folded, his face as grave and solemn as stones that have sermons in them. As you express your surprise at the air of conscious "grace with which the lady drives," your London friend quietly remarks, "Yes, but she is *not* a lady." Unceasingly the carriages roll by, and you are less astonished at the numberless superb equipages or the beauty of the horses, than at the old-world air of the footmen in gold and silver lace, gaudy liveries, spotless linen and snowy silk stockings. Some of the grand old coachmen in full-powdered wigs, decked in all the glory of laced coats and silken calves, held the ribbons with such a conscisus air of imposing grandeur that I willingly accepted them as the tree-pœonias, the most blooming blossoms of this parterre of equipage. It seemed to me that there may be something comfortable in thus hanging all the trappings of station on the backs of coachmen and footmen, if one must be bothered with such things—so that one may lean back quietly in plain clothes in the well-stuffed seat of his private carriage.

But do not let us loiter away all our time in a single scene in Hyde Park. A few steps farther on is Rotten Row (rather an odd name for an elegant place), the chosen arena of fashionable *equestrians.* The English know too well the pleasures of riding, to gallop on horseback over hard pavements, and Rotten Row is a soft circle of a couple of miles, in the park, railed off for this purpose, where your horse's feet have an elastic surface to travel over. Hundreds of fair equestrians, with fathers, brothers, or friends, for companions, are here enjoying a more lively and spirited exercise, than the languid inmates of the carriages we have just left behind us. The English women *rise* in the saddle, like male riders, and at first sight they look awkwardly and less graceful to our eyes—but you soon see that they also sit more firmly and ride more boldly, than ladies on our side of the water.

To stand by and see others *ride*, seems to me to be always too tantalizing to be long endured as a pastime—even where the scene is as full of novelty and variety as this. Let us go on, therefore. This beautiful stream of water, which would be called a pretty "creek" at home, is the Serpentine River, which has been made to meander gracefully through Hyde Park, and wonderfully does its bright waters enhance the beauty of the verdure and the charm of the whole landscape. As we stand on the bridge, and look up and down the river, amid the rich groves and across the green lawns, the city wholly shut out by groves and plantations, how finely one feels the contrast of art and nature to be realized here.

That delicious band of music which you hear now, is in Kensington Gardens, and only a belt of trees and yonder iron gate, separate the latter from Hyde Park. Let us join the crowd of persons of all ages, collected in the great walk, under the shade of gigantic elm trees, to hear the music. It is a well-known air of Donizetti's, and as your eye glances over the company, perhaps some five or six thousand persons, who form the charmingly grouped, out-of-door audience (for the afternoon is a bright one), and as you see the radiant pleasure-sparkle in a thousand happy faces, young and old, who are here enjoying a little pleasant mingling of heaven and earth in an innocent manner, you cannot but be struck with the fact that, if there is a duty belonging to good governments, next to protecting the lives and property of the people, it is that of providing public parks for the pent-up inhabitants of cities.

"Imperial Kensington" is not only more spacious and grand than Hyde Park, but it has a certain antique stateliness, which touches my fancy and pleases me more. The trees are larger and more grove-like, and the broad glades of soft green turf are of a darker and richer green, and invite you to a more private and intimate confidence than any portions of Hyde Park. The grand avenue of elms at the farther part of Kensington Gardens, coming suddenly into it from the farther Bayswater Gate, is one of the noblest geometric groves in any city, and was laid out and planted, I believe, in King William's time. An avenue some hundreds of years old, is always majestic and venerable, and when it adds great extent and fine keeping, like this, is really a grand thing. And yet, perhaps, not one American in fifty that visits Hyde Park, ever gets far enough into the depths of its enjoyment to explore this avenue in Kensington Gardens.

No carriages or horses are permitted in Kensington Gardens, but its broad glades and shadowy lawns are sacred to pedestrians, and are especially the gambol-fields of thousands of lovely children, who, attended by their nurses, make a kind of infant Arcadia of these solemn old groves of the monarch of Dutch tastes. Even the dingy old brick Palace of Kensington, which overlooks one side of the great lawn, cannot chase away the bright dimples from the rosy faces of the charming children one sees here, and the symbols of natural aristocracy—beauty and intelligence—set upon these young faces, were to my eyes a far more agreeable study than those of accident, birth, and fortune, which are so gaudily blazoned forth in Hyde Park.

My London friend, who evidently enjoys our astonishment at the vastness of the London Parks, and the apparent display and real enjoyment they minister to, calculates that not less than 50,000 persons have been out, on foot, on horseback, or in carriages, this afternoon, and adds that upon review days, or other occasions of particular brilliancy, he has known 200,000 persons to be in Hyde Park and Kensington Gardens at once.

You may be weary of parks to-day, but I shall not allow you to escape me without a glance at Regent's Park, another link in the rural scenery of this part of London. Yes, here are *three hundred and thirty-six acres* more of lawn, ornamental plantations, drives and carriage roads. Regent's Park has a younger look than any of the others in the West End of London, having only been planted about twenty-five or thirty years—but it is a beautiful surface, containing a great variety of different scenes within itself. Here are, for instance, the Royal Botanic Garden, with its rich collection of plants and its beautiful flower-shows, which I have already described to you; and the Zoological Garden, some twenty acres in extent, where you may see almost every living animal as nearly as possible in the same circumstances as in its native country. Over the lawns walk the giraffe or cameleopard, led by Arabs in oriental costume; among the leafy avenues you see elephants waddling along, with loads of laughing, half-frightened children on their backs; down in a deep pool of water you peer upon the sluggish hippopotamus; you gaze at the soft eyes of the gazelle as she feeds in her little private paddock, and you feed the black swans that are floating along, with innumerable other rare aquatic birds, upon the surface of glassy lakes of fresh water. And the "Zoological" is just as full of people as Hyde Park, though of a totally different appearance—many students in natural history, some fashionable loungers, chiefly women, more curious strangers, and most of all, boys and girls, feeding their juvenile appetite for the marvellous, by seeing the less astonished animals fed.

And whose are those pretty country residences that you see in the very midst of another part of Regent's Park—beautiful Italian villas and ornamental cottages, embowered in trees of their own, and only divided from the open park by a light railing and belts of shrubbery? These are the villas of certain favored nobles, who have at large cost realized, as you see, the perfection of a residence in town, viz., a country-house in the midst of a great park, which is itself in the midst of a great city. In these favored sites the owners have the luxury of quiet and rural surroundings, usually confined to the country, with the whole of the great world of May Fair and politics within ten or twenty minutes' walk.

And now, having been through more than a *thousand acres* of park scenery, and witnessed the enjoyments of tens of thousands of all classes, to whom these parks are open from sunrise to nine o'clock at night, you will naturally ask me if these luxuries are wholly confined to the West End of London. By no means. In almost all parts of London are "squares"—open places of eight or ten acres, filled with trees, shrubs, grass, and fountains—like what we call "parks" in our cities at home. Besides these, a large new space called the Victoria Park, of two hundred and ninety acres, has been laid out lately in the East part of London, expressly for the recreation and amusement of the poorer classes who are confined to that part of the town.

You see what noble breathing-places London has, within its own boundaries, for the daily health and recreation of its citizens. But these by no means comprise all the rural pleasures of its inhabitants. There are three other magnificent public places within half an hour of London, which are also enjoyed daily by thousands and tens of thousands. I mean Hampton Court, Richmond Park, and the National Gardens at Kew.

Hampton Court is the favorite resort of the middle classes on *holidays*, and a pleasanter sight than that spot on such occasions,—when it is thronged by immense numbers of citizens, their wives and children, with all the riches of that grand old palace, its picture-galleries, halls, and splendid apartments, its two parks and its immense pleasure-grounds thrown open to them, is not easily found. Indeed, a man may be dull enough to care for neither palaces nor parks, for neither nature nor art, but he can scarcely be human, or have a spark of sympathy in the fortunes of his race, if he can wander without interest through these magnificent halls, still in perfect order, built with the most kingly prodigality by the most ambitious and powerful of subjects—Wolsey: halls that were afterwards successively the home of Henry VIII., Elizabeth, James, Charles and Cromwell; halls where Shakspeare played and Sidney wrote, but which, with all their treasures of art, are now the *people's palace* and normal school of enjoyment.

I am neither going to weary you with catalogues of pictures or dissertations upon palace architecture. But I must give you one more impression—that of the magnificent surroundings of Hampton Court. Conjure up a piece of country of diversified rich meadow surface, some five or six miles in circuit; imagine, around the palace, some forty or fifty acres of gardens, mostly in the ancient taste, with pleached alleys (Queen Mary's bower among them), sloping banks of soft turf, huge orange trees in boxes, and a "wilderness" or labyrinth where you may lose yourself in the most intricate perplexity of shrubs; imagine an avenue a mile and a quarter long, of the most gigantic horse-chestnuts you ever beheld, with long vistas of velvet turf and highly-dressed garden scenery around them; imagine other parts of the park where you see on all sides, only great masses and groups of oaks and elms of centuries' growth, and all the freedom of luxuriant nature, with a broad carpet of grass stretching on all sides; with distant portions of the park quite wild-looking, dotted with great hawthorn *trees* of centuries' growth, with the tangled copse and fragrant fern which are the belongings of our own forests, and then fill up the scene in the neighborhood of the palace and gardens as I have before said, on a holiday, with thousands of happy faces, while in the secluded parts of the park the timid deer flits before you, the birds stealthily build their nests, and the insect's hum fills the silent air, and you have some faint idea of the value of such a possession for the population of a great city to pass their holidays in, or to go pic-nic-ing!

I am writing you a long letter, but the *parkomanie* is upon me, and I will not let the ink dry in my pen without a word about Richmond Great Park—also free to the public, and also within the reach of the Londoner who seeks for air and exercise. Richmond Great Park was formerly a royal hunting-ground, but, like all the parks I have mentioned, has been given up to the people—at least the free enjoyment of it. It is the largest of all the parks I have described, being eight miles round, and containing two thousand two hundred and fifty acres. It is a piece of magnificent forest tract —open forest, with grass, tufts of hazel, thorns and ferns, the surface gently undulating, and dotted with grand old oaks—extremely like what you see on a still larger scale in Kentucky. Its solitude and seclusion, within sight of London—are almost startling. The land is high, and from one side of it your eye wanders over the valley of Richmond—with the Thames—here only a silvery looking stream winding through it—a world-renowned view, and one whose sylvan beauty it is impossible to praise too highly. Just in this part of the park, and commanding this superb view, with the towers of Windsor Castle in the distance on one side, and the dome of St. Paul's on the other, and all the antique sylvan seclusion of the old wood around it, stands a modest little cottage—the favorite summer residence of Lord John Russell, the use of which has been given him by his sovereign. A more unambitious looking home, and one better calculated to restore the faculties of an over-worked premier, after a day's toil in Downing-street, it would be impossible to conceive.

I drove through Richmond Great Park in the carriage of the Belgian minister, and his accomplished wife, who was my cicerone, stopped the coachman for a moment near this place, in order that she might point out to me an old oak that had a story to tell. "It was here—just under this tree," she added (her eyes gleaming slightly with womanly indignation as she said it), "that the cruel Henry stood, and saw with his own eyes, the signal made from the Tower of London (five miles off), which told him that Anne Boleyn was at that moment beheaded!" I thanked God that oak trees were longer lived than bad monarchs, and that modern civilization would no longer permit such butchery in a christian country.

I will close this letter with only a single remark. We fancy, not without reason, in New-York, that we have a great city, and that the introduction of Croton water, is so marvellous a luxury in the way of health, that nothing more need be done for the comfort of half a million of people. In crossing the Atlantic, a young New-Yorker, who was rabidly patriotic, and who boasted daily of the superiority of our beloved commercial metropolis over every city on the globe, was our most amusing companion. I chanced to meet him one afternoon a few days after we landed, in one of the great parks in London, in the midst of all the sylvan beauty and human enjoyment, I have attempted to describe to you. He threw up his arms as he recognized me, and exclaimed—"Good heavens! what a scene, and *I* took some Londoners to the steps of the City Hall last summer, to show them *the Park* of New-York!" I consoled him with the advice to be less conceited thereafter in his cockneyism, and to show foreigners the Hudson and Niagara, instead of the City Hall and Bowling Green. But the question may well be asked, Is New-York really not rich enough, or is there absolutely not land enough in America to give our citizens public parks of more than ten acres?

THE END.

The Rococo Garden of Baron Hügel, near Vienna.

www.ingramcontent.com/pod-product-compliance
Lightning Source LLC
LaVergne TN
LVHW021057110826
845150LV00001B/95

* 9 7 8 1 4 2 5 5 6 6 8 7 6 *